Fodor's 2011
LONDON

Fodor's Travel Publications · New York, Toronto, London, Sydney, Auckland
www.fodors.com

W9-CDZ-617

Be a Fodor's Correspondent

Your opinion matters. It matters to us. It matters to your fellow Fodor's travelers, too. And we'd like to hear it. In fact, we *need* to hear it.

When you share your experiences and opinions, you become an active member of the Fodor's community. That means we'll not only use your feedback to make our books better, but we'll publish your names and comments whenever possible. Throughout our guides, look for "Word of Mouth," excerpts of your unvarnished feedback.

Here's how you can help improve Fodor's for all of us.

Tell us when we're right. We rely on local writers to give you an insider's perspective. But our writers and staff editors—who are the best in the business—depend on you. Your positive feedback is a vote to renew our recommendations for the next edition.

Tell us when we're wrong. We're proud that we update most of our guides every year. But we're not perfect. Things change. Hotels cut services. Museums change hours. Charming cafés lose charm. If our writer didn't quite capture the essence of a place, tell us how you'd do it differently. If any of our descriptions are inaccurate or inadequate, we'll incorporate your changes in the next edition and will correct factual errors at fodors.com *immediately*.

Tell us what to include. You probably have had fantastic travel experiences that aren't yet in Fodor's. Why not share them with a community of like-minded travelers? Maybe you chanced upon a beach or bistro or B&B that you don't want to keep to yourself. Tell us why we should include it. And share your discoveries and experiences with everyone directly at fodors.com. Your input may lead us to add a new listing or highlight a place we cover with a "Highly Recommended" star or with our highest rating, "Fodor's Choice."

Give us your opinion instantly at our feedback center at www.fodors.com/feedback. You may also e-mail editors@fodors.com with the subject line "London Editor." Or send your nominations, comments, and complaints by mail to London Editor, Fodor's, 1745 Broadway, New York, NY 10019.

You and travelers like you are the heart of the Fodor's community. Make our community richer by sharing your experiences. Be a Fodor's correspondent.

Happy Traveling!

Tim Jarrell, Publisher

FODOR'S LONDON 2011
Editor: Cate Starmer

Production Editor: Carrie Parker
Maps & Illustrations: Mark Stroud, David Lindroth, *cartographers;* Bob Blake, Rebecca Baer, *map editors;* William Wu, *information graphics*
Design: Fabrizio La Rocca, *creative director;* Guido Caroti, Siobhan O'Hare, *art directors;* Tina Malaney, Chie Ushio, Ann McBride, Jessica Walsh, *designers;* Melanie Marin, *senior picture editor*
Cover Photo: BildagenturHuber/Picture Finders/Fototeca 9x12
Production Manager: Angela L. McLean

COPYRIGHT
Copyright © 2011 by Fodor's Travel, a division of Random House, Inc.

Fodor's is a registered trademark of Random House, Inc.

All rights reserved. Published in the United States by Fodor's Travel, a division of Random House, Inc., and simultaneously in Canada by Random House of Canada, Limited, Toronto. Distributed by Random House, Inc., New York.

ISBN 978–1–4000–0456–0

ISSN 0149–631X

SPECIAL SALES
This book is available at special discounts for bulk purchases for sales promotions or premiums. Special editions, including personalized covers, excerpts of existing books, and corporate imprints, can be created in large quantities for special needs. For more information, write to Special Markets/Premium Sales, 1745 Broadway, MD 6-2, New York, New York 10019, or e-mail specialmarkets@randomhouse.com.

AN IMPORTANT TIP & AN INVITATION
Although all prices, opening times, and other details in this book are based on information supplied to us at press time, changes occur all the time in the travel world, and Fodor's cannot accept responsibility for facts that become outdated or for inadvertent errors or omissions. So **always confirm information when it matters**, especially if you're making a detour to visit a specific place. Your experiences—positive and negative—matter to us. If we have missed or misstated something, **please write to us**. We follow up on all suggestions. Contact the London editor at editors@fodors.com or c/o Fodor's at 1745 Broadway, New York, NY 10019.

PRINTED IN SINGAPORE

10 9 8 7 6 5 4 3 2 1

CONTENTS

Fodor's Features

CONTENTS

MAPS

ABOUT THIS BOOK

Our Ratings

Sometimes you find terrific travel experiences and sometimes they just find you. But usually the burden is on you to select the right combination of experiences. That's where our ratings come in.

As travelers we've all discovered a place so wonderful that its worthiness is obvious. And sometimes that place is so experiential that superlatives don't do it justice: you just have to be there to know. These sights, properties, and experiences get our highest rating, **Fodor's Choice**, indicated by orange stars throughout this book.

Black stars highlight sights and properties we deem **Highly Recommended**, places that our writers, editors, and readers praise again and again for consistency and excellence.

By default, there's another category: any place we include in this book is by definition worth your time, unless we say otherwise. And we will.

Disagree with any of our choices? Care to nominate a place or suggest that we rate one more highly? Visit our feedback center at fodors.com.

Budget Well

Hotel and restaurant price categories from ¢ to $$$$ are defined in the opening pages of chapters 14 and 15. For attractions, we always give standard adult admission fees; reductions are usually available for children, students, and senior citizens. Want to pay with plastic? **AE, D, DC, MC, V** following restaurant and hotel listings indicate if American Express, Discover, Diners Club, MasterCard, and Visa are accepted.

Restaurants

Unless we state otherwise, restaurants are open for lunch and dinner daily. We mention dress only when there's a specific requirement and reservations only when they're essential or not accepted—it's always best to book ahead.

Hotels

Hotels have private bath, phone, TV, and air-conditioning and operate on the European Plan (aka EP, meaning without meals), unless we specify that they use the Continental Plan (CP, with a Continental breakfast), Breakfast Plan (BP, with a full breakfast), or Modified American Plan (MAP, with breakfast and dinner) or are all-inclusive (AI, including all meals and most activities). We always list facilities but not whether you'll be charged an extra fee to use them.

Listings
★	Fodor's Choice
★	Highly recommended
⊠	Physical address
✛	Directions or Map coordinates
⌂	Mailing address
☎	Telephone
🖷	Fax
⊕	On the Web
✉	E-mail
🎫	Admission fee
☉	Open/closed times
Ⓜ	Metro stations
▭	Credit cards

Hotels & Restaurants
🏨	Hotel
↵	Number of rooms
♿	Facilities
⑩	Meal plans
✕	Restaurant
✍	Reservations
🏛	Dress code
↘	Smoking
🍷	BYOB

Outdoors
⛳	Golf
⛺	Camping

Other
♣	Family-friendly
⇨	See also
⊠	Branch address
☞	Take note

Experience
London

LONDON TODAY

So the weather stinks, no one smiles, and it takes far too long to get around—just what is it that makes London such a great place to be?

The World Comes to Town

Londoners are among the least xenophobic in Europe, and with one third of its residents born outside England, London is perhaps the most culturally diverse city on Earth. It's part indifference and part adaptability (heavily sprinkled with tolerance), but Londoners pay precious little attention to outsiders. This is undeniably part of London's charm: without the attentions of strangers, you can lose yourself here like in no other city. With more than 300 languages spoken on its streets—from the hybrid Multicultural London English to Pashto—the city is a terrific tangle of tongues. And as one of Europe's largest cities: whether it's cuisine, music, theater, poetry, or fashion, the outside world converges on London to leave its mark. London's global village can only become increasingly diverse—and unique—as the 2012 Olympics Games approach.

A City of Ideas

The capital of England's knowledge economy, London is foremost a city of ideas and creativity. From literati to glitterati, London is a vibrantly experimental capital and one of the destinations of choice for global culture hounds. Whether it's experimental drama, offbeat literature, street fashion, street performers, sparkling West End productions, cutting-edge art, urban music, or left-field public sculpture, the city is a refreshing haven for the inventive, innovative, and independent-minded. Scores of theaters in the West End make London a powerful magnet for drama enthusiasts, while the city's top-drawer museums embrace an almanac of human wisdom.

The Big Smoke?

London was once notorious for its pea-soup smog, and although a battery of measures has successfully cleaned up its skies the city still has some of the dirtiest air in Europe. Since 2008, the London Low Emission Zone has deterred heavily polluting large vehicles from entering the city area, while the Congestion Charge, charging vehicles £8 per day entering central London, has reduced both traffic and pollution. London's current mayor, Boris Johnson, is a great supporter of further creating bicycle lanes and encouraging Londoners to recycle. Johnson also keeps a close eye on the city's fitness levels, supporting initiatives to combat obesity and

DID YOU KNOW?

■ With more than 7 million residents, London is the most populous city in the European Union, more than twice that of its nearest rival. It's among the most densely populated, too, after Copenhagen, Brussels, and Paris.

■ Up to around £2,000 (nearly $4,000) of taxpayers' money can be used to purchase a wig for a London judge, who often still wears the antiquated accessory. Barristers and solicitors (lawyers) must pay for their own wigs and often buy them used.

■ More than 120 species of fish, including smelt (which locals say has an odor resembling their beloved cucumber sandwiches), live in the Thames. It may look brown because of the sediment, but the Thames is actually Europe's cleanest metropolitan estuary.

promote exercise. Further good news is that only 15% of Londoners smoke cigarettes and in 2007 all enclosed public places (including pubs and restaurants) and places of work became smoke-free. The city's green lungs—its gorgeous and ample parkland—help keep the city oxygenated while Boris Johnson plans to spend £6 million on improving London's open spaces to make this the world's greenest city by 2012.

Have and Have-Nots

For the people who live here, money is what makes London's cogs go around. The credit crunch may have pierced its bubble of prosperity, but in 2009 the U.K. still replaced the U.S. as the world's leading financial center, with London leading the way.

Today, the City contributes about 2.5% of the country's GDP, which highlights the pivotal role it plays in the country's economy. But while its Kazakh oligarchs, Saudi playboys, and cash-splashing freewheelers suggest a city endlessly flaunting its wealth, income disparities are colossal. London remains a reasonably safe city but it pays to keep your wits about you; gang culture and incidents of knife and gun crime conspire to make some neighborhoods a grittier and disadvantaged flip side to the city's flashier boroughs.

Drinking Culture

Although Londoners consume less alcohol than the average British drinker, pub culture is simply indivisible from the London experience. Drinking out can be a pricey pastime but London pubs and bars remain a well-established cornerstone of a good night out, with more than 5,000 watering holes to choose from. Some pubs have roots that poke deep into London's magnificent history; others excel at bringing live music to the drinking masses, while more still put the emphasis on a huge menu of real ales and ciders or first-rate food. The more sophisticated crowd preens in wine bars citywide. Drinking is first and foremost a social occasion where everyone in the group takes turns to buy a round; but be warned, getting your drinks ordered in a crowded London pub can take persistence (and a sharp pair of elbows).

■ The Tube is the world's biggest subway system. With 253 mi of track and 270 stations, it covers more ground than systems in New York, Paris, and Tokyo. More than a billion passenger journeys are made on the network every year.

■ City taxi drivers must pass a training test that requires at least two years of preparation.

Eight of every 10 applicants drop out before completion.

■ London may have been credit-crunched, but the world's most expensive property—a central London flat—recently sold for more than £115 million.

■ The city is also the world's most expensive if you want to park your car. London's Congestion Charge Zone, where vehicles need to pay on weekdays to use the city center streets, is already the world's largest.

■ With electricity generation set to start in 2012, the London Array project will be the world's largest offshore wind farm.

WHAT'S WHERE

The following numbers refer to chapters.

2 **Westminster and Royal London.** This is the place to embrace the "tourist" label. Snap pictures of the mounted Horse Guards, play with the pigeons in Trafalgar Square, and visit stacks of art in the national galleries. It's well worth braving the crowds to wander ancient Westminster Abbey and its historic bounty.

3 **St. James's and Mayfair.** You might not have the wallet for London's most prestigious district, but the window-shopping in Mayfair is free. St. James's is the ultimate enclave of old money and gentleman's London. Here you'll find the noted private members' clubs of Pall Mall, and the starched shirts and cigars of Jermyn Street, where you can shop like the Duke of Windsor.

4 **Soho and Covent Garden.** More sophisticated than seedy these days, the heart of London puts Theaterland, strip joints, Chinatown, and the trendiest of film studios side by side. Nearby Charing Cross Road is a bibliophile's dream, but steer clear of the hectic hordes in Leicester Square, London's answer to Times Square.

5 **Bloomsbury and Legal London.** The literary and left-wing set that made Bloomsbury world famous has left its mark, and the area remains the heart of brainy London. The University of London and the Law Courts are worth a passing glance; stop for a good while in the incomparable British Museum.

6 **The City.** London's Wall Street might be the oldest part of the capital, but thanks to futuristic skyscrapers and a sleek Millennium Bridge, it looks like the newest. Fans of ages gone by won't be disappointed, however: head for the dome of St. Paul's Cathedral, the storybook Tower Bridge, and grisly tales from the Tower of London.

7 **The East End.** Once famed for the 19th-century slums immortalized by Charles Dickens, today the area has become the oh-so-fashionable epicenter of London's contemporary art scene. For the spit-and-sawdust experience of market London on the weekend, dive into the wares at Spitalfields, Petticoat Lane, Brick Lane (popular for curry houses and bagel bakeries), and Columbia Road's much-loved flower market.

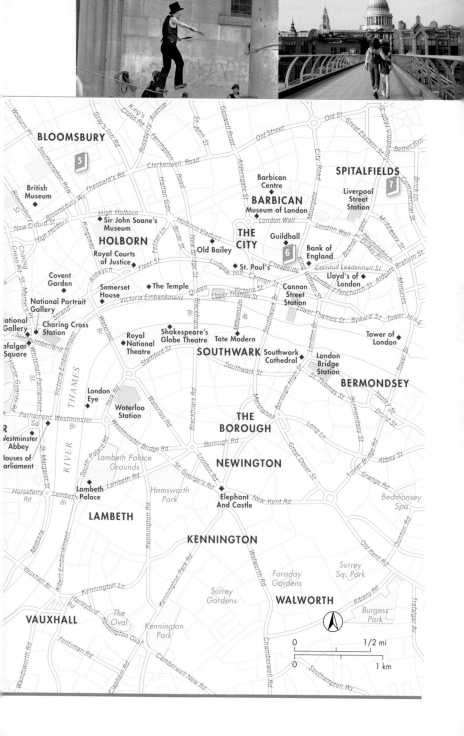

BLOOMSBURY

5

British
Museum

SPITALFIELDS

7

Liverpool
Street
Station

Barbican
Centre

BARBICAN
Museum of London

London Wall

Sir John Soane's
Museum

HOLBORN

**THE
CITY**

Guildhall

Old Bailey

Bank of
England

Royal Courts
of Justice

St. Paul's

Lloyd's of
London

Covent
Garden

Somerset
House

The Temple

Cannon
Street
Station

Leadenhall St

National Portrait
Gallery

National
Gallery

Charing Cross
Station

Royal
National
Theatre

Shakespeare's
Globe Theatre

Tate Modern

Tower of
London

Trafalgar
Square

SOUTHWARK

Southwark
Cathedral

London
Bridge
Station

BERMONDSEY

London
Eye

Waterloo
Station

**THE
BOROUGH**

Westminster
Abbey

Westminster
Sq

Houses of
Parliament

NEWINGTON

Lambeth Palace
Grounds

Hamsworth
Park

Elephant
And Castle

Lambeth
Palace

Bedmonsey
Spa

LAMBETH

KENNINGTON

Faraday
Gardens

Surrey
Sq. Park

VAUXHALL

The
Oval

Kennington
Park

Surrey
Gardens

WALWORTH

Burgess
Park

0   1/2 mi

0   1 km

WHAT'S WHERE

8 The South Bank. Die-hard culture vultures could spend a lifetime here. The Southbank Centre—including the Royal National Theatre and Royal Festival Hall, the National Film Theatre, Shakespeare's Globe, the Design Museum, and the Tate Modern—pretty much seals the artistic deal. Or take it all in from high up on the London Eye.

9 Kensington, Chelsea, and Knightsbridge. Although the many boutiques of the King's Road have lost much of their heady '60s swagger, the museums are as awe-inspiring as ever. The playful Science Museum and the gargantuan Natural History Museum are the most fun for children. For a slightly more affordable alternative to the King's Road, go shopping on High Street Kensington. Or flash your cash at the capital's snazziest department stores, Harrods and Harvey Nichols.

10 Notting Hill and Bayswater. To develop an effortlessly hip London demeanor, hang out in its most coveted residential area. Notting Hill, around Portobello Road, is a trendsetting square mile of multiethnicity, galleries, bijous shops, and see-and-be-seen-in restaurants. Bayswater mixes gaudy Arab fashions and fresh food shops; some think it has

an appealing edginess, others a nouveau-riche élan.

11 Regent's Park and Hampstead. For poetic inspiration, visit Keats House, where the poet penned his immortal "Ode to a Nightingale." Villagelike Hampstead is a must: cozy and wonderful streets, sidewalk cafés, delis, and outdoor swimming on the Heath in "the Lido."

12 Greenwich. Quaint Thames-side streets make for an excellent rummaging ground for trendy antiques. Throw in some brilliant sights, Christopher Wren architecture, and the Greenwich Meridian Line, and you have one of the best excursions beyond the cut-and-thrust of central London.

13 The Thames Upstream. As an idyllic retreat from the city, stroll around London's stately gardens and enjoy a beer close by once-powerful palaces at Chiswick, Kew, Richmond, and Putney. Better yet, take a river cruise along Old Father Thames for views of rolling greenery, and land up at the famous maze of Hampton Court Palace, England's version of Versailles.

PRIMROSE HILL

11

Primrose Hill

REGENT'S PARK

London Zoo

CAMDEN TOWN

KING'S CROSS

BARNSBURY

ISLINGTON

HAGGERSTON

Shoreditch Park

HOXTON

London Canal Museum

King's Cross Station

St. Pancras Station

Euston Station

BLOOMSBURY

SHOREDITCH

Madame Tussauds

Telecom Tower

British Museum & Library

BARBICAN

SPITALFIELDS

Liverpool Street Station

Selfridges

HOLBORN

THE CITY

SOHO

Covent Garden

The Temple

Cannon Street Station

MAYFAIR

Picadilly Circus

HYDE PARK

Tower of London

St. James's Palace

Trafalgar Square

SOUTH BANK

SOUTHWARK

8

THE BOROUGH

London Bridge Station

12

BROMPTON

Buckingham Palace Gardens

WESTMINSTER

Waterloo Station

London Eye

BELGRAVIA

Victoria Station

Tate Gallery

LAMBETH

NEWINGTON

KENNINGTON

WALWORTH

Ronalagh Gardens

Chelsea Embankment

RIVER THAMES

VAUXHALL

The Oval

Kennington Gardens

Surrey Sq. Park

Faraday Gardens

Surrey Gardens

Burgess Park

BATTERSEA PARK

SEE WHAT'S WHERE CENTRAL LONDON

SOUTH LAMBETH

CAMBERWELL

0   1/2 mi

0   1 km

LONDON PLANNER

When to Go

The heaviest tourist season runs mid-April through mid-October, with another peak around Christmas—though the tide never really ebbs. Spring is the time to see the countryside and the royal London parks and gardens at their freshest; fall to enjoy near-ideal exploring conditions. In late summer, be warned: air-conditioning is rarely found in places other than department stores, modern restaurants, hotels, and cinemas in London. Winter can be rather dismal, but all the theaters, concerts, and exhibitions go full speed ahead, and festive Christmas lights bring a glow. For a schedule of festivals, check ⊕ www.visitbritain.com.

When Not to Go

One good time to avoid is the October "half-term," when schools in the capital take a break for a week and nearly all attractions are flooded by children. Arriving at the start of August can be a very busy time, and the weather makes Tube travel a nightmare. And trying to shop in central London the week before Christmas is an insane idea best left only to desperate Londoners who have forgotten to buy presents.

Addresses

Central London and its surrounding districts are divided into 32 boroughs—33, counting the City of London. More useful for navigating, however, are the subdivisions of London into postal districts. Throughout the guide we've given the abbreviated postal code for most listings. The first one or two letters give the location: N means north, NW means northwest, and so on. Don't expect the numbering to be logical, however. (You won't, for example, find W2 next to W3.) The general rule is that the lower numbers, such as W1 or SW1, are closest to the city center.

Getting Around

London is, above all, a walker's city, and will repay every moment you spend exploring on foot. Of course, that may be of diminished appeal when you've got 30 minutes to scramble to the other side of town. Here are other options:

By far the easiest and most practical way to get around is on the Underground, or "Tube." Trains run daily from early morning to night. Buy an Oyster card for £3, which will allow you to use London's transport at a lower cost than using paper tickets. The plastic card can be topped up as often as you want, and your £3 will be reimbursed when you hand the card back. Alternatively, buy a Travelcard pass (from £5.10 per day), which offers unlimited use of the Tube, buses, and the commuter rail. Avoid rush-hour hell—the rest of the day this is a pleasant and quick way to move. Note: The Tube is undergoing a major overhaul. Keep an eye out for information on line closures and alternative routes. Check ⊕ www.tfl.gov.uk for details.

The commuter rail system is an over-ground network that connects outlying districts and suburbs to the center. Prices are comparable to those of the Underground, and you can easily transfer between the Underground and other connecting rail lines at many Tube stations.

Buses crisscross all over, and are a great way to see the city. Their routes are more complicated than the Tube's, but by reading the route posted on the main bus stop and looking for the number and destination on the front of the bus, you won't go far wrong. Service is frequent.

London Hours

Most businesses are closed on Sunday and national ("bank") holidays. Banks are open weekdays 9:30–4:30; offices are generally open 9:30–5:30.

The major national museums and galleries are open daily, with shorter hours on weekends than weekdays. Often they are open late one night a week.

The usual shop hours are Monday–Saturday 9–5:30 and Sunday noon–5. Around Oxford Street, Kensington High Street, and Knightsbridge, hours are 9:30–6, with late-night hours (until 7:30 or 8) on Wednesday or Thursday.

Deal or No Deal?

There's no getting around it: today's exchange rates really maul the pockets of American tourists. But it's much better to accept this fact in advance and factor it into your vacation planning, tailoring outings and trips that will reflect your interests—and your budget.

Often, booking in advance, harnessing low-season deals, and taking advantage of Internet specials for flights and hotel rooms can cut down on costs. London is also great at offering things for free, and the quality of the culture, entertainment, relaxation, and fun to be had in the city means that if you target your spending wisely, you'll go home penny-pinched but satisfied.

What it Costs

	IN LONDON	IN NEW YORK
Pair of theater tickets	£20–£70	$50–$200
Museum admission	Usually free; sometimes £4–£10	Usually $5–$20; sometimes free
Fast-food value meal	£4	$4
Tall latte	£2.15	$3.19
Pint of beer in a pub	£3 and up	$6 and up
1-mi taxi ride before tips	£5	$5
Subway ride within city center	£4 without Oyster or Travelcard	$2.25

How's the Weather?

It's virtually impossible to forecast London weather, but you can be fairly certain that it will *not* be what you expect. It's generally mild—with some savage exceptions, especially in summer. In short, be prepared for anything: layers and an umbrella are your friends. The following are the average daily maximum and minimum temperatures for London.

AVERAGE LONDON
TEMPERATURES

LONDON TOP ATTRACTIONS

Westminster Abbey

(A) Steeped in history, the pillars of this great vaulted hall stand on the final resting place of the men and women who built Britain. Its great Gothic hall continues to play a part in the formation of the kingdom, having hosted nearly every coronation since 1308.

Buckingham Palace

(B) Not the prettiest royal residence, but a must-see for the glimpse it affords of the modern life of the monarchy. The opulence of the state rooms open to the public provides plenty of wow factor, and don't forget the collection of china and carriages at the Queen's Gallery and Royal Mews next door.

St. Paul's Cathedral

(C) No matter how many times you have been before, the scale and elegance of Sir Christopher Wren's masterpiece never fail to take the breath away. Climb the enormous dome, one of the world's largest, to experience the freaky acoustics of the Whispering Gallery, and higher still for fantastic views across London.

Tower of London

(D) The Tower is London at its majestic, idiosyncratic best. This is truly the heart of the kingdom—with foundations dating back nine centuries, every brick tells a story, and the ax-blows and fortunes that have risen and fallen within this turreted mini-city provide an inexhaustible supply of intrigue.

British Museum

(E) If you want to journey through time and space without leaving the confines of Bloomsbury, a visit to the British Museum holds hours of eye-catching artifacts from the world's greatest civilizations, including the Elgin Marbles, the Rosetta Stone, and the Sutton Hoo treasure.

Shakespeare's Globe Theatre

(F) You can catch a Shakespeare play almost every night of the year in London. But standing on a floor of leaves and sawdust in a painstakingly re-created version of the galleried Tudor theater for which he wrote is a special thrill.

Hampton Court Palace

(G) This collection of buildings and gardens so captivated Henry VIII that it became his favorite royal residence. Its Tudor charm, augmented by Wren's touch, and a picturesque upstream Thames location make it a great day out—not even dour Oliver Cromwell, who moved here in 1653, could resist its charms.

Tate Modern

(H) More of an event than the average museum visit, Tate Modern, housed inside a striking 1930s power station, is a hip, immensely successful addition to the London gallery landscape. Passing judgment on the latest controversial temporary exhibit inside the giant turbine hall has become almost a civic duty among art-loving Londoners.

National Gallery

(I) Whatever the collective noun is for a set of old masters—a palette? a canvas?—there are enough here to have the most casual art enthusiast cooing with admiration. When you've finished, enjoy pedestrianized Trafalgar Square on the doorstep of this collection.

London's Central Parks

(J) With London's green spaces so broken up, it seems churlish to pick out only one. The four central parks are all within walking distance: pick St. James's Park for fairy-tale views; Green Park for hillocks and wide boulevards; Regent's Park for its open-air theater and the London Zoo; and Hyde Park for rowing on the Serpentine Lido.

LONDON'S ROYAL LEGACY

Edward the Confessor

(A) Edward (r. 1042–66) came to the throne in 1042 and ordered the construction of the original Westminster Abbey, which was consecrated in 1065, just a week before he died.

William the Conqueror

(B) The Battle of 1066 was won by William (r. 1066–87, House of Normandy) when he shot the then-king Harold through the eye with an arrow at the battle of Hastings. He is credited with starting the building of the White Tower in the Tower of London, though it wasn't completed until after his death.

Henry VIII

(C) A true Renaissance man, Henry (r. 1509–47, House of Tudor) was keen to bring new ideas to the Royal Court. All of Henry's six wives lived at Hampton Court Palace. Henry was desperate for a male heir—the main reason for having two of his wives executed: Anne Boleyn and Catherine Howard.

Queen Mary I

(D) "Bloody Mary" (r. 1553–58, House of Tudor), the Roman Catholic daughter of Henry VIII and his first wife, Catherine of Aragon, persecuted Protestants in an attempt to reverse the Reformation and return England to Catholicism. She imprisoned her half-sister, Elizabeth—daughter of Anne Boleyn—in the Tower, suspecting her of a plot against her, but there was no evidence and Elizabeth came to the throne after her death.

Queen Elizabeth I

(E) The "Virgin Queen" (r. 1558–1603, House of Tudor) never married—perhaps because she thought that any man would try to wrest control from her (though she did move Robert Dudley, Earl of Leicester, into rooms close to her own at Hampton Court). She oversaw and supported a

golden age of playwriting and poetry and famously inspired her troops as they prepared to battle the Spanish Armada.

Charles I

(F) "The Martyr" (r. 1625–49, House of Stuart) is famous for losing the English Civil War, and was beheaded at Banqueting House—a twist of fate as Charles had commissioned the palace to be decorated with paintings showing a monarch being received into heaven.

George III

(G) His frequent bouts of irrational behavior led to the nickname "The Mad One," but George (r. 1760–1820, House of Hanover) is now thought to have suffered from an inherited metabolic illness and often secluded himself at Kew Palace. With the Declaration of Independence in 1776, he lost the American colonies. One of the most cultured monarchs, George donated 65,000 of his books to the British Museum.

Queen Victoria

(H) Famous for the longest reign so far in British history, 63 years, Victoria (r. 1837–1901, House of Hanover) was born in, and spent her childhood at, Kensington Palace, where she learned she would become queen. The Albert memorial is a monument to her beloved husband and the British Empire.

Queen Elizabeth II

(I) The present queen of the United Kingdom and Great Britain and Northern Ireland and Head of the Commonwealth, Elizabeth (r. 1952–present, House of Windsor) is the great-great-granddaughter of Queen Victoria. The Queen lives in Buckingham Palace but also spends time at Windsor Castle, outside the city.

GREAT ITINERARIES

No Time to Spare?

If you're in a hurry, your best bet is to jump on a bus that is heading over the river. You can't beat that combination of classic murky water and the city's skyline.

Crowning Glories

This regal runaround packs more into a day than most cities can offer in a week. Hit Westminster Abbey early to avoid the crowds, then cut through St. James's Park to catch the Changing the Guard at 11:30 AM at Buckingham Palace. (If the palace doors are open, enjoy a peek at royal life.) Take a quick detour to the Tudor delights of St. James's Palace, old haunt of Charles I, before a promenade down the Mall past the Regency glory of Carlton House Terrace and through Admiralty Arch to Trafalgar Square.

■ TIP➜ Get an early start and a hearty breakfast, as this selection of treasures will likely keep you on your feet all day.

After lunch, choose from the canvases of the National Gallery, the Who's Who of the National Portrait Gallery, or a brass rubbing in the crypt of St. Martin-in-the-Fields if the children's interest is flagging. This should leave time for a stately stroll down Whitehall—past Downing Street, Horse Guards Parade, and Banqueting House—to the Houses of Parliament, where you have the option of prebooking a tour or trying to get in to see a debate.

■ TIP➜ Her Majesty's mounted guardsmen make a great photo op—you may even see Prince Harry, a member of the Regiment of the Blues and Royals, responsible for his grandmother's personal protection.

If you have any time or energy left, stroll through Green and Hyde parks to Kensington Palace, home to Queen Victoria in her childhood, and (for aspiring little princesses everywhere) the Royal Ceremonial Dress Collection.

Museum Magic

London has one of the finest collections of museums in the world, and certainly no other comparable city offers so much for free. Many resemble state-of-the-art, hands-on playgrounds; others take a more classical approach. One of the latter is the British Museum in Bloomsbury, an Aladdin's cave of artifacts from across the world that is ideal for either a half- or full-day browse. If you want to bolt on additional visits, pop into the nearby museum of architect Sir John Soane, or the recently refurbished London Transport Museum.

■ TIP➜ The excellent restaurant in the British Museum's Great Court looks down on its library, where Karl Marx would shift uncomfortably, greatly afflicted by boils, as he researched Das Kapital.

Alternatively, South Kensington's "Museum Mile" on Cromwell Road houses the triple whammy of the Victoria & Albert Museum, the Natural History Museum, and the Science Museum, any one of which would make for a substantial half-day's diversion.

Retail Therapy

It's not hard to shop 'til you drop in London's West End. Start with the upscale on New Bond Street to save your frazzled afternoon look for nearby frenetic Oxford Street. Home to (take a deep breath here) Armani, Bulgari, Cartier, Cerruti, Chanel, De Beers, Dolce & Gabbana, Gucci, Jimmy Choo, Prada, Swarovski, Tiffany, and Versace, it's an awesome sweep of expense and elegance.

■ TIP➜ Men should not pass up a chance to browse the shirts and suits on show at nearby Savile Row (famed for its high-

quality tailoring), and accessories on Jermyn Street.

Oxford Street encompasses four Tube stations and is unbeatable for mass-market shopping. Run the gauntlet of high-street designers, cheap odds and ends, department stores, and ferocious pedestrians: it's seriously busy, but you're pretty much guaranteed a buy.

A more sedate but utterly fashionable experience can be found in Knightsbridge, wandering between Harvey Nichols and Harrods department stores. Head south down Sloane Street to Sloane Square and head out along the King's Road, home to boutiques galore and once capital of London's swinging '60s.

■ TIP➜ To catch a glimpse of how to design your home to match your new couture clothes, visit the Conran Shop at 81 Fulham Road, parallel to the King's Road.

To dip into the ever-expanding world of urban chic, try an afternoon in the Portobello street market in Notting Hill, where you can pick up remnants of various bygone ages: glassware, furniture, art, and clothes, from boiler suits to Vietnamese silk dresses. Portobello has wised up to tourist prices in recent years, so a trip out to Spitalfields (covered) market on a Sunday is worth considering, especially for a sample of the East End. For the younger crowd, Camden market still has clubbing wear in spades.

Village People

The easiest village to reach is Hampstead, 20 minutes from the city center by Tube, but a world away in character. It's home to a thriving arts scene, a history of left-wing poets and writers (including John Keats), some of the most gorgeous Georgian houses in London (hence the occasional jibe of "Champagne Socialism"),

and a great range of smart shops, bistros, and French delicatessens.

■ TIP➜ If you're in Hampstead, don't miss the chance to get out onto the Heath, moodier and wilder than many of London's other open spaces.

To the west, leave Richmond behind to get down to the riverside, or head for the vast expanse of the park next door, which breaks all remaining links with city life.

The fantastic views bestowed on Greenwich, southeast of the city center, ensure you never forget how close the city is—and yet this village's nautical past creates an almost seaside feel. The National Maritime Museum and its collection of fine buildings, as well as two very good markets, make it a worthwhile day trip.

To the east, Bethnal Green is a village in the midst of an urban renaissance. Visit the flower market of Columbia Road, the Children's Museum, and the paths along the canal.

■ TIP➜ To appreciate fully how tribal London's villagers can be, try asking which part of the city they come from or live in. The responses you'll get—"Haggerston," "Tufnell Park," "Turnham Green," "Camberwell," "Battersea"—indicate a dizzying array of identities, often consisting only of a few neighboring streets.

THE 2012 OLYMPIC GAMES

After Beijing's mind-boggling display at the 2008 Olympic Games, the baton was passed to London for 2012. London's handover performance at the Beijing Olympics curtain call—featuring a double-decker bus and umbrella-toting commuters—was a typically English affair: slapstick, tongue-in-cheek, and devoid of bombast. Overshadowed by the ambition of Beijing's mesmerising show, some decried its lack of ambition. But it was a confident, offbeat, and fun display that was so very London. The unmistakable message was: come to London and enjoy yourself.

Hotels and Flights

London may have more than 100,000 hotel rooms but you will still need to book your room as far ahead as you can, especially if you want to be near the Olympic Park. Air tickets are also going to be snapped up close to the event.

Getting Around

More than £17 billion has been earmarked for transport development in the run-up to the 2012 Games in this city that sees 20 million trips daily on the transport system. Served by five airports, London already has the world's largest underground system, but pre-Olympics development will see the extension of the East London Line and the Dockland Light Railway, the upgrading and modernization of all underground stations, investment on the Jubilee Line (serving Olympic facilities) to handle extra capacity, and a high-rail link between St Pancras International and Stratford International for the Olympic Park, shuttling spectators to the Games in seven minutes from central London. New cycle and walking lanes are also planned to encourage healthier modes of transportation. London, however, remains one of the most congested cities in Europe, with an average vehicle speed of just under 12 mph.

Buying Tickets

Tickets for the London Olympics 2012 go on sale in 2011 and will generally be available until the start of each event unless sold out. Tickets will include free public transport on the day of the event.

New London?

The 2008 Olympic Games in Beijing further marked the long-heralded shift eastward of the world economic axis. Back in London for the first time since 1948, the Olympic Games return to a nation increasingly at ease with its decreased global stature but just as eager to put on a show. Drawing upon impressive reserves of cosmopolitan verve, creativity, and sheer élan, London aims to host the Olympic Games in striking fashion. While the Beijing Olympics purposefully declared the arrival of a new superpower, the 2012 Olympics will be about showing why London remains one of the world's most-loved and cosmopolitan cities.

The jigsaw-style logo for the London Olympics may have polarised opinion, but the Games have been applauded for their promise to revitalize areas of East London and swing the spotlight of global attention back to town. The Games are also an occasion to showcase some dramatic new architecture. And, Olympic visitors are expected to bring as much as £2.2 billion to the local economy in 2012, fueling the London feel-good factor.

London under Construction

London has focused its Olympic energies on transforming the deprived East London, where the Olympic Park is under construction, but the occasion has been seized upon to overhaul public transport, to showcase some sparkling new

architecture, and to convert some well-known landmarks into Olympic venues.

With the exceptions of Canary Wharf, the Swiss Re Headquarters (the "Gherkin"), the Lloyd's of London building, and the London Eye, London's skyline is typically low-key with little of the brash swagger of, say, Shanghai or Manhattan. But a spectacular crop of new architecture—the 945-foot (288-meter) "Helter-Skelter" Bishopsgate Tower, 740-foot (228-meter) Leadenhall Building "Cheese Grater," and 1,020 foot (310 meters) "Shard of Glass"—is set to inject fresh adrenaline into London's otherwise staid streetscapes and revitalize its skyline.

A curvilinear £303-million piece of eye candy due for completion in 2011, the gorgeous **Aquatics Centre** will be a centerpiece of London's Olympics display. Designed by Iraqi architect Zaha Hadid, the center's wavelike form has been scaled back from original designs, but it remains an impressive and inspirational building.

The **Olympic stadium's** design has divided opinion, with critics making unfavorable comparisons with Beijing's iconic Bird's Nest, but supporters have pointed to the 80,000-capacity stadium's ability to be dismantled as a major plus point.

Olympic Venues

Most big-ticket events will take place in the Olympic Park but some medals will be vied for in more unusual settings, many that are open to the public today.

■ Gymnasts and basketball finalists will be limbering up in the **O2 Arena**, to be temporarily rechristened the **North Greenwich Arena 1**; badminton contestants and rhythmic gymnasts will aim for glory in the North Greenwich Arena 2.

■ The Beach Volleyball competition will be held in **Horse Guard's Parade** in Whitehall, a beach ball's toss from Downing Street and next to St. James's Park.

■ Road Cycling takes to **Regent's Park**. (For great views of the park and Central London head to nearby Primrose Hill.)

■ Football (soccer) matches will kick off in 90-000 seat **Wembley Stadium,** the home of the English National Football team.

■ Triathlon contestants and swimmers in the 10km Open Water event will make a splash in the Serpentine in **Hyde Park.**

■ Lovely **Greenwich Park**—London's oldest Royal Park—is the venue for Equestrian events and Modern Pentathlon.

■ In Woolwich, shooting will be staged at the **Royal Artillery Barracks**, while **Lord's Cricket Ground** will host archery.

■ Tennis can really only be held at one venue—**Wimbledon**—with its famous grass courts, but rowers, canoeists, and kayakers will be heading off to Eton Dorney, near Windsor Castle.

After the Games

Sustainability lies at the heart of the London Olympics, with strong emphasis on mitigating climate change and encouraging healthy living. Plans are in the pipeline to put London's Olympic venues to good use after the games to avoid the usual herd of white elephants. The Olympic Park itself will become a vast urban park—the largest in Europe—with an emphasis on preserving the local environment. Olympics sports facilities are to be converted for the use of sports clubs, and allotment gardens, destroyed during the creation of the Olympic Park, will be restored while the East End will find itself equipped with a fantastic network of transport infrastructure.

FREE (AND ALMOST FREE) THINGS TO DO

The exchange rate may vary, but there's one conversion that'll never change: £0 = $0. Here are our picks for the top free things to do in London.

ART

Many of London's biggest and best cultural attractions are free to enter, and the number of museums offering free entry is staggering. Donations are often more than welcome, and special exhibits usually cost extra.

Major Museums
British Museum
Imperial War Museum
Museum of London
National Gallery
National Maritime Museum, Queen's House, and Royal Observatory
National Portrait Gallery
Natural History Museum
Science Museum
Tate Britain
Tate Modern
Victoria & Albert Museum

Smaller Museums and Galleries
Courtauld Institute Gallery (Permanent Exhibition free on Monday only)
Hogarth's House
Houses of Parliament
Institute of Contemporary Arts (ICA) Gallery
V&A Museum of Childhood
Serpentine Gallery
Saatchi Gallery
Sir John Soane's Museum
Wallace Collection
Whitechapel Art Gallery

CONCERTS

St. Martin-in-the-Fields, St. Stephen Walbrook, and St. James's Church have regular lunchtime concerts, as does St. George Bloomsbury on Sunday, Hyde Park Chapel on Thursday, and St. Giles in the Fields on Friday. There are regular organ recitals at Westminster Abbey.

Of the music colleges, the Royal Academy of Music, the Royal College of Music, the Guildhall, the Trinity College of Music, and the Royal Opera House have regular recitals.

For contemporary ears, the area outside the National Theatre on the South Bank (known as the Djanogly Concert Pitch) reverberates to an eclectic range of music weekdays at 5:45 PM, and on Saturday at 1 PM and 5:45 PM.

You can catch open-mike nights for unsigned acts and singer-songwriters at the River Bar (just south of Tower Bridge) every Wednesday and upcoming jazz stars play a free jam at the Cornerstone, in Covent Garden, every Tuesday. Blues lovers should not miss the legendary John Parry Blues and Rock band jam every Monday at The Globe pub in Hackney. The Palm Tree, in Mile End, is another great East End pub that hosts accomplished local jazz players on weekends, and the Effra, in Brixton, does free jazz most evenings.

FILM, THEATER, AND OPERA

If all seats have been sold, the English National Opera sells standing tickets for the back of the Dress and Upper circles from £10 each. Check at the box office.

Standing-only tickets with obstructed views at the Royal Opera House are between £4 and £14.

"Groundling" standing-only tickets are a traditional way to experience the Globe Theatre from £5.

Sloane Square's Royal Court Theatre, one of the United Kingdom's best venues for new playwriting, has restricted-view, standing-room-only tickets at the downstairs Jerwood Theatre for 10 pence (yes, £0.10), available one hour before the performance.

Prince Charles Cinema in the West End shows weekday movie matinees for £4.

OFFBEAT EXPERIENCES

Go to the Public Record Office in Kew or Islington if you want to track down some ancient branch of the family tree. Even if you don't have any leads, browsing through sheaves of ancient ledgers makes for a fascinating trip down somebody else's memory lane.

London has some of the finest parks in the world, and enjoying them won't cost you a penny. Keen ornithologists can join free bird-watching walks in Hyde Park, and dedicated strollers can take the 7-mi Diana Memorial Walk through Hyde, Green, and St. James's parks.

There are free spectacles throughout the year, but one of the most warmly enjoyed is Guy Fawkes' Night (November 5), when parks throughout the country hold spectacular fireworks displays.

On New Year's Eve thousands of revelers descend on Trafalgar Square and the South Bank to watch more free fireworks. The Underground usually runs for free well into the small hours.

Finally, set aside some time for random wandering. London is a great walking city because so many of its real treasures are untouted: tiny alleyways barely visible on the map, garden squares, churchyards, shop windows, sudden vistas of skyline or park. With comfortable, weatherproof shoes and an umbrella, walking might well become your favorite activity here.

SIGHTSEEING ON THE CHEAP

Join real Londoners on the top deck of a double-decker bus. Routes 9 and 15 also operate shortened Heritage routes on the traditional Routemaster buses. You can use your Oyster card or buy tickets from machines at the bus stops for the following routes:

Bus 11: King's Road, Sloane Square, Victoria Station, Westminster Abbey, Houses of Parliament and Big Ben, Whitehall, Trafalgar Square, the Strand, Fleet Street, and St. Paul's Cathedral.

Bus 12: Bayswater, Marble Arch, Oxford Street, Piccadilly Circus, Trafalgar Square, Horse Guards, Whitehall, Houses of Parliament and Big Ben, Westminster Bridge.

Bus 19: Sloane Square, Knightsbridge, Hyde Park Corner, Green Park, Piccadilly Circus, Shaftsbury Avenue, Oxford Street, Bloomsbury, Islington.

Bus 88: Oxford Circus, Piccadilly Circus, Trafalgar Square, Whitehall, Houses of Parliament and Big Ben, Westminster Abbey, Tate Britain.

MAKING THE MOST OF YOUR POUNDS

England's capital still remains the world's second-most expensive city, but remember that saving can give you a richer experience—you can live like a local if you save like a local.

Although your pocket might feel the pinch, greenbacks can punch above their weight with a few well-chosen tips. Travelers posting on the Travel Talk forums at Fodors.com recommend the following budget-saving tips:

Travel wisely

"The Oyster card is your best bet. You can get the visitor one and use it whenever you come back to London, as they never expire." —genabee6

"To qualify for the 2for1 offers listed at www.daysoutguide.co.uk you must buy a National Rail paper travelcard at any mainline train station. That travelcard will be good for the Tube, Docklands Light Railway, and National Rail trains within the zones covered plus the entire London bus network. Travelcards bought at Tube stations do NOT qualify." —TimS

Thinking with your stomach

"On our first day, we buy some fruit, cheese, crackers, and such, so that we can take something along with us until we're ready to stop for lunch." —Barb_in_Ga

"Other suggestions for lunch include M&S's fantastic food sections. Great sandwiches, fresh baked goods, fruit, even ready-mades that can be heated up elsewhere. The ethnic restaurants, especially in the East End area, Brick Lane, etc., are usually cheaper and very tasty." —nibblette

Save on lodging

"We've rented a centrally located one-bedroom flat for 122 pounds/day, which gives us more space and privacy than a hotel room, at a more reasonable rate. I always rent a flat and it saves me a ton, plus it's nice to wake up and not have to get dressed for your AM cup of coffee or tea and breakfast." —Carrybean

"We intend to rent a flat next time—much more economical. There is more room to relax, and you can save a lot." —Susie50

Sight-see, don't site-spend

"Along with many, many others, www.walks.com does a walk called Legal & Illegal London. The walks guides meet the groups at different Tube stops. They cost £7 and are excellent." —carolyn

"Have just purchased the Historic Royal Palaces family membership, as it gives us free admission to Hampton Court, the Tower, Kew Palace, Kensington and Banqueting House—we will certainly be visiting at least three of those places during our trip, so it seemed like a good deal. Plus, you skip the queues." —needsnow

Shop, but don't drop

"For antiques and collectibles (as well as some more modern creations), Greenwich market is always worth a look." —Jay_G

"The Notting Hill Housing Trust seems to have particularly interesting clothes. Clothes often go to specific, mildly quirky, local charities. There's a store finder at www.charityshops.org.uk." —flanneruk

AFTERNOON TEA

Taking afternoon tea is the height of cool in London right now. From Kate Moss to Cameron Diaz, everyone wants to sit up straight, stick their pinkie out, and sip hot tea in the company of friends and family—and preferably in the warm embrace of an established hotel tea salon.

So, what is afternoon tea, exactly? Well, it means real tea (Earl Grey, English Breakfast, Ceylon, Darjeeling or Assam Indian, or Chinese) brewed in a china pot, and served with china cups and saucers, milk, lemon, and silver spoons, between 3 and 5:30 PM. In particularly grand places, there should be elegant finger foods on a three-tiered silver tea stand: crustless sandwiches on the bottom; fruit scones with Devonshire clotted cream and strawberry jam in the middle; and rich fruitcake, shortbread, patisseries, macaroons, and fancies on top. Tea goers dress up in posh hotels, and conversation (by tradition) avoids politics and religion.

Brown's Hotel. This classic Mayfair townhouse hotel sets the standard at the English Tea Room, where one of London's best-known afternoon teas is served (£35–£48). ⊠ *33 Albermarle St., Mayfair* ☎ *020/7493–6020* ▭ *AE, DC, MC, V* ◔ *Tea weekdays 3–6, weekends 1–6* Ⓤ *Green Park.*

Café at Sotheby's. What could be better than perusing the famous Mayfair auction house before afternoon tea? It's open from 9:30 AM and tends to book up days in advance. Teas are available from £6.50 to £18.75, including toasted tea cakes, scones, and Welsh rarebits. ⊠ *Sotheby's, 34 New Bond St., Mayfair* ☎ *020/7293–5077* ◬ *Reservations essential* ▭ *AE, DC, MC, V* ◔ *Tea weekdays 3–4:45* Ⓤ *Green Park.*

The Dorchester. Amid a maze of marble and gold leaf, afternoon tea in the Promenade is best taken on comfy sofas and to the sound of the resident pianist. Teas are £33.50, £48.50, or £60 for high tea—with light bites like salmon and Cromer crab. Book well ahead. ⊠ *53 Park La.* ☎ *020/7629–8888* ◬ *Reservations essential* ▭ *AE, DC, MC, V* ◔ *Tea daily 2:30 and 4:45* Ⓤ *Hyde Park Corner.*

Fortnum & Mason. Upstairs at the revamped 300-year-old Queen's grocers, three set teas are ceremoniously served: afternoon tea (sandwiches, scones, and cakes: £32), old-fashioned high tea (the traditional nursery meal, with scrambled eggs and salmon: £34), and champagne tea (£42). ⊠ *St. James's Restaurant, 4th fl., 181 Piccadilly, St. James's* ☎ *020/7734–8040* ▭ *AE, DC, MC, V* ◔ *Tea Mon.–Sat. 2–7, Sun. noon–4:30* Ⓤ *Green Park.*

The Ritz. At the Ritz tea is served in the impressive Palm Court, with marble tables and Louis XIV chaises complete with musical accompaniment, giving the last morsel of Edwardian London. Afternoon tea is £37 and champagne tea £48. Reserve two to three months ahead and remember to wear a jacket and tie. ⊠ *150 Piccadilly, St. James's* ☎ *020/7300–2309* ◬ *Reservations essential* ▭ *AE, MC, V* ◔ *Tea daily 11:30, 1:30, 3:30, 5:30, 7:30* Ⓤ *Green Park.*

The Wolsely. This bustling art deco tea salon was inspired by the grand Viennese cafés. Cream teas are well priced at £9.75 or £19.75; you'll find a regularly changing pastry menu. ⊠ *160 Piccadilly, St. James's* ☎ *020/7499–6996* ◬ *Reservations essential* ▭ *AE, DC, MC, V* ◔ *Tea Sun.–Fri. 3:30–6:30, Sat. 3:30–5:30* Ⓤ *Green Park.*

GIVE THE SPORTS SCENE A GO

London will host the 2012 Olympics, but don't expect to see many city inhabitants practicing their javelin throws in Hyde Park.

Sport in the capital comes into its own when it's watched, rather than participated in. You'll most easily witness London's fervent sporting passions in front of a screen in a pub with a pint in hand. And those passions run deep.

If you're lucky enough to score a ticket for a big football match, you'll experience a seething, jeering mass of mockery and rude chants, especially if the opposition happens to be another London team. Amid all the aggression you might also catch a glimpse of why the excitement of English football makes it world sport's hottest media property right now.

And sport does mainly mean football (refer to it as "soccer" at your mortal peril). David Beckham is not alone in being overpaid for kicking a ball around—a generation of footballers live the high life in London, their status somewhere between sporting rock stars and royalty. Cricket, rugby, and tennis briefly impinge on Londoners' sporting horizons at certain times of year, but you're unlikely to see grown men crying at the outcome of matches at Wimbledon, or beating each other up about the Ashes.

Football

The English may not be the very best at football (World Cup winners just once in 1966), but they invented the modern game and the sport is the national obsession. A self-deprecating expectation of failure accompanies the national team's performances, although current squad manager Fabio Capell has injected a new sense of purpose. Some of London's five Premier League football teams are very successful although they rely heavily on non-English players.

It's unlikely you'll be able to get tickets for anything except the least popular Premier League games during the August–May season, despite absurdly high ticket prices (as much as £50 for a standard seat). Lower down football's hierarchical ladder, you'll have a much better chance of seeing a match. If you're engaging the locals in sporting conversation, though, it's imperative to know something about the big teams.

Arsenal is historically London's most successful club, and under the managerial reign of Arsene Wenger they have shed their boring image to become proponents of attractive, free-flowing football while hardly ever employing any English players. ✉ *Emirates Stadium, Dayton Park, London* ☎ *020/7704–4040* ⊕ *www. arsenal.com* Ⓤ *Arsenal.*

Chief rivals to Manchester United in the Premier League, Champions League finalists (2007) **Chelsea** is owned by one of Russia's richest men, who has brought in a bevy of strong players and set his sights on the top spot in the league. ✉ *Stamford Bridge, Fulham Rd., Fulham* ☎ *0871/984–1905* ⊕ *www.chelseafc.com* Ⓤ *Fulham Broadway.*

Tottenham Hotspur, or "Spurs," bitter North London rival of Arsenal, has underperformed for many years, but there are signs of a revival. ✉ *White Hart La., 748 High Rd., Tottenham* ☎ *0844/499–5000* ⊕ *www.tottenhamhotspur.com* Ⓤ *National Rail: White Hart La.*

West Ham, despite the name, is the team of the East End. After a long period of failing to match their past success, the Hammers have created a more consistent team, but one unlikely to claim too many trophies.

✉ *Boleyn Ground, Green St., Upton Park* ☎ *0871/222–2700* ⊕ *www.whufc.com* Ⓤ *Upton Park.*

Cricket

Nominally still the nation's summer sport, cricket has suffered from an unwillingness to drop its stuffy, upper-class traditions. Nevertheless, when the Australians come to play for the Ashes, everyone in the city rediscovers their interest in the game. Postcolonial tensions continue to fester under the surface of the games.

At its best, cricket can be a slow-build of smoldering tension and excitement. At its worst, though, it can be unbearably tedious, as five-day games crawl toward a draw, or as the English weather interferes and rain stops play.

Lord's has been hallowed cricketing turf since 1811. Tickets are hard to come by: obtain an application form and enter the ballot (lottery) to purchase tickets. Forms are sent out in early December or you can apply online. Test Match tickets cost between £25 and £95. County matches (Middlesex plays here) can usually be seen by standing in line on match day. ✉ *St. John's Wood Rd., St. John's Wood* ☎ *020/7432–1000* ⊕ *www.lords.org* Ⓤ *St. John's Wood.*

Horse Racing

The main events of "the Season," as much social as sporting, occur just outside the city.

The Queen attends **Royal Ascot** (✉ *Grand Stand, Ascot, Berkshire* ☎ *0870/727–1234* ⊕ *www.ascot.co.uk*) in mid-June, driving from Windsor in an open carriage for a procession before the plebs. Grandstand tickets, which go on sale in November, cost £56–£66, although some tickets can usually be bought on the day of the race

(generally on Tuesday or Wednesday) for £16. The real spectacle is the crowd itself, and those who arrive dressed inappropriately (jeans, shorts, sneakers) will be turned away from their grandstand seats.

Derby Day (✉ *The Grandstand, Epsom Downs, Surrey* ☎ *0844/579–3004* ⊕ *www. epsomderby.co.uk*), usually held on the first Saturday in June, is the second-biggest social event of the racing calendar. It's also one of the world's greatest horse races, first run in 1780. Tickets are between £20 and £100.

Tennis

The **Wimbledon Lawn Tennis Championships** are famous for the green grass of Centre Court and an old-fashioned insistence on players wearing white. Rain, a perennial hazard even in the last-week-of-June-first-week-of-July timing, has been banished on Centre Court by the addition of a retractable roof. Whether you can get grandstand tickets is literally down to the luck of the draw, because there's a ballot system (lottery) for advance purchase. For more information, see their Web site.

You can also buy entry to roam matches on the outside courts, where even the top-seeded players compete early. Get to Southfields or Wimbledon Tube station as early as possible and get in line. Five hundred show court tickets are also sold, but these usually go to those prepared to stand in line all night. ✉ *Ticket Office, All England Lawn Tennis & Croquet Club, Box 98, Church Rd., Wimbledon* ☎ *020/8944–1066* ⊕ *www.wimbledon.org.*

LONDON LIKE A LOCAL

Those unforgettable London moments usually aren't found in picture-postcard settings like Trafalgar Square, but in far more prosaic locations: at the bar of a friendly pub, amid the clutter of an antiques shop, on a park bench in a smart residential garden, or in a centuries-old church beneath the glass-and-steel towers of The City.

Wander About a Market

London's markets are perfect for an aimless Sunday morning potter, along with locals who aren't quite sure what they're doing there either. The most fun is Portobello, full of great clothes and jewelry from local designers, and plenty of cafés and pubs to drop into along the way.

Discover Pub Culture

Although fashionable coffee shops now dot every street, it's still the pub that Londoners are drawn to the minute the working day finishes. Don't get sucked into the big chains, such as Pitcher and Piano or All Bar One—head instead for the ones with kooky names straight out of a Monty Python sketch. Scuffed carpets, dartboards, and old chaps propping up the bar are all essential.

Go to Any Football Match

London doesn't get much more authentic than a 30,000-strong stadium on match day. In these emotional pressure cookers, thousands of fans come to drink, swear, sing, and live every moment of their team's fortunes. Lower-division games (Barnet, Brentford, Charlton Athletic, Crystal Palace, Millwall, Leyton Orient, or Queens Park Rangers) will be less heavily subscribed and cheaper to watch.

Eat at a Greasy Spoon

The fatty delights of a classic London caff are best sampled after a night's excessive partying. A classic "full English" breakfast will consist of fried bacon, sausage, egg, tomatoes, and mushrooms—and, for the adventurous, black pudding, washed down with a mug of strong tea. Take a selection of red-top tabloid newspapers to peruse for the full effect.

Take a Night Bus Home

Like the street sweepers they overtake, these buses pick up the living leftovers of a thousand different nights out in the capital. Sometimes there are so many stops that it seems it will be dawn before you get to where you want to go, but the endless procession of passengers (and the speed and humor of their banter) is what makes the trip interesting.

Visit a Park

When Londoners need to escape the city, they head for its green spaces. And these will further increase after the 2012 Olympics when the Olympic Park can be included as well. Sometimes it's to read the papers; other times to feed the ducks or play football. The parks boast an incredible range of free events, from music festivals to bird-watching. Favorites include Hyde Park in the west, Regent's Park in the north, Brockwell Park in the south, and Victoria Park in the east.

Party in Hoxton

This neighborhood is no longer the ultra-hip brother-in-charms to Manhattan's Lower East Side that it once was, but maybe it's for the better. Nowadays, the mullet-headed fashionistas and art school dropouts accommodate angular City slickers in the most predictable destination for a guaranteed good night out. Round off your night, or get it going, with a hearty curry on nearby Brick Lane, home to London's Bangladeshi community.

LONDON WITH KIDS

Education Without Yawns

Natural History Museum. It doesn't get much more awe-inspiring than bloodsucking bats, fake earthquakes, and a life-size blue whale. Just make sure you know your diplodocus from your dodo.

Regent's Park Zoo. City? What city? Disappear into the animal kingdom among the enclosures, complete with sessions for kids afraid of spiders (even bird-eating ones!).

Tower of London. Perfect for playing princess in front of the crown jewels. Not so perfect for imagining what becomes of the fairy tale—watch your royal necks.

Science Museum. Special effects, virtual voyages, and interactive galleries: delving into mankind's scientific achievement has never been more hands-on or fun.

V&A Museum. Decorative arts might sound a bit too sophisticated, but weekends at the museum are all set up for children under 12, with fun backpack adventures and design events.

London Dungeon. Gore galore plunges you into murky depths of history, with gruesome rides and special effects scary enough to frighten the coolest of cats.

Performances

Applaud street performers. You can't beat the cacophony of jugglers, fire-eaters, unicyclists, and the human statues tantalizing crowds in Covent Garden.

Enjoy Regent's Park Open Air Theatre. Welcome to the land of fairy dust and magic. Don't miss an evening performance under the stars of *A Midsummer Night's Dream* in summer.

Watch films in 3-D. So they just want to watch television? Blow their minds with the IMAX cinema, Britain's largest screen, which plays fantastical 3-D films to audiences bespectacled in green-and-red glasses.

Sing along to musicals. Move over, Broadway: you can't beat a song and dance number from London's West End.

Activities

Ride the London Eye. Ferris wheel–loving kids will think they've hit the mother lode when they see Europe's biggest observation wheel.

Climb Monument. Those 311 steps up London's tribute to the Great Fire of 1666 are perfect for tiring out hyperactive kids, and the panorama from the top is well worth the climb.

Clamber on the lions. Challenge your child to pick a perch in Trafalgar Square, the capital's tourist hot spot, and climb one of the four tall stone lions at the foot of Nelson's column.

Cruise the Thames. The view from the river puts an entirely different perspective on the city.

Paddle on the Serpentine. Pack a picnic and take a rowboat out into the middle of Hyde Park's famed lake; settle back, and tuck in to lunch.

Lose your kids at Hampton Court. It might be more than 300 years old, but the quest to reach the middle of the world-famous hedge maze remains as challenging as ever.

HISTORICAL PUB WALK

The best way to see London is on foot—and the walk below features some lovely old pubs with a story all their own on both sides of the Thames. If one of the establishments takes your fancy, settle back with a pint and drink in the history.

The South Bank

Just as Chaucer's Canterbury Tales pilgrims did, we start in Southwark. Head west along Borough High Street to the galleried **George Inn**. Mentioned in Dickens's *Little Dorrit*, there has been an inn (where Will Shakespeare drank) here since the 16th century. Back toward London Bridge, wander through **Borough Market**. The sights are packed in here, as you pass **Southwark Cathedral** on your right, the **Golden Hinde** replica, and the **Clink Prison** museum on your way to the **Anchor**. Although it was updated in 2008, it dates from 1775 and is thought to be where writer Samuel Pepys stood as he observed the 1666 fire of London, which he called "a most horrid malicious bloody flame."

Across the Thames

Head over **Southwark Bridge**—with **St. Paul's Cathedral** in your sights—to The City with its financial centers and maze of streets. **Ye Olde Watling** was originally built just before the great fire, and it was destroyed within days. Rebuilt around 1668, again in 1901, and then again in 1947 after the Blitz, it is named after a Roman road, on which it stands.

Down toward Blackfriars Bridge, pass the **College of Arms**, where you can register your heraldic coat of arms. Continue on to the exquisite **Black Friar**. The 19th-century pub's Arts and Crafts interior was remodeled in 1905: the sculptures, mosaics, and metal reliefs all allude to the friars who once lived here.

Head up Blackfriars Lane to the "haunted" **Viaduct Tavern**. Cells in the basement reputedly part of the long-since-demolished Newgate Gaol (where the **Old Bailey Criminal Court** opposite now stands).

Bloomsbury

Walk over Holborn Viaduct into this scholarly neighborhood to **Ye Olde Mitre**, hidden in an alley at the side of Hatton Gardens, dating from 1547 and rebuilt around 1772. A stone mitre from the Bishop of Ely's palace gatehouse is built into one of the walls, and there is also the preserved trunk of a cherry tree that Elizabeth I supposedly danced around.

Turn up Fulwood Place, and if it's open (before 2:30) cut through **Gray's Inn Field**, near legal London's barristers at the Inns of the Court, to the **Lamb**. This Victorian pub, near **Dickens House Museum** and rumored to be one of the author's haunts, has plenty of original fittings, including privacy (or "snob") screens that customers pivot open or closed. Head west along Great Ormond Street to the **Queen's Larder**. When George III was being treated by a doctor who lived in this square, his wife, Queen Charlotte, reputedly rented out the cellar and prepared his meals for him in the 1770s. Just north is the Russell Square tube stop, or you can continue on to the **British Museum** for culture of a different kind.

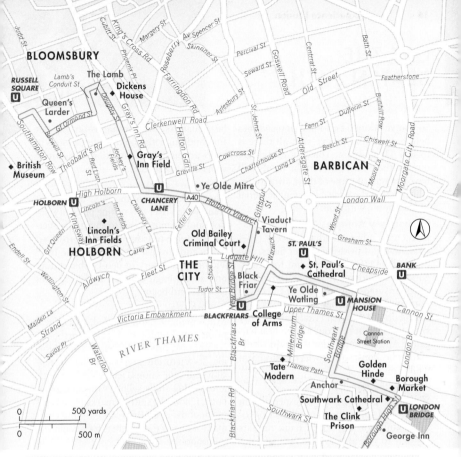

Where to Start:	On the South Bank at the London Bridge Tube/rail station.
Length:	4 mi (about 1.5 hours without stopping). Just part of this walk will give you a taste of the oldest part of London.
Where to Stop:	Russell Square Tube Stations, near the British Museum.
Best Time to Go:	Weekday mornings or afternoons. (Most pubs open late in the morning.)
Worst Time to Go:	Busy summer weekends may be too crowded.
Eating and Drinking:	All the pubs will serve food at lunchtime. Stop when you're hungry or pick up some tasty morsels in Borough Market and stop in either Gray's Inn Fields or Lincoln's Inn Fields for a picnic.
Diversions:	After a pint in The City, consider heading back across the Thames on the Millennium Bridge for an artistic interlude at the Tate Modern. If your legs are sagging from a combination of ale and pavement-stomping, relax on the lawn of Lincoln's Inn Fields, London's largest public square.
Pub Highlights:	The Anchor, Black Friar, George Inn, The Lamb, Queen's Larder, Ye Olde Watling, Ye Olde Mitre

OFF THE BEATEN PATH

So you've "done" London umpteen times before and think you've seen all there is to see? Think again. You just need to get outside the box. Not even the locals will have thought of some of these attractions, which makes them ideal bragging material to take home with you.

Bermondsey Antiques Market

If you want a brush with the cheeky types straight out of British gangster flicks, pop down to this former paradise for stolen goods. An old royal license (now canceled) ensured that stuff bought here did not have to be returned. Small stalls start setting up at 4 AM each Friday; arrive early with a flashlight to scout for the best bargains. An ominous redevelopment of the market beckons, so enjoy its raffish charm while you can.

Reclaim the Beach

When the tides are right, especially in spring and autumn, a small section of the Thames on the South Bank retreats enough to reveal a tiny stretch of sand beach. Cue a *Baywatch*-style celebration, complete with barbecues, music, dancing, and conversation with strangers. Don't forget to bring your own beer.

Smithfields Meat Market

If you're suffering from a little transatlantic jet lag, a visit to London's last remaining meat market, running until dawn on the edge of The City, provides a welcome late-night diversion. It's one of the few places you can see old-fashioned tradesmen at work, buying, selling, and packing all kinds of meat and offal. Nearby pubs have early-morning licenses and, naturally, serve some great cuts of meat.

Vauxhall City Farm

You have probably heard of the London Zoo: this inner-city farm, hidden away just south of the river behind Britain's spy headquarters, offers a hands-on day out for children, with donkey rides, lessons in pony grooming, and milking demonstrations all available.

Highgate Cemetery

The timeless gaze of the stone angels that stand watch over this resting place of London souls is impossible to shrug off. Everlasting home to Communist theorist Karl Marx and novelist George Eliot, the 1839 Victorian cemetery of neo-Gothic statues and sarcophagi, covered by ivy, evokes sadness and beauty.

Brixton Life

Much maligned and avoided, and a focal point of London's African-Caribbean community, Brixton is well worth exploring. Its Victorian streets offer hair-extension and nail salons, jerk chicken joints, and market stalls selling yams and plantains. Ignore the sniffy remarks from types north of the river; Brixton's bars and clubs make it one of the best bets for a night out in London.

Watch a Trial

If you came to London for spectacle, take a trip to a trial at the Old Bailey, the famed criminal court. Stories more twisted and compelling than anything on screen, strange costumes and wigs, command performances—it's true drama, without the West End ticket prices.

Brave a Burlesque

If you find yourself in London but hanker after 1930s Berlin, then the Kit Kat Club–style decadence of burlesque might quench your thirst. It's a risqué combination of cabaret, striptease, and music, definitely for adults only. Try the Tassel Club or Burlesque Bazaar to start.

Millennium Bridge and St. Paul's Cathedral.

THE BUILDING OF LONDON

The past is knit into the very fabric of the lives of Londoners: they live in Regency townhouses, worship in Baroque churches, and chill out in Edwardian-era parks. Unfolding like a gigantic historical pop-up book, London reveals—building by building—the pageant of a nation's history. To make sense of it all, here's a quick architectural tour through time.

Despite invading tribes, an epic fire, and 20th-century bombing, London has always survived, and a surprising amount of yesterday remains visible in its streets today. Starting with remnants of Londinium, the early Roman city contained by a defensive wall some 2,000 years ago, you can trace the city's beginnings. Only pieces of the wall remain, but the name of each entrance to the city has been preserved: Aldgate, Newgate, Bishopsgate, Cripplegate, Aldersgate, and Ludgate.

As commerce grew the city over the centuries, London expanded between two centers of power, Westminster in the west and the Tower in the east. Following both the Great Fire and World War II destruction, the need to rebuild outweighed the desire for sensible street layouts, and often any aesthetic considerations. In fact, London as a whole has rarely been planned, and the financial center is still roughly in the shape of that original Roman wall. London's haphazard streets and alleys are filled with diverse architectural styles side-by-side, each representing a piece of the city's history.

by Janice Fuscoe

TIMELINE

| 56, 64 BC Julius Caesar arrives on Britain's shores | 43 AD–410 AD Roman rule | 61 AD Boudicca attacks and destroys Londinium | | | 600s Anglo-Saxon Lundenwic settlement in Covent Garden area |

| 0 | 250 | 500 | 750 |

(top left) Statue of the Roman Emperor Trajan (r. AD 98–117) outside the largest remaining section of the Roman wall at Tower Hill. (right) Tower of London; (left) Carausius coin struck circa 288–290 AD at the Londinium mint.

Roman Londinium

Pre-410

As the Roman Empire expanded, Britain was conquered and the first city where London now stands began to develop along the Thames. Among many building projects, the Romans enclosed Londinium with a wall to protect against invading tribes after the Celtic warrior queen Boudicca razed the city. Today chunks of the ancient barrier remain in the City, and at the Guildhall art gallery you can see a partial Roman amphitheatre from this time.

■ Visit: Guildhall (Ch. 6), London Wall at Tower Hill Tube station (Ch. 6), Museum of London (Ch. 5)

Saxon and Medieval London

410–1485

Little is known of the 250 years after the Romans left London. Following these "Dark Ages," most medieval houses and bridges were built of timber or wattle and daub and the perishable materials didn't last in the changing city.

England's royalty began building heavily in the capital as a sign of strength and power, focusing on defensive structures. In 1042, the Saxon King Edward the Confessor moved his court and began a church on the site of the current Westminster Abbey, where almost all the monarchs of England have been crowned since. From across the English Channel, William the Conqueror brought Norman architectural styles with him. William built the White Tower; later expanded, the solid castle became the heart of the Tower of London complex. His son and heir William II saw the construction of Westminster Hall, the oldest part of the Palace of Westminster (today's Houses of Parliament). St. Bartholomew's Hospital, founded in 1123, and the Guildhall, a center of commerce from the early 15th century, are among the few buildings that survived the later Great Fire.

■ Visit: Guildhall (Ch. 6), St. Bartholomew's Hospital (Ch. 6), Tower of London (Ch. 6)

1066 William the Conqueror becomes King of England	1240 Parliament sits at Westminster for the first time 1215 Magna Carta	1348 The Black Death	1605 Guy Fawkes's Gunpowder Plot uncovered 1534 Dissolution of the Monasteries	1642–51 Civil War 1666 Great Fire
1000	**1250**		**1500**	**1750**

1

IN FOCUS THE BUILDING OF LONDON

(top left) Painted ceiling of Banqueting House by Peter Paul Rubens; (top right) *The Great Fire of London, with Ludgate and old St Paul's;* (bottom right) St. Paul's Cathedral, built 1675–1708, designed by Christopher Wren

Tudor and Stuart London

1485–1700

As London grew, the Tudor royals influenced the architecture of London not only by creating, but also by destroying. Henry VII continued the expansion of Westminster Abbey and his successor, Henry VIII, resided at Hampton Court. The arts flourished under Elizabeth I, and the original Globe Theatre was built in 1599. Yet many fine medieval churches were torn down as England separated from the Roman Catholic Church.

Architects brought continental ideas to London, notably the influential Italian Palladian style introduced by Inigo Jones. You can see this classical style with it's mathematical proportions and balanced lines at the Queen's House in Greenwich and at Banqueting House, where Charles I was executed following the civil war. Eleven years later, Charles II was restored to the throne, returning from exile in France.

The Great Fire of 1666 destroyed five-sixths of London, but it also wiped out the plague that had ravaged the impoverished and overcrowded population the year before. Sir Christopher Wren was given the Herculean charge of rebuilding London. He wanted to map out a more organized grid for the city, but it was rebuilt on the old haphazard lines. It took Wren 35 years to build his baroque masterpiece, St. Paul's Cathedral. Wren also designed 50 other churches (only 23 still stand, including St. Bride's and St. Stephen Walbrook) and Monument to commemorate the fire. Nicholas Hawksmoor assisted Wren and designed his own highly original churches including the splendid Christ Church in Spitalfields.

■ Visit: Banqueting House (Ch. 2), Christ Church, Spitalfields (Ch. 7), Queen's House, Greenwich (Ch. 12), St. Bride's (Ch. 6), St. Paul's Cathedral (Ch. 6), St. Stephen Walbrook (Ch. 6)

| 1721–42 Robert Walpole, serves as first Prime Minister | 1776 Declaration of American Independence | 1795–1815 Napoleonic Wars | 1837 Queen Victoria comes to the throne |

| 1750 | 1780 | 1810 | 1840 |

(top left) Courtyard of Neo-classical Somerset House, built for George III. (right) The Rotunda of the Victoria and Albert (V&A) Museum with modern Chihuly sculpture; (bottom left) St Martin-in-the-Fields on Trafalgar Square.

Georgian Era

1700–1836

By the beginning of the 18th century, London was the biggest city in Europe and a center of world trade. This growth led to changes in politics, as power moved to a parliamentary system. Increased wealth led to an explosion of art and architecture.

Many different styles flourished—rococo, neo-classical, regency, and gothic revival. The predominant neo-classical, based on the styles of ancient Greece, can be seen in many stately homes. You can admire the elegant Regency terraces around John Nash's Regent's Park.

■ Visit: Regent's Park (Ch. 11), Somerset House (Ch. 4), St. Martin-in-the-Fields (Ch. 2)

Victorian Age

1837–1901

Queen Victoria ruled the British Empire for 63 years. London experienced the growth of wealth, industrialization, and philanthropy; this was also a period of desperate poverty, as depicted in Charles Dickens's novels. At the start of the 19th century the population of the city was over a million; by the end of Victoria's reign it was six million.

This rapid growth required many building programs, from worker housing to even bigger projects such as the bridges, government buildings, and the first subway system in the world. Businessmen, artists, and architects helped create many institutions that still exist

today from the Tate Britain to the Ragged Schools and Foundling hospitals.

The clean, classical lines of the previous era gave way to more elaborate styles—which were considered more "English"—such as the Gothic Revival Houses of Parliament. Other Victorian projects included covered markets, canal locks, arcades, palaces, memorials, museums, theaters, and parks. So much building took place during this period that it's hard to miss the style: look for elaborate, highly decorated architecture.

■ Visit: Burlington Arcade (Ch. 3), Houses of Parliament (Ch. 2), Leadenhall Market in The City (Ch. 6), V&A and Natural History Museum (Ch. 9)

1851 Great Exhibition held in Hyde Park	1901 Death of Queen Victoria	1939–1945 WWII	1951 Festival of Britain
1863 Underground opens		1914–1918 WWI	
1870	1900	1930	1960

1

IN FOCUS THE BUILDING OF LONDON

(left) Theatregoers at The National Theatre on the South Bank of the Thames River; (right) Tower block at Barbican Centre, a 1980s complex of art venues and apartments.

20th-century building

1901–1979

The turn of the 20th century saw wealthy Westminster widening its streets to accommodate the arrival of motor cars and department stores. Even after the First World War, a "live for today" attitude continued among the upper classes, while the poorest Londoners suffered increasing prices and low wages. While modernism—a cultural movement embracing the future and rejecting anything associated with the past—was gathering pace in 1920s Europe, conservative British architecture continued to hark back to traditional influences of ancient Greece and the middle ages.

The WWII devastation of the Blitz bombings changed this and an enormous amount of post-war building was needed quickly. Émigrés such as Hungarian Ernö Goldfinger and Russian-born Berthold Lubetkin brought the modernist architectural movement to London with their high-rise buildings—a solution to the desperate housing shortage. One of the most exciting post-war projects was the 1951 Festival of Britain, celebrating the great inventions of the century. Out of a host of new architecture at the South Bank for this event, only the Royal Festival Hall remains.

Mass-produced concrete, steel, and glass ushered in the brutalist style in the '60s. This outgrowth of modernism can be seen in the Hayward Gallery and National Theatre. It was not a popular style, partly because the use of raw concrete—pioneered in the sunny south of France—looked gray, ugly, and even sinister against the backdrop of wet and windy London.

London's powers-that-be haven't always embraced modernist architecture, and many examples have been torn down. Today some iconic buildings are protected and the massive concrete Barbican Centre finally brought modernism right into the conservative City.

■ Visit: The Barbican Centre (Ch. 6), Hayward Gallery (Ch. 8), National Theatre (Ch. 8), Royal Festival Hall (Ch. 8)

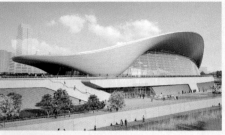

(left) Lloyd's of London by the Richard Rogers Partnership, completed in 1986. (top right) Current design of the London Aquatics Centre by Zaha Hadid. (bottom right) The 2000 Great Court at the British Museum by Sir Norman Foster.

Modern and Millennium London

1980–Present

While the sun may have set on the British empire, London remains a global city, perhaps more now than ever before. The '80s saw changes in economic policy and ambitious building projects, including the Jubilee Line extension to the Underground system. Great business and banking centers reached higher into the sky as London's importance in financial markets increased. London's disused Docklands area got a revitalizing boost with the Canary Wharf development and the DLR (Docklands Light Railway).

Internationally-known architects began to make their mark on the city with creative projects. Known as Tower 42, the NatWest Tower opened in 1980 as the tallest skyscraper in the city—for a great view, head to its bar on the 42nd floor. The Richard Rogers Partnership designed the fabulous 1986 Lloyd's of London building. Sir Norman Foster and his associates have designed the Sackler Galleries at the Royal Academy of Arts, the British Museum's Great Court, City Hall, and the Swiss Re Headquarters (known as the Gherkin).

Building projects to celebrate the Millennium are now so beloved it's hard to imagine London without the pedestrian-only Millennium Bridge and the London Eye.

The "Helter Skelter" Bishopsgate Tower is to be completed in 2012, followed by the Richard Rogers Partnership's "Cheese Grater." Beijing's Olympic Games are a tough act to follow, but the eyes of the world will be on London as the 2012 host city. Everyone's waiting for the curvaceous Aquatics Center designed by world-renowned Zaha Hadid and the 1,016-foot "Shard" designed by Italian Renzo Piano—it will be the tallest building in the EU by 2012; but for future buildings... the sky's the limit.

■ Visit: Canary Wharf (Ch. 12), Lloyd's of London (Ch. 6), Swiss Re (Ch. 6)

Westminster and Royal London

WORD OF MOUTH

"I really, really recommend taking a verger's tour at Westminster Abbey—our guide really made history come alive. If you get to the Abbey when it opens, just sign up for the first tour of the day or you can sign up in advance the previous day."

—azzure

GETTING ORIENTED

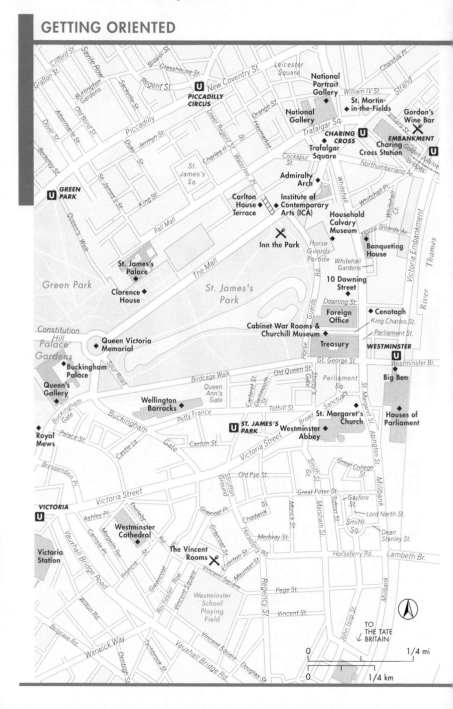

2

Trafalgar Square—easy to access and smack-dab in the center of the action—is a good place to start. Take the Tube to Embankment (Northern, Bakerloo, District, and Circle lines) and walk north until you cross the Strand, or alight at the Charing Cross (Bakerloo and Northern lines) Northumberland Avenue exit. Buses are another great option, as almost all roads lead to Trafalgar Square, which also features on both Routemaster heritage routes London's classic double-deckers.

TOP REASONS TO GO

National Gallery: Visit the outstanding collection of masterpieces, then take in London's historic public gathering place, Trafalgar Square.

Cabinet War Rooms and Churchill Museum: Listen to Churchill's wartime radio addresses to the British people from this cavernous underground wartime hideout.

Changing the Guard: Keep pace with the marching soldiers and bands, resplendent in red and black, as they enact this time-honored ceremony.

Westminster Abbey: Redolent with history, this beautiful Gothic church has been the site of 38 coronations, starting with William the Conqueror in 1066.

Hearing Big Ben: Let its surprisingly familiar chimes waft down as you stroll along the Embankment.

MAKING THE MOST OF YOUR TIME

You could spend a lifetime absorbing the rich history of this part of London. More practically, try to set aside at least two days if you want to dip into the full gamut of attractions without feeling horribly rushed. If Royal London is what you want, make a day of Buckingham Palace or Westminster Abbey, the Queen's Gallery, and the Guards Museum at Wellington Barracks. If you have a more constitutional bent, visit the Houses of Parliament and the Cabinet War Rooms.

FEELING PECKISH?

Gordon's Wine Bar (✉ *47 Villiers St.* ☎ *020/7930–1408* ⊕ *www.gordonswinebar.com*), the oldest in London, is hidden belowground among vaulted brick arches and bathed in candlelight. A range of bottles will suit any budget, and buffet food includes excellent beef. Take your glass outside if the weather's good.

There's great food and drink all year at **Inn the Park** (✉ *St. James's Park* ☎ *020/7451–9999* ⊕ *www.innthepark.com*) and the outdoor pinewood deck makes for fantastic people-watching in the summer.

Or for something different try the **Vincent Rooms** (✉ *Vincent Sq.* ☎ *020/7802–8391* ⊕ *www.westking.ac.uk/vincent/vincent.asp*), the kitchen of a top catering college where tomorrow's hot chefs hone their signature dishes at bargain prices and the menu changes daily.

NEAREST PUBLIC RESTROOMS

If you get caught short in Westminster Abbey, there are paid loos (50p) across the street at the bottom of Victoria Street. Banqueting House and the Queen's Gallery have some of the quietest, most dashing restrooms in London.

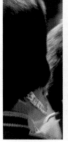

Sightseeing
★★★★★
Nightlife
★★
Dining
★★★
Lodging
★
Shopping
★★

This is postcard London at its best. Crammed with historic churches, grand state buildings, and major art collections, the area unites politics, high culture, and religion. (Oh, and the Queen lives here, too.) World-class monuments such as Buckingham Palace, the Houses of Parliament, Westminster Abbey, and the National Gallery sit alongside lesser-known but lovingly curated museums redolent of British history. If you have time to visit only one part of London, this is it.

Updated by Michelle Rosenberg

Royal London's basic layout can be divided into three distinct areas—Buckingham Palace, Whitehall, and Trafalgar Square—grouped at the corners of triangular St. James's Park.

Trafalgar Square is the official center of London. To its north are two major museums, the **National Gallery** and the **National Portrait Gallery**. From Trafalgar Square two boulevards lead to the seats of very different ideas of governance: **Whitehall** leads to the **Houses of Parliament**, whereas **The Mall**, a wide, pink avenue beyond the stone curtain of **Admiralty Arch**, heads toward the **Queen Victoria Memorial** and **Buckingham Palace**, the sovereign's official residence. Halfway down Whitehall, the Queen's Life Guards sit motionlessly on horses in front of Horse Guards Parade, adjacent to the glorious Banqueting House.

No. 10 Downing Street, diagonally opposite, is home to both the residence and the office of the prime minister. One of the most celebrated occupants, Winston Churchill, is commemorated in the **Cabinet War Rooms & Churchill Museum**, his underground wartime headquarters off Whitehall. Just down the road is the **Cenotaph**, which acts as a focal point for the annual remembrance of those lost in war, and at the end of Whitehall you'll find Parliament Square and the neo-Gothic **Houses of Parliament**, where members of both Houses (Commons and Lords) hold debates and vote on pending legislation.

On Parliament Square's west side is **Westminster Abbey**, a site of daily worship since the 10th century. Poets, political leaders, and 17 monarchs

A BRIEF HISTORY OF WESTMINSTER

The Romans may have gunned for the City, but England's royals went for Westminster. London's future home of democracy started out as Edward the Confessor's palace, when he moved his cramped court west in the 11th century. He founded Westminster Abbey in 1050, where every British monarch has been crowned since. Under the Normans, the palace of Westminster was an elaborate and French-speaking affair. The politicos finally got their hands on it in 1529 (when Henry VII and his court shifted up to the roomier Whitehall Palace), but nearly lost it forever with the Gunpowder Plot of 1605, when Catholic militants attempted to blow the prototypical Parliament to smithereens.

Inigo Jones's magnificent Banqueting House is the only surviving building of Whitehall Palace, and was the setting for the 1649 beheading of Charles I. The Westminster we see today took shape during the Georgian and Victorian periods, as Britain reached the zenith of its imperial power. Grand architecture sprang up, and Buckingham Palace became the principal royal residence in 1837, when Victoria acceded to the throne. Trafalgar Square and Nelson's Column were built in 1843, to commemorate Britain's most famous naval victory, and the Houses of Parliament were rebuilt in 1858 in the trendy neo-Gothic style of the time. The illustrious Clarence House, built in 1825 for the Duke of Clarence (later William IV), is now the home of Prince Charles and Camilla Parker Bowles, Duchess of Cornwall.

are buried in the 13th-century Gothic building. In its shadow is the 16th-century **St. Margaret's Church,** Parliament's "parish church." Heading west along **Birdcage Walk** will bring you to **Buckingham Palace.** The building is open to the public only in summer, but you can see much of the royal art collection in the Queen's Gallery and spectacular ceremonial coaches in the **Royal Mews,** both open all year. Finally, farther south toward Pimlico, **Tate Britain** focuses on prominent British artists from 1500 to today.

TOP ATTRACTIONS

Banqueting House. Built on the site of the original Tudor Palace of Whitehall, which was (according to one foreign visitor) "ill-built, and nothing but a heap of houses," James I commissioned Inigo Jones, one of England's great architects, to undertake a grand building. Influenced during a sojourn in Italy by Andrea Palladio's work, Jones brought Palladian sophistication and purity back to London with him. The resulting graceful and disciplined classical style of Banqueting House, completed in 1622, must have stunned its early occupants. In the quiet vaults beneath, James would escape the stresses of being a sovereign with a glass or two. His son Charles I enhanced the interior by employing the Flemish painter Peter Paul Rubens to glorify his father and the Stuart dynasty in vibrant painted ceiling panels. As it turned out, these allegorical paintings, depicting a wise monarch being received into heaven, were the last thing Charles saw before he was beheaded by Cromwell's Parliamentarians in 1649. But his son Charles II, was able to celebrate the restoration of the monarchy in this same place 20 years later. Banqueting House is also the setting for lunchtime classical concerts, held 1–2 PM. Call, or check the Web site for details. ⊠ *Whitehall, Westminster* ☎ *020/3166–6154 or 020/3166–6155, 020/3166–6153 concert information* ⊕ *www.hrp.org. uk* ✉ *£4.80, includes audio guide, concerts from £17.50* ⊙ *Mon.–Sat. 10–5, last admission 4:30. Closed Christmas wk. Liable to close at short notice for events so calling first is advisable* Ⓤ *Charing Cross, Embankment, Westminster.*

Fodor's Choice ★ **Buckingham Palace.**

See the highlighted listing in this chapter.

Ⓒ ★ **Cabinet War Rooms & Churchill Museum.** It was from this small warren of underground rooms—beneath the vast government buildings of the Treasury—that Winston Churchill and his team directed troops in World War II. Designed to be bombproof, the whole complex has been preserved almost exactly as it was when the last light was turned off at the end of the war. Every clock shows almost 5 PM, and the furniture, fittings, and paraphernalia of a busy, round-the-clock war office are in situ, down to the colored map pins.

During air raids, the leading government ministers met here, and the Cabinet Room is still arranged as if a meeting were about to convene. In the Map Room, the Allied campaign is charted on wall-to-wall maps with a rash of pinholes showing the movements of convoys. In the hub of the room, a bank of different-colored phones known as the "Beauty Chorus" linked the War Rooms to control rooms around the nation. The Prime Minister's Room holds the desk from which Churchill made his morale-boosting broadcasts; the Telephone Room (a converted broom cupboard) has his hotline to FDR. You can also see the restored suite of rooms that the PM used for dining, cooking, and sleeping. Telephonists and clerks who worked 16-hour shifts slept in lesser quarters in unenviable conditions; it would not have been unusual for a secretary in pajamas to scurry past a field marshal en route to a meeting.

An exciting addition to the Cabinet War Rooms is the **Churchill Museum,** which opened in 2005 on the 40th anniversary of his death. Different zones explore his life and achievements—and failures, too—through objects and documents, many of which, such as his personal papers, had never previously been made public. Central to the exhibition is an interactive timeline, with layers of facts, figures, and tales. ⊠ *Clive Steps, King Charles St., Westminster* ☎ *020/7930–6961* ⊕ *cwr. iwm.org.uk* ✉ *£12.95, includes audio tour* ⊙ *Daily 9:30–6; last admission 5* Ⓤ *Westminster.*

A classic photo op: cavalry from the Queen's Life Guard at Buckingham Palace.

Clarence House. The London home of Queen Elizabeth the Queen Mother for nearly 50 years, Clarence House is now the Prince of Wales' and the Duchess of Cornwall's residence. The Regency mansion was built by John Nash for the Duke of Clarence, who found living in St. James's Palace quite unsuitable. Since then it has remained a royal home for princesses, dukes, and duchesses, including the present monarch, Queen Elizabeth, as a newlywed before her coronation. The rooms have been sensitively preserved to reflect the Queen Mother's taste, with the addition of many works of art from the Royal Collection, including works by Winterhalter, Augustus John, and Sickert. You'll find it less palace and more home (for the Prince and his sons William and Harry), with informal family pictures and comfortable sofas. The tour (by timed ticket entry only) is of the ground-floor rooms and includes the Lancaster Room, so called because of the marble chimneypiece presented by Lancaster County to the newly married Princess Elizabeth and the Duke of Edinburgh. Like Buckingham Palace, Clarence House is open only in August and September and tickets must be booked in advance. Visitors should note that there are no public restroom facilities at Clarence House. ⊠ *Clarence House, St. James's Palace, St. James's* ☎ *020/7766–7303* ⊕ *www.royalcollection.org.uk* ⊠ *£8* ☼ *Aug. and Sept.* Ⓤ *Green Park.*

★ **Houses of Parliament.**

See the highlighted listing in this chapter.

☼ **National Gallery.**

Fodor's Choice
★
See the highlighted listing in this chapter.

BUCKINGHAM PALACE

✉ *Buckingham Palace Rd., St. James* ☎ *020/7766–7300* ⊕ *www.royalcollection.org.uk* 💷 *£16.50* ⊗ *Late July–late Sept., daily 9:45–6 (last admission 3:45); times subject to change; check Web site before visiting* Ⓤ *Victoria, St. James's Park, Green Park.*

TIPS

■ Admission is by timed ticket with entry every 15 minutes throughout the day. Allow up to 2 hours.

■ A Royal Day Out ticket, available only in August and September, gives you the regal triple whammy of the Royal Mews, the Queen's Gallery, and the State Rooms, and is valid throughout the day Tickets cost £28.50. Allow 4 hours.

■ Get there by 10:30 to grab a spot in the best viewing section for the Changing the Guard, daily at 11:30 from May until the end of July (varies according to troop deployment requirements) and on alternate days for the rest of the year, weather permitting. www.changing-the-guard.com.

It's rare to get a chance to see how the other half—well, other minute fraction—lives and works. But when the Queen heads off to Scotland on her annual summer holiday (you can tell because the Union Jack flies above the palaceinstead of the Royal Standard), the palace's 19 State Rooms open up to visitors (although the north wing's private apartments remain behind closed doors). With fabulous gilt moldings and walls adorned with masterpieces by Rembrandt, Rubens, and other old masters, the State Rooms are the grandest of the palace's 775 rooms.

HIGHLIGHTS

Inside the palace, the **Grand Hall,** followed by the **Grand Staircase** and **Guard Room,** gives a taste of what's to follow: marble, gold leaf galore, and massive, twinkling chandeliers. Don't miss the theatrical **Throne Room,** with the original 1953 coronation throne, or the sword in **The Ballroom,** used by the Queen to bestow knighthoods and other honors. Royal portraits line the **State Dining Room,** and the **Blue Drawing Room** is splendor in overdrive. The bow-shape **Music Room** features lapis lazuli columns between arched floor-to-ceiling windows, and the alabaster-and-gold plasterwork of the **White Drawing Room** is a suitable crescendo on which to end the tour.

The **Changing the Guard,** also known as **Guard Mounting,** remains one of London's best free shows and culminates in front of the palace. Marching to live bands, the old guard proceeds up the Mall from St. James's Palace to Buckingham Palace. Shortly afterward, the new guard approaches from Wellington Barracks. Then within the forecourt, the captains of the old and new guards symbolically transfer the keys to the palace.

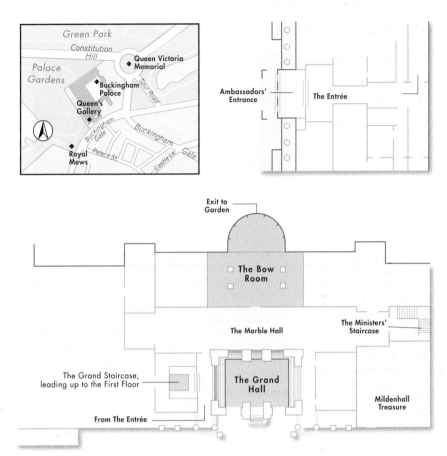

BUCKINGHAM PALACE: GROUND FLOOR

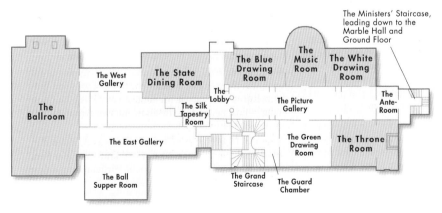

BUCKINGHAM PALACE: FIRST FLOOR

HOUSES OF PARLIAMENT

✉ *St. Stephen's Entrance, St. Margaret St., Westminster* ☎ *020/7219–4272 or 0870/906–3773* ⊕ *www. parliament.uk* ⬚ *Free; £12 summer tours (must book ahead)* ⊙ *Call to confirm hrs* Ⓤ *Westminster.*

If you want to understand some of the centuries-old traditions and arcane idiosyncrasies that make up constitutionless British parliamentary democracy, the Palace of Westminster, as the complex is still properly called, is the place to come. The architecture in this 1,100-room labyrinth impresses, but the real excitement lies in stalking the corridors of power. A palace was first established on the site by Edward the Confessor in the 11th century. William II started building a new palace in 1087, and this gradually became the seat of English administrative power. However, the current building dates from the 19th century, when fire destroyed the rest of the complex in 1834.

HIGHLIGHTS

Visitors aren't allowed to snoop too much, but the **Visitors' Galleries** of the House of Commons do afford a view of democracy in process when the banks of green-leather benches are filled by opposing MPs (members of Parliament). When they speak, it's not directly to each other but through the Speaker, who also decides who will get time on the floor. Elaborate procedures notwithstanding, debate is often drowned out by raucous jeers. When MPs vote, they exit by the "Aye" or the "No" corridor, thus being counted by the party "tellers."

Westminster Hall, with its remarkable hammer-beam roof, was the work of William the Conqueror's son William Rufus. It's one of the largest remaining Norman halls in Europe, and its dramatic interior was the scene of the trial of Charles I.

After the 1834 fire, the **Clock Tower** was completed in 1858, and contains the 13-ton bell known as **Big Ben.** At the southwest end of the main Parliament building is the 323-foot-high Victoria Tower.

TIPS

■ The only tour nonresidents can go on is the paid-for (£12) tour offered when Parliament is in recess, midweek during July, August, September, and October through www.ticketmaster.co.uk.

■ However, nonresidents are able to watch debates when Parliament is in session if they wait in line for tickets. Embassies and High Commissions often have a quota of debate tickets available to their citizens, which can help you avoid long queues. Contact your embassy in London directly for more information

■ If you're pressed for time, queues for the House of Lords are often shorter than for the House of Commons. The easiest time to get into the Commons is during an evening session—Parliament is still sitting if the top of the Clock Tower is illuminated.

■ The most romantic view of the Houses is from the opposite (south) bank, across Lambeth Bridge. It is especially dramatic at night when floodlighted green and gold.

☾ **National Portrait Gallery.** A suitably
Fodor's Choice idiosyncratic collection that pres-
★ ents a potted history of Britain
through its people, past and present, this museum is an essential stop
for all history and literature buffs,
where you can choose to take in a
little or a lot. The spacious, bright

galleries are accessible via a state-of-the-art escalator, which lets you
view the paintings as you ascend to a skylighted space displaying the
oldest works in the Tudor Gallery. At the summit, the Portrait Restaurant, open beyond gallery hours, will delight skyline aficionados.
■ TIP→ Here you'll see one of the best landscapes for real: a panoramic
view of Nelson's Column and the backdrop along Whitehall to the Houses
of Parliament.

Walking through the Photography Gallery, you could be flicking through
the pages of an upmarket celebrity or society magazine for times gone
by. In the Tudor Gallery—a modern update on a Tudor long hall—is a
Holbein cartoon of Henry VIII; Joshua Reynolds's self-portrait hangs in
the refurbished 17th-century rooms, and portraits of notables, including Shakespeare, the Bronte sisters, Jane Austen, and the Queen are
always on display. Other faces are more obscure and will be just as
unknown to you if you're English, because the portraits outlasted their
sitters' fame—not so surprising when the portraitists are such greats as
Reynolds, Gainsborough, Lawrence, Romney, and Hockney. But the
rotating collection's annotation is comprehensive, the layout is easy
to negotiate—chronological, with the oldest at the top—and there's a
separate research center for those who get hooked on particular per-
sonages. Don't miss the absorbing mini-exhibitions in the Studio and
Balcony Galleries; and there are temporary exhibitions in the Wolfson
and Porter galleries, which have ranged from Between Worlds: Voyag-
ers to Britain 1700–1850 to contemporary fashion photography from
Annie Leibovitz and Mario Testino. ⊠ *St. Martin's Pl., Covent Garden*
☏ *020/7312–2463, 020/730–0555 recorded switchboard information*
⊕ *www.npg.org.uk* ⊡ *Free, charge for special exhibitions* ☉ *Mon.–
Wed. and weekends 10–6, Thurs. and Fri. 10–9, last admission 45
mins before closing* Ⓤ *Charing Cross, Leicester Sq.*

★ **The Queen's Gallery.** The former chapel at the south side of Buckingham
Palace is now a temple of art and rare and exquisite objects, acquired
by kings and queens over the centuries. Although Her Majesty herself
is not the personal owner, she has the privilege of holding these works
for the nation. Step through the splendid portico (designed by John
Simpson) into elegantly restrained, spacious galleries whose walls are
hung with some truly great works. An excellent audio guide takes you
through the treasures.

A rough timeline of the major royal collectors starts with Charles I. An
avid appreciator of painters, Charles established the basis of the Royal
Collection, purchasing works by Mantegna, Raphael, Titian, Caravaggio, and Dürer (it was under royal patronage that Rubens painted the
Banqueting House ceiling). During the Civil War and in the aftermath

of Charles's execution, many masterpieces were sold abroad and subsequently repatriated by Charles II. George III, who bought Buckingham House, scooped up a notable collection of Venetian (including Canaletto), Renaissance (Bellini and Raphael), and Dutch (Vermeer) art, and a large number of baroque drawings, in addition to patronizing English contemporary artists such as Gainsborough, Hoppner, and Beechey. He also took a liking to American artist Benjamin West. The Prince Regent, George IV, transformed his father's house into a palace, filling it with fine art from paintings to porcelain. In particular, he had a good eye for Rembrandt, contemporary equestrian

works by Stubbs, and lavish portraits by Lawrence. Queen Victoria had a penchant for Landseer animals and landscapes, Frith's contemporary scenes, and portraits by Winterhalter. Finally, Edward VII indulged Queen Alexandra's love of Fabergé, and many royal tours around the empire produced gifts of gorgeous caliber, such as the Cullinan diamond from South Africa and an emerald-studded belt from India.

The Queen's Gallery displays only a selection from the Royal Collection in themed exhibitions, while more than 3,000 objects reside in museums and galleries in the United Kingdom and abroad: check out the National Gallery, the Victoria & Albert Museum, the Museum of London, and the British Museum. ■TIP➜ The E-gallery provides an interactive electronic version of the collection, allowing the user to open lockets, remove a sword from its scabbard, or take apart the tulip vases. It's probably the closest you could get to eyeing practically every diamond in the sovereign's glittering diadem. ⊠ *Buckingham Palace, Buckingham Palace Rd., St. James's* ☎ *020/7766–7301* ⊕ *www.royal.gov.uk* ☖ *£8.50 with free audio guide, joint ticket with Royal Mews £14.50* ☉ *Daily 10–5:30; last admission 4:30* Ⓤ *Victoria, St. James's Park, Green Park.*

☾ **St. James's Park.** With three palaces at its borders (the Palace of Westminster, the Tudor **St. James's Palace,** and Buckingham Palace), St. James's Park is acclaimed as the most royal of the royal parks. It's London's smallest, most ornamental park, as well as the oldest; it was acquired by Henry VIII in 1532 for a deer park. Henry VIII built the palace next to the park, which was used for hunting only—dueling and sword fights were forbidden. James I improved the land and installed an aviary and zoo (complete with crocodiles). Charles II (after his exile in France, where he admired Louis XIV's formal Versailles Palace landscapes) had formal gardens laid out, with avenues, fruit orchards, and a canal. Lawns were grazed by goats, sheep, and deer, although in the 18th century it became a different kind of hunting ground, for

Fodor's Choice ★

wealthy lotharios looking to pick up nighttime escorts. In the early 19th century John Nash redesigned the landscape in a more naturalistic, romantic style, and if you gaze down the lake toward Buckingham Palace, you can believe you are on a country estate.

About 17 species of birds—including pelicans, geese, ducks, and swans (which belong to the Queen)—now breed on and around Duck Island at the east end of the lake, attracting ornithologists at dawn. Later on summer days the deck chairs (which you must pay to use) are crammed with office workers lunching while being serenaded by music from the bandstands. One of the best times to stroll the leafy walkways is after dark, with Westminster Abbey and the Houses of Parliament rising above the floodlighted lake. The popular Inn the Park restaurant is a wood-and-glass pavilion with a turf roof that blends in beautifully with the surrounding landscape; it's a good stopping place for a meal or a snack on a nice day. ⊠ *The Mall or Horse Guards approach, or Birdcage Walk, St. James's* ⊕ *www.royalparks.gov.uk* ⊙ *Daily 5 AM–midnight* Ⓤ *St. James's Park, Westminster.*

Tate Britain. Although the building is not quite as awe-inspiring as Tate Modern, its younger sister on the south bank of the Thames, Tate Britain's lovely, bright galleries hold only a fraction of the Modern's crowds, making it a pleasant, hands-on place to explore great British art from 1500 to the present. It also hosts the annual Turner Prize exhibition, with its accompanying furor about the state of contemporary art, from about October to January each year. First opened in 1897, funded by the sugar magnate Sir Henry Tate, the museum includes the Linbury Galleries on the lower floors, which stage temporary exhibitions (they can get busy), whereas the upper floors show the permanent collection. Each room has a theme and displays key works by major British artists: Van Dyck, Hogarth, and Reynolds rub shoulders with Rossetti, Sickert, Hockney, and Bacon. Not to be missed is the generous selection of Constable landscapes.

Fodor's Choice ★

The Turner Bequest consists of J. M. W. Turner's personal collection; he left it to the nation on condition that the works be displayed together. The James Stirling–designed Clore Gallery (to the right of the main gallery) opened in 1987 to fulfill Turner's wish, and it should not be missed. You can rent an audio guide with commentaries by curators, experts, and some of the artists themselves.

Craving more art? Step down to the river and take the Tate-to-Tate shuttle boat (dotted with playful Damien Hirst spots) across the Thames to the Tate Modern; it runs between the two museums every 40 minutes. A River Roamer ticket permits additional stops at the London Eye and Tower of London. ⊠ *Millbank, Westminster* ☎ *020/7887–8888, 020/7887–8008 recorded information* ⊕ *www.tate.org.uk/britain* 🎫 *Free, exhibitions £3–£10* ⊙ *Daily 10–5:50, last entry at 5* Ⓤ *Pimlico (signposted 5-min walk).*

NATIONAL GALLERY

✉ *Trafalgar Sq.* ☎ *020/7747-2885* ⊕ *www.nationalgallery.org.uk* 🎟 *Free, charge for special exhibitions* ☉ *Sun.–Thurs. 10–6, Fri. 10–9* Ⓤ *Charing Cross, Embankment, Leicester Square.*

TIPS

■ Color coding throughout the galleries helps you keep track of the period you're immersed in.

■ Begin at an "Art Start" terminal in the Sainsbury Wing or East Wing Espresso Bar. The interactive screens give you access to information on all of the museum's holdings; you can choose your favorites, and print out a free personal tour map.

■ Want some stimulation? Try a free weekday lunchtime lecture, or Ten Minute Talk, which illuminates the story behind a key work of art.

■ One-hour free, guided tours start at the Sainsbury Wing daily at 11:30 and 2:30.

■ If you are eager for even more insight into the art, pick up a themed audio guide, which takes in about 20 paintings.

■ If you visit during school holidays, don't miss special programs and trails for children. There are also free Family Sundays with special talks for children and their parents.

Standing proudly at the top of Trafalgar Square is one of the world's best art collections. The gallery fills the north side of the square, with Nelson's column in the center, with more than 2,300 masterpieces on show, for free.

HIGHLIGHTS

This brief selection is your jumping-off point, but there are hundreds more, enough to fill a full day. In chronological order: (1) **Van Eyck** (circa 1395–1441), *The Arolfini Portrait*—a solemn couple holds hands, the fish-eye mirror behind them mysteriously illuminating what can't be seen from the front view. (2) **Holbein** (1497–1543), *The Ambassadors*—two wealthy visitors from France are depicted surrounded by what were considered luxury goods at the time, such as musical instruments, a book of mathematics, and items for studying astronomy. (3) **Botticelli** (1445–1510), *Venus and Mars*—Mars sleeps, exhausted by the love goddess, oblivious to the lance weilded by mischievous cherubs. (4) **Leonardo da Vinci** (1452–1519), *The Virgin and Child*—this haunting black-chalk cartoon is partly famous for having been attacked at gunpoint, and it now gets extra protection behing glass. (5) **Caravaggio** (1573–1610), *The Supper at Emmaus*—a cinematically lightened, freshly resurrected Christ blesses bread in an astonishingly domestic vision from the master of chiaroscuro. (6) **Constable** (1776–1837), *The Hay Wain*—rendered overfamiliar by too many greeting cards, this is the definitive image of golden-age rural England. (7) **Turner** (1775–1851), *The Fighting Téméraire*—the final voyage of the great French bettleship into a livid, hazy sunset. (8) **Seurat** (1859–91), *Bathers at Asnières*—this static summer day's idyll is one of the pointillist extraordinaire's best-known works.

2

Rather than search for a suitable place in Pimlico or Victoria, you can eat well right at the Tate. The **Tate Britain Café** has drinks, sandwiches, and cakes, and is open daily from 10 AM to 5:30 PM. The **Rex Whistler Restaurant** is almost a destination in itself, with its celebrated Rex Whistler murals and a daily fixed-price three-course lunch menu (around £15) and à la carte choices. Ingredients celebrate British produce, such as Cornish crab, Welsh lamb, organic smoked salmon, and Stilton cheese. Children's portions are available. It's open for lunch Monday through Sunday noon to 3; afternoon tea and breakfast are also served on weekends.

Trafalgar Square. This is literally the center of London: a plaque on the corner of the Strand and Charing Cross Road marks the spot from which distances on U.K. signposts are measured. **Nelson's Column** stands at the heart of the square (which is named after the great admiral's most important victory), guarded by haughty lions designed by Sir Edwin Landseer and flanked by statues of two generals who helped establish the British Empire in India, **Charles Napier** and **Henry Havelock**. The fourth plinth is given over to rotating works by contemporary sculptors. Great events, such as New Year's Eve celebrations, political protests, and sporting triumphs always see the crowds gathering in the city's most famous square.

The commanding open space is built on the grand scale demanded by its central position. From the 13th century, the site housed the royal hawks and falcons until 1530, when these buildings were replaced by stabling for royal horses. This "Great Mews" was demolished in 1830 as part of John Nash's Charing Cross Improvement Scheme. Nash, who envisioned the square as a cultural space open to the public, exploited its natural north-south incline to create a succession of high points from which to look down imposing carriageways toward the Thames, the Houses of Parliament, and Buckingham Palace. Upon Nash's death, the design baton was passed to Sir Charles Barry and then to Sir Edwin Lutyens, and the square was finally completed in 1850. The next major modification was in 2003, when the north side was pedestrianized, providing unimpeded access to the **National Gallery**.

At the southern point of the square, en route to Whitehall, is the **equestrian statue of Charles I.** After the Civil War and the king's execution, Oliver Cromwell, then the leader of the "Commonwealth," commissioned a scrap dealer, brazier John Rivett, to melt the statue. The story goes that Rivett buried it in his garden and made a fortune peddling knickknacks wrought, he claimed, from its metal, only to produce the statue miraculously unscathed after the restoration of the monarchy—and to make more cash reselling it to the authorities. In 1767 Charles II had it placed where it stands today, near the spot where his father was executed in 1649. Each year, on January 30, the day of the king's death, the Royal Stuart Society lays a wreath at the foot of the statue. ⊠ *Trafalgar Sq., Westminster* Ⓤ *Charing Cross.*

Fodor's Choice ★ **Westminster Abbey.** *See the highlighted listing in this chapter.*

The Tate Britain showcases British art from the last 500 years, including contemporary works.

WORTH NOTING

Admiralty Arch. Gateway to the Mall—no, not an indoor shopping center but one of the very grand avenues of London—this is one of the city's stateliest set pieces. On the southwest corner of Trafalgar Square, the arch, which was named after the adjacent Royal Navy headquarters, was designed in 1908–11 by Sir Aston Webb as a two-part memorial to Queen Victoria, along the ceremonial route to Buckingham Palace; the second part is the Victoria Memorial just outside the palace. Passing under one of its five arches—two for pedestrians, two for traffic, and a central arch, opened only for state occasions—the environment changes along with the color of the road, as you leave frenetic Trafalgar Square and go into the Mall (rhymes with the American pronunciation of shall)—the tree-lined boulevard that leads directly to the palace. ⊠ *The Mall, Cockspur St., Trafalgar Sq., Westminster* Ⓤ *Charing Cross.*

Carlton House Terrace. Architect John Nash designed Carlton House, a glorious example of the Regency style. Between 1812 and 1830, under the patronage of George IV (Prince Regent until George III's death in 1820), Nash was the architect of the grand scheme for Regent Street, which started here and ended with the sweep of neoclassical houses encircling Regent's Park. The Prince Regent, who lived at Carlton House, had plans to build a country villa at Primrose Hill (to the north of the park), connected by a grand road—hence Regent Street. Even though it was considered a most extravagant building for its time, Carlton House was demolished after the prince's accession to the throne. Nash's Carlton House Terrace, no less imposing, with white-stucco facades and massive Corinthian columns, was built in its place. It was a smart address and one that prime ministers Gladstone (1856) and Palmerston (1857–75) enjoyed. Today Carlton House Terrace houses the Royal College of Pathologists (No. 2), the Royal Society (No. 6–9), whose members have included Isaac Newton and Charles Darwin, and the Turf Club (No. 5). ⊠ *The Mall, St. James's* Ⓤ *Charing Cross.*

Downing Street. Looking like an unassuming alley but for the iron gates at both its Whitehall and Horse Guards Road approaches, this is the location of the famous **No. 10,** London's modest version equivalent of the White House. The Georgian entrance is deceptive, though, since the old house

BEARSKIN, NOT BUSBY

While on duty, guardsmen are required to remain utterly aloof—they may not speak (some people attempt to make them laugh), may not swat errant flies from their noses, and in theory may not keel over under the weight of their enormous, saunalike hats. Called bearskins (not busbies, as is sometimes incorrectly assumed) after the material from which they are made, the headdress was originally worn by the French Imperial Guard defeated in the Battle of Waterloo in 1815.

now leads to a large mansion behind it, overlooking the Horse Guards Parade. Only three houses remain of the terrace built circa 1680 by Sir George Downing, who spent enough of his youth in America to graduate from Harvard—the second man ever to do so. **No. 11** is traditionally the residence of the chancellor of the exchequer (secretary of the treasury), and **No. 12** is the party whips' office. No. 10 has officially housed the prime minister since 1732. Just south of Downing Street, in the middle of Whitehall, you'll see the **Cenotaph,** a stark white monolith designed in 1920 by Edwin Lutyens to commemorate the 1918 armistice. On Remembrance Day (the Sunday nearest November 11, Armistice Day) it's strewn with red poppy wreaths to honor the dead of both world wars and all British and Commonwealth soldiers killed in action since; the first wreath is laid by the Queen or the senior member of the Royal Family present, and there's a march-past by war veterans, who salute their fallen comrades. ⊠ *Whitehall, Whitehall* Ⓤ *Westminster.*

Household Cavalry Museum. Horse lovers can see working horses belonging to the British Army's two senior regiments, the Life Guards and the Blues and Royals, being tended to in their stable block behind a glass wall. Located in the cavalry's original 17th-century stables, the museum has displays of uniforms and weapons going back to 1661 as well as interactive exhibits on the regiments' current operational roles. In the tack room you can handle saddles and bridles, and try on a trooper's uniform, including its distinctive brass helmet with horsehair plume. ⊠ *Horse Guards, Whitehall* ☎ *020/7930–3070* ⊕ *www.householdcavalrymuseum.org.uk* ✉ *£6* ⊙ *Mar.–Sept., daily 10–6; Oct.–Feb., daily 10–5* Ⓤ *Charing Cross, Westminster.*

Horse Guards Parade. Once the tiltyard of Whitehall Palace, where jousting tournaments were held, the Horse Guards Parade is now notable mainly for the annual Trooping the Colour ceremony, in which the Queen takes the salute, her official birthday tribute, on the second Saturday in June. (Like Paddington Bear, the Queen has two birthdays;

ROYAL ATTRACTIONS

The Queen and the Royal Family attend hundreds of functions a year, and if you want to know what they are doing on any given date, turn to the *Court Circular*, printed in the major London dailies the *Times*, the *Telegraph*, and the *Scotsman*, or check out the Royal Family Web site, ⊕ *www.royal.gov. uk*, for the latest pictures and events. Trooping the Colour is usually held on the second Saturday in June, to celebrate the Queen's official birthday. This spectacular parade begins when she leaves Buckingham Palace in her carriage and rides down the Mall to arrive at Horse Guards Parade at 11 exactly. To watch, just line up along the Mall with your binoculars!

Another time you can catch the Queen in all her regalia is when she and the Duke of Edinburgh ride in state to Westminster to open the Houses of Parliament. The famous gilded black, gilt-trimmed Irish State Coach travels from Buckingham Palace, escorted by the brilliantly uniformed Household Cavalry—on a clear day, it's to be hoped, for this ceremony takes place in late October or early November, depending on the exigencies of Parliament. The Gold State Coach, an icon of fairy-tale glamour, is used for coronations and jubilees only.

But perhaps the most relaxed, least formal time to see the Queen is during Royal Ascot, held at the racetrack near Windsor Castle—a short train ride out of London—usually during the third week of June (Tuesday–Friday). The Queen and members of the Royal Family are driven down the track to the Royal Box in an open carriage, giving spectators a chance to see them. After several races, the Queen invariably walks down to the paddock, greeting race goers as she proceeds.

her real one is on April 21.) There is pageantry galore, with marching bands and throngs of onlookers. Covering the vast expanse of the square that faces Horse Guards Road, opposite St. James's Park at one end and Whitehall at the other, the ceremony is televised. At the Whitehall facade of Horse Guards, the changing of two mounted sentries known as the **Sovereign's Life Guards** provides what may be London's most popular photo opportunity. The ceremony lasts about half an hour. ⊠ *Whitehall, Whitehall* ☎ *020/7930–4832* ⊗ *Queen's mounted guard ceremony Mon.–Sat. 11 AM and 4 PM, Sun. 10 AM and 4 PM* Ⓤ *Westminster*.

QUICK BITES

The Wesley Café (⊠ *Storey's Gate, Westminster* ☎ *020/7222–8010*) is a popular budget haunt for office workers around Westminster, and a good stopping point if you don't want to go farther along Victoria Street in search of food. It's almost opposite Westminster Abbey, in the crypt of Central Hall, a former Methodist church.

Institute of Contemporary Arts (ICA). Behind its incongruous white-stucco facade on the Mall next to the Duke of York steps, the ICA has provided a stage for the avant-garde in performance, theater, dance, visual art, and music since it was established in 1947. There are two cinemas,

three galleries, a great bookshop, a café, a hip bar, and a team of adventurous curators. ⊠ *The Mall, St. James's* ☎ *020/7930–3647* ⊕ *www. ica.org.uk* 🖃 *Free; £8 for cinema screenings* ⊙ *Galleries daily noon– 7, Thurs. until 9* Ⓤ *Charing Cross, Piccadilly Circus.*

QUICK BITES

The ICA Bar and Café has a Modern British menu and windows overlooking the Mall—it's very popular at lunchtime, so come early. Open daily from noon.

PHOTO OP

The best place for a photo opportunity alongside one of the Queen's guardsmen is at St. James's Palace, or try to keep up alongside them during the morning Changing the Guard. They leave St. James's at about 10:50 AM, for Buckingham Palace. Failing that, shuffle up to the mounted horse guards on the Whitehall side, there until 4 PM.

The Mall. This stately, 115-foot-wide processional route sweeping from Admiralty Arch to the Queen Victoria Memorial at Buckingham Palace is an updated 1904 version of the traditional rambling promenade that was used for centuries. The street was originally laid out around 1660 for the game of *paille-maille* (a type of croquet crossed with golf), which also gave the parallel road Pall Mall its name, and it quickly became the place to be seen. Samuel Pepys, Jonathan Swift, and Alexander Pope all wrote about it, and it continued as the beau monde's social playground well into the early 19th century, long after the game had gone out of vogue. ■ TIP➜ Be sure to stroll along the Mall on Sunday when the road is closed to traffic, or catch the bands and troops of the Household Division on their way from St. James's Palace to Buckingham Palace for the Changing the Guard. ⊠ *The Mall, St. James's* Ⓤ *Charing Cross, Green Park.*

☾ **Royal Mews.** Fairy-tale gold-and-glass coaches and sleek Rolls-Royce state cars emanate from the Royal Mews, next door to the Queen's Gallery. The John Nash–designed Mews serves as the headquarters for Her Majesty's travel department (so beware of closures for state visits), complete with the Queen's own special breed of horses, ridden by wigged postilions decked in red-and-gold regalia. Between the stables and riding school arena are exhibits of polished saddlery and riding tack. The highlight of the Mews is the splendid Gold State Coach, not unlike an art gallery on wheels, with its sculpted tritons and sea gods. Mews were originally falcons' quarters (the name comes from their "mewing," or feather shedding), but the horses gradually eclipsed the birds. Royal Collection staff guide tours. ⊠ *Buckingham Palace Rd., St. James's* ☎ *020/7766–7302* ⊕ *www.royalcollection.org.uk* 🖃 *£7.50, joint ticket with Queen's Gallery £14.50* ⊙ *Mar. 28–July 25 and Oct., Sat.–Thurs. 11–4 (last admission 3:15); July–Sept., daily 10–5, no guided tours; last admission 4:15* Ⓤ *Victoria, St. James's Park.*

St. James's Palace. With its solitary sentry posted at the gate, this surprisingly small palace of Tudor brick was once a home for many British sovereigns, including the first Elizabeth and Charles I, who spent his last night here before his execution. Today it's the working office of another Charles—the Prince of Wales. The front door actually opens right onto the street, but he always uses a back entrance to various

Continued on page 70

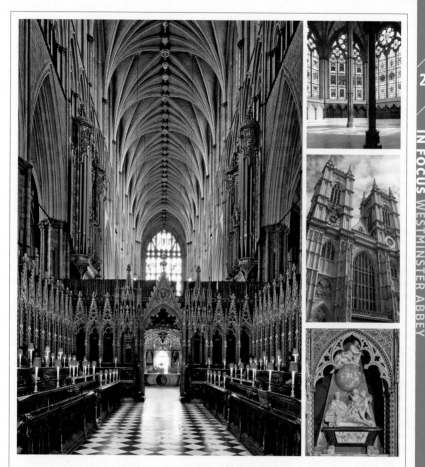

WESTMINSTER ABBEY

A monument to the rich—and often bloody and scandalous—history of Great Britain, Westminster Abbey rises on the Thames skyline as one of the most iconic sites in London.

The mysterious gloom of the lofty medieval interior is home to more than 600 monuments and memorial statues. About 3,300 people, from kings to composers to wordsmiths, are buried in the abbey. It has been the scene of 14 royal weddings and no less than 38 coronations—the first in 1066, when William the Conqueror was made king here.

TOURING THE ABBEY

There's only one way around the abbey, and as there will almost certainly be a long stream of shuffling tourists at your heels, you'll need to be alert to catch the highlights. Enter by the north door.

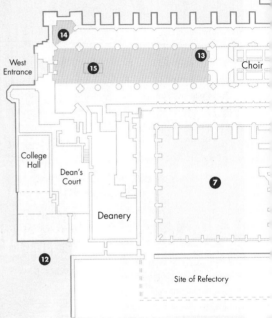

When you enter the church, turn around and look up to see the ❶ **painted-glass rose window**, the largest of its kind.

The ❷ **Coronation Chair**, at the foot of the Henry VII Chapel, has been briefly graced by nearly every regal posterior since Edward I ordered it in 1301. Look for the graffiti on the back of the Coronation chair. It's the work of 18th- and 19th-century visitors and Westminster schoolboys who carved their names there.

The ❸ **Henry VII's Lady Chapel** contains the tombs of Henry VII and his queen, Elizabeth of York. Close by are monuments to the young daughters of James I, and an urn purported to hold the remains of the so-called Princes in the Tower—Edward V and Richard. Interestingly, arch enemies Elizabeth I and her half-sister Mary Tudor share a tomb here. An inscription reads: "Partners both in throne and grave, here rest two sisters, Elizabeth and Mary, in the hope of the Resurrection."

In front of the ❹ **High Altar**, which was used for the funerals of Princess Diana and the Queen Mother, is a black-and-white marble pavement laid in 1268. The intricate Italian Cosmati work contains three Latin inscriptions, one of which states that the world will last for 19,683 years.

The ❺ **Shrine of St. Edward the Confessor** contains the shrine to the pre-Norman king. Because of its great age, you must join a tour with the verger to be admitted to the chapel. (Details are available at the admission desk; there is a small extra charge.)

Geoffrey Chaucer was the first poet to be buried in ❻ **Poets' Corner** in 1400. Other memorials include: William Shakespeare, William Blake, John Milton, Jane Austen, Samuel Taylor Coleridge, William Wordsworth, and Charles Dickens.

A door from the south transept and south choir aisle leads to the calm of the ❼ **Great Cloisters**.

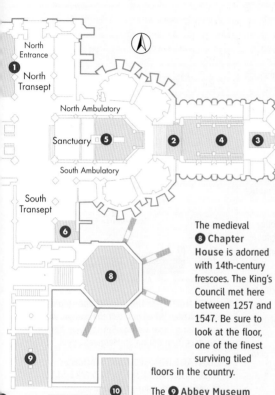

and actual clothing of Charles II and Admiral Lord Nelson (complete with eye patch).

The **❿ Little Cloister** is a quiet haven, and just beyond, the **⓫ College Garden** is a delightful diversion. Filled with medicinal herbs, it has been tended by monks for more than 900 years.

The **⓬ Dean's Yard** is the best spot for a fine view of the massive flying buttresses above.

The medieval **❽ Chapter House** is adorned with 14th-century frescoes. The King's Council met here between 1257 and 1547. Be sure to look at the floor, one of the finest surviving tiled floors in the country.

The **❾ Abbey Museum** includes a collection of deliciously macabre effigies made from the death masks

In the choir screen, north of the entrance to the choir, is a marble **⓭ monument to Sir Isaac Newton.**

⓮ A plaque to Franklin D. Roosevelt is one of the Abbey's very few tributes to a foreigner.

The **⓯ Grave of the Unknown Warrior**, in memory of the soldiers who lost their lives in both world wars, is near the exit of the abbey.

QUIRKY LONDON

Near the Henry VII chapel, keep an eye open for St. Wilgefortis, who was so concerned to protect her chastity that she prayed to God for help and woke up one morning with a full growth of beard.

A BRIEF HISTORY

960 AD Benedictine monastery founded on the site by King Edward and King Dunstan.

1045–65 King Edward the Confessor enlarges the original monastery, erecting a stone church in honor of St. Paul the Apostle. Named "west minster" to distinguish from "east minster" (St. Paul's Cathedral).

1065 The church is consecrated on December 28. Edward doesn't live to see the ceremony.

1161 Following Edward's canonization, his body is moved by Henry III to a more elaborate resting place behind the High Altar. Other medieval kings are later buried around his tomb.

1245–54 Henry III pulls down the abbey and starts again with a new Gothic style influenced by his travels in France. Master mason Henry de Reyns ("of Rheims") constructs the transepts, north front, and rose windows, as well as part of the cloisters and Chapter House.

1269 The new abbey is consecrated and the choir is completed.

1350s Richard II resumes Henry III's plan to rebuild the monastery. Henry V and Henry VII continue as benefactors.

1503 The Lady Chapel is demolished and the foundation stone of Henry VII's Chapel is laid on the site.

1540 The abbey ceases to be used as a monastery.

1560 Elizabeth I refounds the abbey as a Collegiate Church. From this point on it is a "Royal Peculiar," exempt from the jurisdiction of bishops.

1745 The western towers, left unfinished from medieval times, are finally completed, based on a design by Sir Christopher Wren.

1995 Following a 25-year restoration program, saints and allegorical figures are added to the niches on the western towers and around the Great West Door.

PLANNING YOUR DAY

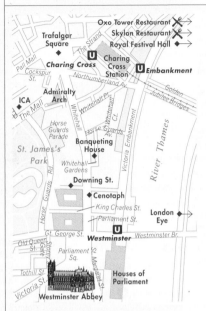

GETTING HERE: The closest Tube stop is Westminster. When you exit the station, walk west along Great George Street, away from the river. Turn left on St. Margaret Street.

CONTACT INFO: ✉ Broad Sanctuary, Westminster SW1 P3PA ☎ 020/7222–5152 🌐 www.westminster-abbey.org.

ADMISSION: Adults: Abbey and museum £15. **Family ticket** (2 adults and 2 children): £30. **Children under 11:** free.

HOURS: The abbey is a house of worship. Services may cause changes to the visiting hours on any given day, so be sure to call ahead.
Abbey: Weekdays 9:30–3:30, Wed. until 6, Sat. 9:30–1:30; closes 1 hr after last admission.
Museum: Daily 10:30–4.
Cloisters: Daily 8–6.
College Garden: Tues.–Thurs., 10–6.
Chapter House: Daily 10:30–4.

WHAT'S NEARBY: To make the most of your day, arrive at the abbey early (doors open at 9:30), then make an afternoon visit to the Parliament buildings and finish with a sunset ride on the **London Eye**. Post-flight, take a walk along the fairy-lit South Bank and have dinner (or a drink in the bar) with a view, at the **Oxo Tower Restaurant** (☎ 020/7803–3888) or the Royal Festival Hall's **Skylon Restaurant** (☎ 020/7654–7800).

Please note that overseas visitors can no longer visit the **Houses of Parliament** during session. However, tours of the buildings are available in August and September. For more information and booking call ☎ 0870/906–3773. Also, it's advisable to prebook tickets for the London Eye. Do this online at www.londoneye.com, or call 0870/990–8883.

IN A HURRY?

If you're pressed for time, concentrate on the following four highlights: the Coronation Chair; Chapter House; Poets' Corner; and Grave of the Unknown Warrior.

THINGS TO KNOW

■ Photography and filming are not permitted anywhere in the abbey.

■ In winter the interior of the abbey can get quite cold; dress accordingly.

■ For an animated history of the museum, join one of the tours that depart from the information desk, tour times vary.

■ Touring the abbey can take half a day, especially in summer, when lines are long.

■ To avoid the crowds, make sure you arrive early. If you're first in line you can enjoy parts of the abbey in relative calm before the mad rush descends.

■ If you want to study up before you go, visit www.westminster-abbey.org, which includes an in-depth history and self-guided tour of the abbey. Otherwise pick up a free leaflet from the information desk.

■ On Sundays the abbey is not open to visitors. Join a service instead. Check the Web site for service times, as well as details of concerts, organ recitals, and special events.

departments of the Royal Household. Matters to ponder as you
look (you can't go in): the palace
was named after a hospital for
women lepers that stood here during the 11th century; Henry VIII
had it built; foreign ambassadors
to Britain are still accredited to the
Court of St. James's even though
it has rarely been a primary royal
residence; the present Queen made
her first speech here; and after the
death of a monarch, the accession

of the new sovereign is announced by the Garter King of Arms from
the Proclamation Gallery overlooking Friary Court. Friary Court out
front is a splendid setting for Trooping the Colour, part of the Queen's
official birthday celebrations. Everyone loves to take a snapshot of the
scarlet-coated guardsman standing sentry outside the imposing Tudor
gateway. Note that the Changing the Guard ceremony at St. James's
Palace occurs only on days when the guard at Buckingham Palace is
changed. See entry for Buckingham Palace for details. ☒ *Friary Court,
St. James's* ⊕ *www.royal.gov.uk* Ⓤ *Green Park.*

St. Margaret's Church. Dwarfed by its neighbor, Westminster Abbey, St.
Margaret's was founded in the 11th century and rebuilt between 1488
and 1523. As the unofficial "parish church" of the Houses of Parliament
it's much sought after for weddings and memorial services—if you're
on the list of VIPs who can use it for such ceremonies. Samuel Pepys,
Chaucer, and John Milton worshipped here, and Winston Churchill was
married here in 1908. The east window celebrates another union, the
marriage of Catherine of Aragon and Henry VIII. ☒ *St. Margaret's St.,
Parliament Sq., Westminster* ☎ *020/7654–4847* ⊕ *www.westminster-
abbey.org/st-margarets* ⊙ *Weekdays 9:30–3:30, Sat. 9–1:30, Sun. 2–5
(entry via east door). Church may close on short notice for services, so
call ahead* Ⓤ *Westminster.*

↻ **St. Martin-in-the-Fields.** One of London's best-loved and most welcoming of churches, has been enhanced both inside and out by expensive
and time-consuming refurbishment work and the building's array of
functions continues unabated. It's a welcome sight for the homeless,
who have sought soup and shelter here since 1914. The church is also
a haven for music lovers; the internationally known Academy of St.
Martin-in-the-Fields was founded here, and a popular program of concerts continues today. (However, although the interior is a wonderful
setting, the wooden benches can make it hard to give your undivided
attention to the music.) The crypt is a hive of lively activity, with a café
and shop, plus the **London Brass-Rubbing Centre,** where you can make
your own life-size souvenir knight, lady, or monarch from replica tomb
brasses, with metallic waxes, paper, and instructions provided from
about £5; and the **Gallery in the Crypt,** showing an exhibition on the
history of the church. St. Martin's is often called the royal parish church,
partly because Charles II was christened here: the small medieval chapel

that once stood on the site, probably used by the monks of Westminster Abbey, gave way to a grand rebuilding, completed in 1726, and James Gibbs's classical temple-with-spire design also became a familiar pattern for churches in early colonial America. Though it has to compete for attention with Trafalgar Square's many prominent structures, its spire is actually slightly taller than Nelson's Column. ⊠ *Trafalgar Sq., Covent Garden* ☎ *020/7766–1100, 020/7839–8362 evening-concert credit-card bookings* ⊕ *www.smitf.org* ⊡ *Concerts £6–£22* ☉ *Mon.–Sat. 8–6, Sun. 8–6 for worship; café Mon.–Wed. 8–8, open until 9 Thurs.–Sat., Sun. 11–6.* Ⓤ *Charing Cross, Leicester Sq.*

ST. MARTIN'S CONCERTS

Evening jazz concerts are held every Wednesday and classical concerts every Thursday–Saturday at 7:30. Tickets are available from the box office in the crypt. Free (but donation appreciated) lunchtime concerts take place Monday, Tuesday, and Friday, 1–2 PM.

QUICK BITES

St. Martin's Café in the Crypt, with its high-arched brick vault, serves full meals, sandwiches, snacks, traditional tea, and wine. The choice here, which includes vegetarian dishes along with Continental and traditional English breakfasts, is one of the best available for such a central location.

☺ **Wellington Barracks.** These are the headquarters of the Guards Division, the Queen's five regiments of elite foot guards (Grenadier, Coldstream, Scots, Irish, and Welsh) who protect the sovereign and patrol her palaces dressed in tunics of gold-purled scarlet and tall bearskin caps. Guardsmen alternate these ceremonial postings with serving in current conflicts, for which they wear more practical uniforms. If you want to learn more about the guards, visit the **Guards Museum,** which has displays on all aspects of a guardsman's life in conflicts dating back to 1642; the entrance is next to the Guards Chapel. Next door is the **Guards Toy Solider Centre,** a great place for a souvenir. ⊠ *Wellington Barracks, Birdcage Walk, Westminster* ☎ *020/7414–3428* ⊕ *www. theguardsmuseum.com* ⊡ *£3* ☉ *Daily 10–4; last admission 3:30* Ⓤ *St. James's Park.*

Westminster Cathedral. Amid the concrete jungle of Victoria Street lies this remarkable neo-Byzantine find, seat of the Archbishopof Westminster, head of the Roman Catholic Church in Britain, and consequently of London's principal Roman Catholic church. Faced with the daunting proximity of Westminster Abbey, the architect, John Francis Bentley, flew in the face of fashion by rejecting neo-Gothic in favor of the Byzantine idiom, which still provides maximum contrast today. The asymmetrical redbrick Byzantine hulk, dating only from 1903, is banded with stripes of Portland stone and abutted by a 273-foot-high bell tower containing Big Edward at the northwest corner, which you can scale by elevator. The interior is still incomplete, but worth seeing for its cavernous, brooding mystery and its rich and colorful marblework. Look out for the stations of the cross (stopping points for prayer or contemplation) by Eric Gill, the glittering mosaic work on the roof of Holy Souls Chapel, and the striking baldachin—the enormous stone canopy standing over the altar and giant cross suspended in front of it. Since his conversion to Catholicism, and a clearer calendar, ex–prime minister Tony Blair has been seen at the church on Sunday mornings. The nave is the widest in the country and is constructed in green marble, which also has a Byzantine connection—it was cut from the same place as the 6th-century St. Sophia's in Istanbul, and was almost confiscated by warring Turks as it traveled across the country. Just inside the main entrance is the tomb of Cardinal Basil Hume, head of the Catholic Church in the United Kingdom for more than 25 years. There's a café in the crypt. ✉ *Ashley Pl., Westminster* ☎ *020/7798–9055* ⊕ *www. westminstercathedral.org.uk* 🖃 *Tower £5* ◷ *Weekdays 7–6, weekends 8–7* Ⓤ *Victoria.*

St. James's and Mayfair

WORD OF MOUTH

"We really liked being based in Mayfair, a very upscale area with many embassies and gorgeous town homes. The kids were impressed at the number of Bentleys, Aston Martins, and Ferraris. It's a short walk to Hyde Park or Green Park, and there are many restaurants and pubs to choose from."

—BelTib

GETTING ORIENTED

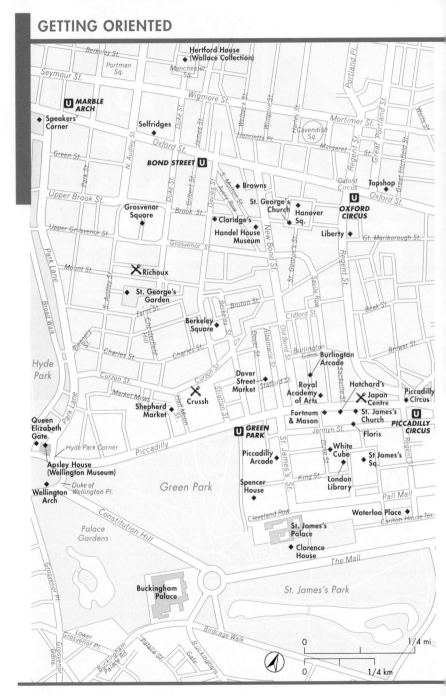

TOP REASONS TO GO

Claridge's Bar: Unwind with afternoon tea at this art deco gem after a shopping spree in Mayfair.

St. James's Church: Raise your spirits at this beautiful masterpiece by Sir Christopher Wren, the site of poet William Blake's baptism.

Fine Shopping: Balance your boutique stores (Stella McCartney, Burberry, Alexander McQueen) with food emporium Fortnum & Mason before relaxing at Waterstone's 5th View with a new book and a glass of wine while enjoying sweeping views at this mega–bookstore café.

Royal Academy of Arts: Visit the Summer Exhibition, usually between June and August, a breathtaking affair showcasing some of the best sculpture and painting in the art world.

St. George's Gardens: Escape from the congestion of central London in this hidden patch of green tucked behind chic Mount Street.

FEELING PECKISH?

Eating healthfully can be a challenge in London, but **Crussh** (⌂ *1 Curzon St., Mayfair* ☎ *020/7629–2554*) on Curzon Street serves excellent juices, smoothies, and soups as well as sandwiches, salads, and wraps to bring across to nearby Green Park.

The **Japan Centre** (⌂ *212–213 Piccadilly, St. James's* ☎ *020/ 7434–4218*), on busy Piccadilly near Piccadilly Circus, has an excellent Japanese deli offering bento boxes and freshly prepared sushi to eat in or take out. There's also a restaurant serving hot Japanese dishes and London's only dedicated tea and sake shop next door.

Since 1909, **Richoux** (⌂ *172 Piccadilly, Mayfair* ☎ *020/7493– 2204*) is an affordable refuge from busy Piccadilly. Simple but well-executed French bistro food is served all day; save room for the excellent pastries.

GETTING THERE

There are three Tube stops on the Central Line that will leave you smack in the center of these neighborhoods: Marble Arch, Bond Street (also Jubilee Line), and Oxford Circus (also Victoria and Bakerloo lines). You can also take the Piccadilly or Bakerloo line to the Piccadilly Circus Tube station, the Piccadilly to the Hyde Park Corner station, or the Piccadilly, Victoria, or Jubilee line to the Green Park station.

The best buses are the 8, which takes in Green Park, Berkeley Square, and New Bond Street, and the 9, one of the few routes that still uses the traditional Routemaster model, which runs along Piccadilly.

MAKING THE MOST OF YOUR TIME

Reserve at least a day to see the sights in St. James's and Mayfair, but choose carefully, as this is one of London's most densely packed, dynamic districts.

The only areas to avoid are the Tube stations at rush hour, and Oxford Street if you don't like crowds.

At all costs, stay away from Oxford Circus around 5 PM, when the commuter rush can, at times, resemble an East African wildebeest migration.

3

| Sightseeing | Smart and stylish Mayfair reflects the shiny affluence of |

Sightseeing
★★★★★

Nightlife
★★★

Dining
★★★★

Lodging
★★★★

Shopping
★★★★

Smart and stylish Mayfair reflects the shiny affluence of London. This is where the city's financial set, British aristocrats, and the international rich live, as well as dine, play, and shop. Meanwhile, more sedate St. James's, with its old-money galleries, restaurants, and gentlemen's clubs, embodies the history and privilege of traditional London.

Updated
by Michelle
Rosenberg

Despite being bounded by four of the busiest streets in London—bustling budget-shopping mecca Oxford Street to the north, traffic artery Park Lane with Hyde Park beyond to the west, and elegant boulevards Regent Street and Piccadilly to the east and south respectively—Mayfair itself is remarkably traffic-free and ideal for walking. Starting at **Selfridges** on Oxford Street, a southward stroll will take you through quiet residential streets lined with Georgian town houses (the area was largely developed in the 17th and 18th centuries).

Mayfair has three grand squares: **Grosvenor Square** and **Berkeley Square** lie to the quieter west side of **Bond Street**, the neighborhood's main luxury shopping street that bisects the area, and **Hanover Square**, with its splendid **St. George's Church** where Handel worshipped, is on the busier eastern side. South of Grosvenor Square is the quiet St. George's Gardens and beyond it the older part of Mayfair, a maze of atmospheric streets and mews.

Leading off Berkeley Square are two of London's most exclusive shopping destinations: **Mount Street** and **Bruton Street**. To the east of New Bond Street, Bruton Street turns into the equally fashionable **Conduit Street**. Between New Bond Street and Regent is **Savile Row**, famous as the source of the world's best made-to-measure suit. At the foot of Savile Row is the **Burlington Arcade** leading to Piccadilly, where you will find the **Royal Academy of Arts**. Architecture buffs will want to see the Christopher Wren–designed **St. James's Church** just across the road. From this side of Piccadilly to Pall Mall, with Green Park to the west and Lower Regent Street to the east, is St. James's, Mayfair's more stealth-wealth neighbor.

A BRIEF HISTORY

The name Mayfair derives from the 15-day May fair that was once held in the web of small streets known as Shepherd Market, but was brought to an end by the upper classes who lived there and felt it was drawing undesirables to their polished part of town. The area was mostly fields and farms belonging to families whose names are commemorated in the surrounding streets—Grosvenor, Burlington, and Berkeley—until it was developed in the early 18th century.

The beautiful St. James's Park, meanwhile, stands as an idyllic emblem of this elite past: it's the oldest royal park in London and all that remains of the royal hunting grounds that once traversed the city to Islington, Marylebone, and Hampstead. Henry VIII acquired the land in 1532 for a deer park.

3

A pedestrian passage alongside the church will take you to **Jermyn Street.** Continue south to **St. James's Square** and **Pall Mall,** with its private clubs tucked away in 18th- and 19th-century patrician buildings. On a more contemporary note, St James's is also home to the **White Cube Gallery,** a leading dealer in modern British art.

At the western end of Piccadilly at Hyde Park corner are two memorials to England's great hero the Duke of Wellington: **Wellington Arch** and the duke's restored London residence, **Apsley House.** From here a northbound bus will take you up Park Lane to **Speakers' Corner** and **Marble Arch.**

TOP ATTRACTIONS

Fodor's Choice
★

Apsley House (Wellington Museum). For Hyde Park Corner read "hero's corner"; even in the subway, beneath the turmoil of traffic, the Duke of Wellington's heroic exploits are retold in murals. The years of war against the French, and the subsequent final defeat of Napoléon at the Battle of Waterloo in 1815 made Wellington—Arthur Wellesley—the greatest soldier and statesman in the land. The house is flanked by imposing statues: opposite is the 1828 Decimus Burton **Wellington Arch** with the four-horse chariot of peace at its pinnacle (open to the public as an exhibition area and viewing platform). Just behind Apsley House, and cast from captured French guns, the legendary **Achilles** statue points the way with thrusting shield to the ducal mansion from the edge of Hyde Park. Next to Apsley House is the elaborate gateway to the royal park, designed and built by Burton at the same time as the Wellington Arch.

Once popularly known as No. 1, London, because it was the first and grandest house at the old tollgate from Knightsbridge village, this was long celebrated as the best address in town. Built by Robert Adam and later refaced and extended, it housed the Duke of Wellington from 1817 until his death in 1852. As the Wellington Museum, it has been

faithfully restored, down to Wellesley's uniforms, weapons, a fine collection of paintings, and his porcelain and plate collections acquired as a result of his military success, such as a Sévres dessert service commissioned by Napoléon for his empress, Josephine. His extensive art collection, much of it presented to him by admirers, includes works by Brueghel, Van Dyck, and Rubens, as well as the famous Veláquez portrait of Pope Innocent X and a portrait of Wellington himself on horseback by Goya. There are also numerous portraits of military comrades, allies, and even his main adversary, Napoléon Bonaparte. The free audio guide highlights the most significant works and the superb décor, notably the stunning Waterloo Gallery, where an annual banquet for officers who fought beside Wellington was held. With its heavily sculpted and gilded ceiling, its feast of old-master paintings on red damask walls, and commanding candelabra, it's a veritable orgy of opulence. Special events take place on the annual Waterloo weekend and occasionally on Waterloo Day (June 18) itself, in addition to other special events throughout the year. Call or check the Web site for details. ✉ *149 Piccadilly, Hyde Park Corner, Mayfair* ☎ *020/7499–5676* ⊕ *www.english-heritage.org.uk* ☻ *Mar.–Oct., Wed.–Sun. and bank holiday Mon. 11–5; Nov.–Feb., Wed.–Sun. 11–4* ⬛ *£5.70, joint ticket with Wellington Arch £6.80* Ⓤ *Hyde Park Corner.*

Bond Street. This world-class shopping haunt is divided into northern "New" (1710) and southern "Old" (1690) halves. You can spot the juncture by a bronzed bench on which Franklin D. Roosevelt sits companionably next to Winston Churchill. On New Bond Street you'll find **Sotheby's,** the world-famous auction house, at No. 35, as well as

Regent Street, home to Liberty department store and Hamleys toy shop, decorated for the holidays.

upscale retailers like Asprey's, Burberry, and Jimmy Choo. There are even more opportunities to flirt with financial ruin on Old Bond Street: flagship boutiques of top-end designers like Chanel, Gucci, and Yves St. Laurent; an array of fine jewelers including Tiffany's; and art dealers Colnaghi, Spink Leger, and Agnew's. **Cork Street,** which parallels the top half of Old Bond Street, is where London's top dealers in contemporary art have their galleries—you're welcome to browse. ✉ *Bond St., Mayfair* Ⓤ *Bond St., Green Park.*

Burlington Arcade. Perhaps the finest of Mayfair's enchanting covered shopping alleys is the second oldest in London, built in 1819 for Lord Cavendish, to stop the hoi polloi from throwing rubbish into his garden at Burlington House, which is behind the arcade. It's still patrolled by top-hatted watchmen called Beadles, who preserve decorum by preventing you from singing, running, or carrying open umbrellas. The arcade is also the main link between the Royal Academy of Arts and its extended galleries at 6 Burlington Gardens. ✉ *Piccadilly, Mayfair* Ⓤ *Green Park, Piccadilly Circus.*

Several of London's most storied and stylish hotels are in Mayfair. Even if you're not staying at one, sample the high life by popping into their glamorous bars for a cocktail—or some afternoon tea. **Claridge's Bar** takes its cue from art deco, as does the Ritz's intimate **Rivoli Bar** and the eponymous **Connaught Bar,** whereas the bar at **Brown's Hotel** is modernist.

Marble Arch. John Nash's 1827 arch, moved to its present location in 1851, stands amid the traffic whirlpool where Bayswater Road segues into Oxford Street, at the top of Park Lane. Search the sidewalk on the traffic island opposite the cinema to find the stone plaque that marks (roughly) the place where the Tyburn Tree stood for four centuries, until 1783. This was London's central gallows, a huge wooden structure with hanging accommodations for 24. Cross over (or under—there are signs to help in the mazelike underpass) to the northeastern corner of Hyde Park to Speakers' Corner. ⊠ *Park La., Mayfair* Ⓤ *Marble Arch*.

Piccadilly Circus. Although it may *seem* like a "circus" with its traffic and the camera-clickers clustered around the steps of **Eros,** the name refers to the five major roads that radiate from it. The origins of "Piccadilly" are from the humble tailor in the Strand named Robert Baker who sold picadils—a stiff ruffled collar all the rage in courtly circles—and built a house with the proceeds. Snobs dubbed his new-money mansion Piccadilly Hall, and the name stuck.

NAPOLEON DYNAMITE

Unmissable, in every sense, is the gigantic Canova statue of a nude (but fig-leafed) Napoléon, which presides over the grand staircase that leads to the many elegant reception rooms. The sculptor chose to present his subject, at the time the most powerful man in Europe, as Mars the Peacemaker, depicting the short and stocky emperor as a classical god more than 11 feet tall with a perfect physique. Even so, Napoléon wasn't happy with either the nudity or the athleticism of Canova's approach and ordered the marble statue to be hidden behind a screen.

Eros, London's favorite statue and symbol of the *Evening Standard* newspaper, is not in fact the Greek god of erotic love at all, but the Angel of Christian Charity, commissioned in 1893 from the young sculptor Alfred Gilbert as a memorial to the philanthropic Earl of Shaftesbury (the angel's bow and arrow are a sweet allusion to the earl's name). Gilbert cast the statue he called his "missile of kindness" in the novel medium of aluminum. Unfortunately, he spent most of his £8,000 fee ensuring the bronze fountain beneath was cast to his specifications. Already in debt, he eventually went bankrupt and fled the country. (Not to worry—he was knighted in the end.) Beneath the modern bank of neon advertisements are some of the most elegant Edwardian-era buildings in town. ⊠ *St. James's* Ⓤ *Piccadilly Circus*.

☺ **Ripley's Believe It Or Not!** London's latest tourist attraction opened in September 2008 and contains four floors of curiosities: natural mutations (an albino alligator), cultural artifacts (Eucadorian shrunken heads), and historic memorabilia (a piece of the Berlin Wall). Objects made by people with too much time on their hands, like the portrait of Princess Diana created from laundry lint or a copy of the Last Supper painted on a grain of rice, are alongside simple pleasures like the second-floor mirror maze. ⊠ *1 Piccadilly Circus, Mayfair* ☎ *020/3238–0022* ⊕ *www. ripleyslondon.com* 🔄 *£21.90* ☉ *Daily 10–midnight*.

Fodor'sChoice ★ **Royal Academy of Arts.** Burlington House was built in the Palladian style for the Earl of Burlington around 1720, and it's one of the few surviving mansions from that period. The chief occupant today is the Royal

Marble Arch was originally a gateway to Buckingham Palace before it was moved to the corner of Hyde Park.

Academy of Arts (RA), and a statue of the academy's first president, Sir Joshua Reynolds, with artist's palette in hand, is prominent in the piazza of light stone with fountains by Sir Phillip King. It's a tranquil, elegant space for sculpture exhibits. Further exhibition space has been afforded with the opening of 6 Burlington Gardens, the old Museum of Mankind, reached through the elegant walkway of Burlington Arcade. The collection houses works by Academicians past and present as well as its most prized piece, the *Taddei Tondo* (a circular bas-relief) by Michelangelo of the Madonna and Child, on display in the Sackler Wing. The RA has an active program of temporary exhibitions; hugely successful exhibitions here have included Van Dyck (1999), a Rodin retrospective (2006), and "Byzantium" (2008). Every June for the past 240 years, the RA has put on its **Summer Exhibition,** a huge and always surprising collection of sculpture and painting by living Royal Academicians and a plethora of other contemporary artists. ⊠ *Burlington House, Piccadilly, Mayfair* ☎ *020/7300–8000, 020/7300–5760 recorded information* ⊕ *www.royalacademy.org.uk* ✉ *From £12; prices vary with exhibition* ☉ *Sat.–Thurs. 10–6, Fri. 10–10* Ⓤ *Piccadilly Circus, Green Park.*

QUICK BITES

The **Royal Academy Restaurant** has hot dishes at lunchtime, very good vegetarian options, and an extensive salad selection that is inexpensive for such a posh location. The walls are covered in Stanley Spencer murals. It's open weekdays 10–5:30, with a dinner menu on Friday from 6:15 to 10:30. For something a little less substantial, have a snack at the Gallery Café, which offers a range of muffins, sandwiches, and pastries. Outdoor tables are available in the summer.

Don't miss the globe-spanning Food Hall in the basement of Sefridges.

★　**Selfridges.** With its row of massive Ionic columns, this huge store was opened three years after Harry Gordon Selfridge came to London from Chicago in 1906. Now Selfridges is comparable to Harrods in size and scope, and, since investing in major face-lift operations, to Knightsbridge's Harvey Nichols in designer cachet. ⊠ *400 Oxford St., Mayfair* ☎ *020/7629–1234* ⊕ *www.selfridges.com* ☉ *Mon.–Sat. 9:30–9, Sun. noon–6* Ⓤ *Marble Arch, Bond Street.*

St. James's Church. Completed in 1684, this was one of the last of Sir Christopher Wren's London churches and his own favorite. It contains one of Grinling Gibbons's finest works, an ornate limewood reredos (the screen behind the altar). The organ is a survivor of Whitehall Palace and was brought here in 1691. A 1940 bomb scored a direct hit here (a garden in the churchyard commemorates Londoners' fortitude during WWII), but the church was subsequently completely restored, albeit with a fiberglass spire. The interior is again showing signs of wear and water damage, and a new restoration project is in the planning stages. It's a lively place, offering all manner of lectures and concerts. The church itself is set back from the street behind a courtyard that hosts different markets: on Tuesday antiques and small collectibles; Wednesday to Saturday arts and crafts. ⊠ *197 Piccadilly, St. James's* ☎ *020/7734–4511, 020/7381–0441 concert program and tickets* ⊕ *www.st-james-piccadilly.org* Ⓤ *Piccadilly Circus, Green Park.*

Wellington Arch. Opposite the Duke of Wellington's mansion, Apsley House, this majestic stone arch surveys the busy traffic rushing around Hyde Park Corner. Designed by Decimus Burton and built in 1828, it was created as a grand entrance to the west side of London and echoes the design of that other landmark gate, Marble Arch. Both were triumphal arches commemorating Britain's victory against France in the Napoleonic Wars, and both were moved after their construction to ease the Victorian traffic situation. The Wellington Arch was constructed at the same time as the Hyde Park's Triumphal Screen (also Burton's design); you'll see the same highly ornamental green gates within the Wellington Arch. Atop the building, the Angel of Peace descends on the quadriga, or four-horse chariot of war. This replaced the Duke of Wellington on his horse, which was considered too large and hence moved to

army barracks in Aldershot. A step inside the arch reveals the stories behind the building and statue, and explores other great arches around the world. Without doubt, the highlight is to walk around the top of the arch and enjoy the brilliant panoramas over the park, including glimpses into the private gardens of Buckingham Palace. ⊠ *Hyde Park Corner, Mayfair* ☎ *020/7930–2726* ⊕ *www.english-heritage.org.uk* ⊡ *£3.50* ⊙ *Apr.–Oct., Wed.–Sun. 10–5; Nov.–Mar., Wed.–Sun. 10–4* Ⓤ *Hyde Park Corner.*

WORTH NOTING

Grosvenor Square. This square (pronounced *Grove*-na) was laid out in 1725–31 and is as desirable an address today as it was then. Americans certainly thought so—from John Adams, the second president, who as ambassador lived at No. 38, to Dwight D. Eisenhower, whose wartime headquarters was at No. 20. Now the massive '60s block of the U.S. Embassy occupies the entire west side, and a British memorial to Franklin D. Roosevelt stands in the center. There is also a memorial to those who died in New York on September 11, 2001. The little brick chapel used by Eisenhower's men during World War II, the 1730 Grosvenor Chapel, stands a couple of blocks south of the square on South Audley Street, with the entrance to pretty **St. George's Gardens** to its left. Across the gardens is the headquarters of the English Jesuits as well as the society-wedding favorite, the mid-19th-century Church of the Immaculate Conception, known as Farm Street Church because of its location. ⊠ *Mayfair* Ⓤ *Bond St.*

☼ **Handel House Museum.** The former home of the composer, where he lived for more than 30 years until his death in 1759, is a celebration of his genius. It's the first museum in London solely dedicated to one composer, and that is made much of with room settings in the contemporary fine Georgian style. You can linger over original manuscripts (there are more to be seen in the British Library) and gaze at portraits—accompanied by live music if the adjoining music rooms are being used by musicians in rehearsal. Some of the composer's most famous pieces were created here, including *Messiah* and *Music for the Royal Fireworks*. To hear a live concert here—there are Thursday evening performances, mostly of baroque music—is to imagine the atmosphere of rehearsals and "salon" music in its day. Handel House makes a perfect cultural pit stop after shopping on nearby Bond and Oxford streets, and if you come on Saturday, there is free admission for kids. The museum occupies both No. 25 and the adjoining house, where life in Georgian London is displayed, and where another musical star, Jimi Hendrix, lived for a brief time in the 1960s, as a blue plaque outside the house indicates—also look for the petite exhibition of photos. Tours of his flat, currently administrative offices and not usually open to the public, are offered twice a year. Phone or check the Web site for details. ⌂ *25 Brook St., entrance in Lancashire Court Mayfair* ☎ *020/7495–1685* ⊕ *www.handelhouse.org* ◱ *£5* ⊙ *Tues.–Sat. 10–6, Thurs. until 8, Sun. noon–6* Ⓤ *Bond St.*

ROYALTY IN AISLE 9

Shoppers and historians alike will enjoy **Fortnum & Mason** at 181 Piccadilly. This old-fashioned fine-foods store feels lifted from another century, with ornate murals decorating the walls, glass cabinets, and brass fixtures casting a dazzling glow all around. Its restaurants, where you can find quintessentially British dishes like Welsh rarebit and a fabulous ice-cream parlor, are beloved of country ladies who've come up for the day. Built in 1788, Fortnum & Mason sent hams to the Duke of Wellington's army and baskets of treats to Florence Nightingale in the Crimea. (It also happens to be the Queen's grocery store.)

★ **Spencer House.** Ancestral abode of the Spencers—Diana, Princess of Wales's family—this is perhaps the finest example of an elegant 18th-century town house extant in London. Reflecting his passion for the Grand Tour and classical antiquities, the first Earl Spencer commissioned architect John Vardy to adapt designs from ancient Rome for a magnificent private palace. Vardy was responsible for the external elevation, including the gorgeous west-facing Palladian facade, its pediment adorned with classical statues, and the ground-floor interiors, notably the lavish Palm Room, which boasts a spectacular screen of columns covered in gilded carvings that resemble gold palm trees. The purpose of the bling-tastic decor was not only to attest to Spencer's power and wealth but also to celebrate his marriage, a love match then rare in aristocratic circles (the palms are a symbol of marital fertility). Midway through construction—the house was built between 1756 and 1766—Spencer changed architects and hired James "Athenian" Stuart, whose designs were based on a classical Greek aesthetic, to decorate the gilded State Rooms on the first floor. These include the Painted Room, the first completely neoclassical room in Europe. In recent years the house has been superlatively restored by Lord Rothschild. The garden, of Henry Holland design, has also been replanted in the 18th- and

Gentleman's shops in St. James specialize in high-quality, handmade goods.

19th-century fashion. The house is open only on Sunday (closed January and August), and only to guided tours. The garden is open some Sundays in summer. Check the Web site for details. ⊠ *27 St. James's Pl., St. James's* ☎ *020/7499–8620* ⊕ *www.spencerhouse.co.uk* ▥ *£9* ☺ *Sept.–Dec. and Feb.–July, Sun. 10:30–5:45, last tour 4:45; tour leaves approx. every 25 mins; tickets on sale Sun. at 10:30* Ⓤ *Green Park.*

St. James's Square. One of London's oldest and leafiest squares was also the most snobbish address of all when it was laid out around 1670, with 14 resident dukes and earls installed by 1720. Since 1841, No. 14—one of the several 18th-century residences spared by World War II bombs—has housed the **London Library,** founded by Thomas Carlyle. With its million or so volumes, it's considered the best private humanities library in the land and is the workplace of some of the city's top writers. You can go in and read famous authors' complaints in the comments book—but not the famous authors' books, unless you take out a £10 day membership. Other notable institutions around the square include the **East India Club** at No. 16, and the **Naval and Military Club** (known as the "In and Out" after the signage on its gateposts) at No. 4. ⊠ *St. James's* ⊕ *www.londonlibrary.co.uk* Ⓤ *Piccadilly Circus.*

St. James's and Mayfair Dining

AT A GLANCE

BUDGET DINING
Golden Hind, Seafood, 73 Marylebone La.

MODERATE DINING
Cecconi's, Italian, 5A Burlington Gardens

Corrigan's Mayfair, Modern British, 28 Upper Gosvenor St.

The Grill at the Dorchester, Modern British, The Dorchester, 53 Park La.

Hibiscus, Modern French, 29 Maddox St.

La Petite Maison, French, 53–54 Brook's Mews

Le Caprice, Modern British, Arlington House, Arlington St.

St. Alban, Mediterranean, 4–12 Regent St.

The Providores & Tapa Room, Asian, 109 Marylebone High St.

Wild Honey, Modern European, 12 George St

The Wolseley, Austrian, 160 Piccadilly

EXPENSIVE DINING
Gaucho Grill, Steak, 25 Swallow St.

Greenhouse, French, 27A Hay's Mews

Hélène Darroze at the Connaught, French, The Connaught, Carlos Pl.

L'Oranger, French, 5 St. James's St.

Le Gavroche, French, 43 Upper Brook St.

Locanda Locatelli, Italian, 8 Seymour St.

Nobu Berkeley Street, Japanese, 15 Berkeley St.

Scott's, Seafood, 20 Mount St.

Sketch, Modern British, 9 Conduit St.

The Square, French, 6–10 Bruton St.

Soho and Covent Garden

WORD OF MOUTH

"The main business for buskers is in the daytime, when the shops and stalls are open. The area is full of interesting-looking shops."
—PatrickLondon

GETTING ORIENTED

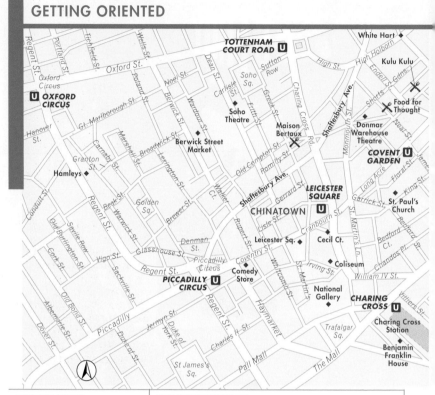

GETTING THERE	TOP REASONS TO GO
For Soho, take any train to the Piccadilly Circus station (on the Piccadilly and Bakerloo lines) or to Leicester Square (Piccadilly and Northern lines), Oxford Circus (Bakerloo, Victoria, and Central lines), or Tottenham Court Road (Northern and Central lines). Get off at Covent Garden on the Piccadilly Line for Covent Garden, and at Embankment (Bakerloo, Northern, District, and Circle lines), Charing Cross (Northern, Bakerloo, and main railway lines), or Temple (District and Circle lines) for the area south of the Strand. More than 30 buses will take you to the Covent Garden area.	**Shaftesbury Avenue:** Take in a show on London's equivalent of Broadway, and snaffle half-price tickets at the Leicester Square kiosk. **Royal Opera House:** Make sure you visit even if you're not going to the opera or ballet for both the beautiful architecture and sheer sense of history. **Courtauld Gallery:** Admire your favorite impressionist painting up close in the Courtauld Gallery, then discover Cranach the Elder's mischievous *Adam and Eve.* **Somerset House:** Watch the skaters and ice-wall climbers on a December evening. Otherwise, try the London Craft Fair, held each autumn in a specially designed pavilion. In summer, dine at the terrace restaurant overlooking the river. **London Transport Museum:** Explore the city's history with interactive installations about its public transport.

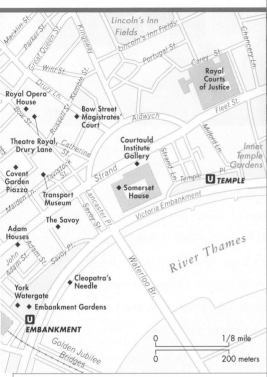

4

MAKING THE MOST OF YOUR TIME

You can comfortably tour all the sights in Covent Garden in a day. Visit the small but perfect Courtauld Gallery on Monday before 2 PM when it's free. That leaves plenty of time to visit the marketplace, watch the street entertainment, and do a bit of shopping, with energy left over for a night on the town (or "on the tiles," as the British say) in Soho.

FEELING PECKISH?

Although they may set out a few tables, the coffee shops and snack bars along the Covent Garden market buildings can be overpriced and of iffy quality. It's usually best to head for Soho when the munchies strike.

Maison Bertaux (⌧ 28 Greek St., Soho ☎ 020/7437–6007) has been around since the end of the 19th century. Decor is spartan, but fab French cakes, tarts, and savory quiches more than make up for that. Nobody's mother ever baked this well.

Kulu Kulu (⌧ 51–53 Shelton St., Covent Garden ☎ 020/7240–5687) offers fresh, good-value sushi. Dishes trundle around on a conveyor belt—ideal if you're pressed for time. There's another branch on Brewer Street in Soho.

Food for Thought (⌧ 31 Neal St., Covent Garden ☎ 020/7836–9072) is always crowded, with hungry customers queuing outside for their delicious range of vegetarian dishes.

GAY LONDON

Old Compton Street in Soho is the epicenter of London's affluent, stylish gay scene. There are some very smart nightclubs in the area.

Madame Jo Jo's (⌧ 8–10 Brewer St. ☎ 020/7724–3040 ⊕ www.madamejojos.com) has been around for nearly 50 years, with a range of different, popular club nights. The club's **Kitsch Cabaret**, which can be booked online, is so popular (with straights as well as gays) that it's booked up weeks in advance.

Sightseeing
★★★
Nightlife
★★★★
Dining
★★★★
Lodging
★★
Shopping
★★★

Once a red-light district, today's Soho delivers more "grown-up" than "adult" entertainment, offering some of London's best nightclubs, live music venues, restaurants, and theaters. By day, this hotbed of media production reverts to the business side of its late-night scene. If Soho is all about showbiz, neighboring Covent Garden, home to the Royal Opera House and Courtald Institute Gallery, is devoted to culture. Both offer an abundance of narrow streets packed with one-of-a-kind shops and lots of character.

Updated
by Michelle
Rosenberg

The narrow, winding streets of Soho lie to the east of Regent Street and to the south of Oxford Street. To the west of Wardour Street, there are lots of interesting small boutiques around Foubert's Place and on Brewer and Lexington streets, which also boast some of London's best-value restaurants. To the east of Wardour Street is nightlife central. At its southern end is gay mecca Old Compton Street and beyond that Shaftsbury Avenue, London's equivalent of Broadway. Between here and **Leicester Square** is London's compact Chinatown. Charing Cross Road, to the east of the square, is famous for its secondhand bookshops, and tiny **Cecil Court** is a pedestrianized passage lined with small antiquarian-book sellers.

To the east of Charing Cross Road lies Covent Garden. Just north of the **Piazza** and the adjoining **Royal Opera House,** busy Long Acre bisects the district on an east–west axis. On the north is a nexus of yet more narrow streets with lots of interesting shops and the **Donmar Warehouse,** one of London's best and most innovative theaters where stars like Nicole Kidman and Ewan McGregor take to the stage. Nearby Monmouth Street is the place to look for innovative fashion. Wellington Street, south of Long Acre, has several reasonably priced restaurants for a quick pretheater bite.

At the end of Wellington Street is the semicircular Aldwych, lined with grand buildings. Moving west down the Strand is the huge 18th-century

DID YOU KNOW

Covent Garden was a convent garden for 300 years before it was a Britain's first planned public square and a fruit and vegetable market. The 1840 market building and the courtyard still teem with shoppers.

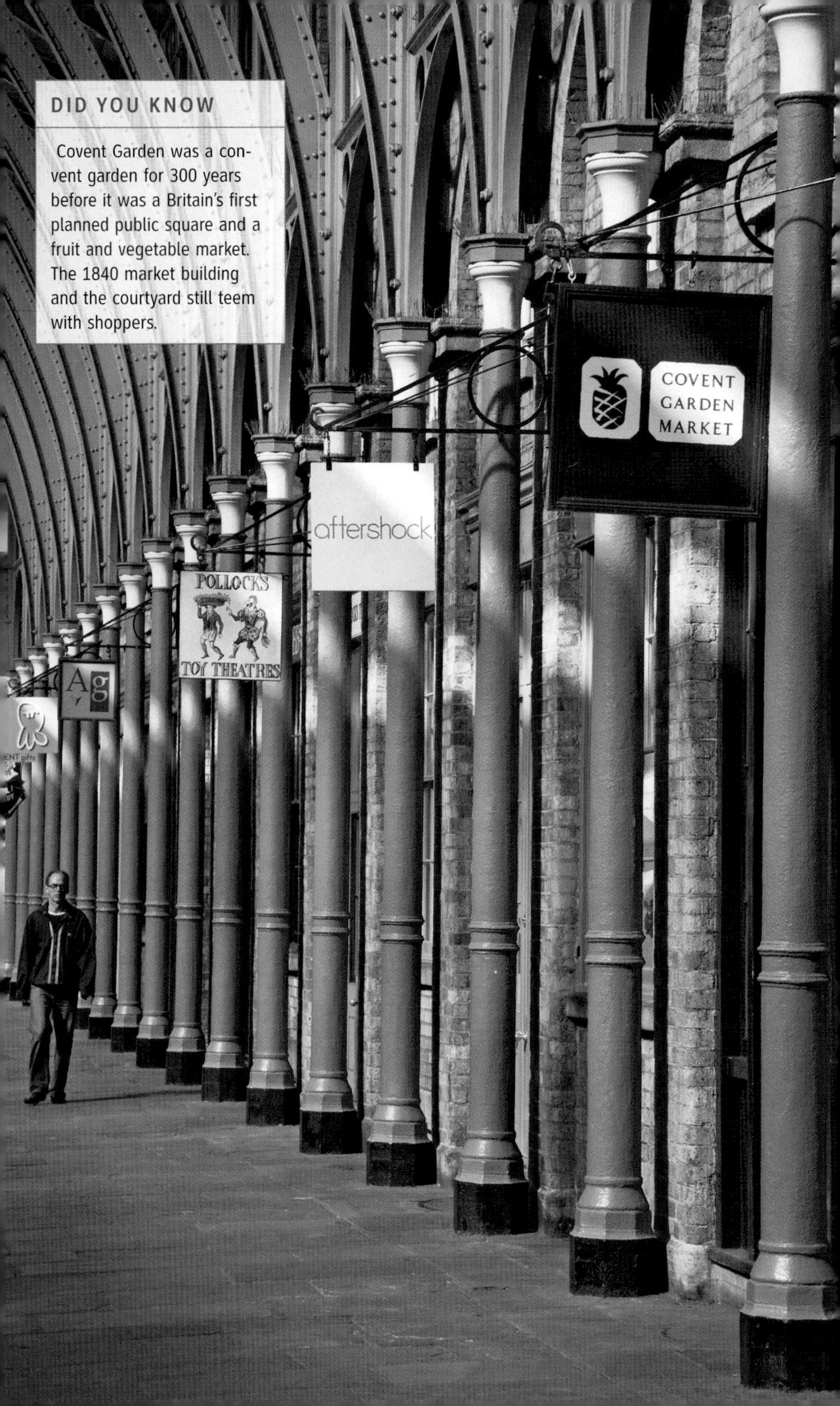
COVENT
GARDEN
MARKET
aftershock
POLLOCK'S
TOY THEATRES
Ag

You can't miss the buskers performing in the streets of Soho and Covent Garden.

piazza of **Somerset House**, which contains the **Courtauld Institute Gallery**. Just behind the Strand are small lanes that will make you feel you've stepped back into the18th and early 19th century. On the way to the verdant **Embankment Gardens** bordering the river, you may pass the **Adam Houses** and the **Benjamin Franklin House**, where the noted statesman lived in the years leading up to the American Revolution.

TOP ATTRACTIONS

Courtauld Institute Gallery. One of London's most beloved art collections, the Courtauld is to your left as you pass through the archway into the grounds of the beautifully restored, grand 18th-century classical **Somerset House**. Founded in 1931 by the textile magnate Samuel Courtauld to house his remarkable private collection, this is one of the world's finest impressionist and postimpressionist galleries, with artists ranging from Bonnard to van Gogh. A déjà-vu moment with Cézanne, Degas, Seurat, or Monet awaits on every wall (Manet's *Bar at the Folies-Bergère* is the star), with bonus post-Renaissance works thrown in. Botticelli, Brueghel, Tiepolo, and Rubens are also represented, thanks to the exquisite bequest of Count Antoine Seilern's Princes Gate collection. German Renaissance paintings, bequeathed in 1947, include the colorful and delightfully wicked *Adam and Eve* by Lucas Cranach the Elder. There are also some bold and bright Fauvist paintings. Don't miss the little café downstairs. The Courtauld Institute of Art (on the other side of the entrance archway) is part of London University and trains art historians and conservators. ⊠ *Somerset House, Strand, Covent Garden* ☎ *020/7848–2526* ⊕ *www.courtauld.ac.uk* ⏴*£5, free Mon.*

A BRIEF HISTORY

Almost as soon as a 17th-century housing development covered what had been a royal park and hunting ground, Soho earned a reputation for entertainment, bohemianism, and cosmopolitan tolerance. When the authorities introduced zero tolerance of soliciting in 1991, the most recent of several attempts to end Soho's sex trade, they cracked down on an old neighborhood tradition that still resurfaces from time to time.

Successive waves of refugees, from French Huguenots in the 1680s followed by Germans, Russians, Poles, Greeks, Italians, and Chinese, settled and brought their ethnic cuisines with them. So when dining out became fashionable after World War I, Soho was the natural place for restaurants to flourish.

In the 1950s and '60s, Soho was London's main artists' quarter and the place to find the top jazz and rock clubs. Among the luminaries who have made their home here are landscape painter John Constable; Casanova; Canaletto, the great painter of Venice; William Blake; and Karl Marx.

Present-day Covent Garden took shape in the 1630s, when Inigo Jones turned what had been agricultural land into Britain's first planned public square. After the Great Fire, it became the site of England's largest fruit-and-vegetable market (the flower market arrived in the 19th century). This, along with the district's many theaters and taverns, gave the area a somewhat dubious reputation, and after the produce market relocated in 1973, the surviving buildings were scheduled for demolition. A local campaign saved them, and the restored market opened in 1980.

10–2, except bank holidays ⊘ *Daily 10–6; last admission 5:30* Ⓤ *Covent Garden, Holborn, Temple.*

★ **Covent Garden Piazza.** The 1840 market building around which Covent Garden pivots is known as the Piazza. Inside, the shops are mostly higher-class clothing chains, plus a couple of cafés and some knick-knack stores that are good for gifts. One particular gem is Benjamin Pollock's Toyshop at No. 44 in the market. Established in the 1880s, it sells delightful toy theaters. There's the superior **Apple Market** for crafts on most days, too. If you turn right, you'll reach the indoor **Jubilee Market,** which, with its stalls of clothing, army-surplus gear, and more crafts and knickknacks, is disappointingly ordinary. In summer it may seem that everyone you see around the Piazza (and the crowds are legion) is a fellow tourist, but there's still plenty of office life in the area. Londoners who shop here tend to head for Neal Street and the area to the left of the subway entrance rather than the touristy market itself. By the church in the square, street performers—from global musicians to jugglers and mimes—play to the crowds, as they have done since the first English Punch and Judy Show, staged here in the 17th century. ⊠ *Covent Garden* Ⓤ *Covent Garden.*

Ⓒ
★ **London Transport Museum.** Housed in the old flower market at the southeast corner of the Covent Garden Piazza, the recently refurbished museum includes the interactive space "Green Futures" that focuses

DID YOU KNOW?

Somerset House was lapped by the River Thames before the Victoria Embankment was built in the 19th century. The neoclassical building's grand courtyard is home to ice skating in winter and dancing fountains in summer.

on the challenge of meeting London's growth in partnership with the environment. As you watch the crowds gawking at the horse trams, steam locomotives, and trolley buses from the past, you're not sure who's enjoying it more, children or adults. This kid-friendly (under 16 admitted free) museum is filled with impressive poster, photograph, and vehicle collections. Food and drink are available at the aptly named Upper Deck café. ⊠ *Covent Garden Piazza* ☏ *020/7379–6344* ⊕ *www. ltmuseum.co.uk* ⊡ *£10* ⊙ *Sat.– Thurs. 10–6 (last admission 5:15), Fri. 11–6 (last admission 5:15)* Ⓤ *Leicester Sq., Covent Garden.*

Royal Opera House. London's premier opera and ballet venue was designed in 1858 by E. M. Barry, son of Sir Charles, the House of Commons architect, and is the third theater on the site. The first theater opened in 1732 and burned down in 1808; the second opened a year later, only to succumb to fire in 1856. The entire building, which has been given a spectacular overhaul, retains the magic of the grand Victorian theater but is now more accessible. The glass-and-steel Floral Hall (so badly damaged by fire in the 1950s it was used only for storing scenery) is the most wonderful feature; you can wander around and drink in (literally, in the foyer café) the interior during the day. The same is true of the Amphitheatre Bar and Piazza concourse, where you can have lunch while looking out at a splendid panorama across the city. There are free lunchtime chamber concerts and lectures, as well as tea dances and occasional free jazz concerts, as part of the policy to dispel the Opera House's elitist tag. ⊠ *Bow St., Covent Garden* ☏ *020/7240–1200* ⊕ *www.royalopera.org* Ⓤ *Covent Garden.*

⊙ Fodor's Choice ★ **Somerset House.** An old royal palace once stood on the site, but it was eventually replaced by this 18th-century building, the work of Sir William Chambers (1726–96), during the reign of George III. It was built to house government offices, principally those of the navy. Now, for the first time in more than 100 years, these gracious rooms are on view, including the Seamen's Waiting Hall and the Nelson Stair. In addition, the Navy Commissioners' Barge has returned to dry dock at the Water Gate. The rooms are on the south side of the building, by the river. The **Courtauld Institute Gallery** occupies most of the north building, facing the busy Strand. In between is the cobbled Italianate courtyard where Admiral Nelson used to walk, the scene of an ice rink in the winter holiday season as well as summer concerts and other cultural events. Cafés and a restored river terrace adjoin the property, and a stone-and-glass footbridge leads up to Waterloo Bridge, which you can walk across

ICE-SKATING

It's hard to beat the skating experience at Somerset House, where during December and January (and sometimes beginning as early as November) a rink is set up in the spectacularly grand courtyard of this central London palace. Check the Web site for current prices; its popularity is enormous, and if you can't get a ticket, other venues such as Hampton Court and the Natural History Museum are following Somerset House's lead in having temporary winter rinks. ☏ 0844/847–1520 ⊕ www. somerset-house.org.uk/icerink.

4

to get to the South Bank. Exhibitions have included works by Renoir and exquisite medieval ivories. A new gallery devoted to contemporary art, design, fashion, architecture, and photography hosts three exhibitions a year. ⌧ *The Strand, Covent Garden* ☎ *020/7845–4600* ⊕ *www. somerset-house.org.uk* 🖻 *Embankment Gallery £5, Courtauld Gallery £5, other areas free* ⊗ *Daily 10–6; last admission 5:30* Ⓤ *Charing Cross, Waterloo, Blackfriars.*

WORTH NOTING

The Adam Houses. All that remains of what was once a regal riverfront row of houses on a 3-acre site, connected by arches and streets below grade, are a few of the structures, but such is their quality that they are worth a detour off the Strand to see. The work of 18th-century Scottish architects and interior designers (John, Robert, James, and William Adam, known collectively as the Adam brothers), the original development was damaged in the 19th century during the building of the embankment, and mostly demolished in 1936 to be replaced by an art deco tower. The original houses still standing are protected, and give a glimpse of their former grandeur. Nos. 1–4 Robert Street and Nos. 7 and 10 Adam Street are the best. At the **Royal Society of Arts** (⌧ *8 John Adam St.* ☎ *020/7930–5115* ⊕ *www.thersa.org* 🖻 *Free* ⊗ *1st Sun. of month, 10–1*), you can see a suite of Adam rooms; no reservations are required. ⌧ *The Strand, Covent Garden* Ⓤ *Charing Cross, Embankment.*

Benjamin Franklin House. Opened to the public for the first time in 2006, this architecturally significant 1730 house is the only surviving residence of American statesman, scientist, writer, and inventor Benjamin Franklin, who lived and worked there for 16 years preceding the American Revolution. The restored Georgian town house has been left unfurnished, the better to show off the original features—18th-century paneling, stoves, beams, bricks, and windows. Older children (under 16 admitted free) particularly enjoy the "Historical Experience," an interactive biography of the Founding Father that is offered on the hour from noon to 4. There's also a glass harmonica (which Franklin invented while living there) and a scholarship center with a complete collection of Franklin's papers. ⌧ *36 Craven St., Covent Garden* ☎ *020/7839–2006, 020/7925–1405 booking line* ⊕ *www.benjaminfranklinhouse.org* 🖻 *£7* ⊗ *Wed.–Sun. noon–5.*

Leicester Square. Looking at the neon of the major movie houses, the fast-food outlets, and the disco entrances, you'd never guess that this square (pronounced Lester) was

> ### CHEAP TICKETS
>
> One landmark certainly worth visiting is the **Society of London Theatre ticket kiosk (TKTS)**, on the southwest corner of Leicester Square, which sells half-price tickets for many of that evening's performances. It's open Monday to Saturday from 10 to 7, and Sunday from noon to 3 PM. One window sells matinee tickets and the other tickets for evening performances, so make sure you join the correct line. Watch out for illegal ticket touts (scalpers), who target tourists around the square.

Leicester Square is home to many cinemas and a half-priced theater ticket booth.

a model of formality and refinement when it was first laid out around 1630. By the 19th century it was already bustling and disreputable, and although today it's not a threatening place, you should still be on your guard, especially at night—any space so full of tourists and people a little the worse for wear is bound to attract pickpockets, and Leicester Square certainly does. Although it retains some residual glamour as the site of red-carpet film premieres, Londoners generally tend to avoid this windswept pedestrianized plaza, crowded as it is with suburban teenagers, wandering backpackers, and mimes. That said, the liveliness can be quite cheering. In the middle is a statue of a sulking Shakespeare, clearly wishing he were somewhere else and perhaps remembering the days when the cinemas were live theaters—burlesque houses, but live all the same. Here, too, are figures of Newton, Hogarth, Reynolds, and Charlie Chaplin. On the northeast corner, in Leicester Place, stands the church of **Notre Dame de France,** with a wonderful mural by Jean Cocteau in one of its side chapels. ✉ *Covent Garden* Ⓤ *Leicester Sq.*

St. Paul's Church. If you want to commune with the spirits of Vivien Leigh, Noël Coward, Edith Evans, or Charlie Chaplin, this might be just the place. Memorials to them and many other theater greats are found in this 1633 work of the renowned Inigo Jones, who, as the King's Surveyor of Works, designed the whole of Covent Garden Piazza (Wren's St. Paul's Cathedral is eastward in the City). St. Paul's has been known as "the actors' church" since the Restoration, thanks to the neighboring theater district and St. Paul's prominent parishioners. (Well-known actors often read the lessons at services, and the church still hosts concerts and small-scale productions.) Fittingly, the opening

Soho and Covent Garden Dining

AT A GLANCE

BUDGET DINING

Baozi Inn, Chinese, 25 Newport Ct.

Bar Italia, Café, 22 Frith St.

Busabe Eathai, Thai, 106–110 Wardour St.

Canela, Portuguese, 33 Earlham St.

Cha Cha Moon, Chinese, 15–21 Ganton St.

Food for Thought, Vegetarian, 31 Neal St.

Maison Bertaux, Café, 28 Greek St.

Wahaca, Mexican, 66 Chandos Pl.

Yauatcha, Chinese, 15 Broadwick St.

MODERATE DINING

Andrew Edmunds, Mediterranean, 46 Lexington St.

Arbutus, Modern British, 63–64 Frith St.

Barrafina, Spanish, 54 Frith St.

Boccadi Lupo, Italian, 12 Archer St.

Côte, French, 124–126 Wardour

Giaconda Dining Room, Modern European, 9 Denmark St.

Great Queen Street, British, 32 Great Queen St.

J Sheekey, Seafood, 28–32 St. Martin's Ct.

Joe Allen, American, 13 Exeter St.

Quo Vadis, Modern European, 26–29 Dean Street

EXPENSIVE DINING

The Ivy, British, 1–5 West St.

L'Atelier de Joël Robuchon, French, 13–15 West St.

Rules, British, 35 Maiden La.

---

scene of Shaw's *Pygmalion* takes place under its Tuscan portico. The western end of the Piazza in front of the portico is a prime pitch for street entertainers, but if they're not to your liking, you can repair to the serenity of the garden entered from King or Bedford streets. ⊠ *Bedford St., Covent Garden* Ⓤ *Covent Garden.*

Theatre Royal, Drury Lane. This is London's best-known auditorium and almost its largest. Since World War II, its forte has been musicals (past ones have included *The King and I*, *My Fair Lady*, *South Pacific*, *Hello, Dolly!*, and *A Chorus Line*)—though David Garrick, who managed it from 1747 to 1776, made its name by reviving the works of the by-then-obscure William Shakespeare. It enjoys all the romantic accessories of a London theater—a history of fires (it burned down three times, once in a Wren-built incarnation), riots (in 1737, when a posse of footmen demanded free admission), attempted regicides (George II in 1716 and his grandson George III in 1800), and even sightings of the most famous phantom of theaterland, the Man in Grey (in the Circle during matinees). ⊠ *Catherine St., Covent Garden* ☎ *020/7494–5000* ⊕ *www. theatre-royal.com* Ⓤ *Covent Garden.*

5

Bloomsbury and Legal London

WORD OF MOUTH

"The British Museum was an anticipated trip highlight for me, one of the main things that drew me to London in the first place. It didn't disappoint. I spent six and a half hours in there, but I am pretty sure I could have spent six and half weeks and not run out of things to look at."

—glenmd

GETTING ORIENTED

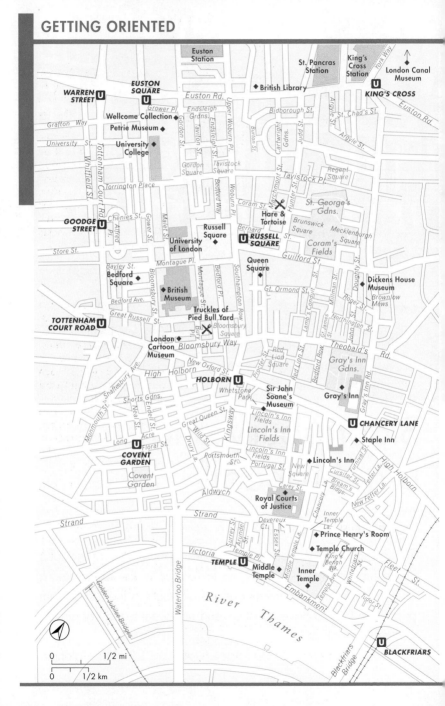

TOP REASONS TO GO

British Museum: It's never too late to start appreciating the treasures here that would take lifetimes to see.

British Library: Lay eyes on the original Magna Carta, an actual Gutenberg Bible, copies of Jane Austen's writings, and Shakespeare's First Folio. According to the library, if you saw five items each day, it would take you a whopping 80,000 years to view the full collection, so start now!

Museum Mile: Stroll along streets lined with independent galleries, antiquarian map shops, and delightful cafés through the area that encompasses many of the city's best museums.

Scholarly London: Visit the Inns of Court for a lesson in law or hang out near the University of London with the day's paper while eavesdropping on political discussions.

FEELING PECKISH?

The Hare and Tortoise Dumpling & Noodle Bar (✉ *11–13 Brunswick Shopping Centre [opposite the Renoir Cinema], Brunswick Square, Bloomsbury* ☎ *020/7278–9799.*) serves scrumptious Asian fast food. This bright café is a favorite with students, and it's easy to see why: ingredients are all natural, the portions are huge, and the bill is always reasonable.

Truckles of Pied Bull Yard (✉ *Off Bury Pl.* ☎ *020/7404–5338*), across Kingsway, toward the British Museum on Bury Place, is a popular chain wine bar and café. Its main attraction is the courtyard, where you can relax away from the museum hustle and bustle. The superb London Review Bookshop is here, too.

SAFETY

Come evening, avoid the region around King's Cross because it's known to be one of London's more unsavory neighborhoods, especially for non-natives who don't know their way about town.

GETTING THERE

You can easily get to where you need to be on foot in Bloomsbury, and the Russell Square Tube stop on the Piccadilly Line leaves you right at the corner of Russell Square. The best Tube stops for the Inns of Court are Holborn on the Central and Piccadilly lines or Chancery Lane on the Central Line. Tottenham Court Road on the Northern and Central lines or Russell Square (Piccadilly Line) are best for the British Museum.

MAKING THE MOST OF YOUR TIME

Bloomsbury can be seen in a day, or in half a day, depending on your interests and your time constraints. If you plan to visit the Inns of Court as well as the British Museum, and you'd also like to get a feel for the neighborhood, then you may wish to devote an entire day to this literary and legal enclave, or come back on another day to visit the British Museum, which can be quite exhausting.

Avoid Bloomsbury in mid-September, when the streets around Russell Square are filled with students moving into housing for the upcoming school session. At other times, it's a pleasure to wander through the quiet, leafy squares, examining historic Blue Plaques or relaxing at a street-side café.

5

Sightseeing
★★★
Nightlife
★★
Dining
★★
Lodging
★★★★
Shopping
★★

The hub of intellectual London, Bloomsbury is anchored by the British Museum and the University of London. As a result, the streets and cafés around Bloomsbury's Russell Square are often crawling with students and professors engaged in heated conversation, and literary agents and academics scan the shelves of the antiquarian bookstores nearby.

Updated by
Jan Fuscoe

Fundamental to the region's spirit of open expression and scholarly debate is the legacy of the "Bloomsbury Group," an elite corps of artists and writers who lived here during the first three decades of the 20th century. **Gordon Square** was at one point home to Virginia Woolf, John Maynard Keynes (both at No. 46), and Lytton Strachey (at No. 51). Much like the Beat poets of San Francisco or the jazz artists of the Harlem Renaissance, they defined their neighborhood as well as an entire era. But perhaps the best-known square in Bloomsbury is the large, centrally located **Russell Square**, with gardens laid out by Humphry Repton, a prominent English landscape designer. Scattered around the **University of London** campus are Woburn Square, Torrington Square, Tavistock Square, and Gordon Square. The unforgettable **British Library** with its vast treasures is a few blocks north, across busy Euston Road.

The area from Somerset House on the Strand, all the way up Kingsway to the Euston Road, is known as London's **Museum Mile** for the myriad historic houses and museums that dot the area. **Charles Dickens Museum**, where the author wrote *Oliver Twist,* is one of the most-visited sites in the area. Artists' studios and design shops share space with tenants near the bright and modern **British Museum**. And guaranteed to raise a smile from the most blasé and footsore tourist is **Sir John Soane's Museum**, which hardly deserves the burden of its dry name.

Bloomsbury also happens to be where London's legal profession was born. In fact, the buildings associated with legal London were some of the few structures spared during the Great Fire of 1666, and so the serpentine alleys, cobbled courts, and historic halls frequented by the city's still-bewigged barristers ooze centuries of history. The massive Gothic-style **Royal Courts of Justice** ramble all the way to the Strand, and the **Inns** of Court—**Gray's Inn, Lincoln's Inn, Middle Temple,** and **Inner Temple**—are where most British trial lawyers have offices to this day. In the 14th century the inns were lodging houses where the barristers lived so that people would know how to easily find them (hence, the label "inn"). Also here are Temple Church, the 500-year-old Prince Henry's Room, and the Staple Inn, one of London's oldest surviving half-timber buildings.

TOP ATTRACTIONS

British Library. Formerly in the British Museum, the collection of around 18 million volumes now has a home in state-of-the-art surroundings, and if you're a researcher, it's a wonderful place to work (special passes are required). The library's treasures are on view to the general public: the Magna Carta, a Gutenberg Bible, Jane Austen's writings, Shakespeare's First Folio, and musical manuscripts by Handel as well as Sir Paul McCartney are on show in the Sir John Ritblat Gallery. Also in the gallery are headphones—you can listen to some of the most interesting snippets in a small showcase of the **National Sound Archive** stored here (it's the world's largest collection, but is not on view), such as the voice of Florence Nightingale and an extract from the Beatles' last tour interview. On weekends and during school vacations there are hands-on demonstrations of how a book comes together. Feast your eyes also on the six-story glass tower that holds the 65,000-volume collection of George III, plus a permanent exhibition of rare stamps. If all this wordiness is just too much, you can relax in the library's piazza or restaurant, or take in one of the occasional free concerts in the amphitheater outside. ✉ *96 Euston Rd., Bloomsbury* ☎ *0870/7412–7332* ⊕ *www.bl.uk* 🎫 *Free, donations appreciated, charge for special exhibitions* ☽ *Mon. and Wed.–Fri. 9:30–6, Tues. 9:30–8, Sat. 9:30–5, Sun. and bank holidays Mon. 11–5* Ⓤ *Euston, Euston Sq., King's Cross.*

British Museum. *See the highlighted listing in this chapter.*

Sir John Soane's Museum. Sir John (1753–1837), architect of the Bank of England, bequeathed his house to the nation on condition that nothing be changed. He obviously had enormous fun with his home: in the Picture Room, for instance, two of Hogarth's *Rake's Progress* series are among the paintings on panels that swing away to reveal secret gallery pockets with even more paintings. Everywhere mirrors and colors play tricks with light and space, and split-level floors worthy of a fairground fun house disorient you. In a basement chamber sits the vast 1300 BC sarcophagus of Seti I, lit by a domed skylight two stories above. (When Sir John acquired this priceless object for £2,000, after it was rejected by the British Museum, he celebrated with a three-day party.) The elegant, tranquil courtyard gardens with statuary and plants are open to the public, and there's a below-street-level passage, which joins two of the courtyards to the museum. Because of the small size of the museum, limited numbers are allowed entry at any one time, so you may have a short wait outside. ✉ *13 Lincoln's Inn Fields, Bloomsbury* ☎ *020/7440–4263* ⊕ *www.soane.org* 🎫 *Free, Sat. tour £5* ☽ *Tues.–Sat. 10–5; also 6–9 on 1st Tues. of month* Ⓤ *Holborn.*

Continued on page 112

THE BRITISH MUSEUM

Anybody writing about the British Museum had better have a large stack of superlatives close at hand: most, biggest, earliest, finest. This is the golden hoard of nearly three centuries of the Empire, the booty brought from Britain's far-flung colonies.

The first major pieces, among them the Rosetta Stone and the Parthenon Sculptures (Elgin Marbles), were "acquired" from the French, who "found" them in Egypt and Greece. The museum has since collected countless goodies of worldwide historical significance: the Black Obelisk, some of the Dead Sea Scrolls, the Lindow Man. And that only begins the list.

The British Museum is a vast space split into 94 galleries, generally divided by continent or period of history, with some areas spanning more than one level. There are marvels wherever you go, and—while we don't like to be pessimistic—it is, yes, impossible to fully appreciate everything in a day. So make the most of the tours, activity trails, and visitors guides that are available.

The following is a highly edited overview of the museum's greatest hits, organized by area. Pick one or two that whet your appetite, then branch out from there, or spend two straight hours indulging in the company of a single favorite sculpture. There's no wrong way to experience the British Museum, just make sure you do!

✉ Great Russell St., Bloomsbury WC1

☎ 020/7323–8000

🌐 www.britishmuseum.org

🎫 Free; donations encouraged. Tickets for special exhibits vary in price.

🕐 Galleries, including special exhibits, Sat.–Wed. 10–5:30, Thurs. and Fri. 10–8:30. Great Court Sun.–Wed. 9–6, Thurs.–Sat. 9 AM–11 PM.

Ⓤ Russell Square, Holborn, Tottenham Court Rd.

(left) The Great Court
(top) *Cradle to Grave* by Pharmacopoeia

MUSEUM HIGHLIGHTS

Ancient Civilizations

The Rosetta Stone. Found in 1799 and carved in 196 BC by decree of Ptolemy V in Egyptian hieroglyphics, demotic, and Greek, it was this multilingual inscription that provided French Egyptologist Jean-François Champollion with the key to deciphering hieroglyphics. *Room 4.*

Colossal statue of Ramesses II. A member of the 19th dynasty (ca. 1270 BC), Ramesses II commissioned innumerable statues of himself—more than any other preceding or succeeding king. This one, a 7-ton likeness of his perfectly posed upper half, comes from his mortuary temple, the Ramesseum, in western Thebes. *Room 4.*

(top) Portland vase
(bottom) Colossal statue of Ramesses II

The Parthenon Sculptures. Perhaps these marvelous treasures of Greece shouldn't be here—but while the debate rages on, you can steal your own moment with the Elgin Marbles. Carved in about 440 BC, these graceful decorations are displayed along with an in-depth, high-tech exhibit of the Acropolis; the **handless, footless Dionysus** who used to recline along its east pediment is especially well known. *Room 18.*

Mausoleum of Halikarnassos. All that remains of this, one of the Seven Wonders of the Ancient World, is a fragmented form of the original "mausoleum," the 4th-century tomb of Maussollos, King of Karia. The highlight of this gallery is the marble forepart of the **colossal chariot horse from the** *quadriga*. *Room 21.*

The Egyptian mummies. Another short flight of stairs takes you to the museum's most popular galleries, especially beloved by children: the Roxie Walker Galleries of Egyptian Funerary Archaeology have a fascinating collection of relics from the Egyptian realm of the dead. In addition to real corpses, wrapped mummies, and mummy cases, there's a menagerie of animal companions and curious items that were buried alongside them. *Rooms 62–63.*

Portland Vase. Made in Italy from cameo glass at the turn of the first century, it is named after the Dukes of Portland, who owned it from 1785 to 1945. It is considered a technical masterpiece—opaque white mythological figures cut by a gem-cutter are set on cobalt-blue background. *Room 70.*

The **Enlightenment Gallery** should be visited purely for the fact that its antiquarian cases hold the contents of the British Museum's first collections—Sir Hans Sloane's natural-history loot, as well as that of Sir Joseph Banks, who acquired specimens of everything from giant shells to fossils to rare plants to exotic beasts during his voyage to the Pacific aboard Captain Cook's *Endeavour*. *Room 1.*

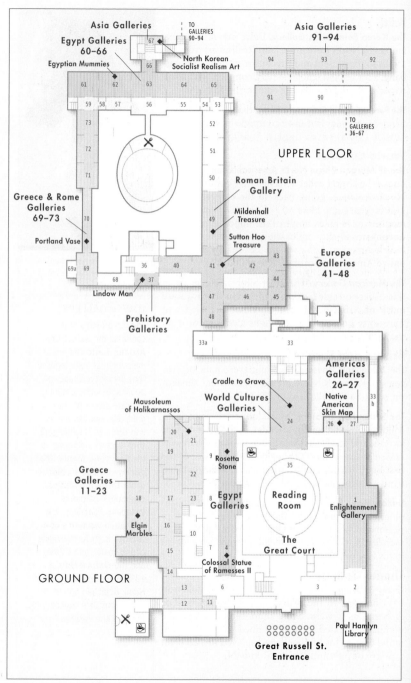

Asia Galleries

Egypt Galleries
60–66

Egyptian Mummies

67

TO GALLERIES
90–94

North Korean
Socialist Realism Art

66

61   62   63   64   65

59 58 57   56   55 54 53

73

52

72

51

71

50

Greece & Rome
Galleries
69–73

70

Roman Britain
Gallery

49

Mildenhall
Treasure

Sutton Hoo
Treasure

Portland Vase

69a 69

68   37

36   40   41   42   43

44

Lindow Man

47   46   45

Prehistory
Galleries

48

34

Asia Galleries
91–94

94   93   92

91   90

TO GALLERIES
36–67

UPPER FLOOR

Europe
Galleries
41–48

33a   33

Americas
Galleries
26–27

Cradle to Grave

World Cultures
Galleries

24

Native
American
Skin Map

33 b

26   27

Mausoleum
of Halikarnassos

20
21

19

22

9   Rosetta
Stone

35

8   Egypt
Galleries

Reading
Room

1
Enlightenment
Gallery

Greece
Galleries
11–23

18   17   23

16   10

Elgin
Marbles

15

7   4

The
Great Court

GROUND FLOOR

14

13   6

3   2

12   11

Colossal Statue
of Ramesses II

Great Russell St.
Entrance

Paul Hamlyn
Library

5

IN FOCUS THE BRITISH MUSEUM

Asia

The Korea Foundation Gallery. Delve into striking examples of **North Korean Socialist Realism art** from the 1950s to the present and a reconstruction of a **sarangbang,** a traditional scholar's study, complete with hanji paper walls and tea-making equipment. *Room 67.*

The Percival David Collection. More than 1400 pieces of Chinese ceramics (the most comprehensive collection outside China) are on display. *Room 95.*

World Cultures

The JP Morgan Chase North American Gallery. This is one of the largest collections of native culture outside North America, going back to the earliest hunters 10,000 years ago. Here a 1775 **native American skin map** serves as an example of the importance of such documents in the exploration and cartography of North America. Look for the beautifully displayed **native American costumes.** *Room 26.*

The Mexican Gallery. The most alluring pieces sit in this collection side by side: a 15th-century **turquoise mask of Xiuhtecuhtli,** the Mexican Fire God and Turquoise Lord, and a **double-headed serpent** from the same period. *Room 27.*

Britain and Europe

The Mildenhall Treasure. This glittering haul of 4th-century Roman silver tableware was found beneath the sod of a Suffolk field in 1942. *Room 49.*

The Sutton Hoo Treasure. Next door to the loot from Mildenhall—and equally splendid, including brooches, swords, and jewel-encrusted helmets—the treasure was buried at sea with (it is thought) Redwald, one of the first English kings, in the 7th century, and excavated from a Suffolk field in 1938–39. *Room 41.*

Lindow Man. "Pete Marsh"—so named by the archaeologists who unearthed the body from a Cheshire peat marsh—was ritually slain, probably as a human sacrifice, in the 1st century and lay perfectly pickled in his bog until 1984. *Room 50.*

Theme Galleries

Living & Dying. The "Cradle to Grave" installation pays homage to the British nation's wellbeing—or ill-being, as it were. More than 14,000 drugs (the number estimated to be prescribed to every person in the U.K. in his lifetime) are displayed in a colorful tapestry of pills and tablets. *Room 24.*

Colossal chariot horse from the *quadriga* of the Mausoleum at Halikarnassos

LOWER GALLERY

The three rooms that comprise the **Sainsbury African Galleries** are of the main interest here: together they present a staggering 200,000 objects, featuring intricate pieces of old ivory, gold, and wooden masks and carvings—highlighting such ancient kingdoms as the Benin and Asante. The displays include a collection of **55 throwing knives;** ceremonial garments including a dazzling pink and green **woman's coif** (*qufiya*) from Tunisia made of silk, metal, and cotton; and the *Oxford Man,* a 1992 woodcarving by Owen Ndou, depicting a man of ambiguous race clutching his Book of Knowledge.

THE NATION'S ATTIC:
A HISTORY OF THE MUSEUM

The collection began when Sir Hans Sloane, physician to Queen Anne and George II, bequeathed his personal collection of curiosities and antiquities to the nation. The collection quickly grew, thanks to enthusiastic kleptomaniacs after the Napoleonic Wars—most notoriously the seventh Earl of Elgin, who obtained the marbles from the Parthenon and Erechtheion on the Acropolis in Athens during his term as British ambassador in Constantinople.

Soon thereafter, it seemed everyone had something to donate—George II gave the old Royal Library, Sir William Hamilton gave antique vases, Charles Townley gave sculptures, the Bank of England gave coins. When the first exhibition galleries opened to visitors in 1759, the trustees agreed to admit only small groups guided by curators. The British Museum quickly became one of the most fashionable places to be seen in the capital, and tickets, which had to be booked in advance, were treated like gold dust.

The museum's holdings quickly outgrew their original space in Montague House. After the addition of such major pieces as the Rosetta Stone and other Egyptian antiquities (spoils of the Napoleonic War) and the Parthenon sculptures, Robert Smirke was commissioned to build an appropriately large and monumental building on the same site. It's still a hot ticket: the British Museum now receives more than 5 million visitors every year.

THE GREAT COURT &
THE READING ROOM

The museum's classical Greek-style facade features figures representing the progress of civilization, and the focal point is the awesome Great Court, a massive glass-roofed space. Here is the museum's inner courtyard (now the largest covered square in Europe) that, for more than 150 years, had been used for storage.

The 19th-century Reading Room, an impressive 106-foot-high blue-and-gold-domed library, forms the centerpiece of the Great Court. The 104,000 ancient tomes are at the British Library until 2012. H.G. Wells, Thomas Hardy, Lord Tennyson, Oscar Wilde, George Orwell, T.S. Elliot, and Beatrix Potter are just a few writers who have used this space as a literary and academic sanctuary over the past 150 years or so. Temporary exhibitions here now include China's Terracotta Army, Hadrian, and Shah 'Abbas.

(above) Reading Room

PLANNING YOUR VISIT

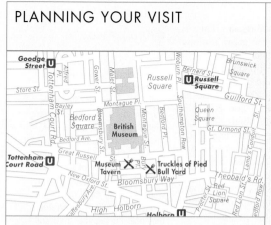

Tours

The **30–40 minute eyeOpener tour (free)** by museum guides does just what it says; ask for details at the information desk. The **90-minute Highlights tour (£8)** runs three times a day. After either of these tours, you can then dip back into the collections that most captured your imagination at your leisure.

An **audio version of the Highlights tour (£3.50)** is a less-animated but perhaps more relaxed way to navigate the galleries. Other audio tours focus on the Enlightenment and the Parthenon sculptures; another is designed for families.

Alternatively, the **Visitor's Guide (£5)** gives a brief but informative overview of the museum's history and is divided into self-guided themed tours.

Before you go, take a look at the online **COMPASS tour** using the museum's navigation tool (www.britishmuseum.org/compass), which allows users to browse past and present exhibits as well as search for specific objects. A children's version can also be found here. Computer stations in the Reading Room offer onsite access to COMPASS.

TIP→ The closest underground station to the British Museum is Russell Square on the Piccadilly line. However, since you will be entering via the back entrance on Montague Place, you will not experience the full impact of the museum's grand facade. To do so, alight at Holborn on the Central and Piccadilly lines or Tottenham Court Road on the Central and Northern lines. The walk from these stations is about 10 minutes.

WITH KIDS

■ Take a look at the "Objects to see with Children" page online. All the items are also on the family audio tour.

■ The Paul Hamlyn Library has trails for kids ages 3 to 5 and 6 to 11. The Ford Centre for Young Visitors has free activity backpacks.

■ Art materials are available for free from information points, where you can also find out about workshops, performances, storytelling sessions, and other free events.

■ Around the museum, there are Hands On desks open daily 11–4, which let visitors handle objects from the collections.

WHERE TO REFUEL

The British Museum's self-service **Gallery Café** gets very crowded but serves an acceptable menu beneath a plaster cast of a part of the Parthenon frieze that Lord Elgin didn't remove. It's open daily, but isn't particularly family friendly.

The **café in the Great Court** keeps longer hours and is a great place to people-watch and admire the spectacular glass roof while you eat your salad and sandwich.

If the weather is nice, exit the museum via the back entrance on Montague Place and amble over to **Russell Square**, which has grassy lawns, water fountains, and a glass-fronted café for post-sandwich coffee and ice cream.

5

IN FOCUS THE BRITISH MUSEUM

WORTH NOTING

Charles Dickens Museum. This is the only one of the many London houses Charles Dickens (1812–70) inhabited that's still standing, and it would have had a real claim to his fame in any case because he wrote *Oliver Twist* and *Nicholas Nickleby* and finished *Pickwick Papers* here between 1837 and 1839. The house looks exactly as it would have in Dickens's day, complete with first editions, letters, and a tall clerk's desk (where the master wrote standing up, often while chatting with visiting friends and relatives). Down in the basement is a replica of the Dingley Dell kitchen from *Pickwick Papers*. A program of changing special exhibitions gives insight into the Dickens family and the author's works, with sessions where, for instance, you can try your own hand with a quill pen. Visitors have reported a "presence" upstairs in the Mary Hogarth bedroom, where Dickens's sister-in-law died. Investigate yourself and decide whether you're spooked—or feel a sense of calm. Christmas is a memorable time to visit, as the rooms are decorated in traditional style: better than any televised costume drama, this is the real thing. ⊠ *48 Doughty St., Bloomsbury* ☏ *020/7405–2127* ⊕ *www.dickensmuseum.com* ☙ *£5* ⊙ *Mon.–Sat. 10–5, Sun. 11–5; last admission 4:30* Ⓤ *Chancery La., Russell Sq.*

> ### WORD OF MOUTH
>
> "[For a nice stroll] head for Temple Tube station and walk east into inner/middle temple. Here you will find an oasis of calm, with just the sound of quill pens being wielded by all the barristers in their chambers. At lunchtime, the gardens of inner temple are open and make a nice spot for a picnic. Then cross over the strand, and wander around the Royal Courts of Justice—if you are interested, they hold the big libel trials and criminal appeals there—just ask at the enquiry desk at the entrance."
> —annhig

Gray's Inn. Although the least architecturally interesting of the four Inns of Court and the one most damaged by German bombs in the 1940s, it still has its romantic associations. In 1594 Shakespeare's *Comedy of Errors* was performed for the first time in its hall—which was restored after World War II and has a fine Elizabethan screen of carved oak. You must make advance arrangements to view the hall, but the secluded and spacious gardens, first planted by Francis Bacon in 1606, are open to the public. ⊠ *Gray's Inn Rd., Holborn* ☏ *020/7458–7800* ⊕ *www. graysinn.org.uk* ☙ *Free* ⊙ *Weekdays noon–2:30* Ⓤ *Holborn, Temple.*

★ **Lincoln's Inn.** There's plenty to see at one of the oldest, best preserved, and most attractive of the Inns of Court—from the Chancery Lane Tudor brick gatehouse to the wide-open, tree-lined, atmospheric Lincoln's Inn Fields and the 15th-century chapel remodeled by Inigo Jones in 1620. ⊠ *Chancery La., Bloomsbury* ☏ *020/7405–1393* ⊕ *www.lincolnsinn. org.uk* ☙ *Free* ⊙ *Gardens weekdays 7–7, chapel weekdays noon–2:30; public may also attend Sun. service in chapel at 11:30 during legal terms* Ⓤ *Chancery La.*

Royal Courts of Justice. Here is the vast Victorian Gothic pile of 35 million bricks containing the nation's principal law courts, with 1,000-odd rooms running off 3½ mi of corridor. And here are heard the most important civil law cases—that's everything from divorce to fraud, with libel in between. You can sit in the viewing gallery to watch any trial you like, for a live version of Court TV. The more dramatic criminal cases are heard at the Old Bailey. Other sights are the 238-foot-long main hall and the compact exhibition of judges' robes. ✉ *The Strand, Bloomsbury* ☎ *020/7947–6000* ⊕ *www.hmcourts-service.gov.uk* ✉ *Free* ⊙ *Weekdays 9–4:30; during Aug. there are no sittings and public areas close at 2:30* Ⓤ *Temple.*

Temple Church. Featuring "the Round"—a rare circular nave—this church was built by the Knights Templar in the 12th century. The Red Knights (so called after the red crosses they wore—you can see them in effigy around the nave) held their secret initiation rites in the crypt here. Having started poor, holy, and dedicated to the protection of pilgrims, they grew rich from showers of royal gifts, until in the 14th century they were charged with heresy, blasphemy, and sodomy, thrown into the Tower, and stripped of their wealth. You might suppose the church to be thickly atmospheric, but Victorian and postwar restorers have tamed its air of antique mystery. Still, it's a very fine Gothic-Romanesque church, whose 1240 chancel ("the Oblong") has been accused of perfection. ✉ *King's Bench Walk, The Temple, Bloomsbury* ☎ *020/7353–8559* ⊕ *www.templechurch.com* ⊙ *Wed.–Sat. 11–4, Sun. 1–4; closures for special services* Ⓤ *Temple.*

University College London. The college was founded in 1826 and set in a satisfyingly classical edifice designed by the architect of the National Gallery, William Wilkins. In 1907 it became part of the University of London, providing higher education without religious exclusion. The college has within its portals the **Slade School of Fine Art,** which did for many of Britain's artists what the nearby Royal Academy of Dramatic Art (on Gower Street) did for its actors. On view inside is a fine collection of sculpture by an alumnus, John Flaxman.

You can also see more Egyptian artifacts, if you didn't get enough at the neighboring British Museum, in the **Petrie Museum** (☎ *020/7679–2884* ⊕ *www.petrie.ucl.ac.uk* ⊙ *Tues.–Fri. 1–5, Sat. 11–2* ✉ *Free, donations appreciated*), accessed from the DMS Watson building. It houses an outstanding, huge collection of fascinating objects of Egyptian archaeology—jewelry, toys, papyri, and some of the world's oldest garments. The South Cloisters contain one of London's weirder treasures: the clothed skeleton of one of the university's founders, Jeremy Bentham, who bequeathed himself to

KING'S CROSS STATION

Known for its 120-foot-tall clock tower, this yellow-brick, Italianate building with large, arched windows was constructed in 1851–52 as the London terminus for the Great Northern Railway. Harry Potter and fellow aspiring wizards took the *Hogwarts Express* to school from the imaginary platform 9¾ (platforms 4 and 5 were the actual shooting site) in the movies based on J.K. Rowling's popular novels. The station has put up a sign for platform 9¾ if you want to take a picture there—but please don't try to run through the wall.

Bloomsbury and Legal London Dining

BUDGET DINING
North Sea Fish Restaurant, Seafood, 7–8 Leigh St.

MODERATE DINING
Galvin Bistrot de Luxe, Bistro, 66 Baker St.

Lemonia, Greek, 89 Regent's Park Rd.

EXPENSIVE DINING
Pied à Terre, French, 34 Charlotte St.

the college. At this writing, plans were afoot to rehouse the museum in purpose-built galleries on three floors of the UCL's future Institute of Cultural Heritage. Check the Web site for more information. ⊠ *Malet Pl., Bloomsbury* Ⓤ *Euston Sq., Goodge St.*

Wellcome Collection. If you fancy something medicinal, sample this quirky collection by U.S. pharmaceutical millionaire and philanthropist Henry Wellcome (1853–1936). Opened in 2007, the museum aims to make medical history and knowledge interesting and accessible to all (though it is not recommended for children under 14). His beloved artifacts, comprising an estimated 1 million items, include Napoleon's toothbrush, Horatio Nelson's razor, and Charles Darwin's walking stick. There are also anatomical models, Peruvian mummies, and Japanese sex aids as well as two permanent exhibitions to inspire debate, Medicine Man and Medicine Now. ⊠ *183 Euston Rd., Bloomsbury* ☎ *020/7611–2222* ⊕ *www.wellcomecollection.org* ✉ *Free* ⊙ *Tues., Wed., Fri., and Sat. 10–6, Thurs. 10–10, Sun. 11–6* Ⓤ *Euston Sq., Euston.*

The City

WORD OF MOUTH

"The Ceremony of The Keys, the formal locking of the gates of the Tower of London, has been carried out every night at 10 PM, for more than 600 years since 1340. Only a few dozen people are admitted . . . apply for the free tickets weeks or months ahead of time. It is a really awesome feeling to witness this solemn ceremony in the dark at the Tower."

—mnapoli

GETTING ORIENTED

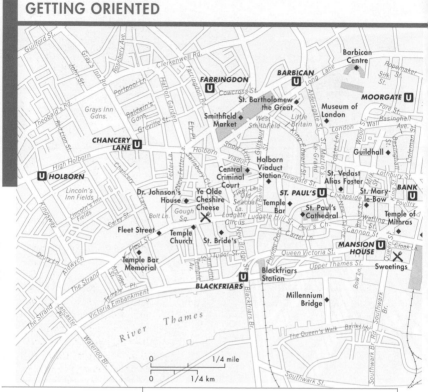

GETTING THERE	TOP REASONS TO GO
The City area is well served by a concentrated selection of Underground stops in London. St. Paul's and Bank are on the Central Line, and Mansion House, Cannon Street, and Monument are on the District and Circle lines. Liverpool Street and Aldgate border The City's eastern edge, whereas Chancery Lane and Farringdon lie to the west. Barbican and Moorgate provide easy access to the theaters and galleries of the Barbican, and Blackfriars, to the south, leads to Ludgate Circus and Fleet Street.	**Monument:** Climb the 311 spiral steps to the top for dizzying views of the London skyline. **St. Paul's Cathedral:** Talk into a wall of the Whispering Gallery and be heard on the opposite side—but wait until it's quiet or you'll hear someone else's secrets. **Tower of London:** Gaze in awe at the stunning Crown Jewels at the center of centuries of royal intrigue. **Museum of London:** Relive the sights and sounds of Roman Londinium. **Shops and The City:** Explore City outfitters and the upscale boutiques of Bow Lane and the Royal Exchange. **Stroll across the Millennium Bridge** between the Tate Modern and St. Paul's and enjoy one of the finest river views in London.

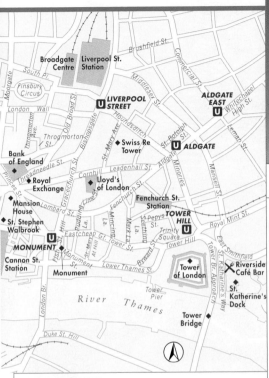

FEELING PECKISH?

The friendly **Riverside Café Bar** (✉ *St. Katherine's Way* ☎ *020/7481–1464*) is one of the few places you're sure to find a good cup of hot chocolate and hot and cold meals, with waterside views of the luxurious yachts and gin palaces moored at the docks.

Sweetings (✉ *39 Queen Victoria St.* ☎ *020/7248–3062*) is not cheap, and closed in the evenings, but it serves one of the best fish lunches in London. Refuel here on Dover sole and Black Velvet, the local brew, and observe the pinstripes at play in their natural habitat.

When you're finished exploring Fleet Street, repair to the famed **Ye Olde Cheshire Cheese** (✉ *145 Fleet St.* ☎ *020/7353–6170*) for a pint of old-fashioned ale and a snack. Parts of the building date from 1667, and it's one of London's best-loved pubs, rightly admired for its roaring log fires and dingy interior, where you can imagine Johnson and Boswell getting together for a literary confab.

MAKING THE MOST OF YOUR TIME

The "Square Mile" is as compact as the nickname suggests, with very little distance between points of interest, making it easy to dip into The City for an afternoon stroll. For full immersion in the Tower of London, however, set aside half a day, especially if seeing the Crown Jewels is a priority. Allow an hour minimum each for the Museum of London, St. Paul's Cathedral, and the Tower Bridge. On weekends, without the scurrying suits, The City is nearly deserted, making it hard to find lunch—and yet this is when the major attractions are at their busiest.

A GOOD WALK

Crossing the Millennium Bridge from the Tate Modern to St. Paul's is one of the finest walks in London for views of the river and the cathedral that towers over it. Dubbed the "blade of light," this shiny aluminum-and-steel construction was the result of a collaboration between architect Norman Foster and sculptor Anthony Caro.

6

DID YOU KNOW?

In The City—the oldest part of London—streets still follow a medieval pattern. Here you can see financial institutions, and notable buildings, like the Bank of England and Lloyd's of London.

Sightseeing
★★★★★
Nightlife
★
Dining
★★★
Lodging
★
Shopping
★★★

The City, as opposed to the city, is the capital's fast-beating financial heart. Easy to walk around, the "Square Mile" also has currency as a religious and political center. St. Paul's Cathedral has looked after Londoners' souls since the 7th century, and the Tower of London—that moat-surrounded royal fortress, prison, and jewel house—has taken care of beheading them.

Updated by
Jan Fuscoe

There are many starting points to explore The City, but **Temple Bar Memorial**, at the top of the Strand, is the site of the only surviving entry point—the gate itself was moved closer to St. Paul's (brick by brick) in 1878 to widen the road. **Fleet Street,** the site of England's first printing press, was the undisputed seat of British journalism until the 1980s. The nearby church of **St. Bride's**, recognizable by its tiered wedding-cake steeple, is another Wren mini-masterpiece and still the church for journalists.

Nestled behind Fleet Street is **Dr. Johnson's House**, former home of the man who claimed that to be bored of London was to be bored of life and author of *Dictionary of the English Language*. Eastward, London's most distinctive building, **St. Paul's Cathedral**, designed by Sir Christopher Wren, has clear views of the **Millennium Bridge**, the pedestrian-only steel suspension bridge that links The City to the South Bank of the Thames. The **Central Criminal Court** (nicknamed **Old Bailey**, and home to London's most intriguing criminal trials) lies to the north, as does the 800-year-old **Smithfield Market**, whose Victorian halls are the site of a daily early morning meat market and the ancient church of **St. Bartholomew the Great** and St. Bartholomew Hospital, both begun in 1123.

The **Museum of London**, where archaeological displays include a portion of the original **Roman Wall** that ringed The City, is a gateway to the modern **Barbican Centre**, a complex of arts venues and apartments. To the southeast lies the **Guildhall**, the site of the only Roman amphitheater in London. Nearby, the church of **St. Mary-le-Bow** and the narrow maze of streets just to its south, around **Bow Lane**, are great shopping haunts.

A BRIEF HISTORY

Rising from the mud of the Thames as the Roman settlement of Londinium, in AD 47, this area marks the beginnings of the capital. It gained immediate momentum as a trading center for materials and goods shipped in from all corners of the fledgling colony. Centuries later, William the Conqueror began building the palace that was to become the Tower of London. It went from being Henry III's defensive shelter in the 13th century to, by Tudor times, the world's most forbidding and grisly prison, where two of Henry VIII's six wives were executed. During the Middle Ages, powerful guilds that nurtured commerce took root, followed by the foundation of great trading companies, such as the Honourable East India Company, which started up in 1600.

The City's history has been punctuated by periods of chaos that have threatened to destroy it. The Great Fire of 1666 was the most serious, sparing only a few of the cramped, labyrinthine streets, where the Great Plague of the previous year had already wiped out a huge portion of the population. Yet the gutted wastelands enabled a new start, driving out the plague-carrying rodents that had menaced London since the Middle Ages and forcing an architectural renaissance, led by Sir Christopher Wren. Further punishment came during the Blitz of World War II, when German bombers destroyed many buildings. Today's eclectic skyline reflects every period of its history, some sublime, some hideous.

6

At the epicenter of The City is a powerful architectural triumvirate: the **Bank of England**, the **Royal Exchange**, and **Mansion House**, where the lord mayor of the City of London (not to be confused with the mayor of London, who works from City Hall on the South Bank) lives and entertains. Nearby are another diverting and historic church, **St. Stephen Walbrook**, and the remains of the **Temple of Mithras**, at one time devoted to Bacchus, Roman god of wine and intoxication. The **Monument** was built to commemorate the Great Fire of London of 1666. Northeast of its 202-foot-high tower are excellent views of two unmissable members of The City skyline: the **Lloyd's of London Building**, and the **Swiss Re Tower**, popularly known as "the Gherkin." From here, the river leads to one of London's most absorbing and bloody attractions, the **Tower of London**. **Tower Bridge** is a suitably giddying finale.

TOP ATTRACTIONS

Monument. Commemorating the "dreadful visitation" of the Great Fire of 1666, this is the world's tallest isolated stone column. It is the work of Sir Christopher Wren and Dr. Robert Hooke, who were asked to erect it "on or as neere unto the place where the said Fire soe unhappily began as conveniently may be." And so here it is—at 202 feet, exactly as tall as the distance it stands from Farriner's baking house in Pudding Lane, where the fire started. The Monument reopened in February 2009 after a two-year restoration project. ✉ *Monument St., The City* ☎ *020/7626–2717* ⊕ *www.themonument.info* ✉ *£2* ⊗ *Daily 9:30–5:30, last admission 5* Ⓤ *Monument.*

Museum of London. If there's one place to get the history of London sorted out, right from 450,000 BC to the present day, it's here—although there's a great deal to sort out: Oliver Cromwell's death mask, Queen Victoria's crinoline gowns, Selfridges' art deco elevators, and the London's Burning exhibition are just some of the goodies. The museum appropriately shelters a section of the 2nd- to 4th-century London wall, which you can view from a window inside. Permanent displays include "London Before London," "Roman London," "Medieval London," and "Tudor London." The lower galleries, dealing with London's history from 1666 until the 21st century, have undergone extensive modernization and will reopen in early 2010. The new vision will also include a section of 21st-century London to explore. The archaeologists and curators at the museum regularly leap from AD to BC, as fresh building work in the city uncovers more treasures. None, though, have been as exciting as the ongoing project of preserving and displaying the Roman amphitheater at the Guildhall, and you can see the rewards of that excavation in the artifacts here. ⊠ *London Wall, The City* ☎ *0870/444–3851* ⊕ *www.museumoflondon.org.uk* ✉ *Free* ⊗ *Mon.–Sat. 10–5:50, Sun. noon–5:50; last admission 5:30* Ⓤ *Barbican, St. Paul's.*

> ## A VIEW TO REMEMBER
>
> At the top of the Monument's 311-step spiral staircase (a better workout than any StairMaster) is a gallery providing fantastic views from the heart of The City that is helpfully caged to prevent suicidal jumps, which were a trend for a while in the 19th century.

Fodor's Choice ★ **St. Paul's Cathedral.** *See the highlighted listing in this chapter.*

Fodor's Choice ★ **Tower Bridge.** Despite its medieval, fairy-tale appearance, this is a Victorian youngster. Constructed of steel, then clothed in Portland stone, the Horace Jones masterpiece was deliberately styled in the Gothic persuasion to complement the Tower next door, and it's famous for its enormous bascules—the 1,200-ton "arms," which open to allow large ships through. This still happens occasionally, but when river traffic was dense, the bascules were raised about five times a day.

The **Tower Bridge Exhibition** is a child-friendly tour where you can discover how one of the world's most famous bridges actually works and then head out onto the walkways for the wonderful city views. First, take in the romance of the panoramas from the east and west walkways between those grand turrets. On the east are the modern superstructures and ships of Docklands, and on the west is the best look at the steel-and-glass "futuristic mushroom" that is Greater London Assembly's City Hall, the Tower of London, St. Paul's, and the Monument. Then it's back down to explore the Victorian engine rooms and discover the inner workings, which you learn about through hands-on displays and films. ⊠ *Tower Bridge Rd., The City* ☎ *020/7403–3761* ⊕ *www.towerbridge. org.uk* ✉ *£6* ⊗ *Daily Apr.–Sept., 10–6:30; Oct.–Mar. 9:30–5:30; last admission 30 mins before closing time* Ⓤ *Tower Hill.*

Fodor's Choice ★ **Tower of London.** *See the highlighted listing in this chapter.*

Continued on page 128

ST. PAUL'S CATHEDRAL

Sir Christopher Wren's maxim "I build for eternity" proves no empty boast.

Sublime, awesome, majestic, and inspirational are just some of the words to describe Wren's masterpiece, St. Paul's Cathedral—even more so now that the restoration for the 300th anniversary is expected to finish in 2010.

This is the spiritual heart of the nation, where people and events are celebrated, mourned, and honored. As you approach the cathedral your eyes are inevitably drawn skyward to the great dome, one of the largest in the world and an amazing piece of engineering. Visit in the late afternoon for evensong, and let the choir's voices transport you to a world of absolute peace in a place of perfect beauty, as pristine as the day it was completed.

TOURING ST. PAUL'S

Enter the cathedral via the main west entrance, and walk straight down the length of the nave to the central Dome Altar. Nobody can resist making a beeline for the dome, so start your tour beneath it, standing dead center on the beautiful sunburst floor, Wren's focal mirror of the magnificent design above. A simple quotation marks the floor "Lector si momentum requiris, circumspice" (Reader if you seek his monument, look around). The dome crowns the center of the cathedral and rises to 364 feet—but save your strength for the "great climb" to get some fantastic views.

THE CATHEDRAL FLOOR

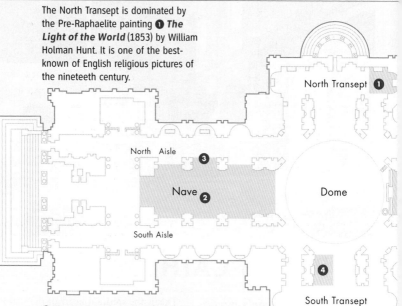

The North Transept is dominated by the Pre-Raphaelite painting ❶ *The Light of the World* (1853) by William Holman Hunt. It is one of the best-known of English religious pictures of the nineteeth century.

❷ **The Nave** is formed of three aisles, and from here you can see right down to the High Altar at the far end of the Choir, more than 100 yards away. Take time to admire the mastery of space and light.

In the north aisle of the Nave is Flax-man's grandiose ❸ **monument to the Duke of Wellington,** who sits astride his faithful charger, Copen-hagen, the horse that carried him through the Battle of Waterloo.

The South Transept displays a ❹ **monument to Admiral Lord Nelson,** Britain's favorite naval hero, with an anchor. Other memorials commemorate the explorer Captain Robert Scott and the darling of British landscape painting J.M.W. Turner.

CELEBRITY STATUS

St. Paul's has witnessed many momentous processions along its checkered nave. The somber state funerals of heroes Admiral Lord Nelson and the Duke of Wellington, and of Sir Winston Churchill, drew huge crowds. It was here, also, that the fairy-tale wedding of Prince Charles and Lady Diana Spencer took place, and the jubilees of Queen Victoria, George V, and the present Queen were celebrated.

6

IN FOCUS ST. PAUL'S CATHEDRAL

The North Choir Aisle features the beautiful **5 gilded gates** by Jean Tijou, perhaps the most accomplished artist in wrought iron of all time, as well as Henry Moore's sculpture **6 *Mother and Child,*** its simple lines complementing the ornate surroundings.

North Choir Aisle

Apse

Choir (Quire)

South Choir Aisle

The South Choir Aisle contains a **7 marble effigy of poet John Donne,** who was Dean of old St. Paul's for his final 10 years (he died in 1631). This is the only statue to have survived the Great Fire of London intact. You can see the scorch marks at the base of the statue.

The Choir contains the **8 Bishop's Throne** or cathedra, hence the name cathedral. Look aloft to the fabulous mosaics. Don't miss the exquisite, delicate carvings by Grinling Gibbons, in particular on the case of the **9 grand organ,** one of the Cathedral's greatest artifacts. It was designed by Wren and played by such illustrious figures as Handel and Mendelssohn.

10 The High Altar, with its glorious canopy, is a profusion of marble and carved and gilded oak.

The Apse is home to the **11 American Memorial Chapel,** which honors the more than 28,000 U.S. soldiers who died while stationed in the U.K. during World War II. The lime-wood paneling incorporates a rocket as a tribute to the United States' achievements in space.

MUSICAL FRICTION

The organ, with its cherubs and angels, was not installed without controversy. The mighty instrument proved a tight fit, and the maker, known as Father Schmidt, and Wren nearly came to blows. Wren was reputed to have said he would not adapt his cathedral for a mere "box of whistles."

THE DOME

The dome is the crowning glory of the cathedral, a must for visitors.

At 99 feet, the ❶ **Whispering Gallery** is reached by 259 spiral steps. This is the part of the cathedral with which you bribe children—they will be fascinated by the acoustic phenomenon: whisper something to the wall on one side, and a second later it transmits clearly to the other side, 107 feet away. The only problem is identifying your whisper from the cacophony of everyone else's. Look down onto the nave from here and up to the monochrome frescoes of St. Paul by Sir James Thornhill.

More stamina is required to reach the ❷ **Stone Gallery**, at 173 feet and 378 steps from ground level. It is on the exterior of the cathedral and offers a vista of the city and the River Thames.

For the best views of all—at 280 feet and 530 steps from ground level—make the trek to the small ❸ **Golden Gallery**, the highest point of the outer dome. A hole in the floor gives a vertiginous view down. You can see the lantern above through a circular opening called the oculus. If you have a head for heights you can walk outside for a spectacular panorama of London.

The top of the dome is crowned with a ❹ **ball and cross**. At 23 feet high and weighing approximately 7 tons, it is the pinnacle of St. Paul's.

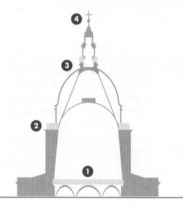

A BRIEF HISTORY

The cathedral is the masterpiece of Sir Christopher Wren (1632–1723), completed in 1710 after 35 years of building and much argument with the Royal Commission. Wren had originally been commissioned to restore Old St. Paul's, the Norman cathedral that had replaced, in its turn, three earlier versions, but the Great Fire left so little of it standing that a new cathedral was deemed necessary.

Wren's first plan, known as the New Model, did not make it past the drawing board; the second, known as the Great Model, got as far as the 20-foot oak rendering you can see here today before it, too, was rejected, whereupon Wren is said to have burst into tears. The third, however, known as the Warrant Design (because it received the royal warrant), was accepted, with the fortunate coda that the architect be allowed to make changes as he saw fit. Without that, there would be no dome, because the approved design had featured a steeple. Parliament felt that building was proceeding too slowly (in fact, 35 years is lightning speed, as cathedrals go) and withheld half of Wren's pay for the last 13 years of work. He was pushing 80 when Queen Anne finally coughed up the arrears.

■ TIP→ To see Wren's Great Model, you must join a Triforium Tour (Mon. and Tues. at 11:30 and 2, Fri. at 2). These one-hour tours include a visit to the library and a glimpse of the famous Geometric staircase. The visit ends in the Trophy Room, where Wren's Great Model is on display. The tour costs £16 per person and includes entry to the cathedral and access to the crypt and galleries. It's best to book in advance by calling 020/7246–8357 or sending an e-mail to visits@stpaulscathedral.org.uk.

THE CRYPT

A visit to the vast crypt is a time for reflection and contemplation, with some 200 memorials to see. If it all becomes too somber, take solace in the café or shop near the crypt entrance.

Here lies ❶ **Admiral Nelson,** killed at the Battle of Trafalgar in 1805. His body was preserved in alcohol for the journey home, and his pickled remains were buried here beneath Cardinal Wolsey's unused 16th-century sarcophagus.

The ❷ **tomb of the Duke of Wellington** comprises a simple casket made from Cornish granite. He is remembered as a hero of battle, but his name lives on in the form of boots, cigars, beef Wellington, and the capital of New Zealand.

Surrounded by his family and close to a plethora of iconic artists, musicians, and scientists, the ❸ **tomb of Sir Christopher Wren** is a modest simple slab.

The beautiful ❹ **O.B.E. Chapel** (dedicated 1960) is a symbol of the Order of the British Empire, an order of chivalry established in 1917 by George V. The theme of sovereign and Commonwealth is represented in the glass panels.

The vast ❺ **treasury** houses the cathedral's plate, although a good deal has been lost or stolen over the centuries—in particular in a daring robbery of 1810—and much of the display comes from other London churches.

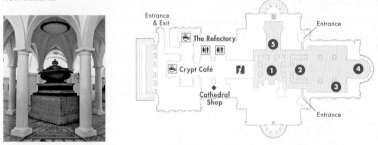

PLANNING YOUR DAY

WHAT'S NEARBY: Stroll over the Millennium Bridge (look back for a great view of St. Paul's) and have lunch at Tate Modern. The restaurant at the top of the gallery has spectacular views of London. ■ TIP➔ **To avoid lines visit early in the morning. For a different experience return for Evensong at 5 PM.**

CONTACT INFO: ⊠ *St. Paul's Churchyard, Ludgate Hill EC4 8AD* ☎ *020/7236-4128* ⊕ *www.stpauls.co.uk* Ⓤ *St. Paul's*

ADMISSION: Adults: £11. **Family ticket** (2 adults, 2 children): £25.50. **Children 7–16:** £3.50.

TOURS: A guided tour of the cathedral, choir, Geometric staircase, and crypt lasts 1½–2 hours and costs £3. Tours start at 10:45, 11:15, 13:30, and 14:00. Multimedia rental guides are included in admission.

HOURS: The cathedral is a house of worship. Services may cause changes to the visiting hours on any given day, so be sure to call ahead.

Cathedral: Mon.–Sat. 8:30–4:30 (last admission at 4).
Shop: Mon.–Sat. 8:30–5, Sun. 10–4:30.
Crypt café: Mon.–Sat. 9–5, Sun. 12–4.

6

IN FOCUS ST. PAUL'S CATHEDRAL

WORTH NOTING

SUMMER FESTIVAL

Every year, for three weeks in June and July, the City of London Festival (⊕ www.colf.org) has numerous walks, dances, street arts, and concerts taking place in buildings that are usually closed to the public, such as St. Paul's Cathedral and Mansion House.

Bank of England. Known for the past couple of centuries as "the Old Lady of Threadneedle Street," after the name appeared in a caption to a political cartoon (which can be seen in the museum), the country's top vault, which has been central to the British economy since 1694, manages the national debt and the foreign exchange reserves, issues banknotes, sets interest rates, looks after England's gold, and regulates the country's banking system. Sir John Soane designed the neoclassical hulk in 1788, wrapping it in windowless walls, which are all that survives of his original building. It's ironic that one of the executives of so sober an institution should have been Kenneth Grahame, author of *The Wind in the Willows*. This and other facets of the bank's history are traced in the Bank of England Museum (entrance is around the corner on Bartholomew Lane). The museum comes to life with the interactive exhibits that chart the bank's more recent history, including the chance to try your hand at controlling inflation, but most visitors still make a beeline for the solid-gold bar that can be stroked and held in the central trading hall (but before you get any ideas, there's security everywhere). ⊠ *Threadneedle St., The City* ☎ *020/7601–5545* ⊕ *www.bankofengland.co.uk* ✉ *Free* ☼ *Weekdays and Lord Mayor's Show day (2nd Sat. in Nov.) 10–5* Ⓤ *Bank, Monument.*

★ **Barbican Centre.** With two theaters; the London Symphony Orchestra and its auditorium; the Guildhall School of Music and Drama; a major art gallery for touring and its own special exhibitions; two cinemas; a convention center; an upscale restaurant, cafés, terraces with fountains, and literary bookshops; and living space in some of the most desirable tower blocks in town, the Barbican is an enormous 1980s concrete maze that Londoners either love or hate. Navigation around the complex is via the yellow lines running, Wizard-of-Oz-like, along the floors, with signs on the walls, although it's still easy to get lost. Actors rate the theater acoustics especially highly, and the steep rake of the seating makes for a good stage view. The dance, music, and theater programs have been transformed into a yearlong fest named BITE, which stands for Barbican International Theatre Events, and encompasses dance, puppetry, and music. The emphasis is on presenting tomorrow's names today, although there are performances by established companies and artists, such as Merce Cunningham. ⊠ *Silk St., The City* ☎ *020/7638–8891* box office ⊕ *www.barbican.org.uk* ✉ *Barbican Centre free, art gallery £6–£8, films £8.50, concerts £6.50–£45, theater £7–£50* ☼ *Barbican Centre Mon.–Sat. 9–11, Sun. and holidays noon–11; gallery Thurs.–Mon. 11–8, Tues. and Wed. 11–6* Ⓤ *Moorgate, Barbican.*

★ **Dr. Johnson's House.** This is where Samuel Johnson lived between 1748 and 1759, compiling his famous dictionary in the attic as his health deteriorated. Built in 1700, the elegant Georgian residence, with its paneled rooms and period furniture, is where the Great Bear (as he was known) compiled his *Dictionary of the English Language*—two early editions of which are among the mementos of Johnson and his friend, diarist, and later, his biographer, James Boswell. ✉ *17 Gough Sq., The City* ☎ *020/7353–3745* ⊕ *www.drjohnsonshouse.org* 💷 *£4.50* 🕑 *May–Sept., Mon.–Sat. 11–5:30; Oct.–Apr., Mon.–Sat. 11–5; closed bank holidays* Ⓤ *Holborn, Chancery La.*

Guildhall. The Corporation of London, which oversees The City, has ceremonially elected and installed its lord mayor here for the last 800 years. The Guildhall was built in 1411, and though it failed to avoid either the 1666 or 1940 flames, its core survived. The Great Hall is a psychedelic patchwork of coats of arms and banners of the City Livery Companies, which inherited the mantle of the medieval trade guilds. Tradesmen couldn't even run a shop without kowtowing to these pro- totypical unions, and their grand banqueting halls, the plushest private dining venues in The City, are testimony to the wealth they amassed. Inside the hall, Gog and Magog, the pair of mythical giants who founded ancient Albion and the city of New Troy, upon which London was said to be built, glower down from their west-gallery grandstand in 9-foot- high painted lime-wood. The hall was also the site of famous trials, including that of Lady Jane Grey in 1553, before her execution at the Tower of London.

To the right of Guildhall Yard is the **Guildhall Art Gallery,** which includes portraits of the great and the good, cityscapes, famous battles, and a slightly cloying pre-Raphaelite section. The construction of the gallery led to the exciting discovery of London's only **Roman amphithe- ater,** which had lain underneath Guildhall Yard undisturbed for more than 1,800 years. It was excavated, and now visitors can walk among the remains, although most of the relics can be seen at the Museum of London, through which guided tours can be booked.

The 1970s west wing houses the **Guildhall Library;** it has mainly City- related books and documents, plus a collection belonging to one of the city livery companies, the Wor- shipful Company of Clockmak- ers, in the **Clockmakers' Museum,** with more than 600 timepieces on show, including a skull-faced watch that belonged to Mary, Queen of Scots. It's one of the most impor- tant horological collections in the country. ✉ *Aldermanbury, The City* ☎ *020/7606–3030, 020/7332–3700 gallery* ⊕ *www.cityoflondon.gov.uk* 💷 *Free; gallery and amphitheater £2.50* 🕑 *Mon.–Sat. 9:30–5; clock- maker museum Mon.–Sat. 9:30– 4:45; gallery Mon.–Sat. 10–5, Sun. noon–4, last admission 4:30 or 3:30* Ⓤ *St. Paul's, Moorgate, Bank, Man- sion House.*

> **WORD OF MOUTH**
>
> "I recommend spending half a day or so around the Strand/ Fleet Street area—on a nice day, you can walk through the Temple (where most London barristers' chambers are), see the ancient Temple church (think crusad- ers and *The Da Vinci Code*) and have lunch in Middle Temple (wear smart clothes and look as if you belong) where at least one Shakespeare play had its first performance—Twelfth Night, I think." —annhig

Interior of the "Inside-Out" Lloyd's of London building, designed by Richard Rogers Partnership.

Old Bailey. If you're lucky, this is the place to watch the real-life drama of justice in action in one of the 16 courtrooms that are open to the public. Previous trials have included those of Crippen and Christie, two of England's most notorious wife murderers, as well as the controversial trial of Oscar Wilde and, less so, the notorious East End gangsters, the Kray twins. The day's hearings are posted on the sign outside, but your best bet is to consult the previous day's tabloid newspapers for an idea of the trials that are making waves. There are security restrictions, and children under 14 are not allowed in; call the information line first. The present-day **Central Criminal Court** is where Newgate Prison stood from the 12th century right until the beginning of the 20th century. Called by the novelist Henry Fielding the "prototype of hell," few survived for long in the version pulled down in 1770. Those who didn't starve were hanged, or pressed to death in the Press Yard, or they succumbed to the virulent gaol (the archaic British spelling of jail) fever. The next model lasted only a couple of years before being torn down by raving mobs during the anti-Catholic Gordon Riots of 1780, to be replaced by the Newgate that Dickens described in several novels, including *Oliver Twist*. The Central Criminal Court replaced Newgate in 1907, and the most famous feature of the solid Edwardian building is the 12-foot gilded statue of Justice perched on top; she was intended to mirror the dome of St. Paul's. ⊠ *Newgate St., The City* ☎ *020/7248–3277 information* ⊕ *www.cityoflondon.gov.uk* ☉ *Public Gallery weekdays 10–1 and 2–4:30 (approx.); line forms at Newgate St. entrance or in Warwick St. Passage; closed bank holidays and day after* Ⓤ *St. Paul's.*

St. Bartholomew the Great. Reached via a perfect half-timber gatehouse atop a 13th-century stone archway, this is one of London's oldest churches. Construction on the church and the hospital nearby was begun in 1123 by Henry I's favorite courtier, Rahere, who caught malaria and, surviving, vowed to dedicate his life to serving the saint who had visited him in his fevered dreams. With the Dissolution of the

> **RISE AND SHINE**
>
> If, for whatever reason, you're thirsting for a drink at 6 AM, head to the pubs around Smithfield market, which are specially licensed to serve early morning pints to market traders (or "bummarees") at the end of a hard day's night.

Monasteries, Henry VIII had most of it torn down; the Romanesque choir loft is all that survives from the 12th century. The ancient church has appeared in *The Other Boleyn Girl, Four Weddings and a Funeral,* and *Shakespeare in Love.* On the other side of the road, the church's namesake **St. Bartholomew's Hospital** (☎ 020/7837–0546 ⊙ Tues.–Fri. 10–4 ☛ *Free*) is home to a small museum displaying scary-looking medical instruments. Take a £5 tour at 2 PM on Friday of the Museum of St. Bartholomew's Hospital (book ahead) and find out how operations were carried out before anesthetics were used. You can also see some Hogarth paintings hanging in the Great Hall. Facing both the church and the museum is Smithfield's meat market. ⊠ *Cloth Fair, West Smithfield, The City* ☎ *020/7606–5171* ⊕ *www.greatsbarts.com* ☛ *Church £4, museum free* ⊙ *Church weekdays 8:30–5 (Nov.–Feb. 8:30–4), Sat. 10:30–4, Sun 8:30–8. Museum Tues.–Fri. 10–4* Ⓤ *Barbican, Farringdon.*

St. Bride's. According to legend, the distinctively tiered steeple of this Christopher Wren–designed church gave rise to the shape of the traditional wedding cake. One early couple inspired to marry here were the parents of Virginia Dare, the first European child born in colonial America in 1587. As St. Paul's (in Covent Garden) is the actors' church, so St. Bride's belongs to journalists, many of whom have been buried or memorialized here. Samuel Richardson—one of the "Fathers of the English Novel," is buried here and by 1664 the crypts were so crowded that diarist Samuel Pepys, who was baptized here, had to bribe the grave digger to "justle together" some bodies to make room for his deceased brother. Now the crypts house a museum of the church's rich history, and a bit of Roman sidewalk. ⊠ *Fleet St., The City* ☎ *020/7427–0133* ⊕ *www.stbrides.com* ☛ *Free* ⊙ *Weekdays 8–6, Sat. 11–3, Sun for services only 10–1 and 5–7:30* Ⓤ *St. Paul's, Blackfriars.*

St. Mary-le-Bow. This church is another classic City survivor; various versions have stood on the site since the 11th century. In 1284 a local goldsmith took refuge here after committing a murder, only to be killed inside the church by enraged relatives of his victim. The church was abandoned for a time afterward, but started up again, and was rebuilt in its current form after the Great Fire. Wren's 1673 incarnation has a tall steeple for a City church (only St. Bride's is taller) and one of the most famous sets of bells around—a Londoner must be born within the sound of the "Bow Bells" to be a true Cockney. The Bow takes its name from the bow-shape arches in the Norman crypt. The garden contains a statue of local boy Captain John Smith, who founded Virginia in 1606 and was later captured by Native Americans. ⊠ *Cheapside, The City* ☎ *020/7248–5139* ⊕ *www. stmarylebow.co.uk* ⊗ *Mon.–Thurs. 7–6, Fri. 7–4* Ⓤ *Mansion House, St. Paul's.*

The Place Below (☎ *020/7329– 0789*), in St. Mary-le-Bow's Norman crypt, is packed with City workers weekdays from 7:30 until 3 for a vegetarian menu covering breakfasts and scrumptious light lunches.

> **DID YOU KNOW?**
>
> The traditional definition of "Cockneys"—East End London residents with their own accent and dialect—is that they were born within hearing distance of the bells of St. Mary-le-Bow church. The Cockney dialect includes rhyming slang (*apples*, as in *apples and pears*, to mean "stairs") and adapting Yiddish words such as *schtum* and *kosher*. In recent years, the term *mockney* has become a lighthearted term of abuse for posh types who try to sound Cockney.

St. Stephen Walbrook. This is the parish church many think is Wren's best, by virtue of its practice dome, which predates the one at St. Paul's by some 30 years, and its celestial atmosphere inside. Yet there's far more to the history of the church than as a dry run for its next-door big brother. There has been a church here since the 7th century, built on the site of an older Roman shrine. Inside the light, airy church, called "the most perfectly proportioned interior in the world" by one admirer, two sights warrant investigation: Henry Moore's 1987 central marble altar, which sits beneath the dome ("like a lump of Camembert," say critics), and, well, a telephone—an eloquent tribute to that savior of souls Rector Chad Varah, who in 1953 founded the Samaritans, givers of phone aid to the suicidal, here. ⊠ *39 Walbrook, The City* ☎ *020/7626–9000* ⊕ *www.ststephenwalbrook.net* ⊗ *Weekdays 10–4* Ⓤ *Bank, Cannon St.*

THE TOWER OF LONDON

The Tower is a microcosm of the city itself—a sprawling, organic hodgepodge of buildings that inspires reverence and terror in equal measure. See the block on which Anne Boleyn was beheaded, marvel at the Crown Jewels, and pay homage to the ravens who keep the monarchy safe.

An architectural patchwork of time, the oldest building of the complex is the fairytale White Tower, conceived by William the Conqueror in 1078 as both a royal residence and a show of power to the troublesome Anglo-Saxons he had subdued at the Battle of Hastings. Today's Tower has seen everything, as a palace, barracks, a mint for producing coins, an armoury, and the Royal menagerie (home of the country's first elephant). The big draw is the stunning opulence of the Crown Jewels, kept on-site in the heavily fortified Jewel House. Most of all, though, the Tower is known for death: it's been a place of imprisonment, torture, and execution for the realm's most notorious traitors as well as its martyrs. These days, unless you count the killer admission fees, there are far less morbid activities taking place in the Tower, but it still breathes London's history and pageantry from its every brick and offers hours of exploration.

TOURING THE TOWER

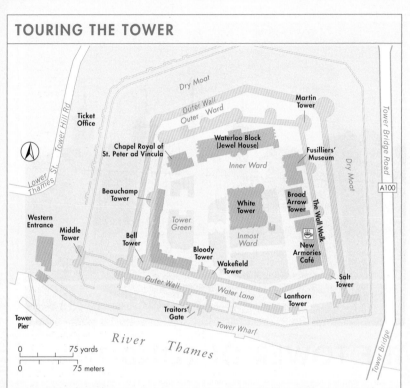

Entry to the Tower is via the **Western Entrance** and the **Middle Tower,** which feed into the outermost ring of the Tower's defenses.

Water Lane leads past the dread-inducing **Traitors' Gate,** the final point of entry for many Tower prisoners.

Toward the end of Water Lane, the **Lanthorn Tower** houses by night the ravens rumored to keep the kingdom safe, and by day a timely high-tech reconstruction of the Catholic Guy Fawkes's plot to blow up the Houses of Parliament in 1605.

The **Bloody Tower** earned its name as the apocryphal site

of the murder of two young princes, Edward and Richard, who disappeared from the Tower after being put there in 1483 by their uncle, Richard III. Two little skeletons (now in Westminster Abbey) were found buried close to the White Tower in 1674 and are thought to be theirs.

The **Beauchamp Tower** housed upper-class miscreants: Latin graffiti about Lady Jane Grey can be glimpsed today on its walls.

Like a prize gem set at the head of a royal crown, the **White Tower** is the centerpiece of the complex. Its four

GOLD DIGGER?

Keep your eyes peeled as you tour the Tower: according to one story, Sir John Barkstead, goldsmith and Lieutenant of the Tower under Cromwell, hid £20,000 in gold coins here before his arrest and execution at the Restoration of Charles II.

towers dominate the Inner Ward, a fitting and forbidding reminder of Norman strength at the time of the conquest of England.

Once inside the White Tower, head upstairs for the **Armouries,** where the big-

Jewel House, Waterloo Barracks

ROYAL BLING

The Crown of Queen Elizabeth, the Queen Mother, from 1937, contains the exotic 105-carat Koh-i-Noor (mountain of light) diamond.

6

IN FOCUS   THE TOWER OF LONDON

TIME KILLERS

Some prisoners managed to keep themselves plenty amused: Sir Walter Raleigh grew tobacco on Tower Green, and in 1561 suspected sorcerer Hugh Draper carved an intricate astronomical clock on the walls of his Salt Tower cell.

gest attraction, quite literally, is the suit of armor worn by a well-endowed Henry VIII. There is a matching outfit for his horse.

Other fascinating exhibits include the set of Samurai armor presented to James I in 1613 by the emperor of Japan, and the tiny set of armor worn by Henry VIII's young son Edward.

The **Jewel House** in Waterloo Block is the Tower's biggest draw, perfect for playing pick-your-favorite-crown

from the wrong side of bulletproof glass. Not only are these crowns, staffs, and orbs encrusted with heavy-duty gems, they are invested with the authority of monarchical power in England, dating back to the 1300s.

Outside, pause at **Tower Green,** permanent departure point for those of noble birth. The hoi polloi were dispatched at nearby Tower Hill. The Tower's most famous female victims—Anne Boleyn, Margaret Countess of Salisbury, Catherine Howard, and Lady Jane Grey—all went this "priviledged" way.

Behind a well-kept square of grass stands the **Chapel Royal of St. Peter ad Vincula,** a delightful Tudor church and final resting place of six beheaded Tudor bodies. ■ TIP➔ **Visitors are welcome for services and can also enter after 4:30 PM daily.**

The **Salt Tower,** reputedly the most haunted corner of the complex, marks the start of the **Wall Walk,** a bracing promenade along the stone spiral steps and battlements of the Tower that looks down on the trucks, taxis, and shimmering high-rises of modern London.

The Wall Walk ends at the **Martin Tower,** former home of the Crown Jewels and now host to the crowns and diamonds exhibition that explains the art of fashioning royal headwear and tells the story of some of the most famous stones.

On leaving the Tower, browse the **gift shop,** and wander the wharf that overlooks the Thames, leading to a picture-postcard view of Tower Bridge.

WHO ARE THE BEEFEATERS?

First of all, they're Yeoman Warders, but probably got the nickname "beefeater" from their position as Royal Bodyguards which entitled them to eat as much beef as they liked. Part of the "Yeoman of the Guard," started in the reign of Edmund IV, the warders have formed the Royal Bodyguard as far back as 1509 when Henry VIII left a dozen of the Yeoman of the Guard at the Tower to protect it.

Originally, the Yeoman Warders also served as jailers of the Tower, doubling as torturers when necessary. (So it would have been a Beefeater tightening the thumb screws, or ratchetting the rack another notch on some unfortunate prisoner. Smile nicely.) Today 36 Yeoman Warders (men and women since 2007), along with the Chief Yeoman Warder and the Yeoman Gaoler, live within the walls of the Tower with their families, in accommodations in the Outer Ward. They stand guard over the Tower, conduct tours, and lock up at 9:53 PM every night with the Ceremony of the Keys.

■TIP➔ Free tickets to the Ceremony of the Keys are available by writing several months in advance; check the Tower Web site for details.

HARK THE RAVENS!

Legend has it that should the hulking black ravens ever leave, the White Tower will crumble and the kingdom fall. Charles II, no doubt jumpy after his father's execution and the monarchy's short-term fall from grace, made a royal decree in 1662 that there should be at least six of the carrion-eating nasties present at all times. There have been some close calls. During World War II, numbers dropped to one, echoing the precarious fate of the war-wracked country. In 2005, two (of eight) died over Christmas when Thor—the most intelligent but also the largest bully of the bunch—killed new recruit Gundolf, named after the Tower's 1070 designer. Pneumonia put an end to Bran, leaving lifelong partner Branwen without her mate.

■DID YOU KNOW?In 1981 a raven named Grog, perhaps seduced by his alcoholic moniker, escaped after 21 years at the Tower. Others have been banished for "conduct unbecoming."

The six that remain, each one identified by a colored band around a claw, are much loved for their fidelity (they mate for life) and their cheek (capable of 440 noises, they are witty and scolding mimics). It's not only the diet of blood-soaked biscuits, rabbit, and scraps from the mess kitchen that keeps them coming back. Their lifting feathers on one wing are trimmed, meaning they can manage the equivalent of a lop-sided air-bound hobble but not much more. For the first half of 2006 the ravens were moved indoors full-time as a preventive measure against avian flu but have since been allowed out and about again. In situ they are a territorial lot, sticking to Tower Green and the White Tower, and lodging nightly by Wakefield Tower. They've had free front-row seats at all the most grisly moments in Tower history—Anne Boleyn's execution included.

■TIP➔ Don't get too close to the ravens: they are prone to pecking and not particularly fond of humans, unless you are the Tower's Raven Master.

And *WHAT* are they wearing?

A **pike** (or halberd), also known as a partisan, is the Yeoman Warder's weapon of choice. The Chief Warder carries a staff topped with a miniature silver model of the White Tower.

Anyone who refers to this as a costume will be lucky to leave the Tower with head still attached to body: this is the **ceremonial uniform** of the Yeoman Warders, and it comes at a cool **£13,000 a throw.**

The black Tudor **bonnet** is made of velvet; the blue undress consists of a felt top hat, with a single Tudor rose in the middle.

This **Tudor-style ruff** helps date the ceremonial uniform, which was first worn in 1552.

Insignia on a Yeoman Warder's upper right arm denote the rank he carried in the military.

The **medals** on a Yeoman Warder's chest are more than mere show: all of the men and women have served for at least 22 years in the armed forces.

This version of the **royal livery** bears the insignia of the current Queen ("E" for Elizabeth) but originally dates from Tudor times. The first letter changes according to the reigning monarch's Christian name; the second letter is always an "R" for *rex* (king) or *regina* (queen).

Slits in the **tunic** date from the times when Beefeaters were expected to ride a horse.

Red socks and **black patent shoes** are worn on special occasions. Visitors are more likely to see the regular blue undress, introduced in 1858 as the regular working dress of the Yeoman Warders.

The **red lines down the trousers** are a sign of the blood from the swords of the Yeoman Warders in their defense of the realm.

6

IN FOCUS THE TOWER OF LONDON

(IN)FAMOUS PRISONERS OF THE TOWER

Anne Boleyn   Lady Jane Grey   Sir Walter Raleigh

Sir Thomas More. A Catholic and Henry VIII's friend and chancellor, Sir Thomas refused to attend the coronation of Anne Boleyn (Henry VIII's second wife) or to recognize the multi-marrying king as head of the Church. Sent to the Tower for treason, in 1535 More was beheaded.

Anne Boleyn. The first of Henry VIII's wives to be beheaded, Anne, who failed to provide the king with a son, was accused of sleeping with five men, including her own brother. All six got the chop in 1536. Her severed head was held up to the crowd, and her lips were said to be mouthing prayer.

Margaret, Countess of Salisbury. Not the best-known prisoner in her lifetime, she has a reputation today for haunting the Tower. And no wonder: the elderly 70-year-old was condemned by Henry VIII in 1541 for a potentially treacherous bloodline (she was the last Plantagenet princess) and hacked to death by the executioner after she refused to put her head on the block like a common traitor and attempted to run away.

Queen Catherine Howard. Henry VIII's fifth wife was locked up for high treason and infidelity and beheaded in 1542 at age 20. Ever eager to please, she spent her final night practicing how to lay her head on the block.

Lady Jane Grey. The nine-days-queen lost her head in 1554 at age 16. Her death was the result of sibling rivalry gone seriously wrong, when Protestant Edward VI slighted his Catholic sister Mary in favor of Lady Jane as heir, and Mary decided to have none of it.

Guy Fawkes. The Roman Catholic soldier who tried to blow up the Houses of Parliament and kill the king in the 1605 Gunpowder plot was first incarcerated in the chambers of the Tower, where King James I requested he be tortured in ever-worsening ways. Perhaps unsurprisingly, he confessed. He met his seriously grisly end in the Old Palace Yard at Westminster, where he was hung, drawn, and quartered in 1607.

Sir Walter Raleigh. Once a favorite of Elizabeth I, he offended her by secretly marrying her Maid of Honor and was chucked in the Tower. Later, as a conspirator against James I, he paid with his life. A frequent visitor to the Tower (he spent 13 years there in three stints), he managed to get the Bloody Tower enlarged on account of his wife and growing family. He was finally executed in 1618 in Old Palace Yard, Westminster.

Josef Jakobs. The last man to be executed in the Tower was caught as a spy when parachuting in from Germany and executed by firing squad in 1941. The chair he sat in when he was shot is preserved in the Royal Armouries' artifacts store.

FOR FURTHER EVIDENCE . . .

A trio of buildings in the Inner Ward, the **Bloody Tower, Beauchamp Tower,** and **Queen's House,** all with excellent views of the execution scaffold in Tower Green, are the heart of the Tower's prison accommodations and home to a permanent exhibition about notable inmates.

TACKLING THE TOWER (without losing your head)

✉ H.M. Tower of London, Tower Hill
☎ 0844/482–7777, 0844/482–7799 tickets
⊕ www.hrp.org.uk 🎫 £17, children 16 and under £9.50, children under 5 free. Family tickets (2 adults, 3 children) £47 ☉ Mar.–Oct., Tues.–Sat. 9–5:30, Sun. and Mon. 10–5:30; last admission at 5. Nov.–Feb., Tues.–Sat. 9–4:30, Sun. and Mon. 10–4:30; last admission at 4
Ⓤ Tower Hill

■**TIP➔ You can buy tickets from automatic kiosks on arrival, or up to seven days in advance at any Tube station. Avoid lines completely and save by booking discounted tickets online.**

MAKING THE MOST OF YOUR TIME: Without doubt, the Tower is worth two to three hours. A full hour of that would be well spent by joining one of the Yeoman Warders' tours (included in admission). It's hard to better their insight, vitality, and humor—they are knights of the realm living their very own fairytale castle existence.

The Crown Jewels are worth the wait, the White Tower is essential, and the Medieval Palace and Bloody Tower should at least be breezed through.

■**TIP➔ It's best to visit on weekdays, when the crowds are smaller.**

WITH KIDS: The Tower's centuries-old cobblestones are not exactly stroller-friendly, but strollers are permitted inside most of the buildings. If you do bring one, be prepared to leave it temporarily unsupervised (the stroller, that is—not your child) outside the White Tower, which has no access. There are baby-changing facilities in the Brick Tower restrooms behind the Jewel House. Look for regular free children's events such as the Knight's school where children can have a go at jousting, sword-fighting, and archery.

■**TIP➔ Tell your child to find one of the Yeoman Warders if he or she should get lost; they will in turn lead him or her to the Byward Tower, which is where you should meet.**

IN A HURRY? If you have less than an hour, head down Wall Walk, through a succession of towers, which eventually spit you out at the Martin Tower. The view over modern London is quite a contrast.

TOURS: Tours given by a Yeoman Warder leave from the main entrance near Middle Tower every half-hour from 10–4, and last about an hour. Beefeaters give occasional 30-minute talks in the Lanthorn Tower about their daily lives. Both tours are free.

AT A GLANCE

The City Dining

BUDGET DINING
E Pellicci, Café, 332 Bethnal Green Rd.

Lahore Kebab House, Pakistani, 2 Umberston St.

Tayyabs, Pakistani, 83 Fieldgate St.

MODERATE DINING
Boundary, French, 2–4 Boundary St.

Canteen, British, 2 Crispin Pl.

L'Anima, Italian, 1 Snowden St.

Moro, Mediterranean, 34–36 Exmouth Market

Plateau, Modern French, 4th Fl., Canada Pl., Canada Square

Simpson's Tavern, British, 38½ Cornhill

Sông Qué Café, Vietnamese, 134 Kingsland Rd.

St John, British, 26 St. John St.

St John Bread & Wine, British, 94–96 Commercial St.

Sweetings, Seafood, 39 Queen Victoria St.

EXPENSIVE DINING
Club Gascon, ModernFrench, 57 West Smithfield

The East End

WORD OF MOUTH

"Spitalfields Market is great for Sunday. Be sure to pop up to Brick Lane for some Indian food after. Or into the Ten Bells for a whiff of Jack the Ripper. Petticoat Lane Market is right there and is also on Sunday mornings."

—gertie3751

GETTING ORIENTED

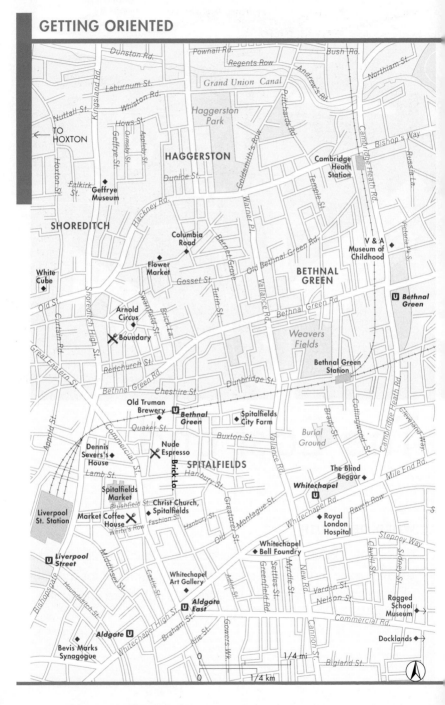

Dunstan Rd.
Pownall Rd.
Regents Row
Bush Rd.
Northiam St.

Laburnum St.
Whiston Rd.
Grand Union Canal
Andrews Rd.
Pritchards Rd.

Nuttall St.
Hows St.
Haggerston Park

Kingsland Rd.
Geffrye St.
Ormsby St.
Appleby St.
Goldsmith's Row

← TO HOXTON

Bishop's Way
Cambridge Heath Rd.
Russia La.

Hoxton St.
HAGGERSTON
Dunloe St.
Cambridge Heath Station

Falkirk St.
Geffrye Museum

Hackney Rd.
Warner Pl.
Temple St.

SHOREDITCH

Columbia Road

Barnet Grove

V & A Museum of Childhood

Flower Market
Gosset St.
Turin St.
Old Bethnal Green Rd.

Victoria Park S.

BETHNAL GREEN

White Cube

Old St.
Shoreditch High St.
Swanfield St.
Bethnal Green Rd.

U Bethnal Green

Arnold Circus
Brick La.
Weavers Fields

Boundary

Great Eastern St.
Curtain Rd.

Redchurch St.
Dunbridge St.
Bethnal Green Station

Bethnal Green Rd.
Cheshire St.

Old Truman Brewery
U Bethnal Green

Quaker St.
Buxton St.
Brady St.
Cottingwood St.
Cleveland Way

Spitalfields City Farm

Burial Ground

Cambridge Heath Rd.

Dennis Severs's House
Nude Espresso

Commercial St.
Brick La.
Hanbury St.
SPITALFIELDS

Lamb St.
The Blind Beggar
Mile End Rd.

Spitalfields Market
Brushfield St.
Christ Church, Spitalfields
Whitechapel
U

Liverpool St. Station
Market Coffee House
Fashion St.
Greatorex St.
Whitechapel Rd.
Royal London Hospital
Raven Row
Stepney Way

White's Row
Hanbury St.
Old Montague St.

U Liverpool Street
Whitechapel Bell Foundry

Bishopsgate
Houndsditch
Middlesex St.
Castle St.
Whitechapel Art Gallery
Adler St.
Settles St.
Greenfield Rd.
Myrtle St.
New Rd.
Cavell St.
Sidney St.

Aldgate East
U

Ragged School Museum →

Bevis Marks Synagogue
Aldgate U
Whitechapel High St.
Braham St.
Gowers Wk.
Varden St.
Nelson St.
Commercial Rd.
Cannon St.

Docklands ◆ →

0   1/4 mi
Bigland St.

0   1/4 km

TOP REASONS TO GO

Geffrye Museum: Stroll around the walled herb garden after a peek into the lives of ordinary Londoners through the years, then have afternoon tea at the glass-fronted museum café.

Market shopping: Take advantage of jet lag to arrive early for Spitalfields or Sunday's Columbia Road flower market.

Brick Lane: Poke about the thrift stores and vintage-clothes shops on (and around) Brick Lane. ⇨ *Also see The East End: London's Best Curries in Where to Eat.*

East End nightlife: Have a hedonistic night out bar- and club-crawling in Hoxton and Shoreditch.

Art Scene: The East End isn't picturesque, but it5s art scene is vibrant, colorful, and exciting—small galleries are interspersed with larger collections.

FEELING PECKISH?

Inside Spitalfields Market is **Canteen** (☎ *0845/686–1122*), an open-floor-plan eatery with long communal tables that serves British dishes made with additive-free ingredients.

For some of the finest coffee in London (by way of New Zealand), go to **Nude Espresso** (⌧ *26 Hanbury St.* ☎ *0780/422–3590*). The best beans, machines, and baristas, are complemented by delicious sandwiches and cakes.

The **Market Coffee House** (⌧ *50–52 Brushfield St.* ☎ *020/7247–4110*) offers sandwiches such as Scotch beef with horseradish and watercress on a roll or bagel, along with fresh soup, ploughman's lunches, and English muffins.

SAFETY

Around the central hubs of Hoxton, Shoreditch, Spitalfields, and Brick Lane, you're unlikely to experience any trouble during daylight hours; even after dark it's relatively safe. However, if you're venturing into Whitechapel or out toward Bethnal Green and Mile End, be on your guard at all times.

GETTING THERE

The best Tube stops to start from are Whitechapel or Aldgate East on the District–Hammersmith & City lines, and Aldgate on the Metropolitan and Circle lines.

MAKING THE MOST OF YOUR TIME

To experience the East End at its most lively, make sure you visit on the weekend—here it's possible to shop, eat, drink, and party your way through a whole 72 hours. Spitalfields Market bustles all weekend, whereas Brick Lane is at its best on a Sunday morning—also the time to visit Columbia Road for its glorious flower market.

If you're planning to explore the East End art scene, pick up a free art map at the Whitechapel Art Gallery (recently expanded) to help you navigate around the many small galleries and art spaces.

As far as nightlife, there's no time limit here. Start after your shopping—Hoxton's bars are your best bet—and finish as far into the following morning as your stamina will allow.

A GOOD WALK

There are some thrilling walks that illustrate the progress of Jack and other murderers around the East End: recommended is the **Blood and Tears Walk: London's Horrible Past** (☎ *020/7625–5155*), led by researcher and actor Declan McHugh, which departs daily from Barbican Tube station.

7

Sightseeing
★★★
Nightlife
★★★★★
Dining
★★★★
Lodging
★
Shopping
★★★★

Made famous by Dickens and infamous by Jack the Ripper, the East End is one of London's most enduringly evocative neighborhoods. It may have fewer conventional tourist attractions but is rich in folk history, architectural gems, and feisty burgeoning culture. Once home to French Huguenots, then Ashkenazi Jews, the area now has a large Bangladeshi community. Since the early 1990s the area has also attracted students and creative media types, lured by the old industrial spaces.

Updated by
Jan Fuscoe

Nowadays the East End is London's most culturally diverse area. Near Whitechapel Road is the **Bevis Marks Spanish and Portuguese Synagogue,** London's oldest synagogue. Farther east, you'll come across the famous **Whitechapel Art Gallery;** the Whitechapel Bell Foundry; and **Brick Lane,** the heart of the Bangladeshi East End, filled with innumerable curry houses and glittering sari shops, and also home to the **Old Truman Brewery,** now converted to studios and gallery space. The Sunday morning junk market on Brick Lane adds further complements to the rewarding vintage-clothes shopping in this area.

Since the East End was heavily bombed in World War II, and subsequently rebuilt with public housing estates, it's not the best-looking part of the capital, although pockets of historic buildings do remain. Nicholas Hawksmoor's masterpiece, **Christ Church, Spitalfields** soars above Fournier Street, alongside some fine early Georgian houses. For a sensory experience of Georgian life, visit **Dennis Severs's House.** Kids enjoy **Spitalfields City Farm** and, to the east in Bethnal Green, the quirky **V&A Museum of Childhood.** Farther east still, toward Mile End, are the former Trinity Almshouses, with the statue of William Booth on the very spot where the first Salvation Army meetings were held, and the notorious **Blind Beggar** pub. The immense **Royal London Hospital** and its museum are just a few yards away.

Today Spitalfields and Shoreditch are London's most exciting bohemian neighborhoods, together with Hoxton, just north of here. There are stylish boutiques (especially on Cheshire Street) and cafés, artists' studios, and galleries in the plentiful old, derelict industrial spaces that were bought up cheaply and have been imaginatively remodeled. **Spitalfields Market,** with its arts and crafts and design booths, is open daily, but the weekends are the most lively. In Shoreditch, **Columbia Road** on Sunday (8–2) gets buried under forests of shrubs and blooms of all shapes and sizes during London's main plant and **flower market.**

The **Geffrye Museum** occupies a row of early-18th-century almshouses, and that bastion of contemporary art, the **White Cube** gallery, lies to the west in the very hip Hoxton Square.

TOP ATTRACTIONS

Bevis Marks Synagogue. This is Britain's oldest and most splendid synagogue. The interior is beautiful, embellished with rich woodwork for the benches and galleries, marble columns, and many plunging brass chandeliers. The wooden ark resembles a Wren-style screen and contains the sacred scrolls of the five books of Moses. When Cromwell allowed the Jews to return to England in 1655 (they had been expelled in 1290), there was no Jewish community, and certainly no place to worship openly. The site chosen to build a new synagogue in 1701 already had religious connections, as the house that stood here before, Burics Marks, was owned by the abbot of Bury St. Edmunds; over the years the name re-evolved. ✉ *Bevis Marks, 2 Heneage La., East End* ☎ *020/7626–1274* ⊕ *www.bevismarks.org* ☉ *Mon., Wed., Thurs. 10:30–2, Tues., Fri. 10:30–1, Sun. 10:30–12:30* Ⓤ *Aldgate East, Liverpool St.*

★ **Geffrye Museum.** Here's where you can discover what life was really like for the general masses in London (and it's different from the grand, high-society town-house interiors of the rich royal boroughs). It's a small museum where you can walk through a series of room sets that re-create everyday domestic interiors from the Elizabethan period through postwar 1950s utility to the present day. Originally, the museum was a row of almshouses for the poor, built in 1716 by Sir Robert Geffrye, former lord mayor of London, that provided shelter for 50 pensioners over the course of 200 years. The houses were rescued from closure by keen petitioners (the inhabitants were relocated to a healthier part of town) and were transformed into the Geffrye Museum in 1914. The former almshouses were restored to their original condition, with most of the internal woodwork intact, including the staircase, upper floors, closets, and paneling. There are also displays on the almshouses' history and on the kinds of people who lived there. To discover more, you can also attend a regular "bring a room to life" talk. The museum's extension wing houses the 20th-century galleries, a lovely café overlooking the garden, and a bookshop stuffed full of great gifts. ⊠ *136 Kingsland Rd., East End* ☎ *020/7739–9893* ⊕ *www.geffrye-museum.org. uk* ⊠ *Free* ⊙ *Tues.–Sat. 10–5, Sun. and bank holidays noon–5* Ⓤ *Old St., then Bus 243; Liverpool St., then Bus 149 or 242.*

Spitalfields Market. There's been a market here since the mid-17th century, but the current version is overflowing with crafts and design shops, stalls, bars, and restaurants (with a pan-world palette, from tapas to Thai), and different-purpose markets every day of the week. Look out for work by young designers, whose one-off accessories make original gifts, and join the office workers for some pie and mash. ■ TIP→ The nearer the weekend, the busier it all gets, culminating in the arts-and-crafts and green market on Sunday—the best day to go. *For more on Spitalfields, see* ⇨ *Chapter 18, Shopping.* ⊠ *Commercial St. between Lamb and Brushfield Sts., East End* ☎ *020/7247–8556* ⊕ *www.visitspitalfields. com* ⊠ *Free* ⊙ *Daily 10–7; market stalls weekdays 10–4, Sun. 9–5* Ⓤ *Liverpool St.*

Ⓒ **V&A Museum of Childhood.** This is the East End outpost of the Victoria & Albert Museum—in fact, this entire iron, glass, and brown-brick building was transported here from South Kensington in 1875. Since then, its contents have grown into the biggest toy collection in the world. The large Dolls' Houses collection is a bit like the Geffrye Museum zapped into miniature, with houses of every period. Each genre of plaything has its own enclosure, so if teddy bears are your weakness, you need waste no time with the train sets or board games. The museum's title is justified in the fascinating galleries on the social history of childhood from baby dolls to Beanie Babies. Don't miss the magnificent 18th-century puppet theater, thought to have been made in Venice to show *commedia dell'arte* (comedy of art) plays. ⊠ *Cambridge Heath Rd., East End* ☎ *020/8983–5200* ⊕ *www.vam.ac.uk/moc* ⊠ *Free* ⊙ *Daily 10–5:45, last admission 5:30* Ⓤ *Bethnal Green.*

★ **Whitechapel Art Gallery.** Founded in 1901, this gallery underwent an ambitious £13 million expansion program that doubled its exhibition space in 2009. The Whitechapel bought the library next door and has created fabulous new galleries alongside facilities for talks, events, film, music, and poetry. The Whitechapel has an international reputation for its shows, which are often on the cutting edge of contemporary art. The American painter Jackson Pollock exhibited here in the 1950s, as did pop artist Robert Rauschenberg in the '60s, and David Hockney had his first solo show here in the '70s. Pick up a free East End art map to help you with the rest of your gallery hopping. ■ TIP→ Late-night music events take place on Friday in the café-bar from 8 PM to 11 PM. ⊠ *77–82 Whitechapel High St., East End* ☎ *020/7522–7888* ⊕ *www. whitechapelgallery.org* ⊠ *Free* ⊙ *Tues.–Sun. 11–6* Ⓤ *Aldgate East.*

EAST END STREET SMARTS

Brick Lane and the narrow streets running off it offer a paradigm of the East End's development. Its population has moved in waves: communities seeking refuge, others moving out in an upwardly mobile direction.

Brick Lane has seen the manufacture of bricks (during the 16th century), beer, and bagels, but nowadays it's becoming the hub of artistic bohemia, especially at the Old Truman Brewery with its calendar of diverse cultural activities. It's also the heart of Banglatown—Bangladeshis make up one-third of the population in this London borough, and you'll see that the surrounding streets have their names written in Bengali—where you find many kebab and curry houses along with shops selling ethnic videos, colorful saris, and stacks of sticky sweets. On Sunday morning the entire street becomes pedestrianized. Shops and cafés are open, and several stalls are set up making it a companion market to the nearby **Petticoat Lane.**

Flower and Dean streets, past the ugly 1970s housing project on **Thrawl Street** (and once the most disreputable street in London) was where Abe Saperstein, founder of the Harlem Globetrotters, was born in 1902.

Fournier Street contains fine examples of the neighborhood's characteristic Georgian terraced houses,

many of them built by the richest of the early-18th-century Huguenot silk weavers (see the enlarged windows on the upper floors). Most of those along the north side of Fournier Street have been restored by conservationists; others still contain textile sweatshops—only now the workers are Bengali.

Wilkes Street, with more 1720s Huguenot houses, is north of the Christ Church, Spitalfields, and neighboring **Princelet Street** was once important to the East End's Jewish community. Where No. 6 stands now, the first of several thriving Yiddish theaters opened in 1886, playing to packed houses until the following year, when a false fire alarm, rung during a January performance, ended with 17 people being crushed to death and so demoralized the theater's actor-founder, Jacob Adler, that he moved his troupe to New York. Adler played a major role in founding that city's great Yiddish theater tradition—which, in turn, had a significant effect on Hollywood.

Elder Street, just off Folgate, is another gem of original 18th-century houses. On the south and east side of Spitalfields Market are yet more time-warp streets that are worth a wander, such as **Gun Street,** where artist Mark Gertler (1891–1939) lived at No. 32.

WORTH NOTING

The Blind Beggar. This is the dark and rather dingy Victorian den of iniquity where Salvation Army founder William Booth preached his first sermon. Also, on the south side of the street stands a stone inscribed HERE WILLIAM BOOTH COMMENCED THE WORK OF THE SALVATION ARMY, JULY 1865, marking the position of the first Sally Army platform; back by the pub a statue of William Booth stands where the first meetings were held. Booth didn't supply the pub's main claim to fame, though. The

Jack the Ripper

Within the shadow of The City walls is London's oldest synagogue, the Bevis Marks, whereas Whitechapel is where the Salvation Army was founded and the original Liberty Bell was forged. However, what everyone remembers most about this area are the Victorian slum streets that were stalked by the most infamous serial killer of all, Jack the Ripper.

At No. 90 Whitechapel High Street once stood George Yard Buildings, where Jack the Ripper's first victim, Martha Turner, was discovered in August 1888. A second murder occurred some weeks later, and Hanbury Street, behind a seedy lodging house at No. 29, is where Jack the

Ripper left his third mutilated victim, "Dark" Annie Chapman. A double murder followed, and then, after a month's lull, came the death on this street of Marie Kelly, the Ripper's last victim and his most revolting murder of all. He had been able to work indoors this time, and Kelly, a young widow, was found strewn all over the room, charred remains of her clothing in the fire grate. Jack the Ripper's identity never has been discovered, although theories abound, including, among others, the cover-up of a prominent member of the British aristocracy, the artist Walter Sickert, and Francis Twomblety, an American quack doctor.

Blind Beggar's real notoriety dates only from March 1966, when Ronnie Kray—one of the Kray twins, the former gangster kings of London's East End underworld—shot dead rival "godfather" George Cornell in the saloon bar. The original Albion Brewery, celebrated home to the first bottled brown ale, was next door. ⊠ *337 Whitechapel Rd., East End* Ⓤ *Whitechapel.*

Christ Church, Spitalfields. This is the 1729 masterpiece of Sir Christopher Wren's associate Nicholas Hawksmoor. Hawksmoor built only six London churches; this one was commissioned as part of Parliament's 1711 "Fifty New Churches Act." The idea was to score points for the Church of England against such nonconformists as the Protestant Huguenots. (It must have worked; in the churchyard, you can still see some of their gravestones, with epitaphs in French.) As the local silk industry declined, the church fell into disrepair, and by 1958 the structure was crumbling, with the looming prospect of demolition. But after 25 years—longer than it took to build—and a huge local effort to gather funds, the structure has been completely restored and is a joy to behold, from the colonnaded portico and tall spire to its bold, strident baroque-style interior. As a concert venue it truly comes into its own. ■ TIP→ If you're lucky enough to be in town during the Spitalfields Festival held every summer and winter, then don't miss the chance to attend a classical concert in this atmospheric ecclesiastical venue. ⊠ *Commercial St., East End* ☏ *020/7377–2440* ☉ *Tues. 11–4, Sun. 1–4* Ⓤ *Aldgate East.*

★ **Dennis Severs's House.** Enter this extraordinary time machine of a house with your imagination primed to take part in the plot. The Georgian terraced house belonged to the eponymous performer-designer-scholar from Escondido, California, who dedicated his life not only to restoring

On Sunday, additional clothing and crafts stalls surround Spitalfields covered market.

his house but also to raising the ghosts of a fictitious Jervis family that might have inhabited it over the course of two centuries. Dennis Severs (1944–99) created a replica of Georgian life, without electricity but with a butler in full 18th-century livery to light the candles and lay the fires—for the Jervises. The 10 rooms are shadowy set pieces of rose-laden Victorian wallpapers, Jacobean paneling, Georgian wing chairs, baroque carved ornaments, "Protestant" colors (upstairs), and "Catholic" shades (downstairs). ■TIP→ The "Silent Night" candlelight tours, each Monday, are the most theatrical and memorable way to "feel" the house; a magical experience relished by both Londoners and out-of-towners. ✉ *18 Folgate St., East End* ☎ *020/7247–4013* ⊕ *www.dennissevershouse.co.uk* 🖃 *£8 for Sun., £5 for Mon. open house; £12 for candlelight Mon. evening* ⊙ *1st and 3rd Sun. of month 2–5, 1st and 3rd Mon. noon–2. Call for hrs for "Silent Night" Mon., reservations essential* Ⓤ *Liverpool Street.*

OFF THE BEATEN PATH

Estorick Collection. West of Hoxton, on the eastern end of the affluent, yuppie borough of Islington, is this small, restored Georgian mansion with an extraordinary collection of early-20th-century Italian art. The works were acquired by Eric Estorick, an American collector and sociologist, who was particularly keen on Italian Futurists; there are works by Balla, Boccioni, and Severini, among others. The downstairs Estorick Caffè is a good place to grab a bite, especially in summer when you can sit outdoors. ✉ *39A Canonbury Sq., off Canonbury Rd., Islington* ☎ *020/7704–9522* ⊕ *www.estorickcollection.com* 🖃 *£5* ⊙ *Wed.–Sat. 11–6, Sun. noon–5* Ⓤ *Highbury & Islington.*

Old Truman Brewery. This is the only one of the former East End breweries still standing. It's a handsome example of Georgian and 19th-century industrial architecture, and in 1873 was the largest brewery in the world. The buildings, which straddle Brick Lane, are a conglomeration of art, craft, and photo studios, and are now established as the capital of cool. The Atlantis Gallery, host of the sell-out Body Worlds exhibition in 2002, is a major

WORD OF MOUTH

"I visited the Dennis Severs's house when I was in London and it has remained one of my top travel experiences to date. It is an 'experience'—for the eyes, the ears (remember the sounds of the kitchen, people in the house and street, etc.?), the smells (cloves in oranges, for one)." —christigpa

focus—visitors were crammed inside to watch a live autopsy as part of the show. Less controversial events include fashion showcases for young, upcoming designers, and fringe events. The Vibe Bar is a hot spot to chill out behind a traditional Georgian facade—it also has a great outdoor space. ⊠ *91 Brick La., East End* ⊕ *www.trumanbrewery. com* Ⓤ *Aldgate East.*

Royal London Hospital. Founded in 1740, the Royal London was once as nasty as its former neighborhood near the Tower of London. Waste was carried out in buckets and dumped in the street; bedbugs and alcoholic nurses were problems; but according to hospital records patients didn't die—they were "relieved." In 1757 the hospital moved to its present site, and the original building forms the core of the one you see today. By then it had become one of the best hospitals in London, and it was enhanced further by the addition of a small medical school in 1785, and again, 70 years later, by an entire state-of-the-art medical college. Thomas John Barnardo, who went on to found the famous Dr. Barnardo's Homes for Orphans, came to train here in 1866. Ten years later the hospital grew to become the largest in the United Kingdom, and now, though mostly rebuilt since World War II, it remains one of London's most capacious. To get an idea of the huge medical leaps forward, walk through the main entrance and garden to the crypt of St. Augustine within St. Philip's Church (alternatively, go directly two blocks south to the entrance on Newark Street), to the **Royal London Hospital Museum** (☉ *Weekdays 10–4:30*), where displays of medical paraphernalia, objects, and documentation illustrate the more-than-250-year history of this East London institution. The museum often closes on short notice, so call before you go. ⊠ *Whitechapel Rd., East End* ☎ *020/7377–7608* ⊕ *www.medicalmuseums.org* ⌂ *Free* ☉ *Hospital and garden daily 9–6* Ⓤ *Whitechapel.*

Ⓒ **Spitalfields City Farm.** This little community farm, squashed into an urban landscape, raises a selection of farm animals, including some rare breeds, to help educate city kids in country matters. A tiny farm shop sells freshly laid eggs and also organic seasonal produce. ⊠ *Buxton St., East End* ☎ *020/7247–8762* ⊕ *www.spitalfieldscityfarm.org* ⌂ *Free* ☉ *Tues.–Sun. 10–4:30* Ⓤ *Aldgate East, Whitechapel, Bethnal Green.*

White Cube. The original White Cube had cramped quarters in genteel St. James's—this outpost was set up to take advantage of the massive

CLOSE UP

The East End Art Scene

It was only inevitable that the once arty Islington area (the N1 postal district, which rubs streets with the less elegant end of the Regent's Canal toward The City, EC1) would become too expensive and gentrified for the artists themselves. Hoxton, on a corner of Islington just off the City Road, with its cheap industrial units and more artisan Georgian–Victorian terraced streets, was the logical next stop.

The seal of boho approval came when Damien Hirst's agent and the most important modern art dealer in town, Jay Jopling, set up the White Cube gallery at 48 Hoxton Square. Impoverished artists, however, are not newcomers to the area—in the 1960s, Bridget Riley set up an outfit here to find affordable studio space for British artists—but the latest wave this side of the millennium has changed the face of this formerly down-at-the-heels neighborhood. It's now undeniably hip to be in Hoxton.

From the Barbican in The City to Whitechapel in the East End, as many as 25 art galleries have opened, showing the latest works of the YBAs (Young British Artists). A spread of trendy real estate has taken a firm grip across the City Road into E1, principally Shoreditch, Spitalfields, and "Banglatown"—the nickname for the neighborhood around Brick Lane where Bengali shops and homes have created a slice of south Asia. Where less-than-glam buildings for the poor (such as the Jewish Soup Kitchen off Commercial Street, Spitalfields) once stood are now loft-style luxury apartments. Boutiques, bars, clubs, and restaurants have followed in their wake, and the Eastside—as it has been coined—is unapologetically brimming with energy.

open spaces of the East End's former industrial units. Damien Hirst (arguably the leader of the Britart phenomenon who gained notoriety for preserving animals in formaldehyde as art, and whose recent auction of work netted a cool $198 million), Tracey Emin, Gilbert and George, Sam Taylor-Wood, and other trailblazers have shown here and gone on to become internationally renowned. The building looks, appropriately enough, like a white cube—it has a glassed-in upper level called "Inside the White Cube," where international guest curators are invited to show their projects. ⊠ *48 Hoxton Sq., Hoxton* ☎ *020/7930–5373* ⊕ *www. whitecube.com* ✏ *Free* ☉ *Tues.–Sat. 10–6* Ⓤ *Old St.*

The South Bank

WORD OF MOUTH

"We did the Eye, buying tickets just before sunset on a clear day and felt it was worth the time and money. Line only took 5–10 minutes. Great experience, even those in our group who had issues with heights soon overcame that. . . . Agree it is so slow moving you won't have a 'ride' experience—it is for the VIEW."

—jeanOH

GETTING ORIENTED

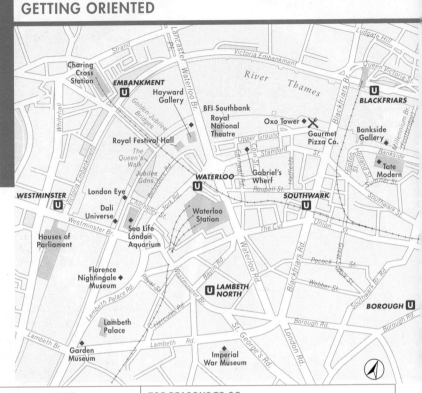

GETTING THERE	TOP REASONS TO GO
For the South Bank use Westminster station on the Jubilee or Northern line, from where you can walk across Westminster Bridge; Embankment on District, Circle, Northern, and Bakerloo lines, where you can walk across Hungerford Bridge; or Waterloo on the Jubilee, Northern, and Bakerloo lines, where it's a five-minute walk to the Royal Festival Hall. In the east, alternatively, use Tower Gateway on the Docklands Light Railway (DLR). London Bridge on the Northern and Jubilee lines is but a five-minute stroll from Borough Market and Southwark Cathedral.	**Golden Jubilee Bridges:** Walk across the footbridge at dusk, then east along a fairy-light embankment toward the Oxo Tower. **Shakespeare's Globe Theatre:** Catch a performance on a summer's eve to be inspired by history while being caught up in a unique theatrical experience. **Royal Festival Hall:** Celebrate the new look of the "people's palace" with a concert or a drink in the foyer. **Tate Modern:** Observe one of the changing installations—always impressive and humbling—in the turbine hall. **Borough Market:** Arrive hungry and gorge your way through stalls of organic produce at London's oldest food market. There's plenty of opportunity to taste the traders' delicious produce on Saturday mornings.

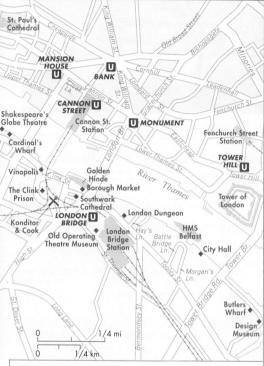

MAKING THE MOST OF YOUR TIME

Don't attempt the South Bank all in one go. Not only will you exhaust yourself, but you will miss out on the varied delights that it has to offer.

The Imperial War Museum demands a couple of hours, with the nearby Garden Museum providing an hour of further distraction.

To take in the South Bank galleries, such as Bankside and the Hayward, you'll need at least a day; the Tate Modern alone deserves a whole morning or afternoon, especially if you want to do justice to both the temporary exhibitions and the permanent collection.

The Globe requires about two hours for the exhibition theater tour and two to three hours for a performance. Finish with drinks or dinner at the Oxo Tower or a stroll west along the riverbank and then across the Golden Jubilee Bridges.

FEELING PECKISH?

At Gabriel's Wharf have a sit-down meal at the **Gourmet Pizza Co.** (⊠ *56 Upper Ground, Gabriel's Wharf,* ☎ *020/7928–3188*) or grab a sandwich or coffee at one of the smaller establishments open during the day here.

For exquisite handmade pastries, along with daily specials such as chicken paella or vegetarian moussaka, stop at the bijou premises of **Konditor & Cook** (⊠ *10 Stoney St.* ☎ *020/7407–5100*), one of the stars of the handful of eateries nearby Borough Market. Alternatively, just dive into the crowds of the market itself and grab something from its many and varied food stalls. It's all good.

SAFETY

At night, it's best to stick to where the action is at the Butler's Wharf and Gabriel's Wharf restaurants, the Oxo Tower, the National Theatre, the National Film Theatre, and the Royal Festival Hall. Stray farther south of the embankment and it quickly begins to feel deserted.

8

Culture, history, sights: the South Bank has it all. Stretching from the Imperial War Museum in the southwest as far as the Design Museum in the east, high-caliber art, music, film, and theater venues are up alongside the likes of an aquarium, a wine museum, historic warships, and a foodie-favorite market. Three structures dominate the skyline: the looming stack of Tate Modern, the distinctive Oxo Tower, and overlooking them all, the London Eye.

Updated by
Janice Fuscoe

For centuries the North London jibe about needing a passport to cross the mighty Thames may have held true. But in the mid-20th century the South Bank emerged as one of the capital's most creative hubs. The reconstructed Shakespeare's Globe Theatre steals the show, but the **Tate Modern** is also a huge draw, a monolithic ex–power station turned museum. The **Southbank Centre** is home to the recently renovated **Royal Festival Hall**, the **Hayward Gallery**, the **BFI Southbank**, and the **National Theatre**. East near **Butlers Wharf**, the ultrachic Design Museum occupies what was once a dingy Dickensian shadowland.

Southwark, the oldest borough in England, was once infamous for being London's outlaw neighborhood. Just across London Bridge, it was conveniently outside the city walls and was therefore the ideal location for the theaters, taverns, and cock-fighting arenas—not to mention brothels—that served as after-hours entertainment in the Middle Ages. Today the **Thames Path** is alive with legal activity, especially in summer, with skateboarders, secondhand-book stalls, and street entertainers. Several footbridges cross the Thames, including the curvaceous **Millennium Bridge,** connecting the Tate Modern to St. Paul's Cathedral, and the **Golden Jubilee Bridges,** with the best view of the Houses of Parliament on the embankment between Westminster and Lambeth bridges. In the shadow of the **Oxo Tower** sits **Gabriel's Wharf,** a small marketplace of shops and restaurants. Sir Francis Drake's ship, the *Golden Hinde,* nestles in Pickfords Wharf and the massive domed **City Hall** lies next to **Tower Bridge.** A millennium project that's a favorite with both Londoners and out-of-towners alike, the **London Eye** is next to the **London Aquarium** and the surrealist museum **Dalí Universe**. The grisly delights of the **Old Operating Theatre Museum** and the **London Dungeon** are favorites for kids. After all this sightseeing, have a drink at **Vinopolis** and grab a bite at the legendary **Borough Market** (the rowdier neighbor of **Southwark Cathedral**). "London's Larder" has become an essential foodie destination, where celebrity chefs go in search of farm-fresh produce.

TOP ATTRACTIONS

Dalí Universe. Here is Europe's most comprehensively arranged collection by master surrealist Salvador Dalí. The many exhibits—from art to sculpture, to furniture, to jewelry—are organized in themes (Sensuality and Femininity, Religion and Mythology, and Dreams and Fantasy), and thus the museum tries to give visitors a reflection of how Dalí thought out his work. There are more than 500 pieces on show, but highlights undoubtedly include the *Mae West Lips Sofa*, the *Lobster Telephone*, and *Spellbound*, a dream sequence, made for the Hitchcock movie of the same name. Although there's much to take in, this museum has a much more commercial flavor and lacks the intimacy of other Dalí museums. ⊠ *County Hall, Riverside Bldg., Westminster Bridge Rd., South Bank* ☎ *0870/744–7485* ⊕ *www.thedaliuniverse.com* ⊠ *£14* ☉ *Daily 9:30–6; last entry 5* Ⓤ *Waterloo, Westminster.*

QUICK BITES

Gabriel's Wharf. This cluster of specialty shops, cafés, and restaurants is part of the Coin Street Community neighborhood and bustles with activity during the daytime. You can rent bicycles here from the London Bicycle Tour Company (☎ 020/7928–6838). ⊠ 56 Upper Ground, South Bank ☎ 020/7021–1686 ⊕ www.coinstreet.org ⊠ Free ☉ Shops and studios Tues.–Sun. 11–6 Ⓤ Blackfriars, Waterloo.

Ⓒ **The Globe Theatre**

Fodor's Choice ★ *See the highlighted listing in this chapter.*

Ⓒ ***Golden Hinde.*** Sir Francis Drake circumnavigated the globe in this little galleon, or one just like it. This exact replica made a 23-year round-the-world voyage—much of it spent along U.S. coasts, both Pacific and Atlantic—and has settled here to continue its educational purpose. Call to confirm opening hours and for information on guided tours. ⊠ *Unit 1 & 2, Pickfords Wharf, Clink St., South Bank* ☎ *0870/011–8700 or 0870/7403–0123* ⊕ *www.goldenhinde.com* ⊠ *£6* ☉ *Daily 10–6* Ⓤ *London Bridge, Mansion House.*

Hayward Gallery. The gray, windowless bunker tucked behind the South-bank Centre concert halls has had to bear the brunt of architectural criticism over the years, but that's changed with a foyer extension that gives more daylight, more space for exhibits, a café, and better access. The highlight of the project is an elliptical mirrored glass pavilion by New York–based artist Dan Graham. Exhibitions here encompass a range of art media, crossing history and cultures, bridging the experimental and established. It's consistently on the cutting edge of new

8

developments in art and critical theory, finding new ways to present the well known, from Picasso to Lichtenstein, and providing a prominent platform for up-and-coming artists. ■TIP➔ A small part of the gallery is always reserved for free exhibitions. ✉ *Southbank Centre, South Bank* ☎ *020/7921–0813* ⊕ *www.hayward.org.uk* ✉ *Varies; usually around £10* ⊘ *Sat.–Thurs. 10–6, Fri. 10–10* Ⓤ *Waterloo.*

⟳ ★ **London Eye.** To mark the start of the new millennium, architects David Marks and Julia Barfield conceived an entirely new vision: a beautiful and celebratory structure that would allow people to see this great city from a completely new perspective—on a giant wheel. As well as representing the turning of the century, a wheel was seen as a symbol

THE ELEPHANT IN THE ROOM

Look at a map of south London, and just below the South Bank you'll see an area called Elephant and Castle. It's not one of London's nicer districts—don't bother visiting—but you might wonder how it got such a fairy-tale name. The most popular story concerns a Spanish princess, betrothed to a prince and sent to England while she was still a little girl. A castle was built for her just outside the city walls, where she was looked after until she was old enough to be married. The name is therefore thought to be a corruption of the Spanish *Infanta de Castile*.

of regeneration and the passing of time. The London Eye is the largest observation wheel ever built and among the top 10 tallest structures in London. The 25-minute slow-motion ride inside one of the enclosed passenger capsules is so smooth you'd hardly know you were suspended over the Thames, moving slowly around. On a clear day you can take in a range of up to 25 mi, viewing London's most famous landmarks from a fascinating angle. If you're looking for a special place to celebrate, champagne and canapés can be arranged ahead of time. ■TIP➔ Buy your ticket online, over the phone, or at the ticket office in advance to avoid the long lines and get a 10% discount. For an extra £10, you can save even more time with a Fast Track flight for which you check in 15 minutes before your "departure." The London Eye sightseeing cruise also departs here for a 40-minute cruise of the Thames. ✉ *Jubilee Gardens, South Bank* ☎ *0870/990–8883* ⊕ *www.londoneye.com* ✉ *£17.50, cruise £12.50* ⊘ *June and Sept., daily 10–9; July and Aug., daily 10–9:30; Oct.–April, daily 10–8* Ⓤ *Waterloo.*

Oxo Tower. Long a London landmark to the insider, the art deco–era Oxo building has graduated from its former incarnations as a power-generating station and warehouse into a vibrant community of artists' and designers' workshops, a pair of restaurants, and five floors of community homes. There's an observation deck for a super river vista (St. Paul's to the east and Somerset House to the west), and a performance area on the first floor, which comes alive all summer long—as does the entire surrounding neighborhood. All the artisans expect you to disturb them whenever they're open, whether buying, commissioning, or just browsing. The biggest draw remains the Oxo Tower Restaurant for a meal or a martini. ✉ *Bargehouse St., South Bank* ☎ *020/7021–1686*

Continued on page 164

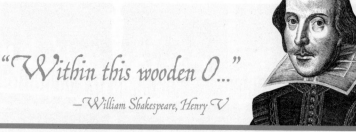

"Within this wooden O..."
—William Shakespeare, Henry V

SHAKESPEARE AND THE GLOBE THEATRE

At Shakespeare's Globe Theatre, they say the Bard does not belong to the British; he belongs to the world. Not a day has gone by since the Restoration when one of his plays isn't being performed or reinterpreted somewhere. But here, at the site of the original Globe, in a painstaking reconstruction of Shakespeare's own open-air theater, is where seeing one of his plays can take on an ethereal quality.

If you are exceedingly well read and a lover of the Bard, then chances are a pilgrimage to his Globe Theatre is already on your list. But if Shakespeare's works leave you wondering why exactly the play is the thing, then a trip to the Globe—to learn more about his life or to see his words come alive—is a must.

The Globe Theatre in Shakespeare's Day

In the 16th and 17th centuries, a handful of theaters—the Rose, the Swan, the Globe, and others whose names are lost—rose above the higgledy-piggledy jumble of rooftops in London's rowdy Southwark neighborhood. They were round or octagonal open-air playhouses, with galleries for the "quality" members of society, and large, open pits for the raucous mobs. People from all social classes, from royalty down to the hoi polloi, shared the communal experience of drama in these places. Shakespeare's Globe was one.

A fire in 1613 destroyed the first Globe, which was quickly rebuilt; however, Oliver Cromwell and waves of other reformers put an end to all the Southwark playhouses in the 1640s. By the time American actor and director Sam Wanamaker visited in 1949, the only indication that the world's greatest dramatist created popular entertainment here was a plaque on a brewery wall. Wanamaker was shocked to find that all evidence of the playwright's legendary playhouse had vanished into air.

And thereby hangs a tale.

Wanamaker's Dream

Over the next several decades, Wanamaker devoted himself to the Bard. He was director of the New Shakespeare Theatre in Liverpool and, in 1959, joined the Shakespeare Memorial Theatre Company (now the Royal Shakespeare Company) at Stratford-upon-Avon. Finally, in the 1970s he began the project

SHAKESPEARE'S ALL-TIME TOP 10

1. *Romeo and Juliet.* Young love, teenage rebellion, and tragedy are the ingredients of the greatest tearjerker of all time.

2. *Hamlet* (*right*). The very model of a modern antihero and origin of the most quoted line of any play: "To be or not to be…"

3. *A Midsummer Night's Dream.* Spells and potions abound as the gods use humans for playthings; lovers' tiffs are followed by happy endings for all.

4. *Othello.* Jealousy poisons love and destroys a proud man.

5. *The Taming of the Shrew.* The eternal battle of the sexes.

6. *Macbeth.* Ambition, murder, and revenge. Evil gets its just reward.

7. *The Merry Wives of Windsor.* A two-timing rascal gets his comeuppance from a pack of hysterically funny gossips.

8. *Richard III.* One of literature's juiciest villains. The whole audience wants to hiss.

9. *The Tempest.* On a desert island, the concerns of men amaze and amuse the innocent Miranda: "Oh brave new world, that has such people in't."

10. *King Lear.* A tragedy of old age, filial love, and grasping, ungrateful children.

that would dominate the rest of his life: reconstructing Shakespeare's theater, as close to the original site as possible.

Today's Globe was re-created using authentic Elizabethan materials and craft techniques—green oak timbers joined only with wooden pegs and mortise-and-tenon joints; plaster made of lime, sand, and goat's hair; and the first thatched roof in London since the Great Fire of 1666. The complex, 200 yards from the site of the original Globe, includes an exhibition center, cafés, and restaurants. (The shell of a 17th-century-style theater, built adjacent to the Globe to a design by Inigo Jones, awaits further funds for completion.)

FUN FACT: Plays are presented in the open air (and sometimes the rain) to an audience of 1,000 on wooden benches in the bays, and 500 "groundlings," who stand on a carpet of hazelnut shells and cinder, just as they did nearly four centuries ago.

The eventual realization of Wanamaker's dream, a full-scale, accurate replica of the Globe, was the keystone that supported the revitalization of the entire district. The new Globe celebrates Shakespeare, his work, and his times, and as an educational trust it is dedicated to making the Bard continually fresh and accessible for new audiences. Sadly, Wanamaker died before construction was completed, in 1997. In Southwark Cathedral, a few hundred yards west of the Globe, a memorial to him stands beside the statue memorializing Shakespeare himself.

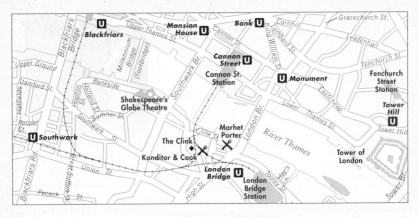

The season of plays is limited to the warmer months, from May to the first week in October, with the schedule announced in late January on the theater's Web site. Tickets go on sale in mid-February. The box office takes phone and mail orders as well as in-person sales, but the most convenient way to buy tickets is online. Book as early as possible.

FUN FACT: "Groundlings"—those with £5 standing-only tickets—are not allowed to sit during the performance. Reserve an actual seat, though, on any one of the theater's three levels, and you can join the "Elizabethan" crowd.

If you do have a seat, you can rent cushions for £1 (or bring your own) to soften the backless wooden benches. A limited number of backrests are also available for rent for £3. The show must go on, rain or shine, warm or chilly—so come prepared for whatever the weather throws at you. Umbrellas are banned, but you can bring a raincoat or buy a cheap Globe rain poncho, which doubles as a great souvenir.

MAKING THE MOST OF YOUR TIME
Give yourself plenty of time: there are several cafés and restaurants, as well as fascinating interactive exhibitions, and theater tours with occasional live demonstrations. Performances can last up to three hours.

SPECIAL EVENT

The Frost Fair, held annually the weekend before Christmas, commemorates several extraordinary winters in the 17th century when the Thames froze over and fairs took place on the ice. It includes street theater, Morris Dancing, sword fighting, and food and crafts stalls. Admission is free, and there is special reduced admission to the Theatre and Exhibition during the fair.

WITH CHILDREN
Childsplay, a program for 8- to 11-year-olds, is held every Saturday during the theatre season. While Mom and Dad enjoy the play, children—helped by actors, musicans, and teachers—learn the background and story and become accustomed to Shakespearean language. By the time they are admitted to the theater for the last 20 minutes of the play, the children have become Shakespeare enthusiasts for life. Workshops start at 1:30 PM and tickets are £12.50; book in advance.

Year-Round at Shakespeare's Globe

Shakespeare's Globe Exhibition is a comprehensive display built under the theater (the entry is adjacent) that provides background material about the Elizabethan theater and about the surrounding neighborhood, Southwark. The exhibition describes the process of building the modern Globe and the serious research that went into it.

FUN FACT: In Shakespeare's day, this was a rough part of town. The Bear Gardens, around the corner from the Globe, was where bear baiting, a cruel animal sport, took place. Farther along, the Clink (now a museum) was the local *gaol* (jail).

Daily live demonstrations include Elizabethan dressing, stage fighting, and swordplay, performed by drama students and stage-fighting instructors from the Royal Academy of Dramatic Art (RADA) and the London Academy of Music and Dramatic Art (LAMDA).

FUN FACT: Many performances are done in Elizabethan dress. Costumes are handmade from period materials—wool, silk, cotton, animal skins, and natural dyes.

Admission also includes a tour of the theater. On matinee days, the tour visits the archaeological site of the nearby (and older) Rose Theatre.

FUN FACT: Shakespeare's casts were all male, with young men and boys playing the female roles. A live demonstration in the costume exhibit shows how this was done—and how convincing it can be.

Visiting the Globe

✉ 21 New Globe Walk, Bankside, South Bank

☎ 020/7401–9919 box office, 020/7902–1400 New Shakespeare's Globe Exhibition

⊕ www.shakespeares-globe.org

🎟 Exhibition & tour £10.50, family ticket (2 adults, 3 children) £28; ticket prices for plays vary (£5–£33)

🕘 Exhibition daily 9–5; plays May—early Oct., call for performance schedule.

Ⓤ Southwark, then walk to Blackfriars Bridge and descend the steps; Mansion House, then cross Southwark Bridge; Blackfriars, then walk across Blackfriars Bridge; St. Paul's, then cross Millennium Bridge.

⊕ *www.oxotower.co.uk* ✉ *Free* ⊗ *Studios and shops Tues.–Sun. 11–6*
Ⓤ *Blackfriars, Waterloo.*

Southwark Cathedral. Pronounced "Suth-uck," this is the second-oldest
Gothic church in London, after Westminster Abbey, with parts dating
back to the 12th century. Although it houses some remarkable memorials,
not to mention a program of lunchtime concerts, it's seldom visited. It was
promoted to cathedral status only in 1905; before that it was the priory
church of St. Mary Overie (as in "over the water"—on the South Bank).
Look for the gaudily renovated 1408 tomb of the poet John Gower, friend
of Chaucer, and for the Harvard Chapel. Another notable buried here is
Edmund Shakespeare, brother of William. ■TIP➜ The Refectory serves
full English breakfasts, light lunches, and tea daily 10–6. ✉ *London Bridge,
South Bank* ☎ *020/7367–6700* ⊕ *www.southwark.anglican.org* ✉ *Free,
suggested donation £4* ⊗ *Daily 8–6* Ⓤ *London Bridge.*

Ↄ **Tate Modern**
Fodor's Choice   *See the highlighted listing in this chapter.*
★

WORTH NOTING

Bankside Gallery. Two artistic societies—the Royal Society of Painter–
Printmakers and the Royal Watercolour Society—have their headquarters here. Together they mount exhibitions of current members' work,
usually for sale, alongside artists' materials and books—a great place
for finding that exclusive, not too expensive gift. There are also regular
themed exhibitions. ✉ *48 Hopton St., South Bank* ☎ *020/7928–7521*
⊕ *www.banksidegallery.com* ✉ *Free* ⊗ *Daily 11–6, call ahead, as hrs
may vary and gallery closes for short periods between exhibitions*
Ⓤ *Blackfriars, Southwark, St. Paul's.*

Ↄ **The Clink Prison**. Giving rise to the term *clink*, or jail, this institution was
originally the prison attached to Winchester House, palace of the Bishops of Winchester until 1626. One of five Southwark establishments, it
was the first to detain women, most of whom were called "Winchester
geese"—a euphemism for prostitutes. They were endemic in Southwark,
especially around the bishops' area of jurisdiction, which was known as
"the Liberty of the Clink" because their graces' solution was to license
prostitution rather than ban it. You'll discover, in graphic detail, how
a grisly Tudor prison would operate on a code of cruelty, deprivation,
and corruption. ✉ *1 Clink St., South Bank* ☎ *020/7403–0900* ⊕ *www.
clink.co.uk* ✉ *£5* ⊗ *Weekdays 10–6, weekends 10–9; last admission 1
hr before closing* Ⓤ *London Bridge.*

Ↄ **Design Museum**. This was the first museum in the world to elevate everyday design and design classics to the status of art by placing them
in their social and cultural context. Fashion, creative technology, and
architecture are explored with thematic displays from the museum's
permanent collection, and temporary exhibitions provide an in-depth
focus on such subjects as the work of great designers such as Charles
Eames and Isamu Noguchi, or thematic shows on the Bauhaus or book
design. The museum looks forward, too, by showcasing innovative contemporary designs and technologies, an area that kids find absorbing

TATE MODERN

✉ *Bankside, South Bank* ☎ *020/7887–8888* ⊕ *www.tate.org.uk/modern* 💷 *Free, charge for special exhibitions* 🕐 *Sun.–Thurs. 10–6, Fri. and Sat. 10–10 (last admission to exhibitions 45 mins before close)* Ⓤ *Blackfriars, Southwark.*

TIPS

■ Don't know where to start? Join one of the free, 45-minute guided tours. Each one covers a different gallery: Poetry and Dream at 11, Material Gestures at noon, States of Flux at 2, and Energy and Process at 3. No need to book; just show up in the appropriate room.

■ Level 4 is devoted to temporary exhibitions, for which there's usually a charge of around £15. Bypass it if you're just here to see the main collection, which is free.

■ Make it a two-for-one art day by taking advantage of the Tate Boat, which ships visitors back and forth between Tate Britain and Tate Modern every 40 minutes.

■ Private "Tate Tours for Two" can be booked online from £100 to £210 including a restaurant meal.

■ An ambitious—and controversial—extension to the front of the Tate Modern is scheduled to open in 2012. No closures had been announced at this writing, but check ahead.

A working power station from 1947 to 1981, this hulking monolith of a building was all but derelict when the Tate adopted it as the home for their modern art collection in the late '90s. And what a magnificent transformation it has been. On permanent display in the galleries are classic works from 1900 to the present day, by Matisse, Picasso, Dalí, Moore, Bacon, Warhol, and the most-talked-about British upstarts. The works are not grouped by artist but are arranged thematically—Landscape, Still Life, and the Nude—on different levels. You could spend a rainy day here exploring the building or, alternatively, come for the latest barnstorming exhibition, which is more often than not a talking point at smart dinner parties across London. Autumn 2010 will see 100 paintings by the French post-impressionist Paul Gauguin. "Gauguin: Maker of Myth" is likely to be a sellout so it's advisable to book tickets and a time slot well in advance.

HIGHLIGHTS

The vast **Turbine Hall** is a dramatic entrance point used to showcase big, audacious installations that tend to generate a lot of publicity. Past highlights include a massive glowing sun, a working spiral slide, and, perhaps most bizarrely, a long crack in the floor.

The **Material Gestures** galleries on Level 3 feature an impressive offering of post–World War II painting and sculpture. Room 7 contains a breathtaking collection of Rothkos and Monets; there are also paintings by Matisse, Pollock, and Picasso, and newer works from the likes of the sculptor Anish Kapoor.

Head to the Restaurant on Level 7 or the Espresso Bar on Level 4 for stunning vistas of the Thames. The view of St. Paul's from the Espresso Bar's balcony is one of the best in London.

8

Borough Market brings hungry shoppers to the London Bridge area every Friday and Saturday.

(there are free activity packs to spark their interest further). All of this is supplemented by a busy program of lectures, events, and talks, including a children's workshop. If you're in need of sustenance, there's the trendsetting Blueprint Café (designed by that most venerated of design gurus, Terence Conran), with its river terrace and superb views. For quicker snacks at a lower price, there's also the museum's own café on the ground floor. Entry to both cafés and the museum store is free. ⊠ *28 Shad Thames, South Bank* ☎ *0870/7403–6933* ⊕ *www.designmuseum. org* ⚏ *£8.50* ☼ *Daily 10–5:45, last admission 5:15* Ⓤ *London Bridge; Tower Hill; DLR: Tower Gateway.*

OFF THE BEATEN PATH **Dulwich Picture Gallery.** A small but distinguished gallery in the London arts scene, Dulwich Picture Gallery (pronounced Dull-ich) was Europe's first purpose-built art museum when it opened in 1811. The permanent collection includes impressive works by Rembrandt, Van Dyck, Rubens, Poussin, and Gainsborough, and it also hosts three major international exhibitions each year. As one British art critic puts it, "we would all travel bravely for a day in Tuscany or Umbria in order to see much less." The gallery also has a lovely café serving meals and drinks. Most of the land around here belongs to Dulwich College, a local boys' school, which keeps strict control over development. Consequently, Dulwich Village feels a bit like a time capsule, with old-fashioned street signs and handsome 18th-century houses strung out along its main street. Take a short wander and you'll find a handful of bijou clothing and crafts stores and the well-manicured Dulwich Park, with lakeside walks and a fine display of rhododendrons in late May. ⊠ *Gallery Rd., Dulwich Village, Southwark* ☎ *020/8693–5254* ⊕ *www.dulwichpicturegallery.org.uk*

✉ *£5–£9. Free guided tours week-ends at 3* ⊘ *Tues.–Fri. 10–5, week-ends 11–5* Ⓤ *National Rail: West Dulwich from Victoria or North Dulwich from London Bridge.*

🕙 **HMS Belfast.** At 613 feet, this is one of the largest and most powerful cruisers the Royal Navy has ever had. It played an important role in the D-Day landings off Nor-mandy, left for the Far East after the war, and has been moored in the relative calm of the Thames since 1971. On board there's a riveting interactive outpost of the **Impe-rial War Museum,** which tells the Royal Navy's story from 1914 to the present and shows you about life on a World War II battleship, from mess decks and bakery to punishment cells, and from opera-

BEDLAM

The Imperial War Museum is in an elegant domed and colonnaded building, erected in the early 19th century to house the Bethlehem Hospital for the Insane, better known as the infamous Bedlam. By 1816, when the patients were moved here, they were no longer kept in cages to be taunted by tourists (see the final scene of Hogarth's *Rake's Progress* at Sir John Soane's Museum for a sense of how horrific it was), since reformers—and George III's madness—had effected more humane standards. Bedlam moved to Surrey in 1930.

tions room to engine room and armaments. At this writing, a major new interactive exhibition on the science and history of shipbuilding is due to run until at least October 2010. ✉ *Morgan's La., Tooley St., South Bank* ☎ *020/7940–6300* ⊕ *www.iwm.org.uk* ✉*£10.70* ⊘ *Mar.–Oct., daily 10–6; Nov.–Feb., daily 10–5; last admission 1 hr before closing* Ⓤ *London Bridge.*

Florence Nightingale Museum. At this writing, the museum is closed and an expanded museum is scheduled to open in May 2010 for the cen-tenary of Florence Nightingale's death. Here you can learn all about the founder of the first school of nursing, that most famous of health-care reformers, "the Lady with the Lamp" known for tending soldiers during the Crimean War (1854–56). ✉ *2 Lambeth Palace Rd., South Bank* ☎ *020/7620–0374* ⊕ *www.florence-nightingale.co.uk* ✉*£5.80* ⊘ *Weekdays 10–5, last admission 4, weekends 10–4:30, last admission 3:30* Ⓤ *Waterloo, Westminster.*

🕙 **Imperial War Museum.** Despite its title, this museum of 20th-century war-★ fare does not glorify bloodshed but emphasizes understanding through evoking what life was like for citizens and soldiers alike through the two world wars and beyond. There's an impressive amount of hard-ware at the main entrance with accompanying interactive material, including a Battle of Britain Spitfire, a German V2 rocket, tanks, guns, and submarines—and from here you can peel off to the various sec-tions of the museum. Sights, sounds, and smells are used to re-create the very uncomfortable Trench Experience in the World War I gallery, which is just as effective as The Blitz Experience in the World War II gallery: a 10-minute taste of an air raid in a street of acrid smoke with sirens blaring and searchlights glaring. There are two galleries of war art on the second floor (by Henry Moore, John Singer Sargent, Stanley Spencer, and William Orpen, to name a few), poetry, photography, and documentary film footage. There's also a permanent Holocaust exhibition, and a Crimes Against Humanity exhibition, which is not suitable for younger children. More recent wars attended by British forces are commemorated, too, in the Victoria and George Cross Gallery. Don't miss the intriguing Secret War Gallery, which charts the history of agents' intrepid work in the wars and the inception of MI5 and MI6, the government's secret services. There's a lovely, bright café where you can rest after your trek south of the river. ⊠ *Lambeth Rd., South Bank* ☎ *020/7416–5000* ⊕ *www.iwm.org.uk* ⊠ *Free (charge for special exhibits)* ⊙ *Daily 10–6* Ⓤ *Lambeth North.*

> ## COMBINATION TICKETS
>
> If you're planning to visit the London Dungeon, Sea Life London Aquarium, and Madame Tussauds, save by booking a combination ticket on any of their Web sites.

☼ **Sea Life London Aquarium.** The curved, colonnaded, neoclassic hulk of County Hall once housed London's local government administration (now at the Norman Foster–designed City Hall building farther downriver by Tower Bridge). Now it's where you can catch a dark and thrilling glimpse of the waters of the world, focused around a superb three-level aquarium full of sharks and stingrays, among other common and rarer breeds. There are also educational exhibits, feeding displays, and hands-on displays—including a tank full of nonvenomous rays that you can touch if they swim near enough—they seem to like having their backs tickled. It's not the biggest aquarium you've ever seen—especially if you've been to SeaWorld—but the exhibit is well arranged, with areas for different oceans, water environments, and climate zones, including a stunning coral reef and rain forest. There are regular feeding times and free talks throughout the day. Look out for new additions to the tanks from the conservation breeding program. ⊠ *County Hall, Riverside Bldg., Westminster Bridge Rd., South Bank* ☎ *0871/663–1678* ⊕ *www.sealife.co.uk* ⊠ *£16* ⊙ *Daily 10–6; last admission 5; mid-July–early Sept. 10–7; last admission 6* Ⓤ *Westminster, Waterloo.*

☼ **London Dungeon.** Here's the goriest, grisliest, most gruesome attraction in town, where realistic waxwork people are subjected in graphic detail to all the historical horrors the Tower of London merely tells you about. Tableaux depict famous bloody moments—like Anne Boleyn's decapitation and the martyrdom of St. George—alongside the torture, murder, and ritual slaughter of lesser-known victims, all to a sound track of screaming, wailing, and agonized moaning. There are displays on the Great Plague, the Great Fire of London, and Jack the Ripper; to add to the fear and fun, costumed characters leap out of the gloom to bring the exhibits to life. Naturally, children absolutely adore this place, but be warned—some nervous kiddies may find it too frightening. ■ TIP➔ Expect long lines on weekends and during school holidays. Booking online will save at least £5. ⊠ *28–34 Tooley St., South Bank* ☎ *0871/7403–7221* ⊕ *www.thedungeons.com* ⊠ *£21.95* ⊙ *Daily; opening times vary slightly, week by week, but generally Sept.–Mar. 10–5; Mar.–Sept. 9:30–6; Aug. 9:30–7; phone to confirm times* Ⓤ *London Bridge.*

The Garden Museum. Before you even go into this rather absorbing little museum, you just know it's going to have a good story behind it. In the

Royal Festival Hall, the heart of the Southbank Centre, is home to many art performances and displays.

mid-1970s, two gardening enthusiasts were looking for the graves of the John Tradescants (the elder and younger), who were adventurous plant collectors, responsible for introducing many familiar blooms to these shores. Their search led them to a medieval church, right next to Lambeth Palace—which, they were horrified to discover, was about to be bulldozed. Inspired to action, they rescued the church and opened this museum, which has built one of the largest collections of historic garden tools, artifacts, and curiosities in the world. The museum also has its own beautiful walled gardens, which are maintained year-round with seasonal plants. One section contains a perfect replica of a 17th-century knot garden; another is devoted entirely to wildflowers. Of course, it's worth a visit to see the church itself, which also contains the tombs of William Bligh, captain of the *Bounty*, and several members of the Boleyn family. An extensive refurbishment in 2008 added a new exhibitions gallery, with temporary displays changing every six months. There's also a green-thumb gift shop and the **Garden Café** serving vegetarian lunches and home-baked cakes. ⊠ *Lambeth Palace Rd., South Bank* ☎ *020/7401–8865* ⊕ *www.gardenmuseum.org.uk* ✉ *£6 (includes garden and all exhibitions)* ⊘ *Daily 10:30–5* Ⓤ *Vauxhall.*

Old Operating Theatre Museum. All that remains of one of England's oldest hospitals, which stood here from the 12th century until 1862, is the room where women went under the knife. The theater was bricked up and forgotten for a century but has been restored into an exhibition of early-19th-century medical practices: the operating table onto which the gagged and blindfolded patients were roped; the box of sawdust underneath for catching their blood; the knives, pliers, and handsaws

The South Bank Dining

MODERATE DINING
Anchor & Hope, Modern British, 36 The Cut

Baltic, Eastern European, 74 Blackfriars Rd.

Chez Bruce, Modern French, 22 Bellevue Rd.

Magdalen, Modern British, 152 Tooley St.

Skylon, Modern European, Royal Festival Hall, Belvedere Rd.

Tom Ilić, Modern European, 123 Queenstown Rd.

the surgeons wielded; and—this was a theater in the round—the spectators' seats. So authentic are the surroundings that they were used in the film *The Madness of King George.* Every Saturday at 11:30 and 2 there are demonstrations of surgical practice. Next door is a sweeter show: the **Herb Garret,** with displays of medicinal herbs used during the same period. ⊠ *9A St. Thomas St., South Bank* ☎ *020/7188–2679* ⊕ *www. thegarret.org.uk* ✉ *£5.60* ⊙ *Daily 10:30–5. Closed Dec. 15–Jan. 5* Ⓤ *London Bridge.*

Vinopolis. Spread over 2 acres between the Globe Theatre and London Bridge, Vinopolis allows you to take a virtual tour of the world's wine cultures and have an opportunity to put your skills to the "taste." Wine tours start at £19.50 and there are a number of packages, including an option that allows you to taste various whiskeys, rums, and absinthes in addition to the wines—and a comedy night on the last Friday of every month. The four restaurants claim to offer more wines by the glass than anywhere else in the city—and there is, of course, a shop. Keep in mind that the last entry is two hours before the scheduled closing time, and that you should allow at least two hours for a tour. ⊠ *1 Bank End, South Bank* ☎ *0870/7940–8300* ⊕ *www.vinopolis.co.uk* ✉ *£19.50* ⊙ *Thurs., Fri. noon–10, Sat. 11–10, Sun. noon–6* Ⓤ *London Bridge.*

Kensington, Chelsea, and Knightsbridge

WORD OF MOUTH

"We also visited the Natural History Museum for what else but the dinos! I really appreciate that these fantastic museums are all free!"

—tongsa

GETTING ORIENTED

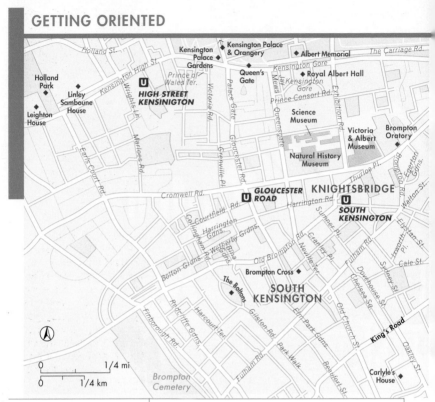

GETTING THERE	TOP REASONS TO GO
There are several useful Tube stations for this area: Sloane Square and High Street Kensington on the District and Circle lines; Earl's Court, Kensington, Knightsbridge, and Hyde Park Corner on the Piccadilly Line; South Kensington and Gloucester Road on the District, Circle, and Piccadilly lines; and Victoria Station on the District, Circle, and Victoria lines.	**The V&A Museum:** Sketch in the sculpture court, where even stools are provided—then have a glass of wine under the Chihuly chandelier.
	Natural History Museum: Watch children catch on that the museum's animatronic T. rex has noticed *them*—and is licking its dinosaur chops. Then see some of those fearsome teeth for real in the dinosaur room.
	Harrods' food halls: Notice the glistening mosaic of fresh fish under the actual mosaic ceilings of these esteemed underground culinary corridors.
SAFETY	**The Proms:** Sing along at the end of a Proms concert in Royal Albert Hall. (Even better: watch the English concertgoers drop their inhibitions and join in, too.)
Kensington, Chelsea, and Knightsbridge are safe areas, but beware of pickpockets in crowded Tube stations and stores.	**King's Road pubs:** Take a rest stop from exploring this most quintessential of London shopping streets. Keep an eye out for Chelsea Pensioners in full red-uniformed regalia.

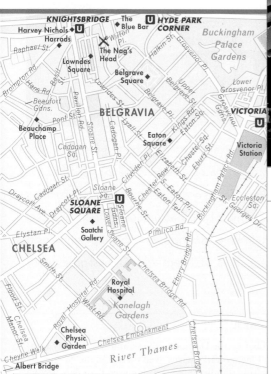

MAKING THE MOST OF YOUR TIME

You could fill three or four days in this borough: a shopping stroll along the length of the King's Road is easily half a day. Add lunch and some time weaving back and forth between the King's Road and the river and you can fill a day. Give yourself a half day, at least, for the Victoria & Albert Museum and a half day for either the Science or Natural History Museum.

FEELING PECKISH?

The Café at the V&A (✉ *Victoria & Albert Museum, Cromwell Rd.* ☎ *020/7942–2500*) serves breakfast, light snacks, tea, and full meals throughout the day, all in a very grand room at modest prices. You can eat in the courtyard if the weather's good, or have a buffet supper on late nights. Stop by just to see the original Arts and Crafts decor, one of William Morris's earliest commissions, with stained-glass panels by Edward Burne Jones.

NEAREST PUBLIC RESTROOMS

Most old-style public restrooms have been replaced by futuristic "autoloos," podlike booths on street corners that usually cost £1 to use. If you're not brave enough to trust their push-button locks (and plenty of locals don't), try Peter Jones or Harvey Nicks department stores, which have several large, clean restrooms that are free to use. You could also try asking for the "loo" in any pub, but be prepared for short shrift if you're not a paying customer.

A GOOD RUN

9

The short circuit around the Thames between Chelsea Bridge and Albert Bridge is a pleasant 1½-mi run. From Chelsea Bridge run west along Chelsea Embankment. The wooded park on the other side is Battersea Park, with its Peace Pagoda in the middle. Turn left across the river on the Albert Bridge. Then turn left into Battersea Park and run along the cinder path beside the river. Now the view is of Chelsea. There are good public bathrooms and drinking fountains in the park. Emerge from the park and turn left across Chelsea Bridge back to the starting point.

Sightseeing
★★★★
Nightlife
★★
Dining
★★★★
Lodging
★★★★
Shopping
★★★★★

The Royal Borough of Kensington & Chelsea (or "K&C" as the locals call it) has always been home to world-famous movers and shakers. There are superb shopping districts, a royal palace, and one of the best concentrations of museums in the world. In Knightsbridge, Britain's reputation as a nation of shopkeepers is well kept—this is *must*-go territory for shopaholics.

KENSINGTON AND CHELSEA

Updated by
Ellin Stein

Chelsea was settled before the Domesday Book and was already fashionable when two of Henry VIII's wives lived there. On the North side of the Thames, over from trendier but less well-heeled Battersea, are the impressive lawns of Wren's **Royal Hospital**. Walking along the Embankment, notice the **Albert Bridge**, a candy-color Victorian confection of a suspension bridge. The bridge, shimmering with thousands of lights, its reflection sparkling on the river, is one of London's great romantic views. **Cheyne Walk**, a lovely street dating back to the 18th century, has **Chelsea Physic Garden**, and **Carlyle's House**, with all their arty and historic associations. The blue plaques commemorating important residents along here are amazing.

Nearby is that most iconic of London shopping streets, the **King's Road** (Charles II's private way from St. James's to Fulham). Leave time in your retail therapy schedule to stop at the recently relocated **Saatchi Gallery**, or explore the tiny Georgian lanes of pastel-color houses that veer off the King's Road to the north—especially **Jubilee Place** and **Burnsall Street,** leading to the hidden "village square" of **Chelsea Green.**

Kensington laid its first royal stake when King William III, fed up with the vapors of the Thames, bought a country place there in 1689 and converted it into **Kensington Palace**. Its **Orangery** is diagonally across the park, with the opulent **Kensington Palace Gardens** running behind it. Londoners call this street Billionaires' Row. Notice that there is no electric street lighting down here; it is still lighted exclusively by old

Victorian gas lamps. Queen Victoria's consort, Prince Albert, added the jewel in the borough's crown when he turned the profits of the Great Exhibition of 1851 into South Kensington's metropolis of museums: **Victoria & Albert Museum (V&A)**, the **Science Museum**, and the **Natural History Museum**. His namesakes in the area include **Royal Albert Hall**, with its bas-reliefs that make it resemble a giant, redbrick Wedgwood pot, and the lavish **Albert Memorial**.

Turn into Derry Street or Young Street and enter **Kensington Square**, one of the most complete 17th-century residential squares in London. Holland Park is about ¾ mi farther west; both **Leighton House** and the **Linley Sambourne House** are nearby as well.

EXPLORING

Albert Memorial. This gleaming, neo-Gothic shrine to Prince Albert created by George Gilbert Scott epitomizes the Victorian era. Albert's grieving widow, Queen Victoria, had this elaborate confection (including a 14-foot bronze statue of the prince) erected on the spot where his Great Exhibition had stood a decade before his early death, from typhoid, in 1861. ✉ *Kensington Gore, Hyde Park, Kensington, Knightsbridge.*

Holland Park. The former grounds of the Jacobean Holland House opened to the public only in 1952. It was originally owned by Sir Walter Cope, the wealthy chancellor of James I, and many treats are to be found within its 60 acres. Holland House itself was nearly flattened by World War II bombs, but the east wing remains, now incorporated into a youth hostel and providing a fantastical stage for the April–September **Open Air Theatre** (☎ *020/7361–3570 box office* ⊕ *www. operahollandpark.com*). The glass-wall Orangery also survived to host art exhibitions and other public events. Next door the former Garden Ballroom has become the upmarket Belvedere restaurant; nearby is a lovely café. From the Belvedere's terrace you see the formal Dutch Garden, planted by Lady Holland in the 1790s with the first English dahlias. North of that are woodland walks; lawns populated by peacocks, guinea fowl, and the odd, awkward emu; a fragrant rose garden; great banks of rhododendrons and azaleas, which bloom profusely in May; a well-supervised children's Adventure Playground; and a Japanese water garden, legacy of the London Festival of Japan. If that's not enough, you can watch cricket on the Cricket Lawn on the south side or tennis on the several courts. ☉ *Daily dawn–dusk* Ⓤ *Holland Park, High Street Kensington.*

★ **Kensington Palace.**

See the highlighted listing in this chapter.

OFF THE
BEATEN
PATH

The Boltons. If you take the Tube to Gloucester Road, you'll be within walking distance of the **Boltons**, two facing crescents of impressive mansions. Built on farmland in the 1850s, the houses were instantly fashionable with the wealthy and famous. A school now stands where Beatrix Potter once lived. Douglas Fairbanks Jr. and Hilaire Belloc have also been residents. Today's mysterious residents may include Arab princes and international bankers—anyone who needs room for a large entourage and can spend around £20 million for a 7- to 10-bedroom home. Continue west along the Old Brompton Road to No. 263–267 and you'll arrive at

9

KENSINGTON PALACE

✉ *The Broad Walk, Kensington Gardens, Kensington* ☎ *0844/482–7799 advance booking, 0844/482–7777 information* ⊕ *www.hrp.org.uk* 🎫 *£12.50* ⊙ *Mar.–Oct., daily 10–6; Nov.–Feb., daily 10–5; last admission 1 hr before closing* Ⓤ *Queensway, Kensington High Street.*

TIPS

■ If you also plan to visit the Tower of London, Hampton Court Palace, Banqueting House, or Kew Palace, consider becoming a member of Historic Royal Palaces. It costs £39 per person, or £77 for a family, and gives you free entry to all five sites for a year.

■ Picnicking is allowed on the benches in the palace grounds. (You can also picnic anywhere in the adjoining Kensington Gardens.)

■ There's a delightful café in the Orangery, near the Sunken Garden. Built for Queen Anne, it's a great place for formal afternoon tea, although you have to book ahead.

■ It's only recently that the palace has made much fuss over its most famous modern resident, the late Diana, Princess of Wales. Commemorative events have included the Field of Flowers—an open-air art installation featuring thousands of dandelion heads arranged into giant flowers.

Not as splendid as Buckingham Palace, or as famous as Hampton Court, Kensington Palace is the most intimate of London's great royal residences. Bought in 1689 by Queen Mary and King William III, whose asthma made it necessary for him to live outside the city, it was converted into a palace by Sir Christopher Wren and Nicholas Hawksmoor. Royals have been living here ever since—former residents include Princess (later Queen) Victoria, Queen Anne, Kings George I and II, and Princess Diana.

HIGHLIGHTS

The **Royal Ceremonial Dress Collection** displays all manner of historic royal garments, ranging from the elegant (gowns belonging to the present Queen, and Princess Diana); to the elaborate (an 18th-century mantua–a dazzling court dress with a 6-foot-wide skirt); and the downright odd (King George III's socks).

The King's Staircase is overlooked by a vast, panoramic trompe l'oeil painting, covering the walls and ceiling with a burst of color. Not all of the figures depicted are courtiers and servants, however; look out for Peter the Wild Boy, a feral child who was something of a celebrity in London during the 1720s.

The King's Gallery was built to display some of the monarch's personal art collection. Many of the paintings here now are copies, but no matter; the room itself is a work of art, with rich red damask walls, intricate gilding, and a beautiful painted ceiling.

The grounds are almost as lovely as the palace itself. Highlights include the Sunken Garden with its fountains and Tudor design that echoes Hampton Court. Unmissable—especially in the spring, when tulips bloom in a riot of color.

the **Troubadour,** a legendary coffee shop–music venue where Bob Dylan performed his first London gig and everyone from Joni Mitchell to Led Zeppelin hung out.

Linley Sambourne House. Filled with delightful Victorian and Edwardian antiques, fabrics, and paintings, the home of *Punch* cartoonist Edward Linley Sambourne in the 1870s is one of the most charming 19th-century London houses extant—small wonder that it was used in Merchant Ivory's *A Room with a View.* An Italianate house, it was the scene for society parties when Anne Messel was in residence in the 1940s. Being Kensington, there's a royal connection, too: her son, Antony Armstrong-Jones, married the late Princess Margaret, and their son has preserved the connection by taking the name Viscount Linley. Admission is by guided tours. Apart from the 11:15 tour on weekends and all Wednesday tours, these are given by costumed actors. ⊠ *18 Stafford Terr., Kensington* ☎ *020/7602–3316* ⊕ *www.rbkc.gov. uk/linleysambournehouse* 🖃 *£6* ☽ *Guided tours Wed. 11:15, 2:15, weekends 11:15, 1, 2:15, 3:30. Closed mid-June–mid-Sept.* Ⓤ *High Street Kensington.*

Natural History Museum.

See the highlighted listing in this chapter.

Fodor'sChoice ★

Royal Albert Hall. This domed, circular 5,223-seat auditorium (as well as the Albert Memorial, opposite) was made possible by the Victorian public, who donated funds for it. More money was raised by selling 1,300 future seats at £100 apiece—not for the first night but for every night for 999 years. Some descendants of purchasers still use them. ■TIP➔ The Royal Albert Hall is best known for its annual July–September BBC Promenade Concerts—the "Proms"—with bargain-price standing (or promenading, or sitting-on-the-floor) tickets sold on the night of the concert. On the last night only, the BBC hosts **Proms in the Park,** a series of free live concerts in Hyde Park and at other locations across the country, which culminate in a big-screen link-up with Royal Albert Hall for the grand finale. ⇨ *For more on Royal Albert Hall, see Arts and Entertainment, Chapter 17.* ⊠ *Kensington Gore, Kensington* ☎ *020/7589–8212* ⊕ *www.royalalberthall.com* 🖃 *Prices vary with event* Ⓤ *South Kensington.*

Royal Hospital, Chelsea. Charles II founded the hospice for elderly and infirm soldiers in 1682; his troops had hitherto enjoyed not so much as a meager pension, and they were growing restive after the civil wars of 1642–46 and 1648. Charles wisely appointed the great architect Sir Christopher Wren to design this small village of brick and Portland stone set in manicured gardens (which you can visit) surrounding the

9

NATURAL HISTORY MUSEUM

✉ *Cromwell Rd., South Kensington* ☎ *020/7942–5000* ⊕ *www.nhm.ac.uk* ✉ *Free* ⊙ *Daily 10–5:50, last admission at 5:30* Ⓤ *South Kensington.*

TIPS

■ "Nature Live" is a program of free, informal talks given by scientists, covering a wildly eclectic range of subjects. They happen every day at 12:30 (also 2:30 on weekends) in the Nature Live Studio, by the Marine Galleries on the ground floor, and in the David Attenborough Studio in the Darwin Centre.

■ The museum has an outdoor ice-skating rink from November to January, and a very popular Christmas fair.

■ Free, daily behind-the-scenes Spirit collection tours of the museum can be booked on the day—although space is limited, so come early. Recommended for children over eight years old.

■ Got kids under seven with you? Check out the museum's "Explorer Backpacks." They contain a range of activity materials to keep the little ones amused, including a pair of binoculars and an explorer's hat. They're free, but you'll need to provide a £25 credit-card deposit.

The outrageously ornate terra-cotta facade of this enormous Victorian museum is strewn with relief panels, depicting living creatures to the left of the entrance and extinct ones to the right. It's an appropriate design, for within these walls lie more than 70 million different specimens. Only a small percentage is on public display, but you could still spend a day here and not come close to seeing everything. The museum is full of cutting-edge exhibits, with all the wow-power and interactives necessary to secure interest from younger visitors.

HIGHLIGHTS

A giant diplodocus skeleton dominates the vaulted, cathedral-like entrance hall, affording you perhaps the most irresistible photo opportunity in the building. It's just a cast, but the **Dinosaur Gallery** (Gallery 21) contains plenty of real-life dino bones, fossils—and some extremely long teeth. You'll also come face to face with a giant animatronic Tyrannosaurus rex—who is programmed to sense when human prey is near and "respond" in character. When he does, you can hear the shrieks of fear and delight all the way across the room.

A dizzyingly tall escalator takes you into a giant globe in the **Earth Galleries**, where there's a choice of levels—and Earth surfaces—to explore. Don't leave without checking out the earthquake simulation in Gallery 61.

The centerpiece of a major expansion is the **Darwin Centre**, opened in 2009 to house some of the (literally) millions of items they don't have room to display, including "Archie," a 28.3-foot giant squid.

Ice-skaters outside the Natural History Museum in South Kensington.

Figure Court—named after the 1682 bronze figure of Charles II dressed up as a Roman general—and the Great Hall (dining room) and chapel. The latter is enhanced by the choir stalls of Grinling Gibbons (who did the bronze of Charles, too), the former by a vast oil of Charles on horseback by Antonio Verrio, and both are open to the public at certain times during the day. There is a small museum here, detailing the history of the resident "Chelsea Pensioners," but it's the building and, of course, the pensioners themselves that are the real attraction. Recognizable by their traditional scarlet frock coats with gold buttons, medals, and tricorne hats, they are all actual veterans, who wear the uniform, and the history it conveys, with a great deal of pride. They celebrate Charles II's birthday—May 29, Founder's Day—by draping oak leaves on his statue and parading around it in memory of a hollow oak tree that expedited the king's miraculous escape from the 1651 Battle of Worcester. Also in May (usually the third week), the **Chelsea Flower Show**, the year's highlight for thousands of garden-obsessed Brits, is held here. Run by the Royal Horticultural Society (☎ *0845/130–4646* ⊕ *www.rhs.org.uk*), this mammoth event takes up vast acreage, and the surrounding streets throng with visitors. ⊠ *Royal Hospital Rd., Chelsea* ☎ *020/7881–5303* ⊕ *www.chelsea-pensioners.org.uk* ⊠ *Free* ☉ *Open daily, times vary by season* Ⓤ *Sloane Sq.*

Saatchi Gallery. Charles Saatchi, who made his fortune building an advertising empire that successfully "rebranded" Margaret Thatcher's Conservative Party, is an astute art collector whose avant-garde acquisitions regularly create headlines. The museum's newest home—its third in 10 years—is at the former Duke of York's HQ, just off the King's Road.

9

CLOSE UP

Historic Plaque Hunt

As you wander around London, you'll see lots of small blue, circular plaques on the sides and facades of buildings, describing which famous, infamous, or obscure but brilliant person once lived there. The first was placed outside Lord Byron's birthplace (now no more) by the Royal Society of Arts. There are around 700 blue plaques, erected by different bodies—you may even find some green ones that originated from Westminster City Council—but English Heritage now maintains the responsibility, and if you want to find out the latest, check the Web site ⊕ *www. english-heritage.org.uk.* Below are some of the highlights:

James Barrie (✉ *100 Bayswater Rd., Hyde Park, W2*); **Robert Browning** (✉ *17 Warwick Crescent, Hyde Park, W2*); **Frederic Chopin** (✉ *4 St. James's Place, St. James's, W1*); **Sir Winston Churchill** (✉ *28 Hyde Park Gate, Kensington, SW7*); **Captain James Cook** (✉ *88 Mile End Rd., Mile End, E1*); **T. S. Eliot** (✉ *3 Kensington Court Gardens, Kensington, W8*); **Benjamin Franklin** (✉ *36 Craven St., Westminster, WC2*); **Mahatma Gandhi** (✉ *20 Baron's Court Rd., West Kensington, W14*); **Jimi Hendrix** (✉ *23 Brook St., Mayfair, W1*); **Alfred Hitchcock** (✉ *153 Cromwell Rd., SW5*); **Wolfgang Amadeus Mozart** (✉ *180 Ebury St., Belgravia, SW1*); **Horatio Nelson** (✉ *103 New Bond St., W1*); **Sir Isaac Newton** (✉ *87 Jermyn St., St. James's, SW1*); **Florence Nightingale** (✉ *10 South St., Mayfair, W1*); **George Bernard Shaw** (✉ *29 Fitzroy Sq., Bloomsbury, W1*); **Percy Bysshe Shelley** (✉ *15 Poland St., Soho, W1*); **H. G. Wells** (✉ *13 Hanover Terrace., NW1*); **Oscar Wilde** (✉ *34 Tite St., Chelsea, SW3*); **William Butler Yeats** (✉ *23 Fitzroy Rd., Camden, NW1*).

Built in 1803, its suitably grand exterior belies an imaginative restoration, which has transformed the interior into 14 gallery exhibition spaces of varying size and shape. Unlike the Tate Modern, there is no permanent collection; instead the galleries are given over to a single exhibition, which normally runs for about three months. Exhibitions have included a highly successful showcase for contemporary Chinese art. ✉ *Duke of York's HQ Building, Kings Rd., Chelsea* ☎ *020/7823–2332* ⊕ *www. saatchigallery.com* 🖾 *Free* ☼ *Open daily 10–6* Ⓤ *Sloane Sq.*

☾ **Science Museum.** This, the third of the great South Kensington museums,
Fodor's Choice stands next to the Natural History Museum in a far plainer build-
★ ing. It has loads of hands-on exhibits, with entire schools of children apparently decanted inside to interact with them; but it is, after all, painlessly educational. Don't dismiss the Science Museum as just for kids, though. Highlights include the Launch Pad gallery, which demonstrates basic scientific principles; *Puffing Billy,* the oldest steam locomotive in the world; and the actual *Apollo 10* capsule. The six floors are devoted to subjects as diverse as the history of flight, space exploration, steam power, medicine, and a sublime exhibition on science in the 18th century. And if the crowds become too much to bear, head down to the basement, where the charmingly low-key Secret Life of the Home exhibit charts the influence of technology on everyday life. Overshadowed by a three-story blue-glass wall, the Wellcome Wing is a recent

annex to the rear of the museum, devoted to contemporary science and technology. It contains a 450-seat IMAX cinema, and the Force-Field ride—an advanced motion simulator that combines seat vibration with other technical gizmos to create such crowd-pleasing effects as flying past an explosion in space. It's worth the £4 price, but not necessarily the excessive wait at busy times—so if the lines are long, head up to the third floor instead, where they have a whole room full of simulators. ■TIP→ If you're a family of at least five, you might be able to get a place on one of the popular new Science Night sleepovers by booking

> ### ARTISTIC CHELSEA
>
> Artists and writers flocked to the area in the 19th century, establishing a creative colony in Cheyne Walk; at one time Turner, Whistler, John Singer Sargent, Dante Gabriel Rossetti, and Oscar Wilde were residents. In the '60s it was the turn of the Rolling Stones and the Beatles; in the '70s Bob Marley wrote "I Shot the Sheriff" in a flat off Cheyne Walk. It's now one of London's most expensive streets, completely unaffordable for latter-day Bob Marleys.

well in advance. Aimed at kids 8–11 years old, these nighttime science workshops offer the chance to camp out in one of the galleries, and include a free IMAX show the next morning. Check the Web site for details. ⊠ *Exhibition Rd., South Kensington* ☎ *0870/870–4868* ⊕ *www. sciencemuseum.org.uk* ⊇ *Free, charge for the cinema shows and special exhibitions* ⊗ *Daily 10–6* Ⓤ *South Kensington.*

Ⓒ **Victoria & Albert Museum.**

Fodor's Choice
★
See the highlighted listing in this chapter.

KNIGHTSBRIDGE

There's no getting away from it. This is shop-'til-you-drop territory of the highest order. With two world-famous department stores, **Harrods** and **Harvey Nichols,** a few hundred yards apart, and every bit of space between and around taken up with designer boutiques, chain stores, and jewelers, it's hard to imagine why anyone who doesn't like shopping would even think of coming here. If the department stores seem overwhelming, **Beauchamp Place** (pronounced Beecham) is a good tonic. It's lined with equally chic and expensive boutiques, but they tend to be smaller, more personal, and less hectic.

Another place to find peace and quiet (of a less expensive kind) is **Brompton Oratory,** the area's ornate and historic Catholic church. If you're lucky, you may catch a rehearsal of the church's famous boys' choir. Or a peaceful stroll in Belgravia may be just the thing. Grand white terraces of aristocratic town houses, part of the Grosvenor estate, are owned by the Dukes of Westminster. Many are leased to embassies, but a remarkable number around **Lowndes Square, Belgrave Square,** and **Eaton Square** remain homes of the discreet, private wealthy. Often, the only people on the streets are professional dog walkers and chauffeurs. Some people call the area near **Elizabeth Street** Belgravia, others Pimlico–Victoria. Either way, now that you've had a break, it's time to shop again, and this street is the place to be.

9

VICTORIA & ALBERT MUSEUM

✉ *Cromwell Rd., South Kensington* ☎ *020/7942–2000* ⊕ *www.vam.ac.uk* ✍ *Free* ⊙ *Sat.–Tues. 10:45–5:45, Fri. 10–10* Ⓤ *South Kensington.*

TIPS

■ The V&A is a notoriously difficult building to navigate, so be sure to pick up a free map. There are stacks of them at each entrance.

■ As a whirlwind introduction, you could take a free one-hour tour at 10:30, 11:30, 1:30, or 3:30. There are also tours devoted just to the British Galleries at 12:30 and 2:30.

■ Public lectures on Friday nights at 7 are delivered by visiting bigwigs from the art or fashion world (from £8). There are free public lectures throughout the week given by museum staff.

■ Whatever time you visit, the sculpture hall (which runs almost the entire length of the ground floor) will be filled with artists, both amateur and professional, sketching the myriad of artworks on display there. Don't be shy: bring a pad and join in.

■ Although the permanent collection is free—and there's enough there to keep you busy for a week—the V&A also hosts high-profile special exhibitions that run for up to three months (from £5).

Always referred to as the V&A, this huge museum is devoted to the applied arts of all disciplines, all periods, and all nationalities. Full of innovation, it's a wonderful, generous place to get lost in. First opened as the South Kensington Museum in 1857, it was renamed in 1899, in honor of Queen Victoria's late husband and has since grown to become one of the country's best-loved cultural institutions.

HIGHLIGHTS

Many collections at the V&A are presented not by period, but by category—textiles, sculpture, jewelry, and so on. Nowhere is the benefit of this more apparent than in the **Fashion Gallery** (Room 40), where formal 18th-century court dresses are displayed alongside the haute couture styles of contemporary designers, creating an arresting sense of visual continuity.

The **British Galleries** (Rooms 52–58), devoted to British art and design from 1500 to 1900, are full of beautiful diversions—among them the Great Bed of Ware (immortalized in Shakespeare's *Twelfth Night*). Here, a series of actual rooms have been painstakingly reconstructed piece by piece after being rescued from historic buildings. These include an ornate music room, and the Henrietta St. Room, a breathtakingly serene parlor dating from 1722.

The **Asian Galleries** (Rooms 44–47) are full of treasures, but among the most striking items on display is a remarkable collection of ornate samurai armor in the **Japanese Gallery** (Room 44). There are also galleries devoted to China, Korea, and the Islamic Middle East. Several new galleries opened in 2009: A Buddhist Sculpture gallery, a new Ceramics gallery, and a Medieval and Renaissance gallery which has the largest collection of works from the period outside of Italy.

World-famous Harrods has been attracting shoppers since 1834.

EXPLORING

Belgrave Square. The square, as well as the streets leading off it, are genuine grand territory and have been since they were built in the mid-1800s. The grand, porticoed mansions were created as town residences for courtiers, conveniently close to Buckingham Palace, just around the corner. These are some of the grandest houses in London, and although many of them are embassies, several are still private homes. Walk down Belgrave Place toward Eaton Place and you pass two of Belgravia's most beautiful mews: Eaton Mews North and Eccleston Mews, both fronted by grand rusticated entrances right out of a 19th-century engraving. ■TIP→ Traffic really whips around Belgrave Square, so be careful.

Brompton Oratory. This is a late product of the mid-19th-century English Roman Catholic revival led by John Henry Cardinal Newman (1801–90), who established the oratory in the 1840s and whose statue you see outside. Architect Herbert Gribble, a previously unknown 29-year-old, won the competition to design the place, an honor that you may conclude went to his head when you see the vast, incredibly ornate interior. It's punctuated by treasures far older than the church itself, like the giant *Twelve Apostles* in the nave, carved from Carrara marble by Giuseppe Mazzuoli in the 1680s and brought here from Siena's cathedral. ⊠ *Brompton Rd., Kensington* ☎ *020/7808–0900* ⊕ *www.bromptonoratory. com* ⧰ *Free* ⧗ *6:30 AM–8 PM* Ⓤ *South Kensington.*

Harrods. Just in case you don't notice it, this well-known shopping destination frames its domed terra-cotta Edwardian outline in thousands of white lights each night (or pink, or green, or pretty much however the mood takes its famously eccentric owner, Mohammed al Fayed). The

9

Dining at a Glance

MODERATE DINING

Aubaine, French, 260–262 Brompton Rd.

Bibendum, Modern British, 81 Fulham Rd.

Boxwood Café, Modern European, The Berkeley, Wilton Pl.

The Pig's Ear, Modern British, 35 Old Church St.

PJ's Bar & Grill, American, 52 Fulham Rd.

Racine, Brasserie, 239 Brompton Rd.

EXPENSIVE DINING

The Capital, French, 22–24 Basil St.

Restaurant Gordon Ramsay, French, 68 Royal Hospital Rd.

Marcus Wareing at the Berkeley, Modern European, The Berkeley, Wilton Pl.

Rasoi Restaurant, Indian, 10 Lincoln St.

Zafferano, Italian, 15 Lowndes St.

Zuma, Japanese, 5 Raphael St.

4.5-acre store's sales weeks are world-class, and inside it's as frenetic as a stock-market floor. Its motto, *Omnia, omnibus, ubique* (Everything, for everybody, everywhere) is not too far from the truth. Don't miss the extravagant Food Hall, with its stunning art nouveau tiling around the meat and poultry section and continuing to the fishmongers' territory, where its glory is rivaled by displays of the sea produce itself. *For more on Harrods, see ⇨ Shopping, Chapter 18.* ⊠ *87–135 Brompton Rd., Knightsbridge* ☎ *020/7730–1234* ⊕ *www.harrods.com* ☉ *Mon.–Sat. 10–8, Sun. 11:30–6* Ⓤ *Knightsbridge.*

Harvey Nichols. This is fashionista central and a must for anyone who has been watching *Absolutely Fabulous,* dahling—in which case you'll already know to call it Harvey Nicks. The Fifth Floor Restaurant, Café, and Bar offer outstanding views and stylish refreshments that attract an equally stylish clientele. *For more on Harvey Nichols, see ⇨ Shopping, Chapter 18.* ⊠ *109–125 Knightsbridge, Knightsbridge* ☎ *020/7235–5000* ⊕ *www.harveynichols.com* ☉ *Mon.–Sat. 10–8, Sun. 11:30–6* Ⓤ *Knightsbridge.*

Notting Hill and Bayswater

WORD OF MOUTH

"I loved the Portobello Road market, Saturday mornings, divided into three sections—the first is near all the permanent antique and craft shops, so it is crafts and jewelry, shawls, trinkets; the second is the food, fruit & veg and flower market; the third is shops and stalls with trendy youthful clothes. Go early!"

—ninastdream

GETTING ORIENTED

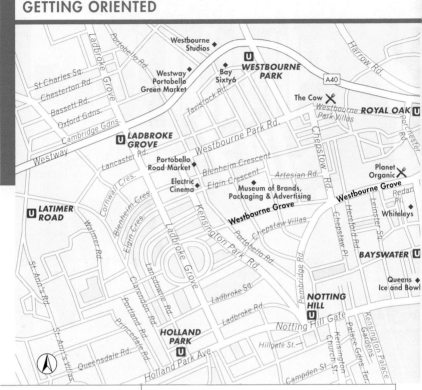

GETTING THERE

For Portobello Market and environs, the best Tube stops are Ladbroke Grove and Westbourne Park (Hammersmith and City lines); ask for directions when you emerge. The Notting Hill stop on the District, Circle, and Central lines enables you to walk the length of Portobello Road on a downhill gradient.

A GOOD WALK

To gape at Notting Hill's grandest houses, stroll over to Lansdowne Road, Lansdowne Crescent, and Lansdowne Square—two blocks west of Kensington Park Row.

TOP REASONS TO GO

Westbourne Grove: People-watch at a sidewalk café in this swank section of the neighborhood.

Portobello Road Market: Seek and ye shall find; go early-morning antiques hunting at London's best and most famous market on Saturday.

Notting Hill shopping: In addition to Portobello Road Market, you can browse for vintage designer pieces at the numerous secondhand and retro clothing stores.

Notting Hill Carnival: Experience the explosion of color, culture, and music that is the Notting Hill Carnival, held over three days every August bank holiday.

Electric Cinema: Catch a movie reclined on a two-seater leather sofa, beer and bar snacks at hand at this restored early 20th-century theatre.

MAKING THE MOST OF YOUR TIME

Saturday is Notting Hill and Portobello Road's most fun and frenetic day. You could easily spend the whole day shopping, eating, and drinking here. The market can get very crowded by noon in nice weather so come early if you are serious about shopping. You may prefer to start at the end of Portobello Road and work backward, using the parks for relaxation after your shopping exertions. Do the same on Friday if you're a flea-market fan.

Sunday, the Hyde Park and Kensington Gardens railings all along Bayswater Road are hung with dubious art, which may slow your progress; this is also the day when the well-heeled locals are out in force, filling the pubs at lunchtime or hitting the parks with their kids if it's sunny.

10

FEELING PECKISH?

A haven for the health conscious, **Planet Organic** (⊠ 42 Westbourne Grove ☎ 020/7727–2227) serves upscale vegetarian meals at nongourmet prices, with a wide selection of specials to take out.

There's cult appeal to the super-value **Churchill Thai Kitchen** (⊠ 199 Kensington Church St., Notting Hill ☎ 020/7792–1246) attached to a traditional English pub swamped in Winston Churchill memorabilia. With large portions of all dishes priced around £7, it's a bargain for this part of town.

SAFETY

At night, be wary of straying too far off the main streets, as it gets "edgier" toward Ladbroke Grove's high-rise estates and surrounding areas. Notting Hill Carnival attracts massive crowds and revelers should be wary of crime.

North of the royal parks, Bayswater is a hub of tourist restaurants and midprice hotels; far more enticing is its famous neighbor to the west, Notting Hill. A trendsetting square mile full of chic bars and restaurants, the style-watching London media has dubbed its well-dressed residents Notting Hillbillies. In the middle of it all is one of the world's great antiques markets, Portobello Road.

Updated by
Jack Jewers

Notting Hill's transformation from poverty-stricken backwater to super-trendy enclave started in the '80s and had reached its peak by the early 2000s—helped, in no small way, by the famous film that bore its name. For the Notting Hill of the film sets (the Travel Bookshop on Blenheim Crescent is Hugh Grant's bookshop in the film *Notting Hill*), head straight for **Westbourne Grove,** replete with chic boutiques and charity shops laden with the castoffs from wealthy residents. The whole area has mushroomed around the **Portobello Road,** with the beautifully restored early-20th-century **Electric Cinema** at No. 191. The famous Saturday antiques market and shops are at the southern end; **Westway Portobello Green Market,** under the Westway overpass, is occupied by bric-a-brac, secondhand threads, and clothes and accessories by young, up-and-coming designers. Nearby on Acklam Road are the **Westbourne Studios,** an office complex with a gallery, restaurant, and bar open to the public, and the capital's best skateboarding park, **Bay Sixty6.**

In Bayswater, the main thoroughfare of **Queensway** is a rather peculiar, cosmopolitan street of ethnic confusion, late-night cafés and restaurants, a skating rink, and the **Whiteleys** shopping-and-movie mall. Nearby **Paddington Station** is the namesake for the marmalade-loving Paddington Bear.

> ## WORD OF MOUTH
>
> "We stopped at Notting Hill and just walked around the back-streets and admired the homes and the plants. I saw an aloe vera plant that stood about 8 feet tall. Amazing. No Hugh Grant sighting, however, and let's face it, that WAS the purpose of this stop."
> —Danna

EXPLORING

⟳ **Hyde Park and Kensington Gardens.**
★ *See the highlighted listing in this chapter.*

★ **Portobello Road.** Tempted by tassels or looking for a 19th-century snuff spoon? Want a Victorian map of Surrey or a dashingly deco party frock? Head to Portobello Road, world famous for its Saturday antiques market (but don't believe the dealer when he swears the Vionnet label just fell off that dress). Actually, the Portobello Market is three markets: antiques, "fruit and veg," and a flea market. If you're coming on Saturday, arrive before 9 AM to find the real treasures in the trash—the crowds can get pretty intense by 10. Lining the sloping street are also dozens of antiques shops and indoor markets, open most days—in fact, serious collectors will want to do Portobello on a weekday, when they can explore the 90-some antiques and art stores in relative peace. *For more on Portobello Road, see* ⇨ *Shopping, Chapter 18.* Ⓤ *Notting Hill Gate, Ladbroke Grove.*

> ### NOTTING HILL CARNIVAL
>
> Loud, colorful, and very, very crowded, the annual Carnival (⊕ *www.nottinghillcarnival.biz*) is a massive event that was started by Afro-Caribbean immigrants in 1965. Held the last weekend in August, it attracts hundreds of thousands of visitors, often young and sometimes raucous. Be aware that crime is rife and has grown in recent years—be careful.

⟳ **Museum of Brands, Packaging and Advertising.** This extraordinary little museum does exactly what it says on the box. Its massive collection of toys, fashion, food wrappers, advertising, and the assorted detritus of everyday life is from all corners of the globe. It's a fascinating and eccentric chronicle of how consumer culture has developed since the Victorian age. ⊠ *2 Colville Mews, Lonsdale Rd., Notting Hill* ☎ *020/7908–0880* ⊕ *www.museumofbrands.com* ⊑ *£5.80* ⊗ *Tues.– Sat. 10–6, Sun. 11–5* Ⓤ *Notting Hill.*

⟳ **Queens Ice and Bowl.** This is London's most central year-round ice-skating rink. The per-session cost, including skate rental, is £10 plus £1.50 skate rental for both adults and children. ⊠ *17 Queensway, Bayswater* ☎ *020/7229–0172* ⊕ *www.queensiceandbowl.co.uk* ⊗ *Daily, Sun.–Fri. 10–6:45, 8–10:45, Sat. 10–6:45, 7:30–10:45* Ⓤ *Queensway.*

10

HYDE PARK AND KENSINGTON GARDENS

Every year millions of visitors descend on the royal parks of Hyde Park and Kensington Gardens, which sit side by side and roll out over 625 acres of grassy expanses that provide much-craved-for respite from London's frenetic pace. The two parks incorporate formal gardens, fountains, sports fields, great picnic spots, shady clusters of ancient trees, and even an outdoor swimming pool.

10

Although it's probably been centuries since any major royal had a casual stroll here—you're more likely to bump into Chris Martin and Gwyneth Paltrow than Her Royal Highness these days—the parks remain the property of the Crown, which saved them from being devoured by the city's late-18th-century growth spurt.

Today the luxury of such wide open spaces continues to be appreciated by the Londoners who steal into the parks before work for a session of tai chi, say, or on weekends when the sun is shining. Simply sitting back in a hired deck chair or strolling through the varied terrain is one of the most enjoyable ways to spend time here.

KENSINGTON GARDENS

At the end of the 17th century, William III moved his court to the impeccably kept green space that is now **Kensington Gardens**. He was attracted to the location for its clean air and tranquillity and subsequently commissioned Sir Christopher Wren to overhaul the original redbrick building, resulting in the splendid **Kensington Palace**.

To the north of the palace complex is the early-20th-century **Sunken Garden**, complete with a living tunnel of lime trees (i.e., linden trees) and golden laburnum.

On western side of the **Long Water** is George Frampton's 1912 *Peter Pan*, a bronze of the boy who lived on an island in the Serpentine and never grew up and whose creator, J.M. Barrie, lived at 100 Bayswater Road, not 500 yards from here.

Back toward Kensington Palace, at the intersection of several paths, is George Frederick Watts's 1904 bronze of a muscle-bound horse and rider, entitled **Physical Energy**. The Round Pond is a magnet for model-boat enthusiasts and duck feeders.

Near the Broad Walk, toward Black Lion Gate, is the **Diana Princess of Wales Memorial Playground**, an enclosed space with specially

Afternoon tea taken at the Orangery, a short walk from the Sunken Garden on the palace grounds, is a quintessentially English experience.

designed structures and areas on the theme of Barrie's Neverland. Hook's ship, crocodiles, "jungles" of foliage, and islands of sand provide a fantasy land for kids—more than 70,000 visit every year. Just outside its bounds is Ivor Innes's *Elfin Oak*, the remains of a tree carved with scores of tiny woodland creatures.

One of the park's most striking monuments is the **Albert Memorial**. This Victorian high-Gothic celebration of Prince Albert is adorned with marble statues representing his interests and amusements.

Diminutive as it may be, the **Serpentine Gallery** has not been afraid of courting controversy with its temporary exhibitions of challenging contemporary works.

Hyde Park was once the hunting ground of King Henry VIII. This stout, bawdy royal more or less stole Hyde Park, along with the smaller St. James's and Green parks, from the monks of Westminster in 1536. The public wasn't to be granted access to Hyde Park's delights until James I came to the throne and opened up limited parts to "respectably dressed" plebeians.

HYDE PARK

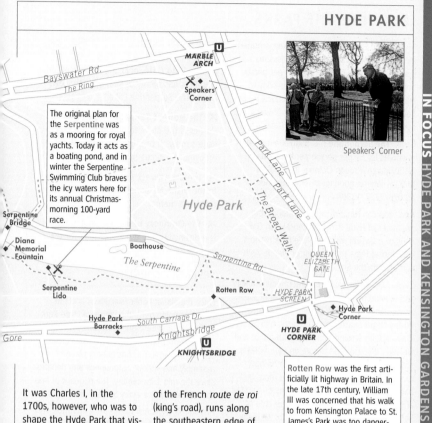

Speakers' Corner

> The original plan for the **Serpentine** was as a mooring for royal yachts. Today it acts as a boating pond, and in winter the Serpentine Swimming Club braves the icy waters here for its annual Christmas-morning 100-yard race.

> **Rotten Row** was the first artificially lit highway in Britain. In the late 17th century, William III was concerned that his walk to from Kensington Palace to St. James's Park was too dangerous, so he ordered 300 lamps to be placed along the route.

It was Charles I, in the 1700s, however, who was to shape the Hyde Park that visitors see today. Once he had created **the Ring** (North Carriage Drive), which forms a curve north of the **Serpentine** and boathouses, Charles allowed the general public to roam free. During the Great Plague of 1665, East Enders and City dwellers fled to the park, seeking refuge from the black bilious disease.

The **Serpentine Bridge**, built in 1826 by George Rennie, marks the boundary between Hyde Park and Kensington Gardens. **Rotten Row**, a corruption

of the French *route de roi* (king's road), runs along the southeastern edge of Hyde Park and is still used by the Household Cavalry, who live at the **Hyde Park Barracks**—a high-rise and a long, low, red block—to the left. This is where the brigade that mounts the guard at Buckingham Palace resides; you can see them at about 10:30 AM, as they leave to perform their duty in full regalia, or await the return of the guard about noon.

On the south side of the 1930s **Serpentine Lido** (open to swimmers from June to September) is the

£3.6 million oval **Diana Memorial Fountain**.

Ever since the 1827 legislation of public assembly, **Speakers' Corner** near Marble Arch has provided an outlet for political debate: on Sundays, it's a spectacle of vehement, sometimes comical, and always entertaining orators.

ENJOYING THE PARKS

Ride. Hyde Park Riding Stables keeps horses for hacking the sand tracks. Group lessons (usually just a few people) are £59 per person per hour. Private lessons are £79 Tuesday–Friday, £95 on weekends. ✉ 63 Bathurst Mews, Bayswater W2 ☎ 020/7723–2813 ⊕ www.hydeparkstables.com Ⓤ Lancaster Gate.

Row. The Serpentine has paddleboats and rowboats for £9 per person per hour, kids £2.50, March through October from 10 AM to 5 PM, later in good weather in summer. ☎ 020/7262–1330).

Run. You can run a **4-mi route** around the perimeter of Hyde Park and Kensington Gardens or a **2½-mi route** in Hyde Park alone if you start at Hyde Park Corner or Marble Arch and encircle the Serpentine.

Skate. On Friday, skaters of intermediate ability and upward meet at 8 PM at the Duke of Wellington Arch, Hyde Park Corner, for the **Friday Night Skate,** an enthusiastic two-hour mass skating session, complete with music and whistles. If you're a bit unsure on your wheels, arrive at 6:30 PM for the free lesson on how to stop. The **Sunday Rollerstroll,** a more laid-back version of the same thing, runs on Sunday afternoons; meet at 2 PM on the east side of Serpentine Road ⊕ www.thefns.com Ⓤ Hyde Park Corner.

Swim. Serpentine Lido is technically a beach on a lake, but a hot day in Hyde Park is surreally reminiscent of the seaside. There are changing facilities, and the swimming section is chlorinated. There is also a paddling pool, sandpit, and kids' entertainer in the afternoons. It's open daily from June through September, 10–5:30; admission £4, ☎ 020/7706–3422 ⊕ www.royalparks.co.uk Ⓤ Knightsbridge.

WHERE TO REFUEL

✗ The **Lido Café**, near the Diana Memorial Fountain, has plenty of seating with views across the Serpentine Lake.

✗ The **Honest Sausage** at Speakers' Corner is the place to grab a free-range sausage sandwich or organic bacon roll before enjoying the circus of debate.

✗ The **Broadwalk Café & Playcafe** next to the Diana Memorial Playground has a children's menu.

✗ The **Orangery** beside Kensington Palace is a distinctly more grown-up affair for tea and cakes.

SPEAKERS' CORNER

Once the site of public executions and the Tyburn hanging trees, the corner of Hyde Park at Cumberland Gate and Park Lane now harbors one of London's most public spectacles: Speakers' Corner. This has been a place of assembly and vitriolic outpourings and debates since the mid-19th century. The pageant of free speech takes place every Sunday afternoon.

Anyone is welcome to mount a soapbox and declaim upon any topic, which makes for an irresistible showcase of eccentricity—one such being the (now-deceased) Protein Man. Wearing his publicity board, the Protein Man proclaimed that the eating of meat, cheese, and peanuts led to uncontrollable acts of passion that would destroy Western civilization. The pamphlets he sold for four decades are now collector's items. Other more strait-laced campaigns have been launched here by the Chartists, the Reform League, the May Day demonstrators, and the Suffragettes.

PRACTICAL INFO

ADMISSION: Free for both parks

HOURS: Kensington Gardens 6 AM–dusk; Hyde Park 5 AM–midnight

CONTACT INFO: ☎ 020/7298–2000, ⊕ www.royalparks.org.uk

GETTING HERE: Ⓤ **Kensington Gardens:** Kensington High Street, Queensway, Lancaster Gate, South Kensington. **Hyde Park:** Hyde Park Corner, Knightsbridge, Lancaster Gate, Marble Arch

EVENTS: Major events, such as rock concerts and festivals, road races, and talks, are regular features of the parks' calendar; check online for what's on during your visit.

Each summer, a different modern architect designs an outdoor pavilion for the contemporary Serpentine Gallery, the venue for outdoor film screenings, readings, and other such cultural soirees.

From June to August, Hyde Park hosts the Royal Parks Summer Festival, with live jazz evenings, opera, and plays all over the park grounds.

(left) Horseback riding, Hyde Park

(top) The Fountains, Kensington Gardens

(bottom) Both parks are lovely year-round, but spring blooms are spectacular.

TOURS: There are **themed guided walks** about once a month, usually on Thursday or Friday afternoons. They are free but must be booked in advance. Check online or call the park offices for dates and details.

A 45-minute tour (£4.50) of the **Albert Memorial** is available. It's held at 2 and 3 PM on the first Sunday of the month from March to December. There's no need to book in advance unless you are part of a big group, in which case call ☎ 020/7495–0916.

Kensington Palace is open for tours from March to October, daily, from 10 to 6 and November to February, daily, from 10 to 5. For tickets (£12.50, price includes audio guide) and information call ☎ 0844/482–7777 or visit ⊕ www.hrp.org.uk.

10

AT A GLANCE

Notting Hill and Bayswater Dining

BUDGET DINING
Mandalay, Asian, 444 Edgware Rd.

MODERATE DINING
Alounak, Middle Eastern, 44 Westbourne Grove

Angelus, French, 4 Bathurst St.

Bumpkin, British, 209 Westbourne Park Rd.

The Cow Dining Room, British, 89 Westbourne Park Rd.

Electric Brasserie, Brasserie, 191 Portobello Rd.

E&O, Asian, 14 Blenheim Crescent

Hereford Road, Modern British, 3 Hereford Rd.

Julie's, British, 135–137 Portland Rd.

Royal China, Chinese, 13 Queensway

EXPENSIVE DINING
The Ledbury, French, 127 Ledbury Rd.

Notting Hill Brasserie, Brasserie, 92 Kensington Park Rd.

Regent's Park and Hampstead

WORD OF MOUTH

"The village of Hampstead could not be more charming. We wandered all about, up and down the hills and lanes, enjoying the architecture all about. Lots of traditional and atmospheric pubs. Hampstead seems a world away, yet there is London in all its glory in the panoramic view below."

—Djkbooks

GETTING ORIENTED

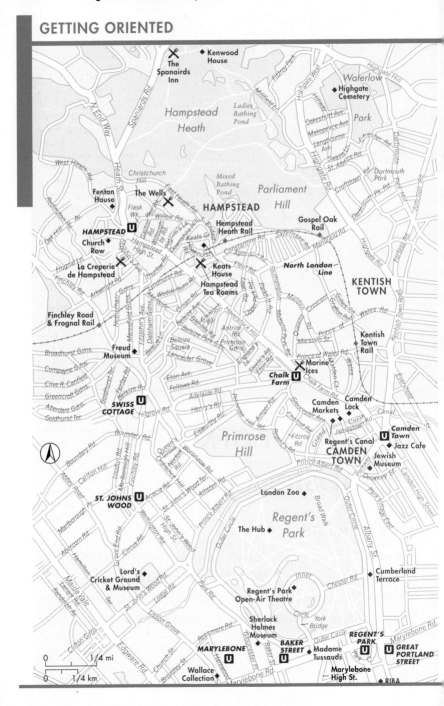

The Spanairds Inn

Kenwood House

Hampstead Heath

Ladies Bathing Pond

Highgate Cemetery

Waterlow

Park

Christchurch Hill

Mixed Bathing Pond

Fenton House

The Wells

HAMPSTEAD

Parliament Hill

Gospel Oak Rail

HAMPSTEAD

Church Row

Flask Wk.

Hempstead Heath Rail

North London Line

KENTISH TOWN

La Creperie de Hampstead

Keats House

Hampstead Tea Rooms

Finchley Road & Frognal Rail

Kentish Town Rail

Freud Museum

Belsize Square

Primrose Gdns.

Broadhurst Gdns.

Companye Gdns.

Clive R. Canfield

Greencroft Gdns.

Aldare Gdns.

Goldhurst Ter.

Marine Ices

SWISS COTTAGE

Chalk Farm

Camden Markets

Camden Lock

Primrose Hill

Regent's Canal

Camden Town

Jazz Cafe

CAMDEN TOWN

Jewish Museum

ST. JOHNS WOOD

London Zoo

The Hub

Regent's Park

Lord's Cricket Ground & Museum

Cumberland Terrace

Regent's Park Open-Air Theatre

Sherlock Holmes Museum

MARYLEBONE

BAKER STREET

Madame Tussauds

REGENT'S PARK

GREAT PORTLAND STREET

Wallace Collection

Marylebone High St.

RIBA

0   1/4 mi

0   1/4 km

TOP REASONS TO GO

Primrose Hill: Tackle the hill on a beautiful day with a friend, a stocked picnic basket, and a blanket, then enjoy the view from the top for a few long hours.

London Zoo: Wander around the new rain-forest lookout and come face-to-face with tiny monkeylike critters the size of your outstretched palm.

Fenton House: Relax in the 300-year-old apple orchard and garden of this handsome Georgian town house.

Wallace Collection: This 18th-century mansion's impressive art collection includes Fragonard's *The Swing.*

Marylebone High Street: Although it's just north of frenetic Oxford Street, you'll feel a whole world away as you wander by the chic restaurants and boutiques.

FEELING PECKISH?

For a substantial but still speedy meal, **La Creperie de Hampstead** (⊠ *Perrin's La. off Hampstead High St., Hampstead* ☎ *020/7372–0081*) serves authentic sweet and savory French crepes from a little cart on the street.

The **Hampstead Tea Rooms** (⊠ *9 South End Rd., Hampstead* ☎ *020/7435–9563*) has been run by the same owners for more than 30 years, selling sandwiches, pies, pastries, and cream cakes, on drool view in the window.

Marine Ices (⊠ *8 Haverstock Hill, Camden Town* ☎ *020/7482–9003*) has a window dispensing London's best ice cream to strollers, and the restaurant offers pasta, pizza, and sundaes near the market at Camden Lock.

SAFETY

It's best to stay out of Hampstead Heath and Regent's Park proper late at night unless there's an event (such as a play or concert) taking place. Camden High Street and the Canal towpath should be avoided after dark.

GETTING THERE

Reaching Hampstead by Tube is as easy as it looks: simply take the Edgware branch of the Northern Line to the Hampstead station, or the overground North London line to Hampstead Heath. The south side of Hampstead Heath can also be reached by the Gospel Oak station on the North London line. To get to Regent's Park, take the Bakerloo Line to Regent's Park Tube station or, for Primrose Hill, the Chalk Farm stop on the Northern Line.

MAKING THE MOST OF YOUR TIME

Depending on your pace and inclination, Marylebone, Regent's Park, and Hampstead can realistically be covered in a day. It might be best to spend the morning in Hampstead, then head south toward Regent's Park and Marylebone in the afternoon so that you're closer to central London come nightfall, if that is where your hotel is located.

A GOOD WALK

There really are no bad walks to be had in Hampstead. Once there, the village is best explored on foot, and Hampstead Heath will lead you by way of marked footpaths on a healthy jaunt through its sprawling green spaces. The neighborhoods around Regent's Park—as well as the park itself—are also best explored on foot.

Sightseeing
★★★★
Nightlife
★★★
Dining
★★
Lodging
★★
Shopping
★★★

London becomes noticeably calmer and greener as you head north from Oxford Street. From the civilized shopping streets of Marylebone, through the well-tended parks of Regent's Park and Primrose Hill up to the open spaces of Hampstead Heath and the handsome Georgian streets of Hampstead itself, this area will provide a taste of how laid-back (moneyed) Londoners can be.

Updated by
Jack Jewers

The residential areas north of Regent's Park are usually considered "leafy" and therefore highly desirable by the garden-loving British. **Hampstead Heath** is a huge swath of countryside in the city, offering spectacular views. At the northern end is **Kenwood House,** a Georgian villa with a remarkable art collection and extensive grounds. To the west of the Heath are the charming streets of Hampstead itself. Here you will find **Fenton House**, a Georgian town house with a period walled garden, and the **Freud Museum**, the last home of the founder of psychiatry.

A walk down Haverstock Hill will bring you to **Primrose Hill**, a manicured green park boasting yet another city panorama. The adjoining "village" of the same name has several fashionable boutiques and restaurants (no chain stores here) popular with the local actors and musicians. To the east of Primrose Hill is lively **Camden Market**, a magnet for every Goth teenager. The **Jewish Museum** traces the history of the Jewish community in Britain and at the **London Canal Museum**, you can take a guided trip through London's slender waterways.

At the bottom of Primrose Hill is the **London Zoo**, at the northern end of **Regent's Park.** From here a westward detour will take you to **Lord's Cricket Ground & Museum**, and continuing south toward Queen Mary's Garden will take you past the **Open-Air Theatre**. Leaving the park on the southern end is to return to the busy urban center. The southeastern exit is near two of London's traditional tourist destinations, the **Sherlock Holmes Museum** and **Madame Tussauds**. The park's southwestern exit takes you onto handsome Portland Place, with its art deco **Royal Institute of British Architects (RIBA)**. To the west of Portland Place is stylish

A BRIEF HISTORY

11

Much like New York City's Greenwich Village, the cliché about the enclaves north of Regent's Park (Primrose Hill, Belsize Park, and Hampstead) is that several of the residents claim to be artists—and yet the cost of a coffee at a café along Regent's Park Road will run you as much as, if not more than, one in central London. In the last decade, real estate prices have skyrocketed, and the elephants of the London Zoo now call some of the best-dressed folks in town neighbors.

In the early 18th century the commercial development of the mineral springs in Hampstead led to its success as a spa; people traveled from miles around to drink the pure waters from Hampstead Wells, and small cottages were hastily built to accommodate the influx. Though the spa phenomenon was short-lived, Hampstead remained a favorite place for many artistic figures whose legacies still permeate the landscape.

Marylebone High Street and, just north of Oxford Street, the **Wallace Collection**, a collection of 17th- and 18th-century art and artifacts housed in an 18th-century mansion.

TOP ATTRACTIONS

🅒
Fodor's Choice
★

Hampstead Heath. For an escape from the ordered prettiness of Hampstead, head to the Heath—unique remnant of London's original countryside with habitats ranging from wide grasslands to ancient woodlands—spread over some 791 acres to the north. Parliament Hill, one of the highest points in London, offers a stunning panorama over the city. There are signposted paths, but these can be confusing. Maps are available from Kenwood House, or the Education Centre near the Lido off Gordon House Road, where you can also get details about the history of the Heath and the flora and fauna growing there. An excellent café near the Athletics Field offers light refreshment under the trees. ✉ *Hampstead* ☎ *020/7482–7073 Heath Information Centre* ⊕ *www.cityoflondon.gov.uk* Ⓤ *Gospel Oak or Hampstead Heath North London Overground Line from Highbury & Islington underground for south of Heath; Hampstead underground, then walk through Flask Walk, Well Walk for east of Heath; Golders Green underground, then Bus 210, 268 to Whitestone Pond for north and west of Heath.*

★ **Highgate Cemetery.** Highgate is not the oldest cemetery in London, but it is probably the best known. When the cemetery was consecrated in 1839, Victorians came from miles around to appreciate the ornate headstones, the impressive tombs, and the view. Such was its popularity that 19 acres on the other side of the road were acquired in 1850, and this additional East Cemetery contains what may be the most visited grave, of Karl Marx, as well as that of George Eliot, among other famous names. Much of the west side's 17 acres were once grounds belonging to Sir William Ashurst, lord mayor of London in 1693. At the summit is the Circle of Lebanon, a ring of vaults built around an ancient cypress tree—a legacy of Ashurst's garden. Leading from it is

HAMPSTEAD PONDS

The Heath's Elysian bathing Ponds—Men's, Ladies' and Mixed—are surrounded by grassy lounging areas. The ponds were originally created in the 17th century when the River Fleet was dammed to create reservoirs. The Ladies' Pond is particularly secluded (though crowded in summer) and open all year, as is the Men's; opening times vary with sunrise and sunset. The Mixed Pond is open May through September, 7 AM to 7 PM. The water in all three is clean and fresh, if murky-looking and bracing. Day tickets are £2.

Less murky is **Parliament Hill Lido**, open year-round. A swim here is £4.30 for the day (Early May–mid-Sept. 7–9:30, adults only in the evening; mid-Sept.–early May 7 AM–12:30 PM). The 1930s swimming pool underwent a £2.9 million refurbishment in 2005. ⊠ *E. Heath Rd., Hampstead* ☎ *020/7485-5757* Ⓤ *Tube or National Rail: Hampstead Heath.*

the Egyptian Avenue, a subterranean stone tunnel lined with catacombs, itself approached by a dramatic colonnade that screens the main cemetery from the road. Both sides are impressive, with a grand (locked) iron gate leading to a sweeping courtyard for horses and carriages. By the 1970s the cemetery had become unkempt and neglected until a group of volunteers, the Friends of Highgate Cemetery, undertook the huge upkeep. Tours are arranged by the Friends, and among the wide variety of interesting statuary—memorials once hidden by overgrowth—they will show you the most notable graves and significant buildings. The west side is accessible only by tour. ■TIP→ Children under eight are not admitted; nor are dogs, tripods, or video cameras. ⊠ *Swains La., Highgate* ☎ *020/8340–1834* ⊕ *www.highgate-cemetery.org* ⊠ *East Cemetery £3, tours £7; Western Cemetery tours £7* ⊗ *Daily; call for opening times, as hrs vary according to whether a funeral service is scheduled. East Cemetery tours, 2:30 PM 1st Sat. of month; Western Cemetery tours weekdays 2 PM, Sat. 11 AM, noon, 1, 2, 3; also 4 PM Apr.–Oct.* Ⓤ *Archway, then Bus 210, 271, or 143 to Highgate Village.*

Keats House. Here you can see the plum tree under which the young Romantic poet composed "Ode to a Nightingale," many of his original manuscripts, his library, and other possessions he managed to acquire in his short life. It was in February 1820 that Keats coughed blood up into his handkerchief and exclaimed, "I know the color of that blood; it is arterial blood. I cannot be deceived in that color. That drop of blood is my death warrant. I must die." He left this house in September, moved to Rome, and died of consumption there, in early 1821, at age 25. There are frequent guided tours and special events, such as poetry readings. A major refurbishment in 2009 saw the house decorated to match its original Regency Style; new exhibition spaces; and a redesign of the gardens, inspired by elements of Keats' poetry, such as "autumn" and "nightingale." ■TIP→ Picnics can be taken into the grounds during the summer. ⊠ *Wentworth Pl., Keats Grove, Hampstead* ☎ *020/7332–3868* ⊕ *www. keatshouse.cityoflondon.gov.uk* ⊠ *£5* ⊗ *Tues.–Sat. 10–noon and 1–5,*

June 1–5 U *Hampstead; North London Line overground: Hampstead Heath from Highbury & Islington.*

☾ ★ **Kenwood House.** This gracious Georgian villa was first built in 1616 and remodeled by Robert Adam between 1764 and 1779. Adam refaced most of the exterior and added the splendid library, which, with its curved painted ceiling, rather garish coloring, and gilded detailing, is the sole highlight of the house for decorative arts and interior design buffs. What is unmissable here is the **Iveagh Bequest,** a collection of paintings that the Earl of Iveagh gave the nation in 1927, including a wonderful Rembrandt self-portrait and works by Reynolds, Van Dyck, Hals, Gainsborough, and Turner. Top billing goes to Vermeer's *Guitar Player,* one of the most beautiful paintings in the world. In front of the house, a graceful lawn slopes down to a little lake crossed by a trompe-l'oeil bridge—all in perfect 18th-century upper-class taste. The rest of the grounds are skirted by Hampstead Heath. ■TIP→ In summer the grounds host a series of popular and classical concerts, culminating in fireworks on the last night. A popular café, the Brew House, is part of the old coach house, and has outdoor tables in the courtyard and terraced garden. ✉ *Hampstead La., Hampstead* ☎ *020/8348–1286* ⊕ *www.english-heritage.org.uk* ☛ *Free* ☾ *House daily except Dec. 24–26 and Jan. 1, 11:30–4. Gardens daily dawn–dusk* U *Golders Green, then Bus 210.*

☾ Fodor's Choice ★ **London Zoo.** The zoo, owned by the Zoological Society of London (a charity), opened in 1828 and peaked in popularity during the 1950s, when more than 3 million people passed through its turnstiles every year. A recent modernization program has seen several big new attractions open up, with a definite focus on wildlife conservation, education, and the breeding of endangered species. A great example of this is the huge BUGS pavilion (Biodiversity Underpinning Global Survival), a self-sustaining, contained ecosystem with 140 species of exotic plants, animals, and creepy-crawlies. By far the biggest new arrival is Gorilla Kingdom, where you can watch the four resident gorillas—Effie, Mjukuu, Bobby, and Zaire—at close range. Also popular is the Clore Rainforest Lookout, home to tiny primates such as marmosets and golden lion tamarins and a large collection of other rain-forest-dwelling creatures. The newly restored Blackburn Pavillion tropical aviary reopened in early 2008, after extensive renovations. This Victorian building houses the largest collection of hummingbirds in the United Kingdom. Other zoo highlights (unchanged over the years, because of English Heritage conservation listing) include the graceful Snowdon Aviary, spacious enough to allow its tenants free flight; and Berthold Lubetkin's 1936 art deco Penguin Pool, currently used for special exhibitions. Don't miss the penguins' new home, though, where feeding time tends to send small

Something will always be in bloom at Queen Mary's Gardens, within the Inner Circle of Regent's Park.

children into raptures. ■**TIP→** For animal encounter sessions with keepers, and feeding times, check the information board at admission. ✉ *Regent's Park* ☎ *020/7722–3333* ⊕ *www.zsl.org* ✉ *£16.90* ⊙ *Nov.–Feb., daily 10–4; Mar.–Oct., daily 10–5:30, last week in Oct. 10–4:30; last admission 1 hr before closing* Ⓤ *Camden Town, then Bus 274.*

★ **Marylebone High Street.** A favorite of style sections everywhere, this street forms the heart of Marylebone Village, a vibrant, upscale residential neighborhood that encompasses the squares and streets around the High Street and nearby Marylebone Lane. It's hard to believe that you're just a few blocks north of Oxford Street as you wander in and out of Marylebone's shops and boutiques. Some noteworthy stops along the way are La Fromagerie (2–4 Moxon Street), an excellent cheese shop; Daunt Books (Nos. 83–84), a travel bookshop; the Saturday afternoon "Cabbages and Frocks" market on the grounds of the St. Marylebone Parish Church, which purveys specialty foods and vintage clothing; and on Sunday 10–2, a large farmers' market in a parking lot just behind the High Street. It becomes less intimate when you get to busy Marylebone Road, but Marylebone Town Hall is worth a look if you're heading that way—perhaps for a stroll in the park or to take the kids to Madame Tussauds. ✉ *Marylebone* Ⓤ *Bond St.*

🕙 **Regent's Park.**
★ *See the highlighted listing in this chapter.*

★ **Wallace Collection.** Assembled by four generations of marquesses of
🕙 Hertford and given to the nation by the widow of Sir Richard Wallace, illegitimate son of the fourth, this collection of art and artifacts is important, exciting, undervisited—and free. As at the Frick Collection

in New York, Hertford House itself is part of the show: the fine late-18th-century mansion, built for the Duke of Manchester, contains a basement floor with educational activities, several galleries, and a courtyard covered by a glass roof, with the upscale Wallace Restaurant.

The first marquess was a patron of Sir Joshua Reynolds, the second bought Hertford House, the third—a flamboyant socialite—favored Sèvres porcelain and 17th-century Dutch painting; but it was the eccentric fourth marquess who, from his self-imposed exile in Paris, really built the collection, snapping up Bouchers, Fragonards, Watteaus, and Lancrets for a song (the French Revolution having rendered them dangerously unfashionable), augmenting these with furniture and sculpture. Richard Wallace continued acquiring treasures after his father's death, scouring Italy for majolica and Renaissance gold, then moving most of it to London. Look for Rembrandt's portrait of his son, the Rubens landscape, Gainsborough and Romney portraits, the Van Dycks and Canalettos, the French rooms, and of course the porcelain. The highlight is Fragonard's *The Swing*, which conjures up the 18th century's let-them-eat-cake frivolity better than any other painting around. Don't forget to smile back at Frans Hals's *Laughing Cavalier* in the Great Gallery or pay your respects to Thomas Sully's enchanting *Queen Victoria*, which resides in a rouge-pink salon (just to the right of the main entrance). ⊠ *Hertford House, Manchester Sq., Marylebone* ☎ *020/7563–9500* ⊕ *www.wallacecollection.org* ☚ *Free* ⊙ *Daily 10–5* Ⓤ *Bond St.*

QUICK BITES

The Wallace Restaurant brings the outside in, in the elegant setting of the glass-roofed courtyard of the Wallace Collection. It's open for breakfast, lunch, and afternoon tea, and for dinner on weekends. The brasserie menu highlights French food from pâtés and cheeses to oysters and succulent steaks. If you don't want to indulge your budget too much, you can just linger over coffee or afternoon tea in the gorgeous surroundings. It's open Sunday–Thursday 10–4:30, Friday and Saturday 10 AM–11 PM.

WORTH NOTING

Ⓒ **Camden Market.** What started life as a small group of clothing stalls in the 1970s has since grown into one of London's biggest tourist attractions. Centered on the Grand Union Canal, this isn't actually a single market, but a vast honeycomb of them that sell just about everything, but mostly crafts, clothing (vintage, ethnic, and young designer), and antiques. Here, especially on weekends, the crowds are dense, young, and relentless. **Camden Lock Market** specializes in crafts, and **Camden Stables Market** is popular with Goth kids and aspiring rock stars. In early 2008, a part of **Camden Canal Market** burned down. There were no casualties, but around 80 smaller stalls were destroyed, as was the famous Hawley Arms pub—a Camden landmark and former hangout for celebrities such as Amy Winehouse and Kate Moss. However, the Lock and Stables Markets were untouched and the Hawley Arms has reopened. *For more on Camden Lock, see* ⇨ *Shopping, Chapter 18.* ⊠ *Camden High St., Camden Town* ⊕ *www.camdenmarkets.org* ⊙ *Daily 10–6* Ⓤ *Camden Town, Chalk Farm.*

REGENT'S PARK

✉ *Marylebone Rd., Regent's Park* ☎ *020/7486–7905* ⊕ *www.royalparks.gov.uk* 🎫 *Free* ⊙ *5AM–dusk* Ⓤ *Baker St., Regent's Park, Great Portland St.*

TIPS

■ Soccer, rugby, tennis, hockey, and softball are all played on the park's many sports grounds. Head up to the area around the Hub (020/7935–2458)—a new, state-of-the-art sports pavilion—to watch some action. You'll have to book in advance if you want to join in, but you're just as likely to find an informal soccer match in progress anywhere in the park, especially on a warm Sunday afternoon.

■ At the Garden Café (Inner Circle, Regent's Park; 020/7935–5729), enjoy breakfast, lunch, or supper on a patio next to the rose gardens, or take away some smoked-salmon bagels and champagne (or cappuccinos) for an elegant picnic.

■ Check the Regent's Park Open-Air Theatre schedule—they have been mounting summer Shakespeare productions here since 1932 (0844/826–4242; www.ope-nairtheatre.org).

■ Don't leave without exploring London Zoo—it's at the very edge of the park on the northeastern side.

Cultivated and formal—compared with the relative wildness of Hampstead Heath—Regent's Park was laid out in 1812 by John Nash, in honor of the Prince Regent (hence the name), who was later crowned George IV. The idea was to re-create the feel of a grand country residence close to the center of town, with all those magnificent white-stucco terraces facing in on the park. Most of Nash's plans were carried out successfully, although the focus of it all—a palace for the prince—was never built. Now it's a destination for sporty types and dog owners—not for nothing did Dodie Smith set her novel *A Hundred and One Dalmatians* in an Outer Circle house. *A Hundred and One Dalmatians* in an Outer Circle house.

HIGHLIGHT

The most famous and impressive of Nash's terraces, **Cumberland Terrace** has a central block of Ionic columns surmounted by a triangular Wedgwood-blue pediment that looks like a giant cameo. The noted architectural historian Sir John Summerson described it as "easily the most breathtaking architectural panorama in London." You can spend a vigorous afternoon rowing about **Regent's Park Boating Lake** (☎ *020/7724–4069*), where rowboats hold up to five adults and cost £6.50 per hour per person. Times vary with seasons and weather. The **Broad Walk** is a good vantage point from which to glimpse the minaret and the golden dome of the **London Central Mosque** on the far west side of the park. As in all London parks, planting here is planned with the aim of having something in bloom in all seasons, but if you hit the park in summer, head first to the Inner Circle. Your nostrils should lead you to **Queen Mary's Gardens,** a fragrant 17-acre circle that riots with 400 different varieties of roses in summer.

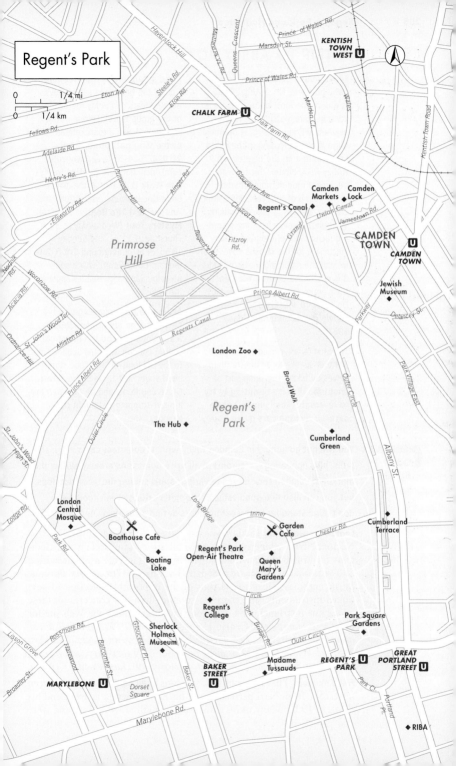

A TRIP TO ABBEY ROAD

For countless Beatlemaniacs and baby boomers, No. 3 Abbey Road is one of the most beloved spots in London. Here, outside the legendary Abbey Road Studios, is the most famous zebra crossing in the world, immortalized on the Beatles' 1969 *Abbey Road* album. This footpath became a mod monument when, on August 8 of that year, John, Paul, George, and Ringo posed—walking symbolically *away* from the recording facility—for photographer Iain Macmillan for the famous cover shot. In fact, the recording facility's Studio 2 is where the Beatles recorded their entire output, from "Love Me Do" onward, including *Sgt. Pepper's Lonely Hearts Club Band* (early 1967).

The studios are closed to the public, but tourists like to Beatle-ize themselves by taking the same sort of photo. ■TIP→ It's tempting to try to re-create "the" photo, but be careful: rushing cars make Abbey Road a dangerous intersection. One of the best—and safer—ways Beatle lovers can enjoy the history of the group is to take one of the smashing walking tours offered by the **Original London Walks** (☎ *020/7624-3978* ⊕ *www.walks. com*), including **The Beatles In-My-Life Walk** (11:20 AM at the Marylebone Underground on Saturday and Tuesday) and **The Beatles Magical Mystery Tour** (Wednesday at 2 PM, Thursday at 11 AM, and Sunday at 10:55 AM at Underground Exit 3, Tottenham Court Road), which cover nostalgic landmark Beatles spots in the city.

Abbey Road is in the elegant neighborhood of St. John's Wood, a 10-minute ride on the Tube from central London. Take the Jubilee Line to the St. John's Wood Tube stop, head southwest three blocks down Grove End Road, and be prepared for a heart-stopping vista right out of Memory Lane.

QUICK BITES

You will not go hungry in Camden Town, with its countless cafés, bars, and pubs, plus appealing restaurants at all price points on Parkway. Within the market at Camden Lock there are various stalls selling the usual hot dogs, but you can also find good value at the stalls selling ethnic food if you don't mind standing as you eat outdoors or find a canalside bench.

Fenton House. This is Hampstead's oldest surviving house. Now a National Trust property, it has fine collections of porcelain and Georgian furniture, along with a superb walled garden, complete with a 300-year-old apple orchard that dates back to the 17th century. Baroque music enthusiasts can join a tour of the important collection of keyboard instruments, and there's a summer series of concerts on these very same instruments on Thursday evenings. Check the Web site for details. ✉ *Hampstead Grove, Hampstead* ☎ *020/7435-3471* ⊕ *www. nationaltrust.org.uk* 💷 *£5.40, garden only £1* ⊙ *Apr.–Oct., Wed.–Fri. 2–5; weekends 11–5; Mar. weekends 2–5 only (hrs vary; call to confirm). Last admission 30 mins before closing* Ⓤ *Hampstead.*

Freud Museum. The father of psychoanalysis lived here for a year, between his escape from Nazi persecution in his native Vienna in 1938 and his death in 1939. Many of his possessions emigrated with him and were

Cover of the Beatles Abbey Road album, with Hampstead's most famous traffic crossing.

set up by his daughter, Anna (herself a pioneer of child psychoanalysis), as a shrine to her father's life and work. Four years after Anna's death in 1982 the house was opened as a museum. It replicates Freud's famous consulting rooms, particularly through the presence of *the* couch. You'll find Freud-related books, lectures, and study groups here, too. ✉ *20 Maresfield Gardens, Hampstead* ☎ *020/7435-2002* ⊕ *www.freud.org. uk* ✉ *£6* ⊗ *Wed.–Sun. noon–5* Ⓤ *Swiss Cottage, Finchley Rd.*

Jewish Museum. After a £10 million refurbishment, the Jewish Museum reopened in March 2010. Here you can follow the history of the Jewish people in Britain from medieval times to the present day, although most of the exhibits date from the 17th century—when Cromwell repealed the laws against Jewish settlement—and later. The collection is spread over four galleries. History: A British Story provides a general overview of British Jewish people over the centuries, through a mix of rare artifacts and interactive displays, including a re-creation of a Victorian street from what was then the Jewish Quarter of East London. The Holocaust Gallery focuses on the incredible story of Leon Greenman (1910–2008), a British Jew who survived six concentration camps—including Auschwitz—and later became a prominent anti-racism campaigner. There are also galleries on modern Judaism, a changing exhibition space, and a free overview of the collection on the ground floor, including a medieval *mikveh* (ritual bath), excavated in 2001. ✉ *Raymond Burton House 129–131 Albert St., Camden Town* ☎ *020/7284-7384* ⊕ *www.jewishmuseum.org.uk* ✉ *£7* ⊗ *Sun.–Thurs. 10–5, Fri. 10–2* Ⓤ *Camden Town.*

PUBS WITH A PAST

Hampstead has some of the most storied pubs in London—although a few have distinctly shady pasts.

The quaintest pub in Hampstead, complete with fireplace and timber frame, is the **Holly Bush** (✉ *22 Holly Mount, Hampstead* ☎ *020/7435–2892*), which dates back to 1807. Tucked away on a side street, with cozy wooden booths inside, it's open until 11 each night and serves traditional English lunches and dinners, often to the accompaniment of live Irish music.

The legendary highwayman Dick Turpin is said to have been born at the **Spaniard's Inn** (✉ *Spaniards Rd.* ☎ *020/8731–8406*), which was once frequented by the likes of Dickens, Shelley, and Stoker. The owners will happily tell you how the latter borrowed one of their many resident ghost stories to furnish the plot of *Dracula*.

A plaque outside the **Wells** (✉ *Well Walk* ☎ *020/7794–3785*) delicately informs visitors that this (now terribly upscale) pub was originally built to provide "facilities for the celebration of unpremeditated and clandestine marriages."

Meanwhile, a much sadder tale is associated with **The Magdala** (✉ *South Hill Park* ☎ *020/7435–2503*), the site of a notorious murder in 1955 for which Ruth Ellis was the last woman in Britain to be hanged. It's a very sedate place these days, but the famous bullet holes near the door have been left untouched.

OFF THE BEATEN PATH

London Canal Museum. Near the recently reopened St. Pancras International train station, in a former ice-storage house, you can learn about the rise and fall of London's once extensive canal network. Children enjoy the activity zone and learning about Henrietta, the museum's horse. Outside, on the Battlebridge Basin, float the gaily painted narrow boats of modern canal dwellers—a few steps and a world away from King's Cross, which was once one of London's least salubrious neighborhoods. The quirky little museum is a half-hour walk along the towpath from Camden Lock—you can download a free audio tour to accompany the walk. ✉ *12–13 New Wharf Rd., King's Cross* ☎ *020/7713–0836* ⊕ *www.canalmuseum.org.uk* ✉ *£3* ☉ *Tues.–Sun. and holiday Mon. 10–4:30; last admission 4. 1st Thurs. of month open to 7:30* Ⓤ *King's Cross*.

Lord's Cricket Ground & Museum. If you can't manage to lay your hands on tickets for a cricket match, the next best thing is to take a tour of the spiritual home of this most English of games. Founded by Thomas Lord, the headquarters of the MCC (Marylebone Cricket Club) opens its "behind the scenes" areas to visitors. You can see the Long Room with cricketing art on display; the players' dressing rooms; and the world's oldest sporting museum, where the progress from gentlemanly village-green game to world-class sport over 400 years is charted. Don't miss the prize exhibit: the urn containing the Ashes (reputedly the remains of a cricket ball presented to the English captain in 1883, a jokey allusion to a newspaper's premature obituary for the death of English cricket published after the home team's defeat by Australia), and even smaller, the poor sparrow that met its death by a bowled ball. More up-to-date is the eye-catching Media Centre building, which achieved high scores in the architectural league. The tour is not available during major matches (it's offered during smaller "county" matches), but the museum remains open to match ticket holders. ✉ *St. John's Wood Rd., St. John's Wood* ☎ *020/7616–8500* ⊕ *www.lords.org* ☕ *£14. Museum only, £5 nonmatch days, £3 match days* ⊘ *Museum Apr.– Sept., daily 9:30–5, except during major matches; Oct.–Mar., daily 11–5 (closes at 4 Fri.). Tours Apr.–Oct., daily 10, noon, and 2; Nov.– Mar., 10 and noon* Ⓤ *St. John's Wood.*

WATER TAXI

British Waterways runs a canal taxi service, offering kayaks that will pick you up and drop you off anywhere on London's canal network, from April through October. Book ahead to take a short hop between Regent's Park and Camden Lock, or a longer sightseeing tour, starting at £5 (☎ 020/8361–3009 ⊕ www.waterscape.com).

☾ **Madame Tussauds.** One of London's busiest sights, this is nothing more and nothing less than the world's premier exhibition of lifelike waxwork models of celebrities. Madame T. learned her craft while making death masks of French Revolution victims, and in 1835 set up her first show of the famous ones near this spot. Top billing still goes to the murderers in the Chamber of Horrors, who stare glassy-eyed at visitors—one from an electric chair, one sitting next to the tin bath where he dissolved several wives in quicklime. What, aside from ghoulish prurience, makes people stand in line to invest in one of London's most expensive museum tickets? It must be the thrill of photo opportunities with Shakespeare, Simon Cowell, and the Queen—all in a single day. ■ **TIP→** Beat the crowds by calling in advance for timed entry tickets, or booking online. ✉ *Marylebone Rd., Regent's Park* ☎ *0870/400–3000 for timed entry tickets* ⊕ *www. madame-tussauds.com* ☕ *From £12.50; prices vary; call or check Web site. Combination ticket with London Eye, London Dungeons, and London Aquarium from £54* ⊘ *Daily 9–6* Ⓤ *Baker St.*

Regent's Park Open-Air Theatre. The theater has mounted productions of Shakespeare productions every summer since 1932; everyone from Vivien Leigh to Jeremy Irons has performed here. Today it also hosts musicals and a Sunday concert series with the likes of KT Tunstall. However, *A Midsummer Night's Dream* is the one to catch—never is that enchanted Greek wood more lifelike than it is here, enhanced by genuine birdsong and a rising moon. The park can get chilly, so bring a blanket; rain stops the play only when heavy. ✉ *Open-Air Theatre, Inner Circle Regent's Park* ☎ *0844/826–4242* ⊕ *www.openairtheatre. org* ☕ *£10–£32* ⊘ *June–mid-Sept., evening performances at 8, matinees at 2:30* Ⓤ *Baker St., Regent's Park.*

Royal Institute of British Architects (RIBA). An art deco gem in elegant Portland Place, RIBA was built by Grey Wornum in 1934. Its distinctive Portland stone facade stands out amid the surrounding 18th-century mansions, and large bronze doors lead to a spacious foyer with a wide marble staircase. There's a wonderful architecture bookstore inside, and you can enjoy your reading in impeccable art deco surroundings

221B Baker Street and "Holmes" himself.

over lunch or coffee in the upstairs café. ⊠ *Park La., 66 Portland Pl., Marylebone* ☎ *0207/580–5533* ⊕ *www.architecture.com* Ⓤ *Regent's Park, Great Portland St.*

QUICK BITES

Dine in art deco splendor at the **RIBA Café & Restaurant** (⊠ **66 Portland Pl., Regent's Park** ☎ **020/7631–0467**) on the first floor of the Royal Institute of British Architects. The café serves excellent salads and sandwiches, and the restaurant offers more-substantial modern European meals. There's a half-covered terrace for alfresco dining in nice weather.

Sherlock Holmes Museum. Outside Baker Street station, by the Marylebone Road exit, is a 9-foot-high bronze statue of the celebrated detective. Keep your eyes peeled, for close by his image, "Holmes" himself, in his familiar deerstalker hat, will escort you to his abode at 221B Baker Street, the address of Arthur Conan Doyle's fictional detective. Inside, Mrs. Hudson, "Holmes's housekeeper," conducts you into a series of Victorian rooms full of Sherlock-abilia. It's all so realistic, you may actually begin to believe that the fictional "great detective" really lived there. ⊠ *221B Baker St., Regent's Park* ☎ *020/7935–8866* ⊕ *www.sherlock-holmes.co.uk* 🎫 *£6* ☉ *Daily 9:30–6* Ⓤ *Baker St.*

WORD OF MOUTH

"The Sherlock Holmes museum is fun for fans and an hour will be more than enough time. Be sure to read the letters in the guest book—some people still seek out his help." —mvor

Greenwich

WORD OF MOUTH

"Greenwich is such a wondrous place to go. I am always amazed when I traipse through the War College's former buildings. The park, the observatory, the Cutty Sark (currently being rebuilt after a fire), the Thames front, the town itself and the market—Greenwich to me was a 3-star site and now even more."

—PalenQ

GETTING ORIENTED

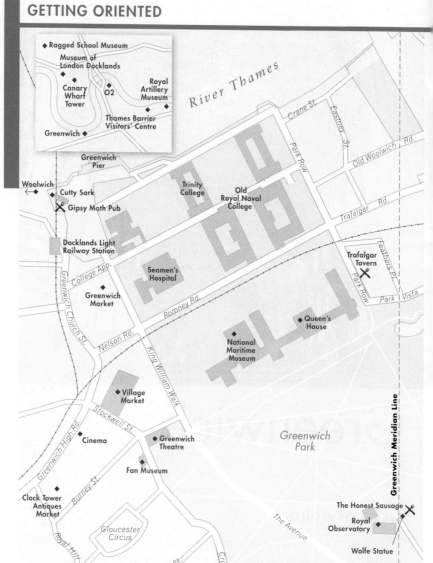

- Ragged School Museum
- Museum of London Docklands
- Canary Wharf Tower
- O2
- Royal Artillery Museum
- Thames Barrier Visitors' Centre
- Greenwich

River Thames

Crane St.

Eastney St.

Old Woolwich Rd.

Greenwich Pier

Woolwich ←

- Cutty Sark
- ✗ Gipsy Moth Pub

Park Row

Trinity College

Old Royal Naval College

Trafalgar Rd.

Feathers' Pl.

Docklands Light Railway Station

College App.

Seamen's Hospital

Greenwich Market

Romney Rd.

Trafalgar Tavern ✗

Park Row

Park Vista

- Queen's House

Greenwich Church St.

Nelson Rd.

King William Walk

- National Maritime Museum

- Village Market

Stockwell St.

GREENWICH FOOT

Greenwich Park

Greenwich High Rd.

- Cinema

- Greenwich Theatre

- Fan Museum

Burney St.

- Clock Tower Antiques Market

Royal Hill

Gloucester Circus

The Avenue

Greenwich Meridian Line

- The Honest Sausage ✗
- Royal Observatory
- Wolfe Statue

King George St.

Croom's Hill

0 _____ 1/8 mile

0 _____ 1/8 kilometer

- Ranger's House

12

TOP REASONS TO GO

Greenwich Meridian Line: Stand astride time at the Royal Observatory and be in the Eastern and Western hemispheres simultaneously.

Old Royal Naval College Chapel: Listen to a lunchtime concert amid neo-Grecian surroundings.

National Maritime Museum: Discover Britain's seafaring past and learn more about the effects the oceans have on the world.

Greenwich Market: Riffle through retro lighting and clothing stalls.

Walk under the Thames to Docklands: Walk through the past in a Victorian tunnel to get a glimpse of the future London in this converted warehouse district. Canary Wharf's financial skyscrapers dominate here, but West India Quay's focus is play, not work.

FEELING PECKISH?

The **Gipsy Moth Pub** (⊠ *60 Greenwich Church St.* ☎ *020/8858-0786*), behind the *Cutty Sark*, is the town's only memorial to another classic ship: the yacht that Sir Francis Chichester sailed single-handedly around the world in the 1960s. The galley here is expensive, but the beer garden makes up for it.

Up by the Royal Observatory is the **Honest Sausage** (⊕ *www. honestsausage.com*), beside the Wolfe monument, serving up delicious homemade organic sausages, and baked potatoes drenched in onion gravy. The views are great, too.

For the best pub in Greenwich, head to the **Trafalgar Tavern** (⊠ *Park Row* ☎ *020/8858-2909* ⊕ *www.trafalgartavern. co.uk*), with excellent views of the Thames. It's a grand place to have a pint and some upscale grub.

GETTING THERE

The zippy "driverless" Docklands Light Railway (DLR) runs to Cutty Sark station from the Sir Norman Foster–designed Canary Wharf and also Bank Tube stations. Or take the DLR to Island Gardens and retrace the steps dockworkers used to take back and forth on the old Victorian Foot Tunnel under the river.

The best way to arrive, however—time and weather permitting—is like a sea admiral of old: by water. Note, though, that this journey takes more than an hour from central London. (⇨ *For more on cruising the Thames, see Chapter 13, The Thames Upstream.*)

MAKING THE MOST OF YOUR TIME

Set apart from the rest of London, Greenwich is worth a day to itself, to make the most of walks in the rolling parklands and to immerse yourself in its richness of maritime art and entertainment. The boat trip takes about an hour from Westminster Pier (next to Big Ben), or 25 minutes from the Tower of London, so factor in enough time for the round-trip. For the crafts markets, a weekend trip is best.

NEAREST PUBLIC RESTROOMS

Duck into the tourist information center (near the Old Royal Naval College), whose loos are free.

Sightseeing
★★★★
Nightlife
★
Dining
★★
Lodging
★
Shopping
★★★

The smart borough of Greenwich is situated on the Greenwich Meridian Line at 0° longitude, the official starting point for every new day, month, and year. The island nation of England—and the district—boasts an incredible maritime history. The world's last remaining tea clipper, the *Cutty Sark* was tragically damaged by fire in 2007, but Greenwich still preserves its unique charm, from its earthy markets to its distinctive Palladian architecture.

Updated by
Jack Jewers

A visit to Greenwich feels like a trip to a seaside town—but one with more than its fair share of historic sites and visitor attractions, all fairly close to one another—that's designated a UNESCO World Heritage Site. The grandiose Christopher Wren–designed **Old Royal Naval Hospital** was originally erected as Greenwich Hospital, a home for veteran sailors. It closed in 1869 and was reincarnated for training young officers; today it's the setting of many a blockbuster period film.

Greenwich was originally home to one of England's finest Tudor palaces, and the birthplace of Henry VIII, Elizabeth I, and Mary I. The masterful Inigo Jones built what is considered the first "classical" building in England in 1616—the **Queen's House,** now housing a collection of fine art. Right next door, the world's largest maritime museum, the **National Maritime Museum,** details stories of Britain's seafaring past and also houses Nelson's bullet-pierced coat from his last battle.

Verdant **Greenwich Park** is London's oldest royal park; here Henry VIII introduced deer so that he could hunt. The **Ranger's House** now houses a private art collection, next door to a beautifully tended rose garden. Atop the park's hill is the **Royal Observatory,** where you can bestride two hemispheres by standing over the **Greenwich Meridian Line** and see a planetarium show.

In town, opposite the Greenwich Theatre, the **Fan Museum** is home to 4,000 fans dating as far back as the 11th century. The **Clock Tower Antiques Market** and the lively **Greenwich Market** keep browsers busy on weekends.

Toward north Greenwich, the hopelessly ambitious Millennium Dome has been successfully rebranded as The O2 and has hosted a reformed Spice Girls, Chris Rock, Prince, and Led Zeppelin in memorable, if wallet-busting, gigs. Now the most popular concert venue in London, it's slated to host the gymnastics events of the 2012 Olympic Games. In the opposite direction, downstream in Woolwich, lies the **Thames Flood Barrier.**

12

FUN FACT

Prance around the lightning-cracked Elizabeth Oak in Greenwich Park and you'll be in good historic company—it's so called after Elizabeth I's own flights of fancy in youth.

TOP ATTRACTIONS

Greenwich Market. Established as a fruit-and-vegetable market in 1700, and granted a royal charter in 1849, the covered market now offers mixed stalls of arts and crafts plus antiques and collectibles on Thursday and Friday and food stalls on Saturday and Sunday. Shopping for handicrafts is a pleasure, as in most cases you're buying directly from the artist. ⊠ *College Approach, Greenwich* ☎ *020/8293–3110* ⊕ *www.greenwichmarket.net* ☉ *Thurs.–Sun. 10–5:30, Wed. 11–6* Ⓤ *DLR: Cutty Sark.*

Clock Tower Antiques Market. The weekend Clock Tower Antiques Market on Greenwich High Road has more vintage shopping, and browsing among the "small collectibles" makes for a good half-hour diversion.

☉ ★ **National Maritime Museum.** Following a millennial face-lift, one of Greenwich's star attractions has been completely updated to make it one of London's most enjoyable museums. Its glass-covered courtyard of beautifully grand stone, dominated by a huge revolving propeller from a powerful frigate, is reminiscent of the British Museum. The collection spans seascape paintings to scientific instruments, interspersed with the heroes of the waves. A permanent Nelson gallery contains the uniform he wore, complete with bloodstain, when he met his end in 1805. Allow at least two hours in this absorbing, adventurous place; if you're in need of refreshment, the museum has a good café with views over Greenwich Park. The **Queen's House** is home to the largest collection of maritime art in the world, including works by William Hogarth, Canaletto, and Joshua Reynolds. Construction was granted by Queen Anne only on condition that the river vista from the house be preserved, and there are few more majestic views in London than Inigo Jones's awe-inspiring symmetry. Completed around 1638, the Tulip Stair, named for the fleur-de-lis–style pattern on the balustrade, is especially fine, spiraling up without a central support to the Great Hall. The Great Hall itself is a perfect cube, exactly 40 feet in all three dimensions, decorated with paintings of the Muses and the Virtues. ⊠ *Romney Rd., Greenwich* ☎ *020/8858–4422* ⊕ *www.nmm.ac.uk* ☜ *Free* ☉ *Daily 10–5; last admission 30 mins before closing* Ⓤ *DLR: Greenwich.*

★ **Old Royal Naval College.** Begun by Christopher Wren in 1694 as a rest home for ancient mariners, it became instead a school for young ones in 1873.

ROYAL OBSERVATORY

✉ *Romney Rd., Greenwich*
☎ *020/8858–4422* ⊕ *www.*
rog.nmm.ac.uk ✆ *Free, plan-*
etarium shows £6 ⊙ *July and*
Aug., daily 10–6; Sept.–June,
daily 10–5; last entry 30
mins before closing Ⓤ *DLR:*
Greenwich.

TIPS

■ A brass line laid among the cobblestones here marks the meridian, one side being the Eastern, one the Western hemisphere. As darkness falls, a funky green laser shoots out across London for several miles, following exactly the path of the meridian line.

■ The Time Ball atop Flamsteed House is one of the world's earliest time signals. Each day at 12:55, it rises halfway up its mast. At 12:58 it rises all the way to the top, and at 1 exactly, the ball falls.

■ The steep hill home to the observatory gives fantastic views across London, topped off with £1-a-slot telescopes to scour the skyline. Time a walk to catch the golden glow of late-afternoon sun on Canary Wharf Tower and head back into Greenwich via the rose garden behind Ranger's House.

■ Youngsters under five are not usually allowed into the auditorium. Tickets can be purchased ahead online.

Since 1884, the ultimate standard for time around the world has been set here: Greenwich is on the prime meridian at 0° longitude. The honor was because of its importance as a site for study of the stars and of the passing of time. Since a redesign in 2007, the observatory has been split into two sites a short walk apart, one dedicated to the wonders of space, the other to mankind's cataloguing of moments.

HIGHLIGHTS

The recently opened south site, not previously accessible to the public, is the location of the enchanting **Peter Harrison Planetarium**, now London's only planetarium, its bronze-clad turret poking out of the ground like a crashed UFO. Shows on black holes and how to interpret the night sky entrance visitors. If you come with children, don't miss the high-technology rooms of the **Astronomy Galleries**, where cutting-edge touch screens and interactive programs give young explorers the chance to run their own space missions to Ganymede, one of Jupiter's moons.

Across the way is **Flamsteed House**, designed by Christopher Wren in 1675 for John Flamsteed, the first Royal Astronomer. A climb to the top of the house reveals the **28-inch telescope**, built in 1893 and now housed inside an onion-shape fiberglass dome. It doesn't compare with the range of modern telescopes, but it is the largest in the United Kingdom, and regular viewing evenings still reveal startling detailed views of the lunar surface. In the **Time Galleries**, linger over the superb workmanship of John Harrison's famous **Maritime Clocks**, H1–H4, which won him the Longitude Prize for solving the problem of accurate timekeeping at sea and greatly improved navigation.

DID YOU KNOW?

Once sailors could deter-
mine their distance from the
Greenwich meridian (Longitude), maritime navigation
was greatly improved. Look
for the brass line marking the
two hemispheres throughout
the cobblestone streets.

Today the University of Greenwich and Trinity College of Music have classes here. Architecturally, you'll notice how the structures part to reveal the **Queen's House** across the central lawns. Behind the college are two more buildings you can visit: the **Painted Hall,** the college's dining hall, derives its name from the baroque murals of William and Mary (reigned 1689–95; William alone 1695–1702) and assorted allegorical figures. James Thornhill's frescoes, depicting scenes of naval grandeur with a suitably pro-British note of propaganda, were painstakingly done over installments in 1708–12 and 1718–26, and were good enough to earn him a knighthood. The hall is still used for dining, making merry, school visits, and weddings today. In the opposite building stands the **College Chapel,** which was rebuilt after a fire in 1779 and is altogether lighter, in a more restrained, neo-Grecian style. ■TIP→ Trinity College of Music holds free classical music concerts in the chapel every Tuesday lunchtime during the school year. ⊠ *Old Royal Naval College, King William Walk, Greenwich* ☎ *020/8269–4747* ⊕ *www.oldroyalnavalcollege.org* ☎ *Free, guided tours £5* ⊙ *Painted Hall and chapel daily 10–5; grounds 8–6* Ⓤ *DLR: Greenwich.*

> **GREENWICH FOOT TUNNEL**
>
> In a brilliant piece of foresight, Greenwich Hospital bought Island Gardens, on the other side of the Thames, in 1849 to prevent anticipated industrial expansion and preserve the view back toward Greenwich. Take the stone spiral steps down into Greenwich Foot Tunnel and head under the Thames (enjoy the echo during the foreboding walk) to Island Gardens, at the southern tip of the Isle of Dogs, for a magnificent view back over the river, of the Old Royal Naval College and Queen's House, framed by the park.

Ↄ **Royal Observatory.**

★ *See the highlighted listing in this chapter.*

WORTH NOTING

Ↄ **Cutty Sark.** At this writing, the famous tea clipper itself remains closed until spring 2011. In addition to repairing the damage from the 2007 fire, the ship is being raised and other work is taking place to make it more accessible to visitors. This sleek, romantic clipper was built in 1869, one of fleets and fleets of similar tall-masted wooden ships that plied oceanic highways of the 19th century, trading in exotic commodities—tea, in this case. The *Cutty Sark* was also the fastest, sailing the China–London route in 1871 in only 107 days. ⊠ *King William Walk, Greenwich* ☎ *020/8858–2698* ⊕ *www.cuttysark.org.uk* Ⓤ *DLR: Cutty Sark.*

Fan Museum. The 2,000 fans here, housed in two restored 1820s buildings opposite the Greenwich Theatre, date from the 17th century onward and make up the world's only such collection. The history and purpose of these objects, often exquisitely crafted from ivory, mother-of-pearl, and tortoiseshell, are explained in satisfying detail. It was the personal vision—and fan collection—of Helene Alexander that brought

Without a central support, the Tulip Stair spirals up to the Great Hall of Queen's House.

it into being, and the workshop and conservation–study center that she has also set up ensure that this anachronistic art has a future. If your interest is really piqued, you can attend fan-making workshops (on the first Saturday of every month only—£20 for the afternoon; call ahead or visit the Web site for booking details). ⊠ *12 Croom's Hill, Greenwich* ☎ *020/8305–1441* ⊕ *www.fan-museum.org* ✉ *£4* ⊗ *Tues.–Sat. 11–5, Sun. noon–5* Ⓤ *DLR: Greenwich.*

Ranger's House. This handsome, early-18th-century villa, which was the Greenwich Park ranger's official residence during the 19th century, is hung with Stuart and Jacobean portraits. But the most interesting diversion is the Wernher Collection, more than 650 works of art with a northern European flavor, amassed by diamond millionaire Julius Wernher at the turn of the 20th century. After making his money in diamond mining, he chose to buy eclectic objects, sometimes beautiful, often downright quirky, like the silver coconut cup now on show in the house. Sèvres porcelain and Limoges enamels, the largest jewelry collection in the country, and some particularly bizarre reliquaries also form part of this fascinating collection. Wernher's American wife, Birdie, was a strong influence and personality during the belle époque, which is easy to imagine from her striking portrait by Sargent. ⊠ *Chesterfield Walk, Blackheath, Greenwich* ☎ *020/8853–0035* ⊕ *www.english-heritage. org.uk* ✉ *£5.70* ⊗ *Apr.–Sept., Mon.–Wed. guided tours only, 11:30 and 2:30, Sun. 11–5; call ahead to confirm* Ⓤ *DLR: Greenwich; no direct bus access, only to Vanbrugh Hill (from east) and Blackheath Hill (from west).*

DID YOU KNOW?

The Docklands Light Rail (DLR) connects former warehouses that have been converted to museums and malls, such as Hay's and Butler's wharves, and the gleaming office buildings of Canary Wharf shown here.

THE DOCKLANDS RENAISSANCE

If it hadn't been for the Thames, Roman Londinium, with its sea link to the rest of the world, would not have grown into a world power. For centuries, life was played out by the riverside, and palaces redolent of Venice—such as Westminster and Whitehall—were built. Dock warehouses sprang up during the 18th century from the trade with the Indies for tea and coffee, spices, and silks. Trade took a gradual downturn after World War II, leading to the docks' degeneration when larger vessels pushed trade farther downriver to Tilbury. It took a driverless railway and Britain's tallest building—Canary Wharf Tower—to start a renaissance. Now, what was once a desolate and dirty quarter near Greenwich is known as the Docklands, a peninsula of waterways with cutting-edge architecture, offices, water-based leisure and cultural activities, restaurants, and bars. Some of the warehouses have been converted into museums and malls, such as Hay's and Butler's wharves.

The best way to explore is on the **Docklands Light Railway (DLR)**, whose elevated track appears to skim over the water past the swanky glass buildings where the railway is reflected in the windows. On foot, however, the Thames Path has helpful plaques along the way, with nuggets of historical information.

The **Museum of London Docklands**, on a quaint cobbled quayside, beside the tower of Canary Wharf, is worth a visit for its warehouse building alone. With uneven wood floors, beams, and pillars, the museum used to be a storehouse for coffee, tea, sugar, and rum from the West Indies—hence the name West India

Quay. The fascinating story of the old port and the river is told using films, together with interactive displays and reconstructions. ✉ *No. 1 Warehouse, West India Quay, Hertsmere Rd., East End* ☎ *020/7001–9844* ⊕ *www.museumindocklands. org.uk* 💷 *£5* ⏲ *Daily 10–6; last admission 5:30* Ⓤ *Canary Wharf; DLR: West India Quay.*

In its time, the **Ragged School Museum** was the largest school in London and a place where impoverished children could get free education and a good meal. The museum re-creates a classroom dating from the 1880s. It's an eye-opener for adults, and fun for kids, who get the chance to work just like Victorian children did in one of the many organized workshops. ✉ *46–50 Copperfield Rd., East End* ☎ *020/8980–6405* ⊕ *www. raggedschoolmuseum.org.uk* 💷 *Free; £2 donation requested for Victorian lessons* ⏲ *Wed. and Thurs. 10–5, 1st Sun. of month 2–5* Ⓤ *Mile End; DLR: Limehouse.*

Farther downstream, adjacent to the old Royal Dockyard at Woolwich, is a brilliant exhibition of the **Firepower Royal Artillery Museum** (✉ *Royal Arsenal, Woolwich* ☎ *020/8855–7755* ⊕ *www.firepower.org.uk* 💷 *£5* ⏲ *Wed.–Sun. 10:30–5* Ⓤ *DLR: Woolwich Arsenal*). Complete with smoke and sound effects, it explores the role of the gunner, from the discovery of gunpowder to the Persian Gulf war. Also on show are tanks and guns—some complete with battle scars. Housed in the old Royal Arsenal leading down to the river shore, its setting provides a powerful sense of the Thames and its lingering effect on the capital's history.

12

OFF THE
BEATEN
PATH

Thames Barrier Visitors' Centre. Learn what comes between London and its famous river—a futuristic-looking metal barrier that has been described as the eighth wonder of the world. Multimedia presentations, a film on the Thames's history, working models, and views of the barrier itself put the importance of the relationship between London and its river in perspective. ⊠ *Unity Way, Eastmoor St., Woolwich* ☏ *020/8305–4188* ⊕ *www.environment-agency.gov.uk* ✉ *£3.50* ☉ *Apr.–Sept., daily 10:30–4:30; Oct.–Mar., daily 11–3:30* Ⓤ *National Rail: Charlton (from London Bridge), then Bus 177 or 180; North Greenwich (Jubilee Line), then Bus 161 or 472.*

The Thames Upstream

WORD OF MOUTH

"Hampton Court . . . has some extremely grand 'palacey' rooms and it's a good place for kids. Lots of grounds to run around and they love the maze. You can take a picnic in with you if you like— or go find one of the pubs on the riverfront for lunch."

—nona1

GETTING ORIENTED

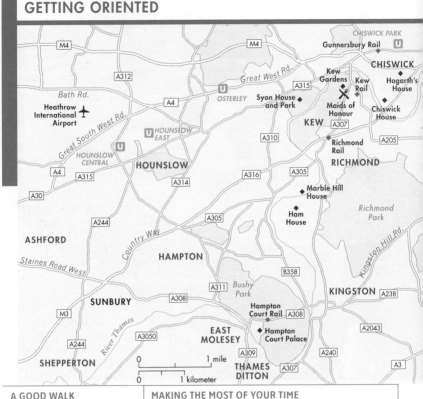

A GOOD WALK	MAKING THE MOST OF YOUR TIME
From Chiswick House, follow Burlington Lane and take a left onto Hogarth Lane—which is anything but a lane—to reach Hogarth's House. Chiswick's Church Street is the nearest thing to a sleepy country village street in all of London. Follow it down to the Thames and turn left at the bottom to reach the 18th-century riverfront houses of Chiswick Mall, referred to by locals as "Millionaire's Row." There are several pretty riverside pubs near Hammersmith Bridge.	Hampton Court Palace requires at least half a day to experience its magic fully, although you could make do with an afternoon at Richmond Park, or a couple of hours for any of the other attractions. Because of the distance between the sights, too much traveling eats into your day. The best option is to concentrate on one of the principal sights, adding in a brisk park visit, one stately home, and a riverside promenade before rounding off with an evening pint.

FEELING PECKISH?

Maids of Honour (✉ 288 Kew Rd., Kew ☎ 020/8940–2752), the most traditional of Old English tearooms, is named for the famous tarts invented here and still baked by hand on the premises. Tea is served Tuesday–Saturday 2:30–5:30. If you want to take some of the lovely cakes and pastries to eat at Kew Gardens or on Kew Green, the shop is open Tuesday–Saturday 9:30–6 and Monday until 1.

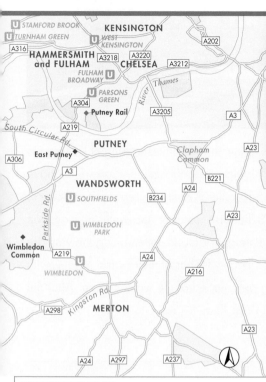

13

GETTING THERE

The District Line is the best of the Tube options, stopping at Turnham Green (in the heart of Chiswick but a fair walk from the houses), Gunnersbury (for Syon Park), Kew Gardens, and Richmond.

For Hampton Court, overland train is your quickest option: South West trains run from Waterloo, also stopping at Chiswick station (best for Chiswick House), Kew Bridge, Richmond (for Ham House), and St. Margaret's (best for Marble Hill House). Silverlink, another overland London service, also stops at Gunnersbury, Kew Gardens, and Richmond.

A pleasant, if slow, way to go is by river. Boats depart upriver from Westminster Pier, by Big Ben, for Kew (1½ hours), Richmond (2–3 hours), and Hampton Court (3–4 hours) several times a day in summer, less frequently from October through March. The boat trip is worth taking only if you make it an integral part of your day out, and be aware that it can get very breezy on the water (⇨ see *A Tour of the Thames*.)

TOP REASONS TO GO

Hampton Court Palace: Get lost in the leafy walls of the palace's maze as dusk falls.

Richmond Park: Take a misty early morning stroll and catch sight of red deer.

Richmond village: Browse the antiques shops and travel back in time.

Kew Gardens: See the earth from above, by visiting Kew's treetop walkway, at the Royal Botanic Gardens.

Thames-side views: Enjoy a pint from the creaking balcony of a centuries-old riverside pub as you watch the boats row home.

NEAREST PUBLIC RESTROOMS

Richmond Park, Kew Gardens, and all the stately homes have public restrooms available.

Sightseeing
★★★★
Nightlife
★★
Dining
★★★
Lodging
★★
Shopping
★★

The upper stretch of the Thames unites a string of lustrous riverside pearls—Chiswick, Kew, Richmond, Putney—taking in friendly streets, horticultural delights, regal magnificence, and Henry VIII's fiendish outdoor labyrinth at Hampton Court Palace. The neighborhoods dotted along the way are as proud of their village-y feel as of their stately history, with many a pleasing pub nestled at the water's edge. After the busyness of the West End, it's easy to forget you're in a capital city.

CHISWICK AND KEW

Updated by
Jack Jewers

Chiswick is the nearest Thames-side destination to central London. It's a low-key district, content with its good run of restaurants, stylish shops, and film-star residents, but it is also proud of the seething moral authority of its most famous son: William Hogarth, one of Britain's best-loved painters, lived here, and tore the fabric of the 18th-century nation to pieces in his slew of satirical engravings. Incongruously stranded among Chiswick's terraced homes are a number of fine 18th-century houses, and a charming little village survives, populated by London's affluent middle-class families.

A mile or so beyond Chiswick is Kew, and the village atmosphere here makes this one of the most desirable areas of outer London. The biggest draw for visitors, though, are the Royal Botanic Gardens.

EXPLORING

Chiswick House. Completed in 1729 by the Earl of Burlington (the Lord Burlington of Burlington House, Piccadilly, home of the Royal Academy, and, of course, the Burlington Arcade) as a country residence in which to entertain friends—who included Pope, Swift, Gay, and Handel—and as a kind of temple to the arts, this is the very model of a Palladian villa, inspired by the Villa Capra near Vicenza in northeastern Italy.

Georgiana, the beautiful Duchess of Devonshire (1757–1806), referred to the house as "my earthly paradise." The house fans out from a central octagonal room in perfect symmetry, guarded by statues of Burlington's heroes, Palladio himself and his disciple Inigo Jones. Burlington was a great connoisseur and an important patron of the arts, but he was also an accomplished architect in his own right, fascinated by—obsessed with, even—the architecture and art of the Italian Renaissance and ancient Rome, with which he'd fallen in love during his Italian Grand Tour. Along with William Kent (1685–1748), who designed the sumptuous interiors (including the Blue Velvet Room with its gilded decoration and intricate ceiling paintings) and the rambling gardens filled with classical temples, statues, and obelisks, Burlington did a great deal toward the dissemination of Palladian ideals around Britain: Chiswick House sparked enormous interest, and you'll see these forms reflected in hundreds of later English stately homes both small and large. It also houses a fabulous collection of paintings and furniture. The gardens are being restored to their 18th-century glory; work started in March 2008 and is scheduled for completion in spring 2010. ⊠ *Burlington La., Chiswick* ☎ *020/8995–0508* ⊕ *www.chgt.org. uk* 🎫 *£4.20* ⊙ *Apr. daily 10–5, May–Oct.; Nov. and Dec. by appointment only* Ⓤ *Turnham Green, Chiswick.*

BOAT RACES

A great place to buy Hogarth prints is at **Fosters** (⊠ *183 Chiswick High Rd.* ☎ *020/8995–2768*), the oldest shop in Chiswick. The shop has its original Georgian frontage, creaking floorboards, and a glorious number of original Victorian novels and essays. It also offers handwritten gift vouchers from £10 to £50,000.

13

Hogarth's House. At this writing, the home of William Hogarth is closed for renovations until at least late 2010 because of fire damage. The satirical painter and engraver, from 1749 until his death in 1764 (his tomb can be found in the cemetery of St. Nicholas's church on Chiswick Mall). ⊠ *Hogarth La., Great West Road, Chiswick* ☎ *020/8994–6757* ⊕ *www.hounslow.info/arts/hogarthshouse* Ⓤ *Turnham Green.*

QUICK BITES

Pubs are the name of the game here at Chiswick's portion of the Thames. Many pubs sit on the bank of the river, offering watery vistas to accompany stout pints of brew. The **City Barge** (⊠ *27 Strand-on-the-Green, Chiswick* ☎ *020/8994–2148*) on the north bank of the Thames has a lovely riverside terrace and honest pub grub. The **Blue Anchor** (⊠ *13 Lower Mall, Hammersmith* ☎ *020/8748–5774*) is a cozy 18th-century watering hole, with rowing memorabilia lining the walls. The **Dove Inn** (⊠ *19 Upper Mall, Hammersmith* ☎ *020/8748–9474*) retains the charm of its 300-plus-year heritage. If you can find a spot on the tiny terrace, it's a tranquil place to watch the energetic oarsmen.

🔄 **Kew Gardens.**
★ *See the highlighted listing in this chapter.*

Kew Palace and Queen Charlotte's Cottage. To this day quietly domestic Kew Palace remains the smallest royal palace in the land. The house and gardens offer a glimpse into the 17th century. Originally known as the Dutch House, it was bought by King George II to provide more room in addition to the White House (another royal residence that used to exist on the grounds) for the extended Royal Family. In spring there's a romantic haze of bluebells. ⊠ *Kew Gardens, Kew* ⊕ *www.hrp. org.uk* ⊒ *£5, in addition to ticket for Kew Gardens* ⊙ *Apr.–Sept., Tues.–Sun. 10–5, Mon. 11–5* Ⓤ *Kew Gardens.*

> **HORSE RIDING**
>
> **Kingston Riding Centre** has stables within minutes of Richmond Park. Private lessons are £34–£45 (half hour) and £61–£87 (one hour). Group lessons and hacks through Richmond Park cost from £38 for one hour, to £63 for 90 minutes. ⊠ *38 Crescent Rd., Kingston-upon-Thames* ☎ *020/8546–6361* ⊕ *www.kingstonridingcentre. com* Ⓤ *Richmond Station, then Bus 371.*

RICHMOND

Named after the palace Henry VII built here in 1500, Richmond is still a welcoming and extremely pretty riverside "village," with many handsome (and expensive) houses, antiques shops, a Victorian theater, London's grandest stately home, and, best of all, the largest of London's royal parks.

EXPLORING

★ **Ham House.** To the west of Richmond Park, overlooking the Thames and nearly opposite the oddly named Eel Pie Island, the house was built in 1610 by Sir Thomas Vavasour, knight marshal to James I, then refurbished later in the century by the Duke and Duchess of Lauderdale, who, although not particularly well regarded (a contemporary called the duchess "the coldest friend and the most violent enemy that ever was known"), managed to produce one of the finest houses in Britain at the time. It's unique in Europe as the most complete example of a lavish Restoration period house, with a restored formal garden, which has become an influential source for other European palaces and grand villas. Produce from the garden can be enjoyed in the café in the Orangery. The library is filled with 17th- and 18th-century volumes; the original decorations in the Great Hall, Round Gallery, and Great Staircase have been replicated; and all the furniture and fittings are on permanent loan from the Victoria & Albert Museum. The gardens and outbuildings (Ice House and Still House) are worth a visit in their own right, and are more conveniently open year-round. A tranquil and scenic way to reach the house is on foot, which takes about 30 minutes, along the eastern riverbank south from Richmond Bridge. ⊠ *Ham St., Richmond* ☎ *020/8940–1950* ⊕ *www.nationaltrust.org.uk* ⊒ *House, gardens, and outbuildings £9* ⊙ *House mid–late Feb. and mid-Mar. to early Nov., Sat.–Wed. noon–4; late Feb. to mid-Mar., weekends noon–4. Gardens all year, Sat.–Wed. 11–5* Ⓤ *Richmond, then Bus 65 or 371.*

KEW GARDENS

✉ *Royal Botanic Gardens, Kew, Richmond, Surrey, TW9 3AB (main entrance is between Richmond Circus and the traffic circle at Mortlake Rd.)* ☎ *020/8332-5655* ⊕ *www.kew.org* ✉ *£13* ⊘ *Feb. and Mar., daily 9:30–5:30; Apr.–Aug., weekdays 9:30–6:30, weekends 9:30–7:30; Sept. and Oct., 9:30–6; Nov.–Feb. 9:30–4:15* Ⓤ *Kew Gardens.*

13

TIPS

■ Guided tours with nature-loving volunteers leave daily from the Guides' desk inside Victoria Plaza at 11 and 2.

■ Can't tell your False acacia from your Corsican pine? The 90-minute Tree Identification Tour leaves from Museum No. 1 (opposite the Palm House) on Saturday at 11:30, £5. Book ahead (020/8332–5604).

■ Fresh air and natural beauty made you peckish? Treat your taste buds to a light tea at the Victoria Terrace Café, dine outside at White Peaks, or go elegant at The Orangery.

■ Hire a Kew Ranger—an interactive handheld GPS that will lead you to highlights, give hints and snippets of history, and even give kids "hunting clues" to keep them occupied. Pick one up from Victoria Gate for £4.95.

Enter Kew Gardens and you are enveloped by blazes of color, extraordinary blooms, hidden trails, magnificent buildings, and centuries of endeavor aimed at getting to grips with the mysteries of plants that entrance, medicate, and excite. Even today academics are hard at work on more than 300 scientific projects across as many acres, researching everything from the cacti of eastern Brazil to the yams of Madagascar. First opened to the public in 1840, Kew has been supported by royalty and nurtured by landscapers, botanists, and architects since the 1720s, and with more than 30,000 species of plants, there is interest and beauty in spades.

Although the plant houses make Kew worth visiting even in the depths of winter (there's also a seasonal garden), the flower beds come into their own in spring and summer.

HIGHLIGHTS

Two great 19th-century greenhouses—the **Palm House** and the **Temperate House**—are filled with exotic blooms, and many of the plants have been there since the final glass panel was fixed into place. The Temperate House, once the biggest greenhouse in the world, today contains the largest greenhouse plant in the world, a Chilean wine palm rooted in 1846. You can climb the spiral staircase to the roof and look down on it and the dense tropical profusion from the walkway. Architect Sir William Chambers built a series of temples and follies, of which the crazy 50-story **Pagoda**, visible for miles around, is the star turn. The Princess of Wales conservatory houses 10 climate zones, and in 2008 the Rhizotron & Xstrata treetop walkway opened—taking you 59 feet up into the air.

Fodor's Choice ★ **Hampton Court Palace.** *See the highlighted listing in this chapter.*

Marble Hill House. On the northern bank of the Thames, almost opposite Ham House, stands another mansion, this one a near-perfect example of a Palladian villa. Set in 66 acres of parkland, Marble Hill House was built in the 1720s by George II for his mistress, the "exceedingly respectable and respected" Henrietta Howard. Later the house was occupied by Mrs. Fitzherbert, who was secretly married to the Prince Regent (later George IV) in 1785. Marble Hill House was restored in 1901 and opened to the public two years later, looking very much like it did in Georgian times, with extravagant gilded rooms in which Ms. Howard entertained famous poets and wits of the age, including Pope, Gay, and Swift. A ferry service operates during the summer from Ham House across the river; access on foot is a half-hour walk south along the west bank from Richmond Bridge. Group tours can be arranged. ⊠ *Richmond Rd., Twickenham, Richmond* ☎ *020/8892–5115* ⊕ *www.english-heritage. org.uk* ⊇ *£4.20* ☉ *Apr.–Oct., Sat. 10–2, Sun. and bank holidays 10–5; Nov., Dec., and Mar., prebooked tours only* Ⓤ *Richmond.*

ↄ **Richmond Park.** Charles I enclosed this one in 1637 for hunting purposes, like practically all the other parks. Unlike the others, however, Richmond Park still has wild red and fallow deer roaming its 2,470 acres of grassland and heath and the oldest oaks you're likely to see—vestiges of the forests that encroached on London from all sides in medieval times. White Lodge, inside the park, was built for George II in 1729. Edward VIII was born here; now it houses the Royal Ballet School. You can walk from the park past the fine 18th-century houses in and around Richmond Hill to the river, admiring first the view from the top. ■TIP➜ There's a splendid, protected view of St. Paul's Cathedral from King Henry VIII's Mound. Established in 1710, it measures 10 mi and is the bane of overenthusiastic town planners. Find it and you have a piece of magic in your sights. ☎ *020/8948–3209* ⊕ *www.royalparks.org.uk* ☉ *Mar.–Sept., daily 7–dusk; Oct.–Feb., daily 7:30–dusk* Ⓤ *Richmond, then Bus 371 or 65.*

QUICK BITES

The White Cross (⊠ *Water Lane, Richmond* ☎ *020/8940–6844*), on the site of a monastery, serves traditional pub grub.

ↄ ★ **Syon House and Park.** The residence of Their Graces the Duke and Duchess of Northumberland, this is one of England's most sumptuous stately homes, and certainly the only one that's near a Tube station. Set in a 55-acre park landscaped by Capability Brown, the core of the house is Tudor—Henry VIII's fifth wife, Catherine Howard, and the extremely short-lived monarch, Lady Jane Grey, made pit stops here before they

HAMPTON COURT PALACE

✉ *Hampton Court Palace, East Molesley, Surrey* ☎ *0844/482–7799* ⊕ *www.hrp.org.uk/hamptoncourtpalace* 🎫 *£14* ⊙ *Apr.–Oct., daily 10–6 (last ticket sold at 5); Nov.–Mar., daily 10–4:30 (last ticket sold at 3:30); check Web site before visiting* Ⓤ *Richmond, then Bus R68; National Rail, South West: Hampton Court Station, 35 mins from Waterloo.*

13

Today the royal palace that sits beside the slow-moving Thames gives you two palaces for the price of one: The magnificent Tudor redbrick mansion that was begun in 1514 by Cardinal Wolsey to impress the young Henry, and the larger 17th-century baroque offering, for which the graceful south wing was designed by Christopher Wren of St. Paul's fame. The first buildings of Hampton Court belonged to a religious order founded in the 11th century and were expanded over the years by its many subsequent residents, none more important than Henry VIII and his six wives. Henry spent a king's ransom (today's equivalent of £18 million or $27.5 million) expanding and refurbishing the palace.

TIPS

■ Avoid the queue and save by buying your tickets online.

■ In a group? Save nearly £10 on admission with a £38 family ticket (two adults, three children).

■ Choose which parts of the palace to explore based on a number of self-guided audio walking tours.

■ In summer months, consider arriving in style by riverboat (see A Tour of the Thames).

■ Come Christmastime, there's ice skating on a rink before the West Front of the palace—an unmissable mixture of pleasantry and pageantry.

■ Special programs, such as cooking demonstrations in the cavernous Tudor kitchens, also make history fun for young royal-watchers.

HIGHLIGHTS

If Tudor takes your fancy, wander through the **State Apartments,** hung with priceless paintings, and on to the wood-beamed magnificence of **Henry's Great Hall,** lined with tapestries and the mustiness of old, before taking in the strikingly azure ceiling of the **Chapel Royal.** Topping it all is the Great House of Easement, a lavatory that could sit 28 people at a time.

Feel a chill in the air? Watch out for the ghost of Henry VIII's doomed fifth wife, Catherine Howard, who literally lost her head yet apparently still screams her way along the **Haunted Gallery.** The latter-day baroque transformers of the palace, William and Mary, maintained beautiful **King's and Queen's Apartments, Georgian Rooms,** and fine collections of porcelain.

Don't miss the world's most famous maze, its ½ mi of pathways among clipped hedgerows still fiendish to negotiate. There's a trick, but we won't give it away here: it's much more fun to go and lose yourself.

AT A GLANCE

Dining at a Glance

BUDGET DINING	MODERATE DINING	EXPENSIVE DINING
Marquess Tavern, Modern British, 32 Canonbury St.	High Road Brasserie, Brasserie, 162–166 Chiswick High Rd.	River Café, Italian, Thames Wharf, Rainville Rd.
Ottolenghi, Café, 287 Upper St.	Princess Victoria, British, 217 Uxbridge Rd.	
	La Trompette, French, 5–7 Devonshire Rd.	

were sent to the Tower—but it was remodeled in the Georgian style in 1761 by famed decorator Robert Adam. He had just returned from studying the sights of classical antiquity in Italy and created two rooms here worthy of any Caesar: the entryway is an amazing study in black and white, pairing neoclassical marbles with antique bronzes, and the Ante-Room contains 12 enormous verd-antique columns surmounted by statues of gold—this, no less, was meant to be a waiting room for the duke's servants and retainers. The Red Drawing Room is covered with crimson Spitalfields silk, and the Long Gallery is one of Adam's noblest creations (it was used by Cary Grant and Robert Mitchum for a duel in the 1958 film *The Grass Is Greener*). Elsewhere on the beautiful, rolling parkland is a Victorian glass conservatory that's famous among connoisseurs for its charm, not surprising as the designer, Charles Fowler, was also responsible for the grand Covent Garden Flower Market. ■TIP➔ On certain bank holidays and Sundays in the summer you can take a miniature steam-train ride in the grounds. ⊠ *Syon Park, Brentford* ☎ *020/8560–0882* ⊕ *www.syonpark.co.uk* ⊠ *£9 for house, gardens, conservatory, and rose garden; £4.50 for gardens and conservatory* ⊗ *House late Mar.–Oct., Wed., Thurs., Sun., and bank holidays 11–5; gardens daily 10:30–dusk; last admission to both 1 hr before closing* Ⓤ *Gunnersbury, then Bus 237 or 267 to Brentlea stop.*

Tower Bridge

A TOUR OF THE THAMES

*"I have seen the Mississippi. That is muddy water.
I have seen the St. Lawrence. That is crystal water.
But the Thames is liquid history."*
—John Burns

The twists and turns of the Thames River through the heart of the capital make it London's best thoroughfare and most compelling viewing point. Once famous for sludge, silt, and sewage, the Thames is now the cleanest city river in the world. Whether you take a river cruise or a leisurely stroll along its banks and bridges, traveling on or alongside the river is an unforgettable way to soak up views of the city.

The Great Conservatory at Syon Park

HAMPTON COURT PALACE TO PUTNEY

Hampton Court Palace is a suitably lavish start or end to any trip on the Thames. The river skirts the grounds, giving magnificent views over the Tudor palace that Henry VIII and his daughter Elizabeth I made home, and continues north to **Kingston Bridge**, starting point for the river voyage of Jerome K. Jerome's *Three Men in a Boat* and home to hectic summer regattas. At **Teddington**, where the poet Alexander Pope and writer Horace Walpole entertained their female admirers in the 18th century, the river turns tidal but remains quiet and unspoiled all the way to **Kew**, passing herons and fine stately homes standing proud on the banks. From **Twickenham Bridge** you round the old deer park (to the south) and **Syon Park** (north), which has belonged to the Duke of Nor-

Waterlily House at Kew Gardens

thumberland's family for centuries. Beyond that is an even greater treat—the UNESCO World Heritage Site of **Kew Botanical Gardens**. All manner of rowboats set up for one, two, four, or eight people pull hard under **Chiswick Bridge** and **Barnes (railway) Bridge**, past the expensive riverside frontage of Chiswick Mall and under **Hammersmith Bridge**, to **Putney** and **Fulham**— smart urban villages facing each other across the banks.

Syon Park

Kew Botanical Gardens

Twickenham Br.

Richmond Landing Stage

Richmond Br.

Marble Hill Park

Eel Pie Island

Teddington

Kingston Br.

Bushy Park

0   1 mi

0   1 km

Hampton Ct. Br.

Hampton Court Palace

Hampton Court Pier

Gunnersbury Park

Kew Br.

Kew Pier

Furnival Gardens

Hammersmith Br.

Temperate House

Chiswick Mall

Barn Elms Water Works

Fulham

Chiswick Br.

Barnes Br.

Bishops Park

Barnes Common

Putney Br.

Hurlingham Park

Wandsworth Park

The stretch between Kew and Hammersmith is real rowing and riverside-pub territory, with a picturesque parade past Strand-on-the-Green by Kew Bridge.

ROWERS' ROW Every spring Britain's oldest universities, Oxford and Cambridge, compete not with their brains but with their brawn, in the **Boat Race**, which began in 1829. The race is 4¼ miles upstream from Putney Bridge to Chiswick Bridge: expect clashing oars, clenched teeth, and the occasional sinking (there have been six). The best views are from Hammersmith at the Surrey bend, which is also where most of the pubs are clustered. ⊕ www.theboatrace.org

A BRIEF HISTORY

An engraving by Claes Van Visscher showing Old London Bridge in 1616, with Southwark Cathedral in the foreground

The Thames has come a long way—and not just from its 344-km (214-mi) journey from a remote Gloucestershire meadow to the sea. In the mid-19th century, the river was dying, poisoned by sewers that flushed into the river. The "Big Stink" was so awful that cholera and typhoid killed more than 10,000 in 1853, and Parliament abandoned sitting in 1858. "The odour is hardly that of frankincense," said one contemporary of the 1884 drought that forced down water levels, leaving elegant Victorian nostrils exposed to slimy ooze on the banks.

Joseph Bazalgette, star civil engineer of his time, was commissioned to design a new sewage system, and by the 1900s nearly all was forgiven. (His efforts did not go unappreciated: Bazalgette was later knighted.) Today 7.2 million people get their drinking water from the Thames River.

WANDSWORTH TO BLACKFRIARS

Parliament

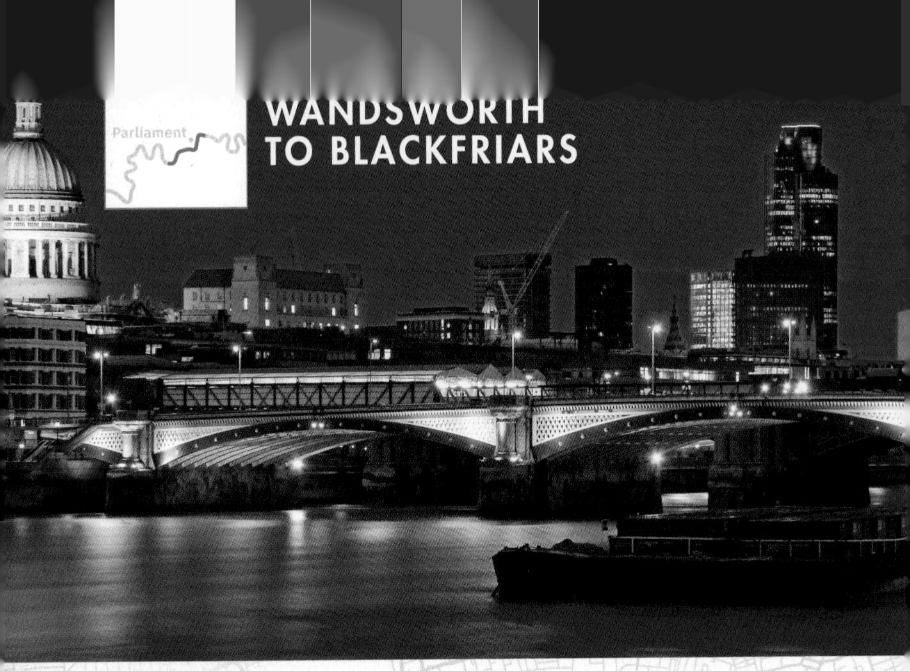

Blackfriars Bridge at night.

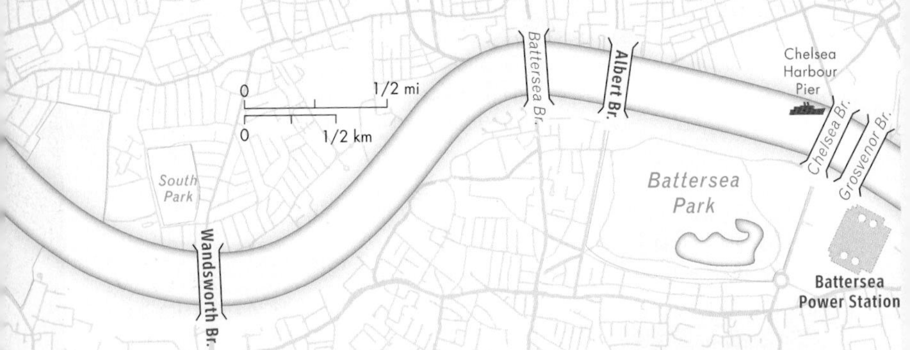

Battersea Br.
Albert Br.
Chelsea
Harbour
Pier
Chelsea Br.
Grosvenor Br.
0
1/2 mi
0
1/2 km
South
Park
Battersea
Park
Battersea
Power Station
Wandsworth Br.

WALKING THE THAMES

Even if you lack sea legs, you can still enjoy the river: not much beats a wander beside London's waterway. The Thames Path (www.nationaltrail.co.uk) follows the river 184 miles, from its source to the flood barriers in Greenwich. Some of the best riverside strolls:

- Hammersmith Bridge to Chiswick Mall
- Golden Jubilee Bridges to the South Bank's Queen's Walk
- Cleopatra's Needle to Parliament along Victoria Embankment
- Tate Modern to St. Paul's over Millennium Bridge

Beyond **Wandsworth Bridge**, the early part of this stretch by Battersea Bridge, rebuilt in 1890, was London's real industrial heartland, the southern side chock full of cottage housing for laborers, artisans at work, and factories.

View from London Eye (left); House's of Parliament (right)

The real treat of this stretch is the view of the **Houses of Parliament** and, beyond that, **Westminster Abbey**. **Victoria Embankment**, stretching all the way from Westminster to Blackfriars, was once all grim mudflats. In 1878 it became the country's first electrically illuminated street, and today its fine architecture, trees, and gardens are perfect strolling territory.

You can't miss the **London Eye**, whose parts were brought down the Thames one by one before being assembled on-location. Look out too for the London Aquarium and the Dalí museum, housed in the baroque-style County Hall.

Cleopatra's Needle, overlooking the Thames by Embankment, dates back to Heliopolis in 1450 BC. Look for World War I shrapnel holes and gouges at the base.

After **Albert Bridge**—glorious at night, with lights like luminescent pearls sweeping down on strings—the Thames is a metropolitan glory of a river, charging through fashionable **Chelsea** and past the now derelict **Battersea Power Station**, under Chelsea, Vauxhall and Lambeth Bridges, with **Lambeth Palace** to the south.

The **Golden Jubilee Bridges** by **Embankment**, two beautifully lit steel-cabled pedestrian walkways, are perfect for reaching the **South Bank**.

Look out for the golden eagle, a monument to World War I RAF fighters, and **Cleopatra's Needle**. For the ultimate double-decker bus-viewing moment, look at **Waterloo Bridge**, once known as Ladies Bridge because it was built by female labor during World War II. The bridge has great views of the South Bank.

Further on is the **Oxo Tower**, whose red-glass letters were designed in 1928 to spell out the brand name while circumventing tight laws on exterior advertising.

By **Blackfriars Bridge**, named after the monks who wore black robes and lived on the north bank during the Middle Ages, the river used to run red by the riverside tanneries and slaughterhouses.

Blackfriars Bridge

MILLENNIUM BRIDGE TO THAMES FLOOD BARRIER

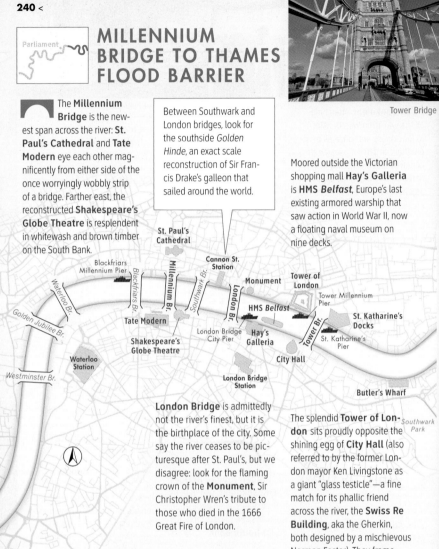

Tower Bridge

The **Millennium Bridge** is the newest span across the river: **St. Paul's Cathedral** and **Tate Modern** eye each other magnificently from either side of the once worryingly wobbly strip of a bridge. Farther east, the reconstructed **Shakespeare's Globe Theatre** is resplendent in whitewash and brown timber on the South Bank.

Between Southwark and London bridges, look for the southside *Golden Hinde*, an exact scale reconstruction of Sir Francis Drake's galleon that sailed around the world.

Moored outside the Victorian shopping mall **Hay's Galleria** is **HMS *Belfast***, Europe's last existing armored warship that saw action in World War II, now a floating naval museum on nine decks.

Blackfriars Millennium Pier
Waterloo Br.
Blackfriars Br.
Golden Jubilee Br.
Millennium Br.
St. Paul's Cathedral
Southwark Br.
Cannon St. Station
London Br.
Monument
Tower of London
Tower Millennium Pier
HMS *Belfast*
St. Katharine's Docks
Tate Modern
London Bridge City Pier
Hay's Galleria
Tower Br.
St. Katharine's Pier
Shakespeare's Globe Theatre
Waterloo Station
Westminster Br.
City Hall
London Bridge Station
Butler's Wharf
Southwark Park

London Bridge is admittedly not the river's finest, but it is the birthplace of the city. Some say the river ceases to be picturesque after St. Paul's, but we disagree: look for the flaming crown of the **Monument**, Sir Christopher Wren's tribute to those who died in the 1666 Great Fire of London.

The splendid **Tower of London** sits proudly opposite the shining egg of **City Hall** (also referred to by the former London mayor Ken Livingstone as a giant "glass testicle"—a fine match for its phallic friend across the river, the **Swiss Re Building**, aka the Gherkin, both designed by a mischievous Norman Foster). They frame the 1894 **Tower Bridge**, a magnificent feat of engineering and style, which leads past the elegant confines of **St. Katharine's Docks**, the trendy restaurants of **Butler's Wharf**, and the **Design Museum**.

LONDON BRIDGE

Viking invaders destroyed London Bridge in 1014, hence the nursery rhyme "London Bridge is falling down." By 1962, London Bridge really was falling down again, its 1831 incarnation unable to take the strain of traffic. It was saved by American tycoon Robert McCulloch, who—possibly confusing the bridge with its much more splendid neighbor, Tower Bridge—bought it in 1968 for $2.46 million and had it shipped, stone by stone, to Lake Havasu in Arizona.

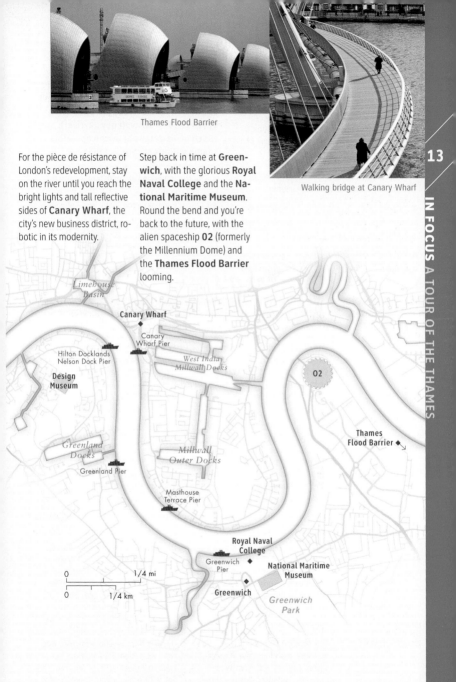

Thames Flood Barrier

Walking bridge at Canary Wharf

For the pièce de résistance of London's redevelopment, stay on the river until you reach the bright lights and tall reflective sides of **Canary Wharf**, the city's new business district, robotic in its modernity.

Step back in time at **Greenwich**, with the glorious **Royal Naval College** and the **National Maritime Museum**. Round the bend and you're back to the future, with the alien spaceship **O2** (formerly the Millennium Dome) and the **Thames Flood Barrier** looming.

Limehouse Basin

Canary Wharf

Canary Wharf Pier

Hilton Docklands Nelson Dock Pier

West India Millwall Docks

O2

Design Museum

Greenland Docks

Thames Flood Barrier

Greenland Pier

Millwall Outer Docks

Masthouse Terrace Pier

Royal Naval College

Greenwich Pier

National Maritime Museum

Greenwich

Greenwich Park

0 ————— 1/4 mi
0 ————— 1/4 km

PLANNING A THAMES BOAT TOUR

"On the smallest pretext of holiday or fine weather the mighty population takes to the boats," wrote Henry James in 1877. You can follow in the footsteps of James, who took a boat trip from Westminster to Greenwich, or make up your own itinerary.

■ Frequent daily tourist-boat services are at their height between April and October.

■ In most cases you can turn up at a pier, and the next departure won't be far away. However, it never hurts to book ahead if you can.

■ Westminster and Tower piers are the busiest starting points, usually with boats heading east.

■TIP➜ For a rundown of all the options, along with prices and timetables, contact **London River Services** (☎ 020/ 7222–1234 ⊕ www.tfl.gov.uk/river), which gives details of all the operators sailing various sections of the river.

■ The trip between Westminster Pier and the Tower of London takes about 30 minutes, as does the trip between the Tower and Greenwich.

■ A full round-trip can take several hours. Ask about flexible fares and hop on/off options at the various piers.

THE BEST WAYS TO EXPERIENCE THE THAMES WHILE...

GOING OFF THE BEATEN PATH (LITERALLY)	020/7928–3132	www.londonducktours.co.uk	£20
	London Ducktours offers sightseeing with a twist—amphibious patrol vehicles used in World War II have been painted like rubber duckies and traverse land and sea.	Departs from the London Eye (on land): Weekdays 10–2 every 30 mins, during the summer months 10–6; weekends 10–4 every 30 mins, during the summer months 10–6.	
SAVING TIME AND MONEY	020/7887–8888	www.tate.org.uk/tatetotate	£5 one-way
	The playfully polka-dotted *Tate Boat* ferries passengers across the river from the Tate Britain to the Tate Modern.	Departs from the pier at either museum: Daily every 40 mins. Approximately 18 mins. one-way.	
IMPRESSING A DATE OR CLIENT	020/7695–1800	www.bateauxlondon.com	£26–£37.50 (lunch), £75–£120 (dinner)
	For ultimate glamour (and expense), look into lunch and dinner cruises with **Bateaux London**, often formal affairs with surprisingly good two- to five-course meals. Variations include jazz brunch cruises on Sundays.	Departs from Embankment Pier for lunch: Apr.–Dec., Wed.–Sat. (also Tues. in Jul. and Aug.), 12; Jan.–Mar., Thur.–Sat., 12; for dinner: Apr.–Dec., daily 7:30; Jan.–Mar., Tue.–Sat., 7:30.	
ENJOYING ON-BOARD ENTERTAINMENT	020/7740–0400	www.citycruises.com	£75
	The *London Showboat* lives up to its name, with four-course meals, snazzy cabaret acts from West End musicals, and after-dinner dancing.	Departs from Westminster Pier: Apr.–Oct., Wed.–Sun. 7:30 PM; Nov., Dec., Mar., Thurs.–Sat. 7:30 PM; Jan.–Feb., Fri.–Sat. 7:30 PM (boarding starts 15 mins. prior to departure). Approximately 3½ hours. Book 48 hours in advance.	

Where to Eat

WORD OF MOUTH

"There are several branches of Wagamama around central London now. Don't be put off by long queues snaking out of the doorways—you won't have to wait long and the food is worth it. Large bowls of Chinese noodle soups or Japanese soba or ramen noodles, stir fries, etc. Not expensive. Long shared tables."

—Kippy

THE SCENE

Updated
by Alex
Wijeratna

London rivals New York, Paris, and Tokyo as one of the best places to eat in the world right now. The sheer diversity of restaurants here is unparalleled. Among the city's 6,700 restaurants are see-and-be-seen hot spots, casual ethnic eateries, innovative gastropubs, and temples to haute cuisine.

To measure London's spectacular culinary rise, note that it was once a common dictum that the British ate to live, whereas the French lived to eat. The best of British food—local, regional, seasonal, and meticulously sourced—is now all the rage and appears on more smart menus by the day. "Nose-to-tail" eating—where every scrap of meat is deemed fair game for the plate—has made a spectacular comeback at St. John in Clerkenwell, and fits perfectly with the new mood of austerity.

Meanwhile, *Hell's Kitchen* star Gordon Ramsay sets the highest bar at his Restaurant Gordon Ramsay in Chelsea, and the rest of the much-lauded haute cuisine scene is dominated by world-class masters. Marcus Wareing roars up on his mentor Ramsay's shoulder at Wareing's self-named place at the Berkeley, Michel Roux Jr. rules the roost at Le Gavroche in Mayfair, Eric Chavot sets a blistering pace at the Capital, Hélène Darroze does it for the girls at the Connaught, and Claude Bosi bosses things at Hibiscus.

For cheap eats, don't miss the city's unofficial dish, the ubiquitous Indian curry. The quality of other international cuisines also has grown in recent years, with London becoming known for its Malaysian, Spanish, Turkish, and North African restaurants. With all of the choices, traditional British food, when you track it down, appears as just one more exotic cuisine in the pantheon.

Whatever eating experience you seek, London can likely deliver. From dirt-cheap street food to posh multicourse meals, the city has become a destination for gustatory adventurers. In this chapter, we've uncovered the best of the best. Dig in, and enjoy!

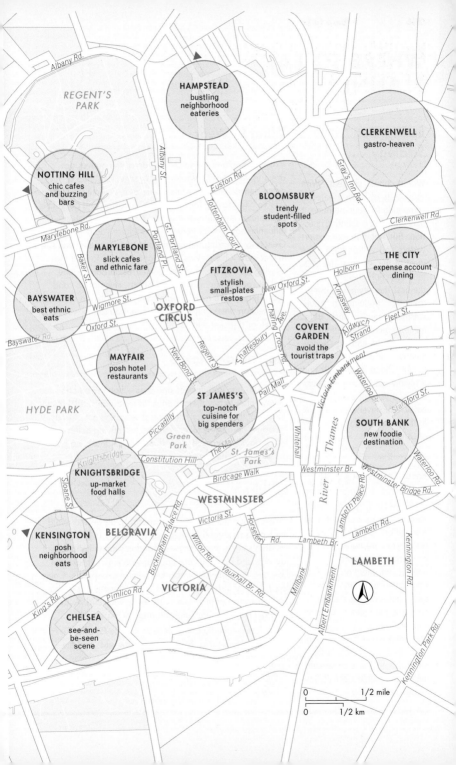

REGENT'S PARK

HAMPSTEAD
bustling neighborhood eateries

CLERKENWELL
gastro-heaven

NOTTING HILL
chic cafes and buzzing bars

BLOOMSBURY
trendy student-filled spots

MARYLEBONE
slick cafes and ethnic fare

FITZROVIA
stylish small-plates restos

THE CITY
expense account dining

OXFORD CIRCUS

BAYSWATER
best ethnic eats

COVENT GARDEN
avoid the tourist traps

MAYFAIR
posh hotel restaurants

HYDE PARK

ST JAMES'S
top-notch cuisine for big spenders

SOUTH BANK
new foodie destination

Green Park

St. James's Park

KNIGHTSBRIDGE
up-market food halls

WESTMINSTER

Thames River

LAMBETH

KENSINGTON
posh neighborhood eats

BELGRAVIA

VICTORIA

CHELSEA
see-and-be-seen scene

Albany Rd.
Albany St.
Euston Rd.
Gray's Inn Rd.
Clerkenwell Rd.
Marylebone Rd.
Portland Pl.
Gt. Portland St.
Tottenham Court Rd.
New Oxford St.
Holborn
Kingsway
Fleet St.
Baker St.
Wigmore St.
Oxford St.
Bayswater Rd.
New Bond St.
Regent St.
Shaftesbury Ave.
Charing Cross Rd.
Aldwych
Strand
Piccadilly
Pall Mall
Victoria Embankment
Waterloo Br.
Stamford St.
Waterloo Rd.
Knightsbridge
Constitution Hill
The Mall
Birdcage Walk
Whitehall
Westminster Br.
Westminster Bridge Rd.
Sloane St.
Victoria St.
Horseferry Rd.
Lambeth Palace Rd.
Lambeth Rd.
Kennington Rd.
Buckingham Palace Rd.
Wilton Rd.
Vauxhall Br. Rd.
Lambeth Br.
Millbank
Albert Embankment
Kennington Park Rd.
King's Rd.
Pimlico Rd.

0   1/2 mile
0   1/2 km

WHERE TO EAT PLANNER

Eating Out Strategy

Where should you eat? With thousands of London eateries competing for your attention, it may seem like a daunting question. But fret not—our expert writers and editors have done most of the legwork. The 100-plus selections here represent the best this city has to offer—from hot pudding to haute cuisine. Search "Best Bets" for top recommendations by price, cuisine, and experience. Sample local flavor in the neighborhood features. Or find a review quickly in the neighborhood listings. Delve in and enjoy. Whichever way you look at it, you're sure to get a taste of London!

Reservations

Plan ahead if you're determined to snag a sought-after reservation. Some renowned restaurants are booked weeks or months in advance. In the reviews, we mention reservations only when they're essential or not accepted, though it's always a good idea to book as far ahead as you can and reconfirm when you arrive in London. Note that some top restaurants also now take credit-card details and charge a penalty fee if you're a no-show.

What to Wear

When in England's style capital, do as the natives do: dress up to eat out. Whatever your style, dial it up a notch. Have some fun while you're at it. Pull out the clothes you've been saving for a "special" occasion and get a little glamorous. As unfair as it seems, the way you look can influence how you're treated—and where you're seated. Generally speaking, jeans and a button-down shirt will suffice at most table-service restaurants in the £ to ££ range. Moving up from there, many pricier restaurants require jackets, and some insist on ties. Shorts, sweatpants, and sports jerseys are rarely appropriate. Note that in reviews we mention dress only when men are required to wear a jacket, or a jacket and tie.

Tipping and Taxes

Do not tip bar staff in pubs and bars—though you can always offer to buy them a drink. In restaurants, tip 10% to 12.5% of the check for full meals if service is not already included; tip a small token if you're just having coffee or tea. If paying by credit card, double-check that a tip has not already been included in the bill.

Children

Unless your children behave impeccably, it's best to avoid the high-class establishments; you're unlikely to find a children's menu there, anyway. London's many Italian restaurants and pizzerias are popular with kids. Or take the little ones to Chinatown for a fun cultural experience. China House serves kids' portions and offers Chinese arts-and-crafts activities from 1 PM to 4 PM every weekend. Activities vary but include magicians and origami experts.

Other family-friendly establishments include Giraffe, Pizza Express, Wagamama, Sticky Fingers, Tootsies, and the pasta chain Carluccio's.

Hours

In London you can find breakfast all day, but it's generally served between 7 AM and 10:30 AM. Workmen's cafés and sandwich bars for office workers are sometimes open from 7 AM, more upscale cafés from 7 AM to 10:30 AM. Lunch is between noon and 2:30 PM. Tea, often a meal in itself, is taken between 3:30 PM and 6 PM, and dinner or supper is typically eaten between 7 PM and 10 PM, though it can be taken earlier. Many ethnic restaurants, especially Indian, serve food until midnight. Sunday is proper lunch day, and some restaurants are open for lunch only. Other restaurants are closed entirely on Sunday and on public holidays. Over the Christmas period, London virtually shuts down and it seems only hotels are prepared to feed travelers. Unless otherwise noted, the restaurants listed in this guide are open daily for lunch and dinner.

Prices

The democratization of restaurants in London has not translated into smaller checks, and London is an extortionate city by global standards. A modest meal for two can easily cost £40, and the £100-a-head meal is not unknown. Damage-control strategies include making lunch your main meal—the top places have bargain midday menus—going for early evening deals, bringing your own wine to an ethnic eatery with a BYOB license, or sharing an à la carte entrée and ordering a second appetizer instead. (Note that an appetizer, usually known as a "starter" or "first course," is sometimes called an "entrée," as it is in France, and that entrées in England are dubbed "main courses" or simply "mains.") Seek out fixed-price menus, and watch for hidden extras on the check, that is, bread or vegetables charged separately.

WHAT IT COSTS IN POUNDS

	£	££	£££	££££	£££££
At Dinner	under £10	£10–£16	£17–£23	£24–£32	over £32

Price per person for an average main course or equivalent combination of smaller dishes at dinner. Note: If a restaurant offers only prix-fixe (set-price) meals, it has been given the price category that reflects the full prix-fixe price.

In This Chapter

14

Credit Cards

American Express, MasterCard, and Visa are accepted in most upscale restaurants, but pubs, small cafés, and indie eateries may take cash only.

Quick Bites

Also look for Quick Bites and Feeling Peckish listings in the neighborhood exploring sections.

BEST BETS FOR LONDON DINING

With thousands of restaurants to choose from, how will you decide where to eat? Fodor's writers and editors have selected their favorite restaurants by price, cuisine, and experience in the Best Bets lists below. In the first column, Fodor's Choice properties represent the "best of the best" in every price category. You can also search by neighborhood for excellent eats—just peruse the following pages. Or find specific details about a restaurant in the full reviews, listed later in the chapter by neighborhood.

Fodor's Choice ★

Anchor & Hope, p. 266
Boxwood Café, p. 269
Boundary, p. 263
Busaba Eathai, p. 282
Giaconda Dining Room, p. 279
Great Queen Street, p. 280
Hélène Darroze at the Connaught, p. 276
Hereford Road, p. 272
J Sheekey, p. 280
La Petite Maison, p. 276
Le Gavroche, p. 276
Marcus Wareing at the Berkeley, p. 270
Moro, p. 265
Scott's, p. 277
St. John, p. 265
Wild Honey, p. 277

Best by Price

£

Busaba Eathai, p. 282
Cha Cha Moon, p. 279
Côte, p. 279
Tayyabs, p. 266
Wahaca, p. 281

££

Anchor & Hope, p. 266
Giaconda Dining Room, p. 279
Great Queen Street, p. 280
Racine, p. 269
Tom Ilić, p. 267

£££

Barrafina, p. 281
Boxwood Café, p. 269
Hereford Road, p. 272
J Sheekey, p. 280
Quo Vadis, p. 280

Wild Honey, p. 277
The Wolseley, p. 278

££££

Boundary, p. 263
The Capital, p. 269
Chez Bruce, p. 266
La Petite Maison, p. 276
St. John, p. 265

£££££

Hélène Darroze at the Connaught, p. 276
Le Gavroche, p. 276
Marcus Wareing at the Berkeley, p. 270
Scott's, p. 277

Best by Cuisine

MODERN BRITISH

Anchor & Hope, p. 266
Hereford Road, p. 272
Great Queen Street, p. 280
Magdalen, p. 267
St. John, p. 265

CHINESE

Baozi Inn, p. 278
Cha Cha Moon, p. 279
Hung Tao, p. 257
Leong's Legends, p. 260
Royal China, p. 272

FRENCH

The Capital, p. 269
Galvin Bistrot de Luxe, p. 262
La Petite Maison, p. 276
Hélène Darroze at the Connaught, p. 276
Marcus Wareing at the Berkeley, p. 270

INDIAN

Hot Stuff, p. 264
Indian Zing, p. 264
Rasoi Restaurant, p. 270
Tayyabs, p. 266
Vama, p. 264

ITALIAN

Bocca di Lupo, p. 282
Cecconi's, p. 275
L'Anima, p. 263
Polpo, p. 260
River Café, p. 271

JAPANESE

Jin Kichi, p. 251
Nobu Berkeley Street, p. 277
Roka, p. 251
Zuma, p. 270

SEAFOOD

Golden Hind, p. 274
J Sheekey, p. 280
Scott's, p. 277
Sweetings, p. 266

SPANISH

Barrafina, p. 281
Dehesa, p. 261
Moro, p. 265
Salt Yard, p. 251
Tapas Brindisa, p. 253

STEAK HOUSE

Electric Brasserie, p. 273
Gaucho Grill, p. 275
Hawksmoor, p. 252
Hereford Road, p. 272
Le Relais de Venise l'Entrecôte, p. 251

THAI AND VIETNAMESE

Busabe Eathai, p. 282
Cicada, p. 252
E&O, p. 273
Sông Qué Café, p. 265

Best by Experience

BRASSERIES

Cecconi's, p. 275
Côte, p. 279
High Road Brasserie, p. 271
PJ's Bar & Grill, p. 267
The Wolseley, p. 278

BRUNCH

Côte, p. 279
High Road Brasserie, p. 271
The Modern Pantry, p. 253

PJ's Bar & Grill, p. 267
Tom's Kitchen, p. 255

BUSINESS DINING

Corrigan's Mayfair, p. 275
The Greenhouse, p. 275
Hibiscus, p. 276
Plateau, p. 265
The Square, p. 277

CELEB SPOTTING

J Sheekey, p. 280
La Petite Maison, p. 276
Nobu Berkeley Street, p. 277
Scott's, p. 277
The Wolseley, p. 278

GASTROPUBS

Anchor & Hope, p. 266
Great Queen Street, p. 280
Marquess Tavern, p. 270
Pig's Ear, p. 268
Princess Victoria, p. 271

GOOD FOR GROUPS

Bumpkin, p. 272
Gaucho Grill, p. 275
Lemonia, p. 262
Tayyabs, p. 266
Zuma, p. 270

GREAT VIEW

Plateau, p. 265
River Café, p. 271
Skylon, p. 267
Tate Modern Restaurant, p. 254

HISTORIC

Maison Bertaux, p. 282
Rules, p. 281

Simpson's Tavern, p. 265
Sweetings, p. 266

HOTEL DINING

The Capital, p. 269
The Grill at the Dorchester, p. 275
Hélène Darroze at the Connaught, p. 276
Alain Ducasse at the Dorchester, p. 258
Marcus Wareing at the Berkeley, p. 270

HOT SPOTS

Bocca di Lupo, p. 282
Boundary, p. 263
Cecconi's, p. 275
Nobu Berkeley Street, p. 277
Scott's, p. 277

LATE-NIGHT DINING

Boxwood Café, p. 269
Cafe Boheme, p. 260
J Sheekey, p. 280
Royal China, p. 272

LOCAL FAVORITES

Chez Bruce, p. 266
La Trompette, p. 271
Lemonia, p. 262
Princess Victoria, p. 271
Tom Ilić, p. 267

LUNCH PRIX-FIXE

Arbutus, p. 281
The Capital, p. 269

Hibiscus, p. 276
Le Gavroche, p. 276
Wild Honey, p. 277

ROMANTIC

Clos Maggiore, p. 261
J Sheekey, p. 280
Rasoi Restaurant, p. 270
Hélène Darroze at the Connaught, p. 276
Scott's, p. 277

QUIET MEAL

Bibendum, p. 269
The Greenhouse, p. 275
L'Oranger, p. 278
Hibiscus, p. 276

SPECIAL OCCASION

Le Caprice, p. 278
Le Gavroche, p. 276
Marcus Wareing at the Berkeley, p. 270
Restaurant Gordon Ramsay, p. 269
Scott's, p. 277

WINE LISTS

Angelus, p. 272
The Greenhouse, p. 275
Princess Victoria, p. 271
Terroirs, p. 261
The Square, p. 277

14

BLOOMSBURY, FITZROVIA, REGENT'S PARK, AND HAMPSTEAD

From the bluestocking and intellectual haunts of Bloomsbury and the chic dining scene of Fitzrovia to the leafy tranquillity of Hampstead, this area offers diverse dining experiences.

Bloomsbury is known as London's literary and academic center with the British Museum, the University of London, Royal Academy of Dramatic Arts, leading hospitals, and numerous bookstores. Although Bloomsbury is known more as a residential area, there are many hotels in Russell Square, which is a convenient central location for visitors. To the west of Bloomsbury, Fitzrovia has striking town houses as well as a wealth of stylish shops, hip bars, and trendy restaurants.

Hampstead village lies in the north of London, and is best described as a leafy, quiet hilltop suburb. This neighborhood is a popular excursion destination for Londoners who want to escape the city with a stroll through peaceful Hampstead Heath to appreciate its meadows and woodland. The area is steeped in artistic and literary history. Now it has the highest concentration of millionaires in Britain, but nonetheless Hampstead has a number of cozy cafés, restaurants, and bustling pubs.

SUNDAY ROAST

Experience classic English flavor at one of Hampstead's homey Georgian pubs: The Wells (✉ *30 Well Walk* ☎ *020/7794–3785* ✛ *2:E1*) serves a traditional Sunday roast with roast beef, Yorkshire pudding, and roasted vegetables for about £16. For the "olde English" pub experience, complete with dim lighting, potbellied stove, and wood-paneled walls, soak up the ambience at the Holly Bush (✉ *22 Holly Mount* ☎ *020/7435–2892* ✛ *1:F1*), housed in a 200-year-old building. The upscale pub fare emphasizes organic and local products, with homemade pies (try beef and Harvey's ale) and a Sunday roast.

DINING TWO WAYS

	SAVE	SPLURGE
French	Le Relais de Venise l'entrecôte (⊠ 120 Marylebone La., Fitzrovia ☎ 020/7486–0878 ✛ 1:H3) is a beloved no-choice steak, fries, and walnut salad Parisian-style brasserie.	L'Autre Pied (⊠ 5–7 Blandford St., Fitzrovia ☎ 020/7486–9696 ✛ 1:G3) showcases chef Marcus Eaves's exemplary Modern French cuisine in an ultrastylish setting.
Gastropub/ Modern European	Konstam at the Prince Albert (⊠ 2 Acton St., Bloomsbury ☎ 020/7833–5040 ✛ 2:D2) cuts down on CO2 and sources 90% of its produce within the M25 London orbital—to inventive and fantastic effect.	Angela Hartnett oversees York & Albany (⊠ 127– 129 Parkway, Regent's Park ☎ 020/7388–3344 ✛ 1:H1), a 1826 John Nash converted coaching house and now swish boutique hotel/ bar/deli and marvelous restaurant.
Japanese charcoal-grilling	Hampstead legend Jin Kichi (⊠ 73 Heath St., Hampstead ☎ 020/7794–6158 ✛ 1:F1) serves traditional char-grilled dishes amid paper lanterns. Meals are reasonably priced and weekend set lunches are £8.250 to £15.10.	Roka (⊠ 37 Charlotte St., Fitzrovia ☎ 020/7580–6464 ✛ 3:C2) has a fabulous robata grill that showcases modern offerings, like black cod or chicken skewers.

DINING BY CUISINE

Bistro
Galvin Bistrot de Luxe, £££
Seafood
North Sea Fish Restaurant, ££
Modern French
Pied à Terre, ££££
Greek
Lemonia, ££

14

GLOBAL TAPAS

The small-plates trend is catching on in London, especially in Bloomsbury and Fitzrovia. Here's where to go: **Fino** (⊠ 33 Charlotte St., Fitzrovia ☎ 020/7813–8010 ✛ 3:C2) serves upscale Spanish tapas in an elegant basement dining room. Select a few dishes or try a set menu. At **Salt Yard** (⊠ 54 Goodge St., Fitzrovia ☎ 020/7637–0657 ✛ 3:B2) the small plates have a Spanish–Italian twist. And **Siam Central** (⊠ 14 Charlotte St., Fitzrovia ☎ 020/7436–7460 ✛ 3:C3) is a popular spot that offers 30 "Thai tapas" for a new spin.

THE CITY, CLERKENWELL, AND SOUTH BANK

Clerkenwell has long been gastro-heaven, but now that The City stays busy weekends, and the South Bank is firmly on the foodie map, the area is a prominent dining destination.

Unrepentant business types troop over to **Hawksmoor** (✉ 157 Commercial St., The City ☎ 020/7247–7392 ✛ 2:H4) for 35-day-aged char-grilled Longhorn steaks. Farther north, there's a more trendy, relaxed vibe, with gastropubs such as the **Peasant** (✉ 240 St. John St., Islington ☎ 020/7336–7726 ✛ 2:F3) attracting media types and nearby City University journalism students. **Cicada** (✉ 132–136 St. John St., Islington ☎ 020/7608–1550 ✛ 2:F3) does consistently high-quality Far Eastern bites at fair prices, and **Moro** (✉ 34–36 Exmouth Market, Islington ☎ 20/7833–8336; see review) is a voguish Iberian stalwart on Exmouth Market.

On the South Bank a short walk from London Bridge Tube, it's possible to eat well on the Thames riverbank at the Design Museum's **Blueprint Café** (✉ Design Museum, 28 Shad Thames, Shad Thames ☎ 020/7378–7031 ✛ 5:H1).

UNDER £10

You can get smoked mackerel superfood salad and pecan pie at "fresh fast food" restaurant **Leon** (✉ 12 Ludgate Circus, Blackfriars ☎ 020/7489–1580 ✛ 2:F5) for less than a tenner. **Tas** (✉ 72 Borough High St., Borough ☎ 020/7403–7200 ✛ 5:H1) serves accessible Turkish food such as grilled spicy sausages and lamb kebabs and has set menus from £8.65. For "olde English" fare, sit at a barrel and quaff half a dozen wild Colchester oysters for £9.30 opposite Borough fruit-and-veg market at **Wright Brothers Oyster & Porter House** (✉ 11 Stoney St., Borough ☎ 020/7403–9554 ✛ 5:H1).

OFF THE TOURIST TRACK

CHEF-CENTRIC CLERKENWELL

The area where the starchiness of The City fades into the relaxed artiness of Islington is a fertile ground for chefs and restaurants. Within walking distance of Farringdon Tube you can find **Club Gascon** (✉ *57 West Smithfield, Clerkenwell* ☎ *020/7796–0600;* see review), serving exquisite southwestern French cuisine, or make your way to the **Clerkenwell Kitchen** (✉ *27–31 Clerkenwell Close, Clerkenwell* ☎ *020/7101–9959* ✛ *2:F3*) where the focus is on organic, seasonal, and sustainable dishes.

Just around the corner, New Zealander Anna Hansen's the **Modern Pantry** (✉ *47–48 St. John's Sq., Clerkenwell* ☎ *020/7553–9210* ✛ *2:F3*) is doing something special with modern fusion food in this calm and clean Georgian all-day pantry and deli on St. John's Square. Farther up, you could easily miss the minimalist white frontage of **St. John** (✉ *26 St. John St., Smithfield* ☎ *020/7251–0848;* see review), but don't—Fergus Henderson's temple to British nose-to-tail carnivorous eating is famed for its no-nonsense approach to offal and all bits in between. Try the signature roast bone marrow–and-parsley salad.

BUSTLING BOROUGH MARKET

Now 250 years old, Borough Market is a favorite with London's top chefs and foodies alike. From Thursday to Saturday, the unassuming location at London Bridge is packed with Londoners and tourists eager to pick up the finest and freshest food in the capital. There are more than 90 stalls, plus shops like **Neal's Yard Dairy** (✉ *6 Park St., Borough* ☎ *020/7367–0799* ✛ *5:H1*), where truckles of Stilton cheese are stacked floor to ceiling. Foodies keen on sampling roast beef with all the trimmings should head to **Roast** (✉ *Floral Hall, Stoney St., Borough Market, Borough* ☎ *020/7940–1300* ✛ *5:H1*). For Spanish Joselito ham, crema Catalana, and Manzanilla sherry, try no-bookings Spanish **Tapas Brindisa** (✉ *18–20 Southwark St., Borough* ☎ *020/7357–8880* ✛ *5:H1*).

14

DINING BY CUISINE

British
Canteen, ££
Simpson's Tavern ££
St. John, £££
St. John Bread & Wine, ££
Café
E Pellicci, £
Eastern European
Baltic, ££
French
Boundary, £££
Italian
L'Anima, £££
Mediterranean
Moro, £££
Modern British
Anchor & Hope, £££
Magdalen, ££
Modern European
Skylon, £££
Tom Ilić, ££
Modern French
Chez Bruce, £££
Club Gascon, ££££
Plateau, £££££
Pakistani
Lahore Kebab House, £
Tayyabs, £
Seafood
Sweetings, £££
Vietnamese
Sông Qué Café, ££

KENSINGTON, CHELSEA, AND KNIGHTSBRIDGE

If you're fabulous, famous, wealthy, or all three, chances are you'll be living—and dining—in one of these neighborhoods among the world-class museums and fantastic shops.

Kensington, Chelsea, and Knightsbridge have some of the city's best restaurants and shops. (Do Gordon Ramsay and Harvey Nichols ring a bell?) Chelsea, made famous in the swinging '60s, is where today's yummy mummies bomb around in Range Rovers, which locals have nicknamed "Chelsea tractors." Known for its shopping, Chelsea's restaurants range from glamorous boîtes to little places ideal for gossip and a bite on the go.

In upscale Knightsbridge, you'll find Harrods department store and the high-end fashion boutiques of Sloane Street, and the restaurants are just as polished as the residents. Come here for an amazing dining experience, but don't expect bargains. Nearby, Kensington is a residential neighborhood with a wider range of restaurants, from little French bistros to funky Vietnamese hideaways.

CULTURAL EATS

The food's almost as good as the art at London's best cultural spaces. Marvel at the masterpieces before bagging a seat with a view at the **National Dining Rooms** (✉ *The National Gallery, Trafalgar Sq., St. James's* ☎ 020/7747–2525 ✛ *5:C1*) for Modern British fare. The stunning view of the Thames is the draw at the **Tate Modern Restaurant** (✉ *Southbank* ☎ 020/7887–8888 ✛ *1:C6*). Try Cornish haddock or peach crumble. Inside the famous auction house, **Cafe at Sotheby's** (✉ *34–35 New Bond St., Mayfair* ☎ 020/7293–5077 ✛ *5:A1*) attracts a classy crowd for spatchcock chicken, and bargain afternoon tea services.

PIT STOPS FOR SHOPPERS

Whether you're looking for a quick bite or a more relaxing meal, there are plenty of options for every budget.

Londoners love **Wagamama** (✉ *Lower ground floor, Harvey Nichols, 109–125 Knightsbridge* ☎ *020/7235-5250* ⊹ *4:F1*) for its healthful, cheap, and cheerful noodles and rice dishes. This branch is inside Harvey Nichols department store.

Savvy shoppers seek out the bargain £8 set lunches and the sensational Modern European cuisine at **Launceston Place** (✉ *1a Launceston Pl., Kensington* ☎ *020/7937-6912* ⊹ *4:B1*), hidden away in Kensington Village.

The closest thing to an authentic American barbecue shack in central London, the **Big Easy** (✉ *332–334 Kings Rd., Chelsea* ☎ *020/7352-4071* ⊹ *4:D4*) serves huge portions of barbecue ribs, Maine lobster, and pulled-pork sandwiches, all washed down by tasty margaritas.

Inside the Sloane Square hotel, the **Chelsea Brasserie** (✉ *7–12 Sloane Sq., Chelsea* ☎ *020/7881-5999* ⊹ *4:G2*) is a buzzy and swish place to have lunch on Sloane Square.

A more casual option is the **Pig's Ear** (✉ *35 Old Church St., Chelsea* ☎ *020/7352-2908; see review*), where you can start with beers in the saloon before enjoying a meal in the dining room. The deep-fried pigs' ears aren't for the fainthearted.

RISING STAR: TOM AIKENS

Tom Aikens was the youngest British chef to be awarded two Michelin stars. His eponymous restaurant (✉ *43 Elystan St., Chelsea* ☎ *020/7584-2003*) is one of the finest in town. It offers unexpected riffs on classic preparations, like John Dory with almonds and sea bass and pistachio.

Tom's Kitchen (✉ *27 Cale St., Chelsea* ☎ *020/7349-0202* ⊹ *4:E3*) is brilliant for breakfast and brunch, with a full English breakfast with all the trimmings for £12.50.

DINING BY CUISINE

American
PJ's Bar & Grill, ££
Brasserie
Racine, £££
French
Aubaine, ££
The Capital, £££££
Restaurant Gordon Ramsay, £££££
Indian
Rasoi Restaurant, ££££
Italian
Zafferano, ££££
Japanese
Zuma, ££££
Modern British
Bibendum, £££
The Pig's Ear, ££
Modern European
Boxwood Café, £££
Marcus Wareing at the Berkeley, £££££

14

NOTTING HILL AND BAYSWATER

Notting Hill or Notting Hell? Notting Hill's trendy atmosphere, designer shops, and oh-so-hip residents, and Bayswater's ethnic eateries, entice Londoners and travelers in droves.

Notting Hill has a reputation as one of London's more fashionable neighborhoods, with numerous boutiques, chic cafés, pâtisseries and restaurants, buzzing bars, and the famous Portobello Road Market's collection of antiques shops, vintage-clothing stands, and delicious food stalls. The gentrification of Notting Hill has led to hordes of bankers and high flyers moving to the area, and hence prices are stratospheric. If you are in London at the end of August, be sure to check out the revelry and fanfare of the multiethnic Notting Hill Carnival street parade—a celebration of West Indian culture.

Bayswater is seedier, more transient, and known for its diversity. This neighborhood's main artery, Queensway, boasts some of the best cheap ethnic restaurants in London. Here, the Greek, Indian, Chinese, and Persian restaurants are all cheek by jowl. Affordable accommodation and shops are plentiful here, making this a popular destination for visitors.

SNACKING SPOT

Portobello Road Market is one of London's most popular outdoor street markets. Get there early on Saturday morning (the market is open 8 AM–6 PM) to beat the crowds. Peruse the antiques and vintage clothes, and when you've built up an appetite, head to the north end of the market for snacks. You'll find fresh fruit and vegetable stands, bakeries, olive and cheese purveyors, and numerous hot food stalls peddling sweet and savory crêpes, hamburgers, wraps, fried prawns, noodles, kebabs, and spicy German sausages.

How to get there: Take the Tube to Ladbroke Grove or Notting Hill Gate station and follow the signs (and crowds).

A GASTROPUB TOUR

These upscale pubs specialize in the kind of high-quality, innovative fare in a low-key bar setting. The **Cow Dining Rooms** (⌂ *9 Westbourne Park Rd., Notting Hill* ☎ *020/7221–0021; see review*) is one of the best-known gastropubs in London. Eat oysters and Guiness at the stylish bar or head upstairs to the slightly more formal dining room. **The Westbourne** (⌂ *101 Westbourne Park Villas, Notting Hill* ☎ *020/7221–1332* ✛ *1:A3*) attracts a good-looking crowd and serves hearty regional food and rustic dishes, with specials like cuttlefish and capers and roast pheasant and bacon. Stop in at cozy **Prince Bonaparte** (⌂ *80 Chepstow Rd., Notting Hill* ☎ *020/7313–9491* ✛ *1:B4*), to try one of their Modern European specialties like beef carpaccio with Parmesan and almonds. The quintessential **Ladbroke Arms** (⌂ *54 Ladbroke Rd., Notting Hill* ☎ *020/7727–6648* ✛ *1:A5*) is an upmarket Sloany neighborhood gastropub. The menu changes frequently, but chocolate fondant is a trademark specialty.

CHEAP EATS

If you're looking for a filling meal that's not too pricey, head to Bayswater. **Alounak** (⌂ *44 Westbourne Grove, Bayswater* ☎ *020/7229–4158* ✛ *1:B4*) is a local favorite featuring superb Iranian cuisine served in a comfortable dining room. **Hung Tao** (⌂ *51 Queensway, Queensway* ☎ *020/7727–5753* ✛ *1:B4*) is unprepossessing but the Chinese soups, noodles, and barbecue pork all pack a punch. **Hereford Road** (⌂ *3 Hereford Rd., Bayswater* ☎ *020/7727–1144; see review* ✛ *1:B4*) serves unfussy British seasonal fare from impeccable sources. Enjoy Middlewhite pork and buttermilk pudding in stylish booths. The expansive **Le Café Anglais** (⌂ *8 Porchester Gardens, Queensway* ☎ *020/7221–1415* ✛ *1:C4*) is a 150-seat Parisian-style rôtisserie. Order Parmesan custard with anchovy toast, or spit-roast chicken with lemon thyme. Weekday lunch is £16.50. Expect a swift queue at no-bookings legend **Royal China** (⌂ *13 Queensway, Queensway* ☎ *020/7221–2535; see review* ✛ *1:B5*) for steaming dim sum.

DINING BY CUISINE

Asian
E&O, £££
Mandalay, £
Brasserie
Electric Brasserie, ££
British
Bumpkin, ££
Julie's, £££
Chinese
Royal China, ££
French
Angelus, £££
Middle Eastern
Alounak, ££
Modern British
The Cow Dining Rooms, £££
Hereford Road, £££
Modern European
Notting Hill Brasserie, ££££
Modern French
The Ledbury, ££££

14

ST. JAMES'S, MAYFAIR, AND MARYLEBONE

Mayfair and St. James's—home to Buckingham Palace and Clarence House, where Prince Charles and Camilla live—have a decidedly old-world, royal feel. Appropriately, most of the restaurants here are fit for a king or queen.

This is where you'll find London's top restaurants, including Le Gavroche, Le Caprice, and L'Oranger—dining experiences that are geared toward a well-heeled, deep-pocketed clientele. Mere mortals should make reservations well in advance to dine at any of these restaurants for dinner. But last-minute tables often crop up, and lunching here can be a great money-saving strategy.

If you're looking for something more low-key and wallet-friendly, head north to Marylebone, where the scenery changes dramatically. Old-world elegance is replaced by funky little cafés and restaurants with an indie spirit. Everything from Moroccan and Turkish to Thai is available here, as well as numerous local favorites. Just follow your nose. Below are a number of places that catch the eye and are doing particularly well.

POSH NOSHING

Some of London's finest restaurants can be found inside its swish hotels. **Alain Ducasse at the Dorchester** (⊠ *53 Park La., Mayfair* ☎ *20/7629–8866* ✥ *1:H6*) oversees intricate modern Franch haute cuisine in a sleek setting at the Dorchester on Park Lane. Admirable Frenchwoman Hélène Darroze shows off virtuoso skills at her self-named dining room at the **Connought** (⊠ *16 Carlos Pl., Mayfair* ☎ *020/3147–7200*; see review), and Marcus Wareing nears perfection at his eponymous cathedral to haute cuisine at the **Berkeley in Knightsbridge** (⊠ *Wilton Pl., Knightsbridge* ☎ *020/7235–1200*; see review).

LONDON'S HOTTEST TABLES

These restaurants are more than just see-and-be-seen hot spots—excellent food adds to the buzz. If you're looking to save, visit at lunch, when the set menu is usually half of what it would cost to eat there at night.

✗ **Great Queen Street:** It's always packed at Covent Garden's top gastropub, which serves old-school British classics in a stripped-down oak-floor-and-table saloon. (⊠ *32 Great Queen St., Covent Garden* ☎ *020/7242–0622, see review* ✛ *3:G4*)

✗ **Giaconda Dining Room:** Try inventive dishes like crispy pigs' trotters and egg mayonnaise at ridiculously low prices at this Australian-run beacon on London's "Tin Pan Alley." (⊠ *9 Denmark St., Soho* ☎ *020/7240–3344, see review* ✛ *3:D4*)

✗ **Wild Honey:** Wild Honey scores with inventive Modern European dishes at knock-down prices in swanky Mayfair. Set lunch comes in at less than £19. (⊠ *12 St. George St., Mayfair* ☎ *020/7758–9160, see review* ✛ *3:A5*)

✗ **Scott's:** The A-list dodge the paparazzi and come here to celebrate. Seafood from stone bass to goujons of lemon sole is enjoyed in a fashionable salon and oyster bar. (⊠ *20 Mount St., Mayfair* ☎ *020/7495–7309, see review* ✛ *1:G5*)

✗ **Hibiscus:** Claude Bosi moved lock, stock, and barrel from Ludlow to Mayfair and now takes London by storm. Feast on Shropshire veal or cherry soufflé. (⊠ *29 Maddox St., Mayfair* ☎ *020/7629–2999, see review* ✛ *3:A5*)

DINING BY CUISINE

Asian
The Providores & Tapa Room, £££

Austrian
The Wolseley, £££

French
Greenhouse, £££££
Hélène Darroze at the Connaught, £££££
La Petite Maison, £££
Le Gavroche, £££££
L'Oranger, ££££
The Square, £££££

Italian
Cecconi's, £££
Locanda Locatelli, ££££

Japanese
Nobu Berkeley Street, ££££

Mediterranean
St. Alban, £££

Modern British
Corrigan's Mayfair, £££
The Grill at the Dorchester, £££
Le Caprice, £££
Sketch, ££££

Modern European
Wild Honey, £££

Modern French
Hibiscus, £££

Seafood
Golden Hind, £
Scott's £££

Steakhouse
Gaucho Grill, ££££

14

SOHO AND COVENT GARDEN

Soho and Covent Garden are the city's playground, an all-day, all-night wonderland of glitz and greasepaint.

This area is London's cultural heart, with media companies and strip clubs, late-night bars, popular musicals, and highbrow theater productions. In the last decade, high rents have forced out seedy businesses and ushered in top-notch restaurants, including **Yauatcha** (⊠ *15–17 Broadwick St., Soho* ☎*020/7494–8888*; see review ✛ *3:C4*) and high-quality Spanish tapas bar **Barrafina** (⊠*54 Frith St., Soho* ☎*020/7813–8016*; see review), a haven for creative modern Iberian food. Because of its popularity with visitors, Soho prices can be absurdly steep: £10 cocktails and £30 main courses are not unheard of. For a quick bite without breaking the bank, head to Chinatown's cobbled streets. The roast pork dim sum or fried tofu and mashed prawns can't fail to delight at the three-story **Leong's Legends** (⊠*4 Macclesfield St., Soho* ☎*020/7287–0288* ✛ *3:D5*) or try the Venetian ciccheti—small dishes—at the **Polpo** bacaro (⊠*41 Beak St., Soho* ☎*020/7734–4479* ✛ *3:B5*).

BARS AND PUBS

Café Boheme (⊠ *13–17 Old Compton St., Soho* ☎ *020/7734–0623* ✛ *3:D5*) has an atmospheric bar, outside tables, and is popular with models, photographers, and the fashion crowd. It's open until 3 AM Monday–Saturday.

Hidden down an unassuming entrance, the **Player** (⊠ *8–10 Broadwick St., Soho* ☎ *020/7494–9125* ✛ *3:C4*) is a trendy Rat Pack–style subterranean cocktail bar that is liked and known by Londoners in the know. One of the best places for a hot romantic date is the elegant champagne bar at **Brasserie Max** inside the Covent Garden Hotel (⊠ *10 Monmouth St., Covent Garden* ☎ *020/7806–1000* ✛ *3:E4*).

MEAL DEALS AND STEALS

PRE- AND POST-THEATER DINING

For a £19.50 romantic French meal deal, head to **Clos Maggiore** (✉ *3 King St., Covent Garden* ☎ *020/7379–9696* ✛ *3:F5*) off the piazza. Race through French artisan charcuterie and "natural" terroirs-based wines at **Terroirs** (✉ *5 William St., Covent Garden* ☎ *020/7036–0660* ✛ *3:E6*). Or try inventive Modern European at **Arbutus** (✉ *63–64 Frith St., Soho* ☎ *020/7734–4545*; see review ✛ *3:D4*), where two courses before 7 ᴘᴍ cost £17.50. **Dehesa** (✉ *25 Ganton St., Soho* ☎ *020/7494–4170* ✛ *3:B5*) near Carnaby Street mixes Italian and Spanish tapas to dazzling effect. The A-list and theater stars head for **J Sheekey** (✉ *28–32 St. Martin's Ct., Covent Garden* ☎ *020/7240–2565*; see review ✛ *3:E6*) post-performance for seafood dishes in a chic salon and oyster bar.

BUDGET EATS AT ANY HOUR

British: At **Mother Mash** (✉ *26 Ganton St., Soho* ☎ *020/7494–9644* ✛ *3:B5*) British pie and mash are £7.95 and come with onion gravy or parsley-sauce "liquor." And there is always a crush at the no-bookings vegetarian **Mildred's** (✉ *45 Lexington St., Soho* ☎ *020/7494–1634* ✛ *3:B5*) canteen, where all mains are less than £9.25.

Pan-Asian: For those who prefer authentic Thai, there's always **Busaba Eathai** (✉ *106–110 Wardour St., Soho* ☎ *020/7255–8686* ✛ *3:C4*), a wildly popular no-bookings Thai canteen with bench seats and shared tables. Exceptional European stews, soups, and cheese and cured meat baguettes pull in the punters at **Fernandez & Wells** (✉ *25 Ganton St., Soho* ☎ *020/7494–4170* ✛ *3:C4*). Vegetarians will love the spread of cheap and exotic fare at the tiny **Yalla Yalla** (✉ *1 Green Ct., Soho* ☎ *020/7287–7663* ✛ *3:C5*). Try baba ghannouj-grilled eggplant purée—or the fatayer pastry filled with spinach, sumac, and pine nuts.

DINING BY CUISINE

14

American
Joe Allen, £££
British
The Ivy, ££££
Rules, ££££
Café
Bar Italia, £
Maison Bertaux, £
Chinese
Baozi Inn, £
Cha Cha Moon, £
Yauatcha, ££££
French
Côte, ££
L'Atelier de Joël Robuchon, £££££
Italian
Bocca di Lupo, £££
Mediterranean
Andrew Edmunds, ££
Mexican
Wahaca, £
Modern British
Arbutus, £££
Great Queen Street, £££
Modern European
Giaconda Dining Room, ££
Quo Vadis, £££
Portuguese
Canela, £
Seafood
J Sheekey, £££
Spanish
Barrafina, £££
Thai
Busabe Eathai, £
Vegetarian
Food for Thought, £

RESTAURANTS

(in alphabetical order by neighborhood)

Use the coordinate (✛ 1:B2) at the end of each listing to locate a site on the corresponding map.

BLOOMSBURY, FITZROVIA, REGENT'S PARK, AND HAMPSTEAD

BLOOMSBURY

£££ ✕ **Galvin Bistrot de Luxe.** The Galvin brothers blaze a trail for the deluxe
BISTRO bistro concept on a no-man's-land stretch of Baker Street. Feted chefs Chris and Jeff forsake Michelin stars and cut loose under the brasserie banner. A more mature crowd enjoys impeccable service in a handsome slate floor and mahogany-paneled salon. There's no finer crab lasagna around, and mains punch above their weight: gilthead bream, stuffed pig's trotter, and the Landaise chicken are all a triumph. The £15.50 set lunch or £17.50 dinners (6–7 PM) are unbeatable. ⊠ *66 Baker St., Bloomsbury* ☎ *020/7935-4007* ⊕ *www.galvinrestaurants.com* ▭ *AE, MC, V* Ⓤ *Baker St.* ✛ *1:G3.*

£ ✕ **North Sea Fish Restaurant.** Come here for the British national dish of
SEAFOOD fish-and-chips—battered cod, thick fries with salt and vinegar, and a dollop of homemade tartar sauce. Note that it's tricky to find: head three blocks south of St. Pancras station and the British Library, then down Judd Street. It has net curtains, velvet seats, and worn carpet, and it's filled with students, pensioners, and academics from the Library's Reading Room. There's freshly caught cod, plaice, haddock, sea bass, and salmon, with mushy peas, as well as dishes like chicken, which you can order grilled. ⊠ *7–8 Leigh St., Bloomsbury* ☎ *020/7387-5892* ▭ *MC, V* ⊗ *Closed Sun.* Ⓤ *Russell Sq.* ✛ *2:C3.*

FITZROVIA

££££–£££££ ✕ **Pied à Terre.** Few places in London can match the precision of Shane
MODERN FRENCH Osborn's haute cuisine at this converted Victorian town house on Charlotte Street in Fitzrovia. The layout may be cramped, but the food's sensational. You'll marvel at poached trout with fennel, rabbit with girolles, and Salt Marsh lamb. The desserts—like salad of peach and strawberries or raspberries and Mascarpone—will knock your socks off. ⊠ *34 Charlotte St., Fitzrovia* ☎ *020/7636-1178* ⊕ *www.pied-a-terre.co.uk* ▭ *AE, MC, V* ⊗ *Closed Sun. No lunch Sat.* Ⓤ *Goodge St.* ✛ *3:C2.*

REGENT'S PARK

££ ✕ **Lemonia.** Primrose Hill's favorite Greek Cypriot restaurant, vine-
GREEK decked and taverna-style Lemonia is large and light, and always packed with hungry North London customers. Besides an endless supply of small-dish *mezédes* starters, there are rustic mains like baked lamb in lemon and beef stewed in wine. Expect hordes of locals, loads of noise, and the occasional mega–film star. Weekday two-course lunch is £9.75. ⊠ *89 Regent's Park Rd., Regent's Park* ☎ *020/7586-7454* ▭ *MC, V* ⊗ *No lunch Sat. No dinner Sun.* Ⓤ *Chalk Farm* ✛ *1:F1.*

THE CITY, CLERKENWELL, AND SOUTH BANK

THE CITY

£££ ✗ **Boundary.** Design guru and veteran restaurateur Sir Terence Conran
FRENCH scores an absolute bull's-eye at Boundary in über-fashionable Hoxton–
Fodor's Choice Shoreditch. A spangly glass-fronted open kitchen and sparkling lighting,
★ acoustics, and Technicolor seats, make this smart 124-seat basement
French brasserie the *glamorati's* east-end destination of choice. The
menu's a wish list of crowd-pleasing dishes designed to impress: shellfish
bisque, escargots à la Bourguignonne, cassoulet Toulousain, lapin à la
moutarde, and steak au poivre. Dover sole comes simply on a white
plate, and desserts like tarte tatin are tasty and reasonably priced. ⊠ *2–4
Boundary St., entrance at 9 Redchurch St., The City* ☎ *020/7729–1051*
⊕ *www.theboundary.co.uk* ⌕ *Reservations essential* ═ *AE, MC, V*
☾ *No lunch Mon.* Ⓜ *Liverpool St.* ✛ *2:H2.*

14

££ ✗ **Canteen.** Posh pies and trendy British classics are executed well at this
BRITISH ultramodern, diner-style canteen in Spitalfields's finance district. With
booths and communal oak tables, a City lunch crowd wolfs down Coronation chicken and savory pies (steak-and-kidney and chicken-and-
tarragon are favorites), with mashed potatoes, greens, or mushy peas.
Finish with blackberry jelly or Eton Mess (strawberries, meringue, and
cream). Everything tastes good and is reasonably priced. ⊠ *2 Crispin
Pl., off Brushfield St., The City* ☎ *0845/686–1122* ⊕ *www.canteen.
co.uk* ═ *AE, MC, V* Ⓤ *Liverpool St.* ✛ *2:H3.*

££££ ✗ **Club Gascon.** Elegant and refined, Club Gascon is one of the sexier
MODERN FRENCH places to dine in London. Maybe it's the leather-wall interior, the cut
flowers, sublime service, or the way the tapas-style southwestern French
cuisine is served (sometimes on a rock rather than on a plate). There's
squab pigeon and roast rabbit, but this restaurant specializes in foie
gras: kick off with duck foie gras with black truffle and finish with it
for dessert, served with grapes. You'll find this French star near the
Smithfield wholesale meat market. ⊠ *57–59 West Smithfield, The City*
☎ *020/7796–0600* ⊕ *www.clubgascon.com* ═ *AE, MC, V* ☾ *Closed
Sun. No lunch Sat.* Ⓤ *Barbican* ✛ *2:F4.*

£ ✗ **E Pellicci.** It's Cockney chitchat and all-day English breakfast at this
CAFÉ century-old family-run landmark café near Brick Lane and Columbia
Road markets. With stained glass, art deco marquetry, and pics auto-
graphed by *EastEnders* TV soap stars, it's the hole-in-the-wall for the
fry-ups that Londoners adore: eggs, bacon, toast, baked beans, black
pudding, and "bubble 'n' squeak" (cabbage and mashed potatoes).
Your arteries may clog up, but at least the wallet survives: almost every-
thing is less than £8 but remember it's cash-only. ⊠ *332 Bethnal Green
Rd., The City* ☎ *020/7739–4873* ═ *No credit cards* ☾ *Closed Sun.*
Ⓤ *Bethnal Green* ✛ *2:H3.*

£££ ✗ **L'Anima.** Brilliant Southern Italian cuisine in a love-it-or-loathe-it
ITALIAN glass-fronted box of a restaurant characterize the scene at L'Anima.
Chef Francesco Mazzei draws inspiration from Sicily, Sardinia, and
Calabria, and works the floor, bar, and clear-fronted kitchen like the
proud owner that he is. Simple, modern dishes like wild mushroom and
black truffle tagliolini are near perfection, as is the baked sea bass—as
succulent as you could wish. Dessert puddings, like peach and Amaretto,

THE EAST END: LONDON'S BEST CURRIES

The East End's Brick Lane is famous for its numerous Bangladeshi curry houses and dodgy sidewalk "curry touts" who encourage you to come inside and dine.

✕ **Aladin** is a local Brick Lane BYOB favorite. Legend has it that HRH Prince Charles stopped by for a chicken tikka masala once. Though lacking in ambience, Aladin makes up for it with low prices and its aromatic curries. Average price of dinner for two: £22. ✉ *132 Brick La.* ☎ *020/7247-8210* ⌂♀ *BYOB* Ⓤ *Aldgate East* ✛ *2:H4.*

✕ **Hot Stuff** in Vauxhall offers some of the best-loved and best-priced curries in London. Run by the Dawood family, it's just a BYOB café with two tables. Home-cooked specials include king prawn biryani, chicken bhuna, and chili paneer. There's wonderful rice, bhagis, naan bread, and creamy dal (spiced lentils). Average price of dinner for two: £24. ✉ *19 Wilcox Rd.* ☎ *020/7720-1480* ⊕ *www.eathotstuff.com* ⌂♀ *BYOB* Ⓤ *Vauxhall* ✛ *5:C6.*

✕ **Indian Zing's** chef-owner Manoj Vasaikar woos the west London curry mafia with updated eclectic Indian cuisine. Start with *rasam* mussels (with garlic and curry leaves), and try Nilgiri lamb or jumbo prawns. Lemon-and-ginger rice and raisin and coconut naan bread are perfect sides. Average price of dinner for two: £45. ✉ *236 King St.* ☎ *020/8748-5959* ⊕ *www.indianzing.co.uk* Ⓤ *Hammersmith* ✛ *1:A6.*

✕ **Rooburoo** is popular throughout north London's Islington neighborhood. It has a reputation for modern spins on classic dishes and is liked by young professionals. Dishes include classic chicken jalfrezi, plus specialties such as Indian wraps and sea-bass fillet in banana leaves. Average price of dinner for two: £30. ✉ *21 Chapel Market* ☎ *020/7278-8100* ⊕ *www.rooburoo.com* Ⓤ *Angel* ✛ *2:E1.*

✕ **Sagar.** Try the Mysare masala dosa pancakes, the cheap thali spreads, and the sweet lassi yogurt drinks at this rated South India vegetarianeateryin Hammersmith. Average price for dinner for two: £23. ✉ *157 King St.* ☎ *020/7741-8563* Ⓤ *Hammersmith, Ravens Court Park* ✛ *1:A5.*

✕ **Vama's** upscale, stylish setting on the King's Road makes it a favorite among Chelsea's trendy crowd. The place has won countless awards and offers its own take on coconut prawn curry, as well as other dishes such as scallop masala and tandoori lamb chops. Average price of dinner for two: £80. ✉ *438 King's Rd.* ☎ *020/7351-4118* ⊕ *www.vama.co.uk* Ⓤ *Sloane Sq., South Kensington* ✛ *4:D5.*

are *belissimo*, and the wines are mainly Italian. ✉ *1 Snowden St., City* ☎ *020/7422-7000* ⊕ *www.lanima.co.uk* ▭ *AE, DC, MC, V* ⊙ *Closed Sun.* Ⓤ *Liverpool St.* ✛ *2:H3.*

£ ✕ **Lahore Kebab House.** Best budget curries in London is the mantra at
PAKISTANI the Lahore Kebab House in run-down Whitechapel. It may be no-frills and BYOB, but the halal Pakistani home-style cooking is cheap and brilliant—popular with Asians and City boys alike. Mutton *tikka*, grilled lamb chops, *tarka daal* lentils, masala fish curry, and *karahi* chicken are

all super-spiced and fiery. A £15-a-head meal knocks spots off anything on offer in nearby Brick Lane's so-called "curry mile." ✉ *2 Umberston St., The City* ☎ *020/7481–9737* ⊕ *www.lahore-kebabhouse.com* ☐ *MC, V* ⛄*BYOB* Ⓤ *Aldgate* ✛ *2:H5.*

£££ ✗ **Moro.** Up from The City, near Clerkenwell and Sadler's Wells con-
MEDITERRANEAN temporary dance theater, is Exmouth Market, a cluster of cute shops,
Fodor's Choice a few delis, an Italian church, and more fine restaurants like Moro.
★ The menu includes a mélange of Spanish and North African flavors. Spiced meats, Serrano hams, salt cod, and wood-fired and char-grilled offerings are the secret to Moro's success. Grilled lamb with marrow and yogurt stands out. Sidle up to the zinc bar, or squeeze into a tiny table and lean in—it's noisy here. But then again, that's part of the buzz. ✉ *34–36 Exmouth Market, The City* ☎ *020/7833–8336* ⊕ *www. moro.co.uk* ⚓ *Reservations essential* ☐ *AE, DC, MC, V* ⊙ *Closed Sun.* Ⓤ *Farringdon* ✛ *2:E3.*

£££ ✗ **Plateau.** Credit crunch or no, Plateau's an excellent venue for a Canary
MODERN FRENCH Wharf business meal. In an all-white space, with tulip-shape chairs and floor-to-ceiling glass windows overlooking Canada Square, Plateau houses a restaurant, rotisserie, two bars, private dining, and outdoor terraces. Food like baked monkfish, wood pigeon with gnocchi, and lamb with sweetbreads are all pricey, but executed well. ✉ *4th fl., Canada Pl., Canada Sq., The City* ☎ *020/7715–7100* ⊕ *www.plateaurestaurant. co.uk* ☐ *AE, DC, MC, V* Ⓤ *Canary Wharf* ✛ *2:H6.*

££ ✗ **Simpson's Tavern.** This historic back-alley City chophouse was founded
BRITISH in 1757 and is as raucous and atmospheric as you'll find. It draws pinstriped City folk, who love the boardinghouse scene and old-school grub: oxtail stew, steak-and-kidney pie, chump chops, potted shrimp, or "stewed cheese" house special (cheese on toast with Béchamel sauce). Brusque service and shared oak bench stalls are part of the charm. Note it's only open weekdays from noon 'til 3. ✉ *38½ Cornhill, at Ball Ct., The City* ☎ *020/7626–9985* ⊕ *www.simpsonstavern.co.uk* ☐ *AE, DC, MC, V* ⊙ *Closed weekends. No dinner* Ⓤ *Bank* ✛ *2:H5.*

££ ✗ **Sông Qué Café.** An urban trawl through Hoxton's trendy boutiques
VIETNAMESE and art galleries is topped off at this amazing-value Vietnamese canteen. Block out the scuzzy Kingsland Road location and the gaudy decor and instead sample a few of the 170 dishes—including green papaya salad, tamarind prawns, Vietnamese pancakes, pork vermicelli, stir-fried tofu, and oodles of *pho* (beef broth with steak and noodles). ✉ *134 Kingsland Rd., The City* ☎ *020/7613–3222* ☐ *MC, V* Ⓤ *Old St.* ✛ *2:H2.*

£££ ✗ **St. John.** Fans travel the world for Fergus Henderson's ultra-Brit-
BRITISH ish nose-to-tail cooking at this stark-white converted smokehouse in
Fodor's Choice Clerkenwell. His chutzpah is galling: one appetizer is pigskin, and oth-
★ ers, like ox heart or pig nose and tail, are marginally less extreme. Dishes like bone marrow and parsley, or chitterlings and dandelion appear stark on the plate but arrive with aplomb. Expect an all-French wine list, plus port. Finish with strawberry trifle and Madeleines. ✉ *26 St. John St., Clerkenwell* ☎ *020/7251–0848* ⊕ *www.stjohnrestaurant. co.uk* ☐ *AE, DC, MC, V* ⊙ *Closed Sun.* Ⓤ *Farringdon* ✛ *2:F4.*

££ ✗ **St. John Bread & Wine.** The canteen cousin of St. John in Clerkenwell
MODERN BRITISH is a winner no matter what meal of the day: have porridge, prunes, and

14

pikelets for breakfast, seed cake and Madeira for "elevenses," beetroot and pickled walnuts for lunch, and smoked sprats for dinner. It's similar to St. John in that you'll find ox heart, pigskin, "blood cake," and duck egg on the menu. You can feast on a whole roast suckling pig that feeds 14. Note it's a handy spot before or after visits to nearby Brick Lane or Old Spitalfields markets. ⊠ *94–96 Commercial St., The City* ☎ *020/7251–0848* ⊕ *www.stjohnrestaurant.co.uk* ▭ *AE, MC, V* U *Aldgate East, Liverpool St.* ✣ *2:H4.*

£££ ╳ **Sweetings.** Established in 1889, Sweetings is a remnant from the
SEAFOOD old imperial City of London heyday. There are some things Sweetings *doesn't* do: reservations, dinner, coffee, weekends. It does, however, do seafood. Not far from St. Paul's cathedral, it's patronized by City gents who drink tankards of Black Velvet (Guinness and champagne) and eat soused herrings, roe on toast, and skate wings with black butter at linen-covered raised counters. The oysters are fresh, and desserts like spotted dick are classic favorites. ⊠ *39 Queen Victoria St., The City* ☎ *020/7248–3062* ⌲ *Reservations not accepted* ▭ *AE, MC, V* ☾ *Closed weekends. No dinner* U *Mansion House* ✣ *2:H6.*

£ ╳ **Tayyabs.** Reckless City financiers, Asians, and medics from the
PAKISTANI Royal London Hospital swamp this high-turnover Pakistani halal curry canteen in Whitechapel. Expect queues after dark, and bear in mind it's BYOB, jam-packed, noisy, and mildly chaotic. Nonetheless, prices are cheap and you can gorge for £15 on minced meat kebabs, karahi chicken, or marinated lamb chops. ⊠ *83 Fieldgate St., The City* ☎ *020/7247–9543* ⊕ *www.tayyabs.co.uk* ⌲ *Reservations not accepted* ▭ *AE, MC, V* 𐰀 *BYOB* U *Aldgate East* ✣ *2:H4.*

SOUTH BANK

££–£££ ╳ **Anchor & Hope.** Great things at friendly prices come from the open
MODERN BRITISH kitchen at this permanently packed, no-reservations, leading gastro-
Fodor's Choice pub on the Cut in Waterloo: pot-roast duck stands out. It's cramped,
★ informal, and highly original, and there are great dishes for groups, like slow-roasted leg of lamb. Expect to share a table, too. ⊠ *36 The Cut, South Bank* ☎ *020/7928–9898* ⌲ *Reservations not accepted* ▭ *MC, V* U *Waterloo, Southwark* ✣ *5:F2.*

££ ╳ **Baltic.** To dine well in South Bank, perhaps after a trip to the Tate
EASTERN Modern, stop into this airy, modern space near Southwark tube. White
EUROPEAN walls, wooden beams, exposed brick, and an amber chandelier make this converted coach house a top spot for modern Eastern European fare. With a Polish and Hungarian bias, Baltic serves fine blinis (with caviar, herring, or smoked salmon), gravlax, potato latkes, leniwe cheese dumplings, and steamed goulash. Dill and rose petal are but two of the dozens of infused vodkas. ⊠ *74 Blackfriars Rd., South Bank* ☎ *020/7928–1111* ⊕ *www.balticrestaurant.co.uk* ▭ *AE, MC, V* U *Southwark* ✣ *5:F2.*

£££ ╳ **Chez Bruce.** Gutsy French cuisine, perfect service, and a neighborhood
MODERN FRENCH vibe make for one of London's favorite restaurants. Take the overland train south of the river to this cozy haunt overlooking Wandsworth Common and expect wonders ranging from old-fashioned braises and daubes to delicious offal and lighter, simply grilled fish dishes. Saddle of rabbit or roast cod and gremolata are immaculately done. The wines

are great, the sommelier is superb, and all in all it's hard to beat. ✉ *2 Bellevue Rd., Wandsworth* ☎ *020/8672–0114* ⊕ *www.chezbruce.co.uk* ⚠ *Reservations essential* ═ *AE, DC, MC, V* ✛ *4:E6.*

££ ✗ **Magdalen.** South of the river between London and Tower bridges, and a hop from the London Assembly headquarters, Magdalen is a beacon of class in an otherwise dowdy part of town. It majors in inventive Modern British cuisine at keen prices; grilled venison (£8), Welsh lamb and chard (£16), lemon sole (£18), and Eton Mess for £5.50 will hardly break the bank. With civilized dark-wood and aubergine surroundings, sit back with a clever 70-bottle wine list that carries 11 by the carafe. ✉ *152 Tooley St., South Bank* ☎ *020/7403–1342* ⊕ *www. magdalenrestaurant.co.uk* ═ *AE, MC, V* ⊙ *No lunch Sat. Closed Sun.* Ⓤ *London Bridge* ✛ *5:H2.*

MODERN BRITISH

£££ ✗ **Skylon.** Located in the Royal Festival Hall, Skylon is *the* Southbank Centre's destination restaurant–bar–grill. Spacious, attractive, and with huge picture windows with spectacular views of the Thames, Skylon guarantees a classy pre- or post-performance meal in the '50s Festival Hall. Against a background of music and performance, concertgoers sip cocktails at the central bar and dine on lamb and couscous at the grill, or quail, spelt risotto, and halibut with squid and chorizo in the restaurant. The food is accomplished, the setting impressive. ✉ *Southbank Centre, Belvedere Rd., South Bank* ☎ *020/7654–7800* ⊕ *www. skylonrestaurant.co.uk* ═ *AE, MC, V* Ⓤ *Waterloo* ✛ *5:D1.*

MODERN EUROPEAN

££ ✗ **Tom Ilić** . The eponymous Serbian-born chef cooks with technical brilliance but charges only neighborhood prices at this haven in Battersea. Big on meat, especially pork, gob-smacked locals lap up dishes like pig's cheek with chorizo, pork, or a trio of lamb with pesto. Desserts like poached rhubarb are highly rated, and set lunches offer outstanding value at £14.50, or £16.95 on Sunday. It's south of the Thames, and best approached by taxi or overland train. ✉ *123 Queenstown Rd., South Bank* ☎ *020/7622–0555* ⊕ *www.tomilic.com* ═ *MC, V* Ⓤ *National Rail: Queenstown Rd. (Battersea)* ✛ *4:H6.*

MODERN EUROPEAN

KENSINGTON, CHELSEA, AND KNIGHTSBRIDGE

CHELSEA

££ ✗ **Aubaine.** Loads of pretty women hang out at Aubaine at Brompton Cross in the summer. They love the distressed gray wooden furniture, cut flowers, in-house pâtisserie, terrace tables, and hot people-watching. Not to mention the figure-friendly Gallic menu, featuring prawn salads, risottos, grilled tuna, eggplant cassoulet, and chicken tartines. Sit by Brompton Road and enjoy the best free catwalk in town. ✉ *260– 262 Brompton Rd., Chelsea* ☎ *020/7052–0100* ⊕ *www.aubaine.co.uk* ═ *AE, MC, V* Ⓤ *South Kensington* ✛ *4:E2.*

FRENCH

££ ✗ **PJ's Bar & Grill.** Enter PJ's and assume the Polo Joe lifestyle: wooden floors and stained glass, a slowly revolving propeller from a 1919 Vickers Vimy flying bomber, and vintage polo gear galore. The place is packed, relaxed, and efficient, and the menu, which includes all-American staples like organic steaks, salads, and brownies, pleases all except vegetarians. PJ's opens late, and the bartenders are pros.

AMERICAN

14

LOCAL CHAINS WORTH A TASTE

When you're on the go or don't have time for a leisurely meal—and Starbucks won't cut it—you might want to try a local chain restaurant or sandwich bar. The ones listed below are well priced and are the best in their category.

✕ **Byron Hamburgers:** Bright and child-friendly, this six-strong line of burger joins storms the market with its delicious Aberdeen Angus Scotch hamburgers and fries. ⊕ www.byronhamburgers.com

✕ **Café Rouge:** A classic 28-strong French bistro chain that's been around for eons and does great prix-fixe deals—so "uncool" that it's now almost fashionable. ⊕ www.caferouge.co.uk

✕ **Carluccio's Caffè:** The Carluccio's chain of 11 all-day Italian café/bar/food shops are freshly sourced, family-friendly, and make brilliant pasta and salad stops on a shopping spree. ⊕ www.carluccios.com

✕ **Ed's Easy Diner:** Overdose on shakes and made-to-order hamburgers at this chain of shiny, retro '50s-theme American diners. ⊕ www.edseasydiner.co.uk

✕ **Le Pain Quotidien:** Try tartine open sandwiches or baguettes and salads at the communal tables. There are 12 branches, including at Eurostar's stunning St. Pancras station. ⊕ www.lepainquotidien.co.uk

✕ **Pizza Express:** Serving classic thin-crust pizzas, Pizza Express is everywhere (there are nearly 100 in London). Soho and Knightsbridge branches have a live jazz program. ⊕ www.pizzaexpress.com

✕ **Pret A Manger:** London's high-street take-out supremo isn't just for store-made sandwiches: there are wraps, noodles, baguettes, sushi, salads, fruit, juices, and tea cakes, too. ⊕ www.pret.com

✕ **Ranoush Juice Bar:** Shawarma kebabs are the draw at these mirrored late-night kebab and juice bars (open 8 AM to 3 AM daily). They also serve falafel, meze, and tabbouleh. ⊕ www.maroush.com

✕ **Strada:** Stop at this 27-strong chain for authentic hand-stretched pizzas baked over a wood fire, plus classic pastas, steaks, and risottos. It's cheap, stylish, and packed. ⊕ www.strada.co.uk

✕ **Tootsies:** This superior burger joint does yummy grilled burgers, fries, salads, steaks, BLTs, and chicken spreads. It's family-friendly, with a children's meal for £5.95. ⊕ www.tootsiesrestaurants.com

✕ **Wagamama:** Londoners drain bowls of noodle soup at this child-friendly chain of high-tech, high-turnover, high-volume Japanese communal canteens. ⊕ www.wagamama.com

Weekend brunch is a must with the wealthy Chelsea jet set. ⊠ *52 Fulham Rd., Kensington* ☎ *020/7581–0025* ⊕ *www.pjsbarandgrill.co.uk* ▭ *AE, MC, V* Ⓤ *South Kensington* ✛ *4:E3.*

££
MODERN BRITISH

✕ **The Pig's Ear.** Heir to the throne Prince William once came with friends and split the bill in the first-floor dining room at this classic gastropub off the King's Road. Elbow in at the crowded ground-floor pub area, or choose a more formal vibe in the dark wood-paneled salon upstairs. You'll find creative dishes on a short menu, like pig's ear, Cornish crab, and braised pork belly, which are all typical, and executed . . . royally. ✉ *35 Old Church St., Chelsea* ☎ *020/7352–2908* ⊟ *AE, MC, V* Ⓤ *Sloane Sq.* ✛ *4:E4.*

££ ✕ **Racine.** There's an upscale buzz at this star of the Brompton Road
BRASSERIE dining scene, not far from the V&A and Harrods, and, Holy Trinity Brompton church. This chic French brasserie excels in doing simple things well—and not overcharging. Classics like melted Raclette cheese, roast quail, and rack of lamb all hit the mark. The £17.50 set lunch or early dinners (6–7:30 PM) are popular. ✉ *239 Brompton Rd., Chelsea* ☎ *020/7584–4477* ⊟ *AE, MC, V* Ⓤ *South Kensington* ✛ *4:E2.*

£££££ ✕ **Restaurant Gordon Ramsay.** Ubiquitous chef Ramsay—of *Hell's Kitchen*
FRENCH fame—oversees a heavenly storm of white beans, lobster, foie gras, and shaved truffles at London's top restaurant in Chelsea. He wins the highest awards here with French classics, where tables are booked months in advance. Splurge on seven courses for £120; dance through a three-course dinner for £90; or waltz through a £45 three-course lunch. ✉ *68 Royal Hospital Rd., Chelsea* ☎ *020/7352–4441* ⊕ *www. gordonramsay.com/royalhospitalroad* ⌔ *Reservations essential* ⊟ *AE, DC, MC, V* ☾ *Closed weekends* Ⓤ *Sloane Sq.* ✛ *4:F4.*

KENSINGTON

£££ ✕ **Bibendum.** Art deco prints and awesome stained-glass windows of
MODERN BRITISH cycling Michelin men set the tone at this former tire showroom and smooth-running London showpiece. Chef Matthew Harris cooks with Euro-Brit flair. Try calves kidney, escargot, risotto, grilled rabbit, Pyrenean lamb, or tripe (just as it ought to be cooked). The £29.50 fixed-price lunch menu is money well spent, especially on Sunday. ✉ *Michelin House, 81 Fulham Rd., Kensington* ☎ *020/7581–5817* ⊕ *www. bibendum.co.uk* ⊟ *AE, DC, MC, V* Ⓤ *South Kensington* ✛ *4:E3.*

KNIGHTSBRIDGE

£££ ✕ **Boxwood Café.** Attached to the Berkeley and in the Gordon Ram-
MODERN say stable, the Boxwood is the best uptown but relaxed place to dine
EUROPEAN in Knightsbridge, with opulent marble, brown, and greens. The New
☾ York–style restaurant is open late (until midnight Thursday–Saturday)
Fodor's Choice and set lunch is useful at £23. Favorite dishes range from Orkney scal-
★ lops to native lobster, and veal burger to knickerbocker glory. Service is top-notch, and you'll find a fashionable buzz. ✉ *The Berkeley, Wilton Pl., Knightsbridge* ☎ *020/7592–1226* ⊕ *www.gordonramsay.com/ boxwoodcafe* ⊟ *AE, MC, V* Ⓤ *Knightsbridge* ✛ *4:G1.*

££££ ✕ **The Capital.** The French haute cuisine is sublime at this legendary
FRENCH clublike hotel dining room that has retained a grown-up atmosphere and formal service since it opened in 1978. Chef Eric Chavot serves impeccable dishes in chic surroundings. Go for exquisite scallops with cucumber jelly, frogs' legs with gnocchi, or turbot and ravioli. Desserts like Jasmine jelly or lemon sorbet are sensational, too. It's two seconds from Harrods, and the £27.50 set lunch is an absolute bargain. ✉ *22–24 Basil St., Knightsbridge* ☎ *020/7589–5171* ⊕ *www.capitalhotel.co.uk* ⊟ *AE, DC, MC, V* Ⓤ *Knightsbridge* ✛ *4:F1.*

14

££££ ✕ **Marcus Wareing at the Berkeley.** Wonder chef Marcus Wareing vies
MODERN to be the best in London at his eponymous restaurant at the Berkeley.
EUROPEAN Opulently designed by David Collins—all clarets, carpet, and burgundy
Fodor's Choice leather seats—Wareing pulls out all the haute cuisine stops with a suc-
★ cession of world-class dishes. Standouts include roast quail with hispi
cabbage; a fine chunk of Scottish halibut with charred leeks or Anjou
pigeon with amaretti. Chocolate moëlleux with banana jelly or orange
crème with spiced brioche are absolutely faultless, and the wine list
includes page after page of famous names. ⊠ *The Berkeley, Wilton Pl.,
Knightsbridge* ☎ *020/7235–1200* ⊕ *www.the-berkeley.co.uk* ⌂ *Reservations essential* ▭ *AE, DC, MC, V* ☾ *Closed Sun. No lunch Sat.*
Ⓤ *Knightsbridge* ✛ *4:G1.*

£££ ✕ **Rasoi Restaurant.** Chef-proprietor Vineet Bhatia showcases the finest
INDIAN new Indian cuisine in London at this tony town-house venue off the
King's Road. Super-seductive and decked with Indian silks, prints, masks,
bells, and ornaments, Bhatia pushes the boundaries with signatures like
wild mushroom rice with tomato ice cream or grilled lobster dusted
with cocoa and sour spices. Don't leave without sampling the warm
chocolate samosas. ⊠ *10 Lincoln St., Knightsbridge* ☎ *020/7225–1881*
⊕ *www.rasoirestaurant.co.uk* ▭ *AE, DC, MC* Ⓤ *Sloane Sq.* ✛ *4:F3.*

£££–££££ ✕ **Zafferano.** Asprey-wearing Belgravians flock to Zafferano, one of
ITALIAN London's leading exponents of Italian *cucina nuova,* not far from Harvey Nichols. The fireworks are in the kitchen, and *what* new-wave
fireworks they are: tuna carpaccio, Fiorentina T-bone steak, pig's cheek
with dumplings, and char-grilled monkfish are all delectable (if not
cheap). The desserts are *delizioso,* too, especially the chocolate tiramisu. ⊠ *15 Lowndes St., Knightsbridge* ☎ *020/7235–5800* ⊕ *www.
zafferanorestaurant.com* ⌂ *Reservations essential* ▭ *AE, DC, MC, V*
Ⓤ *Knightsbridge* ✛ *4:G1.*

£££–££££ ✕ **Zuma.** Hurrah for this buzzy, ever fashionable, Tokyo-style Japanese
JAPANESE restaurant near Harrods. Well lighted and designed, with polished granite, blond wood, exposed pipes, and open timberwork, it includes a sake
bar, robata grill, and sushi counter. Try maki rolls, sea bass sashimi, eel
sushi, black cod, or robata-grilled Wagyu beef. It works well for groups;
grab the "sake sommelier" to help navigate 40 varieties of rice wine
and Japanese spirits. ⊠ *5 Raphael St., Knightsbridge* ☎ *020/7584–1010*
⊕ *www.zumarestaurant.com* ⌂ *Reservations essential* ▭ *AE, DC, MC,
V* Ⓤ *Knightsbridge* ✛ *4:F1.*

GREATER LONDON

NORTH LONDON

£ ✕ **Marquess Tavern.** Hidden among Canonbury's grand garden squares,
MODERN BRITISH this is one of the best gastropubs in town, even if it's outside the city
center. Set in a traditional Victorian boozer, the high-ceilinged, stark-
white dining room is a perfect foil for the British fare. Orkney mussels
starter and mains like haunch of venison or Wilshire trout are all steals.
Chilled plum soup and rice pudding and rhubarb are cheap, too. ⊠ *32
Canonbury St., Islington* ☎ *020/7354–2975* ⊕ *www.marquesstavern.
co.uk* ▭ *AE, MC, V* Ⓤ *Highbury & Islington* ✛ *2:G1.*

£–££ ✕ **Ottolenghi.** Fabulous window displays and a funky all-white interior
CAFÉ characterize this flagship deli–bakery–café in Islington that serves deli-
☺ ciously fresh salads, savories, soups, pastries, and cakes. Sit at shared
tables and tuck into turkey with mint, cumin, and lemon, or opt for
rocket-and-herb salad with pomegranate and feta. Go home with a
takeaway chocolate meringue. ✉ *287 Upper St., Islington* ☎ *020/7288–
1454* ⊕ *www.ottolenghi.co.uk* ▭ *AE, MC, V* ⓤ *Angel* ✛ *2:F1.*

WEST LONDON

££ ✕ **High Road Brasserie.** Ace restaurateur Nick Jones scores with this
BRASSERIE 80-seat all-day Euro brasserie in leafy Turnham Green. French win-
☺ dows, green banquettes, colored tiles, and covered sidewalk dining
provide the setting for comforting favorites at all hours, from steak
tartare and vichyssoise soup to *croque madame* (hot ham and cheese
sandwich topped with a poached egg) and whole moules marinières.
The service is slick, and the buzz is constant. ✉ *162–166 Chiswick High
Rd., Chiswick* ☎ *020/8742–7474* ⊕ *www.highroadhouse.co.uk* ▭ *AE,
MC, V* ⓤ *Turnham Green* ✛ *4:A2.*

£££ ✕ **La Trompette.** Top-notch neighborhood dining doesn't get much bet-
FRENCH ter than this. In outlying Chiswick, La Trompette has a serious west
London following that goes gaga for the elegant food and chic sur-
roundings. A £23.50 weekday lunch might impress with *goujons* (thin
breaded strips) of plaice, saddle of lamb, or bream with tapenade. The
desserts match the mains and the sommelier is charm personified. ✉ *5–7
Devonshire Rd., Chiswick* ☎ *020/8747–1836* ⊕ *www.latrompette.co.uk*
▭ *AE, MC, V* ⓤ *Turnham Green* ✛ *4:A3.*

££ ✕ **Princess Victoria.** This renovated 1829 former gin palace—all light
BRITISH wells, high ceilings, etched glass, and carved wood bars—makes for a
☺ magnificent gastropub setting on a bleak stretch of Shepherd's Bush. With
main courses under £15, top dishes range from steak and triple-cooked
chips to green pea risotto and sea trout and mash. The 400-strong wine
list is overseen by sommelier and co-owner Matt Wilkin, with a focus
on Rhone, Reisling, and Pinot Noir. ✉ *217 Uxbridge Rd., Shepherd's
Bush* ☎ *020/8749–5886* ▭ *MC, V* ⓤ *Shepherd's Bush* ✛ *1:A6.*

££££ ✕ **River Café.** This open-kitchen Italian restaurant sets the standard with
ITALIAN its simple roasts, fresh salads, pastas, and char-grilled meats. Chefs Rose
Gray and Ruth Rogers source ultrafresh, impeccable seasonal ingredients, so expect Tuscan bread soup, handmade nettle-and-ricotta pasta,
and and veal shin with lemon and sage—plus one of London's highest
bills. This is in distant Hammersmith, so if you bag an evening table,
remember that you'll need to book a cab ahead or walk about 10 minutes to the closest Tube. Note that tables are cleared by 11 PM on weekdays, and 11:20 PM Friday and Saturday. ✉ *Thames Wharf, Rainville
Rd., Hammersmith* ☎ *020/7386–4200* ⊕ *www.rivercafe.co.uk* ✍ *Reservations essential* ▭ *AE, DC, MC, V* ⓤ *Hammersmith* ✛ *4:A4.*

14

NOTTING HILL AND BAYSWATER

BAYSWATER

££   ✕ **Alounak.** The food at this lively Persian canteen on Westbourne Grove
MIDDLE EASTERN   may be tried and tested, but swarms still come for the hot bread and
kebabs that emerge from the clay oven by the door. Try chicken kebab
or the *zereshk polo* (chicken with Iranian berries). Take Persian black
tea and sweets, but know that the sour yogurt drinks are not to everyone's taste. ✉ *44 Westbourne Grove, Bayswater* ☎ *020/7229–0416*
🚇 *DC, MC, V* Ⓤ *Queensway* ✛ *1:B4.*

£££   ✕ **Angelus.** Owner, sommelier, and former pro rugby player Thierry
FRENCH   Tomasin scores a converted try at this distinctive French brasserie in
Lancaster Gate. Styled with art deco mirrors and button-back banquettes in a 200-year-old converted former pub, Angelus has a reputation for unrivaled Paris-style brasserie cuisine. The foie gras crème
brûlée, egg cocotte, sole, or quail with bacon are as good as they get.
Light bites, such as beef tartare or banana bread, are served at the bar.
Tomasin is sure to select a classy bottle from the wine list focused mainly
on France. ✉ *4 Bathurst St., Bayswater* ☎ *020/402–0083* ⊕ *www.
angelusrestaurant.co.uk* 🚇 *AE, MC, V* Ⓤ *Lancaster Gate* ✛ *1:D4.*

£££   ✕ **Hereford Road.** Bespectacled chef–co-owner Tom Pemberton mans
MODERN BRITISH   the front-of-house grill at this Bayswater favorite, which specializes
Fodor's Choice   in pared-back best-of-British fare. With an accent on well-sourced
★   regional and seasonal ingredients, many dishes are as uncluttered as
you'll find. Slide into a stylish booth, and gorge on cockles and leeks,
brill with peashoots, or ox cheeks with pickled walnuts. Expect to
see the well-heeled Tory-leaning Notting Hill set. ✉ *3 Hereford Rd.,
Bayswater* ☎ *020/7727–1144* ⊕ *www.herefordroad.org* 🚇 *AE, MC, V*
Ⓤ *Bayswater, Queensway* ✛ *1:B4.*

£   ✕ **Mandalay.** Bargain hunters love this 28-seat Burmese café on Edgware
ASIAN   Road run by the friendly Ally brothers. All dishes are less than £8 and
bookings are recommended. Don't go for atmosphere, romance, or to
impress a date, but instead, focus on the delicious papaya-and-cucum-
ber salad, shrimp fritters, fish curry, and chili king prawns. Completely
stuffed, you'll leave with change from £15. ✉ *444 Edgware Rd., Bayswater* ☎ *020/7258–3696* ⊕ *www.mandalayway.com* 🍴 *Reservations
essential* 🚇 *AE, DC, MC, V* Ⓤ *Edgware Rd.* ✛ *1:E2.*

££   ✕ **Royal China.** The black-and-gold '70s Biba-style decor is half the fun
CHINESE   at this flagship dim sum palace on Queensway. Expect queues and mir-
☺   rored ceilings at this longtime favorite that churns out stacks of dim sum
at a furious pace. Start with dumplings stuffed with pork, squid, duck,
prawns, scallops, or crab, and follow up with spareribs and greens, and
pots of Chinese tea. ✉ *13 Queensway, Bayswater* ☎ *020/7221–2535*
⊕ *www.royalchinagroup.co.uk* 🍴 *Reservations not accepted* 🚇 *AE,
MC, V* Ⓤ *Queensway, Bayswater* ✛ *1:B5.*

NOTTING HILL

££   ✕ **Bumpkin.** Place tongue firmly in cheek at this boisterous country-theme
BRITISH   four-story boho-chic outfit at the scruffier end of Notting Hill. Waitstaff
☺   wear "Country Girl" or "Country Boy" T-shirts in the buzzy ground-floor
brasserie where there's patterned wallpaper, farmhouse cider, and a shared

long wooden table. The British grub is carefully sourced and unashamedly basic—have a chop, cauliflower cheese, fish cakes, leg of lamb, or toad-in-the-hole (sausage in batter). ⊠ *209 Westbourne Park Rd., Notting Hill* ☎ *020/7243–9818* ⊕ *www.bumpkinuk.com* ⌕ *Reservations essential* ⊟ *AE, MC, V* Ⓤ *Notting Hill Gate, Ladbroke Grove* ✛ *1:A3.*

£££ ✕ **The Cow Dining Rooms.** A boho-chic gastropub, the Cow comprises
MODERN BRITISH a faux-Dublin '50s backroom saloon bar that serves Fines de Claires oysters, whelks and winkles, and Dorset crab. Upstairs the chef whips up Brit specialties like Welsh lamb cutlets, English summer salad, black bream, and sea trout and shrimp. Post-recession ex-millionaire Notting Hill locals love the house special in the packed bar: draft Guinness with a pint of prawns and mayonnaise. ⊠ *89 Westbourne Park Rd., Notting Hill* ☎ *020/7221–0021* ⊕ *www.thecowlondon.co.uk* ⊟ *MC, V* Ⓤ *Westbourne Park* ✛ *1:B3.*

£££ ✕ **E&O.** The jet set hang at E&O, one of London's hip scene bars and
ASIAN restaurants, off Portobello Road. E&O means "Eastern and Oriental," and the mix of Chinese, Japanese, Vietnamese, and Thai dishes includes a slew of vegetarian options. Don't skip the lychee martinis, miso black cod, chili tofu, Thai rare beef, or papaya salad. ⊠ *14 Blenheim Crescent, Notting Hill* ☎ *020/7229–5454* ⊕ *www.rickerrestaurants.com/eando* ⊟ *AE, DC, MC, V* Ⓤ *Ladbroke Grove* ✛ *1:A4.*

££ ✕ **Electric Brasserie.** There's no better people-watching than at the Elec-
BRASSERIE tric, a popular hangout from morning to night. Expect oysters, steaks, roasts, chunky sandwiches and seafood platters. The bar's a great place to meet up with friends—or make new ones. Check out the cocktail list, with a broad selection of martinis and champagne cocktails. ⊠ *191 Portobello Rd., Notting Hill* ☎ *020/7908–9696* ⊕ *www.the-electric.co.uk* ⊟ *AE, DC, MC, V* Ⓤ *Notting Hill Gate* ✛ *1:A3.*

£££ ✕ **Julie's.** Does Julie's have a draped-off dining room known as the
BRITISH "G-spot"? The warren of peekaboo alcoves at this cute '70s throwback ooze Victorian sensuality and *allegedly* have witnessed all manner of naughtiness over the years. Royalty and rockers—from Capt. Mark Philips to Mick Jagger—have famously cavorted here. Now it's their children who turn up. The food is pricey and unremarkable, but the old memories abound. Poached lobster with Russian salad, smoked mackerel, pork and Calvados, or tuna and radish are well-liked standards. ⊠ *135 Portland Rd., Notting Hill* ☎ *020/7229–8331* ⊕ *www.juliesrestaurant.com* ⊟ *AE, MC, V* Ⓤ *Holland Park* ✛ *1:A5.*

££££ ✕ **The Ledbury.** Notting Hill's hedge-fund honchos have created a "strong
MODERN FRENCH buy" with this fantastic fine-dining restaurant housed in a high-ceiling room, full of drapes, mirrors, and leather seats. The £60 tasting menu is a tour de force that weaves from scallops with seaweed to Cornish turbot and roast monkfish and marjoram. Finish with passionfruit soufflé with Sauternes ice cream. Excellent service and a confident sommelier round out this winning proposition. ⊠ *127 Ledbury Rd., Notting Hill* ☎ *0207/7792–9090* ⊕ *www.theledbury.com* ⊟ *AE, MC, V* Ⓤ *Westbourne Park* ✛ *1:A4.*

£££–££££ ✕ **Notting Hill Brasserie.** There's something seductive about NHB, with its
MODERN side entrance, twinkle of live jazz piano in the bar, muted conversation,
EUROPEAN African artifacts, mini-armchairs, and friendly service. Set in converted

14

British Food Decoder

In London, local could mean any global flavor, but for pure Britishness, roast beef and Yorkshire pudding top the list. If you want the best-value traditional Sunday lunch, go to a pub. Gastropubs, where Sunday roasts are generally made with top-quality ingredients, are an excellent bet, too. The meat is usually served with crisp roast potatoes and carrots, and with Yorkshire pudding, a savory batter baked in the oven until crisp. A rich, dark, meaty gravy is poured on top.

Other tummy liners include shepherd's pie, made with stewed minced lamb and a mashed-potato topping and baked until lightly browned on top; cottage pie is a similar dish, but made with minced beef instead of lamb. Steak-and-kidney pie is a delight when done properly: with chunks of lean beef and ox kidneys, braised with onions and mushrooms in a thick gravy, and topped with a light puff-pastry crust.

Fish-and-chips, usually battered deep-fried cod or haddock, comes with thick chips, or french fries, as we call them in the States. A ploughman's lunch in a pub is crusty bread, a strong-flavored English cheese with bite (cheddar, blue Stilton, crumbly white Cheshire, or smooth red Leicester), and tangy pickles with a side-salad garnish. For a hot, comforting dessert, seek out a sweet bread-and-butter pudding, made from layers of bread and dried currants baked in cream until crisp. And one can't forgo English cream tea, which consists of scones served with jam and clotted cream, and sandwiches made with wafer-thin slices of cucumber—served as an accompaniment to properly brewed tea.

Victorian town houses, the food is imaginative, with strong and confident flavors. Feeling like fish? Try trout with smoked eel, cod with chorizo, or sole with artichoke. Meat lovers might like the rabbit with pea purée. ⊠ *92 Kensington Park Rd., Notting Hill* ☎ *020/7229–4481* ⊕ *www.nottinghillbrasserie.com* ▭ *AE, MC, V* Ⓤ *Notting Hill Gate* ✛ *1:A4.*

ST. JAMES'S, MAYFAIR, AND MARYLEBONE

MARYLEBONE

£   ✕ **Golden Hind** . You'll find some of the best fish-and-chips in London at

SEAFOOD   the Golden Hind, a British chippy run by Greek Cypriots in a 1914 art deco café, off Marylebone High Street. Locals and tourists alike love the calamari, skate wings, and fish cakes, but it's the perfect—nongreasy—deep-fried or steamed battered cod, plaice, and haddock, the classic Maris Piper chips, and mushy peas that are the big draw. Note it's open noon–3 PM weekdays and 6–10 PM Monday through Saturday. ⊠ *73 Marylebone La., Marylebone* ☎ *020/7486–3644* ▭ *AE, MC, V* ⌁ *BYOB* ☉ *Closed Sun.* Ⓤ *Bond St.* ✛ *1:H3.*

£££   ✕ **The Providores & Tapa Room.** New Zealander Peter Gordon scores

ASIAN   highly with his Pacific Rim fusion food on Marylebone High Street. Have a classy meal in the formal restaurant upstairs or try the packed and more relaxed ground-floor Tapa Room. All sorts of exotica are on the menu, from tamarind and coconut *laksa* (spicy noodle soup) to New Zealand *kumara* (sweet potato). On Sunday morning you'll find the whole of Marylebone village reading the Sunday supplements. New Zealand venison with cassava chips, or Wagyu beef with bone marrow and Parmesan sauce are typical delights. ⊠ *109 Marylebone High St., Marylebone* ☏ *020/7935–6175* ⊕ *www.theprovidores.co.uk* ⊟ *AE, MC, V* Ⓤ *Baker St.* ✛ *1:G3.*

MAYFAIR

£££ ✕ **Cecconi's.** Enjoy all-day buzz at this fashionable Italian brasserie oppo-

ITALIAN site the Royal Academy on Burlington Gardens. Between Savile Row and New Bond Street, the jet set pitch up for breakfast, brunch, and Italian tapas (*cicchetti*) and return for something more substantial later on. Ilse Crawford's green-and-brown interior is a stylish backdrop for classics like veal Milanese, Venetian calves' liver, and tiramisu. Note: It's a cool pit stop during a shopping spree. ⊠ *5A Burlington Gardens, Mayfair* ☏ *020/7434–1500* ⊕ *www.cecconis.co.uk* ⊟ *AE, DC, MC, V* Ⓤ *Green Park, Piccadilly Circus* ✛ *3:A6.*

£££ ✕ **Corrigan's Mayfair.** The nearby streets may be a touch quiet but there's

MODERN BRITISH a warm welcome and a lively scene at Richard Corrigan's flagship haute cuisine venture off Park Lane. This 2008 addition to the Mayfair scene is self-assured and on top of its game. Dark blue banquettes and crisp Irish linen provide a handsome setting for a high-powered clientele who love the lobster Waldorf salad, black bream and spinach, and heartier dishes like rabbit cutlet with dandelion and carrots. There's a chef's table and private dining, and you might see chef Richard Corrigan knocking around. ⊠ *28 Upper Grosvenor St., Mayfair* ☏ *020/7499–9943* ⊕ *www.corriganmayfair.com* ⌕ *Reservations essential* ⊟ *AE, MC, V* Ⓤ *Marble Arch* ✛ *1:G5.*

£££–££££ ✕ **Gaucho Grill.** You'll struggle to find a better steak house than this flag-

STEAKHOUSE ship Argentinian steak emporium off Piccadilly, featuring rump, rib eye, and everything in between. Order your steak *bleu (*rare), or *bien cuit (*well done), and kick back amid the orgy of cowhide furnishings and chandeliers. At this four-floor ode to beef, there's little for vegetarians. ⊠ *25 Swallow St., Mayfair* ☏ *020/7734–4040* ⊕ *www.gauchorestaurants. co.uk* ⊟ *AE, DC, MC, V* Ⓤ *Piccadilly Circus* ✛ *3:B6.*

££££–£££££ ✕ **The Greenhouse.** Tucked amid Mayfair mansions and approached via

FRENCH a spotlighted deck garden, this elegant ground-floor salon is for aficionados of top-class French haute cuisine at any price. Sit by a garden window and feast on Anjou pigeon, Dover sole, John Dory, or Limousin veal. The 90-page wine list has 3,000 bottles, including Château d'Yquem, with 23 served by the glass. ⊠ *27A Hay's Mews, Mayfair* ☏ *020/7499–3331* ⊕ *www.greenhouserestaurant.co.uk* ⌕ *Reservations essential* ⊟ *AE, DC, MC, V* ⊘ *Closed Sun. No lunch Sat.* Ⓤ *Green Park* ✛ *1:H5.*

£££ ✕ **The Grill at the Dorchester.** Traditionalists and modernists alike love

MODERN BRITISH the giant murals of kilted Scottish Highland folk and the tartan carpet, chairs, and banquettes at this most famous of London hotel grills at the Dorchester. Enjoy a showcase of the best of British fare: wild Scottish smoked salmon, Aberdeen Angus beef fillets, Welsh Black rib-eye steaks, Cornish red mullet, Dover sole, whole native lobster, and calves'

14

liver and Wiltshire bacon. All grill orders come with ample servings of chips, new or mashed potatoes, and seasonal vegetables, but remember to leave room for the knockout desserts like brandy soufflé with sage sorbet. ✉ *The Dorchester, 53 Park La., Mayfair* ☎ *020/7629–8888* 🌐 *www.thedorchester.com* ✍ *Reservations essential* ▬ *AE, DC, MC, V* Ⓤ *Hyde Park Corner* ✣ *1:H6.*

££££ FRENCH Fodor's Choice ★ ✕ **Hélène Darroze at the Connaught.** London's crème de la crème flock to Hélène Darroze at the Connaught for exemplary regional French haute cuisine, served in a quintessentially Edwardian wood-paneled hotel dining room. Taking inspiration from Les Landes in southwest France, Darroze sallies forth with a procession of magical dishes. Caviar d'Acquitaine wows with oyster tartare in a stylish martini glass, topped with black caviar jelly and white haricot bean velouté. Spit-roasted and flambéed grouse is served delightfully pink, with duck foie gras, and mini–Brussels sprouts. To finish, enjoy Madagascar chocolate ganache with raspberry sorbet. Note that the prices are high: £32 for lunch, and £85 or £95 for the set dinners. ✉ *The Connaught, Carlos Pl., Mayfair* ☎ *020/3147–7200* 🌐 *www.the-connaught.co.uk* ✍ *Reservations essential* 👔 *Jacket required* ⊙ *Closed Sun. and Mon.* ▬ *AE, DC, MC, V* Ⓤ *Green Park* ✣ *1:H5.*

£££ MODERN FRENCH ✕ **Hibiscus.** Chef and front-of-house Claude and Claire Bosi excel at one of London's finest Modern French restaurants, tucked away on Maddox Street in Mayfair. Wood-paneled and kitted in muted gray and green, gastronomes swoon at the fireworks on the plate. Bosi's effortless cuisine might impress with frogs' leg fricassée, Goosnargh duck breast with wonton, or Lyonnaise tripe with cuttlefish and pig's ear. Lime and olive oil mille-feuille (puff pastry) is bound to send you home happy. ✉ *29 Maddox St., Mayfair* ☎ *020/7629–2999* 🌐 *www.hibiscusrestaurant.co.uk* ▬ *AE, MC, V* ⊙ *No lunch Sat. Closed Sun. and Mon.* Ⓤ *Oxford Circus, Piccadilly* ✣ *3:A5.*

£££ FRENCH Fodor's Choice ★ ✕ **La Petite Maison.** Gwyneth Paltrow blogs that this is her all-time favorite London restaurant, and no wonder—there's nothing on the impeccably well-sourced French Mediterranean and Provençale menu that fails to deliver. Try a crab and lobster salad, a soft Burrata cheese, Datterini tomato and basil spread, or an aromatic baked turbot with artichokes, or chorizo and white wine sauce. Based on the style of the original La Petite Maison in Nice in France, dishes come to the table when they're ready, and friendly staff make for a convivial vibe. ✉ *53–54 Brook's Mews, Mayfair* ☎ *020/7495–4774* 🌐 *www.lpmlondon.co.uk* ▬ *AE, MC, V* Ⓤ *Bond St.* ✣ *1:H4.*

££££ FRENCH Fodor's Choice ★ ✕ **Le Gavroche.** Michel Roux Jr. thrives at this 43-year-old clubby basement haven in Mayfair, which some rate the best formal dining in London. With silver domes and unpriced ladies' menus, Roux's mastery of classic French cuisine dazzles with signatures like foie gras with cinnamon-scented crispy duck pancake, langoustine with Hollandaise sauce, or lamb with flageolets. Desserts, like roast pineapple with white-pepper ice cream, are delightful, too. Weekday set lunch is a relatively affordable treat at £48.60—with a half bottle of wine, water, coffee, and petits fours. ✉ *43 Upper Brook St., Mayfair* ☎ *020/7408–0881* 🌐 *www.le-gavroche.co.uk* ✍ *Reservations essential* 👔 *Jacket required*

☐ *AE, DC, MC, V* ☉ *Closed Sun. and 10 days at Christmas* Ⓤ *Marble Arch* ✢ *1:G5.*

££££ ✕ **Locanda Locatelli.** Celebs like Kate Moss and Victoria Beckham patron-
ITALIAN ize Giorgio Locatelli's glamorous Italian at the Churchill InterContinental. Warmly designed with beige banquettes, convex mirrors, and
cherrywood dividers, the regional Italian food is highly accomplished—
silky risottos, handmade pastas, gorgeous grilled fish, subtle desserts.
Be bold, and try the calves' kidney or Sicilian prawns with risotto,
and lose yourself in the all-Italian wine list. ☒ *8 Seymour St., Mayfair*
☎ *020/7935–9088* ⊕ *www.locandalocatelli.com* ☝ *Reservations essential* ☐ *AE, MC, V* Ⓤ *Marble Arch* ✢ *1:G4.*

££££–£££££ ✕ **Nobu Berkeley Street.** Supermodels, football (soccer) stars, and the For-
JAPANESE mula One crowd pay silly money for new-style sashimi with Peruvian
flair at this so-hip-it-hurts Nobu spin-off near Piccadilly. The beautiful
people go bonkers for miso black cod, California sushi rolls, tuna teri-
yaki, yellowtail, and Wagyu beef. Prices are extreme, but the people-
watching is just *so* good. ☒ *15 Berkeley St., Mayfair* ☎ *020/7290–9222*
⊕ *www.noburestaurants.com* ☐ *AE, MC, V* Ⓤ *Green Park* ✢ *1:H6.*

££££ ✕ **Scott's.** Scott's is so hot that it's where the A-list go to dine. Founded
SEAFOOD in 1851, and renovated and reborn as a glamorous seafood haven and
Fodor's Choice oyster bar, it draws beautiful people who pick at Cumbrae oysters, Red
★ Sea prawns, and Stargazy pie. Standouts like cod with chorizo and pad-
ron peppers are to die for. Prices are high, but don't worry: this really is
the hottest joint in town. ☒ *20 Mount St., Mayfair* ☎ *020/7495–7309*
⊕ *www.scotts-restaurant.com* ☝ *Reservations essential* ☐ *AE, DC, MC,
V* Ⓤ *Bond St.* ✢ *1:G5.*

£££–££££ ✕ **Sketch.** Art-meets-food-meets-fashion at Mourad Mazouz's madcap
MODERN BRITISH gastro-emporium off Regent Street. The all-white Gallery dining room,
a true art gallery by day, serves contemporary cuisine to video projec-
tions and an ambient beat, and turns into a late-night club Wednesday–
Saturday nights, as soon as staff clear the floor. Fashionistas enjoy
tea in the Parlour, and science-based "molecular gastronomy" in the
first-floor Lecture Room. ☒ *9 Conduit St., Mayfair* ☎ *020/7659–4500*
⊕ *www.sketch.uk.com* ☐ *AE, MC, V* ☉ *Closed Sun.* Ⓤ *Oxford Circus*
✢ *3:A5.*

£££££ ✕ **The Square.** Philip Howard's sophisticated set menus, from £30 to
FRENCH £95, include French haute cuisine dishes such as foie gras terrine, calves
sweetbreads with potato rösti, and pork belly with asparagus, followed perhaps by Brillat-Savarin red current cheesecake. The clientele
is mainly corporate types who appreciate impeccable service. There's
a charming sommelier and a long wine list with a particular focus
on Burgundy. ☒ *6–10 Bruton St., Mayfair* ☎ *020/7495–7100* ⊕ *www.
squarerestaurant.org* ☝ *Reservations essential* ☐ *AE, DC, MC, V* ☉ *No
lunch weekends* Ⓤ *Green Park* ✢ *1:H5.*

£££ ✕ **Wild Honey.** Wild Honey's amazing set lunch or early evening deals
MODERN (£18.95–£21.95) are wildly popular. Book ahead at this wood-paneled
EUROPEAN clublike salon, with modern pictures and comfy booths, in swanky
Fodor's Choice Mayfair. Try the tasty Exmouth crab and white peach, Icelandic cod,
★ panna cotta, or signature warm chocolate soup with milk ice cream.
All 50-odd wines are available in third-of-a-bottle carafes. ☒ *12 St.*

14

George St., Mayfair ☎ *020/7758–9160* ⊕ *www.wildhoneyrestaurant. co.uk* ▤ *AE, MC, V* ⊙ *No lunch Sun.* Ⓤ *Oxford Circus* ✛ *3:A5.*

ST. JAMES'S

£££ ✕ **Le Caprice.** Quarter-century-old Le Caprice in St. James's commands
MODERN BRITISH the deepest loyalty of any restaurant in London. Why? Because it gets everything right. It's the celebrity history—think Liz Taylor to Lady Di—the David Bailey prints, the '80s Eva Jiricna interior, perfect service, and appealing menu that sits somewhere between Euro peasant and trendy fashion plate. Sit at the counter and enjoy calves' liver with crispy bacon, red-legged partridge, and Scandinavian iced berries with white chocolate sauce—all served with an ample dollop of celebrity spotting. ⊠ *Arlington House, Arlington St., St. James's* ☎ *020/7629–2239* ⊕ *www.le-caprice.co.uk* ⌨ *Reservations essential* ▤ *AE, DC, MC, V* Ⓤ *Green Park* ✛ *5:A1.*

££££ ✕ **L'Oranger.** French haute cuisine reaches great heights at this aristo-
FRENCH cratic place in St. James's, whether it's scallops with mousse, sea bass with pomegranate, or strawberry frangipane. The dining room is intimate and attractive—polished silver, oak panels, flowers, and French windows—and service is formal. Royal courtiers, business leaders, and the great-and-the-good wallow in the plush surrounds. ⊠ *5 St. James's St., St. James's* ☎ *020/7839–3774* ⊕ *www.loranger.co.uk* ⌨ *Reservations essential* ▤ *AE, DC, MC, V* ⊙ *Closed Sun. No lunch Sat.* Ⓤ *Green Park* ✛ *5:A1.*

£££ ✕ **St. Alban.** South of Piccadilly, close to Theaterland, and with a stylish
MEDITERRANEAN retro-Modern aesthetic, St. Alban is one of the more fashionable places to dine in town. The '60s-airport lounge interior—gray slate walls, turquoise-and-cerise banquettes, carpet, and Michael Craig-Martin murals—is a winning backdrop for the Mediterranean-inspired menu. Try paella, wood-fired pizza, grilled swordfish, or Sardinian fish stew. Pre- and post-theater and Saturday lunch is £17.50. ⊠ *4–12 Regent St., St. James's* ☎ *020/7499–8558* ⊕ *www.stalban.net* ▤ *AE, DC, MC, V* Ⓤ *Piccadilly* ✛ *3:C6.*

£££ ✕ **The Wolseley.** The whole of London seems to enjoy the grand elegance
AUSTRIAN at this Viennese-style grand café on Piccadilly. Framed with black lacquerware, the brasserie begins its long decadent days with breakfast at 7 AM and stays opens until midnight. Linger for beef Tafelspitz, kippers, and kedgeree, or Matjes herrings and Wiener Holstein. For dessert, go for apple strudel or *kaiserschmarren*—a pancake with stewed fruit and raisins. It's known for Viennoiserie pastries and sinful afternoon tea. ⊠ *160 Piccadilly, St. James's* ☎ *020/7499–6996* ⊕ *www.thewolseley. com* ▤ *AE, DC, MC, V* Ⓤ *Green Park* ✛ *1:H6.*

SOHO AND COVENT GARDEN

COVENT GARDEN

£ ✕ **Baozi Inn.** Chairman Mao paraphernalia decorates the walls of this
CHINESE handy Sichuan café on a busy side street in Chinatown. Baozi steamed buns—pork and onion or shrimp and radish—are house specials (£1.50), and there's dragon wonton broth or Chengdu pork dumplings with chili oil (£5.20). Try "ginger juice" spinach (£4.50), or "peace and

happiness" noodle soup, topped with duck, garlic, and Chinese toon tree shoots (£6.50). Tables are cramped, and service is bang, bang, bang! ⊠ *25 Newport Ct., Soho* ☎ *020/7287–6877* ⌾ *Reservations not accepted* ▭ *AE, MC, V* Ⓤ *Leicester Sq.* ✢ *3:E5.*

£
PORTUGUESE

✕ **Canela.** Hidden behind Neal Street in Covent Garden, this laid-back Portuguese–Brazilian café serves savories, pastries, and strong coffee. Portuguese snacks including chicken-stuffed *coxinha* dumplings are £2.50, and mains like *feijoada* (pork and black beans) or bacalhau salt cod with fried potatoes are less than £9. There's a collection of wheat- and gluten-free cakes, and you sit at simple wooden tables. ⊠ *33 Earlham St., Covent Garden* ☎ *020/7240–6926* ⊕ *www.canelacafe.com* ▭ *MC, V* Ⓤ *Covent Garden, Holborn* ✢ *3:E4.*

£
CHINESE

✕ **Cha Cha Moon.** Alan Yau's slump-proof Chinese noodle joint off Carnaby Street charges £7.50 for all mains and sides, so it's no wonder the communal tables are usually crammed like a Hong Kong subway train. Pick wisely from the long menu and you can score a tasty meal for £15. Spring onion pancakes, chili prawn noodles, and eggplant or duck lo mein with broth are good. ⊠ *15–21 Ganton St., Soho* ☎ *020/7297–9800* ⊕ *www.chachamoon.com* ⌾ *Reservations not accepted* ▭ *AE, MC, V* Ⓤ *Oxford Circus* ✢ *3:B5.*

££
FRENCH

✕ **Côte.** Where else can you get a surprisingly good three-course French meal for £11.70? The Côte French brasserie—softly lighted and smoothly decked out with banquettes and Parisian-style round tables—does just the trick, and offers these deals weekdays from 3 until 7. With four choices per course, you'll find all your favorites: Bayonne ham, Les Landes chicken, moules marinière, tuna Niçoise and steak haché. ⊠ *124–126 Wardour, Soho* ☎ *020/7287–9280* ⊕ *www.cote-restaurants. co.uk* ▭ *AE, MC, V* Ⓤ *Tottenham Court Rd.* ✢ *3:C4.*

£
VEGETARIAN

✕ **Food for Thought.** It may only be an unfussy '70s-style subterranean vegetarian café with no liquor license (but BYOB without a corkage fee) on Neal Street, but it's got a cult following, so be prepared to queue down the stairs here in the heart of Covent Garden. You'll find wooden communal tables and a crunchy daily menu of soups, salads, stews, quiches, stir-fries, bakes, and casseroles. Wheat-free, gluten-free, genetically modified–free, and vegan options are available, but note that it closes at 8:30 PM daily, and 5 PM Sunday. ⊠ *31 Neal St., Covent Garden* ☎ *020/7836–9072* ⌾ *Reservations not accepted* ▭ *No credit cards* ⌷ *BYOB* Ⓤ *Covent Garden* ✢ *3:E4.*

££
MODERN
EUROPEAN
Fodor'sChoice
★

✕ **Giaconda Dining Room.** A real find on Denmark Street's "Tin Pan Alley" (think David Bowie, Bob Marley, and the Clash), the Australian-run two-room dining room may seat only 35, but the menu is inspired. Chef Paul Merrony sends out starters—pumpkin risotto, crispy pigs' trotters—and a full range of main entrées for a reasonable cost. Try the fish cakes, salmon and fennel, or hearty dishes like veal kidneys, Italian pork sausage stew, or ham-hock hash with a fried egg on top. Popular puddings such as apricot compote and whipped cream come in at a tasty £6. ⊠ *9 Denmark St., Soho* ☎ *020/7240–3334* ⊕ *www. giacondadining.com* ▭ *AE, MC, V* ⊗ *Closed weekends* Ⓤ *Tottenham Court Rd.* ✢ *3:D4.*

14

£££ ✕ **Great Queen Street.** Expect crowds and a buzz at Covent Garden's
MODERN BRITISH leading gastropub that showcases classic British dishes in a burgundy
Fodor's Choice and bare oak-floor-and-table setting. Old-fashioned dishes like pressed
★ tongue, mackerel, and gooseberry, and mussels and chips may be revived
from a bygone era, but Londoners adore them. Dishes for the whole
table—like seven-hour shoulder of lamb—are highly convivial. There's
little for nonmeat eaters, and no dinner Sunday. ⊠ *32 Great Queen St.,
Covent Garden* ☎ *020/7242–0622* ⌕ *Reservations essential* ▬ *MC, V*
⊘ *No dinner Sun.* Ⓤ *Covent Garden, Holborn* ✛ *3:G4.*

£££–££££ ✕ **The Ivy.** The A-list spurn the Ivy for Scott's and J Sheekey, but it's
BRITISH still hard to bag a table. A mix of daytime TV stars and gawkers dine
on bang bang chicken, salmon fish cakes, and English classics like
shepherd's pie in a handsome wood-paneled salon. For midrange star-
spotting and daytime stars this is a prime spot. If you can't score a
reservation, try walking in for a table at the last moment. ⊠ *1–5 West
St., Covent Garden* ☎ *020/7836–4751* ⊕ *www.the-ivy.co.uk* ⌕ *Reservations essential* ▬ *AE, DC, MC, V* Ⓤ *Covent Garden* ✛ *3:E5.*

£££ ✕ **J Sheekey.** Theater and film stars slip in here as an alternative to Scott's
SEAFOOD or Nobu Berkeley Street. Linked with nearby Theaterland, J Sheekey
Fodor's Choice is one of Londoners' favorite West End haunts. It charms with warm
★ wood paneling, showbiz monochromes, alcove tables, and lava-rock
bar tops. Opt for Arctic herrings, Dover sole, oysters, monkfish, or
famous Sheekey fish pie. Dine at the mirrored bar for the ultimate in
true romance, or enjoy the £24.50 weekend lunch. ⊠ *28–32 St. Martin's
Ct., Covent Garden* ☎ *020/7240–2565* ⊕ *www.j-sheekey.co.uk* ▬ *AE,
DC, MC, V* Ⓤ *Leicester Sq.* ✛ *3:E6.*

£££ ✕ **Joe Allen.** West End theaterland cast and crew flock here after curtain-
AMERICAN fall, but more for the Broadway buzz than the all-American comfort
food. Set in an open–brick wall basement, staff can be distracted, but
the menu's reassuring; goat cheese with blueberry relish is a typical
starter, and mains include barbecue ribs with corn muffins. There are
secret off-menu burgers and Yankee desserts like pecan pie and chocolate brownies, but it's the whiff of greasepaint that everyone adores.
The £18.50 Sunday brunch is a long-running hit. ⊠ *13 Exeter St., Covent Garden* ☎ *020/7836–0651* ⊕ *www.joeallen.co.uk* ⌕ *Reservations
essential* ▬ *AE, MC, V* Ⓤ *Covent Garden* ✛ *3:G5.*

£££££ ✕ **L'Atelier de Joël Robuchon.** Glitterati sit at the counter and graze tapas-
FRENCH style at Joël Robuchon's super-seductive London outpost. Decked out
in plush red and black, counter seating frames the ground-floor open
kitchen, creating a spectacle that is pure culinary theater. Navigate
exquisite French tapas—from frogs' legs and egg cocotte to scallops
and quail with truffle mash. The £105 eight-course tasting menu is a
most decadent way to blow the bank. There's also a bar, and a formal
restaurant, La Cuisine, on the first floor. ⊠ *13–15 West St., Covent
Garden* ☎ *020/7010–8600* ⊕ *www.joel-robuchon.com* ▬ *AE, DC, MC,
V* Ⓤ *Leicester Sq.* ✛ *3:E5.*

£££ ✕ **Quo Vadis.** Home to Karl Marx in the 1850s, and a renowned Soho
MODERN institution since 1924, the revamped Quo Vadis is back to its best.
EUROPEAN Awesome stained-glass windows bathe the ground-floor dining room
in a colorful light as a mixed media–business crowd works its way

through a no-surprises but highly enjoyable Euro brasserie menu. Opt for Piccolo oysters, razor clams, roast chicken, or grilled turbot from the à la carte, or have a pretheater meal for £17.50. ⊠ *26–29 Dean St., Soho* ☎ *020/7437–9585* ⊕ *www.quovadissoho.co.uk* ⊟ *AE, DC, MC, V* Ⓤ *Tottenham Court Rd.* ✥ *3:C4.*

£££–££££
BRITISH

✕ **Rules.** Come, escape from the 21st century. Opened by Thomas Rule in 1798, London's oldest restaurant has hosted everyone from Charles Dickens to Laurence Olivier and the Prince of Wales. This traditional English dining salon has plush red banquettes and lacquered yellow walls crammed with engravings, oil paintings, and Victorian cartoons. Try historic British dishes—steak-and-kidney pie or roast beef and Yorkshire pudding—for a taste of the 18th century. In season, daily specials include game from the restaurant's High Pennines estate. ⊠ *35 Maiden La., Covent Garden* ☎ *020/7836–5314* ⊕ *www.rules.co.uk* ⊟ *AE, MC, V* Ⓤ *Covent Garden* ✥ *3:F6.*

£
MEXICAN

✕ **Wahaca.** Expect a wait for the fab-value Mexican street food at this brightly colored Covent Garden favorite. Mud walls and bench seats make for buzzy basement surroundings, but it's the cheap £3.75–£8.50 tacos, enchiladas, quesadillas, and burritos that pull in the studenty crowds. A £19.50 spread for two will produce a feast of chorizo quesadillas, tacos, slaw, and guacamole, but note that bookings aren't taken and that it's often full by 6:30 PM. ⊠ *66 Chandos Pl., Covent Garden* ☎ *020/7240–1883* ⊕ *www.wahaca.co.uk* ✍ *Reservations not accepted* ⊟ *AE, MC, V* Ⓤ *Charing Cross* ✥ *3:F6.*

SOHO

££
MEDITERRANEAN

✕ **Andrew Edmunds.** Rustic food at realistic prices defines this perpetually jammed, Dickensian, softly lighted romantic Soho restaurant—though it could be larger and the wooden bench seats more forgiving. Tucked away behind Carnaby Street, it's a favorite with the media crowd that come for daily changing, fixed-price lunch menus. Starters and main courses draw on the taste of Ireland, the Mediterranean, and Middle East. Pigeon breast (£5.75), Roquefort soufflé (£6.50), and swordfish with basil mayonnaise (£15) are all hale and hearty. ⊠ *46 Lexington St., Soho* ☎ *020/7437–5708* ✍ *Reservations essential* ⊟ *MC, V* Ⓤ *Oxford Circus, Piccadilly Circus* ✥ *3:C5.*

£££
MODERN BRITISH

✕ **Arbutus.** Serious cuisine at midrange prices has established Arbutus in the winners' enclosure of favorite Soho eateries. The £15.50 three-course lunch or £17.50 pretheater special are bargains of the year. Chef Anthony Demetre might surprise with squid-and-mackerel burger, rabbit cottage pie, or pollack and tomato jam, and finishes off with English trifle. All wines are offered in third-of-a-bottle carafes—a great way to sample new delights. ⊠ *63–64 Frith St., Soho* ☎ *020/7734–4545* ⊕ *www.arbutusrestaurant.co.uk* ⊟ *AE, MC, V* Ⓤ *Tottenham Court Rd.* ✥ *3:D4.*

£££
SPANISH

✕ **Barrafina.** London's top tapas bar on Frith Street in Soho is modeled on Cal Pep in Barcelona and similarly has only a few (23) raised counter seats. It doesn't take bookings and you're likely to queue, but staff are past masters, and the tapas are supreme. Pick at gambas or chorizo, quail, sardines, and octopus, or classics like Jabugo ham and tortilla. You can check out the scene—or who's in the queue—at the

14

live webcam. ⊠ *54 Frith St., Soho* ☎ *020/7813–8016* ⊕ *www.barrafina. co.uk* ⌲ *Reservations not accepted* ═ *AE, MC, V* Ⓤ *Tottenham Court Rd.* ✛ *3:D4.*

£ ✕ **Bar Italia.** This football-mad Frith Street '50s landmark coffee bar
CAFÉ is a 24-hour Soho institution. Grab a cappuccino or macchiato and wolf down a slice of pizza, panettone, or rich chocolate cake at the mirrored counter. The walls are plastered with old pics of Italian singers, sports stars, and movie legends, and it's the *primo numero* spot in London to watch Italy play in soccer's World Cup. ⊠ *22 Frith St., Soho* ☎ *020/7437–4520* ⊕ *www.baritaliasoho.co.uk* ═ *AE, DC, MC, V* Ⓤ *Leicester Sq.* ✛ *3:D5.*

£££ ✕ **Bocca di Lupo.** The place is always packed, the tables are jammed too
ITALIAN close together, and the acoustics are lousy, but everyone loves the buzz and the brilliant regional Italian cuisine. Set in an unlikely street off Soho's red-light district, pile into a succession of small plates and dishes from Bologna to Venato. Try fried anchovies, grilled red prawns, lamb *prosciutto*, cannellini beans, or rustic pork and foie gras sausages. You may not be able to hear your dining companions speak, but at least the amazing milk-free espresso ice cream makes up for the loss. ⊠ *12 Archer St., Soho* ☎ *020/7734–2223* ⊕ *www.boccadilupo.com* ⌲ *Reservations essential* ═ *AE, DC, MC, V* ⊗ *Closed Sun.* Ⓤ *Piccadilly Circus* ✛ *3:C5.*

£ ✕ **Busaba Eathai.** It's top Thai nosh for little moolah at this superior
THAI no-bookings canteen in the heart of Soho. Fitted with bench seats and
Fodor'sChoice hardwood tables, it's no less seductive for the communal dining, rapid
★ service, and fast-moving queue out the front. The menu includes noodles, curries, soups, juices, and stir-fries. Try the chicken with shiitake, cuttlefish curry, or vermicelli with prawns, squid, and scallops. ⊠ *106– 110 Wardour St., Soho* ☎ *020/7255–8686* ⌲ *Reservations not accepted* ═ *AE, MC, V* Ⓤ *Tottenham Court Rd.* ✛ *3:C4.*

£ ✕ **Maison Bertaux.** Romantics cherish this tiny, two-story 1871 French
CAFÉ pâtisserie because nothing's changed in decades. The choux pastry and gooey cakes at this time-warp Soho institution are renowned; the chocolate éclairs, Black Forest gâteaux, and almond croissants always delight. Run by owner and Soho legend Michelle Wade, Maison Bertaux also does a cute tea service and tasty savories, like Dijon slice. Art exhibitions and a theater club are also occasionally pop up here. ⊠ *28 Greek St., Soho* ☎ *020/7437–6007* ═ *No credit cards* Ⓤ *Leicester Sq.* ✛ *3:D5.*

££££ ✕ **Yauatcha.** It's all-day dim sum at this superbly lighted slinky Soho
CHINESE classic. Well designed by Christian Liaigre—with black granite floors, aquarium, candles, and a starry ceiling—the food is a match for the seductive setting. There's wicked dim sum (try prawns or scallops), crispy duck rolls, silver cod, fancy cocktails, and tea and colorful cakes in the first-floor tearoom. Note the quick table turns, and ask to dine in the more romantic basement at night. ⊠ *15 Broadwick St., Soho* ☎ *020/7494–8888* ⊕ *www.yauatcha.com* ⌲ *Reservations essential* ═ *AE, MC, V* Ⓤ *Oxford Circus* ✛ *3:C4.*

London Dining
and Lodging
Atlas

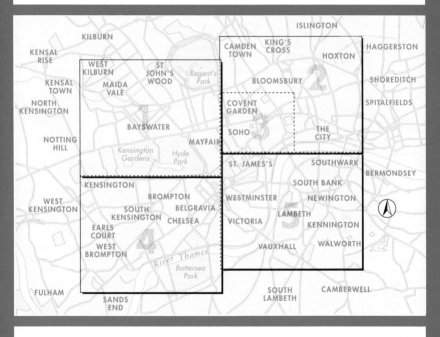

KEY
☐ Hotels
◼ Restaurants
◼ Restaurant in Hotel
Ⓤ **WESTMINSTER** Station London Underground
⇌ National Rail Connection

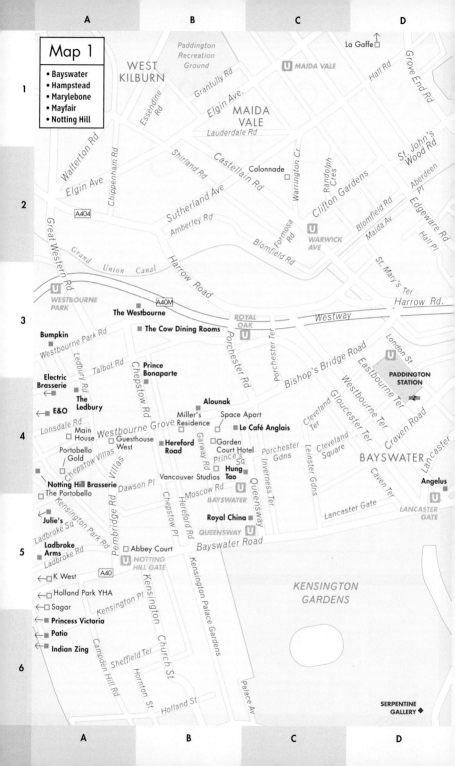

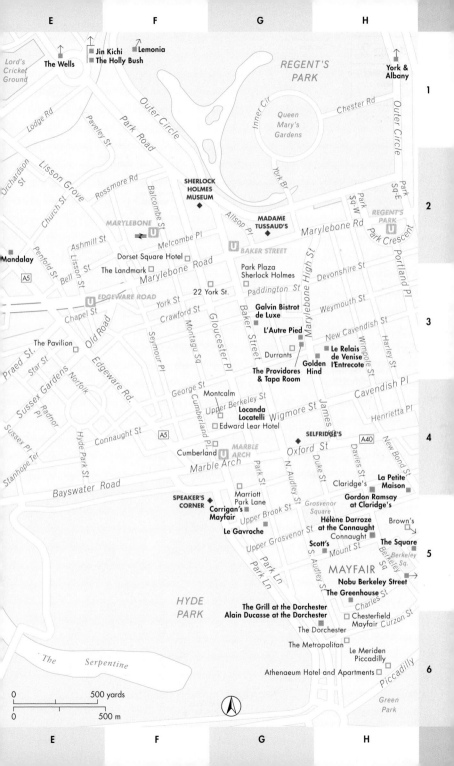

E

Lord's
Cricket
Ground

Lodge Rd

Paveley St

Park Road

Outer Circle

Orchardson St

Lisson Grove

Rossmore Rd

Church St

MARYLEBONE

Ashmill St

Penfold St

Bell St

Lisson St

Mandalay

A5

Balcombe St

Melcombe Pl

Dorset Square Hotel

The Landmark

Marylebone Road

22 York St.

York St

Crawford St

Montagu Sq

Seymour Pl

The Wells

Jin Kichi

Lemonia

The Holly Bush

F

Outer Circle

G

REGENT'S
PARK

Inner Cir

Queen
Mary's
Gardens

Chester Rd

H

York &
Albany

Outer Circle

1

REGENT'S
PARK

Park
Sq-W

Park Crescent

Park
Sq-E

2

SHERLOCK
HOLMES
MUSEUM

Allsop Pl

MADAME
TUSSAUD'S

Marylebone Rd

BAKER STREET

York Br.

Park Plaza
Sherlock Holmes

Paddington St

Galvin Bistrot
de Luxe

Baker Street

L'Autre Pied

Marylebone High St

Devonshire St

Weymouth St

New Cavendish St

Portland Pl

3

Durrants

The Providores
& Tapa Room

Le Relais
de Venise
l'Entrecote

Golden
Hind

Wimpole St

Harley St

Cavendish Pl

Henrietta Pl

The Pavilion

Praed St.

Star St

Sussex Gardens

Radnor
Pl

Sussex Pl

Stanhope Ter

Old Road

Edgeware Rd.

Hyde Park St

Norfolk

Connaught St

A5

Chapel St

EDGEWARE ROAD

George St

Gloucester Pl

Cumberland

Upper Berkeley St

Montcalm

Locanda
Locatelli

Edward Lear Hotel

Cumberland Pl

MARBLE
ARCH

Marble Arch

Wigmore St

James St

SELFRIDGE'S

Oxford St

Duke St

N. Audley St

A40

Davies St

New Bond St

La Petite
Maison

4

Bayswater Road

Marriott
Park Lane

SPEAKER'S
CORNER

Corrigan's
Mayfair

Le Gavroche

Park St

Upper Brook St

Grosvenor
Square

Upper Grosvenor St

Claridge's

Gordon Ramsay
at Claridge's

Hélène Darroze
at the Connaught

Connaught

Scott's

S. Audley St

Mount St

Brown's

The Square

Berkeley
Sq.

Berkeley Sq.

5

HYDE
PARK

Park Ln

Park Ln

MAYFAIR

Nobu Berkeley Street

The Greenhouse

Charles St

The Grill at the Dorchester
Alain Ducasse at the Dorchester

S. Audley St

Chesterfield
Mayfair

Curzon St

The Dorchester

The Metropolitan

Le Meriden
Piccadilly

Piccadilly

Athenaeum Hotel and Apartments

6

The   Serpentine

0   500 yards

0   500 m

Green
Park

E

F

G

H

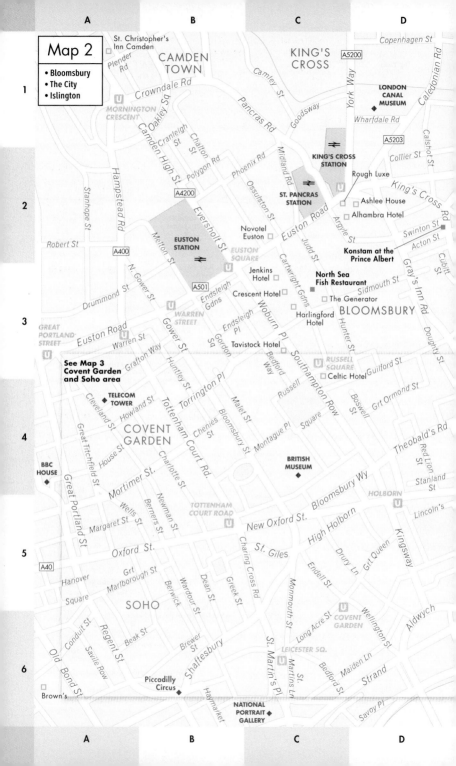

Map 2

- Bloomsbury
- The City
- Islington

A

St. Christopher's Inn Camden

Plender Rd

CAMDEN TOWN

Crowndale Rd

MORNINGTON CRESCENT Ⓤ

Oakley Sq

Camden High St

Cranleigh St

Chalton St

Polygon Rd

Hampstead Rd

Stanhope St

Robert St

A400

Melton St

EUSTON STATION

N. Gower St

Drummond St

A501

Endsleigh Gdns

GREAT PORTLAND STREET Ⓤ

Euston Road

Warren St

Ⓤ

WARREN STREET Ⓤ

Gower St

Grafton Way

See Map 3
Covent Garden
and Soho area

TELECOM TOWER

Cleveland St

Howland St

Huntley St

Torrington Pl

COVENT GARDEN

Great Titchfield St

Goodge St

Mortimer St

Wells St

Berners St

Charlotte St

Newman St

Chenies St

TOTTENHAM COURT ROAD Ⓤ

BBC HOUSE

Great Portland St

Margaret St

Oxford St.

A40

Hanover Square

Grt Marlborough St

Wardour St

Dean St

Berwick

Greek St

SOHO

Conduit St

Savile Row

Regent St

Beak St

Brewer St

Shaftesbury

Old Bond St

Brown's

Piccadilly Circus

Haymarket

B

Pancras Rd

Camley St

Goodsway

Phoenix Rd

Midland Rd

Ossulston St

Eversholt St

EUSTON SQUARE Ⓤ

Euston Road

Novotel Euston

Jenkins Hotel

Cartwright Gdns

Crescent Hotel

Endsleigh Pl

Judd St

Woburn Pl

Gordon Sq

Tavistock Hotel

Bedford Way

Gordon Square

Malet St

Bloomsbury St

Montague Pl

Russell Square

BRITISH MUSEUM

New Oxford St.

St. Giles

Charing Cross Rd

Monmouth St

St. Martin's Pl

LEICESTER SQ.

St. Martins Ln

NATIONAL PORTRAIT GALLERY

C

KING'S CROSS

A5200

York Way

KING'S CROSS STATION

ST. PANCRAS STATION

Rough Luxe

Ashlee House

Alhambra Hotel

Argyle St

Konstam at the Prince Albert

North Sea Fish Restaurant

The Generator

Sidmouth St

Harlingford Hotel

BLOOMSBURY

Hunter St

RUSSELL SQUARE Ⓤ

Celtic Hotel

Guilford St

Boswell St

Grt Ormond St

Theobald's Rd

HOLBORN Ⓤ

High Holborn

Endell St

Drury Ln

Long Acre St

COVENT GARDEN Ⓤ

Wellington St

Bedford St

Maiden Ln

Strand

D

Copenhagen St

Caledonian Rd

LONDON CANAL MUSEUM

Wharfdale Rd

A5203

Collier St

Calshot St

King's Cross Rd

Swinton St

Acton St

Cubitt St

Gray's Inn Rd

Doughty St

Red Lion St

Stanland St

Lincoln's

Kingsway

Grt Queen

Aldwych

Savoy Pl

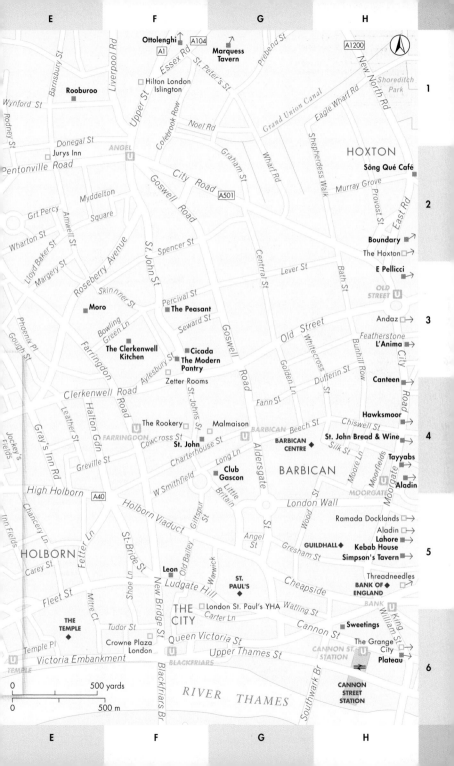

E   F   G   H

Barnsbury St

Wynford St

Rodney St

Liverpool Rd

Ottolenghi ↑ A104
A1

Essex Rd

St. Peter's St

Marquess Tavern

Prebend St

A1200

Shoreditch Park

Upper St

Hilton London Islington

Colebrook Row

Noel Rd

Grand Union Canal

Eagle Wharf Rd

New North Rd

1

Rooburoo

Donegal St

ANGEL Ⓤ

Pentonville Road

Myddelton

Grt Percy

Jurys Inn

Amwell St

City Road

Graham St

Wharf Rd

Shepherdess Walk

HOXTON

Sông Qué Café

Goswell Road

A501

Murray Grove

Provost St

East Rd

2

Wharton St

Square

St. John St

Spencer St

Central St

Lever St

Boundary

The Hoxton

Bath St

E Pellicci

Lloyd Baker St

Margery St

Roseberry Avenue

Skinnner St

Percival St

Moro

Bowling Green Ln

The Peasant

Seward St

Goswell

Old Street

Whitecross St

OLD STREET Ⓤ

Andaz

Featherstone

3

Phoenix Pl

Gough St

Farringdon

The Clerkenwell Kitchen

Aylesbury St

Cicada
The Modern Pantry

Road

Golden Ln

Bunhill Row

L'Anima

Canteen

City

St. John's St

Zetter Rooms

Dufferin St

Clerkenwell Road

Fann St

Hawksmoor

Road

Leather St

Halton Gdn

The Rookery

Malmaison

FARRINGDON Ⓤ

BARBICAN Ⓤ

Beech St

Chiswell St

St. John Bread & Wine

4

Jockey's Fields

Gray's Inn Rd

Greville St

Cowcross St

St. John

Charterhouse St

Long Ln

BARBICAN CENTRE

Silk St

Moore Ln

Moorfields

Tayyabs

Aladin

High Holborn

A40

Holborn Viaduct

Club Gascon

W Smithfield

Little Britain

Aldersgate

BARBICAN

London Wall

Wood St

MOORGATE Ⓤ

Moorgate

Chancery Ln

Fetter Ln

St-Bride St

Giltspur St

Warwick

Angel St

Gresham St

GUILDHALL ◆

Ramada Docklands

Aladin

Lahore Kebab House

Simpson's Tavern

5

HOLBORN

Carey St

Leon

Old Bailey

ST. PAUL'S ◆

Cheapside

BANK Ⓤ

Threadneedles

BANK OF ◆ ENGLAND

Fleet St

Mitre Ct

Shoe Ln

New Bridge St

Ludgate Hill

London St. Paul's YHA

THE CITY

Carter Ln

Watling St

Cannon St

Sweetings

BANK

King William St

The Grange City

THE TEMPLE ◆

Tudor St

Crowne Plaza London

Queen Victoria St

Upper Thames St

CANNON ST. STATION

Plateau

6

TEMPLE Ⓤ

Victoria Embankment

Blackfriars Br

BLACKFRIARS Ⓤ

Southwark Br

CANNON STREET STATION

RIVER   THAMES

0   500 yards

0   500 m

E   F   G   H

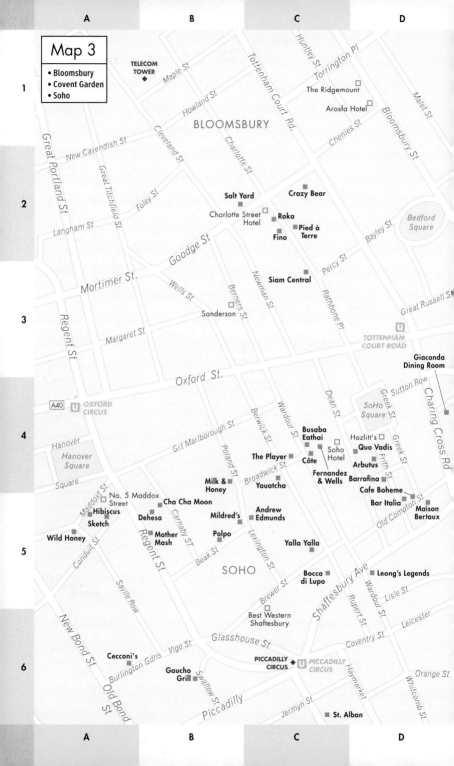

Map 3

- Bloomsbury
- Covent Garden
- Soho

A **B** **C** **D**

1

TELECOM TOWER

Maple St

Huntley St

Torrington Pl

Tottenham Court Rd.

The Ridgemount

Arosfa Hotel

Howland St

Chenies St

Malet St

Bloomsbury St

BLOOMSBURY

New Cavendish St

Cleveland St

Charlotte St

Great Portland St

Great Titchfield St

2

Foley St

Salt Yard

Crazy Bear

Langham St

Charlotte Street Hotel

Roka

Fino

Pied à Terre

Bayley St

Bedford Square

Mortimer St.

Goodge St

Wells St

Berners St

Newman St

Siam Central

Percy St

Rathbone Pl

3

Margaret St

Regent St

Sanderson

Great Russell St

TOTTENHAM COURT ROAD

Oxford St.

Giaconda Dining Room

Sutton Row

4

A40

OXFORD CIRCUS

Hanover Square

Hanover Square

Grt Marlborough St

Berwick St

Wardour St

Dean St

SoHo Square

Greek St

Charing Cross Rd

Busaba Eathai

Hazlitt's

Quo Vadis

The Player

Côte

Soho Hotel

Arbutus

Frith St

Fernandez & Wells

Barrafina

Poland St

Broadwick St

Milk & Honey

Yauatcha

Cafe Boheme

Bar Italia

Maddox St

No. 5 Maddox Street

Cha Cha Moon

Andrew Edmunds

Old Compton St

Maison Bertaux

5

Hibiscus

Sketch

Dehesa

Carnaby St

Mildred's

Lexington St

Wild Honey

Conduit St

Mother Mash

Polpo

Beak St

Yalla Yalla

Regent St

SOHO

Bocca di Lupo

Shaftesbury Ave

Leong's Legends

Wardour St

Lisle St

Savile Row

Brewer St

Rupert St

Leicester

Best Western Shaftesbury

Glasshouse St

Coventry St

6

New Bond St

Cecconi's

Burlington Gdns

Vigo St

Gaucho Grill

Swallow St

PICCADILLY CIRCUS

PICCADILLY CIRCUS

Haymarket

Orange St

Whitcomb St

Old Bond St

Piccadilly

Jermyn St

St. Alban

A **B** **C** **D**

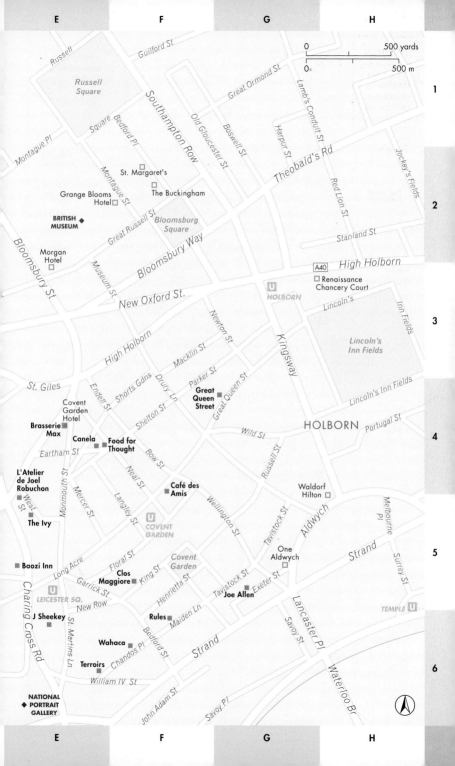

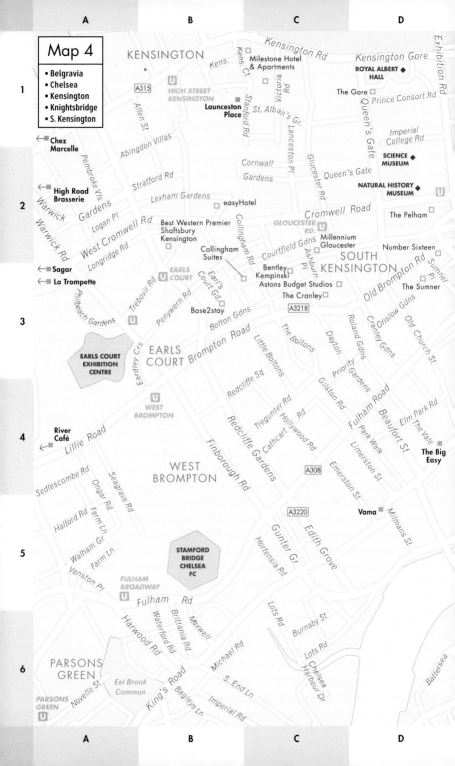

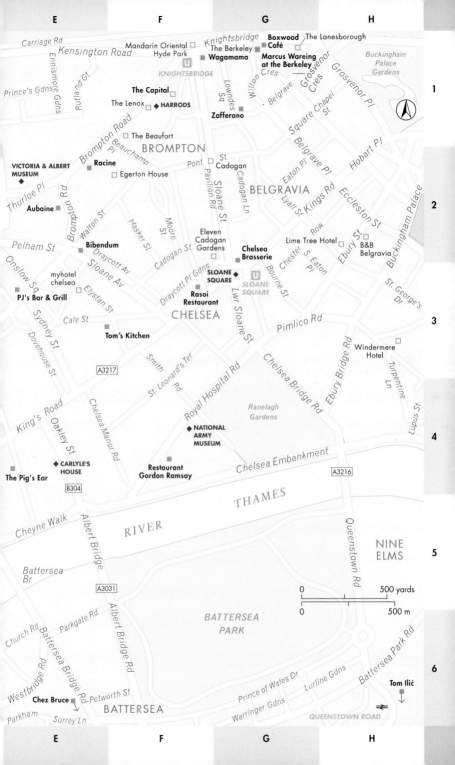

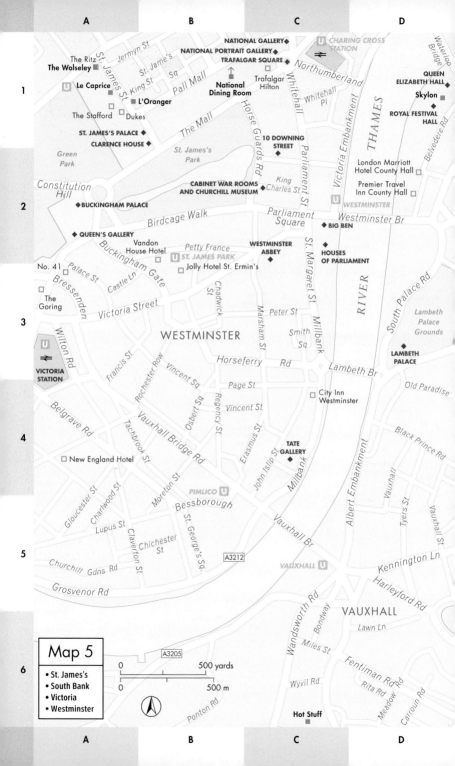

Where to Stay

WORD OF MOUTH

"You'll get many different opinions on what area is 'best' to stay in. Really, anywhere in zone 1, you'll be within several minutes' Tube or bus ride to whatever you want to see. (The Underground system is laid out in concentric circles, with the 'bull's-eye' being zone 1, the next ring zone 2 . . . out to zone 6.)"

—jent103

THE SCENE

Updated
by Christi
Daugherty

You'll find many things in London hotels: luxury, extraordinary service, and incredible views. But one thing you'll look long and hard for is a bargain. Rooms have traditionally been expensive, and the wild swings of the exchange rate make it hard to predict just how much you'll end up paying. Meanwhile, the London hotel market is focusing on luxury, luxury, luxury. Five-star hotels close, renovate, and reopen with increased prices at a dizzying pace. If it's any consolation, London does luxury better than just about any city, so you'll get your money's worth.

For those on more moderate budgets, the situation is in transition. The city is still struggling to develop a solid base of moderately priced high-quality hotels. Two places that have opened in recent years—the Hoxton and Guesthouse West—are great options in this category. The Hoxton even has special online sales that bring room rates down to an astonishing £1 per night. A newly attractive alternative are hotels in the Premier and Millennium chains, which offer sleek, modern rooms, lots of modern conveniences, and sales that frequently bring room prices well below £100 a night. The Best Western Premier Shaftesbury Kensington and Millennium Gloucester are both good examples.

At the budget level, small bed-and-breakfasts still dominate, although most are quite battered and basic. An alternative to that is the easyHotel chain, with its tiny, bright orange "pod" rooms. There's also the more sophisticated (and more expensive) base2stay, which falls somewhere between budget and not so much. And even at the very bottom of the price scale, accommodations can be unexpectedly trendy—just look at the slick simplicity of the Generator hostel.

WHERE SHOULD I STAY?

	NEIGHBORHOOD VIBE	PROS	CONS
Bloomsbury, Holborn, Hampstead, and Islington	Diverse area that is part bustling business center, and part tranquil respite with tree-lined streets and meadows.	Easy access to Tube, and 15 minutes to city center; major sights, like British Museum are here; buzzing nightlife in Islington.	Busy streets filled with honking trucks and roving students; the area around King's Cross can be sketchy—avoid it at night.
The City and South Bank	London's financial district, where most of the city's banks and businesses are headquartered.	Central location with easy transportation access; great hotel deals in South Bank; many major sights nearby.	It can be as quiet as a tomb after 8 PM; many nearby restaurants and shops close over the weekend.
East End	Increasingly trendy area east of the town center, with a great arts scene.	Great for art lovers, shoppers, and business execs with meetings in Canary Wharf.	Still a transitional area, parts of Hoxton can be a bit dodgy at night; 20-minute Tube ride from central London.
Kensington, Chelsea, and Knightsbridge	This is one of London's most upscale neighborhoods and a center of London's tourist universe. A glittering galaxy of posh department stores, boutiques, and fabulous hotels.	Diverse hotel selection; great area for meandering walks; superb shopping district. London's capital of high-end shopping with Harrods; easy Tube access; gorgeous architecture.	Depending on where you are, the nearest Tube might be a hike; residential area might be too quiet for some. Few budget hotel or restaurant options; beware of pickpockets in crowded Tube stations; not many sights here.
Notting Hill and Bayswater	Plenty of hotel options in an upscale, trendy area favored by locals and tourists.	Hotel deals abound in Bayswater; gorgeous greenery in Hyde Park; great shopping districts.	Few budget lodging options; residential areas may be too quiet at night for some.
Soho and Covent Garden	A tourist hub with endless entertainment on the streets and in theaters and clubs—it's party central for young adults.	Buzzing area with plenty to see and do; late-night entertainment abounds; wonderful shopping district.	The area tends to be noisy at night; few budget hotels; keep your wits about you at night, and watch out for pickpockets.
Westminster and Victoria	This historic section, aka "Royal London," is home to major tourist attractions like Buckingham Palace.	Central area near tourist sites; easy Tube access; considered a safe area to stay.	Mostly expensive lodging options; few restaurants and entertainment venues nearby.

15

WHERE TO STAY PLANNER

Lodging Strategy

Where should you stay? With hundreds of London hotels, it may seem like a daunting question. But it doesn't have to be. The 120-plus selections here represent the best this city has to offer—from the most-for-your-money budget motels to the sleekest designer hotels. Scan "Best Bets" on the following pages for top recommendations by price and experience. Or peruse the reviews. To find one quickly, search by neighborhood, then alphabetically. Happy hunting!

Need a Reservation?

Yes. Hotel reservations are an absolute necessity when planning your trip to London, so book your room as far in advance as possible. Fierce competition means properties undergo frequent improvements. When booking inquire about any ongoing renovations lest you get a room within earshot of noisy construction. In this ever-changing city, travelers can find themselves temporarily, and most inconveniently, without amenities they'd expected, such as room service or spa access, if their hotel is upgrading.

Checking In

Typical check-in and checkout times are 2 PM and noon, respectively. Many flights from North America arrive early in the morning, but having to wait six hours for a room after arriving jet-lagged at 8 AM isn't the ideal way to start a vacation. Alert the hotel of your early arrival; large hotels can often make special early check-in arrangements, but be prepared to drop off your bags and strike out for some weary early sightseeing.

Hotel Quality

Note that rooms can vary considerably in a single hotel. If you don't like the room you're given, ask to see another. Hotels often renovate room by room—you might find yourself allocated a dark, unrenovated room, whereas a bright, newly decorated room awaits just down the hall.

Breakfast

Most hotels include breakfast in the price of the room. In England, though, breakfast is almost always exactly the same—one fried egg, two sausage links, two slices of bacon, grilled tomato slice, sautéed mushrooms, and toast. This is known as the "full English." In most small hotels and all B&Bs, this is the only hot breakfast available. Pancakes, French toast, waffles, and omelets are not common here, and only the most expensive hotels will offer anything along those lines. Luckily, virtually all accommodations also offer packaged cereals, muffins, yogurt, and fresh fruit, so when the sausage-and-bacon brigade begins to get you down, go Continental.

Note: if breakfast is automatically included in a hotel's rate, we've noted it at the end of each review (CP for continental breakfast daily and BP for full breakfast daily).

Facilities

The lodgings listed are the cream of the crop in each price category. All available facilities are mentioned, but some do cost extra. When pricing accommodations, always ask what's included. Modern hotels usually have air-conditioning, but B&Bs and hotels in older buildings often do not, and it is generally not the norm in London. You should specify if you wish to have a double bed. All hotels listed have private baths unless otherwise noted. Whatever the price, *don't* expect a room that's large by American standards. As in most of Europe, space is at a premium here.

Prices

Many central London hotels—particularly those in The City, Bloomsbury, and Holborn—are popular with business travelers and offer significant discounts for weekend stays. Almost all major properties have steeply discounted rates in the off-season. If you're planning to visit in the fall, winter, or early spring, start monitoring online prices a few months before your trip and book whenever you see a good rate. Chains such as Hilton, Premier, and Millennium are known for their low-season sales in which prices can be as little as half the normal rate.

The farther you go out of the city center, the better the deal. New hotels in far east and west London are cheaper than those in the center of town, but you'll spend a bit more time on the Tube every day. ■TIP→ The Visit London Accommodation Booking Service (☎020/7932–2020, ⊕ www. visitlondon.com) offers a best-price guarantee.

WHAT IT COSTS IN POUNDS

	£	££	£££	££££	£££££
For Two People	under £80	£80–£140	£141–£200	£201–£300	over £300

Prices are for two people in a standard double room in high season, V.A.T. included.

In This Chapter

15

Lodging Alternatives

If you're looking for a better deal, or more choices, consider a flat (apartment) rental, hostel, University Residence Halls, or bed-and-breakfast. Some of these options include at least one meal or access to a kitchen, also lowering your dining budget.

BEST BETS FOR LONDON LODGING

Fodor's offers a selective listing of high-quality lodging experiences at every price range, from the city's best budget motel to its most sophisticated luxury hotel. Here, we've compiled our top recommendations by price and experience. The very best properties—in other words, those that provide a particularly remarkable experience in their price range—are designated in the listings with the Fodor's Choice logo.

Fodor'sChoice ★

Athenaeum Hotel, p. 327
Claridge's, p. 331
The Connaught, p. 328
The Generator, p. 302
The Hoxton, p. 312
Mandarin Oriental Hyde Park, p. 319
Number Sixteen, p. 317
One Aldwych, p. 332
Renaissance Chancery Court, p. 308
The Rookery, p. 310
The Stafford, p. 332
Zetter Rooms, p. 308

Best by Price

£

easyHotel, p. 315
The Generator, p. 302
St. Christopher's, p. 311

££

Harlingford Hotel, p. 303
Morgan Hotel, p. 303

£££

Athenaeum Hotel, p. 327
Best Western Premier Shaftesbury Kensington, p. 314
Guesthouse West, p. 324
The Hoxton, p. 312
Miller's Residence, p. 325
Number Sixteen, p. 317
Zetter Rooms, p. 308

££££

Charlotte Street Hotel, p. 302
Claridge's, p. 331
Colonnade, p. 322
Grange City, p. 309
The Rookery, p. 310

£££££

The Connaught, p. 328
Mandarin Oriental Hyde Park, p. 319
One Aldwych, p. 332
Renaissance Chancery Court, p. 308
The Stafford, p. 332

Best by Experience

BEST SPAS

The Bentley, p. 314
Claridge's, p. 331
One Aldwych, p. 332
Renaissance Chancery Court, p. 308

HISTORIC HOTELS

The Cadogan, p. 313
Claridge's, p. 331
The Dorchester, p. 329
The Rookery, p. 310

BEST BREAKFAST

The Dorchester, p. 329
K West, p. 324
Milestone Hotel & Apartments, p. 316
The Rookery, p. 310

BUSINESS TRAVELERS

Crowne Plaza London–The City, p. 309
Grange City, p. 309
Threadneedles, p. 310
Zetter rooms, p. 308

BEST CONCIERGE

The Connaught, p. 328
The Dorchester, p. 329
The Lanesborough, p. 319
Mandarin Oriental Hyde Park, p. 319

MOST KID-FRIENDLY

Best Western Shaftesbury, p. 331
City Inn Westminster, p. 336
No. 5 Maddox Street, p. 331
Premier Travel Inn County Hall, p. 311

MOST ROMANTIC

Number Sixteen, p. 317
The Pelham, p. 317
The Rookery, p. 310
The Stafford, p. 332

HOTELS

(in alphabetical order by neighborhood)

Use the coordinate (✣ 1:B2) at the end of each listing to locate a site on the corresponding map.

BLOOMSBURY, HAMPSTEAD, HOLBORN, AND ISLINGTON

BLOOMSBURY

£ ⊡ **Alhambra Hotel.** One of the best bargains in Bloomsbury, this family-run hotel has singles as low as £50 and doubles as low as £60. Rooms are small and the look is dated, but they're definitely good value. All rooms have a TV, all guests have access to free Wi-Fi, and tea/coffee-makers are available on request. It's not fancy, but it certainly is cheap. **Pros:** low price; great location. **Cons:** decor's a bit old-fashioned; no frills here. ⊠ *17–19 Argyle St., Bloomsbury* ☎ *020/7837–9575* ⊕ *www. alhambrahotel.com* ⤳ *52 rooms* ⚲ *In-room: no a/c, no phone, Wi-Fi. In-hotel: parking (paid)* ⊟ *AE, MC, V* ⊙ *BP* Ⓤ *King's Cross* ✣ *2:C2.*

££ ⊡ **Arosfa Hotel.** The friendly owners and an interesting historical tidbit (the property once was the home of pre-Raphaelite painter Sir John Everett Millais) set this B&B apart from the Gower Street hotel pack. Rooms are simple and comfortable in white and pastel shades. Those at the back are far quieter and overlook the hotel's pleasant garden, although even at the front, the double glazing somewhat tames the din of the students from nearby University College London. **Pros:** good location for museums and theaters. **Cons:** price a bit high for what you get; few services. ⊠ *83 Gower St., Bloomsbury* ☎ *020/7636–2115* ⊕ *www.arosfalondon.com* ⤳ *15 rooms* ⚲ *In-room: no a/c, Wi-Fi. In-hotel: bar* ⊟ *MC, V* ⊙ *BP* Ⓤ *Goodge St.* ✣ *3:D1.*

££–£££ ⊡ **The Buckingham.** This Georgian town house near Russell Square is a great bargain for the money. Its spacious, well-designed rooms are all studios and suites. Each has its own tiny kitchenette, giving you an alternative to eating in restaurants every night. All have marble-and-granite bathrooms and plenty of amenities. Staff are friendly, and the location is an easy walk from the British Museum and Covent Garden. **Pros:** great location; small kitchens free you from restaurants. **Cons:** no room service. ⊠ *11–13 Bayley St., Bedford Sq., Bloomsbury* ☎ *020/7636–2474* ⊕ *www.grangehotels.com* ⤳ *17 rooms* ⚲ *In-room: no a/c, Internet. In-hotel: bar* ⊟ *MC, V* Ⓤ *Tottenham Court Rd.* ✣ *3:F2.*

£ ⊡ **Celtic Hotel.** Run by the people behind the former St. Margaret's guest-house, the Celtic takes the same approach to keep this budget B&B popular. Rooms are simple and basic, but comfortable. The hotel is currently undergoing renovation (a room at a time), and rooms that have been redone are agreeably decorated with a modern look. However, those that haven't are still old-fashioned and dark, with cheap curtains and bedspreads. Bathrooms are tiny, but have everything you need. Hotel workers are friendly and helpful, and can guide you to good restaurants and pubs nearby. The best advertisement for this hotel is the fact that so many of the guests are regulars who come back again and again, drawn by the location near the British Museum and London's

15

West end. **Pros:** good prices; friendly service; handy location at the edge of Bloomsbury. **Cons:** don't come expecting luxury; no hotel Web site means you can't book rooms online. ✉ *61-63 Guildford St., Bloomsbury* ☎ *0207/837–6737* ➦ *35 rooms* ⚮ *In-room: no a/c, no phone, no TV. In-hotel: Wi-Fi* ▭ *MC, V* ¶❍❘ *BP* Ⓜ *Russell Sq.* ✥ *2:C3.*

££££–£££££   🛏 **Charlotte Street Hotel.** On a busy street in the media hub around Soho, this hotel fuses the modern and traditional with real style. Bedrooms are beautifully decorated with unique printed fabrics by designer and owner Kit Kemp. Each bathroom is lined with gleaming granite and oak, with walk-in showers and deep baths, and a flat-screen TV so you can catch up on the news while you soak with exclusive products by London perfumer Miller Harris. The restaurant, Oscar, is excellent for European cuisine, and the bar is a trendy local hangout. There's a public screening room for the Sunday-night dinner-and-film club or you might want to read a paper by the fire in the spacious drawing room. **Pros:** elegant, luxurious; great location. **Cons:** the popular bar can be noisy; reservations are necessary for the restaurant. ✉ *15 Charlotte St., Bloomsbury* ☎ *020/7806–2000; 800/553–6674 in U.S.* ⊕ *www.charlottestreethotel. com* ➦ *44 rooms, 8 suites* ⚮ *In-room: safe, refrigerator, DVD, Wi-Fi. In-hotel: restaurant, room service, bar, gym, laundry service* ▭ *AE, DC, MC, V* Ⓤ *Goodge St.* ✥ *3:C2.*

££   🛏 **Crescent Hotel.** Located on one of Bloomsbury's grand old squares, the Crescent is a friendly, attractive B&B. Rooms are small and simply decorated in cheery colors, and breakfast is big and hearty. Bathrooms are tiny and utilitarian—some have a bath and shower, others only a bath, so if you have a preference, ask when you book. You can use the tennis courts and private gardens in the square—great for picnics on a sunny day. **Pros:** lovely, convenient location; friendly staff. **Cons:** basic decor; no elevator. ✉ *49–50 Cartright Gardens, Bloomsbury* ☎ *020/7383–2054* ⊕ *www.crescenthoteloflondon.com* ➦ *27 rooms, 10 with bath* ⚮ *In-room: no a/c, Internet. In-hotel: tennis court* ▭ *MC, V* ¶❍❘ *BP* Ⓤ *Russell Sq.* ✥ *2:C3.*

£   🛏 **The Generator.** This is where the young, enthusiastic traveler comes
Fodor's Choice   to find fellow partyers. It's also the cleverest youth hostel in town. Set
★   in a former police barracks, the decor makes the most of the bunk beds and dim lighting. The Internet café provides handy brochures. The Generator Bar has cheap drinks and a rowdy crowd, and the Fuel Stop cafeteria provides inexpensive meals. There are singles, twins, and dormitory rooms, each with a washbasin, locker, and free bed linens. Prices run from £20 to £35 per person. **Pros:** funky, youthful attitude; great location. **Cons:** bar is crowded and noisy; party atmosphere is not for everyone. ✉ *MacNaghten House, Compton Pl. off 37 Tavistock Pl., Bloomsbury* ☎ *020/7388–7666* ⊕ *www.generatorhostels.com* ➦ *214 beds* ⚮ *In-room: no a/c, no phone, no TV. In-hotel: restaurant, bars, Internet terminal, parking (paid)* ▭ *MC, V* ¶❍❘ *CP* Ⓤ *Russell Sq.* ✥ *2:C3.*

££–£££   🛏 **Grange Blooms Hotel.** Part of the reliable Grange hotels chain, this white Georgian town-house hotel offers a pleasant home away from home in a building just around the corner from the British Museum. Rooms are not too tiny by London standards, and those in the back of the hotel look out onto a leafy green garden. Decor in public areas is a bit stuffy with bright carpeting, curtains, and sofas, but only in a pleasant, traditional way. Service is excellent, with a concierge and porter always on hand to help. You can get good deals by booking in advance through the Web site, and on the whole, it's good value for the money. **Pros:** great location; good prices if you book early. **Cons:** bathrooms could use an upgrade; outdated decor; no elevator. ✉ *7 Montague St., Bloomsbury* ☎ *020/7323–1717* ⊕ *www.grangehotels.com* ⤴ *26 rooms, 1 suite* ⚘ *In-room: no a/c, Internet. In-hotel: restaurant, room service, bar, some pets allowed* ⊟ *AE, DC, MC, V* Ⓤ *Russell Sq.* ✛ *3:F2.*

££ 🛏 **Harlingford Hotel.** The Harlingford is by far the sleekest and most contemporary of the Cartwright Gardens hotels. Bold color schemes and beautifully tiled bathrooms enliven the family-run place. Bedrooms aren't big, but they're attractive, quiet, and comfortable. Public rooms are similarly small but perfectly appointed. With space for four, the quad rooms are a good choice for traveling families. For those who tire of eggs and sausage every morning, the hotel promises a choice of 10 kinds of cereal. **Pros:** good location; friendly staff; breakfast included. **Cons:** rooms are quite small; bathrooms are tiny. ✉ *61–63 Cartwright Gardens, Bloomsbury* ☎ *020/7387–1551* ⊕ *www.harlingfordhotel.com* ⤴ *43 rooms* ⚘ *In-room: no a/c, Internet. In-hotel: bar, tennis court* ⊟ *AE, DC, MC, V* ⦿| *BP* Ⓤ *Russell Sq.* ✛ *2:C2.*

££ 🛏 **Jenkins Hotel.** This small, moderately priced hotel has a classic Georgian exterior that belies its simply designed interior. The old-fashioned but pleasant enough budget hotel is done in blues and whites. Bathrooms and rooms are small, but it has everything needed for a good night's rest with no frills. **Pros:** good location for theaters and restaurants. **Cons:** basic decor; thin mattresses. ✉ *45 Cartwright Gardens, Bloomsbury* ☎ *020/7387–2067* ⊕ *www.jenkinshotel.demon.co.uk* ⤴ *13 rooms* ⚘ *In-room: no a/c, safe, refrigerator, Internet* ⊟ *MC, V* ⦿| *BP* Ⓤ *Russell Sq., King's Cross, Euston* ✛ *2:C3.*

££ 🛏 **Morgan Hotel.** This family-run Georgian row-house hotel is a handy option for those traveling on a budget—but don't expect many bells or whistles. Rooms are basic but attractive—the best are the little apartments (£££), which give you a bit more space to move around in and have a tiny kitchen. Downstairs, the small, paneled breakfast room is the kind of space real-estate agents would describe as "cozy." Rooms have sunny decor; some have floor-to-ceiling windows, and the ones in the back overlook the British Museum. **Pros:** double and triple rooms are spacious by London standards; handy for the museum and West End theaters. **Cons:** mattresses are quite thin, as are walls. ✉ *24 Bloomsbury St., Bloomsbury* ☎ *020/7636–3735* ⊕ *www.morganhotel.co.uk* ⤴ *15 rooms, 5 apartments* ⚘ *In-room: a/c (some), refrigerator (some), Internet* ⊟ *MC, V* ⦿| *BP* Ⓤ *Tottenham Court Rd, Russell Sq.* ✛ *3:E2.*

£ 🛏 **The Ridgemount.** Mere blocks away from the British Museum and London's West End theaters, this guesthouse has clean and neat rooms at a bargain. The public areas, especially the family-style breakfast room, are rather sweetly cluttered Victorian-style parlors. Rooms are plainly decorated and not all have private bathrooms, but some overlook a leafy garden. **Pros:** good location near the museums. **Cons:** guest-

Fodor'sChoice ★

The Generator

Renaissance Chancery Court

Zetter Rooms

The Rookery

The Hoxton

Number Sixteen

Fodor's Choice ★

Mandarin Oriental Hyde Park

Athenaeum Hotel and Apartments

The Connaught

Claridge's

The Stafford

One Aldwych

room decor is basic; no customer services; cheapest rooms have shared bathrooms. ⊠ *65 Gower St., Bloomsbury* ☎ *020/7636–1141* ⊕ *www. ridgemounthotel.co.uk* ⟿ *32 rooms, 15 with bath* ♿ *In-room: no a/c, no phone* ▭ *MC, V* ⦿⌶ *BP* Ⓤ *Goodge St.* ✛ *3:D1.*

£££   ⊞ **Rough Luxe.** London's quirkiest hotel is, as its name implies, a strange combination of budget hotel and swanky luxury. In a 19th-century building near King's Cross train station in a neighborhood locals would describe as "dodgy," its rooms have been renovated to keep bits of their old battered walls and flooring in place so that the elegant new beds, designer lighting, and original artwork are cast in stark relief. All rooms have Skype-equipped mobile phones, rather than landlines. Some rooms share bathrooms, but all baths have been fully renovated with lovely touches (claw-foot tubs, designer sinks) alongside remnants of the old, torn wallpaper. The whole effect is so extraordinary that the hotel is regularly featured in designer magazines. Certainly its chutz-pah is impressive, given that prices are high while bathrooms are often shared and services few. **Pros:** art and design lovers will be dazzled; it's all very avant-garde. **Cons:** not everybody likes avant-garde; no restaurant or bar; neighborhood is a bit scary. ⊠ *1 Birkenhead St., Bloomsbury* ☎ *0207/837–5338* ⊕ *www.roughluxe.co.uk* ⟿ *10 rooms* ♿ *In-room: no a/c , no TV (some), Wi-Fi. In-hotel: Wi-Fi* ▭ *MC, V* Ⓜ *Kings Cross* ✛ *2:C2.*

£££££   ⊞ **Sanderson.** This surreal "urban spa" is housed in a converted 1950s textile factory with a lobby that looks like a design museum: billowy fab-rics serve as bathroom doors, and bedrooms have sleigh beds. The furni-ture is a mix of over-the-top Louis XV and postmodern pieces. Exercise addicts find Agua (the "holistic bath house") and the indoor-outdoor fitness classes to be just what the doctor ordered. The Asian-influenced restaurant Suka merges Malaysian and British cuisine. The elegantly landscaped courtyard forms a romantic retreat in the city, especially late at night, by candlelight. **Pros:** popular with design mavens; your every whim gratified. **Cons:** "designer cool" can be self-consciously hip; bar and restaurant are so exclusive it's hard to get in. ⊠ *50 Berners St., Bloomsbury* ☎ *020/7300–1400* ⊕ *www.sandersonlondon.com* ⟿ *150 rooms* ♿ *In-room: a/c, safe, DVD, Wi-Fi. In-hotel: restaurant, room service, bars, gym, spa, laundry service, parking (paid)* ▭ *AE, DC, MC, V* Ⓤ *Oxford Circus, Tottenham Court Rd.* ✛ *3:B3.*

£–££   ⊞ **Tavistock Hotel.** This big, sprawling hotel off Russell Square makes for a convenient and affordable base from which to explore the British Museum and London's West End. The rooms are small and simply fur-nished, but clean and quiet with tea/coffeemakers. The hotel itself has plenty of amenities, including a relaxed bar and restaurant. Although it has an amazing art deco foyer, it won't win any style awards, but it's a solid choice when money is an issue. **Pros:** affordable option in a great location near the British Museum. **Cons:** it's huge and a bit old-fashioned; the elevators are creaky. ⊠ *Tavistock Sq., Blooms-bury* ☎ *020/7278–7871 reservations, 020/7636–8383 hotel* ⊕ *www. imperialhotels.co.uk* ⟿ *343 rooms* ♿ *In-room: no a/c In-hotel: restau-rant, bar* ▭ *MC, V* ⦿⌶ *CP* Ⓤ *Russell Sq.* ✛ *2:C3.*

LONDON CHAIN HOTEL PRIMER

England has a number of hotel chains—worth considering—some are moderately priced, others are luxurious. Here's a quick run-down of our favorites:

Premier Inns: This widespread chain features medium-size, moderately priced hotels. They're known for their attractive if bland look, and for frequent sales, which keep prices cheap. ⊕ www.premierinn.com

Millennium: Similar in style to Premier Inns, Millennium (and its other brand, Copthorne) hotels are targeted at both business and leisure travelers. They offer well-designed rooms with plenty of gadgets and have frequent sales. ⊕ www.millenniumhotels.co.uk

Malmaison: With lavish, elegant small hotels around the country, this upscale chain offers luxurious designer style, good restaurants, and trendy bars. ⊕ www.malmaison.com

Grange Hotels: This chain includes a good mix of large and small hotels, with reliable (if somewhat dull) neutral decor, good service, and plenty of gadgets for business travelers. Prices vary, although most are moderately priced. ⊕ www.grangehotels.com

myhotel: A small chain of pricey boutique hotels, with a designer decor, trendy bars, and a modern approach, myhotels offer reliable comfortable and service, if you don't mind the price tag. ⊕ www.myhotels.com

easyhotel: One of the first chains to bring so-called "pod hotels" to London, the easyhotel chain specializes in very cheap (less than £40 a night for a double) rooms that offer all the basics, but are teeny-tiny, and have no extras at all. ⊕ www.easyhotel.com

15

HAMPSTEAD

££ 🖼 **La Gaffe.** Italian Bernardo Stella has welcomed people back to these early-18th-century row houses, a short walk up one of Hampstead's magnificent hills, for more than 20 years. His restaurant has been going for nearly 40 years. Make no mistake: rooms are tiny, with showers only, but many have canopy or four-poster beds, and all are sweetly designed. In the enclosed courtyard there's a raised summer patio. **Pros:** pretty area of town; friendly guesthouse. **Cons:** a bit of a journey to central London; few services; no elevator. ⊠ 107–111 Heath St., Hampstead ☎ 020/7435–8965 ⊕ www.lagaffe.co.uk ⤳ 18 rooms, 3 suites ⌂ In-room: no a/c. In-hotel: restaurant, bar, laundry facilities, parking (free) ⊟ AE, MC, V ⊠⊙⊨ CP ⓤ Hampstead ✛ 1:D1.

HOLBORN

£ 🖼 **Ashlee House.** This may be a hostel, but it attracts visitors of all ages and is quite popular with older budget travelers, thanks to the lack of a curfew and a 24-hour reception desk. It has all the necessary hostel amenities, including shared kitchen, free luggage storage, guided walking tours, and an Internet station. Staff are as cheerful as the decor, which is all sunny yellows and vivid pinks. Prices (per person) range from £9 for a dorm room to £26 for a double. **Pros:** great location for theaters and restaurants; friendly staff. **Cons:** few amenities. ✉ *261 Gray's Inn Rd., Holborn* ☎ *020/7833–9400* ⊕ *www.ashleehouse.co.uk* ↝ *26 rooms, 175 beds* ⚬ *In-room: no a/c, no phone, no TV. In-hotel: bar, laundry facilities, Internet terminal* ▤ *MC, V* ¶◯| *CP* Ⓤ *King's Cross* ✛ *2:C2.*

££££ — **Renaissance Chancery Court.** This landmark structure, built by the
Fodor's Choice — Pearl Assurance Company in 1914, houses a beautiful Marriott hotel.
★ — So striking is the architecture that the building was featured in the film *Howards End.* The spacious bedrooms are popular with business travelers and the decor has a masculine edge—lots of leather and dark-red fabrics, with luxurious mattresses. The day spa in the basement is a peaceful cocoon. There's marble everywhere, from the floors in public spaces and the massive staircase to the in-room bathrooms. The restaurant, Pearl, is known for its Modern European cuisine, and the bar, in an old banking hall, has elegant soaring ceilings. **Pros:** gorgeous space; your every need catered to. **Cons:** area is deserted at night and on weekends. ✉ *252 High Holborn, Holborn* ☎ *020/7829–9888* ⊕ *www. marriott.com* ↝ *343 rooms, 14 suites* ⚬ *In-room: a/c, safe, refrigerator, Internet. In-hotel: restaurant, room service, bar, gym, spa, laundry service* ▤ *AE, MC, V* Ⓤ *Holborn* ✛ *3:G3.*

£££–££££ — **Zetter Rooms.** By day, nothing but business suits buzz through the
Fodor's Choice — area between Holborn and Clerkenwell. By night, though, the ties are
★ — loosened and it's all oh-so-trendy. One of London's latest "it" hotels, Zetter reflects both personalities. The dizzying five-story atrium, art deco staircase, and slick European restaurant are your first indications of what to expect at this converted warehouse: a breath of fresh air (and a little space) in London's mostly Victorian hotel scene. Rooms are smoothly done up in soft dove gray and vanilla fabrics, and the views of the city from the higher floors are wonderful. **Pros:** big rooms; lots of gadgets; free broadband in rooms. **Cons:** recently increased prices mean this place is no longer a bargain; rooms with good views cost more. ✉ *86–88 Clerkenwell Rd., Holborn* ☎ *020/7324–4444* ⊕ *www. thezetter.com* ↝ *59 rooms* ⚬ *In-room: a/c, safe, refrigerator, DVD, Internet. In-hotel: restaurant, room service, bar, laundry service* ▤ *AE, MC, V* Ⓤ *Farringdon* ✛ *2:F3.*

ISLINGTON

£££–££££ — **Hilton London Islington.** Next door to the Islington Business Design
Centre, this hotel is sleek and modern, standing out starkly in historic Islington. The hotel has standard, good-size rooms with all the usual amenities meant to soothe the soul of the business traveler. For guests with time for aesthetics, the rooms higher up have panoramic views. **Pros:** lots of amenities for business travelers; handy restaurant and bar. **Cons:** not many amenities for leisure travelers. ✉ *53 Upper St., Islington* ☎ *020/7354–7700* ⊕ *www.hilton.co.uk/islington* ↝ *183 rooms, 6 suites* ⚬ *In-room: a/c, safe, Internet. In-hotel: 3 restaurants, room service, bar, gym, spa* ▤ *AE, DC, MC, V* ¶◯| *BP* Ⓤ *Angel* ✛ *2:F1.*

THE CITY AND SOUTH BANK

THE CITY

£££££ ⛨ **Crowne Plaza London—The City.** The shell of an old stationery warehouse, on the former site of Henry VIII's Bridewell Palace, is now in its "nth" reincarnation as a polished hotel. Don't let its all-business appearance and financial-district location put you off. It's just paces away from the Tube, and soundproof windows block out City noise. At night, the soundproofing is wasted, as the neighborhood is very quiet, so you'll have to go elsewhere for a party scene. Minimalist rooms are smaller than at a typical Crowne Plaza but reasonable by London standards. Head down to the hotel's Michelin-starred restaurant, Refettorio, for high-quality rustic Italian cuisine by acclaimed chef Giorgio Locatelli. **Pros:** good prices available with advance booking; lots of amenities in rooms. **Cons:** neighborhood is busy during the day and quiet at night. ✉ *19 New Bridge St., The City* ☎ *0870/423–4901* ⊕ *www.crowneplaza. com* ⌨ *203 rooms, 14 suites* ⌂ *In-room: a/c, safe, refrigerator, DVD (some), Internet, Wi-Fi. In-hotel: restaurant, room service, bar, gym, laundry service, parking (paid)* Ⓤ *Blackfriars* ✛ *2:F6.*

££££ ⛨ **Grange City.** With an eye on business, this sleek hotel in London's City has everything the workaholic needs to feel right at home—chic bedrooms subtly decorated in creams and chocolates, modern furnishings, plenty of space (by London standards), broadband and direct-dial phones, and more. The women-only wing has extra amenities ranging from more powerful hair dryers to extra-secure doors with peepholes and chain locks. Ladies (and gentlemen) can exercise in the hotel's magnificent columned swimming pool, and then linger over sushi at the Koto Japanese Restaurant or sip cocktails in the Isis Lounge. **Pros:** good-size rooms; very safe for female travelers. **Cons:** location is a bit off the tourist track. ✉ *8–14 Cooper's Row, The City* ☎ *020/7863–3700* ⊕ *www.grangehotels.com* ⌨ *307 rooms* ⌂ *In-room: a/c, safe, refrigerator, Internet. In-hotel: 2 restaurants, room service, bar, pool, gym, spa, laundry service* ▭ *AE, MC, V* Ⓤ *Tower Hill, Aldgate, Monument* ✛ *2:H6.*

£ ⛨ **London St. Pauls YHA.** On the doorstep of this hostel are St. Paul's Cathedral and the Millennium Bridge that leads to the Tate Modern. Once a choir school, the hostel has an oak-panel chapel that's now a meeting room. Most of the rooms have four to eight beds, but there are a few singles, doubles, and triples. **Pros:** very friendly place; safe and central. **Cons:** bustling atmosphere can keep you up nights; geared to the young. ✉ *36 Carter La., The City* ☎ *0845/371–9012* ⊕ *www.yha. org.uk* ⌨ *193 beds* ⌂ *In-room: no a/c, no phone, no TV. In-hotel: restaurant, bar, laundry facilities, Internet terminal* ▭ *AE, MC, V* ⍉ *BP* Ⓤ *St. Paul's* ✛ *2:F5.*

££££ ⛨ **Malmaison.** Part of a small chain of well-regarded U.K. boutique hotels, this Clerkenwell address is filled with elegant furnishings, clean lines, and all the electronic extras. Stylish rooms are well decorated in neutral cream and beige, and have huge comfortable beds and CD systems with a library of music on demand, as well as satellite TVs and free broadband. The hotel prides itself on fast, high-quality room service, so breakfast in bed can be a pleasure. **Pros:** luxurious rooms; excellent

15

service. **Cons:** neighborhood is off the tourist track; area can be quiet at night. ⊠ *18-21 Charterhouse Sq., The City* ☎ *020/7012–3700* ⊕ *www. malmaison.com* ↝ *95 rooms, 2 suites* ⚷ *In-room: a/c, safe, refrigerator, Internet. In-hotel: restaurant, room service, bar, gym, laundry service* ▭ *AE, MC, V* ⍿⦶ *CP* Ⓤ *Barbican, Farringdon* ✛ *2:F4.*

££££
Fodor's Choice
★

🏠 **The Rookery.** This is an extraordinary hotel, where each beautiful double room is decorated with a lavish, theatrical flair and an eye for history. Many have four-poster beds, and each has a claw-foot bathtub, antique carved wooden headboard, and period furnishings, including exquisite salvaged pieces. In the Rook's Nest, the hotel's duplex suite, you can relax in an antique bath in the corner of the bedroom or enjoy a magnificent view of The City's historic buildings. The conservatory, with its small patio garden, is a relaxing place to unwind. Great deals are available here in the winter. **Pros:** beautiful, quirky space; helpful staff. **Cons:** area is quiet at night and busy during the day. ⊠ *12 Peter's La., at Cowcross St., The City* ☎ *020/7336–0931* ⊕ *www.rookeryhotel. com* ↝ *30 rooms, 3 suites* ⚷ *In-room: a/c, safe, refrigerator, Internet. In-hotel: room service, bar, laundry service, parking (paid)* ▭ *AE, DC, MC, V* Ⓤ *Farringdon* ✛ *2:F4.*

£££££
🏠 **Threadneedles.** The elaborate building housing this grand hotel is a former bank, and the vast old banking hall has been beautifully adapted along with its luxurious marble and mahogany panels. Rooms are a good size for London, with modern bathrooms, big comfortable beds, and neutral coffee and cream colors, with dashes of deep burgundy. Given its location in the financial district, it's no surprise that this place looks as if it were custom-designed to please business travelers. Steep discounts are available by booking online in advance. **Pros:** lap of luxury; excellent service. **Cons:** a bit stuffy for some tastes; The City is very quiet at night. ⊠ *5 Threadneedle St., The City* ☎ *020/7657–8080* ⊕ *www.theetoncollection.com* ↝ *63 rooms, 6 suites* ⚷ *In-room: a/c, safe, refrigerator, DVD, Wi-Fi. In-hotel: restaurant, room service, bar, laundry service* ▭ *AE, DC, MC, V* Ⓤ *Bank* ✛ *2:H5.*

SOUTH BANK

£££–££££
🏠 **London Bridge Hotel.** Just steps away from the London Bridge rail and Tube station, this thoroughly modern, stylish hotel is popular with business travelers, but leisure travelers find it just as handy. Most of the South Bank's attractions are within easy walking distance, and it's a short stroll to London Bridge station to catch the Tube. Each diminutive but sleek room is understated and contemporary, with a calming, neutral decor. Three spacious two-bedroom apartments (£££££) come with kitchen, living room, and dining room. **Pros:** great for the arty South Bank; good deals available on its Web site in the off-season. **Cons:** small rooms, even smaller bathrooms. ⊠ *8–18 London Bridge St., South Bank* ☎ *020/7855–2200* ⊕ *www.london-bridge-hotel.co.uk* ↝ *138 rooms, 3 apartments* ⚷ *In-room: a/c, safe, kitchen (some), refrigerator, Wi-Fi (free). In-hotel: restaurant, room service, bar, gym, laundry service, parking (paid)* ▭ *AE, DC, MC, V* Ⓤ *London Bridge* ✛ *5:H1.*

£££££
🏠 **London Marriott Hotel County Hall.** This grand hotel has what many want—a view of the London Eye and the Houses of Parliament across the Thames. The building is a mammoth, spectacular, pedimented, and

columned affair with bronze doors and marble lobby. Rooms have been renovated in recent years, and most have a warm modern decor, with beige and taupe fabrics and walls. The views are lovely, the fabrics are luxurious, and it's got all the businesslike bells and whistles you could ever want. **Pros:** handy location for South Bank arts scene; great gym. **Cons:** decor is overdone; breakfasts are rather pricey. ⊠ *County Hall, Westminster Bridge Rd., South Bank* ☎ *020/7928–5200* ⊕ *www. marriott.com* ⤵ *200 rooms* ⌂ *In-room: a/c, safe, refrigerator, Wi-Fi. In-hotel: 2 restaurants, room service, bars, pool, gym, spa, laundry service, parking (paid)* ▭ *AE, DC, MC, V* Ⓤ *Westminster* ✥ *5:D2.*

££ 🛏 **Premier Travel Inn County Hall.** It might be near the riverfront, but any view of the Thames from this hotel is blocked by the nearby Marriott. Still, it's got a handy location near the London Eye, and you get a decent value here. Rooms are not very big, but they're nicely decorated, and the staff are helpful. Best of all for families on a budget are the foldout beds that let you accommodate two kids at no extra charge. **Pros:** good location for the South Bank; bargains to be had if you book in advance. **Cons:** denied great views by other buildings nearby; limited services. ⊠ *Belvedere Rd., South Bank* ☎ *0870/238–3300* ⊕ *www. premiertravelinn.com* ⤵ *313 rooms* ⌂ *In-room: no a/c, Internet. In-hotel: 2 restaurants, bar, parking (paid)* ▭ *AE, DC, MC, V* Ⓤ *Westminster* ✥ *5:D2.*

££ 🛏 **Premier Travel Inn Southwark.** This excellent branch of the Premier Travel Inn chain is a bit out of the way on the South Bank, but it sits on a quiet cobbled lane, and is ideally located for visiting the Tate Modern or the Globe Theatre. Rooms are simply decorated, and all have the chain's signature 6-foot-wide beds (really two 3-foot-wide beds zipped together). Ask for a room away from the elevators, which can be a little noisy. **Pros:** great location for the South Bank; quiet street. **Cons:** small rooms; limited customer services. ⊠ *34 Park St., South Bank* ☎ *020/7089–2580 or 0870/990–6402* ⊕ *www.premiertravelinn.com* ⤵ *56 rooms* ⌂ *In-room: a/c, Internet. In-hotel: parking (paid)* ▭ *AE, DC, MC, V* Ⓤ *London Bridge* ✥ *5:H1.*

£ 🛏 **St. Christopher's.** Named for the patron saint of travelers, St. Christopher's Inn is the headquarters of a small, reliably good hostel chain. It's actually made up of three hostels: the quiet Orient Espresso (above a coffee shop), the historic Inn, and party-hearty Village. You check into all of them at the St. Christopher's Inn. All the hostels are within walking distance, and all are cheap and cheerful, with swipe-card security and shared bathrooms. Along with the usual hostel offerings, it has the added benefit of a rooftop sauna and open-air hot tub. Orient Espresso also has a women-only wing. The sports bar in St. Christopher's Village is a good place to meet other travelers. **Pros:** friendly; clean; safe. **Cons:** lively party scene might be too much for some. ⊠ *161–165 Borough High St., South Bank* ☎ *020/7407–1856* ⊕ *www.st-christophers.co.uk* ⤵ *166 beds at Village, 50 beds at the Inn, 36 beds at Orient Espresso; all without bath* ⌂ *In-room: no a/c, no phone, no TV. In-hotel: restaurant, bar, laundry facilities, Wi-Fi (free)* ▭ *MC, V* ❚❘ *CP* Ⓤ *London Bridge, Borough* ✥ *5:H2.*

15

children. Bathrooms are small but well designed. The air-conditioned rooms are not big, but have a stylish, modern look with white walls and bedding, and dark throws and pillows. Tiny kitchenettes give you alternatives to another restaurant meal. Its "arrival base" system allows you to use a room before

WORD OF MOUTH

"My preference for London has been the South Kensington area, for its proximity to museums, Knightsbridge shopping, and some good local pubs." —maytraveller

your check-in time for £15 an hour. **Pros:** attractive rooms; handy mini-kitchens; good location. **Cons:** prices are a bit high for what you get; bathrooms are very tiny. ⊠ *25 Courtfield Gardens, South Kensington* ☎ *020/7244–2255, 800/511–9821 in U.S.* ⊕ *www.base2stay.com* ↗ *67 rooms* ♿ *In-room: a/c, kitchen, Internet* ▭ *MC, V* Ⓤ *Earls Court Station* ✛ *4:B3.*

£££££   ⚓ **The Bentley.** This opulent hotel is an elegant escape in Kensington. Housed in a creamy-white Victorian building, its lobby is a gorgeous explosion of marble, with high ceilings and chandeliers. The bedrooms are almost palatial in size (by London standards), with silk wallpaper, golden furnishings, and fine marble bathrooms with whirlpool baths—some have steam rooms. The restaurant serves modern British cuisine with Continental touches, and Malachite is a quiet bar for a brandy after dinner. The staff is obliging, and the marble Turkish steam room is a unique haven from the stresses of the day. **Pros:** luxurious rooms; gorgeous spa; great location. **Cons:** can be a bit stuffy; old-fashioned style won't please everyone. ⊠ *27–33 Harrington Gardens, South Kensington* ☎ *020/7244–5555* ⊕ *www.thebentley-hotel.com* ↗ *52 rooms, 12 suites* ♿ *In-room: a/c, safe, refrigerator, DVD, Internet. In-hotel: restaurant, room service, bar, gym, spa, laundry service, parking (paid), some pets allowed* ▭ *AE, D, MC, V* Ⓤ *Gloucester Rd.* ✛ *4:C3.*

£££   ⚓ **Best Western Premier Shaftesbury Kensington.** Just steps from Earl's Court Tube station at the edge of Kensington, this hotel offers a lot for your money. Its look is fresh and relaxing, with cool grays and earth tones in the guest rooms, and firm queen-size beds. Bathrooms are small but handsome, with modern bowl sinks, towel warmers, and big walk-in showers. Staff are friendly and helpful. **Pros:** rates are as low as half price in the off-season and for early bookings; free Wi-Fi. **Cons:** rooms are quite small; reservations do get lost here, so bring your confirmation number. ⊠ *33–37 Hogarth Rd., Kensington* ☎ *020/7370–6831* ⊕ *www.bestwestern.co.uk* ↗ *133 rooms* ♿ *In-room: a/c, safe, refrigerator, Wi-Fi. In-hotel: restaurant, room service* ▭ *AE, MC, V* ⦿*BP* Ⓤ *Earl's Court* ✛ *4:B3.*

£££–££££   ⚓ **Collingham Suites.** In an attractive Georgian building in Kensington, the Collingham is filled with suites and small apartments. All the rooms are tastefully decorated in contemporary style, with neutral carpets and a creamy pallet. Rooms are spacious by London standards, and most have separate living rooms and kitchens. All suites are set up to insure that business travelers are well taken care of, so there's free Wi-Fi, and lots of space to work. **Pros:** plenty of space; the two- and three-bedroom apartments are good for families. **Cons:** high price for

columned affair with bronze doors and marble lobby. Rooms have been renovated in recent years, and most have a warm modern decor, with beige and taupe fabrics and walls. The views are lovely, the fabrics are luxurious, and it's got all the businesslike bells and whistles you could ever want. **Pros:** handy location for South Bank arts scene; great gym. **Cons:** decor is overdone; breakfasts are rather pricey. ✉ *County Hall, Westminster Bridge Rd., South Bank* ☎ *020/7928–5200* ⊕ *www.marriott.com* ↵ *200 rooms* ⚹ *In-room: a/c, safe, refrigerator, Wi-Fi. In-hotel: 2 restaurants, room service, bars, pool, gym, spa, laundry service, parking (paid)* ▭ *AE, DC, MC, V* Ⓤ *Westminster* ✛ *5:D2.*

££ 🏨 **Premier Travel Inn County Hall**. It might be near the riverfront, but any
Ⓒ view of the Thames from this hotel is blocked by the nearby Marriott. Still, it's got a handy location near the London Eye, and you get a decent value here. Rooms are not very big, but they're nicely decorated, and the staff are helpful. Best of all for families on a budget are the foldout beds that let you accommodate two kids at no extra charge. **Pros:** good location for the South Bank; bargains to be had if you book in advance. **Cons:** denied great views by other buildings nearby; limited services. ✉ *Belvedere Rd., South Bank* ☎ *0870/238–3300* ⊕ *www.premiertravelinn.com* ↵ *313 rooms* ⚹ *In-room: no a/c, Internet. In-hotel: 2 restaurants, bar, parking (paid)* ▭ *AE, DC, MC, V* Ⓤ *Westminster* ✛ *5:D2.*

££ 🏨 **Premier Travel Inn Southwark**. This excellent branch of the Premier Travel Inn chain is a bit out of the way on the South Bank, but it sits on a quiet cobbled lane, and is ideally located for visiting the Tate Modern or the Globe Theatre. Rooms are simply decorated, and all have the chain's signature 6-foot-wide beds (really two 3-foot-wide beds zipped together). Ask for a room away from the elevators, which can be a little noisy. **Pros:** great location for the South Bank; quiet street. **Cons:** small rooms; limited customer services. ✉ *34 Park St., South Bank* ☎ *020/7089–2580 or 0870/990–6402* ⊕ *www.premiertravelinn.com* ↵ *56 rooms* ⚹ *In-room: a/c, Internet. In-hotel: parking (paid)* ▭ *AE, DC, MC, V* Ⓤ *London Bridge* ✛ *5:H1.*

£ 🏨 **St. Christopher's**. Named for the patron saint of travelers, St. Christopher's Inn is the headquarters of a small, reliably good hostel chain. It's actually made up of three hostels: the quiet Orient Espresso (above a coffee shop), the historic Inn, and party-hearty Village. You check into all of them at the St. Christopher's Inn. All the hostels are within walking distance, and all are cheap and cheerful, with swipe-card security and shared bathrooms. Along with the usual hostel offerings, it has the added benefit of a rooftop sauna and open-air hot tub. Orient Espresso also has a women-only wing. The sports bar in St. Christopher's Village is a good place to meet other travelers. **Pros:** friendly; clean; safe. **Cons:** lively party scene might be too much for some. ✉ *161–165 Borough High St., South Bank* ☎ *020/7407–1856* ⊕ *www.st-christophers.co.uk* ↵ *166 beds at Village, 50 beds at the Inn, 36 beds at Orient Espresso; all without bath* ⚹ *In-room: no a/c, no phone, no TV. In-hotel: restaurant, bar, laundry facilities, Wi-Fi (free)* ▭ *MC, V* ⓘ◉⏐ *CP* Ⓤ *London Bridge, Borough* ✛ *5:H2.*

15

EAST LONDON

£££   🏨 **Andaz.** This swanky, upscale hotel owned by the Hyatt group opened in late 2007 and has been making headlines for its modern, masculine design and unconventional approach. Instead of checking in at a desk, guests sit in a lounge while a staff member with a handheld computer takes their information. Rooms are sparsely decorated with designer furniture, and most important, intensely comfortable beds. Most have white walls, charcoal floors, and ruby-red touches. Rooms have Wi-Fi, MP3 docking stations, and "healthy minibars" stocked with nuts, fruit, and yogurt. The 1901 restaurant is exquisite, with marble floors and modern chandeliers, and the champagne bar is popular with city workers. **Pros:** nice attention to detail; guests can borrow an iPod from the front desk; no standing in line to check in. **Cons:** sparse decor is not for all. ✉ 40 Liverpool St., East London 🕾 020/7961–1234 ⊕ london. liverpoolstreet.andaz.hyatt.com ⇨ 267 rooms ⏦ In-room: a/c, safe, Wi-Fi. In-hotel: restaurant, room service, bar, gym, laundry service, parking (paid) ⊟ MC, V Ⓤ Liverpool St. ✢ 2:H3.

£££   Fodor's Choice   ★   🏨 **The Hoxton.** This trendy, East London hotel sits in the eponymous neighborhood and is designed to reflect the funky galleries and small boutiques for which the area is known. It claims to combine a country-lodge lifestyle with true urban living, and to that end its lobby has both crackling fires and cool cocktails, and the comfortable guest rooms have Frette linen sheets, down comforters, and free Wi-Fi. The design throughout is contemporary—but not so modern as to be absurd. There's still wood furniture and soft carpets. The bar is popular with local office workers, and the Hoxton Grille restaurant combines American steak-house style with French bistro chic. All rooms come with a free healthful breakfast of yogurt and fruit. **Pros:** cool-looking place; every night five rooms in this hotel are priced at £1, but you'll need to join the mailing list. **Cons:** restaurant and bar can be crowded in the evening; area is a bit off the beaten tourist track. ✉ 81 Great Eastern St., East London 🕾 020/7550–1000 ⊕ www.hoxtonhotels.com ⇨ 205 rooms ⏦ In-room: a/c, safe, Internet, Wi-Fi. In-hotel: restaurant, room service, bar ⊟ AE, MC, V ⏃⎮ BP Ⓤ Old St. ✢ 2:H2.

£££   🏨 **Ramada Hotel and Suites Docklands.** Built in a dramatic waterfront location, this modern hotel is in the rejuvenated London Docklands in East London. Many rooms have water views, and others have views of the city. Rooms are sleek and modern, geared at business travelers, with Wi-Fi, large desks, data ports, and personal voice mail. The hotel's restaurants and bars are handy, although there's plenty to choose from these days in Docklands. **Pros:** waterfront views; big discounts for weekend bookings. **Cons:** area is very quiet on weekends; about a 20-minute Tube ride to central London. ✉ ExCel, 2 Festoon Way, Royal Victoria Dock, East London 🕾 020/7540–4820 ⊕ www.ramadadocklands.co.uk ⇨ 224 rooms ⏦ In-room: a/c, safe, Internet. In-hotel: restaurant, room service, bar, gym ⊟ AE, MC, V ⏃⎮ BP Ⓤ Old St. ✢ 2:H5.

KENSINGTON, CHELSEA, AND KNIGHTSBRIDGE

CHELSEA

££££–£££££   ☐ **The Cadogan.** This is one of London's most historically naughty hotels. It was once the home of Lillie Langtry, a scandalous actress and King Edward's mistress in the 1890s. Her home was turned into a hotel, where Oscar Wilde stayed in 1895 (in Room 118) when he was arrested for "indecency" with a young man. A recent overhaul means much of the hotel's old stuffiness is gone—elegant golds and creams have replaced fussy florals. The drawing room has rich wood paneling and deep, comfortable armchairs, and is a good place for tea and people-watching, as is the small, sophisticated bar. Breakfast includes healthful cereals and fruits alongside decadent pastries. **Pros:** luxurious but not stuffy; friendly staff; great location for shopping. **Cons:** rooms are quite small, as are the bar and restaurant. ⊠ *75 Sloane St., Chelsea* ☎ *020/7235–7141* ⊕ *www.cadogan.com* ⤴ *65 rooms* ⌂ *In-room: a/c, refrigerator, Wi-Fi. In-hotel: restaurant, room service, bar, tennis courts, laundry service* ⊟ *AE, MC, V* Ⓤ *Sloane Sq.* ⊹ *4:F2.*

£££–££££   ☐ **myhotel chelsea.** This small, chic hotel tucked away down a Chelsea side street is a charmer. Rooms are bijou small but sophisticated, with mauve satin throws atop crisp white down comforters. Tiny bathrooms are made cheery with pale-pink granite countertops. Flat-screen TVs, DVD players, and Wi-Fi keep you digital. The beauty is in the details here—there's no restaurant, but the fire-warmed bar serves light meals and tea. There's no pool, but there's a spa. The guest library lends DVDs and books, and is a quiet place to relax. It claims to use feng shui principles in its design—good luck will be yours! **Pros:** stylish rooms made for relaxation; good advance deals on its Web site. **Cons:** tiny rooms; no restaurant. ⊠ *35 Ixworth Pl., Chelsea* ☎ *020/7225–7500* ⊕ *www.myhotels.com* ⤴ *45 rooms, 9 suites* ⌂ *In-room: a/c, safe, refrigerator, DVD, Wi-Fi. In-hotel: room service, bar, gym, spa, laundry service, some pets allowed* ⊟ *AE, D, MC, V* Ⓤ *South Kensington* ⊹ *4:E3.*

KENSINGTON

££–£££   ☐ **Astons Apartments.** Three redbrick Victorian town houses on a quiet residential street hold Astons's comfortable studios and apartments. All are simple and small but well designed with tiny kitchenettes, and the apartments (£££) have marble bathrooms and other extra touches as well. Some sleep families of four; others are barely big enough for two people. The decor has a modern, blond-wood look, and it all makes a nice alternative to normal hotel rooms. **Pros:** kitchenettes free you from restaurant tyranny; rooms are well designed. **Cons:** furnishings look a bit cheap; few customer services. ⊠ *31 Rosary Gardens, South Kensington* ☎ *020/7590–6000, 800/525–2810 in U.S.* ⊕ *www.astons-apartments.com* ⤴ *43 rooms, 12 suites* ⌂ *In-room: no a/c, safe, kitchen, refrigerator, Internet. In-hotel: parking (paid), some pets allowed* ⊟ *AE, MC, V* Ⓤ *Gloucester Rd.* ⊹ *4:D3.*

££–£££   ☐ **base2stay.** In a creamy white Georgian town house in chic Kensington, this hotel promises a new approach—a near-budget hotel. Prices are just above budget and just below moderate. Rooms are mostly comfortable doubles, but some have bunk beds, for traveling friends or children. Bathrooms are small but well designed. The air-conditioned rooms are not big, but have a styl-ish, modern look with white walls and bedding, and dark throws and pillows. Tiny kitchenettes give you alternatives to another restaurant meal. Its "arrival base" system allows you to use a room before

your check-in time for £15 an hour. **Pros:** attractive rooms; handy mini-kitchens; good location. **Cons:** prices are a bit high for what you get; bathrooms are very tiny. ⊠ *25 Courtfield Gardens, South Kensington* ☎ *020/7244–2255, 800/511–9821 in U.S.* ⊕ *www.base2stay.com* ⤳ *67 rooms* ⌂ *In-room: a/c, kitchen, Internet* ▭ *MC, V* ⓤ *Earls Court Station* ✛ *4:B3.*

£££££   🏨 **The Bentley.** This opulent hotel is an elegant escape in Kensington. Housed in a creamy-white Victorian building, its lobby is a gorgeous explosion of marble, with high ceilings and chandeliers. The bedrooms are almost palatial in size (by London standards), with silk wallpaper, golden furnishings, and fine marble bathrooms with whirlpool baths—some have steam rooms. The restaurant serves modern British cuisine with Continental touches, and Malachite is a quiet bar for a brandy after dinner. The staff is obliging, and the marble Turkish steam room is a unique haven from the stresses of the day. **Pros:** luxurious rooms; gorgeous spa; great location. **Cons:** can be a bit stuffy; old-fashioned style won't please everyone. ⊠ *27–33 Harrington Gardens, South Kensington* ☎ *020/7244–5555* ⊕ *www.thebentley-hotel.com* ⤳ *52 rooms, 12 suites* ⌂ *In-room: a/c, safe, refrigerator, DVD, Internet. In-hotel: restaurant, room service, bar, gym, spa, laundry service, parking (paid), some pets allowed* ▭ *AE, D, MC, V* ⓤ *Gloucester Rd.* ✛ *4:C3.*

£££   🏨 **Best Western Premier Shaftesbury Kensington.** Just steps from Earl's Court Tube station at the edge of Kensington, this hotel offers a lot for your money. Its look is fresh and relaxing, with cool grays and earth tones in the guest rooms, and firm queen-size beds. Bathrooms are small but handsome, with modern bowl sinks, towel warmers, and big walk-in showers. Staff are friendly and helpful. **Pros:** rates are as low as half price in the off-season and for early bookings; free Wi-Fi. **Cons:** rooms are quite small; reservations do get lost here, so bring your confirmation number. ⊠ *33–37 Hogarth Rd., Kensington* ☎ *020/7370–6831* ⊕ *www.bestwestern.co.uk* ⤳ *133 rooms* ⌂ *In-room: a/c, safe, refrigerator, Wi-Fi. In-hotel: restaurant, room service* ▭ *AE, MC, V* ⦿ *BP* ⓤ *Earl's Court* ✛ *4:B3.*

£££–££££   🏨 **Collingham Suites.** In an attractive Georgian building in Kensington, the Collingham is filled with suites and small apartments. All the rooms are tastefully decorated in contemporary style, with neutral carpets and a creamy pallet. Rooms are spacious by London standards, and most have separate living rooms and kitchens. All suites are set up to insure that business travelers are well taken care of, so there's free Wi-Fi, and lots of space to work. **Pros:** plenty of space; the two- and three-bedroom apartments are good for families. **Cons:** high price for

what you get; no in-house restaurant or bar. ✉ *26–27 Collingham Gardens, Kensington* ☎ *0207/244–8677* ⊕ *www.collinghamapartments. com* ↝ *26 rooms* ♿ *In-room: a/c, kitchen, refrigerator, Wi-Fi* ▭ *MC, V* Ⓜ *Gloucester Rd.* ✛ *1:G4.*

££££ 🖭 **The Cranley.** Old-fashioned British propriety is the overall feeling here at this small, Victorian town-house hotel. High ceilings, huge windows, and a pale, creamy color scheme make the bedrooms light and bright. Antique desks and four-poster or half-tester beds give the place historic authenticity. Even the bathrooms have traditional Victorian fittings—although the plumbing is completely modern. Afternoon tea and evening canapés are complimentary and tasty. **Pros:** good-size rooms; friendly staff. **Cons:** steep stairs into lobby; no restaurant. ✉ *10–12 Bina Gardens, South Kensington* ☎ *020/7373–0123* ⊕ *www.thecranley. com* ↝ *29 rooms, 5 suites, 4 apartments* ♿ *In-room: a/c, safe, Internet. In-hotel: parking (paid)* ▭ *AE, DC, MC, V* Ⓤ *Gloucester Rd.* ✛ *4:C3.*

£ 🖭 **easyHotel.** This budget hotel opened in 2005 as London's first "pod hotel." Crammed into a big white town house are 34 tiny rooms, all with a double bed, private bathroom, and little else. Each is brightly decorated in the trademark orange and white of the easyGroup (which includes the budget airline easyJet). The idea behind the hotel is to provide high-quality basics (bed, sink, shower, and toilet) for little money. The small reception desk can't offer much in terms of service, and if you want your room cleaned while you stay, it's an additional £10 a day. The concept continues to be a huge hit—easyHotel is fully booked months in advance and has opened additional branches at Heathrow Airport, as well as near Victoria and Paddington stations and elsewhere in Kensington. Check the Web site for all locations. **Pros:** amazing price; safe and pleasant space. **Cons:** not for the claustrophobic; six floors, no lift; everything costs extra, from a TV in your room to fresh towels; no customer services. ✉ *14 Lexham Gardens, Kensington* ☎ *020/7216– 1717* ⊕ *www.easyhotel.com* ↝ *34 rooms* ♿ *In-room: no a/c, no phone* ▭ *MC, V* Ⓤ *Gloucester Rd.* ✛ *4:B2.*

££££–£££££ 🖭 **Eleven Cadogan Gardens.** This aristocratic, late-Victorian, gabled town house has a clubby feel—there's no sign, just a simple 11 above the door. That can be explained, as it's not only a hotel but also a private members club. All rooms have recently been redone in dark, sophisticated tones by interior designer Paul Davies. He's lavished silk and chiffon on them and dimmed the lights, but the hotel has lost a little of its old personal touch. The best rooms are at the back, overlooking a private garden. **Pros:** small size means you get personal attention; lobby is great for people-watching. **Cons:** some might consider it over-designed; lots of stairs and tiny elevators; not great for those with mobility issues. ✉ *11 Cadogan Gardens, Sloane Sq., South Kensington* ☎ *020/7730– 7000* ⊕ *www.number-eleven.co.uk* ↝ *62 rooms* ♿ *In-room: a/c, safe, refrigerator, Internet. In-hotel: room service, bar, gym, laundry service, Internet terminal* ▭ *AE, DC, MC, V* Ⓤ *Sloane Sq.* ✛ *4:G2.*

££££–£££££ 🖭 **The Gore.** Just down the road from the Albert Hall, this gorgeous, friendly hotel has a luxurious mixture of the comfortable and the extraordinary. The lobby evokes a wealthy estate from centuries past, and upstairs most rooms are spacious and decorated in calming neutral

15

tones with rich fabrics. A handful of rooms are spectacular: one is a Tudor fantasy with minstrel gallery, stained glass, and four-poster bed, another—the "Judy Garland"—is done up in over-the-top Hollywood style. **Pros:** small scale means the staff can lavish attention on you; spacious rooms. **Cons:** price has gone up in recent years, making this only for those with deep pockets. ☒ *189 Queen's Gate, Kensington* ☎ *020/7584–6601* ⊕ *www.gorehotel.com* ↰ *50 rooms* ♿ *In-room: no a/c, safe, refrigerator, Wi-Fi. In-hotel: restaurant, room service, bar, laundry service* ▭ *AE, DC, MC, V* Ⓤ *Gloucester Rd.* ✛ *4:D1.*

£   🏠 **Holland Park YHA.** In a 1970s addition to a grand Jacobean mansion, this is the most historic and pastoral of London's youth hostels. Clean, bright, modern dorm rooms overlook the wooded park, where peacocks strut around the Kyoto Gardens. High Street Kensington and civilization are just a few steps away. Inexpensive lunches and dinners are available in the cheerful canteen. **Pros:** friendly and bright; beautiful setting. **Cons:** can be a bit boisterous, with a youthful atmosphere. ☒ *Holland Walk, Kensington* ☎ *0845/371–9122* ⊕ *www.yha.org.uk* ↰ *200 beds* ♿ *In-room: no a/c, no phone, no TV. In-hotel: bar, tennis courts, laundry facilities, Internet terminal* ▭ *AE, MC, V* ⏁ *BP* Ⓤ *High Street Kensington* ✛ *1:A5.*

£££–££££   🏠 **Kensington House Hotel.** This refurbished 19th-century town house off High Street Kensington has streamlined rooms with a creamy, contemporary look. All have large windows and plenty of light, and comfortable beds with luxurious fabrics and soft comforters. Rear guest rooms have views of trees and mews houses, and all rooms have extras such as tea/coffeemakers and bathrobes. **Pros:** attractive design; relaxing setting; free Wi-Fi. **Cons:** rooms are small; bathrooms are minuscule; the elevator is Lilliputian. ☒ *15–16 Prince of Wales Terr., Kensington* ☎ *020/7937–2345* ⊕ *www.kenhouse.com* ↰ *41 rooms* ♿ *In-room: no a/c, safe, Wi-Fi. In-hotel: room service, bar, laundry service, parking (paid)* ▭ *AE, DC, MC, V* ⏁ *CP* Ⓤ *High Street Kensington* ✛ *4:C1.*

£££££   🏠 **Milestone Hotel & Apartments.** This pair of intricately decorated Victorian town houses overlooking Kensington Palace and Gardens is an intimate, luxurious alternative to the city's more famous high-end hotels. Great thoughtfulness goes into the hospitality, and everything is possible in this special place. You'll be offered a drink upon arrival and, if you so desire, you can return to a post-theater midnight snack in your room or leave with a picnic basket for the park across the street. Each sumptuous room is full of antiques; many have canopied beds. A favorite is the Ascot Room, which is filled with elegant hats of the kind worn at the famous races. **Pros:** beautiful space; big rooms. **Cons:** service can be a bit stuffy (it seems you're not expected to do anything for yourself). ☒ *1 Kensington Ct., Kensington* ☎ *020/7917–1000* ⊕ *www.milestonehotel. com* ↰ *45 rooms, 12 suites, 6 apartments* ♿ *In-room: a/c, safe, kitchen (some), refrigerator, DVD, Wi-Fi. In-hotel: 2 restaurants, room service, bar, gym, laundry service, some pets allowed* ▭ *AE, DC, MC, V* Ⓤ *High Street Kensington* ✛ *4:C1.*

£££   🏠 **Millennium Gloucester.** Refurbished in 2007, the hotel has a sleek lobby with polished wood columns, a warming fireplace, and glittering chandeliers. Guest rooms are done in neutral creams and earth tones, and blond-wood desks and leather chairs have a blandly masculine look. The hotel is popular with business travelers, so rooms come equipped with satellite TV and broadband. Bathrooms are relatively small but have all you need. There are two bars and several restaurants, which means you don't have to go out if you'd prefer to stay in. **Pros:** good deals available if you book in advance. **Cons:** public areas and restaurant can get crowded. ⊠ *4–18 Harrington Gardens, Kensington* ☎ *020/7373–6030* ⊕ *www.millenniumhotels.co.uk/ millenniumgloucester* ⇗ *143 rooms* ⌂ *In-room: a/c, safe, refrigerator, Wi-Fi. In-hotel: restaurant, room service* ▭ *AE, MC, V* ⏐○⏐ *BP* Ⓤ *Gloucester Rd.* ✛ *4:C2.*

£££–££££
Fodor's Choice
★

🖭 **Number Sixteen.** In a white-portico row of Victorian houses, close to the South Kensington Tube and a short walk from the Victoria & Albert Museum, Number Sixteen is a lovely luxury guesthouse. Rooms are spacious and have marble- and oak-clad bathrooms. The style is not so much interior-designed as understated—new furniture and modern prints are juxtaposed with weighty oil paintings and antiques. The staff is friendly, so lingering in the drawing rooms is a pleasure, and drinks are served in the leafy garden in summer. **Pros:** just the right level of helpful service; decor is gorgeous. **Cons:** there's no restaurant; very small elevator. ⊠ *16 Sumner Pl., South Kensington* ☎ *020/7589–5232, 800/553–6674 in U.S.* ⊕ *www.firmdale.com* ⇗ *42 rooms* ⌂ *In-room: no a/c (some), safe, refrigerator, Wi-Fi. In-hotel: room service, bar, laundry service* ▭ *AE, MC, V* ⏐○⏐ *CP* Ⓤ *South Kensington* ✛ *4:D3.*

££££–£££££

🖭 **The Pelham.** Museum lovers flock to this sweet hotel across the street from the South Kensington Tube station. The Natural History, Science, and V&A museums are all a short stroll away, as is the King's Road. At the end of a day's sightseeing, settle down in front of the fireplace in one of the two snug drawing rooms with their honor bars. The stylish, contemporary rooms by designer Kit Kemp have sash windows and marble bathrooms. Some top-floor rooms have sloping ceilings and casement windows. Downstairs, the Bistro Fifteen offers a contemporary take on British cuisine. **Pros:** great location for museum-hopping; gorgeous bathrooms. **Cons:** top-floor rooms are not for the tall! ⊠ *15 Cromwell Pl., South Kensington* ☎ *020/7589–8288, 888/757–5587 in U.S.* ⊕ *www.pelhamhotel.co.uk* ⇗ *47 rooms, 4 suites* ⌂ *In-room: a/c, safe (some), refrigerator, Wi-Fi. In-hotel: restaurant, room service, bar, parking (paid)* ▭ *AE, MC, V* Ⓤ *South Kensington* ✛ *4:D2.*

£££

🖭 **The Sumner.** This elegant Georgian town house on a quiet residential street is the kind of place where you can feel yourself relaxing the minute you enter. Guest rooms are painted in neutral tones with splashes of rich color, and the interior design has a modern flair—even the fruit bowl is arranged creatively. There's plenty here for the gadget lover, including flat-screen TVs and free broadband. If the weather is good, relax in the small garden; in winter, warm your feet by the fire. In the morning, take breakfast in the sunny conservatory. **Pros:** small enough that the staff know your name. **Cons:** services are limited but prices high. ⊠ *5 Sumner Pl., South Kensington* ☎ *020/7723–2244* ⊕ *www.thesumner.com* ⇗ *20 rooms* ⌂ *In-room: a/c, refrigerator, Internet. In-hotel: room service, parking (paid)* ▭ *AE, MC, V* ⏐○⏐ *BP* Ⓤ *South Kensington* ✛ *4:D3.*

15

KNIGHTSBRIDGE

££££ ⊡ **The Beaufort.** At this elegant, modern-style boutique guesthouse, you get many amenities for your money. Guests have a front-door key, access to the honor bar in the drawing room, and an in-room music system with CDs and radio. The high-ceilinged, contemporary rooms have muted, sophisticated colors. Rates include flowers, fruit, chocolates, cookies, and water in your room; free e-mail and Wi-Fi, and movies via the TV; tea in the drawing room; and admission to a local health club. Junior suites include a free one-way airport transfer. Four of the rooms have wrought-iron balconies. **Pros:** gorgeous decor; friendly. **Cons:** standard doubles are much smaller than the price might indicate. ⊠ *33 Beaufort Gardens, Knightsbridge* 🖀 *020/7584–5252* 🖷 *800/584–7764 in U.S.* ⊕ *www.thebeaufort.co.uk* ⤴ *20 rooms, 7 suites* ⚄ *In-room: a/c, safe, Wi-Fi. In-hotel: room service, bar, laundry service* ⊟ *AE, DC, MC, V* ⏧⊙⏧ *CP* ⓤ *Knightsbridge* ✛ *4:F1.*

£££££ ⊡ **The Berkeley.** The elegant Berkeley is increasingly known for its luxurious, modern approach, which culminates in its splendid penthouse swimming pool. The big bedrooms have either swags of William Morris prints or art deco touches. All have sitting areas and ample luxury, including CD/DVD players, and Floris toiletries in the big marble bathrooms. Dining venues include Marcus Wareing's high-class Pétrus restaurant, Gordon Ramsay's excellent and extremely popular Boxwood Café, the eclectic and sumptuous Blue Bar (popular with celebrities), and the whimsical Caramel Room where morning coffee and decadent doughnuts are served to slim ladies who look as if they've never eaten such a thing in their lives. **Pros:** lavish luxury; attentive service; handy location for shopping. **Cons:** stratospheric prices; you'll need designer clothes to fit in here. ⊠ *Wilton Pl., Belgravia* 🖀 *020/7235–6000, 800/637–2869 in U.S.* ⊕ *www.the-berkeley.com* ⤴ *103 rooms, 55 suites* ⚄ *In-room: a/c, safe, refrigerator, DVD, Internet. In-hotel: restaurant, room service, bar, pool, gym, spa, laundry service, parking (paid)* ⊟ *AE, DC, MC, V* ⓤ *Knightsbridge* ✛ *4:G1.*

£££££ ⊡ **The Capital.** This is a true boutique hotel, with subtle, elegant decor, spacious rooms, and understated service. Formerly a private house, it demonstrates impeccable taste: fine-grain woods, original prints, and soothing, country-chic furnishings. Ask for a front-facing room to get more space. Nothing is ever too much here—mattresses are handmade, sheets are 450-thread count, bathrooms are marble. The Capital Restaurant is a famous gathering place of the rich and famous—its two Michelin stars mean that you'll need to book your table well in advance. **Pros:** beautiful space; handy for shopping at Harrods. **Cons:** you'll pay dearly for this luxury. ⊠ *22–24 Basil St., Knightsbridge* 🖀 *020/7589–5171, 800/926–3199 in U.S.* ⊕ *www.capitalhotel.co.uk* ⤴ *40 rooms, 8 suites* ⚄ *In-room: a/c, safe, refrigerator, Internet. In-hotel: restaurant, room service, bar, laundry service, parking (paid), some pets allowed* ⊟ *AE, DC, MC, V* ⓤ *Knightsbridge* ✛ *4:F1.*

££££ ⊡ **Egerton House.** This utterly peaceful, small hotel specializes in a traditional concept of luxury. Recenty refurbished bedrooms are lavishly decorated with luxurious fabrics in rich colors. Some have pleasant views overlooking the gorgeous gardens in back. The two drawing rooms are good places to write letters or relax with a drink from the honor bar. **Pros:** staff are helpful; location is great for Knightsbridge shopping. **Cons:** some find the decor fussy. ✉ *17–19 Egerton Terr., Knightsbridge* ☎ *020/7589–2412, 877/955–1515 in U.S.* ⊕ *www. egertonhousehotel.co.uk* ⤵ *23 rooms, 6 suites* ⚒ *In-room: a/c, refrigerator, Internet. In-hotel: room service, bar, laundry service, parking (paid)* ☰ *AE, DC, MC, V* Ⓤ *Knightsbridge, South Kensington* ✛ *4:F2.*

£££££ 🏨 **The Lanesborough.** Royally proportioned lounges distinguish this luxury hotel, now part of the St. Regis group. Everything exudes richness—moiré silk, magnificent antiques and oil paintings, handwoven carpets. To check in, sign the visitors' book, then retire to your room, where you can nibble the complimentary fruit, sip the bottled water, and be served by a personal butler. If you yearn for a bygone age and are willing to spend, spend, spend, this hotel is for you. **Pros:** lap of luxury; your every whim is fulfilled. **Cons:** prices are extraordinary; not everybody likes constantly hovering service. ✉ *Hyde Park Corner, Belgravia* ☎ *020/7259–5599, 800/999–1828 in U.S.* ⊕ *www.lanesborough. com* ⤵ *49 rooms, 46 suites* ⚒ *In-room: a/c, safe, refrigerator, Wi-Fi. In-hotel: restaurant, room service, bar, gym, laundry service, parking (paid)* ☰ *AE, DC, MC, V* Ⓤ *Hyde Park Corner* ✛ *4:G1.*

££££ 🏨 **The Levin.** This posh boutique hotel created by the people behind the Capital Hotel is owned by luxury-loving oenophiles. Expect smooth, duck-egg-blue walls, hyper-modern furnishings, and a champagne bar in every room. Yes, that's right—each room has its own selection of pricey splits of bubbly, along with all the mixings (and directions) for making champagne cocktails. Downstairs, the relaxed Le Metro Bar & Brasserie serves French and English classics (steak frites, sausages and mash) paired with an outstanding wine list. Located next door to Harrods, shopping locations don't get any more prime than this. **Pros:** your own champagne bar; sauntering to Harrods. **Cons:** no elevator; no bargains here. ✉ *28 Basil St., Knightsbridge* ☎ *020/7589–6286* ⊕ *www. thelevinhotel.co.uk* ⤵ *12 rooms, 1 suite* ⚒ *In-room: a/c, DVD, Internet. In-hotel: restaurant, bar, parking (paid)* ☰ *AE, V* ❡*CP* Ⓤ *Knightsbridge* ✛ *4:F1.*

£££££

Fodor's Choice

★

🏨 **Mandarin Oriental Hyde Park.** Stay here, and the three greats of Knightsbridge—Hyde Park, Harrods, and Harvey Nichols—are on your doorstep. Built in 1880, the Mandarin Oriental is one of London's most elegant hotels. Bedrooms are Victorian but with hidden high-tech gadgets and luxurious touches like Frette linen duvets, fresh orchids, and delicate chocolates. Miles of marble were used to fill the grand entrance. The Park restaurant, glittering Foliage restaurant, and quirky Mandarin Bar all attract Europe's jet setters. The service here is legendary and there's a butler on every floor, should you, for example, need a bit of help with the pillow menu. **Pros:** amazing views of Hyde Park; excellent service. **Cons:** nothing here comes cheap; you must dress for dinner (and lunch and breakfast). ✉ *66 Knightsbridge, Knightsbridge* ☎ *020/7235–2000* ⊕ *www.mandarinoriental.com* ⤵ *177 rooms, 23 suites* ⚒ *In-room: a/c, safe, refrigerator, DVD (some), Wi-Fi. In-hotel: 2 restaurants, room service, bar, gym, spa, laundry service, parking (paid)* ☰ *AE, DC, MC, V* Ⓤ *Knightsbridge* ✛ *4:F1.*

15

APARTMENT RENTALS & HOME EXCHANGES

APARTMENT RENTALS

For a home base that's roomy enough for a family and that comes with cooking facilities, consider renting furnished "flats" (what apartments are called in Britain). These can save you money, especially if you're traveling with a group. If you're interested in home exchange, but don't feel like sharing, some home-exchange directories list rentals as well. If you want to deal directly with local agents, get a personal recommendation from someone who has used the company; there's no accredited rating system for apartment-rental standards like the one for hotels.

International Agents

Hideaways International (✉ 767 Islington St., Portsmouth, NH ☎ 603/430–4433 or 800/843–4433 ⊕ www.hideaways.com) offers boutique hotels, tours, and cruises. Its offerings in London are extremely exclusive. Annual membership is $195.

Interhome (✉ 1990 N.E. 163rd St., Suite 110, North Miami Beach, FL ☎ 305/940–2299 or 800/882–6864 ⊕ www.interhome.us) has dozens of rather pricey, but luxurious, flats all over London with £3,000 per week being a not unusual price.

Villanet (✉ 1251 N.W. 116th St., Seattle, WA ☎ 206/417–3444 or 877/250–4366 ⊕ www.rentavilla. com) has hundreds of flats in residential neighborhoods all over London, with prices starting at £75 per person per night.

The Villas International (✉ 4340 Redwood Hwy., Suite D309, San Rafael, CA ☎ 415/499–9490 or 800/221–2260 ⊕ www.villasintl.com)

agency has exclusively priced flats all over London that start around £1,800 per week—some sleep up to 10 people.

Local Agents

Acorn Apartments (✉ Ground Fl., 19 Bedford Pl. ☎ 020/7636–8325 ⊕ www.acorn-apartments.co.uk) offers attractive small central apartments starting at around £90, however the Web site is not very good and it may be easier to call for information.

The Apartment Service (✉ 5 Francis Grove, Wimbledon ☎ 020/8944–1444 ⊕ www.apartmentservice.com) specializes in executive apartments for business travelers in and around the City, so prices are high, but so is the level of quality. Prices start at around £80 per night, although most apartments are around £180.

At Home in London (✉ 70 Black Lion La., Hammersmith ☎ 020/8748–1943 ⊕ www.athomeinlondon. co.uk ⊟ MC, V) has rooms in private homes in Knightsbridge, Kensington, Mayfair, Chelsea, and West London. Prices average around £75 a night per room, making this a great alternative to budget hotels.

Bulldog Club (✉ 14 Dewhurst Rd., Kensington ☎ 0870/803–4414, 877/727–3004 in U.S. ⊕ www. bulldogclub.com ⊟ AE, MC, V ☞ There's a 2.5% fee for using a credit card; debit cards incur no fees; the full price of the room must be paid in advance. Check their cancellation policies carefully) offers delightful little London flats in Knightsbridge, Kensington, and Chelsea. Many properties are available for about £100 per night with full English breakfasts.

Stay in the properties of Londoners who are temporarily away with **Coach House London Vacation Rentals** (✉ *2 Tunley Rd., Balham* ☎ *020/8133-8332* ⊕ *www.rentals.chslondon.com* ☐ *AE, MC, V ☞ Payment by credit card only; 10% deposit required*). Attractive apartments and houses are primarily in Notting Hill, Kensington, and Chelsea, and most cost around £115 per night. The minimum booking of three nights is a bit limiting, though, and you must make a substantial security deposit (usually between £200 and £1,000), which is returned after your stay.

Landmark Trust (☎ *01628/825-925* ⊕ *www.landmarktrust.org.uk*) has London apartments in unusual and historic buildings, prices start at around £100 a night, but many buildings require a minimum stay of seven days.

Uptown Reservations (☎ *020/7937-2001* ⊕ *www.uptownres.co.uk*) accepts only upscale addresses, and specializes in hosted homes or apartments for Americans, often business executives. Nearly all the homes on its register are in Knightsbridge, Belgravia, Kensington, and Chelsea. Prices start at £550 per week. There's limited information on their Web site; bookings must be made over the phone. A nonrefundable deposit is required.

Additionally, travelers at Fodors.com recommend these rental services:

"I've used **London Guest Suites** (⊕ *www.londonguestsuites.com*) many times and like them. They have rentals of all lengths. I also just booked a flat at **A Place Like Home** (⊕ *www.aplacelikehome.co.uk*)" —carrybean

"We stayed in 1 Sloane Ave. and were extremely happy and pleased with the apartment and the company **The Apartments** (⊕ *www.theapartments.co.uk*)" —jrecm

"Try the biggest rental site in Europe: **Holiday-Rentals from Home Away** (⊕ *www.holiday-rentals.co.uk*)" —travel_tomato

"Check out **VRBO** (⊕ *www.vrbo.com*), lots of London listings, and **Farnum-Christ** (⊕ *www.farnum-christ.com*) which is a high-ish end agency with some wonderful flats." —janisj

"I've used **London Connections** (⊕ *www.londonconnections.com*) several times and I've been very pleased." —Tinathread

HOME EXCHANGES

If you would like to exchange your home for someone else's, join a home-exchange organization, which will send you its updated listings of available exchanges for a year and will include your own listing in at least one of them. It's up to you to make specific arrangements.

Exchange Clubs

HomeLink International (✉ *Box 47747, Tampa, FL 33647* ☎ *954/566-2687 or 800/638-3841* ⊕ *www.homelink.org*); $115 yearly for a listing and online access.

Intervac U.S (✉ *Box 590504, San Francisco, CA94159* ☎ *800/756-4663* ⊕ *www.intervacus.com*); $95 yearly for a listing and online access.

15

NOTTING HILL AND BAYSWATER

BAYSWATER

££££ 🏠 **Colonnade.** Near a canal filled with colorful narrow boats, this lovely town house rests in a quiet, residential area known as "Little Venice." From the Freud suite (Sigmund visited regularly in 1938) to the rooms with four-poster beds or balconies, you'll find rich brocades, velvets, and antiques. It's a former home, so each room is different; some are split-level. Extra touches in each include bathrobes and slippers, bowls of apples, and CD players. The 1920s elevator and the Wedgwood fireplace in the lobby add to the historic style of the place, but the new tapas bar is pleasantly modern. **Pros:** beautifully decorated; Frette sheets; frequent online sales that can cut the price by £100. **Cons:** a bit far from popular sights; rooms are quite small. ⊠ *2 Warrington Crescent, Bayswater* ☎ *020/7286–1052* ⊕ *www.theetoncollection.com* ⌨ *15 rooms, 28 suites* ♿ *In-room: a/c, safe, Internet. In-hotel: restaurant, room service, bars, laundry service, parking (paid), some pets allowed* ⊟ *AE, DC, MC, V* Ⓤ *Warwick Ave.* ✛ *1:C2.*

£–££ 🏠 **Garden Court Hotel.** This small hotel is formed from two 19th-century town houses in a quiet garden square. Each room has a character of its own, some with original Victorian fittings. Note that all the rooms are individually decorated—some are nicer than others. Rooms with toilet and shower cost an extra £30, and a hot breakfast also ups the bill. The little, lush garden is a lovely hideaway when the sun shines. **Pros:** lovely garden; lots of charm; new elevator makes the upper floors more pleasant. **Cons:** not all rooms have private baths; some rooms need updating. ⊠ *30–31 Kensington Gardens Sq., Bayswater* ☎ *020/7229–2553* ⊕ *www.gardencourthotel.co.uk* ⌨ *12 rooms, 10 with bath* ♿ *In-room: no a/c. In-hotel: bar, Wi-Fi hotspot, some pets allowed* ⊟ *MC, V* ❙◯❙ *BP* Ⓤ *Bayswater, Queensway* ✛ *1:B4.*

££ 🏠 **The Pavilion Hotel.** This eccentric Victorian town house calls itself the Pavilion *Fashion Rock 'n' Roll* Hotel, and that should give you an idea that this is a trendy address for fashionistas, actors, and musicians. Often used for fashion shoots, the kitsch bedrooms veer wildly from Moroccan fantasy (the "Casablanca Nights" room) to acres of plaid ("Highland Fling") and satin ("Enter the Dragon"). You'll take some photos of your own here. Triples and family rooms are ideal for groups looking for space *and* style. **Pros:** small and friendly; great for arty types. **Cons:** few guest services; neighborhood has little for visitors. ⊠ *34–36 Sussex Gardens, Bayswater* ☎ *020/7262–0905* ⊕ *www.pavilionhoteluk.com* ⌨ *30 rooms* ♿ *In-room: no a/c, DVD (some), Internet. In-hotel: room service, bar, laundry service, parking (paid)* ⊟ *AE, D, MC, V* ❙◯❙ *CP* Ⓤ *Paddington, Edgware Rd.* ✛ *1:E3.*

££–£££ 🏠 **Space Apart.** This Georgian hotel near Hyde Park is a great find. Its 30 studio apartments have all been recently renovated in stellar style. Each is done in soothing tones of white and gray, with polished wood floors and attractive modern kitchenettes equipped with all you need to make small meals. The standard rooms are quite small, but premium rooms cost only £20 more and give you much more space to play with. Bathrooms are new and modern, although they are not big. The location is handy, and the value for money here is really impressive. **Pros:**

HOSTELS AND UNIVERSITIES

Bargains are undeniably hard to find in London, but if you don't mind sharing bathrooms, TVs, and sofas with a few hundred of your newest friends, you can save a lot of cash.

HOSTELS

No matter what your age, you can save on lodging costs by staying at hostels. In some 4,500 locations in more than 70 countries around the world, Hostelling International (HI), the umbrella group for a number of national youth-hostel associations, has single-sex, dorm-style beds and, at many hostels, rooms for couples and family accommodations. Membership in any HI national hostel association, open to travelers of all ages, allows you to stay in HI-affiliated hostels at member rates; one-year membership is about $28 for adults; hostels charge about $10–$30 per night. Members have priority if the hostel is full; they're also eligible for other discounts.

Contacts Hostelling International—Canada (✉ 205 Catherine St., Suite 400, Ottawa, Ontario ☎ 613/237–7884 or 800/663–5777 ⊕ www.hihostels.ca). **Hostelling International—USA** (✉ 8401 Colesville Rd., Suite 600, Silver Spring, MD ☎ 301/495–1240 ⊕ www.hiusa.org). **YHA England and Wales** (✉ Trevelyan House, Dimple Rd., Matlock, Derbyshire, UK ☎ 0162/959–2700 ⊕ www.yha.org.uk).

UNIVERSITY RESIDENCE HALLS

University student dorms (Halls of Residence) can be ideal for single travelers as well as those on a tight budget who want to come to London in summer when deals on other lodgings are scarce. Walter Sickert Hall has year-round lodging in its "executive rooms" (six single and three twin), and breakfast is even delivered to your room. Beds are usually available for a week around Easter, and from mid-June to mid-September in all the university accommodations around town. As you might expect, showers and toilets are shared, and there are no bellhops to carry your bags or concierges to answer your questions.

Contacts City University Hall of Residence: Walter Sickert Hall (✉ Graham St. ☎ 020/7040–8037 ⊕ www.city.ac.uk/ems) has rooms starting at £20 per person, per night. **London School of Economics Vacations** (☎ 020/7955–7575 ⊕ www.lsevacations.co.uk) costs £50 for a double without a toilet and £72 for a double with a toilet. You can choose from a variety of rooms in their many halls of residence around London. **University College London** (✉ Residence Manager, Campbell House, 5–10 Taviton St. ☎ 020/7679–2000 ⊕ www.ucl.ac.ukresidences) costs £35–£50 for a double and is open from mid-June to mid-September.

15

the price is right; the larger suites have space for four people. **Cons:** no in-house restaurant or bar; minimum two-night stay required. ✉ 32–37 *Kensington Gardens Square, Bayswater* ☎ 0207/908–1340 ⊕ *www.aparthotel-london.co.uk* ⊷ *30 rooms* ⌂ *In-room: a/c, no phone, kitchen, refrigerator, Internet* ⊟ *MC, V* Ⓜ *Bayswater* ⊕ *1:4B.*

££ ⊞ **Vancouver Studios.** This little hotel in a heritage-listed Victorian town house is perfect for those wanting a home away from home. All rooms are like efficiency apartments, with mini-kitchens and microwaves, and you can even preorder groceries, which are stocked in your mini-refrigerator upon arrival. Each studio has daily maid service as well as room service. Some rooms have working fireplaces, and one opens onto the leafy, paved garden. **Pros:** more space than a hotel room; unique little apartments. **Cons:** a bit out of the way; a bargain only if several people share the space. ⊠ *30 Prince's Sq., Bayswater* ☎ *020/7243–1270* ⊕ *www.vancouverstudios.co.uk* ⌁ *45 studios* ♿ *In-room: no a/c, kitchen, refrigerator, DVD, Wi-Fi. In-hotel: room service, bar, laundry facilities, laundry service, parking (paid)* ▭ *AE, DC, MC, V* Ⓤ *Bayswater, Queensway* ✛ *1:B4.*

NOTTING HILL

£££ 🏨 **Guesthouse West.** This hip hotel offers high-class chic at moderate prices. They almost get it right. The minimalist decor and technology—cool black-and-white photos and flat-screen TVs—are stylish. Rooms, however, are truly tiny, and there's no room service. The child-friendly restaurant is packed with locals, and the bar is a beautiful homage to the 1930s. The hotel's relationship with a local spa provides guests with discounts, and there are guaranteed seats for shows at the small Gate Theatre. **Pros:** sophisticated decor; lots of gadgets. **Cons:** a bit out of the way; tiny rooms; no room service. ⊠ *163–165 Westbourne Grove, Notting Hill* ☎ *020/7792–9800* ⊕ *www.guesthousewest.com* ⌁ *20 rooms* ♿ *In-room: a/c, DVD, Wi-Fi. In-hotel: restaurant, bar, parking (paid)* ▭ *AE, MC, V* Ⓤ *Notting Hill Gate* ✛ *1:A4.*

£££–££££ 🏨 **K West.** The proudly edgy K West is hidden away inside a feature-less glass-and-steel building near the Shepherd's Bush Tube stop, just outside Notting Hill. This is a grown-up place popular with business types and young couples, and *not* geared toward families with kids. Suites have two-person baths and drawers with "adult entertainment" supplies. Dark wood, soft suede, and sleek beige walls combine to create a designer look in the bedrooms. And the minimalist style extends to the all-white hotel bar, dubbed the K Lounge, and the hotel restaurant "Kanteen." **Pros:** sleek, modern decor; funky attitude. **Cons:** a bit off the tourist track; not for kids. ⊠ *Richmond Way, Shepherd's Bush* ☎ *020/8008–6600* ⊕ *www.k-west.co.uk* ⌁ *216 rooms, 6 suites* ♿ *In-room: a/c, safe, DVD, Wi-Fi. In-hotel: restaurant, room service, bar, gym, spa, laundry service, Internet terminals (free), parking (paid)* ▭ *AE, DC, MC, V* ⍟ *CP* Ⓤ *Shepherd's Bush* ✛ *1:A5.*

££–£££ 🏨 **Main House.** A brass lion door knocker marks Main House's Victorian front door, typical of Notting Hill. With just four rooms, this hotel offers nothing but a good night's sleep in a Victorian home. Furnished with clean white linens, polished wood floors, modern furniture, and Asian art, it is uncluttered and delightfully spacious. The tiny urban terrace is a great place for stargazing or reading the morning paper. A day rate at the local health club is available, too. **Pros:** unusual option; great location. **Cons:** few rooms mean it books up far in advance; no room service. ⊠ *6 Colvile Rd., Notting Hill* ☎ *020/7221–9691* ⊕ *www. themainhouse.com* ⌁ *4 rooms* ♿ *In-room: a/c (some), Wi-Fi (some). In-hotel: bicycles, laundry service, parking (paid)* ▭ *MC, V* ⍟ *CP* Ⓤ *Notting Hill Gate* ✛ *1:A4.*

££££–££££ 🛏 **Miller's Residence.** From the moment you ring the bell and are ushered up the winding staircase flanked by antiques and curios, you know you've entered a realm where history is paramount. The building is so packed with Jacobean, Victorian, Georgian, and Tudor antiques that if it weren't so elegant it might remind you of your grandmother's attic. Run by Martin Miller of *Miller's Antique Price Guides* fame, this town house serves as his home, gallery, and B&B. Sip a complimentary evening cocktail in the long, candlelit drawing room with fireplace while mixing with other guests or the convivial staff. **Pros:** extraordinary-looking place; great for antiques fans. **Cons:** quirky hotels are not for everyone; few amenities; no room service. ✉ *111A Westbourne Grove, Notting Hill* ☎ *020/7243–1024* ⊕ *www.millersuk.com* ⇨ *6 rooms, 2 suites* ⌂ *In-room: no a/c, Internet. In-hotel: bar, laundry service* ⊟ *AE, DC, MC, V* ⦿*CP* Ⓤ *Notting Hill Gate* ✣ *1:B4.*

££££–£££££ 🛏 **The Portobello.** One of London's most famous hotels, the little Portobello (formed from two adjoining Victorian houses) is seriously hip and attracts scores of celebrities. It's a quirky place, decorated with utter abandon. In your (small but stylish) room, you're likely to find an assortment of antiques, luxurious fabrics, statues, and bizarre bric-a-brac. Some rooms have balconies and claw-foot bathtubs. Room 16 has an extraordinary Victorian "bathing machine" that actor Johnny Depp is said to have once filled with champagne for Kate Moss, a former flame. **Pros:** stylish; great for celebrity-spotting; good location. **Cons:** most rooms are quite small; may be too eccentric for some. ✉ *22 Stanley Gardens, Notting Hill* ☎ *020/7727–2777* ⊕ *www.portobello-hotel.co.uk* ⇨ *24 rooms* ⌂ *In-room: no a/c (some), safe, refrigerator, Internet. In-hotel: restaurant, room service, bar* ⊟ *AE, MC, V* ⊘ *Closed 10 days at Christmas* ⦿*CP* Ⓤ *Notting Hill Gate* ✣ *1:A5.*

££–£££ 🛏 **Portobello Gold.** This no-frills B&B in the heart of the Portobello Road antiques area is on the floor above the pub and restaurant of the same name. Flat-screen TVs are mounted on the wall, and the beds take up almost the entire tiny room in the doubles. The best of the bunch is the split-level apartment (£££—sleeps six) with roof terrace, small kitchen, and soothing aquarium. The casual restaurant serves international food and has a great wine list, all at reasonable prices. There's free Wi-Fi in guest rooms as well as an Internet café that charges £1 per half hour. **Pros:** great location; free Internet access in rooms. **Cons:** rooms are tiny; no elevator. ✉ *95–97 Portobello Rd., Notting Hill* ☎ *020/7460–4910* ⊕ *www.portobellogold.com* ⇨ *6 rooms, 1 apartment* ⌂ *In-room: a/c, Wi-Fi. In-hotel: restaurant, room service, bar* ⊟ *MC, V* ⦿*CP* Ⓤ *Notting Hill Gate* ✣ *1:A4.*

ST. JAMES'S, MAYFAIR, AND MARYLEBONE

MARYLEBONE

££££–£££££ 🛏 **Dorset Square Hotel.** A fine pair of Regency town houses with design ideas high-end home magazine subscribers would love, this hotel is small but perfectly formed. Rooms are certainly not big, but they're all beautifully decorated and each has its unique, luxurious style. Staff are subdued, but friendly. The beds are swathed in Frette linens and stacked

15

with goose-down pillows. This quirky, personable place is ideal for those looking for something elegant, but unique. The first-floor balconied Coronet rooms are the largest. **Pros:** friendly, approachable luxury; some rooms have four-poster beds. **Cons:** rooms are small; bathrooms are very small indeed. ⊠ *40 Dorset Sq., Marylebone* ☎ *020/7723–7874* ⊕ *www.dorsetsquare.co.uk* ⇗ *35 rooms, 3 suites* ⌂ *In-room: a/c, safe (some), refrigerator, DVD, Internet, Wi-Fi. In-hotel: restaurant, room service, bar, laundry service, parking (paid), some pets allowed* ⊟ *AE, MC, V* Ⓤ *Baker St.* ✦ *1:F3.*

£–££   🏠 **Edward Lear Hotel.** Named after a 19th-century poet famed for writing things nobody could really understand, this charming hotel occupies two historic town houses dating to the end of the 18th century. One was once the home of the eponymous writer, and his sweetly nonsensical words decorate the walls, including "The Owl and the Pussycat." Rooms are small and basic, with thin bedspreads and cream walls. Bathrooms are nothing fancy, and not all rooms have a private bath, so specify when you book if you have a preference. Downstairs the sitting rooms are casual and a bit battered. Also, bedrooms facing the street can be noisy—light sleepers should ask for rooms at the back. **Pros:** great price for such a good location. **Cons:** decor is plain; mattresses are a bit thin; rooms are tiny. ⊠ *28–30 Seymour St., Marylebone* ☎ *020/7402–5401* ⊕ *www.edlear.com* ⇗ *31 rooms* ⌂ *In-room: no a/c, Internet* ⊟ *MC, V* ⎮◎⎮ *BP* Ⓤ *Marble Arch* ✦ *1:F4.*

£££££   🏠 **The Landmark.** This is one of London's grande dame hotels. Rich
☾   fabrics in neutral tones make the rooms welcoming and elegant. The lovely, eight-story atrium Winter Garden is overlooked by odd-numbered rooms. Even standard rooms here are among the largest in London and have white-marble bathrooms with plush robes. It's worth mentioning that despite all this lavishness, this is one of the few grand London hotels that doesn't force you to dress up. **Pros:** amazing levels of luxury; spacious rooms. **Cons:** busy neighborhood outside; very traditional decor. ⊠ *222 Marylebone Rd., Marylebone* ☎ *020/7631–8000* ⊕ *www.landmarklondon.co.uk* ⇗ *299 rooms, 47 suites* ⌂ *In-room: a/c, safe, refrigerator, Internet. In-hotel: 2 restaurants, bars, pool, gym, spa, laundry service* ⊟ *AE, DC, MC, V* Ⓤ *Marylebone* ✦ *1:F3.*

£££   🏠 **Park Plaza Sherlock Holmes Hotel.** This was once a rather ordinary Hilton, until somebody noticed its location and had the idea of making it a boutique hotel. Add a beautiful bar for a bit of local buzz, and—presto!—the place took off like a rocket. You might say it was elementary. With wood floors and leather furniture, the bar is relaxing; rooms have a masculine edge with lots of earth tones, pinstripe sheets, and hyper-modern bathrooms stocked with fluffy bathrobes. Still, overall, it's a handsome option near the good shopping of Marylebone High Street. Rooms are equipped with international electrical outlets, including those that work with American equipment. **Pros:** nicely decorated; good location for fans of shopping and Holmes. **Cons:** have to walk through the bar to get to reception; not well soundproofed from noisy street. ⊠ *108 Baker St., Marylebone* ☎ *020/7486–6161* ⊕ *www. sherlockholmeshotel.com* ⇗ *119 rooms* ⌂ *In-room: a/c, safe, refrigerator, Wi-Fi. In-hotel: restaurant, room service, bar, gym, spa* ⊟ *AE, DC, MC, V* Ⓤ *Baker St.* ✦ *1:G3.*

£ ⓘ **St. Christopher's Inn Camden.** In bustling, hippie Camden Town just north of the center of London, this branch of the local hostel and backpacker hotel chain is perfectly situated for wandering around Camden Lock and Camden Market. The decor is in the usual cheap-and-cheery hostel style, and is kept in good condition. There's no curfew, and you get key-card security and 10% off in the raucous Belushi's bar on the ground floor. Rooms range from doubles to 10-bed dorms; linens are free. **Pros:** clean; friendly; well located for Camden's busy

15

nightlife. **Cons:** a bit noisy and boisterous. ☒ *48–50 Camden High St., Camden Town* ☎ *020/7407–1856* ⊕ *www.st-christophers.co.uk* ⏎ *52 beds, some without bath* ♿ *In-room: no a/c, no phone, no TV. In-hotel: restaurant, bar, laundry facilities, Internet terminal* 🟰 *MC, V* ⅠⓄⅠ*CP* Ⓤ *Camden Town, Mornington Crescent* ✛ *2:A1.*

MAYFAIR

££ ⓘ **22 York Street.** This Georgian town house has a cozy, family feel with polished pine floors and plenty of quilts and antiques. Pride of place goes to the central, communal dining table where guests share a varied Continental breakfast. A living room with tea/coffeemaker is at your disposal as well. The homey bedrooms are individually furnished in charming white and cream tones. Triples and family rooms for four are available. **Pros:** handy guesthouse in a great location for shoppers. **Cons:** price is a bit steep for what is, in the end, a glorified B&B. ☒ *22 York St., Mayfair* ☎ *020/7224–2990* ⊕ *www.22yorkstreet.co.uk* ⏎ *10 rooms* ♿ *In-room: no a/c. In-hotel: bar* 🟰 *AE, MC, V* ⅠⓄⅠ*CP* Ⓤ *Baker St.* ✛ *1:G3.*

£££–££££   ⓘ **Athenaeum Hotel and Apartments.** This grand hotel overlooking Green
Fodor's Choice   Park offers plenty for the money. Rooms are both comfortable and lav-
★   ishly decorated, with deeply comfortable Hypnos beds, plasma-screen television systems, luxurious fabrics, and original contemporary artworks. If you need more space, you can choose one of its apartments instead. (These occupy a row of Georgian town houses next to the main hotel buildings, and each has separate living, dining, and sleeping spaces; and tiny, fully equipped kitchenettes.) The spa downstairs is available only to guests, ensuring you can always get an appointment. The elegant restaurant serves butter-rich European cuisine, and a full afternoon tea here (£26) is an elegant experience. Breakfasts are luxurious and varied, with endless Continental and cooked options. **Pros:** peaceful park views; handy for Buckingham Palace and Piccadilly; great value for elegant setting. **Cons:** some rooms could use a decor update; bathrooms are almost all small. ☒ *116 Piccadilly, Mayfair* ☎ *020/7640–3333* ⊕ *www.athenaeumhotel.com* ⏎ *111 rooms, 46 suites and apartments* ♿ *In-room: a/c, safe, kitchen (some), DVD,*

Wi-Fi. *In-hotel: restaurant, room service, bar, gym, spa* ▭ *AE, MC, V* ⏅| *BP* Ⓤ *Green Park* ⊹ *1:H6.*

££££££   ⊡ **Brown's.** Founded in 1837 by James Brown, Lord Byron's "gentleman's gentleman," this hotel, made up of 11 Georgian town houses, holds a treasured place in London society. Lounges and dining rooms are chic and contemporary. Everything is done up in cool neutral tones of coffee and cream; all guest rooms have an office space; and marble bathrooms have high-end bath products. No expense has been spared here, and if you stay here, you will not be spared expense either. The staff is exceedingly professional and helpful; nothing is too much trouble for them. **Pros:** elegant space; attentive service. **Cons:** everything costs here. ✉ *34 Albemarle St., Mayfair* ☎ *020/7493–6020* ⊕ *www. brownshotel.com* ⤲ *88 rooms, 29 suites* ⌂ *In-room: a/c, safe, refrigerator, DVD, Internet. In-hotel: 2 restaurants, room service, bar, gym, spa* ▭ *AE, DC, MC, V* Ⓤ *Green Park* ⊹ *1:H5.*

£££–££££   ⊡ **Chesterfield Mayfair.** Set deep in the heart of Mayfair, this four-star hotel is the former town house of the Earl of Chesterfield. The welcoming wood-and-leather public rooms match the dark-wood furnishings in the tiny bedrooms, which are done in burgundy, browns, and forest green. Lounges and restaurants have free Wi-Fi, although rooms are limited to broadband access. There are bargains to be had if you book online in advance, and the service is excellent. Dinner at the award-winning Butler's Restaurant is a must. **Pros:** friendly, laid-back. **Cons:** prices are a bit high; some rooms are very small. ✉ *35 Charles St., Mayfair* ☎ *020/7958–7729, 877/955–1515 in U.S.* ⊕ *www.chesterfieldmayfair. com* ⤲ *101 rooms, 9 suites* ⌂ *In-room: a/c, safe (some), Internet, Wi-Fi. In-hotel: 2 restaurants, room service, bar, gym, laundry service* ▭ *AE, DC, MC, V* Ⓤ *Green Park* ⊹ *1:H5.*

££££££   ⊡ **The Connaught.** Many of the classic Connaught touches (the grand oak
Fodor's Choice   staircase, for example, and the small, elegant bars) remain, but the hotel
★   has an elegant, modern look since a thorough 2007 renovation. Guy Oliver–designed rooms are done in smooth taupes and creams, though some are still on the small side. Bathrooms are also small, but have the latest gadgets. Hélène Darroze at the Connaught brings the titular Michelin-starred Parisian chef to London for the first time, opened in 2008. The walls of the newly redesigned hotel bar are, quite literally, platinum plated. **Pros:** this is a legendary hotel; great for star-spotting. **Cons:** you pay a lot for that history; bathrooms are tiny. ✉ *Carlos Pl., Mayfair* ☎ *020/7499–7070* ⊕ *www.the-connaught.co.uk* ⤲ *92 rooms* ⌂ *In-room: a/c, safe, refrigerator, DVD, Wi-Fi. In-hotel: 2 restaurants, room service, bars, gym, laundry service, Internet terminal, parking (paid)* ▭ *AE, DC, MC, V* Ⓤ *Bond St.* ⊹ *1:G5.*

££££££   ⊡ **Cumberland.** Perched on Oxford Street at the top of Park Lane, the Cumberland is a hotel behemoth. A sleek, elegant design, and a virtually all-white lobby with soaring ceilings and art in clear glass cases make this an attractive space. With 900 guest rooms, this is certainly no small hotel. All the rooms have modern decor in soothing shades of beige and cream. Rooms show good attention to detail—from the Egyptian cotton bed linens to the plasma-screen TVs, but they vary in size. Some are quite large, but ordinary double rooms are very small.

It has three restaurants (one of them headed by British TV chef Gary Rhodes) and two bars, all of which are as highly priced as the rooms. **Pros:** some rooms are spacious; those on upper floors have good views. **Cons:** basic double rooms are small; you're just a number in such a giant hotel; price is high for what's available. ⊠ *Great Cumberland Place, Mayfair* ☎ *0871/200–1595* ⊕ *www.cumberlandhotel-london. co.uk* ↜ *900 rooms* ☒ *In-room: a/c, safe, Internet. In-hotel: 2 restaurants, room service, bars, gym, laundry service* ═ *AE, MC, V* Ⓤ *Marble Arch* ✛ *1:G4.*

£££££   ⊡ **The Dorchester.** Few hotels this opulent manage to be as personable. The glamour level is off the scale: 1,500 square yards of gold leaf and 1,100 square yards of marble. Bedrooms (some not as spacious as you might expect) have Irish linen sheets on canopied beds, brocades, velvets, and Italian marble and etched-glass bathrooms with exclusive toiletries created by Floris. Furnishings throughout are English country-house style, with more than a hint of art deco, in keeping with the original 1930s building. The hotel has embraced modern technology, and employs "e-butlers" to help guests figure out the advanced Web TVs in the rooms. There are three elegant-to-the-point-of-fussy restaurants, including one helmed by Alain Ducasse, which is always making headlines. **Pros:** historic luxury; lovely views of Hyde Park; top-notch star-spotting. **Cons:** traditional look is not to all tastes; prices are high. ⊠ *Park Lane, Mayfair* ☎ *020/7629–8888* ⊕ *www.thedorchester.com* ↜ *195 rooms, 55 suites* ☒ *In-room: a/c, safe, DVD, Internet. In-hotel: 3 restaurants, bar, gym, spa, laundry service, parking (paid)* ═ *AE, DC, MC, V* Ⓤ *Marble Arch, Hyde Park Corner* ✛ *1:H5.*

£££   ⊡ **Durrants.** A stone's throw from Oxford Street and the smaller, posher shops of Marylebone High Street, Durrants sits on a quiet corner not far from the Wallace Collection. It's a tasteful option, with old-English wood paneling, leather armchairs, and patterned carpet. Note: bedrooms at the back of the hotel are smaller than those at the front, but also quieter and air-conditioned. The building has served as a hotel since the late 18th century. **Pros:** comfortable; relaxed base for exploring. **Cons:** not all rooms are air-conditioned; some rooms are quite small. ⊠ *26–32 George St., Mayfair* ☎ *020/7935–8131* ⊕ *www.durrantshotel. co.uk* ↜ *87 rooms, 5 suites* ☒ *In-room: no a/c (some), Internet. In-hotel: restaurant, room service, bar, laundry service* ═ *AE, MC, V* Ⓤ *Bond St.* ✛ *1:G3.*

£££££   ⊡ **InterContinental London Park Lane.** The InterContinental London Park Lane, overlooking busy Hyde Park Corner and the Queen's back garden, offers luxurious rooms that appeal to the high-end business traveler. The bedrooms are comfortable and slightly masculine, incorporating dark woods, with rich curtains and bedspreads. There are also top-brand electronics. Several of the suites are "themed," bearing clever titles like "The Cinema," which has its own screening room, and "The London," a self-contained minimalist loft. **Pros:** central location; business facilities; full-service spa. **Cons:** Muzak in lobby; no outward views from standard rooms. ⊠ *One Hamilton Pl., Park Lane, Mayfair* ☎ *0871/423–4901* ⊕ *www.intercontinental.com* ↜ *447 rooms* ☒ *In-room: a/c, safe, DVD, Internet. In-hotel: 2 restaurants, room service,*

15

bar, gym, spa, laundry service, Internet terminal, parking (paid) ▭ *AE, DC, MC, V* Ⓤ *Hyde Park Corner* ✛ *1:H6.*

££££ ⚏ **Marriott Park Lane.** The ornate facade and beautiful interior of this swanky Marriott date to 1919. Today its useful location at the Oxford Street end of Park Lane gives access to great shopping on Bond Street and lovely strolls through Hyde Park. In spite of its size, the hotel has a boutique feel. The sizeable bedrooms are standard Marriott fare, with neutral decor, comfortable mattresses, and lots of business accoutrements. The 140 Park Lane bar has its own cocktail, the Crantini 140, a heady mix of white cranberries, vodka, and Cointreau. **Pros:** great location; big bedrooms. **Cons:** a bit nondescript, very busy streets outside. ✉ *140 Park La., Mayfair* ☏ *020/7493–7000* ⊕ *www.marriott. co.uk* ↩ *148 rooms, 9 suites* ⚏ *In-room: a/c, safe, refrigerator, Internet, Wi-Fi. In-hotel: restaurant, room service, pool, gym, spa, laundry service* ▭ *AE, DC, MC, V* Ⓤ *Marble Arch* ✛ *1:G4.*

££££ ⚏ **The Metropolitan.** Home to Nobu and the chic Met bar, this supertrendy hotel is a popular address for visiting fashion, music, and media folk. The lobby is sleek, white, and modern, as are the bedrooms, which are designed by Keith Hobbs and have identical minimalist taupe-and-white furnishings paired with vivid purple carpets. The best rooms overlook Hyde Park, but all rooms have a groovy refrigerator hiding the latest alcoholic and health-boosting beverages. In-house restaurant Nobu is famed for its exclusivity (book your table at the same time as your room). **Pros:** perfect for the style-conscious; sweeping views of London's most famous parks. **Cons:** some guests find it pretentious. ✉ *Old Park La., Mayfair* ☏ *020/7447–1000, 888/272–3002 in U.S.* ⊕ *www.metropolitan.co.uk* ↩ *137 rooms, 18 suites* ⚏ *In-room: a/c, safe, refrigerator, DVD (some), Internet. In-hotel: restaurant, room service, bar, gym, laundry service, parking (paid)* ▭ *AE, DC, MC, V* Ⓤ *Hyde Park Corner* ✛ *1:H6.*

££££ ⚏ **The Montcalm.** A traditional grand hotel at the edge of Park Lane, the Montcalm gears itself at both business travelers and leisure travels in search of luxury. It might have a modern look, but it has an old-fashioned attitude; it's the kind of place that calls a gym a "gym recreation area." Rooms are contemporary, though, decorated in tones of toffee and cream, with comfortable king sized beds. The marble bathrooms are not big, but they do have soothing rain showers. All rooms have free Wi-Fi, MP3 docking stations, and free fresh fruit and bottled water. The bar, Barre Noire, is a pleasant place to meet a few locals over a martini, and the Vetro restaurant specializes in Italian cuisine. The small spa—"wellness centre"—has a workout pool, and relaxing treatment rooms where you can have the day's cares worked out of your shoulders by somebody else. **Pros:** Great location off Park Lane; dedication to luxury and comfort. **Cons:** Old-fashioned approach might seem stuffy to some. ✉ *34–40 Great Cumberland Street, Mayfair* ☏ *0207/402–4288* ⊕ *www.montcalm.co.uk* ↩ *170 rooms* ⚏ *In-room: a/c, safe, refrigerator (some), DVD, Wi-Fi. In-hotel: restaurant, room service, bar, pool, gym, spa, laundry service* ▭ *AE, MC, V* ⦿ *BP* Ⓜ *Marble Arch* ✛ *1:G4.*

£££££ 🖫 **No. 5 Maddox Street.** It doesn't get more boutique than this. With 12 luxury suites, each filled with everything you could ever need, this hotel is a great option for those who tire quickly of traditional travel. Room service caters to every whim, delivering groceries and lending out CDs, DVDs, or even a bicycle. Deluxe suites have balconies and working fireplaces. All rooms are decorated with subtle, Asian-inspired touches like bamboo and delicate art. The tiny kitchens are stocked with everything from cookies to herbal tea. Guests have access to a nearby health club. **Pros:** handy kitchens get you out of restaurants; everything can be delivered to your door. **Cons:** you can feel isolated, as there's no communal lobby. ⌧ *5 Maddox St., Mayfair* ☎ *020/7647–0200* ⊕ *www. living-rooms.co.uk* ↪ *12 suites* ⌂ *In-room: a/c, safe, kitchen, refrigerator, DVD, Wi-Fi. In-hotel: room service, laundry service, parking (paid)* ▭ *AE, DC, MC, V* Ⓤ *Oxford Circus* ✛ *3:A5.*

ST. JAMES'S

££££ 🖫 **Best Western Shaftesbury.** This Best Western chain in the midst of historic London does an admirable job of fitting in, while using as much chrome and frosted glass as anybody could ask for. Complimentary newspapers are scattered about, and bedrooms are ultramodern, with neutral rugs, white walls, dark curtains, and sleek furniture. The price reflects all this effort, so it's not the typical Best Western bargain, but it's pleasant and ideally situated in the heart of theaterland. **Pros:** free broadband in all rooms; great location for theaters, shopping, and museums. **Cons:** the price is clearly based on its location, rather than its amenities; rooms are tiny. ⌧ *65–73 Shaftesbury Ave., Piccadilly* ☎ *020/7871–6000, 866/891–7710 in U.S.* ⊕ *www.shaftesburyhotel. co.uk* ↪ *69 rooms* ⌂ *In-room: a/c, DVD, Internet* ▭ *AE, MC, V* Ⓤ *Piccadilly Circus* ✛ *3:C5.*

££££–£££££ 🖫 **Claridge's.** Stay here, and you're staying at a hotel legend with one
Fodor's Choice of the world's classiest guest lists, founded in 1812. The friendly, liv-
★ eried staff is not in the least condescending, and the rooms are never less than luxurious. Enjoy a cup of tea in the lounge, or retreat to the stylish bar for cocktails—or, better, to Gordon Ramsay's inimitable restaurant. The bathrooms are spacious (with enormous showerheads), as are the bedrooms (with soothing, modern decor in tones of taupe and cream). The grand staircase and magnificent elevator complete with sofa and driver are equally glamorous. Perhaps Spencer Tracy said it best when he remarked that, when he died, he wanted to go not to heaven, but to Claridge's. **Pros:** serious luxury everywhere—this is an old-money hotel. **Cons:** it's a bit pretentious—the guests in the hotel bar can be almost cartoonishly snobbish. ⌧ *Brook St., St. James's* ☎ *020/7629–8860, 866/599–6991 in U.S.* ⊕ *www.claridges. co.uk* ↪ *203 rooms* ⌂ *In-room: a/c, safe, DVD, Wi-Fi. In-hotel: restaurant, bar, gym, spa, laundry service, parking (paid)* ▭ *AE, DC, MC, V* Ⓤ *Bond St.* ✛ *1:H4.*

£££££ 🖫 **Dukes.** This small, exclusive hotel in a discreet cul-de-sac recently underwent a renovation that changed it from Edwardian to contemporary in one fell swoop. Ample natural light brightens rooms decorated in shades of cream and chocolate. The hotel's trump card is that, for such a central location, it's remarkably peaceful. **Pros:** low-key elegance;

15

peaceful oasis. **Cons:** can be a bit quiet for some; price is rather high for what's available. ✉ *35 St. James's Pl., St. James's* ☎ *020/7491–4840, 800/381–4702 in U.S.* ⊕ *www.dukeshotel.co.uk* ⤳ *78 rooms, 12 suites* ⚱ *In-room: a/c, safe, refrigerator, DVD (some), Wi-Fi. In-hotel: restaurant, bar, gym, spa, laundry service, parking (paid)* ▭ *AE, DC, MC, V* Ⓤ *Green Park* ✥ *5:A1.*

££££££ 🖬 **The Stafford.** This is a rare find: a posh hotel that is equal parts ele-
Fodor'sChoice gance and friendliness. It's hard to check in without meeting the gre-
★ garious manager, and his unshakable cheeriness must be infectious, for the staff are also upbeat and helpful. The location is one of the few peaceful spots in the area, down a small lane behind Piccadilly. Its 13 adorable carriage-house rooms are installed in the 18th-century stable block; each individually decorated room has a cobbled mews entrance and gas-fueled fireplace, exposed beams, iPod dock, and CD player. The popular little American Bar has ties, baseball caps, and toy planes hanging from the ceiling. **Pros:** great staff; big, luxurious rooms; quiet location. **Cons:** traditional decor is not to all tastes; men must wear jackets in the bar. ✉ *St. James's Pl., St. James's* ☎ *020/7493–0111* ⊕ *www.thestaffordhotel.co.uk* ⤳ *81 rooms* ⚱ *In-room: a/c, Internet. In-hotel: restaurant, bar* ▭ *AE, DC, MC, V* Ⓤ *Green Park* ✥ *5:A1.*

SOHO AND COVENT GARDEN

COVENT GARDEN

£££££ 🖬 **Covent Garden Hotel.** In the midst of boisterous Covent Garden, this hotel is now the London home-away-from-home for a mélange of off-duty celebrities, actors, and style mavens. With painted silks, *style anglais* ottomans, and 19th-century Romantic oils, the public salons are perfect places to decompress over a glass of sherry from the bar. Guest rooms are *World of Interiors* stylish, each showcasing matching-but-mixed couture fabrics to stunning effect. For £35, the popular Saturday-night film club includes dinner in the brasserie and a film in the deluxe in-house cinema. **Pros:** great for star-spotting, and movie buffs. **Cons:** you can feel you don't matter if you're not a film star. ✉ *10 Monmouth St., Covent Garden* ☎ *020/7806–1000, 800/553–6674 in U.S.* ⊕ *www.firmdale.com* ⤳ *55 rooms, 3 suites* ⚱ *In-room: a/c, safe, DVD, Wi-Fi. In-hotel: restaurant, room service, gym, spa, laundry service* ▭ *AE, MC, V* Ⓤ *Covent Garden* ✥ *3:E4.*

£££££ 🖬 **One Aldwych.** An understated blend of contemporary and classic
Fodor'sChoice results in pure, modern luxury here. Flawlessly designed inside an
★ Edwardian building, One Aldwych is coolly eclectic, with an artsy lobby, feather duvets, Italian linen sheets, and ample elegance. It's the ultimate in 21st-century style, from the free, hotel-wide Wi-Fi, down to the gorgeous swimming pool in the health club. Suites have amenities such as a private gym, a kitchen, and a terrace. Breakfast is made with organic ingredients. The pool at One Aldwych has underwater speakers that play music you can hear only when you dive in. **Pros:** understated (and underwater) luxury. **Cons:** all this luxury doesn't come cheap. ✉ *1 Aldwych, Covent Garden* ☎ *020/7300–1000* ⊕ *www.onealdwych.co.uk* ⤳ *93 rooms, 12 suites* ⚱ *In-room: a/c, safe, kitchen (some), refrigerator, Wi-Fi. In-hotel: 2 restaurants, room service, bars, pool, gym, spa,*

BED-AND-BREAKFASTS

You can stay in small, homey B&Bs for an up-close-and-personal brush with city life (Arosfa Hotel), or find yourself in what is really a modern guesthouse, where you never meet the owners (B&B Belgravia). The main benefit of staying in a B&B is that the price is usually cheaper than a hotel room of comparable quality, and you receive more personal service. The limitations may be few in number, but can be off-putting for some: although you can sometimes arrange for daily maid service, there is no restaurant or bar, and no concierge should you have a question. If you book a room in a privately owned house through an agency, prices start as low as £70 a night, and go up for more central neighborhoods and larger and more luxurious homes. It's a nice option, both for seasoned travelers and for those trying to travel well without busting their budgets. Search the Web and call around to find the place that's right for you.

Contacts Host & Guest Service (✉ 103 Dawes Rd., Fulham ☎ 0870/220–2640 ⊕ www.host-guest.co.uk ▭ MC, V ☞ Full payment in advance) can find you a room in London as well as the rest of the United Kingdom. It's a great way to find bargains, knowing that all have been vetted by the agency, but the Web site functionality is a bit creaky. The long-established family-run agency **London B&B** (✉ 437 J St., Suite 210, San Diego, CA ☎ 800/872–2632 ⊕ www.londonbandb.com ☞ 30% deposit required) has some truly spectacular—and some more modest—homes in central London. Most cost between $130–$150 per night. You can check many of them out online, but you still have to call even to find out prices.

15

laundry service, parking (paid) ▭ AE, MC, V Ⓤ Charing Cross, Covent Garden ✛ 3:G5.

££££ 🏨 **Trafalgar Hilton.** This fresh, contemporary hotel defies the Hilton norm. The rooms here, in either sky-blue or beige color schemes, keep many of the 19th-century office building's original features, and some have floor-to-ceiling windows with extraordinary views of Trafalgar Square and the city. Twenty-one rooms are split-level, with upstairs space for chilling out with a CD or DVD and sleeping space below. Bathrooms have deep baths, full-size toiletries, eye masks, and mini-TVs. Go up to the roof garden for spectacular views of the Houses of Parliament, Westminster Abbey, and the London Eye. Better yet, ask for Room 303 to enjoy these exquisite views in privacy. **Pros:** amazing views; spacious rooms. **Cons:** prices never seem to drop, even in the off-season. ✉ 2 Spring Gardens, Covent Garden ☎ 020/7870–2900 ⊕ www.hilton.co.uk 🛏 127 rooms, 2 suites ♿ In-room: a/c, safe, DVD, Internet. In-hotel: restaurant, room service, bar, laundry service, parking (paid) ▭ AE, DC, MC, V Ⓤ Charing Cross ✛ 5:C1.

£££££ 🏨 **Waldorf Hilton.** After a massive overhaul, the Waldorf has frosted glass, white marble, and understated bedrooms. The "Art + Tech" rooms cater to modern travelers' demands with plasma-screen TVs, complimentary fruit, herbal teas, and soft drinks, as well as safes with laptop chargers. The "contemporary" rooms have retained period features while incorporating all the new gadgets. The elegant restaurant and bar make for memorabe evenings. **Pros:** tradition meets modern life comfortably here. **Cons:** prices are quite high for a Hilton. ✉ *Aldwych, Covent Garden* ☎ *020/7836–2400* ⊕ *www.hilton.co.uk* ⤵ *303 rooms* ⚷ *In-room: a/c, safe, refrigerator, Internet. In-hotel: restaurant, room service, bar, pool, gym, spa, laundry service, parking (paid)* ⊟ *AE, DC, MC, V* Ⓤ *Charing Cross* ✛ *3:H5.*

SOHO

££££   ☷ **Hazlitt's.** Three connected early-18th-century houses, one of which was the last home of essayist William Hazlitt (1778–1830), make up this charming Soho hotel. It's a disarmingly friendly place, full of personality but devoid of certain modern amenities (as the owners say, "In 1718 there were no elevators, and there still aren't"). Robust antiques are everywhere, most beds are four-posters, and every bathroom has a Victorian claw-foot tub. There are tiny sitting rooms, wooden staircases, and more restaurants nearby than you could visit in a year. **Pros:** great for art and antiques lovers; truly beautiful and relaxed. **Cons:** no in-house restaurant; no elevators. ✉ *6 Frith St., Soho* ☎ *020/7434– 1771* ⊕ *www.hazlittshotel.com* ⤵ *20 rooms, 3 suites* ⚷ *In-room: a/c, Wi-Fi. In-hotel: room service, laundry service, parking (paid), some pets allowed* ⊟ *AE, DC, MC, V* Ⓤ *Tottenham Court Rd.* ✛ *3:D4.*

££££–£££££   ☷ **Soho Hotel.** This redbrick, loftlike boutique hotel's public rooms are boldly designed with bright colors and big artworks, but the large bedrooms are calmer, most with neutral, beige-and-cream tones, or subtle, sophisticated pinstripes, all offset by modern furniture. The bar and restaurant, Refuel, is one of the city's hot spots, and there are movie-screening rooms downstairs, in case the wide-screen TVs in the rooms aren't big enough. **Pros:** small and sophisticated; comfortable beds. **Cons:** bar can be crowded and noisy on weeknights. ✉ *4 Richmond Mews, off Dean St., Soho* ☎ *020/7559–3000* ⊕ *www.sohohotel.com* ⤵ *85 rooms, 6 apartments* ⚷ *In-room: a/c, DVD, Internet. In-hotel: room service, gym* ⊟ *AE, MC, V* Ⓤ *Tottenham Court Rd.* ✛ *3:C4.*

WESTMINSTER AND VICTORIA

VICTORIA

££   ☷ **B&B Belgravia.** This modern guesthouse a short walk from Victoria Station has cool all-white decor—white chairs and walls, white pillars and desks, white linens and towels. It all looks a bit ethereal, which is what they're aiming for. Rooms are small but beds are comfortable, and at least nothing you're wearing will clash. There's a modern, open-plan lounge where a fire crackles away in the winter. It's a good place to grab a cup of tea (always available) and check your e-mail on the free computer. **Pros:** free Wi-Fi; nice extras like free use of a laptop in the hotel lounge; coffee and tea always available. **Cons:** bathrooms and rooms are small; no hotel restaurant or bar. ✉ *64–66 Ebury St., Victoria* ☎ *020/7259–8570* ⊕ *www.bb-belgravia.com* ⤵ *17 rooms* ⚷ *In-room: no a/c, Wi-Fi* ⊟ *AE, DC, MC, V* ⧉|CP Ⓤ *Knightsbridge* ✛ *4:H2.*

££££–£££££   ☷ **The Goring.** Buckingham Palace is just around the corner, and visiting VIPs use the Goring as a convenient, suitably dignified base for royal occasions. The hotel, built in 1910 and now run by third-generation Gorings, retains an Edwardian style. It would never be described as "modern," with striped wallpaper and floral curtains combined with patterned carpets and brass fittings. But it is luxurious and welcoming all the same. **Pros:** comfortable beds; spacious rooms. **Cons:** decor is a bit fussy. ⊠ *15 Beeston Pl., Grosvenor Gardens, Victoria* ☎ *020/7396–9000* ⊕ *www.thegoring.com* ⤳ *68 rooms, 6 suites* ⟂ *In-room: a/c, safe, Internet. In-hotel: restaurant, room service, bar, gym, laundry service, parking (paid)* ⊟ *AE, DC, MC, V* Ⓤ *Victoria* ✛ *5:A3.*

££–£££ 🛏 **Lime Tree Hotel.** On a street filled with budget hotels, the homey Lime Tree stands out for its gracious proprietors, the Davies family, who also act as concierges. The flowery, comfortable rooms include tea/coffeemakers. The triples and quads are suitable for families, but children under five are not allowed. The simple breakfast room covered with notes and gifts from former guests opens onto a garden. **Pros:** friendly and cheap; great location. **Cons:** some rooms are up several flights of stairs, and there's no elevator. ⊠ *135–137 Ebury St., Victoria* ☎ *020/7730–8191* ⊕ *www.limetreehotel.co.uk* ⤳ *25 rooms* ⟂ *In-room: no a/c, safe, Wi-Fi. In-hotel: no kids under 5* ⊟ *MC, V* �“❘ *BP* Ⓤ *Victoria* ✛ *4:H2.*

££ 🛏 **New England Hotel.** This family-run B&B in a 19th-century town house is cheap(ish) and cheerful. The power showers, comfortable beds, and electronic key cards are pluses, but there's nothing fancy about the interior, and the bright color scheme is possibly too cheerful for some. View this as a fallback option if other, better budget places are booked up. **Pros:** handy location; friendly owners. **Cons:** a bit battered; prices a little high for what you get. ⊠ *20 St. George's Dr., Victoria* ☎ *020/7834–8351* ⊕ *www.newenglandhotel.com* ⤳ *25 rooms* ⟂ *In-room: no a/c, Internet. In-hotel: parking (paid)* ⊟ *AE, DC, MC, V* �“❘ *BP* Ⓤ *Victoria* ✛ *5:A4.*

£££££ 🛏 **No. 41.** This luxurious abode's designer credentials are everywhere, from the unusual tiled floors to the extraordinary furnishings drawn from every corner of the globe. Even the entrance is unique: you walk into a guests-only elevator and are swept up to the fifth-floor lobby. Rooms, some of them split-level, are complete with high-tech gadgets to keep you in touch with the office back home. When you're not working, you can relax on the butter-soft leather sofa in front of the fireplace, recline on the exquisite bed linens and feather duvets, or luxuriate in the marble bath. A "whatever, whenever" button on the telephone connects you with the helpful, amiable staff who provide exactly that. **Pros:** unique place; lots of technology in gorgeous rooms; great service. **Cons:** the unusual design is not for everyone. ⊠ *41 Buckingham Palace Rd., Victoria* ☎ *020/7300–0041* ⊕ *www.41hotel.com* ⤳ *14 rooms, 4 suites* ⟂ *In-room: a/c, safe, Internet. In-hotel: room service, bar, laundry service, parking (paid)* ⊟ *AE, DC, MC, V* ❘❘ *CP* Ⓤ *Victoria* ✛ *5:A3.*

££ 🛏 **Windermere Hotel.** This sweet little hotel will not let you forget that it stands on the site of London's first B&B, which opened here in 1881. It's draped in charmingly sunny floral fabrics, which look appropriate on the antique beds. Bathrooms are thoroughly modern, and the attached restaurant, small though it may be, is actually quite good. It's

15

a decent option if you can't get a discount rate at a plusher hotel for the same price. **Pros:** attractive rooms; good location. **Cons:** price is a bit high for what you get; rooms and bathrooms are tiny; there's no elevator. ⊠ *142–144 Warwick Way, Victoria* ☎ *020/7834–5163* ⊕ *www. windermere-hotel.co.uk* ✍ *22 rooms* ⚲ *In-room: a/c, Internet. In-hotel: room service, bar, Wi-Fi* ▬ *MC, V* Ⓤ *Victoria* ✛ *4:H3.*

WESTMINSTER

££££   🛏 **City Inn Westminster**. In a rather stark steel-and-glass building steps
🕐   from the Tate Britain, this member of a small U.K. chain has some rooms with spectacular views of Big Ben and the London Eye. Extras like floor-to-ceiling windows and flat-screen TVs complement the contemporary, monochrome guest rooms. Cots, baby baths, Nickelodeon, special menus, and baby food are all on tap for kids. The restaurant and bar serve Modern British cooking. **Pros:** amazing views; lots of high-tech toys including iMac computers. **Cons:** with more than 400 rooms, you're just a number. ⊠ *30 John Islip St., Westminster* ☎ *020/7630–1000* ⊕ *www.cityinn.com* ✍ *444 rooms, 16 suites* ⚲ *In-room: a/c, safe, DVD, Wi-Fi. In-hotel: restaurant, room service, bar, gym, laundry service, parking (paid)* ▬ *AE, MC, V* Ⓤ *Pimlico* ✛ *5:C4.*

££–£££   🛏 **Jolly Hotel St. Ermin's**. The hotel is just a short stroll from Westminster Abbey, Buckingham Palace, and the Houses of Parliament. An Edwardian anomaly in the shadow of modern skyscrapers, it's set on a tiny cul-de-sac courtyard. The lobby is an extravaganza of Victorian stylings like cake-frosting stuccowork in shades of baby blue and creamy white. Sadly, guest rooms are much more ordinary and not likely to be much to write home about. The hotel's restaurant is an ornately carved 19th-century Jacobean-style salon, and one of the most magnificent rooms in which to dine in London. **Pros:** amazing lobby; great location near Buckingham Palace. **Cons:** rooms are a bit small and plain. ⊠ *2 Caxton St., Westminster* ☎ *020/7222–7888* ⊕ *www.jollyhotels.it* ✍ *277 rooms, 8 suites* ⚲ *In-room: a/c, safe (some), refrigerator, Internet. In-hotel: restaurant, room service, bar, laundry service, parking (paid)* ▬ *AE, DC, MC, V* Ⓤ *St. James's Park* ✛ *5:B3.*

£–££   🛏 **Vandon House Hotel**. Popular with students, backpackers, and families on a budget, this simply decorated hotel is close to Westminster Abbey and Buckingham Palace. Singles and some twin rooms share bathrooms, but the rest have bathrooms with a shower only. Family rooms include a double bed and camp-style bunk bed, which could result in scuffles over who sleeps where. It's nothing fancy, but it's a friendly little place. **Pros:** handy location; comfortable beds. **Cons:** simple decor; few extras. ⊠ *1 Vandon St., Westminster* ☎ *020/7799–6780* ⊕ *www.vandonhouse. com* ✍ *32 rooms* ⚲ *In-room: no a/c, Wi-Fi. In-hotel: bar, laundry service* ▬ *MC, V* ⦿ *CP* Ⓤ *St. James's Park* ✛ *5:B3.*

Pubs and Nightlife

WORD OF MOUTH

"London has two types of pubs. One is the local where neighbors visit. The second is an open type hosting casual visitors. Inquire at your hotel about a local. Be prepared to buy a round. At the casual bar, ask for a recommendation of a beer or ale. Ask at your hotel for a nearby pub with the best pub grub."

—GSteed

PUBS AND NIGHTLIFE PLANNER

Getting Around

If you're out past 12:30 AM, the best way to get home is by taxi (the Tube stops running around 12:30 AM Monday–Saturday and midnight on Sunday). The best place to hail a taxi is at the front door of one of the major hotels; you can also have the staff at your last stop of the evening call one for you.

Liquor Laws, Smoking Laws

In 2005, England relaxed its licensing laws and as many as 5,200 drinking establishments in London extended their opening hours. The new era marks the most notable change of laws that required most pubs to close at 11 PM. And although it's controversial, the new development translates into only a modest increase in overall licensing hours; most still close at 11, and others at midnight or a few short hours later.

A bigger change to many has been the 2007 law that bans smoking inside any public building. Many in the nightlife industry opposed the changes, worried that it would have a negative effect on their businesses. On the other hand, London's venues have become much more family-friendly and healthier as a result.

Can I Take My Kids to the Pub?

As pubs increasingly emphasize what's coming out of the kitchen rather than what's flowing from the tap, whether or not to bring the kids has become a frequent question. The law dictates that patrons must be 18 years of age or older to drink alcohol in a pub.

Children 14 to 17 may enter a pub but are not permitted to purchase or drink alcohol, and children under 14 are not permitted in the bar area of a pub unless the pub has a "Children's Certificate" and they are accompanied by an adult. In general, however, pubs have a section set aside for families and welcome well-behaved children, especially during the day. If possible, it's best to call ahead—the bar staff will fill you in on their children's policy.

What to Wear

As a general rule, you can dress as you would for an evening in New York City; however, you see fewer people in the upscale London nightspots wearing jeans and sneakers. British women are also prone to baring a bit more skin, so that sparkly, backless top you were saving for a Caribbean soirée might be just as suitable for a night out in London, weather permitting. In general, people are more likely to dress down than up for a trip to a gig or to the pub.

What's Happening Now

There are several Web sites, in addition to the print publications *The Evening Standard, Time Out London, Where London,* and *In London,* that will tell you who's playing where and when. Check out ⊕ *www.londontown.com,* ⊕ *www.allinlondon.co.uk,* ⊕ *www.viewlondon.co.uk,* or ⊕ *www.london.net/nightlife.*

REGENT'S PARK

HAMPSTEAD
villagey pubs for long Sunday lunches

CLERKENWELL
urban cutting edge

NOTTING HILL
arty but smart and rich-hip drinking holes

BLOOMSBURY
heritage, learning, bowling

HOXTON
arty and on the pulse

Albany Rd.

Albany St.

Gt. Portland St.

Portland Pl.

Euston Rd.

Tottenham Court Rd.

Gray's Inn Rd.

Clerkenwell Rd.

Marylebone Rd.

Baker St.

Wigmore St.

FITZROVIA
secret chic

New Oxford St.

Holborn

Kingsway

Fleet St.

OXFORD CIRCUS

Oxford St.

Bayswater Rd.

SOHO
lowlife and highlife, music and dance

COVENT GARDEN
a drink before the show

Charing Cross Rd.

Strand

MAYFAIR
wine and spirits

New Bond St.

Regent St.

Shaftesbury Ave.

HYDE PARK

ST JAMES'S
jacket required

Pall Mall

Victoria Embankment

Waterloo Bridge

Stamford St.

SOUTH BANK
real ale, real food

Waterloo Rd.

Piccadilly

Green Park

The Mall

St. James's Park

Whitehall

River Thames

KNIGHTSBRIDGE
hotel bar martinis

Knightsbridge

Constitution Hill

Birdcage Walk

WESTMINSTER

Westminster Br.

Westminster Bridge Rd.

Sloane St.

HAMMERSMITH
relaxed and upmarket, evenings by the river

BELGRAVIA
hidden mews gems

Victoria St.

Horseferry Rd.

Lambeth Palace Rd.

Lambeth Br.

Lambeth Rd.

Kennington Rd.

Buckingham Palace Rd.

Wilton Rd.

Vauxhall Br. Rd.

Millbank

LAMBETH

VICTORIA

Pimlico Rd.

King's Rd.

CHELSEA
sophisticated and moneyed

Albert Embankment

Kennington Park Rd.

0		1/2 mile

0		1/2 km

Updated by
Kiki Deere

London is a veritable utopia for excitement junkies, culture fiends, and those who—simply put—like to party. Virginia Woolf once wrote of London, "I step out upon a tawny-colored magic carpet . . . and get carried into beauty without raising a finger. The nights are amazing, with all the white porticoes and broad silent avenues. And people pop in and out, lightly, divertingly, like rabbits."

Most who visit London will, like Woolf, be mesmerized by the city's energy, which reveals itself in layers. Whether you prefer a romantic evening at the opera, rhythm and blues with fine French food, the gritty guitar riffs of East London, a pint and gourmet pizza at a local gastropub, or swanky cocktails and sushi at London's sexiest lair, the U.K. capital is sure to feed your fancy.

PUBS

Even today, competing with a thoroughly modern entertainment industry, the traditional pub is still a vital part of British life. It also should be a part of the visitor's experience, as there are few better places to meet Londoners in their local habitat. There are thousands of pubs in London—ever fewer of which still have original Victorian etched glass, Edwardian panels, and art nouveau carvings. The list below offers a few pubs selected for central location, historical interest, a pleasant garden, music, or good food, but you might just as happily adopt your own temporary "local."

Pubs in the capital are changing: 90-year-old licensing laws have finally been modernized, gastropub fever is sweeping London, and smoking in all pubs has been illegal since 2007. At many places, char-grills are installed in the kitchen out back and nouveau pub grub, such as Moroccan chicken, is on the menu. Regardless of what you eat, however, you'll definitely want to order a pint.

■TIP→ Remember that what Americans call beer, the British call lager, often beers from continental Europe. However, the real pub drink is "bitter," usually served at cellar temperature (that is, cooler than room temperature but not actually chilled). There's a movement to protect the traditional British cask-conditioned ale that is much less gassy. There are also plenty of other

WORD OF MOUTH

"My favorite pub in London is the Black Friar. The beer's good and the pub is an absolutely gorgeous art nouveau masterpiece. It is a cathedral of drink, no joke. Crowded immediately after work, not at other times." —fnarf999

potations: Irish stouts like Guinness and Murphy's are thick, pitch-black brews you'll either love or hate; ciders, ranging from sweet to dry, are made from apples (Magner's cider, served over ice, is now ubiquitously fashionable); shandies are a mix of lager and lemonade (lemon soda). Discuss your choice of drink with the barman, turn to your neighbor, raise the glass, and utter that most pleasant of toasts, "Cheers."

Admiral Codrington. Named after a hero of the Napoleonic Wars, this smart pub was once the most popular meeting place for the upwardly mobile of Sloane Square (Lady Diana Spencer is said to have been a regular in her teaching days). The "Admiral Cod," as it's known, now houses a modern restaurant where excellent English fare is served at lunch and dinnertime (treat yourself to a delicious raspberry soufflé to finish). Activity at the island bar centers on the wine list; well-off Chelsea residents pack the bare wood interior on weekend evenings. ⊠ *17 Mossop St., Chelsea* ☎ *020/7581–0005* ⊕ *www.theadmiralcodrington. co.uk* Ⓤ *South Kensington.*

Anchor. Near the Southwark Bridge, this historic pub is today best known as a place to enjoy the riverside views. ⊠ *34 Park St., South Bank* ☎ *020/7407–1577* Ⓤ *London Bridge.*

Fodor's Choice ★ **Anchor & Hope.** One of London's most popular gastropubs, the Anchor & Hope doesn't take reservations (except for Sunday lunch), meaning queuing would-be diners snake around the red-walled, wooden-floored pub, kept happy by some good real ales and a fine wine list as they wait for hours for a table. The food is old-fashioned English (think salt cod, tripe, and chips) with a few modern twists. ⊠ *36 The Cut, South Bank* ☎ *020/7928–9898* Ⓤ *Southwark.*

Black Friar. A step from Blackfriars Tube stop, this spectacular pub has an Arts-and-Crafts interior that is entertainingly, satirically ecclesiastical, with inlaid mother-of-pearl, wood carvings, stained glass, and marble pillars all over the place. In spite of the finely lettered temperance tracts on view just below the reliefs of monks, fairies, and friars, there is a nice group of ales on tap from independent brewers. ⊠ *174 Queen Victoria St., The City* ☎ *020/7236–5474* Ⓤ *Blackfriars.*

Blue Anchor. This unaltered Georgian pub has been seen in the movie *Sliding Doors* and was the site where *The Planets* composer Gustav Holst wrote his *Hammersmith Suite.* Sit out by the river, or shelter inside with a good ale. ⊠ *13 Lower Mall, Hammersmith* ☎ *020/8748– 5774* ⊕ *www.blueanchorlondon.com* Ⓤ *Hammersmith.*

16

Camden Arms. On the site of the last fatal duel in Britain, this funky-yet-chill place has plenty of interesting features. Check out the ornate spiral staircase after a good pint of beer. House tunes spun by DJs pervade this pub–lounge every Friday night, and often on Saturdays. Modern cocktails are served alongside Thai cuisine. ⊠ *1 Randolph St., Camden* ☎ *020/7267–9829* ⊕ *www.thecamdenarms.com* Ⓤ *Camden.*

Fodor'sChoice
★
The Cat's Back. A few minutes' walk from the river at Putney Bridge, a short Tube ride into zone 2 from Central London, this is probably one of the most imaginative and cheery pubs in London; eclectic paintings plaster the walls, and the candlelighted interior gives the place a welcoming and homey feel. The newly opened restaurant upstairs supports local artists. The place goes crazy in the evenings when live music is played, from folk to African beats, with relaxed and friendly locals merrily singing away while having a pint or two. There's also a little beer garden at the back. ⊠ *86–88 Point Pleasant, East Putney, Wandsworth* ☎ *0208/877–0818* Ⓤ *East Putney, Putney Bridge.*

Fodor'sChoice
★
The Cow. Guinness and oysters are a specialty in this friendly, unpretentious, Irish pub right near Portobello Road. They also sell Cuban cigars, though you can't smoke in the bar. The food is excellent, with dishes like fish stews and casseroles of autumn mutton, as is the service, and the atmosphere is warm, welcoming, and always buzzing. ⊠ *89 Westbourne Park Rd., Notting Hill* ☎ *020/7221–0021* ⊕ *www.thecowlondon.co.uk* Ⓤ *Royal Oak, Westbourne Park.*

Cricketers. This fantastically traditional pub in one of London's wealthiest neighborhoods offers curry nights on Wednesday. It's also a fine place for a Pimm's (a British gin-based liquor). ■**TIP**➜ On a summer's day, Cricketers makes a sublime vantage point for the cricket and the frolicking that take place on Richmond Green. ⊠ *Maids of Honour Row, the Green, Richmond* ☎ *020/8940–4372* Ⓤ *Richmond.*

The Crown. Away from the moneyed bustle of Upper Street, this is a quieter, more refined version of Islington pub life. Etched glass, an open fire, a nice selection of beer on tap, and good food make this well worth seeking out in the neighborhood. ⊠ *116 Cloudesley Rd., Islington* ☎ *020/7837–7107* Ⓤ *Angel.*

De Hems. London's only Dutch pub, straddling Chinatown and Shaftesbury Avenue, was founded in 1902. Lindeboom and Fruli (strawberry beer) are on tap, among numerous other tasty and strong Dutch and Belgian beverages. Interestingly named Netherlands dishes, such as *bitterballen* (deep-fried meatballs) and *vlammetjes* (spicy spring rolls), are on the menu, and the place is almost always lively—sometimes bustling—up to the midnight closing time. ⊠ *11 Macclesfield St., Chinatown* ☎ *020/7437–2494* Ⓤ *Piccadilly Circus.*

Dove Inn. Read the list of famous ex-regulars, from Charles II and Nell Gwyn to Ernest Hemingway, as you wait for a beer at this smart, comely, and very popular 16th-century riverside pub by Hammersmith Bridge. It's the smallest bar in Britain—have a look at the Guinness World Records plaque. After a few pints you can practice your singing skills to the English patriotic song that was composed here, "Rule, Britannia!" If the Dove is too full, stroll upstream along the bank to the Old Ship or the Blue Anchor. ■TIP➜ Please note, after 8 PM you must be 18 to be admitted to this pub. ✉ *19 Upper Mall, Hammersmith* ☎ *020/8748–9474* Ⓤ *Hammersmith.*

Engineer. A gastropub before anyone knew what the term meant, the children-friendly Engineer has an upscale restaurant area (serving breakfast, lunch, and dinner), a stylish carved wooden bar with some good beers on tap, and a garden as well. Expect fresh-cut flowers, a modern British menu on the chalkboard, and lots of young, beautiful people. ✉ *65 Gloucester Ave., Primrose Hill* ☎ *020/7722–0950* ⊕ *www. the-engineer.com* Ⓤ *Chalk Farm.*

French House. In the pub where the French Resistance convened during World War II , Soho hipsters and eccentrics rub shoulders now with theater people and the literati—more than shoulders, actually, because this tiny, tricolor-waving, photograph-lined pub is almost always packed. Note that in French style, only half-pints of beer are served here. ✉ *49 Dean St., Soho* ☎ *020/7437–2799* ⊕ *www.frenchhousesoho. com* Ⓤ *Tottenham Court Rd.*

The George Inn. This Southwark pub has quite a history: Shakespeare drank here, Dickens featured it in his writing, and it's the last galleried inn in London. ✉ *77 Borough High St., South Bank* ☎ *020/7407–2056* Ⓤ *London Bridge.*

Harp. This is the sort of friendly little local you might find on some out-of-the-way backstreet, except that it's right in the middle of town, between Trafalgar Square and Covent Garden. As a result, the Harp can get crowded, but the squeeze is worth it for the real ales (eight traditional ales are now available) and a no-frills menu of British sausages, cooked behind the bar. ✉ *47 Chandos Pl., Covent Garden* ☎ *020/7836– 0291* Ⓤ *Charing Cross.*

The Holly Bush. A short walk up the hill from Hampstead Tube station, the friendly Holly Bush was once a country pub before London spread this far north. It retains something of a rural feel—there's even a shoe polish machine by the entrance. Separate rooms with stripped wooden floors and an open fire make it an intimate place to enjoy great ales and organic and free-range pub food. Try the homemade pork scratchings and pickled eggs. ✉ *22 Holly Mount, Hampstead* ☎ *020/7435–2892* ⊕ *www.hollybushpub.com* Ⓤ *Hampstead.*

Island Queen. This sociable Islington pub with ornate windows and warm, red decor has home-cooked food and a cozy upstairs lounge. There's a wine club on Mondays, with very reasonably priced house wine, and a challenging quiz night on Tuesdays. Relax on the soft sofas with a Belgian beer or one of the guest ales. Playwright Joe Orton frequented the place; he lived—and died, murdered by his lover—on the very same street. ✉ *87 Noel Rd., Islington* ☎ *020/7354–8741* ⊕ *www. theislandqueenislington.co.uk* Ⓤ *Angel.*

Fodor's Choice ★ **Jerusalem Tavern.** Owned by the well-respected St. Peter's Brewery from Suffolk, the Jerusalem Tavern is one-of-a-kind, small and endearingly eccentric. Ancient Delft-style tiles meld with wood and concrete in a converted watchmaker and jeweler's shop dating back to the 18th century. The beer, both bottled and on tap, is some of the best available

16

Market Porter pub is directly across from foodie favorite Borough Market.

anywhere in London. It's often busy, especially after work. ✉ *55 Britton St., Clerkenwell* ☎ *020/7490–4281* Ⓤ *Farringdon.*

★ **The Lamb.** Charles Dickens and his contemporaries drank here, but today's enthusiastic clientele make sure this intimate pub avoids the pitfalls of feeling too old-fashioned. For private chats at the bar, you can close the delicate etched-glass "snob screen" to the bar staff, opening it only when you fancy another pint. ✉ *94 Lamb's Conduit St., Bloomsbury* ☎ *020/7405–0713* Ⓤ *Russell Sq.*

Lamb & Flag. This refreshingly un-gentrified 17th-century pub was once known as the Bucket of Blood because the upstairs room was used as a ring for bare-knuckle boxing. Now it's a friendly—and bloodless— pub, serving food (lunch only) and real ale. It's on the edge of Covent Garden, off Garrick Street. ✉ *33 Rose St., Covent Garden* ☎ *020/7497– 9504* Ⓤ *Covent Garden.*

The Lowlander. Calling itself a "Belgian and Dutch beer café," Lowlander is a world away from English café culture. There are 15 beers on tap, with at least 40 bottled options available to order from the long wooden tables. Exceptionally helpful staff are on hand to guide you, and Belgian fries with mayonnaise help absorb some of the alcohol. ✉ *36 Drury La., Covent Garden* ☎ *020/7379–7446* ⊕ *www.lowlander.com* Ⓤ *Covent Garden, Holborn.*

★ **Market Porter.** Opposite Borough Market, this atmospheric pub opens at 6 AM for the stallholders, and always seems busy. Remarkably, it manages to remain a relaxed place, with helpful staff and happy customers spilling out onto the road right through the year. The wide selection of real ales is lovingly tended. ✉ *9 Stoney St., South Bank* ☎ *020/7407–2495* ⊕ *www.markettaverns.co.uk* Ⓤ *London Bridge.*

Mayflower. An atmospheric 17th-century riverside inn with exposed beams and a terrace, this is practically the very place from which the Pilgrims set sail for Plymouth Rock. ✉ *117 Rotherhithe St., South Bank* ☎ *020/7237–4088* Ⓤ *Rotherhithe.*

★ **Museum Tavern.** Across the street from the British Museum, this friendly and classy Victorian pub makes an ideal resting place after the rigors of the culture trail. Karl Marx unwound here after a hard day in the Library. He could have spent his *Kapital* on any of seven well-kept beers available on tap. ✉ *49 Great Russell St., Bloomsbury* ☎ *020/7242–8987* Ⓤ *Tottenham Court Rd.*

★ **The Nag's Head.** It's best not to upset the landlord in this classic little mews pub in Belgravia—he runs a tight ship, and no cell phones are allowed. If that sounds like misery, the lovingly collected Victorian artifacts (including antique penny arcade games), high-quality beer, and old-fashioned pub grub should make up for it. ✉ *53 Kinnerton St., Belgravia* ☎ *020/7235–1135* Ⓤ *Hyde Park Corner.*

16

Princess Louise. This fine, popular pub has over-the-top Victorian interior-glazed tiles and intricately engraved glass screens that divide the bar area into cozy little annexes. It's not all show, either: there's a good selection of excellent-value Yorkshire real ales. ✉ *208 High Holborn, Holborn* ☎ *020/7405–8816* Ⓤ *Holborn.*

Prospect of Whitby. Named after a ship, this is London's oldest riverside pub, dating from around 1520. Once upon a time it was called the Devil's Tavern because of the lowlife criminals—thieves and smugglers—who congregated here. Ornamented with pewter ware and nautical objects, this much-loved "boozer" is often pointed out from boat trips up the Thames. ✉ *57 Wapping Wall, East End* ☎ *020/7481–1095* Ⓤ *Wapping.*

The Queen's Larder. The royal reputation of this very small pub is rumored to be from the Queen Charlotte's cooking for her "mad" husband, George III, when he was being treated at the square. ✉ *1 Queen's Sq., Bloomsbury* ☎ *020/7837–5627* ⊕ *www.queenslarder. co.uk* Ⓤ *Russel Sq.*

The Running Horse. Wood paneling gives this smart Mayfair pub an authentic feel, although the bright art deco lights may seem a bit out of place. Pub grub is served, and it's a pleasant stopover during your jaunt around the elegant neighborhood. ✉ *50 Davies St., Mayfair* ☎ *020/7493–1275* Ⓤ *Bond St.*

The Sherlock Holmes. This pub used to be known as the Northumberland Arms, and Arthur Conan Doyle popped in regularly for a pint, in the days before old black-and-white Basil Rathbone films played on loop on the pub's television. It figures in *The Hound of the Baskervilles,* and you can see the hound's supposed head and plaster casts of its huge paws among other Holmes "memorabilia" in the bar. Even if you're not a Conan Doyle fan, the beer is excellent. ✉ *10–11 Northumberland St., Westminster* ☎ *020/7930–2644* ⊕ *www.sherlockholmespub. com* Ⓤ *Charing Cross.*

Spaniards Inn. Ideal as a refueling point when you're on a Hampstead Heath hike, this historic oak-beam pub has a gorgeous garden, scene of the tea party in Dickens's *Pickwick Papers*. Dick Turpin, the highwayman, frequented the inn. Before Dickens's time, Shelley, Keats, and Byron hung out here as well. It's extremely popular, especially on Sunday, when Londoners roll in. It's also very dog friendly—there's even a dog wash in the garden. ⊠ *Spaniards Rd., Hampstead* ☎ *020/8731–8406* ⊕ *www.thespaniardshampstead.co.uk* Ⓤ *Hampstead.*

Viaduct Tavern. This pub's "haunted" reputation stems from its proximity to the former Newgate Gaol, which once stood across the street. Cells in the basement can be seen with a free tour before or after the lunchtime rush and before 5 PM. ⊠ *126 Newgate St., The City* ☎ *020/600–1863* ⊙ *Closed weekends* Ⓤ *St. Paul's.*

★ **White Hart**. This elegant, family-owned pub on Drury Lane is one of the best places to mix with cast and crew of the stage. A female-friendly environment, a cheery skylight above the lounge area, a late license, and above-average pub fare make the White Hart a particularly sociable spot for a drink. ⊠ *191 Drury La., Covent Garden* ☎ *020/7242–2317* ⊕ *www.whitehartdrurylane.co.uk* Ⓤ *Holborn, Covent Garden, Tottenham Court Rd.*

Fodor'sChoice
★ **White Horse**. This pub in well-to-do Parson's Green has a superb menu with a beer or wine chosen to match each dish. Open early for weekend brunch, the "Sloaney Pony" (named for its wealthy Sloane Square clientele) is enormously popular and a place to find many a Hugh Grant and Liz Hurley look-alike. In the summer delicious barbecues are rustled up on the patio. The manager is an expert on cask-conditioned ale, with as many as eight (and 40 beers) on tap, and there are more than 75 wines. ⊠ *1–3 Parson's Green, Parson's Green* ☎ *020/7736–2115* ⊕ *www.whitehorsesw6.com* Ⓤ *Parson's Green.*

Ye Olde Cheshire Cheese. Yes, it's a tourist trap, but it's also an extremely historic pub (it dates from 1667, the year after the Great Fire of London), and it deserves a visit for its sawdust-covered floors, low wood-beam ceilings, and the 14th-century crypt of Whitefriars' monastery under the cellar bar. This was the most regular of Dr. Johnson's and Dickens's *many* locals. ⊠ *145 Fleet St., The City* ☎ *020/7353–6170* Ⓤ *Blackfriars.*

Ye Olde Mitre. Hidden off the side of 8 Hatton Gardens, this cozy pub's roots go back to 1547, though it was rebuilt around 1772. ⊠ *1 Ely Ct., The City* ☎ *020/7405–4751* Ⓤ *Chancery La.*

Ye Olde Watling. This busy corner pub has been rebuilt at least three times since 1666. One of its incarnations was supposedly as a hostel for Christopher Wren's workmen while nearby St Paul's was being built. ⊠ *29 Watling St., The City* ☎ *020/248–8935* Ⓤ *Mansion House.*

NIGHTLIFE

As is true of nearly all cosmopolitan centers, the pace with which bars and clubs go in and out of fashion is mind-boggling. The phenomenon of absinthe has been replaced by bourbon's bite and the frenzy for the perfect cocktail recipe, and the dreaded velvet rope has been usurped by the doorbell-ringing mystique of members-only drinking clubs. The understated glamour of North London's Primrose Hill, which makes movie stars feel so at ease, might be considered dull by the über-trendy club goers of London's East End, and the price of a pint in Chelsea would be dubbed blasphemous by the musicians and poets of racially diverse Brixton. Meanwhile, some of the city's most talked-about nightlife spots are turning out to be those attached to some of its best restaurants and hotels—no wonder, when you consider the increased popularity of London cuisine in international circles. Moreover, the gay scene in London continues to flourish.

Whatever your pleasure, however your whim turns come evening, chances are you'll find what you're looking for in London's ever-changing arena of activity and invention.

BARS

Today the London bar scene is known for its bizarre blends, its pioneering panache, and its highly stylish regulars. Time was, bars in London were just a stopover in an evening full of fun—perhaps the pub first, then a bar, and then it's off to boogie the night away at the nearest dance club. These days, however, bars have become less pit stops and more destinations in themselves. With the addition of dinner menus, DJs, dance floors, and the still-new later opening hours, people now stay into the wee small hours of the morning at many of London's most fashionable bars. From exotic spaces designed to look like African villages to classic art deco creations to cavernous structures housed in old railway stations, London's bar culture is as diverse as it is delicious.

All Star Lanes. One of London's most chic bars is an unlikely combination—it's in a sleek, underground, retro bowling alley in the heart of literary Bloomsbury. Here, surrounded by 1950s Americana, you can sit on the red leather seats and choose from the largest selection of bourbons in London. There are also locations in Bayswater and Brick Lane. ⌧ *Victoria House, Bloomsbury Pl., Bloomsbury* ☎ *020/7025–2676* ⊕ *www.allstarlanes.co.uk* ⊗ *Mon.–Wed. 5 PM –11:30 PM, Thurs. 5–midnight, Fri. and Sat. noon–2 AM, Sun. noon–11* Ⓤ *Holborn.*

★ **American Bar.** Festooned with a chin-dropping array of club ties, signed celebrity photographs, sporting mementos, and baseball caps, this sensational hotel cocktail bar has superb martinis. ■**TIP**➔ Jacket required. ⌧ *Stafford Hotel, 16–18 St. James's Pl., St. James's* ☎ *020/518–1253* ⊕ *www.thestaffordhotel.co.uk* ⊗ *Weekdays 11:30–11, weekends noon–11* Ⓤ *Green Park.*

Babalou. Inside the crypt of a church, this intimate vaulted bar with North African overtones has restaurant and lounge areas. Brixton hipsters shake it up to top DJs spinning the decks, and knock back fancy cocktails at the bar. There's live music on Friday night. ⌧ *Brixton Hill, under St. Matthew's Church, Brixton* ☎ *020/7738–3366* ⊕ *www. babalou.net* ⊗ *Fri. and Sat. 8 PM–5 AM* Ⓤ *Brixton.*

16

Beach Blanket Babylon. In a Georgian house in Notting Hill, close to Portobello Market, this always-packed bar is distinguishable by its eclectic indoor-outdoor spaces with Gaudí-esque curves and snuggly corners—like a fairy-tale grotto or a medieval dungeon. Its sister restaurant-bar recently opened in Shoreditch. ☒ *45 Ledbury Rd., Notting Hill* ☏ *020/7229–2907* ⊕ *www.beachblanket.co.uk* ⊗ *Mon.–Sat. noon–midnight, Sun. noon–11:30 PM* Ⓤ *Notting Hill Gate.*

Bedford and Strand. The wine bar is enjoying something of a renaissance in London, and this is one of the best of a new generation. It's sunk atmospherically down below the streets of Covent Garden, with dark wood and hanging shades; the wine list is short but well chosen, the service is faultless, and the bistro food is created with plenty of care. ☒ *1A Bedford St., Charing Cross* ☏ *020/7836–3033* ⊕ *www.bedford-strand.com* ⊗ *Weekdays noon–midnight, Sat. 5:30 PM–midnight* Ⓤ *Charing Cross.*

Big Chill Bar. Gritty urban chic combines with a rural festival feel at this laid-back East London venue. English grub is available and, as you'd expect from the organizers of one of the country's best music festivals, the tunes are top-notch. ☒ *Dray Walk, off Brick La., Shoreditch* ☏ *020/7392–9180* ⊕ *www.bigchill.net* ⊗ *Weekdays noon–midnight, weekends noon–1AM.*

The Blue Bar at the Berkeley Hotel. With low-slung gray-blue walls this hotel bar is ever so slightly sexy. Immaculate service, an excellent cocktail list—try the Sex in the City—and a trendy David Collins design, make this an ideal spot for a secretive tête-à-tête, complete with jazzy music in the background. ☒ *Wilton Pl., Knightsbridge* ☏ *020/291–1680* ⊕ *the-berkeley.co.uk* ⊗ *Weekdays 4 PM–1 AM, Sat. 3 PM–1 AM, Sun. 4–11 PM* Ⓤ *Knightsbridge.*

Cafe des Amis. This relaxed basement wine bar near the Royal Opera House is the perfect pre- or post-theater spot, popular among musicians and performers alike—and a friendly enough place to go on your own. More than 30 wines are served by the glass, along with a good selection of cheeses and plates of charcuterie as well as more substantial dishes for those with more of an appetite (there's also a French restaurant with a Mediterranean twist on the ground floor serving everything from moules marinieres to risotto). Opera buffs will enjoy the performance and production prints on the walls. ☒ *11–14 Hanover Pl., Covent Garden* ☏ *020/7379–3444* ⊕ *www.cafedesamis.co.uk* ⊗ *Mon.–Sat. 11:30 AM–1 AM* Ⓤ *Covent Garden.*

Cafe Kick. Table football dominates this friendly place, with Portuguese beers and Brazilian cocktails consumed over many football games. Homemade soups and hot pots make it a good lunchtime stop, but it's at night that it really comes alive. There are three football tables—buy a token from the bar for 80p—and it's usually winner stays on, though you can ring ahead to reserve a table. ☒ *43 Exmouth Market, Clerkenwell* ☏ *020/7837–8077* ⊕ *www.cafekick.co.uk* ⊗ *Mon.–Thurs. noon–11 PM, Fri. and Sat. noon–midnight. Closed Sun. in winter* Ⓤ *Angel or Farringdon.*

Cinnamon Club. In the basement of what was once Old Westminster Library, the bar of this contemporary Indian restaurant (treat yourself to

Order a pint at the 17th-century Lamb & Flag pub in Covent Garden.

a superb curry) has Bollywood scenes playing on a large screen, Asian-theme cocktails (mango mojitos, Delhi mules), delicious bar snacks, and a clientele that includes fashionable young politicos. ⊠ *The Old Westminster Library, Great Smith St., Westminster* ☎ *020/7222-2555* ⊕ *www.cinnamonclub.com* ⊗ *Mon.–Sat. 6–11:45 PM* Ⓤ *Westminster.*

Fodor'sChoice
★
Claridge's Bar. This elegant Mayfair meeting place remains unpretentious even when it brims with beautiful people. The bar has an art deco heritage made hip by the sophisticated touch of designer David Collins. A library of rare champagnes and brandies as well as a delicious choice of traditional and exotic cocktails—try The Flapper or the Black Pearl—will occupy your taste buds. Request a glass of vintage Cristal in the Macanudo Fumoir. ⊠ *55 Brook St., Mayfair* ☎ *020/7629-8860* ⊕ *www.claridges.co.uk* ⊗ *Mon.–Sat. noon–1 AM, Sun. noon–midnight* Ⓤ *Bond St.*

Fodor'sChoice
★
Cocoon. Pan-Asian restaurant Cocoon transforms itself into a sophisticated lounge bar (with DJ) Thursday through Saturday until 3 AM. Soft curves give the tastefully modern place a bubbly feel, and contrasting levels of lighting blend intimacy with a vibrant atmosphere. Nibble away on one of chef Ricky Pang's original dishes while you sip on some of London's best cocktails, all with an Asian twist—try the Love & Rockets. ⊠ *65 Regent St., St. James's* ☎ *020/7494-7600* ⊕ *www.cocoon-restaurants.com* ⊗ *Thurs.–Sat. 11 PM–3 AM* Ⓤ *Piccadilly Circus.*

Fodor'sChoice
★
Crazy Bear. This sexy basement bar with cowhide stools and croc-skin tables feels like Casablanca in Fitzrovia. As you enter Crazy Bear, a spiral staircase leads to a mirrored parlor over which presides a 1947 Murano chandelier. But don't let the opulence fool you: waitstaff here

are warm and welcoming to an all-ages international crowd abuzz with chatter. A new chef means the menu now advertises drinks and dumplings. ✉ *26–28 Whitfield St., Fitzrovia* ☎ *020/7631–0088* ⊕ *www. crazybeargroup.co.uk* ⊘ *Sun.–Wed. noon–midnight, Thurs.–Sat. noon–1 AM* Ⓤ *Goodge St.*

 Dogstar. This popular South London hangout is frequented by local hipsters and counterculture types. It was the first DJ bar in the world and has since enjoyed a fabulous reputation. The vibe at this "surrealist boudoir" is unpretentious, with top-name DJs playing cutting-edge sounds every night. (free Tuesday–Thursday). ✉ *389 Coldharbour La., Brixton* ☎ *020/7733–7515* ⊕ *www.antic-ltd.com/dogstar* ▱ *Free–£5* ⊘ *Tues.– Thurs. 4 PM–2 AM, Fri. 4 PM–4 AM, Sat. noon–4 AM, Sun. noon–2 AM* Ⓤ *Brixton.*

Harlem. Backed by music producer Arthur Baker (the Elbow Room), Harlem re-creates New York in more ways than one, not the least of which is its size: the two rooms together equal the dimensions of an average Manhattan apartment. However, funky DJs, fresh tunes, and reasonably priced drinks—not to mention the great soul food served in the first-floor restaurant—give Harlem a vibe all its own. ✉ *78 Westbourne Grove, Westbourne Grove* ☎ *020/7985–0900* ⊕ *www. harlemsoulfood.com* ⊘ *Weekdays 5 PM–2:30 AM, Sat. 10 AM–2:30 AM, Sun. 10 AM–midnight* Ⓤ *Westbourne Park.*

Hoxton Square Bar & Kitchen. The rectangular concrete bar, reminiscent of a Swedish airport hangar, has long, comfortable sofas, plate-glass windows at the front and back, and outdoor tables overlooking leafy Hoxton Square. In the converted Lux cinema next door, there's a designated restaurant area serving venison and the like. The music policy here is "anything but house," and creative types give the place good business. ✉ *2–4 Hoxton Sq., Hoxton* ☎ *020/7613–0709* ⊕ *www. hoxtonsquarebar.com* ⊘ *Mon. 11 AM–midnight, Tues.–Thurs. 11 AM–1 AM, Fri. and Sat. 11 AM–2 AM, Sun. 11 AM–12:30 AM* Ⓤ *Old St.*

Le Beaujolais. Around 60 lovingly selected French wines are available here, where you can snack on olives, charcuterie, and homemade *croque monsieur* (grilled ham and cheese) sandwiches while snug and warm under the bottle-laden ceiling as a funky blues sound track plays. It's a romantic little spot and can get crowded just before theater performances, but it has room again once the shows begin. ✉ *25 Litchfield St., Leicester Square* ☎ *020/7836–2955* ⊘ *Weekdays noon–11, Sat. 5–11* Ⓤ *Leicester Sq.*

Long Bar at Sanderson Hotel. The 80-foot-long shimmering white onyx island bar in the Philippe Starck–designed Sanderson Hotel attracts a cliquish and trendy crowd. The large but welcoming outdoor area exudes a Zen-like feel, with soothing running water mixed with dim lighting and decorative vegetation providing a truly relaxing experience. For a more intimate and romantic setting, the hotel's **Purple Bar** serves excellent chocolate martinis. ✉ *50 Berners St., Fitzrovia* ☎ *020/7300– 1444* ⊕ *www.sandersonlondon.com* ⊘ *Mon. 11 AM–1 AM, Tues. and Wed. 11 AM–1:30 AM, Thurs.–Sat. 11 AM–3 AM, Sun. noon–10:30 PM* Ⓤ *Oxford Circus.*

★ **Nordic.** With shooters called "Husky Poo" and "Danish Bacon Surprise" and crayfish tails and meatballs on the smorgasbord menu, Nordic takes its Scandinavian feel the whole way. This secluded, shabby-chic bar serves many couples cozied up among travel brochures promoting the Viking lands. If you can't decide what to drink, the cocktail roulette wheel on the wall may help. ✉ *25 Newman St., Soho* ☎ *020/7631–3174* ⊕ *www.nordicbar.com* ⊙ *Mon.–Thurs. noon–11 PM, Fri. noon–midnight, Sat. 6 PM–midnight* Ⓤ *Tottenham Court Rd.*

The Mint Leaf Bar. Renowned for its long bar, this restaurant's bar–lounge has more than 500 spirits and serves more than 1,000 well-prepared cocktails. Nibbles and light snacks with an Indian twist are available, and if you're up for some more substantial spicy food, treat yourself to a meal at the sophisticated restaurant. There is also a sister bar and restaurant located in Angel Court in The City. ✉ *Suffolk Place, Haymarket* ☎ *020/7930–9020* ⊕ *www.mintleafrestaurant.com* ⊙ *Mon.–Wed. noon–midnight; Thurs. and Fri. noon–1 AM; Sat. 5 PM–1 AM; Sun. 6 PM–midnight* Ⓤ *Piccadilly Circus.*

Potemkin. More than 100 vodkas and some great cocktails are available at this modern Russian bar. Friendly staff happily suggest where to start, and mixed pickles and other Russian fare is available to accompany your drinks. ✉ *144 Clerkenwell Rd., Clerkenwell* ☎ *020/7278–6661* ⊕ *www.potemkin.co.uk* ⊙ *Weekdays noon–11 PM, Sat. 6–11* Ⓤ *Farringdon, Chancery La.*

★ **Salon Bar £ L'Atelier.** Renowned chef Joel Robuchon's intimate, relaxed, and elegant bar with red undertones is in the same premises as his L'Atelier and La Cuisine restaurants. New cocktails await you, as the drink menu changes every six months, with new flavors and textures sure to entice your taste buds. If you're feeling generous, treat yourself to an unforgettable dinner at the restaurant pre- or post-drinks—try the Fois Gras Chaud. ✉ *13–15 West St., Leicester Square* ☎ *020/7010–8600* ⊕ *www.joel-robuchon.com* ⊙ *Mon.–Sat. 2:30 PM–2 AM, Sun. 2:30 PM–10:30 PM* Ⓤ *Leicester Sq.*

Sketch. At this esoteric living room bar one seat never looks like the next. A patisserie during the day, the exclusive Parlour Bar exudes plenty of rarefied charm while the intimate East Bar at the back is reminiscent of a sci-fi film set. ✉ *9 Conduit St., Soho* ☎ *020/7659–4500* ⊕ *www.sketch.uk.com* ⊙ *Parlour Bar Mon.–Thurs. 6:30–10 PM, Fri. and Sat. 6:30–9 PM, members only after 9 PM; East Bar Mon.–Thurs. 6 PM–1 AM, Fri. and Sat. 6 PM–2 AM* Ⓤ *Oxford Circus.*

16

COMEDY AND CABARET

From renowned comedians such as Eddie Izzard to amateurs who try their luck on stage, there are plenty of comedy and cabaret acts to keep you entertained all night long.

Amused Moose. This Soho basement/retro nightclub is widely considered the best place to see breaking talent as well as household names doing "secret" shows. Ricky Gervais, Eddie Izzard, and Russel Brand are among those who have graced this stage, and every summer a handful of the Edinburgh Fringe comedians preview here. The bar is open late (and serves food), and there's a DJ and dancing until 5 AM after the show. Tickets are often discounted with a printout from their Web site, and shows are mainly on Saturday. ⊠ *Moonlighting, 17 Greek St., Soho* ☎ *020/7287-3727* ⊕ *www.amusedmoose.com* ✉ *£9 and up* ⊗ *Doors open at 7:30 PM* Ⓤ *Tottenham Court Rd.*

Banana Cabaret. This huge, vibrant pub is one of London's finest comedy venues. Well worth the trek, it's only 100 yards from Balham station, and there's a minicab office close by for those tempted to make a long night of it. ⊠ *Bedford Pub, 77 Bedford Hill, Balham* ☎ *020/682-8940* ⊕ *www.bananacabaret.co.uk* ✉ *£13–£16* ⊗ *Fri. 7:30 PM–2 AM, Sat. 7 PM–2 AM* Ⓤ *Balham.*

Canal Café Theatre. Famous comics and cabaret stars perform every night of the week in this intimate, canal-side venue. The long-running News-Revue is a topical song-and-sketch show every night, Thursday–Sunday. ⊠ *Bridge House, Delamere Terr., Little Venice* ☎ *020/7289-6054* ⊕ *www.canalcafetheatre.com* ✉ *£5–£11* ⊗ *Mon.–Sat. 7:30–11, Sun. 7–10:30* Ⓤ *Warwick Ave., Royal Oak, Paddington.*

Comedy Café. In addition to lots of stand-up comedy, this popular dive in trendy Hoxton has a grill menu, a free open mike on Wednesday, and late-night disco on Saturday night. ⊠ *66 Rivington St., Shoreditch* ☎ *020/7739-5706* ⊕ *www.comedycafe.co.uk* ✉ *Free–£15* ⊗ *Wed. and Thurs. 7–midnight, Fri. 6–11, Sat. 6 PM–1 AM* Ⓤ *Old St.*

★ **Comedy Store**. Known as the birthplace of alternative comedy, this is where the United Kingdom's funniest stand-ups have cut their teeth before being launched onto prime-time TV. Comedy Store Players, a team with six comedians doing improvisation with audience suggestions, entertain audiences on Wednesday and Sunday; the Cutting Edge team steps in every Tuesday; and on the last Monday of every month the King Gong show (£5) hits the stage, where amateur comedians try their luck. Thursday, Friday, and Saturday have the best stand-up acts. There's also a bar with food. ■TIP→ Tickets can be booked through Ticketmaster or over the phone. Note that children under 18 are not admitted to this venue. ⊠ *1A Oxendon St., Soho* ☎ *0844/847-1728* ⊕ *www. thecomedystore.co.uk* ✉ *£13–£18* ⊗ *Shows daily 8 PM, with extra shows Fri. and Sat. at midnight* Ⓤ *Piccadilly Circus, Leicester Sq.*

Fodor's Choice ★ **Soho Theatre**. This innovative theater's programs include comedy shows by established acts and up-and-coming comedians. The bar downstairs, Café Lazeez, stays open until 11:30 on Sunday through Thursday, and until 1 AM Saturday. Check local listings or the Web site for what's on, and book tickets in advance. ⊠ *21 Dean St., Soho* ☎ *020/7478-0100* ⊕ *www.sohotheatre.com* ✉ *£10–£22.50* ⊗ *Mon.–Sat. usually 7–11 although show times vary* Ⓤ *Tottenham Court Rd.*

DANCE CLUBS

The city that practically invented raves is always on the verge of creating something new, and on any given night there's a club playing the latest in dance music. Because London is so ethnically diverse, the tunes

Cargo dance club is a huge venue for live music of all types.

that emanate from the DJ box are equally varied—an amalgamation of sounds infusing drum 'n' bass, hip-hop, deep house, Latin house, breakbeat, indie, and R&B.

The club scene here ranges from mammoth-size playgrounds like Fabric and Cargo to more intimate venues where you can actually hear your friends talk. Check the daily listings in *Time Out* for "club nights," which are theme nights that take place the same night every week, sometimes at the same clubs but often shifting locations. Another good way to learn about club nights is by picking up flyers in your favorite bar.

Cargo. Housed under a series of old railway arches, this vast brick-wall bar, restaurant, dance floor, and live-music venue pulls a young, international crowd with its hip vibe and diverse selection of music. Long tables bring people together, as does the food, which draws on global influences and is served tapas-style. ⊠ *83 Rivington St., Shoreditch* ☎ *020/7739–3440* ⊕ *www.cargo-london.com* ✉ *Free–£20* ⊗ *Mon.–Thurs. noon–1 AM, Fri. noon–3 AM, Sat. 6 PM–3 AM, Sun. 1 PM–midnight* Ⓤ *Old St.*

Fabric. This sprawling subterranean club is now a firm fixture on the London scene. "Fabric Live" hosts drum 'n' bass, dubstep, and hip-hop crews and live acts on Friday; international big-name DJs play slow, sexy bass lines and cutting-edge music on Saturday. The devastating sound system and "bodysonic" dance floor ensure that bass riffs vibrate through your entire body. ■TIP→ Get there early to avoid a lengthy queue, and don't wear a suit. ⊠ *77A Charterhouse St., East End* ☎ *020/7336–8898* ⊕ *www.fabriclondon.com* ✉ *£13–£16* ⊗ *Fri. 10 PM–6 AM, Sat. 11 PM–8 AM, Sun. 11 PM–6 AM* Ⓤ *Farringdon.*

★ **KOKO.** This Victorian theater, formerly known as Camden Palace, has seen acts from Charlie Chaplin to Madonna, and genres from punk to rave. Updated with lush reds not unlike a cockney Moulin Rouge, this is still one of London's most stunning venues. Sounds of live indie rock, cabaret, funky house, and club classics keep the big dance floor moving, even when it's not heaving. ⊠ *1A Camden High St., Camden Town* ☎ *0870/432–5527* ⊕ *www.koko.uk.com* ☏ *£3–£20* ☉ *Opening hrs vary, depending on shows* Ⓤ *Mornington Crescent.*

Mass. In what was previously St. Matthew's Church, but is now an atmospheric club with Gothic overtones, winding stone steps lead to the main room, where an extended balcony hangs over the dance floor. An unpretentious and friendly crowd dances, on rotating club nights, to reggae, drum 'n' bass, and R&B. ⊠ *Brixton Hill, St. Matthew's Church, Brixton* ☎ *020/7738–7875* ⊕ *www.mass-club.com* ☏ *£5–£20* ☉ *Wed. and Thurs. 10 PM–2 AM, Fri. and Sat. 9 PM–6 AM* Ⓤ *Brixton.*

Ministry of Sound. It's more of an industry than a club, with its own record label, online radio station, and international DJs. The stripped-down warehouse-style club has a super sound system and pulls in the world's most legendary names in dance. There are chill-out rooms, two bars, and three dance floors. ⊠ *103 Gaunt St., South Bank* ☎ *020/740–8600* ⊕ *www.ministryofsound.com* ☏ *£6–£20* ☉ *Fri. 10:30 PM–6 AM, Sat. 11 PM–7 AM* Ⓤ *Elephant & Castle.*

★ **Notting Hill Arts Club.** Rock stars like Liam Gallagher and Courtney Love have been seen at this small basement club-bar. An alternative crowd swills beer to eclectic music that spans Asian underground, hip-hop, Latin-inspired funk, deep house, and jazzy grooves. What it lacks in looks it makes up for in mood. ⊠ *21 Notting Hill Gate, Notting Hill* ☎ *020/7460–4459* ⊕ *www.nottinghillartsclub.com* ☏ *Free–£8* ☉ *Weekdays 7 PM–2 AM, Sat. 4 PM–2 AM, Sun. 4 PM–1 AM* Ⓤ *Notting Hill Gate.*

Pacha. London's version of the Ibizan superclub is in a restored 1920s dance hall next to Victoria Coach Station. The hedonistic surroundings include a (smoking) roof terrace for alfresco clubbing and a new state-of-the-art VIP room. The crowd is slightly older than average and stylish, but not necessarily as moneyed as you might expect. ⊠ *Terminus Pl., Victoria* ☎ *0845/371–4489* ⊕ *www.pachalondon.com* ☏ *£15–£20* ☉ *Fri. and Sat. 10 PM–5 AM* Ⓤ *Victoria.*

333. The last word in dance music for the trendy Shoreditch crowd. Fashionable bright young things dance to drum 'n' bass, twisted disco, and underground dance genres. There are three floors, each with its own theme. You can chill on leather sofas at the relaxed Mother Bar upstairs, open from 8 PM daily, which always has DJs. ⊠ *333 Old St., East End* ☎ *020/7739–5949* ⊕ *www.333mother.com* ☏ *Free–£10* ☉ *Fri. and Sat. 10 PM–3 AM, bar Mon.–Sun., 8 PM–3 AM* Ⓤ *Old St.*

Fodor'sChoice
★ **Vendome Mayfair.** This recently opened classy club draws a trendy crowd for house music, colorful furnishings, and futuristic designs with '70s retro disco decor. The revolving DJ booth at the center of the club, the Renaissance-like entrance, the individually themed booths, and the faux snakeskin banisters shout out pure decadence. ⊠ *85 Piccadilly, Mayfair*

☎ *020/495–2595* ⊕ *www.vendomemayfair.com* ✉ *£20* ⊙ *Mon., Tues., and Thurs. 10 PM–3 AM, Fri. and Sat. 10 PM–4 AM.*

ECLECTIC MUSIC

The eclectic music scene in London is constantly becoming more mish-mashed—the electro scene has evolved into the "nu rave" scene, and the constant arrival of new bands adds to the capital's already diverse music scene.

The Borderline. This important small venue has a solid reputation for booking everything from metal to country and beyond. Oasis, Pearl Jam, Blur, Sheryl Crow, PJ Harvey, Ben Harper, Jeff Buckley, and Counting Crows have all played live here. ⊠ *Orange Yard off Manette St., Soho* ☎ *0844/847–2466* ⊕ *www.meanfiddler.com* ✉ *£6–£25* ⊙ *Mon.–Sat. 7 PM–3 AM, Sun. 7–10:30 PM* Ⓤ *Tottenham Court Rd.*

Dingwalls. This midsize venue in the Camden Lock warehouses caters to the full spectrum of musical tastes—country, jazz, blues, folk, indie, and world beat. ■ TIP➔ Note that on Friday and Saturday it becomes a comedy club, Jongleurs. ⊠ *Middle Yard, Camden Lock off Camden High St., Camden Town* ☎ *020/7267–1577* ⊕ *www.dingwalls.com* ✉ *£5–£20* ⊙ *Sun.–Thurs. 7:30 PM–11 PM* Ⓤ *Camden Town.*

93 Feet East. Knowing nods greet the bands in this cool but friendly independent venue, with a courtyard out back for taking a breather or partaking in weekend barbecues. Up-and-coming guitar groups and blues acts find their way here, house DJs get you moving, and live hip-hop crews shake you off your seat with hefty bass lines. ⊠ *150 Brick La., East End* ☎ *020/7247–3293* ⊕ *www.93feeteast.co.uk* ✉ *Free–£10* ⊙ *Mon.–Thurs. 5–11 PM, Fri. 5 PM –1 AM, Sat. noon–1 AM, Sun. noon–10:30 PM* Ⓤ *Aldgate East.*

Fodor's Choice ★ **O2 Academy Brixton.** This legendary Brixton venue has seen it all—mods and rockers, hippies and punks. Despite a capacity for almost 5,000 people, this refurbished Victorian hall with original art deco fixtures retains a clublike charm; it has plenty of bars and upstairs seating. ⊠ *211 Stockwell Rd., Brixton* ☎ *020/7771–3000* ⊕ *www.brixton-academy.co.uk* ✉ *£10–£50* ⊙ *Opening hrs vary* Ⓤ *Brixton.*

O2 Shepherd's Bush Empire. Once a grand old theater and former BBC TV studio, this intimate venue with fine balcony views now hosts a great cross section of mid-league U.K. and U.S. bands. ⊠ *Shepherd's Bush Green, Shepherd's Bush* ☎ *020/8354–3300* ⊕ *www.shepherds-bush-empire.co.uk* ✉ *£10–£35* ⊙ *Opening hrs vary* Ⓤ *Shepherd's Bush.*

100 Club. Since it opened in 1942, all the greats have played here, from Glenn Miller and Louis Armstrong on down to the best traditional jazz artists, British and American blues, R&B, and punk. This cool, inexpensive club now reverberates to rock, indie, and R&B—as well as jazz, of course. You can still take jitterbug and jive lessons from the London Swing Dance Society. ⊠ *100 Oxford St., Soho* ☎ *020/7636–0933* ⊕ *www.the100club.co.uk* ✉ *£7–£15* ⊙ *Mon. 7:30–midnight, Tues.–Thurs. 7:30–11, Fri. 7:30 PM–12:30 AM, Sat. 7:30 PM–2 AM, Sun. 7:30–11* Ⓤ *Oxford Circus, Tottenham Court Rd.*

16

The Thameside Bulls Head has live jazz every night.

12 Bar Club. This rough-and-ready acoustic club hosts notable singer-songwriters. Four different acts of new folk, contemporary country, blues, and even ska and punk perform each night in the intimate venue. There's a good selection of bottled beer and gastropub food here. ✉ *22–23 Denmark Pl., West End* ☎ *020/7240–2622* ⊕ *www.12barclub.com* ✉ *£3–£10* ⊙ *Fri. and Sat. 7 PM–3 AM, Sun. 6 PM–12:30 AM. Café serves food 9–9* Ⓤ *Tottenham Court Rd.*

★ **Union Chapel.** This beautiful old chapel has excellent acoustics and sublime architecture. The beauty of the space and its impressive multicultural programming have made it one of London's best musical venues, especially for acoustic shows. Performers have included Björk, Beck, and Goldfrapp, though now you're more likely to hear lower-key alternative country, world music, and jazz. ✉ *Compton Terr., Islington* ☎ *020/7226–1686* ⊕ *www.unionchapel.org.uk* ✉ *Free–£25* ⊙ *Opening hrs vary* Ⓤ *Highbury & Islington.*

JAZZ AND BLUES

Jazz in London is highly eclectic. You can expect anything from danceable, smooth tunes played at a supper club to groovy New Orleans–style blues to exotic world-beat rhythms, which can be heard at some of the less central venues throughout the capital. London hosts the **London Jazz Festival** (⊕ *www.londonjazzfestival.org.uk*) in November, which showcases top and emerging artists in experimental jazz. The **Ealing Jazz Festival** (⊕ *www.ealing.gov.uk*), at the end of July, claims to be the biggest free jazz event in Europe.

Ain't Nothin' but . . . The Blues Bar. The name sums up this bar that whips up a sweaty environment. Local musicians, as well as some notable names, squeeze onto the tiny stage. There's good bar food of the chili-and-gumbo variety. Most weekday nights there's no cover. ✉ *20 Kingly St., Soho* ☎ *020/7287–0514* ⊕ *www.aintnothinbut.co.uk* ✉ *Free–£5* ⊙ *Mon.–Wed. 6 PM–1 AM, Thurs. 6 PM–2 AM, Fri. 5 PM–3 AM, Sat. 3 PM–3 AM, Sun. 3 PM–midnight* Ⓤ *Oxford Circus.*

★ **Bull's Head**. Its pleasant location (right on the Thames) and the big-name musicians who jam here regularly make the excursion to Bull's Head worthwhile. Jazz-and-blues shows start nightly at 8:30 PM (1 PM and 8.30 PM on Sunday). ■**TIP**➔ They also offer more than 60 wines, 40 malt whiskies, Thai food, and English grub at lunchtime. ✉ *373 Lonsdale Rd., Barnes Bridge, Barnes* ☎ *020/8876–5241* ⊕ *www.thebullshead. com* ✉ *£6–£12* ⊙ *Daily noon–midnight* Ⓤ *Hammersmith, then Bus 209 to Barnes Bridge.*

Dover Street Restaurant & Jazz Bar. Put on your blue-suede shoes and prepare to dance the night away—that is, after you've feasted from the French Mediterranean menu. Fun for dates as well as groups, Dover Street Restaurant has three bars, a DJ, and a stage with the latest live bands performing everything from jazz to soul to R&B, all this encir-cling linen-covered tables with a friendly staff catering to your every whim. ✉ *8–10 Dover St., Mayfair* ☎ *020/7491–7509* ⊕ *www.doverst. co.uk* ✉ *Free–£15* ⊙ *Mon.–Thurs. noon–3 PM and 5:30 PM–3 AM, Fri. noon–3 PM and 7 PM –3 AM, Sat. 7 PM–3 AM* Ⓤ *Green Park.*

★ **Jazz Café**. A palace of high-tech cool in bohemian Camden—it remains an essential hangout for fans of both the mainstream end of the rep-ertoire and hip-hop, funk, rap, and Latin fusion. Book ahead if you want a prime table overlooking the stage, in the balcony restaurant. ✉ *5 Pkwy., Camden Town* ☎ *020/7688–8899 restaurant reservations, 0870/060–3777 standing tickets* ⊕ *www.jazzcafe.co.uk* ✉ *£10–£25* ⊙ *Daily 7 PM–2 AM* Ⓤ *Camden Town.*

Fodor'sChoice **Pizza Express Jazz Club Soho**. One of the capital's most ubiquitous pizza
★ chains also runs a great Soho jazz venue. The dimly lighted restaurant hosts top-quality international jazz acts every night. The Italian-style thin-crust pizzas are good, too, though on the small side. ✉ *10 Dean St., Soho* ☎ *0845/602–7017* ⊕ *www.pizzaexpresslive.com* ✉ *£10–£25* ⊙ *Daily from 11:30 AM for food; music 7:30 PM–11 PM* Ⓤ *Tottenham Court Rd.*

Ronnie Scott's. Since the '60s, this legendary jazz club has attracted big names. It's usually crowded and hot, the food isn't great, and service is slow—but the mood can't be beat, even since the sad departure of its eponymous founder and saxophonist. Reservations are recommended. ✉ *47 Frith St., Soho* ☎ *020/7439–0747* ⊕ *www.ronniescotts.co.uk* ✉ *£20–£36 nonmembers, 20% off for members, annual membership £165* ⊙ *Mon.–Sat. 6 PM–3 AM, Sun. 6:30 PM–11 PM* Ⓤ *Leicester Sq.*

606 Club. Expect a civilized Chelsea club that showcases mainstream and contemporary jazz by well-known British-based musicians. ■**TIP**➔ You must eat a meal in order to consume alcohol, so allow for an extra £20. Reservations are advisable. Sunday lunchtime jazz takes place one or

16

twice a month; call ahead. ⊠ *90 Lots Rd., Chelsea* ☎ *020/7352–5953* ⊕ *www.606club.co.uk* ✉ *£8–£12 music charge added to bill* ⊘ *Mon. 7:30 PM–12:30 AM, Tues.–Thurs. 7 PM–12:30 AM, Fri. and Sat. 8 PM–1:30 AM, Sun. 7 PM–midnight* Ⓤ *Earl's Court, Fulham Broadway.*

ROCK

Ever since the Beatles hit the world stage in the early 1960s, London has been at the epicenter of rock and roll. The city is a given stop on any burgeoning or established band's international tour. These days, since rock clubs have been granted later licenses, many shows now go past 11 PM. Fans here are both loyal and enthusiastic. It is, therefore, a good idea to buy show tickets ahead of time. The "Gigs and Tickets" section on ⊕ *www.nme.com* is a comprehensive search engine where you can easily book tickets online; *Time Out* is another good source for upcoming shows.

★ **Barfly Club.** At one of the finest small clubs in the capital, punk, indie guitar bands, and new metal rock attract a nonmainstream crowd. Weekend club nights upstairs host DJs (and live bands) who rock the decks. The Baryfly's sister club, **The Fly,** is on New Oxford Street. ⊠ *49 Chalk Farm Rd., Camden Town* ⊠ *36/38 New Oxford St.* ☎ *020/7424–0800* ⊕ *www.barflyclub.com* ✉ *£5–£8* ⊘ *Mon. and Tues. 7–midnight, Wed. and Thurs. 7 PM–2 AM, Fri. and Sat. 7 PM–3 AM* Ⓤ *Camden Town, Chalk Farm.*

The HMV Forum. The best medium-to-big-name rock performers consistently play at the 2,000-capacity club. It's a converted 1920 art deco cinema, with a balcony overlooking the dance floor. Consult the Web site for current listings. ⊠ *9–17 Highgate Rd., Kentish Town* ☎ *020/7428–4099* ⊕ *www.kentishtownforum.com* ✉ *£12–£25* ⊘ *Opening hrs vary, depending on concert schedule* Ⓤ *Kentish Town.*

Water Rats. This high-spirited pub hosted Bob Dylan on his 1963 tour, as well as the first Oasis gig. Alt-country, hip-hop, and indie guitar bands thrash it out most nights of the week. ⊠ *328 Gray's Inn Rd., Euston* ☎ *020/7837–7269* ⊕ *www.themonto.com* ✉ *£6 and up* ⊘ *Mon.–Sat. noon–11:30* Ⓤ *King's Cross.*

THE GAY SCENE

The U.K. capital's gay and lesbian culture is as thriving as it is in New York or Los Angeles, with Soho serving as the hub of gay London. Clubs in London cater to almost every desire, whether that be the suited-up Tommy Hilfiger–look-alike scene, cruisers taking on dingy dives, flamboyant drag shows, lesbian tea dances, or themed fetish nights. There's also a cornucopia of queer theater and performance art that runs throughout the year. Whatever your tastes, you'll be able to satisfy them with a night on the town in London.

Choices are admittedly much better for males than females here; although many of the gay clubs are female-friendly, those catering strictly to lesbians are in the minority. The National Film Board puts on the Gay and Lesbian Film Festival in March (⊕ *www.llgff.org.uk*).

Pride London in June (an annual event encompassing a parade, sports, art, comedy, theater, music, cabaret, and dance) welcomes anyone and everyone, and had more than half a million participants in 2008 . This extravagant pageant spirals its way through London's streets, with major events taking place in Trafalgar Square and Leicester Square, then culminates in Victoria Embankment with ticketed parties continuing on afterward (⊕ *www.pridelondon.org* for details).

For up-to-date listings, consult *Time Out* (⊕ *www.timeout.com/london/ gay*), *Boyz* (⊕ *www.boyz.co.uk*), *Gay Times* (⊕ *www.gaytimes.co.uk*), *Attitude* (⊕ *www.attitude.co.uk*), or the lesbian monthly *Diva* (⊕ *www. divamag.co.uk*).

Online resources include Rainbow Network (⊕ *www.rainbownetwork. com*).

BARS, CAFÉS, AND PUBS

Most bars in London are gay-friendly, though there are a number of cafés and pubs that are known as gay hangouts after-hours. Here's a listing of just a few, some of which serve drinks until 3 AM (11 PM on Sunday).

Box. True to its name, this modern, industrial-chic café–bar is small and square. It's a staple on the preclub circuit and gets packed to the hilt with muscular men. For peckish punters, food is served until 9 PM (except on Saturday until 5 PM) daily. ⊠ *32–34 Monmouth St., Soho* ☎ *020/7240–5828* ⊕ *www.boxbar.com* ⊗ *Weekdays noon–11, weekends noon–10:30* Ⓤ *Leicester Sq.*

Candy Bar. The United Kingdom's first girls' bar is intimate, chilled, and cruisey, with DJs mixing the latest sounds. Pole dancing and striptease are now also features on some nights. Men are welcome only as guests. ⊠ *4 Carlisle St., Soho* ☎ *020/7494–4041* ⊕ *www.candybarsoho.com* ⊜ *£3 after 9 PM Thurs., £5 after 9 PM Fri., £6 after 9 PM Sat.* ⊗ *Mon.– Thurs. noon–midnight, Fri. and Sat. noon–2 AM, Sun. 5–11* Ⓤ *Tottenham Court Rd.*

The Edge. *Poseurs* are welcome at this hip hangout. Straight groovers mingle with gay men over the four jam-packed floors. In summer, sidewalk tables provide an enviable view of Soho's daily street theater. ⊠ *11 Soho Sq., Soho* ☎ *020/7439–1313* ⊕ *www.edgesoho.co.uk* ⊜ *£2 after 10 PM only on Fri. and Sat.* ⊗ *Mon.–Sat. noon–1 AM, Sun. noon–11:30* Ⓤ *Oxford Circus.*

Fodor'sChoice ★ **Friendly Society.** This haute moderne hot spot hops with activity almost any night of the week; the basement feels a bit like something out of *Star Trek* with its white-leather pod seats. The place is known for being gay yet female-friendly. ⊠ *79 Wardour St., Soho* ☎ *020/7434–3805* ⊗ *Weekdays 4–11, Sat. 2–11, Sun. 2–10:30* Ⓤ *Leicester Sq.*

Rupert Street. For smart boyz, this gay chic island among the sleaze has a lounge feel with brown-leather sofas and floor-to-ceiling windows. It's crowded and cruisey at night with preclubbers, civilized and cafélike by day: a good spot for brunch. Traditional British food is served until 10 PM. ⊠ *50 Rupert St., Soho* ☎ *020/7494–3059* ⊕ *www.rupertstreet.com* ⊗ *Mon.–Wed. noon–11, Thurs.–Sat. noon–11:30, Sun. noon–10:30* Ⓤ *Leicester Sq., Piccadilly Circus.*

16

CLUBS

Many of London's best gay dance clubs are in mixed clubs like Fabric on themed nights designated for gays. Almost all dance clubs in London are gay-friendly, but if you want to cruise or mingle only with other gays, it's best to call ahead or check Web-site listings.

BJ's White Swan. A longtime fave with the girls, this is a very camp and fun Sunday ballroom, Latin, line-dance, time-warp disco. The amateur strip competition on Wednesday is for men only, and there are cabarets on the weekends. Free entry Tuesday, Wednesday, and Thursday. ⊠ *BJ's White Swan, 556 Commercial Rd., East End* ☎ *020/7780–9870* ⊕ *www.bjswhiteswan.com* 🖃 *Fri. and Sat. £5, Sun. £2* ⊙ *Tues.–Thurs. 9 PM–2 AM, Fri. and Sat. 9 PM–4 AM, Sun. 6:30–midnight* Ⓤ *Aldgate East, DLR: Limehouse.*

Fodor's Choice ★ **Heaven.** With by far the best light show on any London dance floor, Heaven is unpretentious, loud, and huge, with a labyrinth of rooms, bars, and live-music parlors. Friday and Saturday nights there's a gay comedy night (£10 in advance, 7–10 PM). If you go to just one club, Heaven should be it. ⊠ *The Arches, Villiers St., Covent Garden* ☎ *020/7930–2020* ⊕ *www.heaven-london.com* 🖃 *£4–£12* ⊙ *Mon. 11 PM–6 AM, Tues.–Thurs. 11 PM–5 AM, Wed. 10:30 PM–4 AM, Fri. 11 PM–5 AM, Sat. 10:30 PM–5 AM* Ⓤ *Charing Cross, Embankment.*

★ **The Shadow Lounge.** This fabulous little lounge and dance club glitters with faux jewels and twinkling fiber-optic lights over its sunken dance floor, which comes complete with pole for those inclined to do their thing around it. It has a serious A-list celebrity factor, with the glamorous London glitterati camping out in the VIP booth. Members are given entrance priority when the place gets full, especially on weekends, so show up early or prepare to queue. Free entry on Monday. ⊠ *5 Brewer St., Soho* ☎ *020/7287–7988* ⊕ *www.theshadowlounge.co.uk* 🖃 *£5–£10* ⊙ *Mon.–Sat. 10 PM–3 AM* Ⓤ *Leicester Sq.*

Trade. This London institution among the hedonistic muscle boys is now more than a decade old, and begins when many clubs are closing. The Trade brand has events all over the country—check online for dates. Most of the London events take place at The Ministry of Sound. ■TIP→ Its schedule is irregular, so check the Web site for dates. ☎ *020/7609–8364* ⊕ *www.tradeuk.net* 🖃 *£15 in advance (book at www.ticketweb.co.uk), £18 at door* ⊙ *Days vary, 6 AM–4 PM*

Arts and Entertainment

WORD OF MOUTH

"We bought standing-room tickets to the Proms which go on sale a couple of hours before the concert. You don't really stand but sit on the floor in the top gallery. It's like a big picnic. It was fun!"

—Marija

ARTS AND ENTERTAINMENT PLANNER

What's on Now

To find out what's showing now, the weekly magazine *Time Out* (£2.99, issued every Tuesday) is invaluable. The *Evening Standard* carries listings, many of which are available online at ⊕ *www.thisislondon.co.uk*. London's widely available free newspapers are also worth checking out, as are many Sunday papers, and the Saturday *Independent, Guardian,* and *Times.* You can pick up the free fortnightly *London Theatre Guide* from hotels and tourist-information centers.

There are hundreds of small private galleries all over London with interesting work by famous and not-yet-famous artists. The bimonthly free pamphlet "new exhibitions of contemporary art" (⊕ *www.newexhibitions. com*), available at most galleries, lists and maps nearly 200 art spaces in London. Expect to pay around £10 for entry into touring exhibitions, but most permanent displays and commercial galleries are free.

Top 5 for the Arts

Stand with the "plebs" in Shakespeare's Globe Theatre. There are seats, but to really experience theater Shakespearean-style you should stand in the yard, with the stage at eye level (plus it's a bargain at £5).

Visit the latest grand art installation in the Turbine Hall at the Tate Modern. The enormity of the Tate's central space either intimidates or inspires artists challenged to fill it.

Catch a world-class performance at the Proms. There's a surprisingly down-to-earth atmosphere among the elated company at these great concerts.

Enjoy a night at the National Film Theatre. Mingle with the real aficionados at screenings of foreign, classic, or experimental films.

Watch a Hollywood star in a West End production. Film stars often come to London to boost their artistic credibility in small-scale theaters.

Top 5 Theater Deals

Behind the pillars. Many theaters and concert halls sell discounted seats with restricted views.

Matinees. Afternoon performances are almost always a better value than evening ones.

Previews. Tickets to shows are usually less expensive in the first few weeks of their run, before the critics have had their say.

Mondays. Most cinemas, and some theaters, including the Royal Court, have a reduced-price ticketing policy on Monday.

Standing. The Globe Theatre and the Proms are the two most prominent occasions where remaining upright saves you money.

Updated by
Kiki Deere

Shakespearean theater and contemporary musicals, enormous art installations and tiny Renaissance portraits, magnificent operas and cutting-edge physical theater—if you're into going out, London will suit your fancy.

The arts in London have acquired some shiny new buildings and renovated homes, especially south of the river. Herzog and de Meuron's magnificent Tate Modern, in what was once the Bankside Power Station, is now cemented as one of the city's big attractions, and there's already an enormous extension planned.

The Tate has enlivened London's contemporary art scene and, along with the reopened Royal Festival Hall, provides the main focus for a rejuvenated South Bank.

Whether you prefer your art classical or modern, or as a contemporary twist on a time-honored classic, you'll find that London's vibrant cultural scene holds its own on the world stage. There are international theater festivals, innovative music festivals, and cutting-edge seasons of postmodern dance. Divas sing original-language librettos at the Royal Opera House, Shakespeare's plays are brought to life at the reconstructed Globe Theatre, and challenging new writing is produced at the Royal Court. Whether you feel like the lighthearted extravagance of a West End musical or the next shark-in-formaldehyde at the White Cube, the choice is yours.

DANCE

Dance fans in London can enjoy the classicism of the world-renowned Royal Ballet, as well as innovative works by several contemporary dance companies—including Rambert Dance Company, Matthew Bourne's New Adventures, and the Wheeldon Company—and scores of independent choreographers. The English National Ballet and visiting international companies perform at the Coliseum and at Sadler's Wells, which also hosts various other ballet companies and dance troupes. Encompassing the newly refurbished Royal Festival Hall, the Southbank Centre has a seriously good contemporary dance program that hosts top international companies and important U.K. choreographers, as well as

Random Dance Company performs at Sadler's Wells.

multicultural offerings ranging from Japanese Butoh and Indian Kathak to hip-hop. The Place and the Lilian Bayliss Theatre at Sadler's Wells are where you'll find the most daring, cutting-edge performances.

The biggest annual event is **Dance Umbrella** (☎ *0208/741–4040* ⊕ *www.danceumbrella.co.uk*), a five-week season in October and November that hosts international and British-based artists at various venues across the city.

The following theaters are the key dance venues. Also check ⊕ *www.londondance.com* for current performances and fringe venues.

The London Coliseum. Opera is mainly performed here, along with ballet in the summer and Christmas season. The English National Ballet (⊕ *www.ballet.org.uk*) and other dance companies are sometimes on stage in this restored Edwardian baroque theater (1904) with a magnificent auditorium and a rooftop glass dome with a bar and great views. ⊠ *St. Martin's La., Covent Garden* ☎ *020/7632–8300* ⊕ *www.eno.org* Ⓤ *Leicester Sq.*

Peacock Theatre. Sadler's Wells's West End annex, this modernist theater near the London School of Economics focuses on younger companies and shows in popular dance genres like flamenco, tango, and hip-hop. ⊠ *Portugal St., Holborn* ☎ *0844/412–4322* ⊕ *www.sadlerswells.com/peacock* Ⓤ *Holborn.*

The Place. The Robin Howard Dance Theatre is London's only theater dedicated to contemporary dance, and with tickets between £5 and £15 it's good value, too. Resolution! is the United Kingdom's biggest platform event for new choreographers. ⊠ *17 Duke's Rd., Bloomsbury* ☎ *020/7121–1100* ⊕ *www.theplace.org.uk* Ⓤ *Euston.*

Fodor's Choice
★
Royal Opera House. The renowned Royal Ballet performs classical and contemporary repertoire in this spectacular state-of-the-art Victorian theater. ✉ *Bow St., Covent Garden* ☎ *020/7304–4000* ⊕ *www.roh.org. uk* Ⓤ *Covent Garden.*

Fodor's Choice
★
Sadler's Wells. This gleaming building opened in 1998, the seventh on the site in its 300-year history, and is devoted to presenting leading classical and contemporary dance companies. The Random Dance Company is in residence, and the Wheeldon Company performs here half the time, when they're not in the United States. The little Lilian Bayliss Theatre here has more left-field pieces. ✉ *Rosebery Ave., Islington* ☎ *0844/412–4300* ⊕ *www.sadlers-wells.com* Ⓤ *Angel.*

Southbank Centre. A diverse and exciting season of international and British-based contemporary dance companies is presented in the Queen Elizabeth Hall, Purcell Room, and Royal Festival Hall. ✉ *Belvedere Rd., South Bank* ☎ *0844/875–0073* ⊕ *www.southbankcentre.co.uk* Ⓤ *Waterloo, Embankment.*

CLASSICAL MUSIC

Whether it's a concert by cellist Yo-Yo Ma or a Mozart requiem by candlelight, it's possible to hear first-rate musicians in world-class venues almost every day of the year. The London Symphony Orchestra is in residence at the Barbican Centre, although other top orchestras—including the Philharmonia and the Royal Philharmonic—also perform here. The Barbican also hosts chamber-music concerts, with celebrated orchestras such as the City of London Sinfonia. Wigmore Hall, a lovely venue for chamber music, is renowned for its song recitals by up-and-coming young singers. The Southbank Centre has an impressive international music season, held in the Queen Elizabeth Hall and the small Purcell Room as well as in the Royal Festival Hall, now completely refurbished. Full houses are rare, so even at the biggest concert halls you should be able to get a ticket for £12. If you can't book in advance, arrive at the hall an hour before the performance for a chance at returns.

■TIP→ Lunchtime concerts take place all over the city in smaller concert halls, the big arts-center foyers, and churches; they usually cost less than £5 or are free, and feature string quartets, singers, jazz ensembles, or gospel choirs. St. John's, Smith Square, and St. Martin-in-the-Fields are popular locations. Performances usually begin about 1 PM and last one hour.

Classical-music festivals range from the stimulating avant-garde **Meltdown** (⊕ *www.rfh.org.uk/meltdown*) curated each year by a prominent musician—recently Patti Smith or David Bowie—at the Southbank Centre in June to church hall recitals including the **Spitalfields Festival** (⊕ *www.spitalfieldsfestival.org.uk*), a program of recitals held in beautiful, historic East End churches in June and December, and the monthlong **City of London Festival** (⊕ *www.colf.org*) in the Square Mile during the summer. A great British tradition since 1895, the **Henry Wood Promenade Concerts** (more commonly known as the "Proms" ⊕ *www. bbc.co.uk/proms*) run eight weeks, from July to September, at the Royal Albert Hall. Despite an extraordinary quantity of high-quality concerts, it's renowned for its (atypical) last night: a madly jingoistic display of

17

singing "Land of Hope and Glory," Union Jack–waving, and general madness. For regular Proms, tickets run £5–£90, with hundreds of standing tickets for £5 available at the hall on the night of the concert. ■ TIP➔ The last night is broadcast in Hyde Park on a jumbo screen, but even here a seat on the grass requires a paid ticket that can set you back around £25.

Barbican Centre. Home to the London Symphony Orchestra (⊕ *www. lso.co.uk*) and frequent host of the English Chamber Orchestra and the BBC Symphony Orchestra, the Barbican has an excellent season of big-name virtuosos. ⊠ *Silk St., East End* ☎ *020/7638–8891 box office* ⊕ *www.barbican.org.uk* Ⓤ *Barbican, Moorgate.*

Cadogan Hall. Formerly a church, Cadogan Hall has been turned into a spacious concert venue where the English Chamber Orchestra performs regularly. ⊠ *5 Sloane Terr., Kensington* ☎ *020/7730–4500* ⊕ *www. cadoganhall.com* Ⓤ *Sloane Sq.*

★   **Royal Albert Hall.** Built in 1871, this splendid iron-and-glass–dome auditorium hosts music programs in a wide range of genres, including top-flight pop artists, as well as being the home of Europe's most democratic music festival, the Proms. The hall is also open daily for daytime guided tours (£8). ⊠ *Kensington Gore, Kensington* ☎ *020/7589–8212* ⊕ *www. royalalberthall.com* Ⓤ *South Kensington.*

St. James's Church. The organ was brought here in 1691 after fire destroyed its former home, the Palace of Whitehall. St. James's holds regular classical-music concerts and free lunchtime recitals Monday, Wednesday, and Friday at 1:10 PM (free but donations suggested). ⊠ *197 Piccadilly, St. James's* ☎ *020/7381–0441 concert program and tickets* ⊕ *www.st-james-piccadilly.org* Ⓤ *Piccadilly Circus, Green Park.*

St. John's, Smith Square. This baroque church behind Westminster Abbey offers chamber music and organ recitals as well as orchestral concerts September through July. There are occasional lunchtime recitals for £8. ⊠ *Smith Sq., Westminster* ☎ *020/7222–1061* ⊕ *www.sjss.org.uk* Ⓤ *Westminster.*

★   **St. Martin-in-the-Fields.** Popular lunchtime concerts (free but £3.50 donation suggested) are held in this lovely 1726 church, as are regular evening concerts. ■ TIP➔ Stop for a snack at the Café in the Crypt. ⊠ *Trafalgar Sq., Covent Garden* ☎ *020/7766–1100* ⊕ *www.stmartin-in-the-fields.org* Ⓤ *Charing Cross.*

Southbank Centre. After a £90 million refurbishment, the Royal Festival Hall reopened in 2007 with large-scale choral and orchestral works in newly improved acoustic surroundings. Both the Philharmonia and the London Philharmonic orchestras are based here. Another £20 million has been spent on the rest of the Southbank Centre, where other venues host smaller-scale music performances; the Queen Elizabeth Hall has chamber orchestras and top-tier soloists, and in the intimate Purcell Room you can listen to chamber music and solo recitals. ⊠ *Belvedere Rd., South Bank* ☎ *0844/847–9910* ⊕ *www.southbankcentre.org.uk* Ⓤ *Waterloo.*

THE ARTS FOR FREE

MUSEUMS AND GALLERIES

Few if any other cities in the world equal the number of free art venues offered in London. Most of the city's museums and galleries do not charge entrance fees. The monthly *Galleries* magazine, available from galleries themselves or online at ⊕ *www.artefact.co.uk*, has listings for all private galleries in the capital.

CONTEMPORARY MUSIC

Brixton's Dogstar pub has a great selection of DJs playing for free on weekday evenings. Ain't Nothing But.the Blues Bar in Soho has live music most nights, often without a cover charge, and pubs such as the Monarch and the Hawley Arms near Camden Market offer the chance to see tomorrow's indie stars today. The largest of the music superstores, such as Virgin Piccadilly and HMV Oxford Street, have occasional live performances of pop and rock bands, often to accompany album or single launches.

CLASSICAL MUSIC AND JAZZ

The Barbican, the Royal National Theatre, and the Royal Opera House often have free music in their foyers or in dedicated spaces, usually of high standard. On the South Bank, free festivals and special performances often take place alongside the river.

Many of London's world-class music colleges give free concerts several times a week. The Royal Academy of Music and the Royal College of Music often have free recitals. St. Martin-in-the-Fields has free lunchtime concerts, as does Christchurch Spitalfields. Other churches, including Westminster Abbey, St. James's Piccadilly, and St. Paul's in Covent Garden, also have frequent free music. For the Proms, which run from July to September at the Royal Albert Hall, good seats are expensive, but hundreds of standing tickets are available at £5: not quite free, but a good value.

DRAMA AND PERFORMANCE ARTS

Look out for occasional festivals where innovative performances take place on the South Bank. Check the newspapers and *Time Out* for upcoming performances.

PARK LIFE

London's parks come to life in summer with a wide-ranging program of music, dance, and visual arts (⊕ *www.royalparks.gov.uk* for details or ☎ *020/7298–2000*). There are several summer festivals in London parks, some with lots of big-name pop stars, like the O2 Wireless festival in Hyde Park and the somewhat more indie Lovebox Weekender in Victoria Park. Notable art fairs are October's Frieze in Regent's Park (⊕ *www.friezeartfair.com*) and the Affordable Art Fair in Battersea Park (⊕ *www.affordableartfair.com*).

RADIO AND TELEVISION

With so much broadcast material made in London, much of it recorded in front of live audiences, there are often opportunities to watch a free quiz show, current-affairs debate, comedy, or even drama. Check the BBC Web site for forthcoming recordings (⊕ *www.bbc.co.uk/tickets*). **Hat Trick Productions** (☎ *020/184–7777* ⊕ *www.hattrick.co.uk*) makes a number of good comedy programs, including the satirical current-affairs program *Have I Got News for You.*

17

Wigmore Hall. Hear chamber music and song recitals in this charming hall with near-perfect acoustics. Don't miss the midmorning Sunday concerts (11:30 AM). ⊠ *36 Wigmore St., Marylebone* ☏ *020/7935–2141* ⊕ *www.wigmore-hall.org.uk* Ⓤ *Bond St.*

Kings Place. This airy new concert venue, opened in October 2008—the first in London for 25 years—by the Eurostar terminal in King's Cross, is the permanent home of the London Sinfonietta and the Orchestra of the Age of Enlightenment. It offers weeklong programs by musicians in a range of genres, and the London Chamber Music Society performs Sunday concerts. ⊠ *90 York Way, King's Cross* ☏ *0207/520–1490* ⊕ *www.kingsplace.co.uk* Ⓤ *King's Cross.*

FILM

There are many wonderful movie theaters in London and several that are committed to nonmainstream and repertory cinema, in particular the National Film Theatre. Now almost 50 years old, the **Times BFI London Film Festival** (⊕ *www.lff.org.uk*) brings hundreds of films made by masters of world cinema to London for 16 days each October into November, accompanied by often-sold-out events. The smaller, avant-garde **Raindance Film Festival** (⊕ *www.raindance.co.uk*) highlights independent filmmaking, September into October.

West End movie theaters continue to do good business. Most of the major houses, such as the Odeon Leicester Square and the Empire, are in the Leicester Square–Piccadilly Circus area, where tickets average £12. Monday and matinees are often cheaper, at around £6–£10, and there are also fewer crowds.

Check out *Time Out,* one of the London papers, or ⊕ *www.viewlondon.co.uk* for listings.

Ⓒ **Barbican.** In addition to Hollywood films, obscure classics and film festivals with Screen Talks are programmed in the three cinemas here. Saturday Family Film Club has adventure and animation to please all ages. ⊠ *Silk St., East End* ☏ *020/7382–7000 information, 020/7638–8891 box office* ⊕ *www.barbican.org.uk/film* Ⓤ *Barbican.*

BFI London IMAX Cinema. The British Film Institute's glazed drum-shape IMAX theater has the largest screen in the United Kingdom (approximately 75 feet wide and the height of five double-decker buses) playing state-of-the-art 2-D and 3-D films. ⊠ *1 Charlie Chaplin Walk, South Bank* ☏ *0870/787–2525* ⊕ *www.bfi.org.uk/imax* Ⓤ *Waterloo.*

Ⓒ
★ **BFI Southbank.** With easily the best repertory programming in London, the three cinemas and studio at what was previously known as the National Film Theatre are effectively a national film center run by the British Film Institute. They show more than 1,000 titles each year, favoring art-house, foreign, silent, overlooked, classic, noir, and short films over Hollywood blockbusters. After a recent rejuvenation and expansion, the center also has a gallery, bookshop, and "mediatheque," where visitors can watch film and television from the National Archive. This is one of the venues for the Times BFI London Film Festival; throughout the year there are minifestivals, seminars, and guest

The Proms at Royal Albert Hall have standing tickets for £5 on the night of the concerts.

speakers. ■TIP→ Members (£40) get priority bookings (useful for special events) and £1.40 off each screening. ⊠ *Belvedere Rd., South Bank* ☎ *020/7633–0274 information, 020/7928–3232 box office* ⊕ *www.bfi. org.uk* Ⓤ *Waterloo.*

★ **Curzon Soho.** This comfortable cinema runs an artsy program of mixed repertoire and mainstream films. There are also branches in Mayfair, Bloomsbury, Chelsea, and Richmond. Members (£25) get discounts. ⊠ *99 Shaftesbury Ave., Soho* ☎ *0871/703–3988* Ⓤ *Piccadilly Circus, Leicester Sq.* ⊠ *38 Curzon St., Mayfair* ☎ *0871/703–3989* ⊕ *www. curzoncinemas.com* Ⓤ *Green Park.*

Ⓒ **The Electric Cinema.** This refurbished Portobello Road art house screens ★ mainstream and international movies. The emphasis is on comfort, with leather sofas, armchairs, footstools, and mini–coffee tables for your tapas-style food and wine. Saturday matinees for kids are popular. ⊠ *191 Portobello Rd., Notting Hill* ☎ *020/7908–9696* ⊕ *www. electriccinema.co.uk* Ⓤ *Ladbroke Grove, Notting Hill Gate.*

Ⓒ **Everyman Cinema Club.** Kick off your shoes, curl up on the large comfy sofas, and have tapas and champagne brought to you in front of classic, foreign, cutting-edge, and almost-new Hollywood titles. This venue also screens the Metropolitan Opera live from New York, and is a popular place for Hampstead denizens to bring their kids. ⊠ *5 Holly Bush Vale, Hampstead* ☎ *0870/066–4777* ⊕ *www.everymancinema. com* Ⓤ *Hampstead.*

ICA Cinema. Underground and vintage movies are shown in the avant-garde Institute of Contemporary Arts. ⊠ *The Mall, St. James's*

London's Royal Opera House is also home to the Royal Ballet and an in-house orchestra.

☎ *020/7930–0493 information, 020/7930–3647 box office* ⊕ *www.ica. org.uk* Ⓤ *Piccadilly Circus, Charing Cross.*

☺ **Prince Charles Cinema.** This repertory cinema right off Leicester Square offers a chance to catch up with independent features, documentaries, and even blockbusters you may have missed, and tickets are only £5 and under. This is where the "sing-along" screening originated— you can come in character and warble along to *The Sound of Music* and *Hairspray.* ✉ *7 Leicester Pl., Soho* ☎ *0207/494–3654* ⊕ *www. princecharlescinema.com* Ⓤ *Leicester Sq., Piccadilly Circus.*

Riverside Studios Cinema. The selection at this converted movie studio showing repertory cinema changes almost daily. Admission fees are reasonable; £7.50 gets you entrance to a double bill. ✉ *Crisp Rd., Hammersmith* ☎ *020/8237–1111* ⊕ *www.riversidestudios.co.uk* Ⓤ *Hammersmith.*

Tricycle Theatre. Expect the best of new British, European, and World Cinema, as well as films from the United States. There are occasional Irish, black, and Asian film festivals, as well as a year-round program of film-related activities for children. Discounted cinema tickets are available on Mondays. ✉ *269 Kilburn High Rd., Kilburn* ☎ *020/7328–1900 information, 020/7328–1000 box office* ⊕ *www.tricycle.co.uk* Ⓤ *Kilburn.*

OPERA

The two key players in London's opera scene are the Royal Opera House (which ranks with the Metropolitan Opera House in New York) and the more innovative English National Opera (ENO), which presents

English-language productions at the London Coliseum. Only the Theatre Royal, Drury Lane, has a longer theatrical history than the Royal Opera House—the third theater to be built on the site since 1858.

Despite occasional performances by the likes of Björk, the Royal Opera House struggles to shrug off its reputation for elitism and ticket prices that can rise to £210. It is, however, more accessible than it used to be—the cheapest tickets are just £4. Conditions of purchase vary; call for information. Prices for the ENO are generally lower, ranging from around £12 to £80. You can get same-day balcony seats for as little as £5.

Almeida Opera is a festival that often showcases cutting-edge opera. In summer, the increasingly adventurous Opera Holland Park presents the usual chestnuts alongside some obscure works under a newly enlarged canopy in leafy Holland Park.

International touring companies often perform at Sadler's Wells, the Barbican, the Southbank Centre, and Wigmore Hall, so check the weekly listings for details.

★ **Almeida Theatre.** The Almeida Opera Festival in July has an adventurous program of new opera and musical theater. ✉ *Almeida St., Islington* ☎ *020/7359–4404* ⊕ *www.almeida.co.uk* Ⓤ *Angel.*

English National Opera. Despite financial problems, ENO continues to produce innovative opera for lower prices than the Royal Opera House. The company is based at the London Coliseum, one of the city's largest and most venerable theaters. ✉ *St. Martin's La., Covent Garden* ☎ *0871/911–0200* ⊕ *www.eno.org* Ⓤ *Leicester Sq.*

★ **Glyndebourne.** Fifty-four miles south of London, Glyndebourne is one of the most famous opera houses in the world. Six operas are presented from mid-May to late August. The best route by car is the M23 to Brighton, then the A27 toward Lewes. There are regular trains from London (Victoria) to Lewes with coach connections to and from Glyndebourne. Call the information office for recommended trains for each performance. ✉ *Lewes* ☎ *01273/815–000* ⊕ *www.glyndebourne.com.*

Opera Holland Park. In summer, well-loved operas and imaginative productions of relatively unknown works are presented under a spectacular new canopy against the remains of Holland House, one of the first great houses built in Kensington. Ticket prices range from £10 to £54, with 1,200 tickets offered free to young people ages 9–18 every season. Tickets go on sale in April. ✉ *Holland Park, Kensington High St., Kensington* ☎ *0845/230–9769* ⊕ *www.operahollandpark.com* Ⓤ *Kensington High St., Holland Park.*

Fodor's Choice
★ **Royal Opera House.** Original-language productions are presented in this extravagant theater, also home to the Royal Ballet. Tickets range in price from £4 to £210. ■ TIP➔ It may be worth showing up on the morning of a performance to purchase a same-day seat, of which 67 are offered. The box office opens at 10 AM, but queues for popular productions can start as early as 7 AM and unsold tickets are offered at half price four hours before a performance. There are free lunchtime recitals most Mondays in the Linbury Studio Theatre or the Crush Room (arrive early to get a ticket—between 11 AM and noon), and three summer

17

concerts are broadcast live to a large screen in Covent Garden Piazza. ✉ *Bow St., Covent Garden* ☎ *020/7304–4000* ⊕ *www.royalopera.org* Ⓤ *Covent Garden.*

THEATER

In London the play really *is* the thing, ranging from a long-running popular musical like *Mamma Mia!,* a groundbreaking reworking of Pinter, imaginative physical theater from an experimental company like *Complicite,* a lavish Disney spectacle, or a small fringe production above a pub. West End glitz and glamour continue to pull in the audiences, and so do the more innovative productions. Only in London will a Tuesday matinee of the Royal Shakespeare Company's *Henry IV* sell out a 1,200-seat theater.

In London the words radical and quality, or classical and experimental are not mutually exclusive. The Royal Shakespeare Company (⊕ *www. rsc.org.uk*) and the National Theatre (⊕ *www.nationaltheatre.org.uk*) often stage contemporary versions of the classics. The Almeida, Battersea Arts Centre (BAC), Donmar Warehouse, Royal Court Theatre, Soho Theatre, and Old Vic attract famous actors and have excellent reputations for new writing and innovative theatrical approaches. These are the venues where you'll see an original production before it becomes a hit in the West End or on Broadway (and for a fraction of the cost.)

The London theater scene remains vibrant throughout the summer months. Open-air productions of Shakespeare are particularly well served, whether in the faithful reconstruction of the Elizabethan Globe Theatre or under the stars in Regent's Park's Open Air Theatre. Theater festivals such as **Lift** (⊕ *www.liftfest.org.uk*), the London International Festival of Theatre, and **B.I.T.E.** *(Barbican International Theater Events* ⊕ *www.barbican.org.uk)* provide the chance to see international and cutting-edge companies throughout the year.

Theatergoing isn't cheap. Tickets less than £10 are a rarity, although designated productions at the National Theatre have seats at this price. At the commercial theaters you should expect to pay from £15 for a seat in the upper balcony to at least £25 for a good one in the stalls (orchestra) or dress circle (mezzanine). However, last-minute returns available on the night may provide some good deals. Tickets may be booked through ticket agents, at individual theater box offices, or over the phone by credit card. Be sure to inquire about any extra fees—prices can vary enormously, but agents are legally obliged to reveal the face value of the ticket if you ask. All the larger hotels offer theater bookings, but they tack on a hefty service charge. ■TIP➔ Be very wary of ticket touts (scalpers) and unscrupulous ticket agents outside theaters and working the line at TKTS (a half-price ticket booth)—they try to sell tickets at five times the price of the ticket at legitimate box offices (and you'll pay a stiff fine if caught buying a scalped ticket).

Ticketmaster (☎ *0844/277–4321, +44 161/385–3211 from outside the U.K.* ⊕ *www.ticketmaster.co.uk*) sells tickets to a number of different theaters, although they charge a booking fee. You can book tickets in the United States through **Keith Prowse** (✉ *234 W. 44th St., Suite 1000,*

New York, NY ☎ *800/669–8687* ⊕ *www.keithprowse.com).* For discount tickets, **Society of London Theatre** (☎ *020/7557–6700* ⊕ *www. tkts.co.uk*) operates TKTS, a half-price ticket booth on the south-west corner of Leicester Square, and sells the best available seats to performances at about 25 theaters. It's open Monday–Saturday 10–7, Sunday noon–3; there's a £3 service charge (included in the price). Major credit cards are accepted.

★ **Almeida Theatre.** This Off–West End venue premieres excellent new plays and exciting twists on the classics. Hollywood stars often perform here. ⊠ *Almeida St., Islington* ☎ *020/7359–4404* ⊕ *www.almeida. co.uk* Ⓤ *Angel, Highbury & Islington.*

★ **BAC.** Battersea Arts Centre has a reputation for producing innovative new work. Check out Scratch, a night of low-tech cabaret theater by emerging artists where the audience provides feedback on works-in-progress. Tuesday shows usually have pay-what-you-can entry. ⊠ *176 Lavender Hill, Battersea* ☎ *020/7223–2223* ⊕ *www.bac.org.uk* Ⓤ *British Rail: Clapham Junction.*

Barbican Centre. Built in 1982, the Barbican Centre puts on a number of performances by British and international theater companies as part of its year-round **B.I.T.E.** (Barbican International Theatre Events), which also features groundbreaking performance, dance, drama, and musical theater. ⊠ *Silk St., The City* ☎ *020/7638–8891* ⊕ *www.barbican.org. uk* Ⓤ *Barbican.*

Fodor's Choice ★ **Donmar Warehouse.** Hollywood stars often perform here in diverse and daring new works, bold interpretations of the classics, and small-scale musicals. It works both ways, too—former director Sam Mendes went straight from here to directing *American Beauty.* ⊠ *41 Earlham St., Covent Garden* ☎ *0844/871–7624* ⊕ *www.donmarwarehouse.com* Ⓤ *Covent Garden.*

★ **Hackney Empire.** The history of this treasure of a theater is drama in its own right. Charlie Chaplin is said to have appeared here during its days as a thriving variety theater and music hall in the early 1900s. Recently refurbished, it now hosts traditional family entertainment and variety shows, opera, musical theater, dance, and drama, often with a multi-cultural slant. ⊠ *291 Mare St., Hackney* ☎ *020/8985–2424* ⊕ *www. hackneyempire.co.uk* Ⓤ *National Rail: Hackney Central.*

★ **National Theatre.** When this theater opened in 1976, Londoners generally felt the same way about the low-slung, multilayered "Brutalist" block the color of heavy storm clouds (designed by Sir Denys Lasdun) as they would feel a decade later about the Barbican Centre. Prince Charles described the building as "a clever way of building a nuclear power station in the middle of London without anyone objecting." But whatever its merits or demerits as a feature on the landscape, the

17

Royal National Theatre's interior spaces are definitely worth a tour. Interspersed with the three theaters, the 1,120-seat Olivier, the 890-seat Lyttelton, and the 300-seat Cottesloe, is a multilayered foyer with exhibitions, bars, and restaurants, and free entertainment. Musicals, classics, and new plays are performed by a top-flight company. Some shows offer £10 ticket deals. ✉ *Southbank Centre, Belvedere Rd., South Bank* ☎ *020/7452–3000 box office, 0207/452–3400 information* ⊕ *www.nationaltheatre.org.uk* 🎫 *Tour £5.90* ⊙ *Foyer Mon.–Sat. 9:30 AM–11 PM; 75-min tour backstage up to 6 times daily weekdays, twice on Sat., often on Sun.* Ⓤ *Waterloo.*

Novello Theatre. Dating back to 1905 and refurbished a century later, the Novello specializes in popular contemporary musicals and serves as the Royal Shakespeare Company's London base. ✉ *Aldwych, Covent Garden* ☎ *0844/482–5170* ⊕ *www.delfontmackintosh.co.uk* Ⓤ *Covent Garden, Temple.*

The Old Vic. American actor Kevin Spacey is the artistic director of this grand 1818 Victorian theater. Legends of the stage have performed here, including John Gielgud, Vivien Leigh, Peter O'Toole, Richard Burton, Judi Dench, and Laurence Olivier, who called it his favorite theater. After decades of financial duress threatening to shut it down, the Old Vic is now safely under the ownership of a dedicated trust, though Spacey's production record has been uneven. ✉ *The Cut, Southwark* ☎ *0844/871–7628* ⊕ *www.oldvictheatre.com* Ⓤ *Waterloo.*

Fodor's Choice ★ Open Air Theatre. On a warm summer evening, classical theater in the pastoral and royal Regent's Park is hard to beat for magical adventure. Enjoy a supper before the performance, a bite during the intermission on the picnic lawn, or drinks in the spacious bar. ✉ *Inner Circle, Regent's Park* ☎ *0844/826–4242* ⊕ *www.openairtheatre.org* Ⓤ *Baker St., Regent's Park.*

★ Royal Court Theatre. Britain's undisputed epicenter of new writing, the RCT is now 50 years old and continues to produce gritty British and international drama. ■TIP→ Don't miss the best deal in town—10-pence standing tickets go on sale one hour before each performance, and there are £10 tickets on Monday. ✉ *Sloane Sq., Chelsea* ☎ *020/7565–5000* ⊕ *www.royalcourttheatre.com* Ⓤ *Sloane Sq.*

Fodor's Choice ★ Shakespeare's Globe Theatre. This faithful reconstruction of the open-air playhouse where Shakespeare worked and wrote many of his greatest plays re-creates the 16th-century theatergoing experience. Standing room in the "pit" right in front of the stage costs £5. The season runs April through October. ⇨ *For more on Shakespeare's Globe Theatre, see Chapter 8.* ✉ *21 New Globe Walk, Bankside, South Bank* ☎ *020/7401–9919* ⊕ *www.shakespeares-globe.org* Ⓤ *Southwark, then walk to Blackfriars Bridge and descend steps; Mansion House, then cross Southwark Bridge; Blackfriars, then walk across Blackfriars Bridge; St. Paul's, then cross Millenium Bridge.*

Soho Theatre. This sleek theater in the heart of Soho is devoted to fostering new writing and is a prolific presenter of work by emerging writers and comedy performance. ✉ *21 Dean St., Soho* ☎ *0207/478–0100* ⊕ *www.sohotheatre.com* Ⓤ *Tottenham Court Rd.*

⟲ **Tricycle Theatre**. The Tricycle is committed to the best in Irish, African-Caribbean, Asian, and political drama, and the promotion of new plays. ✉ *269 Kilburn High Rd., Kilburn* ☎ *020/7328–1000* ⊕ *www.tricycle. co.uk* Ⓤ *Kilburn.*

Young Vic. Ensconced in a new home near Waterloo, big names perform here alongside young talent, often in daring, innovative productions of classic plays. ✉ *66 The Cut, Waterloo, South Bank* ☎ *020/922–2922* ⊕ *www.youngvic.org* Ⓤ *Waterloo.*

CONTEMPORARY ART

In the 21st century, the focus of the city's art scene has shifted from the past to the future. Helped by the prominence of the Tate Modern, London's contemporary art scene has never been so high profile. In publicly funded exhibition spaces like the Barbican Gallery, the Hayward Gallery, the Institute of Contemporary Arts, and the Serpentine Gallery, London now has a modern-art environment on a par with Bilbao and New York. Young British Artists (YBAs, though no longer as young as they once were) Damien Hirst, Tracey Emin, and others are firmly planted in the public imagination. The celebrity status of British artists is in part thanks to the annual Turner Prize, which always stirs up controversy in the media during a monthlong display of the work, usually at Tate Britain.

Depending on whom you talk to, the Saatchi Gallery is considered to be either the savior of contemporary art or the wardrobe of the emperor's new clothes. It recently reopened in the former Duke of York's barracks off Chelsea's Kings Road.

The South Bank's Tate Modern may house the giants of modern art, but East London is where the innovative action is. There are dozens of galleries in the fashionable spaces around Old Street, and the truly hip have already moved even farther east, to areas such as Bethnal Green. The Whitechapel Art Gallery and Jay Jopling's influential White Cube in Hoxton Square remain at the epicenter of the new art establishment and continue to show exciting work by emerging British artists.

On the first Thursday of every month, more than 100 museums and galleries of East London stay open 'til late (more information at ⊕ *www. firstthursdays.co.uk*). For information about upcoming events and new young British artists visit ⊕ *www.murmurart.com*).

Barbican Centre. Innovative exhibitions of 20th-century and current art and design are shown in the Barbican Gallery and the **Curve** (▨ *Usually free*). More than just an art gallery, the Barbican Centre also hosts music events, films, and talks of an artistic slant, as well as theater. ✉ *Silk St., The City* ☎ *020/7638–8891* ⊕ *www.barbican.org.uk* ▨ *Prices vary with exhibition (some free), tickets cheaper if booked online in advance* ⊙ *Mon., Fri., Sat., and Sun. 11* AM*–8* PM*, Tues. and Wed. 11–6, Thurs. 11* AM*–10* PM Ⓤ *Barbican.*

★ **Hayward Gallery.** This modern art gallery is a classic example of 1960s Brutalist architecture. It's part of the Southbank Centre and is one of London's major venues for contemporary art exhibitions. ✉ *Belvedere*

Dominique Gonzalez-Foerster's sculpture TH.2058, in the Turbine Hall of the Tate Modern.

Rd., Southbank Centre, South Bank ☎ *0844/875–0073* ⊕ *www.hayward.org.uk* 🖃 *Prices vary with exhibition (some free)* ⊗ *Sat.–Thurs. 10–6, Fri. 10–10* Ⓤ *Waterloo.*

Institute of Contemporary Arts. Housed in an elegant John Nash–designed Regency terrace, the ICA's two galleries have changing exhibitions of contemporary visual art. The ICA also programs performance, film, new media, literary talks, and photography. There's an arts bookstore, cafeteria, and bar. ⊠ *Nash House, The Mall, St. James's* ☎ *020/7930–3647* ⊕ *www.ica.org.uk* 🖃 *Free* ⊗ *Mon.–Wed. noon–11 PM, Thurs.–Sat. noon–1 AM, Sun. noon–9 PM* Ⓤ *Charing Cross.*

Lisson. Owner Nicholas Logsdail represents about 40 blue-chip artists, including minimalist Sol Lewitt and Dan Graham, at arguably the most respected gallery in London. The gallery is most associated with New Object sculptors like Anish Kapoor and Richard Deacon, many of whom have won the Turner Prize. A branch down the road at 29 Bell Street features work by younger, up-and-coming artists. ⊠ *52–54 Bell St., Marylebone* ☎ *020/7724–2739* ⊕ *www.lissongallery.com* 🖃 *Free* ⊗ *Weekdays 10–6, Sat. 11–5* Ⓤ *Edgware Rd., Marylebone.*

★ **Photographer's Gallery.** Britain's first photography gallery brought world-famous photographers like André Kertesz, Jacques-Henri Lartigue, and Irving Penn to the United Kingdom, and continues to program cutting-edge and provocative photography. The prestigious annual Deutsche Börse Photography Prize is exhibited and awarded here annually. There is a print sales room, a bookstore, and a café. ⊠ *16-18 Ramillies St., off Oxford St.* ☎ *020/7831–1772* ⊕ *www.photonet.org.uk* 🖃 *Free* ⊗ *Tues.,*

The Tate Modern's vast spaces are a reminder of its former life as a power station.

Wed., and Sat. 11 AM–6 PM, Thurs. and Fri. 11 AM–8 PM, Sun. noon–6 PM ⓤ *Oxford Circus.*

Riflemaker. Located in London's oldest public building and a former Georgian riflemaker's workshop, this gallery exhibits ambitious works by emerging artists, having housed debuts by Francesca Lowe, Chosil Kil, Jaime Gili, and Jamie Shovin. ✉ *79 Beak St., Soho* ☎ *020/7439–0000* ⊕ *www.riflemaker.org* ⊙ *Weekdays 10 AM–6 PM, Sat. noon–6 PM* ⓤ *Piccadilly Circus, Oxford Circus.*

Royal Academy. Housed in an aristocratic mansion and home to Britain's first art school (founded in 1768), the academy is best known for its blockbuster special exhibitions—like the record-breaking Monet, and the controversial Sensation drawn from the Saatchi collection. The annual Summer Exhibition has been a popular London tradition since 1769. ✉ *Burlington House, Mayfair* ☎ *020/7300–8000* ⊕ *www.royalacademy.org.uk* ✉ *From £8, prices vary with exhibition* ⊙ *Daily 10–6, except Fri. 10–10* ⓤ *Piccadilly Circus.*

Saatchi Gallery. Charles Saatchi's ultramodern gallery devoted to leading contemporary artists has reopened in all 70,000 square feet of the Duke of York's HQ building in Chelsea in 2008 complete with a new bookshop and café-bar. ✉ *Duke of York's HQ, Sloane Sq., Chelsea* ☎ *020/7823–2332* ⊕ *www.saatchi-gallery.co.uk* ✉ *Free* ⊙ *Daily 10 AM–6 PM* ⓤ *Sloane Sq.*

Serpentine Gallery. Built in 1934 as a tea pavilion in Kensington Gardens, the Serpentine has an international reputation for exhibitions of modern and contemporary art. Man Ray, Henry Moore, Andy Warhol, Bridget Riley, Damien Hirst, and Rachel Whiteread are a few of the artists who have had exhibits here. The annual Summer Pavilion, designed by a different leading architect every year, is always worth catching. ⊠ *Kensington Gardens, South Kensington* ☎ *020/7402–6075* ⊕ *www.serpentinegallery.org* 🎫 *Free* ☉ *Daily 10–6* Ⓤ *South Kensington, Lancaster Gate.*

Fodor'sChoice **Tate Modern.** This converted power station is one of the largest modern-
★ art galleries in the world, so give yourself ample time to take it all in. The permanent collection includes work by all the major 20th-century artists, though only a fraction is shown at any one time. There are also blockbuster touring shows and solo exhibitions of international artists. ■ TIP→ The bar on the top floor has gorgeous views overlooking the Thames and St. Paul's Cathedral. ⊠ *Bankside, South Bank* ☎ *020/7887–8888* ⊕ *www.tate.org.uk* 🎫 *Free–£12.50* ☉ *Sun.–Thurs. 10–6, Fri. and Sat. 10–10* Ⓤ *Southwark, St. Paul's, London Bridge.*

Victoria Miro Gallery. This important commercial gallery has exhibited some of the biggest names on the British contemporary art scene—Chris Ofili, the Chapman brothers, and Peter Doig, to name a few. It also brings in exciting new talent from abroad. ⊠ *16 Wharf Rd., Islington* ☎ *020/7336–8109* ⊕ *www.victoria-miro.com* 🎫 *Free* ☉ *Tues.–Sat. 10–6* Ⓤ *Old St., Angel.*

★ **White Cube.** Jay Joplin's influential gallery is housed in a 1920s light-industrial building on Hoxton Square. Many of its artists are Turner Prize stars—Hirst, Emin, Hume, et al.—and many live in the East End, which supposedly has the highest concentration of artists in Europe. Farther west, White Cube has a second gallery in a striking building in Mason's Yard, St. James's. ⊠ *48 Hoxton Sq., Hoxton* ☎ *020/7930–5373* ⊕ *www.whitecube.com* 🎫 *Free* ☉ *Tues.–Sat. 10–6* Ⓤ *Old St.*

★ **Whitechapel Art Gallery.** Established in 1897, this independent East End gallery is one of London's most innovative and consistently interesting. Jeff Wall, Bill Viola, Gary Hume, and Janet Cardiff have exhibited here. Closed Mondays. ⊠ *80–82 Whitechapel High St., Shoreditch* ☎ *020/7522–7888* ⊕ *www.whitechapel.org* 🎫 *Free* ☉ *Tues., Wed., Fri.–Sun. 11* AM*–6* PM, *Thurs. 11* AM*–9* PM Ⓤ *Aldgate East.*

Shopping

WORD OF MOUTH

"[Each market is] really quite different: Camden is a little edgier and perhaps cooler—there's more furniture and goods; Spitalfields is largely clothes, pictures, food, and curios."

—geoffthelobster

SHOPPING PLANNER

Top Shops

Portobello Road Market. Whether you are a serious antiques buyer or just want to browse the stalls and people-watch, Portobello Road is London's most dynamic market.

Liberty. In a Tudor-style building, Liberty has an outstanding collection of clothing crafted from its famous prints and furniture, as well as cutting-edge fashion.

Dover Street Market. Run by Comme des Garcons designer Rei Kawakubo, this concept store is a combination art gallery and department store, and also hosts design retrospectives.

Hamleys. With floor after floor of treasures for every child on your list, this is *the* London toy shop.

Mint. Fans of contemporary furniture and housewares should head to Mint, which showcases the work of both leading and up-and-coming designers.

Rellik. Celebs like Sienna Miller love Rellik for its superb collection of vintage clothing, ranging from classic Dior to Ossie Clark and Vivienne Westwood.

Opening Hours

Most shops are open from about 9:30 or 10 AM to 6 or 6:30 PM. Some may open at 11 and stay open until 7. Because shop hours, particularly for the smaller shops, are varied, it's a good idea to phone ahead. Stores that have late shopping—and not all do—are usually open until 7 or 8 PM on Wednesday or Thursday only. Most department stores stay open late during the week. On Sunday, many shops open between 11 AM and noon and close at 5 or 6 PM. Most stores are open on Sunday in December for the Christmas season.

A Word About Service

American standards of customer service are rare in London—salespeople can seem abrupt or rude, but don't take it personally.

Watch Your Language

Locals like to say that Brits and Americans are separated by a common language. Here are a few confusing terms to watch for when out and about in the shops:

Pants means underwear. Every other type of long-legged bottoms (except jeans) are called **trousers.**

Knickers are ladies' undies. If you want pantyhose, ask for **tights.**

Jumper means sweater—unless it's a cardigan, in which case it's often shortened to **cardie.** If you ask for a **sweater,** you may be offered a sweatshirt.

Men use **braces** to hold up their trousers; in England **suspenders** is another word for garters.

If you want some Adidas or Nike-type athletic shoes, ask for **trainers,** not sneakers.

Don't ask for a **pocketbook** or a **purse** if you mean a handbag—the former will be incomprehensible, and the latter will produce a coin purse.

Nightgowns are usually abbreviated to **nighties** and bathrobes are always **dressing gowns.**

CAMDEN TOWN
cheap
second-hand
and club gear

CLERKENWELL
a historical
hotspot for
crafts and design

**HOXTON &
SHOREDITCH**
edgy young
designers

MARYLEBONE
small shops
in village-like
setting

NOTTING HILL
antiques, vintage
clothing, and
boho boutiques

**OXFORD
CIRCUS**
global flagships,
department stores,
and street style
on Carnaby

SOHO
books abound
on Charing
Cross Road

**COVENT
GARDEN**
an urban-wear
mecca around
Seven Dials

MAYFAIR
catwalk names
on Bond St.,
trad tailors on
Savile Row

ST JAMES'S
old-fashioned
specialists, from
hatters to
shirtmakers

KNIGHTSBRIDGE
luxe labels
and, of course,
Harrods

CHELSEA
the King's Rd.
spans fashion
to furniture

REGENT'S
PARK

BLOOMSBURY

BAYSWATER

HYDE PARK

BELGRAVIA

WESTMINSTER

LAMBETH

VICTORIA

Green
Park

St. James's
Park

Thames

River

Albany Rd.
Park Rd.
Lisson Grove
Marylebone Rd.
Baker St.
Edgware Rd.
Wigmore St.
Oxford St.
Bayswater Rd.
Kensington Rd.
Knightsbridge
Brompton Rd.
Sloane St.
King's Rd.
Pimlico Rd.
Albany St.
Euston Rd.
Gt. Portland St.
Portland Pl.
Tottenham Court Rd.
New Oxford St.
Regent St.
New Bond St.
Charing Cross Rd.
Shaftesbury
Pall Mall
Piccadilly
The Mall
Constitution Hill
Birdcage Walk
Buckingham Palace Rd.
Victoria St.
Wilton Rd.
Vauxhall Br. Rd.
Horseferry Rd.
Millbank
Gray's Inn Rd.
Holborn
Kingsway
Aldwych
Strand
Waterloo Br.
Victoria Embankment
Whitehall
Westminster Br.
Lambeth Palace Rd.
Lambeth Br.
Albert Embankment

0   1/2 mile
0   1/2 km

KNIGHTSBRIDGE, CHELSEA, AND SOUTH KENSINGTON

All the big British brands like Burberry and Pringle are here, as well as the big department stores like Harvey Nichols and Harrods. If you're a design buff or love antiques, then make a beeline to Chelsea.

These are some of most exclusive shopping areas in London, so expect to find yummy mummies with money to burn, Russian heiresses, and celebrities—along with plenty of chauffeur-driven Bentleys idling outside stores. Start at the top of Sloane Street, which has all the big designer names, and as you head into South Kensington, you'll find more independent boutiques and plenty of cafés and restaurants that are perfect for a shopping break. Even if your bank account has fewer zeros than you'd like, wander down the King's Road to check out the home design and antiques shops. You never know, you might just score a bargain, and at the very least, you'll come away feeling design-inspired. King's Road also has plenty of High-street chains, like Oasis, Whistles, and Warehouse, which are gentler on the wallet.

BEST TIME TO GO

Weekends are crowded, so try to hit the shops mid-week for a calmer experience. On the other hand, people-watching is part of the true K&C experience, so take your time and soak it all up. The bi-annual sales, in January and July, make shops busy no matter what the day.

BEST FIND FOR YOUR BEST FRIEND

For something affordable in these neighborhoods, pick up a beautifully packaged bottle of Grapefruit or Wild Fig & Cassis perfume at Jo Malone. A box of correspondence cards from Smythson is another classic gift.

REFUELING

Chic ladies sip lattes and nibble on goat-cheese tarts or a salad Nicoise at **Aubaine**, a simple and elegant French café and boulangerie. For something more substantial, tuck into a hearty meal at the gastropub **Admiral Codrington**, known as "The Cod" to the locals. You can't go wrong with an order of crispy fish-and-chips served with chive butter, or salmon and crab cakes, all washed down with beer or a bottle of wine.

WHAT YOU'LL WANT

BEST OF THE BRITISH

Harvey Nichols. The capital's best department store is a must.

Jimmy Choo. Every woman needs a pair of sexy, sky-high Jimmy Choos.

Pringle of Scotland. There's nothing dowdy here. The traditional plaids still crop up, but the latest designs are edgy and cool.

Vivienne Westwood. Her World's End boutique, with the crazy clock outside, is where it all started.

TRENDSETTERS

Myla. Scores of trendy Londoners stock up on the sexy lingerie and swimwear here.

Bruce Oldfield. Come for an Oscar-worthy couture gown or a glam wedding dress.

Marie-Chantal. For exclusive baby and children's clothing fit for a prince—or a princess.

All Saints. Limited stock and fresh-from-the-catwalk designs here mean original looks—you won't be walking around looking like everyone else.

18

ST. JAMES'S AND MAYFAIR

CLOTH SOLD BY THE METRE

If you love old-fashioned tailoring and shops that seem unchanged since Victorian times, then hit one of the many traditional shops in St. James's and Mayfair.

Mayfair is one of the most elegant places to shop in London—not only because of the big-name designers who have their flagships here, but because the cobblestone streets and hushed atmosphere add to the exclusivity. Serious fashionistas can make their way through Nicole Fahri, Armani, Versace, and Ralph Lauren on Bond Street and New Bond Street before heading to tiny South Molton Street, which is home to Browns and plenty of great shoe stores. But for shoppers who aren't as big on the latest catwalk fashions, spend an afternoon on St. James's Jermyn Street, which has a lost-in-time quality and carries on the tradition of producing high-quality handmade shirts, hats, and suits. The area is also home to Savile Row, which is synonymous with handmade suits—this is where Prince Charles and rocker David Bowie have had their clothing made. And if the budget won't stretch for a suit or a pair of shoes, head to the food section of Fortnum & Mason to stock up on beautifully packaged teas or jams.

BEST TIME TO GO

Because this area covers some of the most exclusive shopping streets in the capital, don't expect huge crowds. South Molton Street can get a bit busy, whereas the area around Jermyn Street is extremely quiet. Many of the independent stores are closed on Sunday.

BEST FIND FOR YOUR DAD

Long-established shirt-maker **Hilditch & Key** makes bespoke and ready-to-wear dress shirts. If your budget won't run to bespoke, pick up a formal shirt from **Thomas Pink** or **Charles Tyrwhitt**.

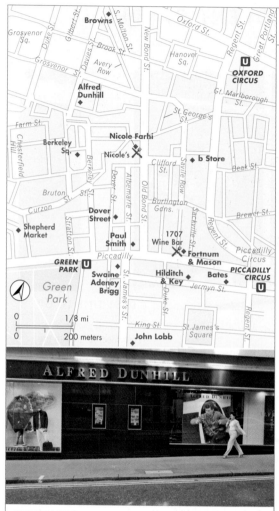

WHAT YOU'LL WANT

DESIGNER CHIC

b store. Models flock here for the ever-changing stock of clothing and accessories by emerging talent.

Browns. This mini–department store stocks big names as well as plenty of up-and-coming designers.

Dover Street Market. Alongside Alber Elbaz and Alaia fashion, expect to see art exhibits and one-off events at this concept store.

Paul Smith. Known for his classics-with-a-twist, his furniture and curio shop has the same quirky design ethos.

OLD SCHOOL

Alfred Dunhill. Shop here for driving accessories and leather goods, or just for a cigar and a shave.

Bates Gentlemen's Hatter. Try a top hat, bowler, flat cap, or a classic Panama hat.

John Lobb. This exclusive store has been making shoes for royalty and celebrities for hundreds of years.

Swaine Adeney Brigg. Get the complete English gentlemen look here, including a walking stick, umbrella, and tweed coat.

18

REFUELING

Nicole's restaurant in the basement of the Nicole Farhi shop is ideal for a quick lunch between purchases. The two-story restaurant was designed by Ms. Farhi, as was the menu, which features modern British cuisine with a California twist. For the quickest service, head to the upper level; reservations are recommended for the more formal dining room. Or pop in for a glass of wine at the **1707 Wine Bar** inside Fortnum & Mason. The elegant lower level is part of the recent 300th-birthday expansion and just one of four restaurants in the Queen's grocery store.

SOHO AND COVENT GARDEN

Although primarily known for theaters today and naughty-entertainment in the past, Soho and Covent Garden are chock-full of independent boutiques and some of the best High-street chain brands stores.

Some people never make it past the covered market area of Covent Garden (which is fine for a browse through the stalls), but to find the really interesting boutiques, head off one of the smaller streets in the area. Monmouth Street is becoming one of the best areas for independent boutiques. Some of the bigger names in fashion, like Ted Baker, Radley, and Camper, have set up shop on the pretty, cobblestone Floral Street, and Earlham Street is a happy mishmash of stalls and shops. Brighten your day with some fresh flowers at the low-key Wild Bunch or before getting ready to flex your credit card.

BEST TIME TO GO

It's almost always crowded, so go with the flow—or get there early in the morning.

BEST FIND FOR YOUR ANGLOPHILE FRIEND

Couldn't make it to Scotland this trip? Leave room in your luggage for a bottle or two of single-malt whisky from **Milroy's of Soho**, which stocks whiskies from every distillery in Scotland. Or stop by the **Tea House** on Neal Street, which sells more than 100 varieties of tea along with pots and mugs to make the perfect brew.

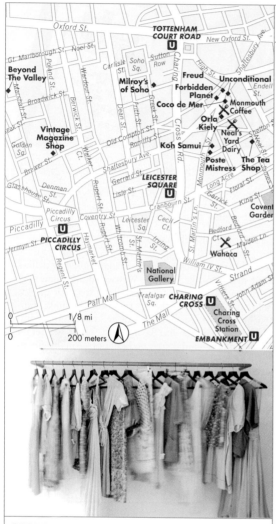

WHAT YOU'LL WANT

HIGH FASHION

Beyond the Valley. Stop here for one-of-a-kind jewelry, fashion, and art from up-and-coming designers.

Coco de Mer. Lingerie, sleepwear, and erotic books fill this beautiful space.

Koh Samui. This small boutique is always stocked with the latest dresses, trousers, and accessories.

Poste Mistress. This shoe shop has the look of a girly boudoir, and carries designs from Pucci to Jil Sander.

QUIRKY COOL

Forbidden Planet. Secret sci-fi geek? Stop by one of the world's biggest retailers of sci-fi and comic book merchandise.

Freud. All the housewares are designed in-house, and they also specialize in Charles Rennie Mackintosh furniture.

Orla Kiely. Her distinctive accessory designs have leaf patterns and plenty of eye-popping colors.

Unconditional. Come here if you like eccentric, urban, cool looks, along with funky jewelry.

Vintage Magazine Shop. Looking for a copy of *Vogue* from the '60s? You'll find it here, along with comics and memorabilia.

18

REFUELING

Wahaca serves up dishes inspired by Mexican street food. The wait for a bench seat is worth it, and you'll have money left over to continue shopping your way through Covent Garden. If you just want a caffeine jolt, head to **Monmouth Coffee**, which roasts all its own beans, or pick up some cheese to nibble on from **Neal's Yard Dairy.**

Updated by
Kiki Deere

London is one of the best shopping cities in the world, as well as one of the most expensive. But whether you are looking for furniture or a fine cashmere scarf, bespoke shoes or a funky frock, London will not disappoint.

Although it's impossible to pin down one particular look that defines the city, homegrown designers like Vivienne Westwood, Matthew Williamson, Paul Smith, and Alice Temperley stand out for their quirky, eccentric designs. London is, after all, the city that brought punk, miniskirts, and Mod fashion to the world. But if you're after a more traditional look, head to Jermyn Street and Savile Row, which still retain their old-world look and feel—and there's no better place in the city to buy custom-made shirts and suits. If your budget won't stretch to Savile Row, no problem. The city's High Street chain stores like Topshop, Oasis, Reiss, and FCUK are great places to pick up designs straight from the catwalk, at a fraction of the price. And don't forget London's markets, known for their size, variety, and sheer street theater.

Apart from bankrupting yourself, the only problem you may encounter is exhaustion. London's shopping districts are spread out all over the city, so do like the locals do. Plan your excursion with military precision, taking in only one or two areas in a day, and stop for a hearty lunch and glass of wine or a pint in a pub.

ANTIQUES

Investment-quality items or lovable junk—London has lots. For the best range of merchandise, and plenty of character, try markets first. Some say that Portobello Road has become a bit of a tourist trap, but if you acknowledge that it's a circus and get into the spirit, it's a lot of fun, if expensive. Kensington Church Street and the shops along the King's Road have some of the best antiques in the city, but the prices are high, unless you're willing to wake up early and try your luck at the Lots Road Auction, near the swish Chelsea Design Center. Less stratospheric, an antiques enclave has sprung up around Alfie's Antique Market in Marylebone; the small shops lining Church Street sell everything from

CLOSE UP

Know Your Shopping Personality

"What's the best place to shop in London?" is an unanswerable question, akin to "How long is a piece of string?" There are thousands of shops in the city, and dozens of neighborhoods worth shopping in. Identify your shopping personality to narrow your choices for a successful outing.

Whirlwind. If you're after a one-stop shopping experience, head to one of London's biggest department stores. Selfridges and Liberty are near the Bond Street and Oxford Circus Tube stations, and Harvey Nichols and Harrods share Knightsbridge Tube.

Fashionista. When only the top designers will do, start at Harvey Nichols, in Knightsbridge, then take in the designer boutiques along Sloane Street before boarding the Tube for Green Park. From there, head up New and Old Bond streets, finishing at Fenwick. If you still have time and energy, aim for South Molton Street or St. Christopher's Place W1 for more fashion boutiques.

Eclectic. If you don't want to be pinned down and like beautiful

workmanship and originality, start at Liberty on Regent Street, then head for either the Holland Park/Notting Hill or Marylebone neighborhoods. Both provide enough idiosyncratic lifestyle shops for hours of browsing.

Funky and Avant-Garde. For cutting-edge fashion and housewares, head east to the city's coolest neighborhoods, chiefly Hoxton and Shoreditch. Walk around Spitalfields and Brick Lane, which have excellent markets. Then work your way north to Hoxton and Shoreditch, which are chock-full of independent stores—start at Columbia Road.

Easygoing. If you want to pop in and out of a variety of shops, as well as avoid the crowds around Oxford Street, head to the King's Road in Chelsea. You'll find department store Peter Jonesa, Marks & Spencer, and plenty of High-street chains, as well as independent boutiques. Another good bet is High Street Kensington for the big chains like Topshop, Oasis, and Warehouse.

large-scale 19th-century English and European furniture to art deco ceramics and vintage shop fittings.

Listed here is a selection of the hundreds of stores to whet your appetite.
■ TIP→ Opening times vary: many places that are open on the weekend will close Monday or Tuesday.

★ **Alfie's Antique Market.** A large and exciting labyrinth on four floors, it has dealers specializing in anything and everything, but particularly in vintage clothing, decorative accessories, and furniture. Highlights include the fabulous collection of cocktail dresses and kitsch bar accessories at The Girl Can't Help It, and Vincenzo Caffarrella's spectacular Italian lighting. There's also a rooftop restaurant if you need a coffee break. In addition to the market, this end of Church Street is lined with excellent antiques shops. ⊠ *13–25 Church St., Marylebone* ☏ *020/7723–6066* ☺ *Closed Sun. and Mon.* Ⓤ *Edgware Rd.*

Antiquarius. Just a short walk from Sloane Square on the King's Road is an indoor antiques market with around 100 stalls selling collect-ibles, including items that won't bust your baggage allowance but may empty your bank account: art deco brooches, vintage costume jewelry, old pocket watches, silver salt cellars, and so on. ⊠ *131–141 King's Rd., Chelsea* ☎ *020/7823–3900* ⊘ *Closed Sun.* Ⓤ *Sloane Sq.*

Grays Antique Market. More than 100 dealers under one roof special-ize in everything from Sheffield plate to Asian antiquities, although the majority of stalls focus on jewelry. Bargains are not impossible, and proper pedigrees are guaranteed. Also try Grays in the Mews around the corner—it has less-expensive merchandise, including the large Bib-lion bookshop and excellent vintage clothing at Vintage Modes. ⊠ *58 Davies St., Mayfair* ☎ *020/7629–7034* ⊘ *Closed Sun.* Ⓤ *Bond St.* ⊠ *1–7 Davies Mews, Mayfair* ☎ *020/7629–7034* Ⓤ *Bond St.*

★ **London Silver Vaults.** Housed in a basement vault, this extraordinary space holds stalls from more than 30 silver dealers. Products range from the spectacular to the over-the-top, but you can also pick up smaller items, from a set of Victorian cake forks to a teaspoon or candlesticks. ■TIP→ **As an especially cool feature, most of the silver merchants actually trade out of room-size, underground vaults, originally rented out to London's upper crust to store their valuables.** ⊠ *53–64 Chancery La., Holborn* ☎ *020/7242–3844* ⊘ *Closed Sat. after 1, and Sun.* Ⓤ *Chancery La.*

APPLIED ARTS AND HANDICRAFTS

London, with its prestigious design colleges, multiple design fairs, and myriad galleries, is a magnet for artisans and craftspeople in glass, textiles, jewelry making, ceramics, metal, leather, and woodwork. Open-studio weekends (usually late May/early June and late Novem-ber/early December) allow you to buy direct from makers. Two of the most convenient are Craft Central, formerly the Clerkenwell Green Association (⊕ *www.craftcentral.org.uk*), and Cockpit Arts (⊕ *www. cockpitarts.com*).

Designers Guild. Tricia Guild's exuberantly colored modern fabrics, wall-papers, paints, furniture, and bed linens have inspired several decades' worth of home owners and apartment dwellers, and her soft-furnish-ings book has taught many a budget-conscious do-it-yourselfer how to reupholster a sofa or make lined draperies. The shop also stocks con-temporary furniture, wallpapers, and home accessories by other design-ers. ⊠ *267–271 and 275–277 King's Rd., Chelsea* ☎ *020/893–7620* ⊘ *Closed Sun.* Ⓤ *Sloane Sq.*

★ **Lesley Craze Gallery.** This serene gallery displays jewelry by some 100 young designers from around the world, with a strong British bias, featuring both precious and semiprecious stones. There's also a textiles room showcasing unusual and colorful handmade scarves, bags, and cushions. Prices are reasonable. ⊠ *33–35A Clerkenwell Green, East End* ☎ *020/7608–0393* ⊙ *Closed Sun.; open Mon. in Nov. and Dec. only* Ⓤ *Farringdon.*

Oxo Tower. Many varied artisans have to pass rigorous selection procedures to set up in the prime riverside workshops where they make, display, and sell their work. The workshops are glass walled, and you're welcome to explore, even if you're just browsing. There are around 30 studios, spread over two floors. The Oxo Tower Restaurant & Brasserie on the top floor is noisy and expensive, but with its fantastic view across the river, it's worth popping up for a drink. There's also a public terrace where you can take in the view. ⊠ *Barge House St., South Bank* ☎ *020/7401–2255* ⊙ *Closed Mon.* Ⓤ *Southwark, Blackfriars, Waterloo.*

BEAUTY

Skin-care junkies and perfume fans will be hard-pressed to walk away empty-handed from some of London's best beauty emporiums. Visitors should try to visit at least one of London's most venerable perfumeries— the old-school favorites Floris or Penhaligon, as well as newcomers like Miller Harris. London's organic pioneer, Neal's Yard Remedies, is still going strong but has plenty of competition from brands like the Cow Shed.

18

Content. Fans of organic beauty products should pop into Content. The store itself was built from organic, recycled products and resembles an old-fashioned apothecary. All the products carried are organic and chemical-free, and packaging is kept to a minimum. Content stocks face and body lotions, perfume, and cosmetics, and some of the brands carried include Dr. Haushka, Saaf, Jane Iredale, and Jo Wood organics. ⊠ *14 Bulstrode St., Marylebone* ☎ *020/3075–1006* Ⓤ *Bond St.*

Fodor's Choice **Floris.** One of the most beautiful shops in London, Floris boasts gleam-
★ ing glass-and-Spanish-mahogany showcases from the Great Exhibition of 1851. As well as beautifully packaged soaps, bath essences, perfumes, and its famous rose-scented mouthwash, gift possibilities include goose-down powder puffs and cut-glass atomizers. Queen Victoria used to dab her favorite Floris fragrance on her lace handkerchief. True to its origins as a barbershop, Floris makes shaving products as well as scents for both men and women. ⊠ *89 Jermyn St., St. James's* ☎ *020/7930–2885* ⊙ *Closed Sun.* Ⓤ *Piccadilly Circus.*

Jo Malone. London's own passionate perfumer and cosmetician began blending scents and creams in the 1990s, and now has shops around the world. In addition to selling heavenly scented products in elegantly simple, modern packaging, the shop also does facials and Fragrance Combining consultations. There are similar services at the 23 Brook

LONDON'S SPA SCENE

Although a bout of nonstop shopping is an ideal way to spend a day, the city's depth and breadth of shops may leave you feeling ready for a spa treatment or two. Or consider treating yourself to a full day of pampering. London's spas have come a long way in the past few years, although locals still don't take grooming to the same level as their New York counterparts. Whether you are looking for a quickie pedicure or an afternoon wallowing in treatments, there are plenty of options. ■TIP→ Always check to see if service is included in the treatment; if it isn't, a 10% tip is considered adequate.

For all-out luxury, try the tranquil **Spa at Chancery Court** (⊠ *252 High Holborn, Holborn* ☎ *020/7829–7058* ⊕ *www.spachancerycourt. com* Ⓤ *Holborn*) with its limestone walls, wooden floors, and orchids. Everything here is done well and done big, including the relaxation and changing rooms. Choose from a jet-lag treatment or Reiki, to an eight-handed massage or facials using E'Spa products.

The tiny **Pacifica Day Spa** (⊠ *1 Courtnell St., Notting Hill* ☎ *020/7243–1718* ⊕ *www. pacificadayspa.co.uk* Ⓤ *Notting Hill Gate*) has a soothing, Asian-theme design. Although the relaxation area is spartan and the four treatment rooms are small, the extensive spa menu makes up for this. Therapists uses Dermalogica and Elemis products for facials and massages, or treat your feet to a yoga pedicure, which includes reflexology.

Tucked away in tony Holland Park is the sleek **Cowshed Clarendon Cross** (⊠ *119 Portland Rd., Holland Park* ☎ *020/7078–1944* ⊕ *www. cowshedonline.com* Ⓤ *Holland Park*)— the brand's first stand-alone spa. Enjoy a smoothie or lunch at the ground-floor kitchen before heading off to your of salt scrub, speedy pedicures, or deep tissue massage.

If your budget will allow it, head to the **Mandarin Oriental Spa** (⊠ *Mandarin Oriental Hyde Park, 66 Knightsbridge, Knightsbridge* ☎ *020/7838–9888* ⊕ *www. mandarinoriental.com* Ⓤ *Knightsbridge*). Instead of booking a specific treatment, book a slot of time and allow the therapist to come up with a tailor-made program. Don't miss the Amethyst Crystal Steam Room or the Zen Colour Therapy Relaxation room.

In a hurry? Book an express facial or massage at the chic **Spa Illuminata** (⊠ *63 South Audley St., Mayfair* ☎ *020/7499–7777* ⊕ *www. spailluminata.com* Ⓤ *Bond St., Green Park*). If you have time to linger, don't miss the lavishly tiled steam rooms, funky zebra-stripe chairs, and marble floors. Illuminata facials use products from Decleor and Carita.

Street shop in Mayfair W1. ⊠ *150 Sloane St., Chelsea* ☎ *0870/192–5121* Ⓤ *Sloane Sq.*

Liz Earle Naturally Active Cosmetics. Former writer and broadcaster Liz Earle is one of the biggest names in British beauty, yet before she opened this Chelsea shop in 2007, her affordable, botanical-based skin-care line was available only via mail order, or from an outlet at her Isle of Wight company. The remarkably effective products have a devoted following—magazine beauty editors among them. ✉ *38–39 Duke of York Sq., King's Rd., Chelsea* ☎ *020/7730–9191* Ⓤ *Sloane Sq.*

Miller Harris. This luxury perfume brand is the brainchild of Lyn Harris, who started with just four classic scents in 2000 and has expanded her range to 20. She sources her rare ingredients from all over the world, and customers can also work with Harris to create a bespoke scent—a process that takes up to six months. Her Mayfair flagship store houses a scent library, perfect for relaxing while choosing your perfume. ✉ *21 Bruton St., Mayfair* ☎ *020/7629–7750* Ⓤ *Bond St.*

BOOKS AND PRINTS

Charing Cross Road has long been a center of London bookselling, but books are big business in London and the trade spreads into many corners of the city. Every decent London High street has its Waterstone's, Borders, or local independent, some complete with coffee shops and, in some cases, even cocktail bars. Bloomsbury, around London University and the British Museum, is good territory for used books and eccentric specialists.

GENERAL

18

Daunt Books. The most beautiful Daunt branch is the Edwardian store in Marylebone. The travel section is housed in a dramatic oak room, illuminated by a lofty conservatory roof and stained-glass windows. Guidebooks, poetry, and other literature are organized by country. There's also an excellent children's section and, at the front, biography and fiction are piled on tables for eclectic browsing. There are branches in Belsize Park, Hampstead, and Holland Park. ✉ *83 Chelsea, Marylebone High St., Marylebone* ☎ *020/7224–2295* Ⓤ *Baker St.*

Fodor's Choice ★ **Foyles.** A quirky, labyrinthine, family-run business, this store was founded in 1903 by the Foyle brothers, after they failed the civil service exam. Today Foyles' five floors carry almost every title imaginable. One of London's best sources for textbooks, the store stocks everything from popular fiction to military history, sheet music, medical tomes, opera scores, and fine arts. Store-within-a-store Ray's Jazz has a cool café, and there's even a piranha tank on the children's floor. In 2005, a branch opened in the South Bank, followed by a concession within Selfridges department store and an outpost in St. Pancras International, home of Eurostar. ✉ *113–119 Charing Cross Rd., Soho* ☎ *020/440–3212* Ⓤ *Tottenham Court Rd.* ✉ *Royal Festival Hall, South Bank* ☎ *020/7437–5660* Ⓤ *Waterloo.*

Fodor's Choice ★ **Hatchards.** This is London's oldest bookshop, open since 1797 and beloved by writers themselves (customers have included Oscar Wilde,

Rudyard Kipling, and Lord Byron) thanks to its cozy, independent character. Independence, however, is a matter of appearance only—Hatchards is owned by the same corporate giant as the omnipresent Waterstone's chain. Nevertheless, you can revel in its old-fashioned charm while perusing the well-stocked shelves lining the winding stairs. The staff has retained old-fashioned helpfulness, too. ✉ *187 Piccadilly, St. James's* ☎ *020/7439–9921* Ⓤ *Piccadilly Circus.*

John Sandoe Books, Ltd. More than 25,000 books fill the three dollhouse-size floors (and are also stacked on the stairs) of an 18th-century house. Organization? Forget it! Only the staff know where anything is, as books are crammed on the stairs, around the stairs, and on various tables. But staffers are knowledgeable, friendly, and full of great recommendations. Local writers, including William Boyd and Arabella Boxer, among others, are regulars and contribute to the shop's annual short publications. This is bookselling the way it used to be. ✉ *10 Blacklands Terr., Chelsea* ☎ *020/7589–9473* Ⓤ *Sloane Sq.*

Waterstone's. For book buying as a hedonistic leisure activity, the monster-size store by Piccadilly Circus caters to all tastes. Sip a gin-and-tonic or get a bite while browsing through a book and admiring the view from the top floor until 9 PM at the 5th View Bar & Food. Waterstone's is the country's leading book chain, and they've pulled out all the stops to make this, their flagship, as comfortable and relaxed as a bookstore can be. ✉ *203–206 Piccadilly* ☎ *020/7851–2400* Ⓤ *Piccadilly Circus.*

SPECIALTY

Books for Cooks. It may seem odd to describe a bookshop as delicious-smelling, but between the products of its test kitchen and its regularly scheduled cooking workshops, Books for Cooks is hard to resist. Just about every world cuisine is represented on its shelves, along with the complete lineup of celebrity-chef editions. You can sample lunch dishes, cakes, and coffee at one of a handful of tables in the back. ■TIP➔ Before you come to London, visit the shop's Web site, www.booksforcooks. com, to sign up for a cooking class. ✉ *4 Blenheim Crescent, Notting Hill* ☎ *020/7221–1992* ◷ *Closed Sun. and Mon.* Ⓤ *Notting Hill Gate, Ladbroke Grove.*

Gay's the Word. Open since 1979, this is London's leading gay and lesbian bookshop. Thousands of titles, from literature and thoughtful nonfiction to erotica, and even detective novels, fill the shelves. The shop is a well-loved fixture on the scene, and often hosts discussion groups, readings, and other events. ✉ *66 Marchmont St., Bloomsbury* ☎ *020/7278–7654* ◷ *Closed Sun. morning* Ⓤ *Russell Sq.*

Stanfords. When it comes to encyclopedic coverage, there simply cannot be a better travel-book and map shop on the planet. Stanfords is packed with a comprehensive selection of map and travel-book series. Whether you're planning a day trip to Surrey or an adventure to the South Pole, this should be your first stop. ✉ *12–14 Long Acre, Covent Garden* ☎ *020/7836–1321* Ⓤ *Covent Garden.*

RARE AND ANTIQUARIAN

The English gentleman's library, with its glass-front cabinets full of rare leather-bound books, may be a film and literary cliché, but there's no denying that London is one of the world's great centers for rare-book collectors. There's still quite a concentration of used bookstores on Charing Cross Road, with additional book and print specialists tucked away in Cecil Court, a pedestrian alley linking it with St. Martin's Lane. (See ⊕ *www.cecilcourt.co.uk* for a full list of the shops in this unique enclave.) Other well-respected specialists reside in Mayfair.

★ **Grosvenor Prints.** London's largest collection of 17th- to early-20th-century prints includes a good selection of rare, early Americana. The main emphasis is on London views and architecture as well as sporting and decorative prints. It's an eccentric collection, with prices ranging from £5 into the thousands. ⊠ *19 Shelton St., Covent Garden* ☎ *020/7836–1979* ⊗ *Closed Sun.* Ⓤ *Covent Garden.*

Maggs Brothers Ltd. How could any book lover resist a shop with such a deliciously Dickensian name? In a Georgian town house in one of Mayfair's elegant squares, Maggs was established in 1853, and is one of the world's oldest and largest rare-book dealers. Shop staff act as advisers to important collectors, but they are, nonetheless, friendly and helpful to all interested visitors. ⊠ *50 Berkeley Sq., Mayfair* ☎ *020/7493–7160* ⊗ *Closed weekends* Ⓤ *Green Park.*

Simon Finch Rare Books Ltd. This unsnobbish dealer spans all periods, from Babylonian tablets to modern first editions. English history and literature, medical texts, and photography are among the eclectic specialties. ⊠ *Floors 1–4, 26 Brook St.* ☎ *020/7499–0974* ⊗ *Closed weekends* Ⓤ *Bond St.*

18

CLOTHING

London is one of the world's fashion capitals, and every designer you've ever heard of is available. But it's the city's eccentric street style that gives fashion here its edge. London women may not look as soignée as French or Italian women, but many are daring and colorful fashion risk-takers. This is where the trends that show up on the European catwalks really begin.

What makes London clothes shopping so much fun—for both men and women—is that you can buy high-quality traditional British clothing, bespoke tailoring, today's best fashion labels, delicious vintage clothing, and outrageous directional street style without traveling farther than a couple of Tube stops.

ACCESSORIES

Whether you're looking for a sturdy umbrella, a traditional hat, or a bag that will last a lifetime, London's specialists are known for their high level of craftsmanship—and today's designers draw on centuries of expertise.

★ **Anya Hindmarch.** Exquisite leather bags and personalized, printed canvas totes are what made Hindmarch famous, along with her hit 2007 "I'm Not A Plastic Bag" eco-creation. Her designs are sold at Harrods and Harvey Nichols, but in her stores, you can see her complete collection of bags and shoes, and have your own photograph immortalized on a bag from a choice of sizes and styles. There are also branches around the corner on Pont Street (bespoke store), on Bond Street in Mayfair, and Ledbury Road in Notting Hill. ✉ *157–158 Sloane St., Knightsbridge* 🕿 *020/7730–0961* Ⓤ *Sloane Sq., Knightsbridge.*

★ **Bernstock Speirs.** Paul Bernstock and Thelma Speirs turn tradition on its head—their street-smart trilbies and knitted hats, featuring unusual colors and quirky details, have caught the eye of Liam Gallagher and Kylie Minogue. ✉ *234 Brick La., Spitalfields/East End* 🕿 *020/7739–7385* Ⓤ *Liverpool St., Bethnal Green.*

Connolly. Connolly used to produce the leather for Rolls-Royces and Aston Martins, and that heritage lives on in its deluxe motoring accessories, from sleek luggage to an espresso machine designed for your car. Today the brand is owned by fashion designer Joseph Ettedgui, and the Andree Putman–designed shop sells a broad range of luxurious clothing and accessories for men and women, including butter-soft leather and suede jackets, wallets, and driving gloves. ✉ *41 Conduit St., Mayfair* 🕿 *020/7439–2510* ☾ *Open Sun. in Dec. only* Ⓤ *Oxford Circus, Bond St.*

James Lock & Co. Ltd. Need a silk opera hat, a flat-weave Panama, or a traditional tweed flat cap? James Lock of St. James's has been making hats from its cozy little shop since 1676, and has dressed the heads of Admiral Lord Nelson, Jackie Onassis, Frank Sinatra, and, recently, hip young musicians and models. ✉ *6 St. James's St., St. James's* 🕿 *020/7930–5849* ☾ *Closed Sun.* Ⓤ *Green Park, Piccadilly Circus.*

James Smith & Sons Ltd. This has to be the world's ultimate umbrella shop, and a must for anyone interested in real Victorian London. The family-owned shop has been in business since 1857 in the same New Oxford Street corner, and sells every kind of umbrella, cane, and walking stick imaginable. The decor is unchanged since the 19th century; you will feel as if you have stepped back into time. If the umbrellas are out of your price range, James Smith also sells smaller accessories and handmade wooden bowls. ✉ *Hazelwood House, 53 New Oxford St., Bloomsbury* 🕿 *020/7836–4731* ☾ *Closed Sun.* Ⓤ *Tottenham Court Rd., Holborn.*

★ **Lulu Guinness.** Famous for her flamboyant themed bags (memorable designs include a satin "bucket" topped with roses and an elaborately beaded red snakeskin "lips" clutch), which are like pieces of sculpture, Guinness also showcases vintage-inspired vanity cases, shoes, beauty products, and bed linens in this fabulous little shop, which is just as whimsical as her designs. ✉ *3 Ellis St., Chelsea* 🕿 *020/7823–4828* ☾ *Closed Sun.* Ⓤ *Sloane Sq.*

Mulberry. This luxury goods company has produced many a season's It bag, including the Roxanne and the Bayswater. In addition to the leather handbags, Mulberry also produces gorgeous leather accessories, from wallets to luggage. In 2008 the company unveiled its first line of

LONDON SHOPPING STEALS AND DEALS

Although London has never been known as a budget shopping destination, when the pound is strong, prices can seem stratospheric. No matter what currency you are using, there are still bargains to be had, as long as you know where, and when, to look. To get the maximum mileage out of your cash, visit during the widespread biannual sales, which kick off in late June and just after Christmas, and last about a month. For the best choices and biggest discounts, head to a department store such as Selfridges.

Fashion insiders attend the many sales held throughout the year, from big warehouse clearances, such as the Designer Warehouse Sales (⊕ www.designerwarehouse-sales.com) and Designer Sales UK (⊕ www.designersales.co.uk), to individual designers' sample sales—check out ⊕ www.fashionconfidential.co.uk or ⊕ www.dailycandy.com/london for information, and to register for updates. London outlets, such as Browns Labels for Less, Paul Smith Sale Shop, and the Joseph Sale Shop on the King's Road, offer year-round designer bargains.

If you're not fussy about labels, there are even more choices. **Primark**

(✉ 499 Oxford St., Oxford St. ☎ 020/7495–0420 Ⓤ Marble Arch) is fantastic for low-cost, high-fashion clothing. The huge, two-story Oxford Street flagship is the best place to shop, although keep in mind you get what you pay for; some of the fabrics and finishes betray their low prices. If you don't mind paying a little more, try **COS** (✉ 222 Regent St., Mayfair ☎ 020/7478–0400 Ⓤ Oxford Circus). Short for Collection of Style, this store is the upscale sibling of Swedish chain H&M, offering classic separates for men and women in fine fabrics such as linen, silk, and cashmere. The look is grown-up and subtle, and the prices are in line with mid-range British chains. You may think having a suit custom-made in the city famous for its tailoring traditions is beyond your means, but there are less costly options away from hallowed Savile Row. Contemporary tailors **Pokit** (✉ 53 Lamb's Conduit St., Bloomsbury ☎ 020/7430–9782 ⊙ Closed Sun. Ⓤ Holborn) offer sharp but comfortable made-to-measure suits for men and women from just £500. And if your budget is tighter, you can score a secondhand Savile Row suit at Old Hat (⇨ see Vintage London).

shoes. Aside from the New Bond Street flagship, there are branches in Knightsbridge and Notting Hill. The boutique-size store at St. Christopher's Place, W1, stocks accessories only. ✉ 41–42 New Bond St., Mayfair ☎ 020/7491–3900 Ⓤ Bond St.

Philip Treacy. Treacy's magnificent hats are annual showstoppers on Ladies Day at the Royal Ascot races and regularly grace the glossy magazines' society pages. Part Mad Hatter, part Cecil Beaton, Treacy's creations always guarantee a grand entrance. In addition to the extravagant, haute couture hats handmade in the atelier, ready-to-wear hats and bags are also for sale. ✉ 69 Elizabeth St., Belgravia ☎ 020/7730–3992 ⊙ Closed Sun. Ⓤ Sloane Sq.

★   **Swaine Adeney Brigg.** This shop has been selling practical supplies for country pursuits since 1750. Not just for the horsey set, the store has golf umbrellas, walking sticks, and hip flasks—all beautifully crafted and ingenious. Or pick up your own Poet Hat, the iconic hat worn by Harrison Ford in every "Indiana Jones" film, and which the company has been making since the 1890s. On a frosty morning, you shouldn't be without the umbrella with a slim tipple-holder flask secreted inside the stick. Traditional menswear (tweeds, cashmere sweaters, and Herbert Johnson hats) are downstairs. ⊠ *54 St. James's St., St. James's* ☏ *020/7409–7277* ☾ *Closed Sun.* Ⓤ *Green Park.*

CHILDREN'S WEAR

Several of the lower-price adult chains, including H&M, Next, Monsoon, Primark, and Zara, have cheap and cheerful children's lines. In select Jigsaw branches, Jigsaw Junior has classics with a twist for girls. London parents swear by no-nonsense department store John Lewis, on Oxford Street, W1, for fair prices and high-quality goods. But if you're looking for something more than run of the mill, expect to pay for it.

Marie Chantal. If you love beautiful, tasteful clothes for babies and children, head to this boutique that is the brainchild of Princess Marie-Chantal of Greece. As you'd imagine, the look is regal and the price is high. Materials used include silk, linen, and Liberty prints. ⊠ *148 Walton St., South Kensington* ☏ *020/7838–1111* Ⓤ *South Kensington.*

Rachel Riley. Looking for traditional English style on a small scale? Riley's expensive vintage-inspired collection includes classics like duffel coats, cashmere booties, and floral dresses for girls and teens. Mothers who love the Riley look can pick up coordinating outfits for themselves. ⊠ *14 Pont St., Knightsbridge* ☏ *020/7259–5969* Ⓤ *Knightsbridge* ⊠ *82 Marylebone High St., Marylebone* ☏ *020/7935–7007* Ⓤ *Baker St., Bond St.*

GENERAL   **Aimé.** French-Cambodian sisters Val and Vanda Heng-Vong launched this shop to showcase the best of French clothing and housewares design. Expect to find fashion by Isabel Marant, Antik Batik, and APC. You can also pick up scents by Esteban and a well-edited collection of ceramics. Just next door at 34 Ledbury Road, Petit Aimé sells children's clothing. ⊠ *32 Ledbury Rd., Notting Hill* ☏ *020/7221–7070* Ⓤ *Notting Hill Gate.*

Aquascutum. Known for its trench coats (worn by Churchill, no less), Aquascutum also offers clothing for men and women in classic British style. The men's suits and sweaters are timeless, and the women's collection has become surprisingly funky, offering fresh takes on overcoats and items like tunics and jersey dresses. The brand is also available at Harrods, Selfridges, and other big department stores around town. ⊠ *100 Regent St., Soho* ☏ *020/7675–8200* Ⓤ *Piccadilly Circus.*

b Store. Some people regard b Store as the best little clothing boutique in London. Located at the end of Savile Row, b Store couldn't be farther away in terms of style from the traditional tailors down the street. Head here for cutting-edge pieces from avant-garde designers such as Diana Brinks and Ute Ploeir, plus the store's quirky own-label shoes. ⊠ *24A*

Savile Row, Mayfair ☎ *020/7734–6846* ⊗ *Closed Sun.* Ⓤ *Piccadilly Circus, Oxford Circus.*

Brora. The knitwear is cozy, but the taste temperature is cool in this contemporary cashmere emporium for men, women, and kids. There are dressed-up camisoles, sweaters and cardigans, adorable baby ensembles, plus noncashmere items such as picnic blankets and scarves. There are branches in Notting Hill, Marylebone, Islington, and Wimbledon. ✉ *344 King's Rd., Chelsea* ☎ *020/7352–3697* Ⓤ *Sloane Sq.*

Burberry. A few years ago, Burberry was the victim of its own success, with the company's ubiquitous plaid appearing on everything from baseball hats to baby strollers and bikinis. These days, the brand has cultivated a more rock-and-roll image, featuring fetishy boots and tough-edge leather jackets in some catwalk collections. The raincoats are still a classic buy, along with the plaid scarves in every color imaginable. If you're up for a trek, there's a huge factory outlet in Hackney on Chatham Place with clothing for men, women, and children, as well as accessories, at half price and less. There are also branches at Brompton Road in Knightsbridge and Regent Street in Soho. ✉ *21–23 New Bond St., Mayfair* ☎ *020/3367–3000* Ⓤ *Piccadilly Circus.*

Fodor's Choice ★ **Dover Street Market.** Visiting this six-floor emporium isn't just about buying; with its arty displays and eccentric mix of merchandise, it is as fascinating as any gallery. The creation of Comme des Garçons' Rei Kawakubo, it showcases all of the label's collections for men and women alongside other designers such as Lanvin, Alaïa, and exclusive Japanese lines, plus curiosities including antique medical specimens, avant-garde art books, and vintage couture. You never know what you will find, which is half the fun. ■TIP→ An outpost of the Rose Bakery on the top floor makes a handy pit stop. ✉ *17–18 Dover St., Mayfair* ☎ *020/7518–0680* ⊗ *Closed Sun.* Ⓤ *Green Park.*

18

Egg. Tucked away in a residential mews a short walk from Harvey Nichols, this shop is the brainchild of Maureen Doherty, once Issey Miyake's right-hand person. Minimalist, unstructured styles for men and women in natural fabrics, such as silk, cashmere, and antique cotton, have an artisanal quality. The shop is a former Victorian dairy, and garments are casually hung on hooks or folded on wooden tables in the simple, white space. The price tags, however, are anything but humble. Unusual ceramics and jewelry are also on display. ✉ *36 Kinnerton St., Knightsbridge* ☎ *020/7235–9315* ⊗ *Closed Sun. and Mon.* Ⓤ *Knightsbridge.*

★ **Junky Styling.** This brand was launched by designers Annika Sanders and Kerry Seager, who "deconstructed" old clothing when they wanted something unique to wear clubbing. They recycled traditional suits and shirts into wild outfits, and the business grew from there. The highly original (and eco-friendly) garments, for both men and women, are funky but retain the sophistication of their tailored origins. ⊠ *12 Dray Walk, The Old Truman Brewery, 91 Brick La., Spitalfields/East End* ☎ *020/7247–1883* Ⓤ *Liverpool St., Aldgate East.*

★ **The Laden Showroom.** Sienna Miller, Victoria Beckham, and Noel Gallagher are among the celebs who regularly check out new talent at this East End showroom for young designers. The store retails the work of more than 55 new designers, some selling one-off items—so the look you find is likely to be exclusive. ⊠ *103 Brick La., Spitalfields/East End* ☎ *020/7247–2431* Ⓤ *Liverpool St., Whitechapel.*

Margaret Howell. These quintessentially English clothes are low-key and understated while managing to look utterly contemporary. Howell mixes impeccable British tailoring and traditional fabrics (linen, cashmere, tweed) with relaxed modern cuts. A fan of 20th-century household design, the designer also showcases vintage Ercol furniture at her boutique. ⊠ *34 Wigmore St., Marylebone* ☎ *020/7009–9006* ⊘ *Closed Sun.* Ⓤ *Oxford Circus* ⊠ *111 Fulham Rd., Chelsea* ☎ *020/7591–2255* Ⓤ *South Kensington.*

★ **Paul Smith.** British classics with colorful and irreverent twists define Paul Smith's collections for both women and men. Beautifully tailored men's suits in exceptional fabrics might sport flamboyant linings or unusual detailing. Women's lines tend to take familiar and traditional British ideas and turn them on their heads with humor and color. Accessories, including wallets, scarves, diaries—and even a soccer ball—in his signature rainbow stripes make great gifts. There are several branches, including a Notting Hill mansion at 120–122 Kensington Park Road, W11; a small, funky outpost at 13 Park Street, SE1, near Borough Market; a vintage furniture shop at 9 Albemarle Street in Mayfair; and, not far away, a sale shop at 23 Avery Row, W1. There is also a ladies' and men's shoes and accessories shop on Marylebone High Street. ⊠ *40–44 Floral St., Covent Garden* ☎ *020/7379–7133* Ⓤ *Covent Garden.*

The Shop at Bluebird. The "concept store" has come to London. The brainchild of the couple behind popular womenswear brand Jigsaw, this 10,000-square-foot space in the old Bluebird garage brings together fashion, furniture, books, and music—all chosen for style and originality. It's worth visiting for the displays alone, which change regularly, although the funky ceiling-light installation of more than 1,000 bulbs seems to be a constant feature. After browsing, unwind with a treatment at the on-site spa or have a bite at Terence Conran's restaurant in the same complex. ■ **TIP→** It's a good 20 minutes' walk from the nearest Tube station at Sloane Square, so catch a No. 11 or No. 22 bus along the King's Road. ⊠ *350 King's Rd., Chelsea* ☎ *020/7351–3873* Ⓤ *Sloane Sq.*

MENSWEAR

All the stores listed in General Clothing have good selections of menswear, especially the sublime Paul Smith. The department stores listed in this chapter have good menswear departments, but Selfridges and Liberty deserve special mentions for interesting designer offerings. London's Savile Row tailors are still the spot where a man orders a bespoke suit once he has really "arrived," but British style has loosened up considerably in recent years. Ozwald Boateng, with his sharp designs, and colorful suitings and linings, is typical of the new wave of bespoke tailors. Those with more flash than cash should hotfoot it to the trend-setting fashion chains: Topman, Reiss, and Zara.

★ **Bamford & Sons.** The men's and boys' wear at Bamford & Sons combines the British heritage of tailoring and fabrics with a suave modernity. Dashing city wear, romantically nonchalant country clothes, plus fine leather and cashmere accessories are all available. There is also a small but exquisite women's collection (showcased fully at the new Brompton Cross branch). The store at 44 Pimlico Road houses a Daylesford Organic café in the basement, with a complete line of sleekly packaged organic foodstuffs from owner Lady Carole Bamford's Cotswold farm, plus an adjacent garden shop. ✉ *31 Sloane Sq., Chelsea* ☎ *020/7881–8010* Ⓤ *Sloane Sq.* ✉ *The Old Workshop, 79–81 Ledbury Rd., Notting Hill* ☎ *020/7792–9350* Ⓤ *Notting Hill Gate.*

Gieves and Hawkes. One of the grandest of grand old names for London bespoke tailoring, this company made its name outfitting Britain's Royal Military officers and still supplies bespoke military uniforms. Prices for a bespoke suit start around £3,600, or choose an off-the-peg design starting at around £600. ✉ *1 Savile Row, Mayfair* ☎ *020/7434–2001* Ⓤ *Piccadilly Circus.*

Hackett. If J. Crew isn't preppy enough for you, try Hackett. Started as a posh thrift shop, Hackett once recycled cricket flannels, hunting pinks, Oxford brogues, and similar British wear. Now it makes its own attire, and it has become a genuine—and very good—gentlemen's outfitter. The look is traditional and classic, and some of the best buys include polo shirts, corduroys, and stripey scarves. ✉ *Main store: 137–138 Sloane St., Knightsbridge* ☎ *020/7730–3331* Ⓤ *Sloane Sq.*

★ **Ozwald Boateng.** Ozwald Boateng's (pronounced Bwa-teng) is one of the funkiest tailors working on Savile Row. His made-to-measure suits in eye-popping colors (even the more conservative suits sport bright silk linings), luxurious fabrics, and leading-edge styling are worn by rock and club-land luminaries including Jamie Foxx, Mick Jagger, and Laurence Fishburne. ✉ *30 Savile Row, Mayfair* ☎ *0207/437–2030* ◷ *Closed Sun.* Ⓤ *Piccadilly Circus.*

Thomas Pink. The chain still makes some of the best dress shirts around for both men and women in fine fabrics such as Sea Island and Egyptian cotton. Bespoke shirts for men are available at the Jermyn Street branch. ✉ *85 Jermyn St., St. James's* ☎ *020/7930–6364* Ⓤ *Green Park, Piccadilly Circus.*

★ **Turnbull & Asser.** This is *the* custom shirtmaker, dripping exclusivity from every fiber—after all, Prince Charles is a client and James Bond wears the shirts on film. At least 28 separate measurements are taken, and the cloth, woven to their specifications, comes in 1,000 different patterns—the cottons feel as good as silk. The first order must be for a minimum of six shirts, starting from £180 each. There are less expensive, though still exquisite, ready-to-wear shirts available as well as jackets, cashmeres, suits, ties, and accessories like pajamas. ✉ *71–72 Jermyn St., St. James's* ☎ *020/7808–3000* ◷ *Closed Sun.* Ⓤ *Green Park.*

18

WOMEN'S WEAR

As one of the world's great fashion capitals, London has shops to dress you in style—whether your taste is trendy or traditional, and your budget rummage or royal. High-street chains like Miss Selfridge, Top-shop, New Look, and All Saints take aim at the young, adventurous, and slim; Hobbs, Whistles, and Jaeger provide updated classics for the more sophisticated; and fashion-oriented department stores—Harvey Nichols, Harrods, Selfridges, Liberty, Fenwick—cater to women of all ages and tastes. The hottest names on the London catwalks have their headquarters here—Alexander McQueen's flagship store is at 4–5 Old Bond Street, Mayfair W1, and, nearby, Stella McCartney's collections are showcased in a town house at 30 Bruton Street.

★ **Agent Provocateur.** Created by Vivienne Westwood's son, these shops purvey sexy, naughty-but-nice lingerie in gorgeous fabrics and lace. The original shop is in the almost-red-light area of Soho, but there are now branches across the city—and across the Atlantic. Selections are available in Selfridges. ⊠ *16 Pont St., Knightsbridge* ☎ *020/7235–0229* ⊗ *Closed Sun.* Ⓤ *Knightsbridge, Sloane Sq.*

★ **Browns.** This shop—actually a series of small shops on South Molton Street—was a pioneer designer boutique in the 1970s and continues to talent-spot the newest and best around. You may find the windows showcasing the work of top graduates from this year's student shows or displaying well-established designers such as Marni, Chloé, Juyna Watanabe, Yves Saint Laurent, Dries Van Noten, or Anne Demeule-meester. The men's store at No. 23 has a similar selection, whereas Browns Focus, across the street at Nos. 38–39, showcases young, hip designs and denim. Browns also has its own label, a bargain outlet at No. 50, and a designer bridal boutique at 11–12 Hinde Street, W1. There is also a smaller boutique at 6C Sloane Street, and another at 59 Book Street, off New Bond Street, which solely sells shoes. ⊠ *23–27 S. Molton St., Mayfair* ☎ *020/7514–0000* Ⓤ *Bond St.*

Coco Ribbon. It's the chic boutique that caters to very girly girls. This is, after all, the shop that pioneered the Panty Postman (regular monthly deliveries arrive by mail) and sells women's clothing, cosmetics, and accessories. Coco Ribbon carries designers including Rebecca Taylor, Sass and Bide, and Jasmine di Milo, as well as selling its own branded line of cashmere. ⊠ *21 Kensington Park Rd., Notting Hill* ☎ *020/7229–4904* Ⓤ *Notting Hill Gate.*

Fenwick (⊠ *63 New Bond St., Mayfair* ☎ *020/7629–9161* Ⓤ *Bond St.*) is a haven of realistically priced fashion in a shopping area where most things cost the earth. Five floors of chic clothes and accessories for men and women, lingerie, and home furnishings highlight lesser-known and emerging designers from all over Europe.

★ **Jigsaw.** Popular with women in their twenties through forties, Jigsaw toes the line between trendy and classic (a bit like Banana Republic). Prices are reasonable for feminine dresses, practical T-shirts, and knit-wear in high-quality fabrics and distinctive yet subtle colors. There are several other branches are around town. Girls get in on the act, too, with their own line, Jigsaw Junior. ⊠ *The Chapel, Duke of York Sq., King's Road* ☎ *020/730–4404* Ⓤ *Sloane Sq.*

★ **Koh Samui.** Named for a Thai island resort, this shop stocks designer clothes for the kind of hip young woman who thinks nothing of flying there for a week's detox at the drop of a hat. On the rails are the likes of Marc Jacobs, Matthew Williamson, and Balenciaga, plus hot young design talent and select vintage pieces. ⊠ *65–67 Monmouth St., Covent Garden* ☎ *020/7240–4280* Ⓤ *Covent Garden.*

Luella. The brainchild of ex–fashion editor Luella Bartley, this brand will appeal to fans of quirky British humor. Her collection, of which Kate Moss and singer Lily Allen are fans, is chic and playful. Expect dresses with plenty of volume, skinny jeans, and short shorts. ⊠ *25 Brook St., Mayfair* ☎ *020/7518–1830* ◷ *Closed Sun.* Ⓤ *Bond St.*

Nicole Farhi. Busy women willing to invest in quality value Nicole Farhi's softly tailored, functional dresses and separates. The style manages to be contemporary yet timeless, making these standbys in many a working woman's wardrobe. Of the numerous locations, the New Bond Street store sells clothes for both men and women, but the full men's collection is available at the Floral Street branch. ⊠ *158 New Bond St., Mayfair* ☎ *020/7499–8368* Ⓤ *Bond St.* ☞ *Men's Collection:* ⊠ *11 Floral St., Covent Garden* ☎ *020/7497–8713* Ⓤ *Covent Garden.*

Orla Kiely. The Irish designer is probably best known for her bags and wallets with signature leaf print, but her appealingly simple retro-tinged prints (cars, mugs, leaves, abstracts) grace everything from dresses to lamp shades—all showcased in this airy flagship store. There are also nonpatterned clothes in her youthful, trend-led collection. ⊠ *31 Monmouth St., Covent Garden* ☎ *020/7240–4022* Ⓤ *Covent Garden.*

Rigby & Peller. Those who love luxury lingerie shop here for brands like Prima Donna and Aubade, as well as R&P's own line. If the right fit eludes you, and you fancy being fitted by the Queen's corsetiere, have a bra made to measure (from around £309). Most of the young royal and aristo women buy here, not just because the store holds the royal appointment, but because the quality is excellent and the service much friendlier than you might expect. There are a number of stores across town, all of which are open on Sunday except the Conduit Street shop. ⊠ *13 Kings Rd., Chelsea* ☎ *0845/076–5545* Ⓤ *Sloane Sq.*

Fodor'sChoice
★ **Topshop.** This London standby has successfully made the transition from "cheap and cheerful" to genuine fashion hot spot with afford-able prices. Plenty of foreign fashion editors make Topshop their first port of call when visiting. Clothing and accessories are geared to the younger, trendy end of the market (although women who are young at heart find plenty of wearable items here), and the aim is to copy runway trends as fast as possible—although the store also has its own catwalk line, Topshop Unique. Every season, a changing array of front-of-the-pack designers create small collections for the in-store Boutique, and there are further lines from affordable independent designers. Innova-tions, such as personal style advisers and an on-site "blow-dry bar," are constantly being introduced. Topman brings the same fashion approach to clothing for younger men. ■TIP➜ If the crowds become too much,

18

VINTAGE LONDON

The trend for vintage clothing on both sides of the Atlantic shows no sign of letting up, and the British, with their love of theatrical style, have embraced it with particular gusto. Many boutiques have integrated vintage items into their stock. Liberty, Selfridges, and Topshop all have vintage sections. You can find retro from the recent past at Camden Market or on the fringes of Portobello Road and Brick Lane/Spitalfields. Here are some of the best specialist shops:

Absolute Vintage is a warehouse of handpicked items from the 1930s through the 1980s, but the specialty here is shoes. The shop has the largest collection of vintage shoes in the United Kingdom (more than 1,000 pairs). Best of all, prices are reasonable. ✉ *15 Hanbury St., Spitalfields/East End* ☎ *020/7247–3883* Ⓤ *Whitechapel, Liverpool St.*

Beyond Retro stocks more than 10,000 vintage items for men and women. From cowboy boots to bowling shirts to prom dresses, they've got the largest collection of American retro in the United Kingdom. ✉ *110–112 Cheshire St., Spitalfields/East End* ☎ *020/7613–3636* Ⓤ *Whitechapel, Bethnal Green Rail.*

Old Hat. One for the boys, this shop is jam-packed with secondhand suits, overcoats, and all manner of gentlemanly accoutrements. Look for tailoring by illustrious Savile Row names at a fraction of their original price. ✉ *66 Fulham High St., Fulham* ☎ *020/7610–6558* ◷ *Closed Sun.* Ⓤ *Putney Bridge.*

Orsini is a tiny but choice boutique. Eveningwear with Hollywood-style glamour is the trademark here,

with clothes from the 1920s to the 1970s. Victoria Beckham is a fan. ✉ *76 Earl's Court Rd., Kensington* ☎ *020/7937–2903* Ⓤ *Earl's Court, High Street Kensington.*

Every piece of clothing at **Palette London** is in immaculate condition, which can save a lot of digging. Owner Mark Ellis sells Ossie Clark, Missoni, Pucci, and Chanel from the '40s up until the '90s. ✉ *21 Canonbury La., Islington* ☎ *020/7288–7428* Ⓤ *Islington.*

Fodor's Choice **Rellik** is favored by the likes of Kate Moss and began as a street stall on Portobello Road. Today vintage hunters looking to splurge can find a selection of YSL, Chanel, and Dior, as well as items from lesser-known designers. Prices from £30 to £1,000. ✉ *8 Golborne Rd., Ladbroke Grove* ☎ *020/8962–0089* Ⓤ *Westbourne Park.*

Rokit consists of two shops along Brick Lane that stock everything from handbags and ball gowns to jeans, military, and Western wear, and the ever-changing collection spans from the 1920s to the 1990s. Magazine and rock stylists love it. There are also branches in Camden and Covent Garden. ✉ *101 and 107 Brick La., Spitalfields/East End* ☎ *020/7375–3864* Ⓤ *Aldgate East.*

Virginia, Virginia Baker's collection of vintage clothing, may be the best in London. Dresses, hats, and accessories from early Victorian (circa 1850) to the early 1930s are available. These are wearable collectors' items and priced accordingly. ✉ *98 Portland Rd., Clarendon Cross, Holland Park/Notting Hill* ☎ *020/7727–9908* ◷ *Closed Sun.; open Sat. by appointment only* Ⓤ *Holland Park.*

head to one of the smaller Topshops in town, such as the Kensington High Street branch. ✉ *214 Oxford St., Soho* ☎ *020/927–7634* Ⓤ *Oxford Circus* ✉ *42–44 Kensington High St., Kensington* ☎ *020/7938–1242* Ⓤ *High Street Kensington.*

Vivienne Westwood. This is where it all started: the pompadour-punk ball gowns, Lady Hamilton vest coats, and foppish landmark get-ups are the core of Westwood's first

> ## ROYAL WARRANT
>
> Many stores carry items with the Royal Warrant seal (even some sugar brands). Though not personally endorsed by the royals, it does mean that the palace has used the item for five consecutive years—and it could enliven a gift for royal-watchers.

boutique in Chelsea, where you can still buy ready-to-wear (mainly the more casual Anglomania diffusion line and exclusive Worlds End label based on the archives) under the spinning clock. The designer still represents the apex of high-style British couture. Head for the Conduit Street flagship for all the collections. The small Davies Street boutique sells only the Gold Label and made-to-measure couture. ✉ *44 Conduit St., Mayfair* ☎ *020/7439–1109* Ⓤ *Oxford Circus* ☞ *Original boutique:* ✉ *430 King's Rd., Chelsea* ☎ *020/7352–6551* ☉ *Closed Sun.* Ⓤ *Sloane Sq.* ✉ *6 Davies St., Mayfair* ☎ *020/7629–3757* ☉ *Closed Sun.* Ⓤ *Bond St.*

DEPARTMENT STORES

★ **Browns.** Launched in the '70s, mini-department store Browns caters to the very label-conscious customer. You will find men's and women's fashion from Alexander McQueen and Marni and Chloe, as well as lesser-known designers like Nicholas Kirkwood and jewelry by Muriel Grateau. The beauty department is also worth a look, especially for hard-to-find brands like London cult favorite Vaishaly, a facialist to celebs like British chef Nigella Lawson. ✉ *24–27 South Molton St., Mayfair* ☎ *020/7514–0000* Ⓤ *Bond St.*

Fodor'sChoice **Harrods.** This Knightsbridge institution is an encyclopedia of luxury
★ brands, with more than 300 departments and 20 restaurants spread over 1 million square feet. If you approach Harrods as a tourist attraction rather than a fashion store, you won't be disappointed: focus on the spectacular food halls, the huge ground-floor perfumery, the marble-clad accessory rooms, and the theme park–like EgyptianRoom—at the bottom of the nearby escalator there's a tacky shrine to Diana and Dodi. ■TIP➜ Be prepared to brave the crowds (avoid visiting on Saturday if you can), and be prepared to pay if you want to use the bathroom on some floors. ✉ *87–135 Brompton Rd., Knightsbridge* ☎ *020/7730–1234* Ⓤ *Knightsbridge.*

★ **Harvey Nichols.** Whereas tourists flock to Harrods, true London fashionistas shop at Harvey Nichols, or Harvey Nicks as it's called. The fashion and accessories departments are outstanding, carrying designs from Prada to 3.1 Phillip Lim. The furniture and housewares are equally gorgeous (and pricey), but bargains abound during the twice-annual sales in January and July. The Fifth Floor restaurant is a place to see and be seen, but if you're after a quick bite, pick up a sandwich and some

18

chocolates from the Foodmarket or Daylesford Organic. ✉ *109–125 Knightsbridge, Knightsbridge* ☎ *020/7235–5000* Ⓤ *Knightsbridge.*

Fodor's Choice
★

Liberty. With a wonderful black-and-white mock-Tudor facade, Liberty is a peacock among the chain-store pigeons on Regent Street. In the 19th century, Liberty's designers, leaders in the art nouveau, Arts and Crafts, and aesthetic movements, created classic fabric and home-furnishing designs. Those Liberty prints are still world famous today, and grace fashionable goods, from silk kimonos to embossed leather bags, wallets, and photo albums. Inside, the store is a labyrinth of nooks and crannies stuffed with goodies. The carpet and furniture departments are worth a look even if you're not buying. The jewelry and accessories departments contrast the unusual and bohemian with deluxe international labels. Fashion, for men and women, focuses on quality and beautiful fabric. ✉ *Regent St., Mayfair* ☎ *020/7734–1234* Ⓤ *Oxford Circus.*

Marks & Spencer. You'd be hard-pressed to find a Briton who doesn't have something in their closet from Marks & Spencer (or "Marks and Sparks" as it's affectionately known). This major chain whips up classic, dependable clothing for men, women, and children. It occasionally scores a fashion hit with its Per Una and Autograph lines, but the best buys here are the classics, such as cashmere and wool sweaters, socks and undies, and (don't laugh) machine-washable suits. The food department at M&S is consistently superb, and a great place to pick up a sandwich or premade salad on the go. (Look for their M&S Simply Food stores all over town.) The Marble Arch branch is the flagship, and has a fast stock turnover, but the 173 Oxford Street location also has an extensive fashion department. ✉ *458 Oxford St., Marble Arch* ☎ *020/7935–7954* Ⓤ *Marble Arch* ✉ *173 Oxford St., Oxford Circus* ☎ *020/7437–7722* Ⓤ *Oxford Circus.*

Fodor's Choice
★

Selfridges. This giant, bustling store is giving Harvey Nicks a run for its money as London's leading fashion department store. It's packed to the rafters with clothes for everyone in the family, from midpriced lines to the latest catwalk names. The store continues to break ground with its striking modern design—especially the men's and women's high-fashion Superbrands sections, and the ground-floor Wonder Room, which showcases extravagant jewelry and unusual gifts. The frenetic cosmetics department is, according to the store, the largest in Europe. There are so many zones with pulsating music that merge into one another—from fashion to sports gear to audio equipment—that you practically need a map. ■TIP➔ Take a break with a glass of wine from the Wonder Bar, or pick up some rare tea in the Food Hall as a gift. ✉ *400 Oxford St., Oxford Street* ☎ *0800/123–400* Ⓤ *Bond St.*

FOOD AND DRINK

London excels at posh nosh, and the selection has gotten even bigger with European integration—but be prepared to pay quite a lot for it. The Food Halls at Harrods are internationally famous, almost as much for the beautiful displays and ceramic-tile ceilings as for the packaged teas, chocolates, biscuits, fresh produce, fish, and game. Selfridges is less daunting but more international in its selection, and the grande dame of London food halls is Fortnum & Mason. Marks & Spencer, almost as well known for its high-quality ready-made meals as its undies, has M&S Simply Food stores around town.

Berry Bros. & Rudd. Although wine is sold in British supermarkets and there are decent High-street chains for wine (like Oddbins and Nicolas), try Berry Bros. & Rudd for special bottles and a unique shopping experience. A family-run wine business since 1698, "BBR" stores its vintage bottles and casks in vaulted cellars that are more than 300 years old. The shop is charmingly quirky and the staff is extremely knowledgeable—and not snooty if your budget isn't huge. ☒ *3 St. James's St., St. James's* ☎ *020/7396–9600* ⊕ *www.bbr.com* ⊙ *Closed Sun.* Ⓤ *Green Park.*

Charbonnel et Walker. Britain's master chocolatier since 1875, this Mayfair shop specializes in traditional sweets (violet and rose-petal creams, for example) and was serving up beautifully packaged, high-quality chocolates long before most of the fashionable new brands appeared. ■TIP➜ Some of their "drawing room" boxes are real works of art, and their drinking chocolate—coarsely grated fine chocolate in a tin—is worth carrying home in a suitcase. ☒ *One The Royal Arcade, 28 Old Bond St., Mayfair* ☎ *020/7491–0939* ⊙ *Closed Sun.* Ⓤ *Green Park.*

Fortnum & Mason. Although it's the Queen's grocer, this store is, paradoxically, the most egalitarian of gift shops. It has plenty of irresistibly packaged luxury foods, stamped with the gold BY APPOINTMENT crest, for less than £5, which make ideal gifts. Try the teas, preserves (unusual products include rose-petal jelly), condiments, chocolate, tins of pâté, Gentleman's Relish (anchovy paste), or a box of Duchy Originals oatcakes—like Paul Newman, the Prince of Wales has gone into the retail food business. Fortnum's celebrated its tercentenary in 2007 with a major refurbishment—although the impeccably mannered staff still sport traditional tailcoats. The gleaming food hall spans two floors, and there's also a sleek wine bar designed by David Collins. The rest of the store is devoted to upscale gifts, toiletries, and housewares, and there are four more restaurants to choose from, including an indulgent ice-cream parlor. ☒ *181 Piccadilly, St. James's* ☎ *020/7734–8040* Ⓜ *Green Park.*

Fodor's Choice ★

L'Artisan du Chocolat. Praised by top chefs Gordon Ramsay and Heston Blumenthal, L'Artisan raises chocolate to an art form. Its abstract "Couture" chocolates are infused with fruits, nuts, and spices (including such exotic flavorings as Szechuan pepper and tobacco). It is also one of the few chocolate shops in the world that makes liquid salted caramels. Leave the kiddies at home, though; this shop is total wish fulfillment for grown-up chocolate lovers. ☒ *89 Lower Sloane St., Chelsea* ☎ *020/7824–8365* Ⓤ *Sloane Sq.*

★ **Paxton & Whitfield.** This is the most venerable of London's cheese shops, in business for more than 200 years. The fabulous aromas come from some of the world's greatest cheeses, including many British varieties, stacked on straw on refrigerated shelves or laid out on a marble-top counter. Samples are set out for tasting. British ham, pâtés, condiments,

18

preserves, and wines are also stocked, and the staff will advise on the best bottle to complement your cheese. ✉ *93 Jermyn St., St. James's* ☎ *020/7930–0259* ✆ *Closed Sun.* Ⓤ *Piccadilly Circus, Green Park.*

The Vintage House. If whisky is more to your taste than wine, you may want to visit the Vintage House, which has the country's largest selection of single malts (more than 1,400), many notable for their age. The shop is open late—to 11 PM most nights. ✉ *42 Old Compton St., Soho* ☎ *020/7437–2592* Ⓤ *Piccadilly Circus, Leicester Sq.*

HOME DECOR

London's main department stores have just about everything you might need; John Lewis, on Oxford Street, W1, is especially good for practical items, such as kitchen equipment. Terence Conran no longer owns Habitat, but his good-design-on-a-budget philosophy is still apparent. For something more unusual, head to Cheshire Street in the East End. Independent home-design shops have sprouted up here over the past few years, including the wonderfully British Labour & Wait, which sells stylish yet practical goods. Most are open only on weekends, when the Brick Lane and Spitalfields markets bring customers to the area.

Cath Kidston. If you love chintz and bright patterns, then stop by Cath Kidston. Her signature look is bright, girly prints—ginghams, polka dots, and miles and miles of roses—pasted over everything in sight, from ceramics and bed linens to fine china, stationery, and dog beds. There are a few clothing and nightwear lines for women and children, along with handbags and totes, but everything in this shop is basically a canvas for Kidston's sugary prints. ✉ *28–32 Shelton St., Covent Garden* ☎ *020/7836–4803* Ⓤ *Covent Garden.*

★ **Conran Shop.** This is the domain of Sir Terence Conran, who has been informing British taste since he opened Habitat in the '60s. (Although no longer associated with Habitat, the stores are still a bastion of clean, unfussy modernist design—check out the flagship on Tottenham Court Road.) Home enhancers from furniture to stemware—both handmade and mass produced, by famous names and young designers—are displayed in a suitably gorgeous building that is a modernist design landmark in its own right. Both the flagship store and the branch on Marylebone High Street, Marylebone, W1, are bursting with great gifts ✉ *Michelin House, 81 Fulham Rd., Chelsea* ☎ *020/7589–7401* Ⓤ *South Kensington.*

Fodor'sChoice
★ **Mint.** Owner Lina Kanafani has scoured the globe to stock an eclectic mix of furniture, art, ceramics, and home accessories. Mint also showcases works by up-and-coming designers and sells plenty of limited edition and one-off pieces. If you don't want to ship a couch home, consider a miniature flower vase or a handmade ceramic pitcher. ✉ *2 North Terrace* ☎ *020/225–2228* Ⓤ *Bond St.*

TwentyTwentyOne. Open since 1996, TwentyTwentyOne showcases the best in both modern and vintage furniture. There are design classics like a chaise longue from Le Corbusier, as well curvy daybeds from designer Jacob Pringiers. The kids' range is particularly cool, such as the plastic

BRING A BIT OF ENGLAND HOME

To avoid panic-buying a bulk pack of Cadbury chocolate or "My sister went to London." T-shirt at Heathrow, it's wise to plan your gift purchasing with care. For everything under one roof, unique department store Liberty is hard to beat—here, you'll find everything from exquisite Miller Harris fragrances by British perfumer Lyn Harris to small leather goods embossed with the famous Liberty prints. Fortnum & Mason is also a good bet for traditional offerings, such as leather-covered hip flasks and its beautifully packaged biscuits, teas, and unusual condiments. For the menfolk back home, consider some traditional shaving cream from Geo. F. Trumper. The museum shops are also bursting with original gift ideas, from Britart books and posters at Tate Modern to double-decker bus models and Tube-map mouse mats at the recently refurbished London Transport Museum. Also check out the craft showrooms listed under Applied Arts & Handicrafts for truly unique items. The shops below will further inspire—and are all close to each other for easy browsing.

A. Gold. All the foodstuffs sold in this Dickensian-looking shop, occupying an old milliner's premises near Spitalfields Market, are sourced or grown in the United Kingdom. A bottle of mead, a jar of English wildflower honey, or Somerset brandy are all great Brit gifts. Stylish gift baskets and old-fashioned picnic hampers are available. ⊠ *42 Brushfield St., East End* ☎ *020/7247–2487* Ⓤ *Liverpool St.*

Geo F. Trumper. If you don't have time for an old-fashioned hot towel shave here, pick up some accessories to take home for yourself and as a gift. The Extract of West Indian Lime is a popular, zingy aftershave, or pick up a Coconut Oil Shaving Soap, which comes in a hand-turned wooden bowl. There is also a store at 9 Curzon Street in Mayfair. ⊠ *20 Jermyn St., St. James's* ☎ *020/7734–1370* ⊘ *Closed Sun.* Ⓤ *Piccadilly Circus.*

Labour & Wait. Although household items like colanders and clothespins may not sound like ideal souvenirs, this shop may make you reconsider. The owners are on a mission to revive functional, old-fashioned British goods, such as enamel kitchenware, "Brown Betty" glazed teapots, Guernsey sweaters, and vintage Welsh blankets. ⊠ *18 Cheshire St., East End* ☎ *020/7729–6253* ⊘ *Closed Mon., Tues., Thurs.* Ⓤ *Aldgate East, Liverpool St.*

National Trust Gift Shop. If you can't get to one of the country houses owned by the Trust, then this shop–information center in the old Blewcoat School is the next best thing. The infinitely original and covetable gifts include neat pots of preserves, chocolate, china, books, body-care products, and more, whose origins and design are based upon the Trust houses and estates around the nation. ⊠ *23 Caxton St., Westminster* ☎ *020/7222–2877* ⊘ *Closed weekends* Ⓤ *St. James's Park.*

Shelf. On the same street as Labour & Wait, this gift shop, run by a pair of artist/designers, sells stationery, books, small household items, and original artworks and oddities made in London and Europe. ⊠ *40 Cheshire St., East End* ☎ *020/7739–9444* ⊘ *By appointment only Mon.–Thurs.* Ⓤ *Aldgate East, Liverpool St.*

18

elephants designed by the Eames brothers, and small accessories like tote bags and cushion covers will easily fit into your luggage. ⊠ *274 Upper St., Islington* ☎ *020/7288–1996* Ⓤ *Highbury & Islington.*

CHINA AND GLASS

English bone china is legendary, and the famous brands—Royal Doulton, Spode, Wedgwood, Minton, and the like—are still made in England, most in the Staffordshire towns around Stoke-on-Trent known as "The Potteries." The top brands are all over London, and Harrods and Selfridges both have excellent selections.

Emma Bridgewater. Look here for fun and funky casual plates, mugs, jugs, and breakfast tableware embellished with polka dots, hens, hearts and flowers, amusing mottoes, or matter-of-fact labels (sugar or coffee). ⊠ *81A Marylebone High St., Marylebone* ☎ *020/7486–6897* Ⓤ *Baker St., Regent's Park.*

Thomas Goode. This spacious luxury homeware shop has been at the same smart Mayfair address since 1827. The china, silver, crystal, and linens are either of the store's own design and manufacture or are simply the best that money can buy. Originally, customers here were mainly international royals and heads of state. The store still holds three royal warrants, but anyone who can afford it can have their own bespoke set of china. ■TIP→ If such luxury is beyond you, visit anyway for the shop's archive of antique plates and those designed for royalty, including a pattern for Charles and Diana's wedding. ⊠ *19 S. Audley St., Mayfair* ☎ *020/7499–2823* Ⓤ *Green Park, Marble Arch.*

JEWELRY

If you are suddenly overcome with the need to invest in serious rocks, London won't let you down. All the major international players are here: Cartier, Tiffany, Bulgari, Fred, Boucheron, De Beers, Van Cleef and Arpels, Graff, David Morris, and Britain's own Mappin & Webb among them. Bond Street, in particular, is good hunting grounds for megawatt stocking fillers. ■TIP→ Bargain hunters who know their gems head for Hatton Garden, London's traditional diamond center. It's lined with small, independent dealers. For a selection of unusual designer jewelry under one roof, try Liberty, Selfridges, or Fenwick. Widespread chain Links of London is a good bet for unfussy sterling silver and gold pieces, especially charm bracelets and cufflinks, and Lesley Craze Gallery is strong on handcrafted jewelry.

★ **Asprey.** Exquisite jewelry and gifts are displayed in a discreet and very British environment at the "global flagship" store, designed by Lord Foster and British interior designer David Mlinaric. The setting oozes money, good taste, and comfort. If you're in the market for an immaculate 1930s cigarette case, a crystal vase, a lizard-bound diary, or a pair of pavé diamond and sapphire earrings, you won't be disappointed. Bespoke jewelry is available as well. ⊠ *167 New Bond St., Mayfair* ☎ *020/7493–6767* Ⓤ *Green Park*

★ **Butler & Wilson.** Long before anybody ever heard the word bling, this shop was marketing the look—in diamanté, colored rhinestones, and crystal—to movie stars and secretaries alike. Specialists in bold costume jewelry, they've added semiprecious stones to the collections and the look is anything but subtle, so it may not suit all tastes unless you're in the market for a rhinestone Union Jack pin. Even if you're not a fan, the shop is worth a visit for its vintage (and vintage-influenced) clothes, once used only to display the jewelry. There's also another shop at 20 South Molton Street. ✉ *189 Fulham Rd., Chelsea* ☎ *020/7352–8255* Ⓤ *South Kensington.*

Garrard. Formally known as "Garrard, the Crown Jeweler," this is the company that, since Queen Victoria's day, has set the Kohinoor diamond into more than one royal crown. Many of the company's jewels can be found in the Tower of London. Today, the focus is on diamonds and precious gems in simple, classic settings, and the store also sells silver accessories. Although some collections such as Knightrider and the Wings line (featuring winged hoop earrings and pendants) are definitely bling, tradition rules, and you can still drop in to pick up a jeweled tiara. ✉ *24 Albemarle St., Mayfair* ☎ *0870/871–8888* Ⓤ *Green Park.*

★ **Kabiri.** A dazzling array of exciting contemporary jewelry by emerging and established designers from around the world is packed into this small shop. There is something to suit most budgets and tastes, from flamboyant statement pieces to subtle, delicate adornment. Look out for British talent Johanne Mills, Scott Stephen, and Tatty Devine, among many others. ✉ *37 Marylebone High St., Marylebone* ☎ *020/7224–1808* Ⓤ *Baker St., Regent's Park.*

18

MUSIC

Although their supremacy is increasingly challenged by Internet downloads, global megastores such as HMV and Zavvi (formerly Virgin Megastore) are still busy. There are also specialty stores galore for cutting-edge music mixed by club DJs, and for stocking up your own collection of good old-fashioned vinyl. ■**TIP→ Consider that CDs cost anywhere from 10% to as much as 50% more in the United Kingdom than they do in North America. So look for the kind of music you really can't find at home.** Long-standing independent record-shop enclave Berwick Street, in Soho, W1, has seen some recent closures, but several shops remain, including the wide-ranging Sister Ray (Nos. 34–35), and Vinyl Junkies (No. 94), and there are more dotted in surrounding streets. Camden Market is also good for a browse through secondhand and independent music stores.

BM Soho. House, drum 'n' bass, electro, dubstep—this shop (formerly Blackmarket Records) stocks the hottest club music around. They carry some CDs, but this is really a shop for vinyl lovers. ⊠ *25 D'Arblay St., Soho* ☎ *020/7437–0478* Ⓤ *Oxford Circus, Tottenham Court Rd.*

MDC Music & Movies. Perfectly placed for music lovers attending concerts at the Royal Festival Hall, classical specialist MDC also stocks jazz and world music. Staff here, and at sister shop MDC Opera next to the ENO Coliseum, are knowledgeable and helpful. ⊠ *Festival Riverside, Royal Festival Hall, South Bank* ☎ *020/7620–0198* Ⓤ *Waterloo.*

Music & Video Exchange. This store—actually a conglomeration of several shops on Notting Hill Gate—is a convenient destination for seekers of unusual and mainstream chart music as well as classical and pop. Rare records and CDs are upstairs, the soul and dance branch is at No. 42, and the classical branch is at No. 36. There are also branches in Soho, Greenwich, and Camden. ⊠ *38 Notting Hill Gate, Notting Hill* ☎ *020/7243–8574* Ⓤ *Notting Hill Gate.*

★ **Rough Trade East.** Whereas some London record stores are struggling, this veteran indie-music specialist seems to have gotten the formula right—in 2007 it opened this spacious new East End branch that's as much a hangout as a shop, complete with a stage for live gigs, a café, and even Internet access. ⊠ *Dray Walk, Old Truman Brewery, 91 Brick La., East End* ☎ *020/7392–7788* Ⓤ *Liverpool St.*

SHOES

It's no accident that Manolo Blahnik, the star footwear designer, made his name in London and still chooses to live here. The man who has shod fashionable women from Audrey Hepburn to Kate Moss and the *Sex and the City* girls still trades from his original shop in Chelsea, off the King's Road. Jimmy Choo is another "native son" who began his career quietly in London's East End before Tamara Mellon turned his name into a global luxury brand. The British capital is still a hotbed of shoemaking talent: Georgina Goodman, Beatrix Ong, and Rupert Sanderson are some of the most exciting names of the moment. Stop in at one of the King's Road branches of Office, Kurt Geiger, or Kate Kuba for British-designed shoes at slightly more affordable prices.

★ **Beatrix Ong.** This young designer trained under Jimmy Choo, and her collection is just as sexy and bold. Her Burlington Arcade shops sells a ready-to-wear collection of strappy sandals and stilettos, and brides-to-be are also well catered to. ⊠ *Jaeger, 200/206 Regent St.* ☎ *020/979–1100 Ext. 4* Ⓤ *Oxford Circus.*

Emma Hope. The signature look at Emma Hope is vintage inspired. Mules and kitten-heel shoes have exquisite embroidery and beading. The ballet flats will appeal to those who favor comfort, but the filigree stilettos and bejeweled court shoes are the real showstoppers. Her stores also stock shoes and accessories for men. ⊠ *207 Westbourne Grove, Notting Hill* ☎ *020/7313–7490* Ⓤ *Notting Hill Gate.*

Georgina Goodman. Former fashion stylist Georgina Goodman's original, colorful designs for women have been praised by the great Manolo himself. Featuring such signature flourishes as hand-painted leather and unusual heel shapes, her footwear is influenced by, but not enslaved to, current fashion. The pretty flat "slippers" in seasonally changing materials are affordable best sellers. ✉ *44 Old Bond St., Mayfair* ☎ *020/7493–7673* ☉ *Closed Sun.* Ⓤ *Green Park*.

Jimmy Choo. It's the name on every supermodel's and fashion editor's feet, even though it's Tamara Mellon who launched and owns the company. The brand's exquisite, elegant designs combine luxurious materials and details with shapes (pointy toes and slim high heels are signatures) that are classic enough to have fashion staying power—essential given the prices. The handbags are also a hit with fans. ✉ *32 Sloane St., Knightsbridge* ☎ *020/7823–1051* Ⓤ *Knightsbridge*.

★ **Manolo Blahnik.** Blink and you'll miss the discreet sign of this little shoe shop. Here, in the heart of Chelsea, the man who single-handedly managed to revive the sexy stiletto and make it classier than ever has been trading since 1973. It's a must for shoe lovers with a healthy budget. If you're wearing your Manolos, hop on a bus or into a cab—the nearest Tube is about a mile and a half away. ✉ *49–51 Old Church St., Chelsea* ☎ *020/7352–3863* ☉ *Closed Sun.* Ⓤ *Sloane Sq.*

Office. Inexpensive but imaginative takes on catwalk looks are the stock in trade at this popular chain. Styles for men and women feature trend-conscious shapes and funky patterns and finishes. Upscale sibling stores Poste (✉ *10 S. Molton St., W1*) and Poste Mistress (✉ *61–63 Monmouth St., Covent Garden WC2*) stock cutting-edge designer shoes for men and women, respectively. ✉ *57 Neal St., Covent Garden* ☎ *020/7379–1896* Ⓤ *Covent Garden*.

★ **Rupert Sanderson.** Designed in London and made in Italy, Sanderson's elegant shoes have been a huge hit in fashion circles. Ladylike styles, bright colors, smart details, and a penchant for peep toes are signature elements. Prices reflect the impeccable craftsmanship. There's now a tiny outpost next to Harrods at 2A Hans Road, SW3. ✉ *33 Bruton Pl., Mayfair* ☎ *0207/491–2220* ☉ *Closed Sun.* Ⓤ *Bond St., Green Park*.

18

STATIONERY AND GRAPHIC ARTS

Whether you're looking for monogrammed calling cards or a pretty box of note cards to bring back as a gift, you're in luck. At the top of the range is Smythson, where many a socialite and celebrity have their personal stationery made, and shops like Paperchase are crammed with brightly colored notebooks and writing accessories.

Green & Stone. This fabulous cave of artists' materials, papers, art books, easels, and mannequins is one of the longest-running shops on the King's Road, with a distinguished arts pedigree. It began life in 1927 as part of the Chenil Gallery, under the directorship of Augustus John and George Bernard Shaw. At the current location since 1934, it also has a framing service, antique paint boxes, and artists' tools. ✉ *259 King's Rd., Chelsea* ☎ *020/7352–0837* Ⓤ *Sloane Sq.*

Paperchase. The stationery superstore of London, it sells writing paper in every conceivable shade and in a dozen mediums. There are lovely cards, artists' materials, notebooks, and loose stationery. The three-floor store has a café. Other branches in London include 289 King's Road, and 13 The Piazza, Covent Garden. ✉ *213–215 Tottenham Court Rd., Bloomsbury* ☎ *020/7467–6200* Ⓤ *Goodge St.*

★ **Smythson of Bond Street.** Hands down, this is the most elegant stationer in Britain. No hostess of any standing would consider having a leather-bound guest book made by anyone else, and the shop's distinctive pale-blue–page diaries and social stationery are British through and through. Bespoke stationery sets come with a form and a sample so that recipients can personalize their gift. Smythson also produces a small range of leather handbags and purses. There are branches on Sloane Street, in Harvey Nicks, Harrods, and at Selfridges. ✉ *40 New Bond St., Mayfair* ☎ *020/7629–8558* Ⓤ *Bond St., Green Park.*

TOYS AND MODELS

If you're traveling with kids in tow, there are plenty of shops that cater to children. Forget about taking them to check out the latest game system; London is the place to shop for traditional toys like soldiers, puppets, and teddy bears.

Armoury of St. James's. The fine toy soldiers and military models in stock here are collectors' items. Painted and mounted knights only 6 inches high can cost more than £1,200 (though figures start at a mere £7.50 for a Beefeater). Besides lead and tin soldiers, the shop has regimental brooches, porcelain figures, military memorabilia, and military antiques. ✉ *17 Piccadilly Arcade, St. James's* ☎ *020/7493–5082* ☉ *Closed Sun.* Ⓤ *Piccadilly Circus, Green Park.*

Benjamin Pollock's Toyshop. This independently owned Covent Garden shop carries on in the tradition of its founder and namesake, who sold "theatrical sheets" for toy theaters from the mid-19th century to his death in 1937. Robert Louis Stevenson was a fan who wrote, "If you love art, folly, or the bright eyes of children, speed to Pollock's." Magical toy theaters are the main stock in trade, but nostalgic puppets, mechanical toys, and zoetropes are also available. ✉ *44 The Market, Covent Garden Piazza* ☎ *020/7379–7866* Ⓤ *Covent Garden.*

Fodor's Choice
★ **Hamleys.** Every London child puts a trip to Hamleys at the top of his or her wish list. A Regent Street institution, the shop has demonstrations, a play area, a café, and every cool toy on the planet—as soon as it's launched. The huge stock, including six floors of toys and games for children and adults, ranges from traditional teddy bears to all the latest technological gimmickry. It's a mad rush at Christmastime, but Santa's grotto is one of the best in town. ✉ *188–196 Regent St., Soho* ☎ *0871/704–1977* Ⓤ *Oxford Circus.*

TO MARKET, TO MARKET

Londoners love a good market. With their cluttered stalls and crowds of people, they are a visible reminder that, in this world of global chain stores and supermarkets, London is still, in many respects, an Old World European city.

Every neighborhood has its cluster of fruit, vegetable, and flower stalls, or its weekend car-boot sales—gigantic garage sales where ordinary people pay a fiver for the privilege of selling their castoffs. Some, like Broadway Market in London Fields, run for miles. Others, like Brixton Market, Europe's biggest Caribbean-food market, featuring more than 300 stalls, specialize in ethnic ingredients and products. Still others crop up in the most unexpected places: on Berwick Street in the heart of Soho, for example, media moguls, designers, ad execs, actors, dancers, and ladies of the night mingle over the punnets of strawberries, wedges of cheddar, and slabs of wet fish.

The big specialty markets, traditionally open on weekends, are not only great for the occasional bargain but also for people-watching, photo ops, and all around great days out. And though the markets are popular with visitors, they aren't tourist traps. In fact, browsing the London markets is one of the few activities in London where natives and tourists mix and enjoy themselves as equals.

PORTOBELLO ROAD MARKET

🕐 Sat. 8 AM–6 PM

✉ Portobello Rd., Notting Hill

Ⓤ Ladbroke Grove (Hammersmith & City Line), Notting Hill (District, Circle, or Central Line)

☞ Antiques, fruits and vegetables, vintage clothing, household goods

★ **Fodor's Choice** **London's most famous market** still wins the prize for the all-around best. It sits in a lively multicultural part of town; the 1,500-odd antiques dealers don't rip you off (although you should haggle where you can); and it stretches over a mile, changing character completely as it goes.

The southern end is lined with antiques shops and arcades; the middle, above Elgin Crescent, is where locals buy fruits and vegetables. This middle area was the setting for the lovely sequence in the movie *Notting Hill* where Hugh Grant walks along the market and through the changing seasons. The section near the elevated highway (called the Westway) has the best flea market in town, with vintage-clothing stores along the edges. Here, young designers sell their wares in and around the Portobello Green arcade. After that, the market trails off into a giant rummage sale of the kinds of cheap household goods the British call tat.

Some say Portobello Road has become a bit of a tourist trap, but if you acknowledge that it's a circus and get into the spirit, it's a lot of fun. Perhaps you won't find many bargains, but this is such a cool part of town that just hanging out is a good enough excuse to come. There are some food and flower stalls throughout the week, but to see the market in full swing, Saturday is the only day to come.

A PORTOBELLO DAY

In good weather the market gets very crowded by midday. For a Londoner's day at Portobello, come as early as you can (7 AM) and enjoy the market when the traders have time for a chat and you can actually get near the stalls. By 10:30 you'll have seen plenty of the market and can stop for a late breakfast or brunch at the **Electric Brasserie** (✉ 191 Portobello Rd. ☎ 020/7908–9696), next to the area's famous Electric Cinema. If you still have the will to shop, move on to the less crowded boutiques along Westbourne Grove, Blenheim Crescent, or Ledbury Road.

BOROUGH MARKET

🕐 Thurs. 11–5, Fri. noon–6, Sat. 8–5

✉ Borough High St., South Bank

Ⓤ London Bridge (Jubilee or Northern Line),

🍽 Cheese, olives, coffee, baked goods, meats, fish, fruits, vegetables

★ **There's been a market** in Borough since Roman times. This one, spread under the arches and railway tracks leading to London Bridge Station, is the successor to a medieval market once held on London Bridge. Post-millennium, it has been transformed from a noisy collection of local stalls to a trendy foodie center. Named the best market in London by a local magazine and the best market in Britain by a national newspaper, the Farmers Market held on Thursdays (some stalls), Fridays and Saturdays has attracted some of London's best merchants of comestibles. Fresh coffees, gorgeous cheeses, olives, and baked goods complement the organically farmed meats, fresh fish, fruit, and veggies.

Don't make any other lunch plans for the day; celebrity chef Jamie Oliver's scallop man cooks them up fresh from the Dorset coast at Shell Seekers; wild boar sausages sizzle on a grill, and there is much more that's tempting to gobble on the spot. There are chocolates, preserves, and Mrs. Bassa's handmade Indian condiments to take home, but the best souvenirs are the memories. If you'd rather eat sitting down, pop into the sleek reaturant Roast, which specializes in local seasonal food—much of it purchased at the market.

A BARGAIN DAY ON THE SOUTH BANK

Combine a visit to the Tate Modern (free) and a walk across the Millennium Bridge from the Tate to St. Paul's with a Thames-side picnic of goodies foraged at Borough Market. There are gourmet breads and farmhouse cheeses from France and Italy.

Or how about a wedge of Stinking Bishop cheese (Wallace and Gromit's favorite) from Neal's Yard Dairy? Fishmonger Applebee's serves up freshly sautéed garlic prawns in a wrap with chili and crème fraîche.

A PUB RIGHT OUT OF DICKENS

On the way back to Borough Tube station, stop for a pint at the **George Inn** (✉ 77 Borough High St., Southwark SE1 ☎ 020/7407-2056 Ⓤ London Bridge), mentioned by Dickens in *Little Dorrit*. This 17th-century coaching inn was a famous terminus in its day, and is the last galleried inn in London. Now owned by the National Trust, it is leased to a private company and still operates as a pub.

THE EAST END MARKETS

Brick Lane. The noisy center of the Bengali community is a hubbub of buying and selling. Sunday stalls have food, hardware, household goods, electrical goods, books, bikes, shoes, clothes, spices, and saris. The CDs and DVDs are as likely as not to be counterfeit, and the bargain iron may not have a plug—so be careful. But people come more to enjoy the ethnic buzz, eat curries and Bengali sweets, or indulge in salt beef on a bagel at Beigel Bake, London's 24-hour bagel bakery, a survivor of the neighborhood's Jewish past. Brick Lane's activity spills over into nearby Petticoat Lane Market with similar goods but less atmosphere.

From Brick Lane it's a stone's throw to the **Columbia Road Flower Market**. It's only 52 stalls, but markets don't get much more photogenic than this. Flowers, shrubs, bulbs, trees, garden tools, and accessories are sold wholesale. The local cafés are superb.

Stop to smell the roses and have Sunday brunch on Columbia Road before plunging into **Spitalfields**. The covered market (once London's wholesale meat market) is at the center of this area's boho revival. The original building has been restored to its Victorian splendor, and a modern shopping complex that respects its character has been developed around it, with a covered area housing additional stalls. Wares include crafts, retro clothing, handmade rugs, soap, and cakes. And, from Spanish tapas to Thai satays, it's possible to eat your way around the world.

BRICK LANE
🕓 Sun. 8 AM–2 PM

✉ Brick La., East End

Ⓤ Aldgate East (Hammersmith & City or District Line), Liverpool Street (Hammersmith & City, District, or Circle Line)

☞ Food, hardware, household goods, electric goods, books, bikes, shoes, clothes, spices, saris

COLUMBIA ROAD FLOWER MARKET
🕓 Sun. 8–4

✉ Columbia Rd., East End

Ⓤ Old Street (Northern Line)

☞ Flowers, shrubs, bulbs, trees, garden tools, accessories

SPITALFIELDS
🕓 Stalls Thurs., Fri. 10–4, Sun. 9–5. Restaurants weekdays 11 AM–11 PM, Sun. 9–5. Retail shops daily 11 AM–7 PM.

✉ Brushfield St., East End

Ⓤ Liverpool St. (Hammersmith & City, Circle, or Bakerloo Line), Aldgate East (Hammersmith & City or District Line)

☞ Crafts, foods, vintage clothing, rugs, soap, cakes

BERMONDSEY ANTIQUES MARKET

- 🕐 Fri. 4 AM–about 1 PM
- ✉ Long La. and Bermondsey Sq., South Bank
- Ⓤ London Bridge (Jubilee or Northern Line), Borough (Nothern Line)
- ☞ Antiques (silverware, paintings, furniture)

Come before dawn and bring a flashlight to bag a bargain antique at this famous market. Dealers arrive as early as 4 AM to snap up the best bric-a-brac and silverware, paintings, objets d'art, fine arts, and furniture. The early start grew out of a wrinkle in the law under which thieves could sell stolen goods with impunity in the hours of darkness when provenance could not be ascertained. That law was changed, and the market has been shrinking ever since.

What should be one of London's most important antiques markets is in decline and in desperate need of a significant rebrand to survive. The recent establishment of the Saturday morning Bermondsey Farmer's Market, as well as the 2009 redevelopment of Bermondsey Square (⊕ www.bermondseysquare.co.uk) should attract more customers to the Antiques Market. The square now includes a hotel, an arthouse cinema, shops, and restaurants.

THE CAMDEN MARKETS

CAMDEN MARKET
🕐 Daily 9:30 AM–6 PM

CAMDEN LOCK MARKET, STABLES MARKET, AND CANAL MARKET
🕐 Daily 10–6

ELECTRIC MARKET
🕐 Sun. 10–5

- ✉ Camden Town
- Ⓤ Camden Town, Chalk Farm (Northern Line)
- ☞ Vintage clothing, antiques, jewelry, candlesticks, ceramics, mirrors, toys

This area's actually several markets gathered around a pair of locks in the Regent's Canal. Camden Lock Market proper began in 1973 on the site of a former timber yard. The lock studios attracted artists with reasonable rents and gave customers the chance to see goods being made. Today, the market includes some of London's most creative types, with products designed on site and market stalls offering a spectacular array of merchandise: vintage and new clothes, antiques and junk, jewelry and scarves, candlesticks, ceramics, mirrors, and toys.

The markets on Camden High Street (both outdoors and within the Electric Ballroom) mainly sell cheap T-shirts, secondhand clothes, and tacky pop-culture paraphernalia; it's best to head to Camden Lock and Stable Markets. Though much of the merchandise is youth oriented, the markets have a lively appeal to aging hippies, fashion designers, and anyone with a taste for the bohemian who doesn't mind crowds and a bit of a madhouse scene. Don't miss the Horse Hospital (weekends only) for quirky antiques dealers.

THE GREENWICH MARKET

On weekends, the focus is on crafts, while on Wednesdays it's on fresh produce and housewares, on Thursdays and Fridays it's on antiques: china, old books, cameras, vintage clothing, marine memorabilia, and other curiosities. On weekends, the Village Market down the road offers yet more flea-market miscellany and cheap goods. Less crowded than Camden, less touristy than Covent Garden, this part-indoor, part-outdoor market is surrounded by interesting shops and close to historic sites. If you make a day of it, you can see the Greenwich Observatory and stand on Longitude 0 (marked in brass and stone in front of the observatory). But, sadly, due to setbacks in the Cutty Sark's restoration after fire damage in Spring 2007, the famous tea clipper will be closed until Spring 2011.

🕑 Wed. 11 AM–6 PM
Thurs.–Sun. 10–5:30 PM

✉ Greenwich High Rd., Greenwich

Ⓤ DLR: Cutty Sark for Maritime Greenwich

☞ Antiques, arts, crafts, books, toys, paraphernalia

Know-How

■ **TWO MARKET TIPS TO REMEMBER→** In the end, if you like something and you can afford it, it's worth buying; you're the best judge of that. But it's annoying to buy an "English antique" only to find the Made in China label when you get home. To avoid disappointment:

Look for hallmarks. A lot of what passes for English silver is plate or outright fake. English gold and silver must, by law, be marked with hallmarks that indicate their material and the year in which they were made. Books of hallmarks are inexpensive to buy in London bookshops.

Buy crafts items directly from the makers. Ceramicists, jewelers, needleworkers and other artisans often sell their own work at markets. Besides buying the item, you may have a conversation worth remembering.

■ **MARKET ETIQUETTE →** You've probably heard that you're expected to bargain with the market traders to get the best price. That's true to a degree, but London markets are not Middle Eastern souks, and most bargaining is modest. Unless you are an expert in the item you want to buy and really know how low you can go, don't offer a ridiculously low price. Instead ask the dealer, "Is that the best you can do?" If the dealer is willing to bargain, he or she will suggest a slightly lower price, maybe 10% less. You might try to get another 10% off and end up meeting in the middle.

Side Trips from London

WORD OF MOUTH

"You can do many day trips. Places like Windsor, Hampton Court, Greenwich, Warwick Castle, Canterbury, Cambridge, Bath, and Salisbury (and the list goes on) are very easy to get to via train from London."

—Lori

SIDE TRIPS FROM LONDON PLANNER

Getting Around

Normally the towns covered in this chapter are best reached by train. Bus travel costs less, but can take twice as long. However, train routes throughout Britain are often subject to delays. Wherever you're going, plan ahead: check the latest time-tables before you set off, and try to get an early start. ⇨ *Also see Travel Smart London.*

Station Tips

You can reach any of London's main-line train stations by Tube. London's bus stations can be confusing for the uninitiated. Here's a quick breakdown:

Victoria Coach Station is on Buckingham Palace Road: it's a five-minute walk from Victoria Tube station. This is where to go for coach departures; arrivals are at a different location, a short walk from here.

Victoria Bus Station is where many of the local London bus services arrive and depart, and is directly outside the main exits of the train and Tube stations.

Green Line Coach Station is on Bulleid Way (in front of the Colonnades Shopping Centre on Buckingham Palace Road) and is the departure point for most Green Line and Megabus services.

Visitor Information

Bath (☎ 0906/711–2000 50p per minute, 0844/847–5257 from outside U.K. ⊕ www.visitbath.co.uk). **Brighton** (☎ 0906/711–2255 50p per minute ⊕ www.visitbrighton.com). **Cambridge** (☎ 0871/226–8006, 1223/464732 from outside U.K. ⊕ www.visitcambridge.org). **Canterbury** (☎ 01227/378100 ⊕ www.canterbury.co.uk). **Oxford** (☎ 01865/252–2000 ⊕ www.visitoxford.org). **Stratford-upon-Avon** (☎ 0870/160–7930 ⊕ www.shakespeare-country.co.uk). **Windsor** (☎ 01753/743900 ⊕ www.windsor.gov.uk).

To Get To . . .

	TAKE THE TRAIN FROM . . .	TAKE THE BUS FROM . . .
Bath	Paddington (90 minutes; half-hourly departures)	Victoria Coach Station (3 hours, 50 minutes; hourly departures)
Brighton	Victoria (1–1½ hours; half hourly) or London Bridge (95 minutes; departures every 15 minutes)	Victoria Coach (2 hours; hourly)
Cambridge	King's Cross (1 hour; hourly)	Victoria Coach (about 2 hours; hourly)
Canterbury	Victoria (85 minutes; hourly)	Victoria Coach (1 hour, 50 minutes; hourly)
Oxford	Paddington (55 minutes; half-hourly)	Victoria Coach (1 hour, 40 minutes; half-hourly)
Stratford-upon-Avon	Paddington (2 hours, 20 minutes); Marylebone (2½ hours); or Euston (2½ hours)	Victoria Coach (3 hours; about 3 times daily)
Windsor	Paddington (40 minutes; hourly) or Waterloo (1 hour; hourly)	Green Line Coach Station (1½ hours)

Updated by
Ellin Stein

London is exciting and entertaining, but it's not all Britain has to offer. If you have even one day to spare, head out of the city. A train ride past hills dotted with sheep, a stroll through a medieval town, or a visit to one of England's great castles could make you feel as though you've added another week to your vacation.

Londoners are undeniably lucky. Few urban populations enjoy such glorious—and easily accessible—options for day-tripping. England is extremely compact, and the train and bus networks, although somewhat inefficient and expensive compared with their European counterparts, are extensive and user-friendly.

Although you could tackle any one of the towns in this chapter on a frenzied day trip—heavy summer crowds make it difficult to cover the sights in a relaxed manner—consider staying for a day or two. You'd then have time to explore a very different England—one blessed with quiet country pubs, tree-lined lanes, and neatly trimmed farms. No matter where you go, lodging reservations are a good idea from June through September, when foreign visitors saturate the English countryside.

19

BATH

115 mi (185 km) west of London.

"I really believe I shall always be talking of Bath . . . I do like it so very much. Oh! Who can ever be tired of Bath?" says Catherine Morland in Jane Austen's *Northanger Abbey*. Today thousands of visitors heartily concur. A remarkably unsullied Georgian city with remnants of its Roman occupation, Bath looks as if John Wood (circa 1705–54), its chief architect; "Beau" Nash (1674–1762), its principal dandy; and Jane Austen (1775–1817) might still be seen strolling on the promenade. Stepping out of the train station puts you right in the center, and Bath is compact enough to explore on foot. A single day is sufficient for you to take in the glorious yellow-stone buildings, tour the Roman baths,

The Great Bath had a vaulted ceiling in Roman times.

and stop for tea, though it will give you only a brief hint of the cultural life that thrives in this vibrant town.

EXPLORING

Bath Abbey was commissioned by God. Really. The design came to Bishop Oliver King in a dream, and was built during the 15th century. Look up at the fan-vaulted ceiling in the nave and the carved angels on the restored West Front. In the **Heritage Vaults** is a museum of archaeological finds, with a scale model of 13th-century Bath. ⊠ *Abbey Churchyard* ☏ *01225/422462* ⊕ *www.bathabbey.org* ✉ *Abbey free, suggested donation £2.50; Heritage Vaults free* ⊘ *Abbey Apr.–Oct., Mon.–Sat. 9–6, Sun. 1–2:30 and 4:30–5:30; Nov.–Mar., Mon.–Sat. 9–4:30, Sun. 1–2:30 and 4:30–5:30. Heritage Vaults Mon.–Sat. 10–4.*

★ Among Bath's remarkable architectural achievements is the **Circus** (⊠ *Intersection of Brock, Gay, and Bennett Sts.*), a perfectly circular ring of three-story stone houses designed by John Wood. The painter Thomas Gainsborough (1727–88) lived at No. 17 from 1766 to 1774.

On the east side of Bath's Circus are thrills for Austen readers: her much-mentioned **Assembly Rooms,** where the upper class would gather for concerts and dances. Within the rooms is the **Fashion Museum,** which displays fashions from the 17th through 21st century. Allow at least an hour to tour the museum. ⊠ *Bennett St.* ☏ *01225/477173* ⊕ *www.fashionmuseum.co.uk* ✉ *£7, combined ticket with Roman Baths £14.50* ⊘ *Mar.–Oct., daily 10:30–5; Nov.–Feb., daily 10:30–4; last admission 1 hr before closing.*

One of the most famous landmarks of the city, **Pulteney Bridge** (⌂ *Off Bridge St. at Grand Parade*), was the great Georgian architect Robert Adam's sole contribution to Bath. In its way, the bridge is as fine as the only other bridge in Europe with shops lining either side: the Ponte Vecchio in Florence.

Fodor's Choice
★
The **Pump Room and Roman Baths** are among the most popular sights outside London. The Romans set about building the baths here around the healing spring of the English goddess Aquae Sulis in AD 60, after wars with the Britons had laid the city to waste. The site became famous as a temple to Minerva, the Roman goddess of wisdom. Legend has it that the first taker of these sacred waters was King Lear's leprous father, Prince Bladud, in the 9th century BC. (Yes, it's claimed he was cured.) The British added the Pump Room—oft-described in Austen's works, and now beautifully restored—in the 18th century. You can drink the spa waters here, or have a more agreeable cup of tea. Below the Pump Room is a museum of quirky objects found during excavations. Allow at least 90 minutes for the museum. ⌂ *Abbey Churchyard* ☎ *01225/477785* ⊕ *www.romanbaths.co.uk* ✉ *Sept.–June £10.50, July and Aug. £11, combined ticket with Fashion Museum £14.50* ☉ *Mar.–June, Sept., and Oct., daily 9–5; July and Aug., daily 9–9; Nov.–Feb., daily 9:30–4:30; last admission 1 hr before closing.*

Fodor's Choice
★
The 18th-century **Royal Crescent** is the most famous site in Bath, and you can't help but see why. Designed by John Wood the Younger, it's perfectly proportioned and beautifully sited, with sweeping views over parkland. A marvelous museum at **Number 1 Royal Crescent** shows life as Beau Nash would have lived it circa 1765. ⌂ *1 Royal Crescent* ☎ *01225/428126* ⊕ *www.bath-preservation-trust.org.uk* ✉ *£5* ☉ *Mid-Feb.–Oct., Tues.–Sun. 10:30–5; Nov., Tues.–Sun. 10:30–4; last admission 30 mins before closing.*

QUICK
BITES

Sally Lunn's Refreshment House & Museum (⌂ *4 N. Parade Passage* ☎ *01225/461634*) claims to be Bath's oldest house (1482). It's famous for the Sally Lunn bun, a light, semisweet bread served with sweet or savory toppings. The cellars hold a museum where you can view the old foundation of the house, plus the original kitchen.

Thermae Bath Spa. This complex of buildings—one from 2006, others dating back to the Regency—houses a spa built on the site of Britain's only natural thermal springs. The naturally heated, open-air rooftop pool offers views over the city as well as a swim. ⌂ *Hot Bath St.* ☎ *01225/331234* ⊕ *www.thermaebathspa.com* ✉ *From £22* ☉ *New Royal Bath, daily 9 AM–10 PM, last admission 7:30. Cross Bath, 10–8, last admission 6:30.*

19

WHERE TO EAT

££–£££
CONTINENTAL
✕ **5 Restaurant.** Just over the Pulteney Bridge from the center of town, this airy bistro, decorated with plants and framed posters, is an ideal spot for a light lunch. The regularly changing modern French and Mediterranean menu includes tasty homemade soups, crostini of goat cheese

and cherry tomatoes, and grilled rib of beef with a red-wine sauce. ⊠ *5 Argyle St.* ☎ *01225/444499* ⊕ *www.no5restaurant.co.uk* ⊟ *AE, DC, MC, V.*

BRIGHTON

52 mi (83 km) south of London.

Ever since the Prince Regent first visited in 1783, Brighton has been England's most exciting seaside city, and today it's as eccentric and cosmopolitan as ever. With its rich cultural mix—Regency architecture, an amusement pier, specialty shops, a large gay community, sidewalk cafés, lively arts, and, of course, the odd and exotic Royal Pavilion—Brighton is a truly extraordinary city by the sea. For most of the 20th century the city was known for its tarnished allure and faded glamour. Happily, a young, bustling spirit has given a face-lift to this ever-popular resort, which shares its city status with neighboring Hove, as genteel a retreat as Brighton is abuzz.

EXPLORING

In the 1850s, the British fell in love with elaborate piers jutting out over the sea and containing, bizarrely, tiny amusement parks.

★ Arguably the most beautiful of them all, **Brighton Pier,** which opened in 1899, followed in the quirky tradition. And today, the white, frilly structure still holds a crowded maze of arcade rooms, cafés and fried-food stalls, and amusement-park rides—including a roller coaster that seems to plummet off the end of the structure. Down the beach from Brighton Pier are the remains of **West Pier** (☎ *01273/321499* ⊕ *www.westpier. co.uk*). Built in 1866, it was the more upscale of Brighton's piers and was for many years the most recognizable landmark of the city. Sadly, storms and fires have ravaged the structure over the last 30 years, leaving only a charred skeleton. Plans have been approved for construction of a £20-million Space Needle–style observation tower where the graceful Victorian structure once touched the shore. Called i360, the tower will carry passengers up 400 feet in a glass pod. After some delays, it's now scheduled to open in 2011. ⊠ *Waterfront along Madeira Dr.* ☎ *01273/609361* ⊕ *www.brightonpier.co.uk* ☜ *Free, costs of rides vary* ⊙ *June–Aug., daily 9 AM–midnight; Sept.–May, daily 10–10.*

The heart of Brighton is the **Steine** (pronounced *steen*), a long, narrow park close to the seafront. This was an open, grassy area with a stream running through it where fishermen dried their nets until the surrounding neighborhood became fashionable in the second half of the 18th century.

Fodor's Choice The most remarkable building on the Steine is unquestionably the ★ extravagant, fairy-tale **Royal Pavilion.** Built by architect Henry Holland in 1787 as a simple seaside villa, the Pavilion was transformed by John Nash between 1815 and 1823 for the Prince Regent (later George IV), who favored an exotic, Eastern design with opulent Chinese interiors. When Queen Victoria came to the throne in 1837, she disapproved of

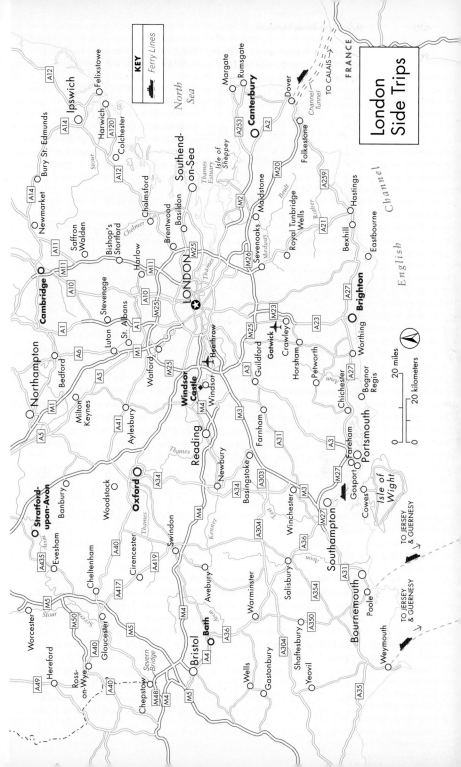

the palace and planned to demolish it. Fortunately, the local council bought it from her, and after a lengthy process of restoration the Pavilion looks much as it did in its Regency heyday. Take particular note of the spectacular **Music Room,** styled as a Chinese pavilion, and the **Banqueting Room,** with its enormous flying-dragon gasolier, or gaslight chandelier, a revolutionary

invention in the early 19th century. The gardens, too, have been restored to Regency splendor, following John Nash's naturalistic design of 1826. ⊠ *Old Steine* ☎ *01273/290900* ⊕ *www.royalpavilion.org.uk* 🗐 *£9.50* ☉ *Oct.–Mar., daily 10–5:15; Apr.–Sept., daily 9:30–5:45; last admission 45 mins before closing.*

The grounds of the Royal Pavilion contain the **Brighton Museum and Art Gallery,** whose buildings were designed as a stable block for the Prince Regent's horses. The museum, which recently underwent a £10 million face-lift, has particularly interesting art nouveau and art deco collections. Look out for Salvador Dalí's famous sofa in the shape of Mae West's lips, and pause at the Balcony Café for its bird's-eye view over the 20th-century Art and Design collection. ⊠ *Royal Pavilion Gardens* ☎ *01273/290900* ⊕ *www.brighton.virtualmuseum.info* 🗐 *Free* ☉ *Tues.–Sun. 10–5. Closed Mon. except public holidays.*

The **Lanes** (⊠ *Bordered by West, North, East, and Prince Albert Sts.*), a maze of alleys and passageways, once held the homes of fishermen and their families. Closed to vehicular traffic, those cobbled streets are now the city's shopping hot spot, filled with interesting restaurants, boutiques, and antiques shops. Seafood restaurants and pubs line the heart of the Lanes, at Market Street and Market Square.

🔄 **Volk's Electric Railway,** built by inventor Magnus Volk in 1883, was the first public electric railroad in Britain. In summer you can take the 1-mi trip along Brighton Beach. ⊠ *Madeira Dr.* ☎ *01273/292718* 🗐 *£1.70 one-way, £2.70 round-trip* ☉ *Late Mar.–Sept., weekdays 10–5, weekends 10–6.*

WHERE TO EAT

££–£££   ✕ **Due South.** Arguably the first high-quality dining option on Brigh-
SEAFOOD   ton's seafront, Due South is really making waves on Brighton's food scene. The menu features clever, classic game and seafood dishes, with locally sourced organic fruit and vegetables. ⊠ *139 Kings Road Arches* ☎ *01273/821218* ⊕ *www.duesouth.co.uk* 🗖 *AE, MC, V.*

££–£££   ✕ **English's of Brighton.** One of the few old-fashioned seafood havens left
SEAFOOD   in England is buried in the Lanes in three fishermen's cottages. It's been a restaurant for more than 150 years and a family business for more than 50. You can eat succulent oysters and other seafood dishes at the counter or take a table in the smart restaurant section. The restaurant's popularity means it's usually busy, and service can sometimes be slow.

⊠ *29–31 East St.* ☎ *01273/327980* ⊕ *www.englishs.co.uk* ▭ *AE, DC, MC, V.*

££–£££
MODERN BRITISH

✕**Havana.** The mock-Cuban building, high ceilings, rattan chairs, tan leather furnishings, and sophisticated food at Havana might make you think you're in London. Don't let that deter you, however—this place is a pleasure. Expect modern twists on British classics: the red mullet fillet, for example, is served with a crispy asparagus tart. The chic bar area is a perfect place to rest your feet at the end of the day. ⊠ *32 Duke St.* ☎ *01273/773388* ⊕ *www.havana.uk.com* ▭ *AE, MC, V.*

££
VEGETARIAN
★

✕**Terre à Terre.** This inspiring vegetarian restaurant is popular, so come early for a light lunch, or book a table for an evening meal. Ravioli stuffed with butternut squash and feta, served with *cavoloneno* and walnut salsa should satisfy most palates, and dishes have names to match their culinary inventiveness, such as Fundamentally Fungus and Thai One On. ⊠ *71 East St.* ☎ *01273/729051* ⊕ *www.terreaterre.co.uk* ▭ *Reservations essential* ▭ *AE, DC, MC, V* ☺ *Closed Mon.*

CAMBRIDGE

60 mi (97 km) north of London.

With the spires of its university buildings framed by towering trees and expansive meadows, its medieval streets and passages enhanced by gardens and riverbanks, the city of Cambridge is among the loveliest in England. The city predates the Roman occupation of Britain, but the university was not founded until the 13th century. There's disagreement about the birth of the university: one story attributes its founding to impoverished students from Oxford, who came in search of eels—a cheap source of nourishment. Today a healthy rivalry persists between the two schools.

This university town may be beautiful, but it's no museum. Even when the students are on vacation, there's a cultural and intellectual buzz here. It's a preserved medieval city of some 109,000 souls and growing, dominated culturally and architecturally by its famous university (whose students make up around one-fifth of the inhabitants), and beautified by parks, gardens, and the quietly flowing River Cam. A quintessential Cambridge pursuit is punting on the Cam (one occupant propels the narrow, square-end, flat-bottom boat with a long pole), followed by a stroll along the Backs, the left bank of the river fringed by St. John's, Trinity, Clare, King's, and Queens' colleges, and by Trinity Hall.

VISITING THE COLLEGES
College visits are certainly a highlight of a Cambridge tour, but remember that the colleges are private residences and workplaces, even when school isn't in session. Each is an independent entity within the university; some are closed to the public, but at others you can see the chapels, dining rooms (called halls), and sometimes the libraries, too. Some colleges charge a small fee for the privilege of nosing around. All are closed during exams, usually from mid-April to late June, and the opening hours often vary. Additionally, all are subject to closures at short notice, especially King's; check the Web sites in advance. For

details about visiting specific colleges not listed here, contact **Cambridge University** (☎ *01223/337733* ⊕ *www.cam.ac.uk*).

By far the best way to gain access without annoying anyone is to join a walking tour led by an official Blue Badge guide—in fact, many areas are off-limits unless you do. The two-hour tours (£8.50–£10) leave Monday–Saturday from the **Tourist Information Centre,** Sunday October–March from outside the Tourist Office. (✉ *The Old Library, Wheeler St.* ☎ *0871/226–8006, 1223/464732 from abroad* ⊕ *www.visitcambridge. org* ⊗ *May–Sept., weekdays 10–5:30, Sat. 10–5, Sun. 11–3; Oct.–Apr., weekdays 10–5:30, Sat. 10–5. Tours: Oct.–Mar., Mon.–Sat. 11:30 and 1:30, Sun. 1:30; Apr.–June, Sept., daily 11:30 and 1:30; July and Aug., daily 10:30, 11:30, 1:30, and 2:30).*

EXPLORING

Emmanuel College (1584) is the alma mater of one John Harvard, who gave his books and his name to the American university. A number of the Pilgrims were Emmanuel alumni; they named Cambridge, Massachusetts, after their onetime home. ✉ *St. Andrew's St.* ☎ *01223/334200* ⊕ *www.emma.cam.ac.uk* ☜ *Free* ⊗ *Daily 9–6.*

FodorsChoice One of England's finest art galleries, the **Fitzwilliam Museum** houses
★ an outstanding collection of art, as well as striking antiquities from ancient Egypt, Greece, and Rome. Highlights include two large Titians, an extensive collection of French impressionist paintings, and many paintings by Matisse and Picasso. The gallery holds occasional free classical music concerts. ✉ *Trumpington St.* ☎ *01223/332900* ⊕ *www. fitzmuseum.cam.ac.uk* ☜ *Free* ⊗ *Tues.–Sat. 10–5, Sun. noon–5.*

FodorsChoice **King's College** (1441) is notable as the site of the world-famous Gothic-
★ style **King's College Chapel** (built 1446–1547). Some deem its great fan-vaulted roof, supported by a delicate tracery of columns, the most glorious example of Perpendicular Gothic in Britain. It's the home of the famous choristers, and, to cap it all, Rubens's *Adoration of the Magi* is tucked away behind the altar. The college's Back Lawn leads down to the river, from which the panorama of college and chapel is one of the university's most photographed views. ✉ *King's Parade* ☎ *01223/331212* ⊕ *www.kings.cam.ac.uk* ☜ *£5* ⊗ *Term time, weekdays 9:30–3:30, Sat. 9:30–3:15, Sun. 1:15–2:15; out of term, Mon.–Sat. 9:30–4:30, Sun. 10–5. Hrs may vary; call in advance or see Web site.*

Pembroke College (1347) has delightful gardens and bowling greens. Its chapel, completed in 1665, was the architect Christopher Wren's first commission. ✉ *Trumpington St.* ☎ *01223/338100* ⊕ *www.pem.cam. ac.uk* ☜ *Free* ⊗ *Daily 9–3.*

In 1284 the Bishop of Ely founded **Peterhouse College,** Cambridge's smallest and oldest college. Take a tranquil walk through its former deer park, by the river side of its ivy-clad buildings. ✉ *Trumpington St.* ☎ *01223/338200* ⊕ *www.pet.cam.ac.uk* ☜ *Free* ⊗ *Daily 9–5 (groups 1–5).*

★ **Queens' College**—Originally established in 1447 as the College of St. Bernard's, one of Cambridge's most eye-catching colleges was re-founded a year later by Margaret of Anjou, queen of Henry VI, and then re-founded again in 1475 by Elizabeth, queen of Edward IV—hence the new name.

Cross over the Cam via the **Wooden Bridge,** also known as the Mathematical Bridge. A popular myth tells of how it was built by Isaac Newton without any binding save gravity, then dismantled by curious scholars eager to learn Sir Isaac's secret. However, the bridge wasn't actually put together until 1749, 22 years after Newton's death. ⊠ *Queens' La.* ☎ *01223/335511* ⊕ *www.queens.cam.ac.uk* ☞ *£2.50, free Nov.–mid-Mar., closed during exams—call for info* ۞ *Mid-Mar.–Sept., 10–4:30; Oct.–mid-Mar., daily 1:45–4:30.*

The only Cambridge College founded by townspeople (in 1352) is **Corpus Christi College,** whose beautiful, serene, 14th-century Old Court is the oldest college quadrangle in Cambridge. The college's Parker Library contains one of the world's finest collections of medieval manuscripts. ⊠ *Trumpington St.* ☎ *01223/338000* ⊕ *www.corpus.cam.ac.uk* ☞ *Free* ۞ *Daily 2–4.*

St. John's College (1511), the university's second largest, has noted alumni (Wordsworth studied here), a series of beautiful courtyards, and two of the finest sights in town: the **School of Pythagoras,** the oldest house in Cambridge; and the 1831 **Bridge of Sighs,** a replica of its Venetian counterpart. The windowed, covered stone bridge reaches across the Cam to the mock-Gothic New Court (1825–31). The New Court cupola's white crenellations have earned it the nickname "the wedding cake." ⊠ *St. John's St.* ☎ *01223/338600* ⊕ *www.joh.cam.ac.uk* ☞ *£3* ۞ *Mar.–Oct., daily 10–5:30; Nov.–Feb., weekends 10–4.*

Fodor'sChoice
★
Trinity College was founded by Henry VIII in 1546, and has the largest student population of all the colleges. It's also famous for having been attended by Byron, Thackeray, Tennyson, Bertrand Russell, Nabokov, Nehru, and 31 Nobel Prize winners. Many of Trinity's features reflect its status as one of Cambridge's largest colleges, not least its 17th-century "great court," scene of the university race in *Chariots of Fire.* Don't miss the wonderful library by Christopher Wren, where you can see a letter written by alumnus Isaac Newton with early notes on gravity, and A. A. Milne's handwritten manuscript of *The House at Pooh Corner.* ⊠ *Trinity St.* ☎ *01223/338400* ⊕ *www.trin.cam.ac.uk* ☞ *£3 Mid-Mar.–Oct.* ۞ *College daily 10–5; library weekdays noon–2, Sat. in term time 10–noon; hall and chapel open to visitors, but hrs vary.*

19

WHERE TO EAT

£
CAFÉ
✕**Fitzbillies.** Usually filled with students' visiting parents, this traditional café is famous for its exceptionally sticky Chelsea buns (if you don't want to sit down, the bakery next door has the same pastries to take away). It also serves filling and tasty lunches, afternoon teas, and dinners with such dishes as risotto, confit of duck salad, and goat cheese and sweet shallot tart. ⊠ *52 Trumpington St.* ☎ *01223/352500* ⊕ *www. fitzbillies.co.uk* ⊟ *AE, MC, V.*

££££   ✕ **Midsummer House.** In fine weather the gray-brick Midsummer House's
ECLECTIC   conservatory, beside the River Cam, makes for a memorable lunchtime
★   jaunt. Choose from a selection of innovative French and Mediterranean dishes. You might get braised turbot, a smoked-eel salad, or grilled
pigeon adorned with inventively presented vegetables. ⊠ *Midsummer
Common* ☎ *01223/369299* ⊕ *www.midsummerhouse.co.uk* ⊲ *Reservations essential* ⊟ *AE, MC, V* ⊗ *Closed Sun. and Mon. No lunch Tues.*

CANTERBURY

60 mi (97 km) southeast of London.

A bustling medieval cathedral town, charming Canterbury has good
shopping, plenty of history, and just enough to see in a day—making it
an ideal day trip from London.

As you might remember from high-school English classes spent studying
Chaucer's *Canterbury Tales*, the height of Canterbury's popularity came
in the 12th century, when thousands of pilgrims flocked here to see the
shrine of Archbishop (and later Saint) Thomas à Becket, murdered when
four knights misunderstood King Henry II's complaints about the "troublesome priest." The humble ancient buildings that served as pilgrims'
inns still dominate the streets of Canterbury's pedestrian center.

Dig a little deeper and there's evidence of prosperous society in the Canterbury area as early as the Bronze Age (around 1000 BC). Canterbury
was an important Roman city, as well as an Anglo-Saxon center in the
Kingdom of Kent; it's currently headquarters of the Anglican Church.
The town remains a lively place, a fact that has impressed visitors since
1388, when Chaucer wrote his stories.

EXPLORING

You can easily cover Canterbury in a day. The 90-minute journey southeast from London's Victoria Station leaves plenty of time for a tour of
the cathedral, a museum visit or two, and (if the weather's right) a walk
around the perimeter of the old walled town. Canterbury is bisected
by a road running northwest, along which the major tourist sites are
clustered. This road begins as St. George's Street, then becomes High
Street, and finally turns into St. Peter's Street.

If you're seeing several sights while in town, consider purchasing an
Attractions Passport from the visitor center. It costs £19 and gives
you admission to the Canterbury Cathedral, the Canterbury Tales, St.
Augustine's Abbey, and another museum of your choice.

On St. George's Street a lone church tower marks the site of **St. George's
Church**—the rest of the building was destroyed in World War II—where
playwright Christopher Marlowe was baptized in 1564.

★   The **Canterbury Roman Museum** is below ground level, in the ruins of the
original Roman town. There's a colorful restored Roman mosaic pave-
ment and a hypocaust (the Roman version of central heating), as well
as a display of excavated objects. Get a feel for what it once looked
like via the computer-generated reconstructions of Roman buildings.

Canterbury Cathedral, the destination of Chaucer's pilgrims in *The Canterbury Tales*.

✉ *Butchery La.* ☎ *01227/785575* ⊕ *www.canterbury-museums.co.uk* 🎫 *£3.10* 🕙 *June–Oct., Mon.–Sat. 10–4, Sun. 1:30–4; Nov.–May, Mon.– Sat. 10–4.*

Mercery Lane, with its medieval-style cottages and massive, overhanging timber roofs, runs right off Canterbury High Street and ends in the tiny **Buttermarket**, a square that was known in the 15th century as the Bullstake: animals were tied here for baiting before slaughter at market. Today it's a town square surrounded by small bars and restaurants, and is often crowded with people visiting the cathedral.

The immense **Christchurch Gate**, built in 1517, leads into the cathedral close. As you pass through, look up at the sculpted heads of two young figures: Prince Arthur, elder brother of Henry VIII, and the young Catherine of Aragon, to whom he was betrothed. After Arthur's death, Catherine married Henry. Her inability to produce a male heir after 25 years of marriage led to Henry's decision to divorce her, creating an irrevocable breach with the Roman Catholic Church and altering the course of English history.

Fodor'sChoice ★ The massive heart of the town, towering **Canterbury Cathedral** was the first of England's great Norman cathedrals. The nucleus of worldwide Anglicanism, the Cathedral Church of Christ Canterbury (its formal name) is a living textbook of medieval architecture.

The cathedral was only a century old, and still relatively small in size, when Thomas à Becket, the Archbishop of Canterbury, was murdered here in 1170. An uncompromising defender of ecclesiastical interests, Becket had angered his friend Henry II, who supposedly exclaimed, "Who will rid me of this troublesome priest?" Thinking they were carrying out the king's wishes, four knights burst in on Becket in one of the church's side chapels, chased him through the halls, and stabbed him to death. Two years later Becket was canonized, and Henry II's subsequent penitence helped establish the cathedral as the undisputed center of English Christianity.

Becket's tomb, destroyed by Henry VIII in 1538 as part of his campaign to reduce the power of the Church and confiscate its treasures, was one of the most extravagant shrines in Christendom. In **Trinity Chapel**, which held the shrine, you can still see a series of 13th-century stained-glass windows illustrating Becket's miracles. The actual site of Becket's murder is down a flight of steps just to the left of the nave, and marked with a simple sign that says only "Becket." If time permits, be sure to explore the **Cloisters, the Crypt,** and the small monastic buildings north of the cathedral. ⊠ *Cathedral Precincts* ☎ *01227/762862* ⊕ *www.canterbury-cathedral.org* ⌨ *£7.50; free for services* ⊘ *Easter–Sept., Mon.–Sat. 9–6, Sun. 12:30–2:30; Oct.–Easter, Mon.–Sat. 9–5:30, Sun. 12:30–2:30. Last entry 30 mins before closing. Restricted access during services.*

To learn more about Chaucer's quirky pilgrims on their way to Canterbury, visit **The Canterbury Tales,** an audiovisual (and occasionally olfactory) dramatization of 14th-century English life. You'll "meet" Chaucer's pilgrims at the Tabard Inn near London and view tableaux illustrating five tales. In the summer, actors in period costumes play out scenes from the town's history. ⊠ *St. Margaret's St.* ☎ *01227/784600* ⊕ *www.canterburytales.org.uk* ⌨ *£7.75* ⊘ *Nov.–Feb., daily 10–4:30; Mar.–June, Sept., and Oct., daily 10–5; July and Aug., daily 9:30–5.*

★ The medieval Poor Priests' Hospital is now the site of the **Museum of Canterbury** (previously the Canterbury Heritage Museum). Its exhibits provide an excellent overview of the city's history and architecture from Roman times to World War II, although the displays are a strange mix of the serious (the Blitz) and the silly (cartoon characters Bagpuss and Rupert Bear). It also touches on the mysterious death of the 16th-century poet and playwright Christopher Marlowe. It's definitely child-friendly—kids can even look at "medieval poo" under a microscope. Visit early in the day to avoid the crowds. ⊠ *20 Stour St.* ☎ *01227/475202* ⊕ *www.canterbury-museums.co.uk* ⌨ *£3.60* ⊘ *Jan.–May and Oct.–Dec., Mon.–Sat. 11–5; June–Sept., Mon.–Sat. 11–5, Sun. 1:30–5; last admission at 4.*

☾ Only one of the city's seven medieval gatehouses survives, complete with twin castellated towers; it now contains the **West Gate Museum.** Inside are medieval bric-a-brac and armaments used by the city guard, as well as more contemporary weaponry. Built in the 14th century, the building became a jail in the 15th century, and you can view the prison cells. Climb to the roof for a panoramic view of the city spires. Because it's accessed by spiral stone stairs, this museum is only for those without mobility problems. ⊠ *St. Peter's St.* ☎ *01227/789576* ⊕ *www.canterbury-museums.co.uk* ⌨ *£1.30* ⊘ *Mon.–Sat. 11–12:30 and 1:30–3:30; last admission 15 mins before closing. Closed Christmas wk.*

Perhaps the best view of Canterbury's medieval past comes from following its 13th- and 14th-century **medieval city walls,** which were themselves built on the line of the original Roman walls. Those to the east have survived intact, towering some 20 feet high and offering a sweeping view of the town. You can access these from a number of places, including Castle and Broad streets.

Augustine, England's first Christian missionary, was buried in 597 at **St. Augustine's Abbey,** one of the oldest monastic sites in the country. When Henry VIII seized the abbey in the 16th century, he destroyed some of the buildings and converted others into a royal manor for his fourth wife, Anne of Cleves. A free interactive audio tour vividly puts events into context. The abbey is the base for Canterbury's biennial Sculpture Festival (held in odd-number years). Contemporary sculpture is placed on the grounds, and in other locations in the city, May through August. ⊠ *Longport* ☎ *01227/767345* ⊕ *www.english-heritage.org.uk* ✉ *£4.30* ☺ *Apr.–June, Wed.–Sun. 10–5; July and Aug., daily 10–6; Sept.–Oct., weekends 11–5; Nov.–Mar., weekends 11–4.*

☺ Dane John Gardens (the name is a corruption of *donjon,* French for a castle keep) offers a children's maze and a historic monument, **Dane John Mound,** the remains of a Norman fortress that formed part of the city defenses and today offers excellent cathedral views.

WHERE TO EAT

££–£££ FRENCH ★ ✕ **Café Belge.** The magnificent beamed barn roof of this older building remains, but the interior—stripped wooden floors, and white walls enlivened by modern art—specializes in mussel dishes with Belgian beer. ⊠ *89–90 St. Dunstan's St.* ☎ *01227/768222* ═ *AE, MC, V.*

£ BRITISH ✕ **City Fish Bar.** Long lines and lots of satisfied finger-licking attest to the deserved popularity of this excellent fish-and-chips outlet in the center of town. Everything is freshly fried, the batter is crisp, and the fish is tasty; the fried mushrooms are also surprisingly good. It closes at 7. ⊠ *30 St. Margaret's St.* ☎ *01227/760873* ═ *No credit cards.*

£–££ BRITISH ✕ **Duck Inn.** About 5 mi outside of Canterbury, this lovely, low-roof traditional pub is a great favorite among regular visitors to the city. Its pleasant rural location yields a bit of country charm, and dishes such as game pies are delightfully traditional. The name is said to come from the fact that the beams above the entrance are so low that you must duck as you enter or risk bashing your head. ⊠ *Pett Bottom, near bridge* ☎ *01227/830354* ═ *No credit cards.*

£–££ BRITISH ★ ✕ **Weavers.** In one of the Weavers' Houses (the Weavers were Huguenots and Walloons who fled persecution in continental Europe in the 16th and 17th centuries) on the River Stour, this popular restaurant in the center of town is an ideal place to revel in the Tudor surroundings and feast on generous portions of British comfort food. Traditional pies and grills, seafood, and pasta dishes are served along with a good selection of wines. Ask for a table in the more sedate ground-floor dining area. ⊠ *1 St. Peter's St.* ☎ *01227/464660* ═ *AE, MC, V.*

OXFORD

62 mi (100 km) northwest of London.

HERE'S WHERE

The Bodleian Library's Divinity School, open to the public, is a superbly vaulted room dating to 1462, which acted as Hogwarts in *Harry Potter and the Sorcerer's Stone*. The dining hall at Christ Church College should look familiar to fans as well—it was used as the model for the Hogwarts dining hall.

The university that educated former Prime Minister Tony Blair, former President Bill Clinton, and writers J. R. R. Tolkien, Percy Bysshe Shelley, Oscar Wilde, W. H. Auden, and C. S. Lewis is the heart and soul of the town. Its fabled "dreaming spires" can be seen for miles around, and it's not at all unusual to see robed students rushing to class or harried dons clutching mortarboards as they race to exams on bicycles. Dating from the 12th century, Oxford University is older than Cambridge, and the city is bigger and more cosmopolitan than its competitor to the east. It's satisfyingly filled with hushed quadrangles, chapels, canals, rivers, and vivid gardens. Bikes are inevitably propped against picturesque wrought-iron railings, and students propel flat-bottom boats down the little River Cherwell with long poles. (It's harder than it looks, but you can rent a punt yourself at the foot of Magdalen Bridge.)

In the end, though, central Oxford is also a bit of an illusion. Outside of the eminently photographable university area, it's a major industrial center, with sprawling modern suburbs and large car and steel plants around its fringes.

VISITING THE COLLEGES

The same concerns for people's work and privacy hold here as in Cambridge. Note that many of the colleges and university buildings are closed around Christmas (sometimes Easter, too) and on certain days from April to June for exams and degree ceremonies.

If you have limited time, get a detailed map from the tourist office and focus on selected sights. The Oxford University Web site (⊕ *www.ox.ac. uk*) is a great source of information if you're planning to go it alone.

Guided city walking tours (both themed and general) leave the **Oxford Tourist Information Centre** at different times throughout the day. ⊠ *15–16 Broad St.* ☎ *01865/252200* ⊕ *www.visitoxford.org* ☎ *£7* ☉ *Mon.–Sat. 9:30–5, Sun. 10–4.*

EXPLORING

Any Oxford visit should begin at its very center—a pleasant walk of 10 minutes or so east from the train station—with the splendid **University Church of St. Mary the Virgin** (1280). Climb 127 steps to the top of its 14th-century tower for a panoramic view of the city. ⊠ *High St.* ☎ *01865/279111* ⊕ *www.university-church.ox.ac.uk* ☎ *Church free, tower £3* ☉ *Church admission Sept.–June, Mon.–Sat. 9–5, Sun. noon–5; July and Aug., Mon.–Sat. 9–6, Sun. noon–6; tower only—daily noon–5; last admission to tower 30 mins before closing.*

Radcliffe Camera, an unmissable circular library at Oxford University.

Fodor's Choice
★ Among Oxford's most famous sights, the gorgeous, round **Radcliffe Camera** (1737–49) is the most beautiful of the buildings housing the extensive contents of the august **Bodleian Library.** The baroque domed rotunda with an octagonal base sits in a lovely square where your photographic instincts can run riot. Not many of the 6-million-plus volumes are on view to those who aren't dons, but you can see part of the collection if you call ahead to book a regular or self-guided audio tour. Note that children under 11 are not admitted. ⊠ *Broad St.* ☎ *01865/277224* ⊕ *www.shop.bodley.ox.ac.uk* ✉ *Bodleian self-guided audio tour £2.50; 1-hr guided tour £6, extended guided tour £12* ⊙ *Weekdays 9–5; Divinity School weekdays 9–5, Sat. 9–4:30, Sun. 11–7 (admission £1).*

★ The **Sheldonian Theatre,** built between 1664 and 1668, was Sir Christopher Wren's first major work (the chapel at Pembroke College was his first commission). The theater, which he modeled on a Roman amphitheater, made his reputation. It was built as a venue for the university's public ceremonies, and graduations are still held here—entirely in Latin, as befits the building's spirit. Outside is one of Oxford's most striking sights—a metal fence topped with stone busts of 18 Roman emperors (modern reproductions of the originals, which were eaten away by pollution). ⊠ *Broad St.* ☎ *01865/277299* ⊕ *www.sheldon.ox.ac.uk* ✉ *£2* ⊙ *Mar.–Oct., Mon.–Sat. 10–12:30 and 2–4:30; Nov.–Feb., Mon.–Sat. 10–12:30 and 2–3:30. Closed for 10 days at Christmas and Easter and for degree ceremonies and events.*

Outside the "new" (they're actually Victorian) college gates of prestigious **Balliol College** (1263), a cobblestone cross in the sidewalk marks the spot where Archbishop Cranmer and Bishops Latimer and Ridley were burned in 1555 for their Protestant beliefs. The original college gates (rumored to have existed at the time of the scorching) hang in the library passage, between the inner and outer quadrangles. ⊠ *Broad St.* ☎ *01865/277777* ⊕ *www.balliol.ox.ac.uk* ⌧ *£1* ⊘ *Daily 2–5, or dusk if earlier.*

★ The **chapel of Trinity College** (1555) is an architectural gem—a tiny place with a delicately painted ceiling, gorgeously tiled floor, and elaborate wood carvings on the pews, pulpit, and walls. Some of the superb carvings were done by Grinling Gibbons, a 17th-century master carver whose work can also be seen in Hampton Court Palace and St. Paul's Cathedral, and who inspired the 18th-century cabinetmaker Thomas Chippendale. ⊠ *Broad St.* ☎ *01865/279900* ⊕ *www.trinity.ox.ac.uk* ⌧ *£1.50* ⊘ *Daily 10–noon and 2–4, or dusk if earlier.*

Fodor'sChoice
★ The **Ashmolean Museum**, founded in 1683, is one of Britain's oldest public museums. Some of the world's most precious art objects are stashed here—drawings by Michelangelo and Raphael, European silverware and ceramics, a world-class numismatic collection, and Egyptian, Greek, and Roman artifacts. in the completely renovated museum and new additional buildings opened in November 2009. ⊠ *Beaumont St.* ☎ *01865/278000* ⊕ *www.ashmolean.org* ⌧ *Free* ⊘ *Tues.–Sat. 10–5, Sun. noon–5.*

St. John's College (1555), former Prime Minister Tony Blair's alma mater, is worth a stop for its historic courtyards, world-renowned symmetrical gardens, and its library, where you can view some of Jane Austen's letters and an illustrated 1483 edition of *The Canterbury Tales* by the English printer William Caxton. ⊠ *St. Giles* ☎ *01865/277300* ⊕ *www.sjc.ox.ac.uk* ⌧ *Free* ⊘ *Daily 1–5, 1–dusk in winter.*

College members, but not visitors, can enter the university's largest college via **Tom Gate.** This massive gatehouse is surmounted by Christopher Wren's **Tom Tower, which** contains Great Tom, a giant clock that strikes each hour with high and low notes.

★
☾ **Christ Church College.** Traditionally called "the House" by its students, Christ Church has the largest quadrangle in town. This is where Charles Dodgson, better known as Lewis Carroll, was a math don; a shop across from the parkland (known as "the meadows") on St. Aldate's was the inspiration for the shop in *Through the Looking Glass.* Don't miss the 800-year-old chapel, or the Tudor dining hall, with its portraits of former students—John Wesley, William Penn, and six of the 13 prime ministers who attended the college. ⊠ *St. Aldate's* ☎ *01865/276492* ⊕ *www.chch.ox.ac.uk* ⌧ *£6.30* ⊘ *Weekdays 9–5, Sun. 2:30–5. Dining hall weekdays 2:30–5 during school year. Last admission 30 mins before closing.*

WHERE TO EAT

££–£££
CONTINENTAL
★ ✕ **Brasserie Blanc.** Raymond Blanc's Conran-designed brasserie is sophisticated even by London standards. The top British chef populates his menu with modern European and regional French dishes: you might see steamed Loch Fyne mussels in a white wine–and-cream sauce, or a Barbary duck breast in black cherry sauce. At £12 for two courses

or £14 for three, the prix-fixe lunch is an incredible value, and well worth the short walk north of the town center. ✉ *71–72 Walton St.* ☎ *01865/510999* ⊕ *www.brasserieblanc.com* ⚐ *Reservations essential* ▭ *AE, DC, MC, V.*

£   ✕ **Grand Café.** In a lovely 1920s building, this inexpensive café looks as if
CAFÉ   it should cost the world. Golden tiles, carved columns, and antique marble floor fill the place with charm, and the menu of tasty sandwiches, salads, and tarts, as well as perfect coffee drinks and desserts, make it a great place for lunch or an afternoon break. At night it puts away its menus and transforms itself into a popular cocktail bar. ✉ *84 High St.* ☎ *01865/204463* ⊕ *www.thegrandcafe.co.uk* ▭ *AE, DC, MC, V.*

£   ✕ **Pizza Express.** Many people are surprised to discover that this uniquely
ITALIAN   situated restaurant in the former sitting room of the 15th-century Golden Cross—Shakespeare's stopover lodging on his frequent trips from Stratford to London—is part of a nationwide chain. Creativity is encouraged here, so vegetarians, vegans, and meat eaters alike can enjoy inventing their own dream pizzas. A terrace is open in summer, but be sure to check out the medieval paintings and friezes inside the restaurant before heading out. ✉ *8 The Golden Cross, Cornmarket St.* ☎ *01865/790442* ⊕ *www.pizzaexpress.com* ▭ *AE, DC, MC, V.*

STRATFORD-UPON-AVON

104 mi (167 km) north of London.

Stratford-upon-Avon has become adept at accommodating the hordes of people who stream in for a glimpse of William Shakespeare's world. Filled with all the distinctive, Tudor half-timber buildings your heart could desire, this is certainly a handsome town. But it can feel, at times, like a literary amusement park, so if you're not a fan of the Bard, you'd probably do better to explore a historic English market town.

It's difficult to avoid feeling like a herd animal as you board the Shakespeare bus, but tours like City Sightseeing's **Stratford and the Shakespeare Story** (✉ *Pen and Parchment pub, Bridgefort* ☎ *01789/412680* ⊕ *www. city-sightseeing.com* 🎟 *£11*), with a hop-on, hop-off route around the five Shakespeare Birthplace Trust properties (two of which are out of town), can make a visit infinitely easier if you don't have a car.

It's worth purchasing a combined ticket to the **Shakespeare's Birthplace Trust properties,** which include Shakespeare's Birthplace Museum, Nash's House, Hall's Croft, Anne Hathaway's Cottage, and the Shakespeare Countryside Museum. The ticket, which is valid for one year and is available at any of the properties, costs £17 for all the sites, or £12 for the three in-town properties (not including Anne Hathaway's Cottage and Mary Arden's House). Note that you cannot buy a ticket for just one of the in-town sites. ☎ *01789/204016* ⊕ *www.shakespeare.org.uk.*

19

EXPLORING

Most visitors to Stratford start at **Shakespeare's Birthplace Museum.** The half-timber building in which Shakespeare was born in 1564 is a national treasure. It was owned by his descendants until the 19th century, and it became a national memorial in 1847. It's been furnished and decorated with simple whitewashed walls and brightly colored fabrics that were popular in Shakespeare's time. All the textiles have been hand-dyed using period methods. The revamped visitor center tells the story of Shakespeare's life in great detail, which makes a good starting point for any tour of Stratford. ⊠ *Henley St.* ☎ *01789/204016* ⊕ *www.shakespeare.org.uk* ✉ *£12, includes admission to Nash's House and Hall's Croft* ☉ *Apr.–Oct., daily 9–5; Nov.–Mar., daily 10–4.*

WORD OF MOUTH

"Most visitors have only enough time in a hectic schedule to walk from the coach park or train station through the center to the Birthplace. If they stayed for longer and visited Anne Hathaway's Cottage by *walking* from the center (15 minutes) across the fields where undoubtedly Shakespeare walked, or visited Charlecote Park, a beautiful Elizabethan house by the Avon, they might return home with happier memories of Stratford-upon-Avon!"   —bellini

Nash's House contains an exhibit charting the history of Stratford, against a backdrop of period furniture and tapestries. The main attraction is really the extravagant gardens around the adjacent remains of **New Place,** the home where Shakespeare spent his last years, and where he died in 1616. A gorgeous Elizabethan knot garden, based on drawings of gardens from Shakespeare's time, grows around the remaining foundation of the house, which was destroyed in 1759 by its last owner, the Reverend Francis Gastrell, in an attempt to stop the tide of visitors. ⊠ *Chapel St.* ☎ *01789/204016* ⊕ *www.shakespeare.org.uk* ✉ *£12, includes admission to Shakespeare's Birthplace and Hall's Croft* ☉ *Nov.–Mar., daily 11–4; Apr.–Oct., daily 10–5.*

★ **Hall's Croft** is Stratford's most beautiful Tudor town house. This was—almost definitely—the home of Shakespeare's daughter Susanna and her husband, Dr. John Hall. It's outfitted with furniture of the period and the doctor's dispensary. The walled garden is delightful. ⊠ *Old Town St.* ☎ *01789/204016* ⊕ *www.shakespeare.org.uk* ✉ *£9, includes admission to Shakespeare's Birthplace and Nash's House* ☉ *Nov.–Mar., daily 11–4; Apr.–Oct., daily 10–5.*

"Shakespeare's church," the 13th-century **Holy Trinity,** is fronted by a beautiful avenue of lime trees. Shakespeare is buried here, in the chancel. The bust of the Bard is thought to be an authentic likeness, executed a few years after his death. ⊠ *Trinity St.* ☎ *01789/266316* ✉ *Church free, chancel £1.50* ☉ *Mar., Mon.–Sat. 9–5, Sun. noon–5; Apr.–Sept., Mon.–Sat. 8:30–6, Sun. noon–5; Oct., Mon.–Sat. 9–5, Sun. noon–5; Nov.–Feb., Mon.–Sat. 9–4, Sun. 12:30–5; last admission 20 mins before closing.*

Fodor's Choice
★ The **Royal Shakespeare Theatre** on the bank of the Avon is the home of the Royal Shakespeare Company in Stratford, but after a massive renovation project began in 2007, the Main Theatre, along with the smaller **Swan Theatre** in the same building, has been closed to the loyal fans who usually fill its seats for several productions a year. At this writing, productions are scheduled to be back in the Main Theatre in 2011 and the building itself will be open as of late 2010. But never fear: you

can still see the latest Royal Shakespeare Company productions at the excellent temporary Courtyard theater until the new space is fully operational. Check the Web site to see what's going to be on during your visit. It's always best to book in advance, but day-of-performance tickets are usually available. ⊠ *Waterside* ☎*0844/800–1110 ticket hotline, 0844/800–1117 information, 0844/800–1114 tours and events* ⊕ *www.rsc.org.uk.*

STRATFORD ENVIRONS

The two remaining stops on the Shakespeare trail are just outside Stratford.

★ **Anne Hathaway's Cottage,** the early home of the playwright's wife, is a picturesque thatched cottage restored to reflect the comfortable middle-class Hathaway life. You can walk here from town—it's just over a mile from central Stratford. ⊠ *Cottage La., Shottery* ☎ *01789/204016* ⊕ *www.shakespeare.org.uk* 🎫 *£6.50* ⊙ *Apr.–Oct., daily 9–5; Nov.–Mar., daily 10–4.*

↻ **Mary Arden's Farm** uses 16th-century methods to grow food on its working farm. This stop is great for kids, who can see the lambs and calves, listen as the farmers explain their work in the fields, and watch the cooks prepare food in the Tudor farmhouse kitchen. This site was formerly referred to as Mary Arden's House, and believed to be where Shakespeare's mother grew up. In late 2000, research findings based on newly discovered real-estate records revealed that the real **Mary Arden's Farm,** hitherto known as Glebe Farm, was actually nearby and (thankfully) already owned by the Shakespeare Birthplace Trust. ⊠ *Wilmcote* ☎ *01789/204016, 01789/293455 for information on special events* ⊕ *www.shakespeare.org.uk* 🎫 *£8; children £5* ⊙ *Nov.–Mar. daily 10–4; Apr.–Oct., daily 10–5.*

↻ Some 8 mi north of Stratford in the medieval town of Warwick, **War-**
★ **wick Castle** fulfills the most clichéd Camelot daydreams. This medieval, fortified, much-restored, castellated, moated, landscaped (by Capability Brown) castle, now managed by the experts at Madame Tussauds, is a true period museum—complete with dungeons and a torture chamber, state rooms, and the occasional battle reenactment or joust. Note: It gets very crowded in summer, when lines for tickets, as well as food and drink, can be long, so it's not for those looking for a quiet, historic retreat to explore. Tickets are cheaper if purchased in advance on the Web site, and you'll also avoid some lines. ⊠ *Castle La. off Mill St., Warwick* ☎ *01926/495421, 08704/422000 24-hr information line* ⊕ *www.warwick-castle.co.uk* 🎫 *£17.95–£22.95* ⊙ *Apr.–Sept., daily 10–6; Oct.–Mar., daily 10–5; last admission 30 mins before closing.*

19

Stratford-upon-Avon honors Shakespeare's Birthday with an annual procession.

WHERE TO EAT

£–££
BRITISH
✗ **The Black Swan/The Dirty Duck.** The only pub in Britain to be licensed under two names (the more informal one came courtesy of American GIs who were stationed here during WWII), this is one of Stratford's most celebrated pubs—it has attracted actors since the 18th-century thespian David Garrick's days. A little veranda overlooks the theaters and the river here. Along with a pint of bitter, it's a fine place to enjoy English grill specialties, as well as braised oxtail and honey-roasted duck. You can also choose from an assortment of bar meals. ⊠ *Waterside* ☎ *01789/297312* ▭ *AE, MC, V.*

££
BRITISH
✗ **Lambs of Sheep Street.** Sit downstairs to appreciate the hardwood floors and oak beams of this local epicurean favorite; upstairs, the look is more contemporary. The updates of tried-and-true dishes include salmon cakes with wilted spinach, and roast neck of lamb. Daily fish specials keep the menu seasonal, and the desserts are fantastic. A £11.50 fixed-price lunch is a good deal for two courses. ⊠ *12 Sheep St.* ☎ *01789/292554* ⊕ *www.lambsrestaurant.co.uk* ☖ *Reservations essential* ▭ *MC, V.*

££–£££
BRITISH
✗ **Oppo.** Hearty, warming meals are offered at this informal, family-friendly restaurant in a 16th-century building on the main dining street near the theaters. The American and modern European dishes on the menu win praise from the locals. Try the roasted chicken. ⊠ *13 Sheep St.* ☎ *01789/269980* ⊕ *www.theoppo.co.uk* ▭ *MC, V.*

WINDSOR CASTLE

24 mi (39 km) west of London.

The tall turrets of Windsor Castle, believed to be the world's largest inhabited castle, can be seen for miles around. The grand stone building is the star attraction in this quiet medieval town—though Eton College, England's most famous public school, is also just a lovely walk away across the Thames. The castle is the only royal residence to have been in continuous royal use since the days of William the Conqueror, who chose this site to build a timber stockade soon after his conquest of Britain in 1066. It was Edward III in the 1300s who really founded the castle: he built the Norman gateway, the great Round Tower, and the State Apartments. Charles II restored the State Apartments during the 1600s, and, during the 1820s George IV—with his mania for building—converted what was still essentially a medieval castle into the palace you see today.

> **DID YOU KNOW?**
>
> The Queen uses Windsor often—it's said she likes it much more than Buckingham Palace—spending most weekends here, often joined by family and friends. You know she's in when the Royal Standard is flown above the Round Tower but not in when you see the Union Jack.

EXPLORING

The massive citadel of **Windsor Castle** occupies 13 acres, but the first part you notice on entering is the **Round Tower,** on top of which the Standard is flown and at the base of which is the 11th-century Moat Garden. Passing under the portcullis at the Norman Gate, you reach the **Upper Ward,** the quadrangle containing the State Apartments—which you may tour—and the sovereign's Private Apartments. Processions for foreign heads of state and other ceremonies take place here, as does the Changing of the Guard when the Queen is in residence. A short walk takes you to the Lower Ward, where the high point is the magnificent **St. George's Chapel,** home of the Order of the Garter, the highest chivalric order in the land, founded in 1348 by Edward III. Ten sovereigns are buried in the chapel—a fantastic Perpendicular Gothic vision 230 feet long, complete with gargoyles, buttresses, banners, swords, and choir stalls. This is also where royal weddings take place.

The **State Apartments** are as grand as Buckingham Palace's and have the added attraction of a few gems from the Queen's vast art collection: choice canvases by Rubens, Rembrandt, Van Dyck, Gainsborough, Canaletto, and Holbein; da Vinci drawings; Gobelin tapestries; and lime-wood carvings by Grinling Gibbons. The entrance is through a grand hall holding cases crammed with precious china—some still used for royal banquets. Don't miss the outsize suit of armor, made for Henry VIII, in the armory. Make sure you take in the magnificent views across to Windsor Great Park, which are the remains of a former royal hunting forest.

19

☯ One unmissable treat is **Queen Mary's Dolls' House,** a 12:1 scale, seven-story palace with electricity, running water, and working elevators, designed in 1924 by Sir Edwin Lutyens. The detail is incredible—even the diminutive wine bottles hold the real thing. ⊠ *Windsor Castle* ☎ *020/7766–7304 tickets, 01753/831118 opening hours* ⊕ *www. royalcollection.org.uk* ✉ *£15.50 (£41 family ticket) for Precincts, State Apartments, Gallery, St. George's Chapel, Albert Memorial Chapel, and Queen Mary's Dolls' House; £8.50 when State Apartments are closed* ☯ *Mar.–Oct., daily 9:45–5:15, last admission at 4; Nov.–Feb., daily 9:45–4:15, last admission at 3; St. George's Chapel closed Sun. except to worshippers. Hrs vary; check Web site.*

★ The splendid redbrick Tudor-style buildings of **Eton College,** founded in 1440 by King Henry VI, border the north end of High Street. During the college semesters, schoolboys dress in their distinctive striped trousers, swallow-tailed coats, and stiff collars to walk to class—it's all terrifically photogenic. The Gothic **Chapel** rivals St. George's at Windsor in size and magnificence, and is both austere and intimate. The **Museum of Eton Life** has displays on the school's history. Admission to the school is with a prebooked guided tour only. ⊠ *Main entrance off Eton High St.* ☎ *01753/671177* ⊕ *www.etoncollege.com* ✉ *£6 short tour, £8 extended tour* ☯ *Tours mid-Mar.–Sept., daily at 2 and 3:15. Closed Mon. and Tues. and Thurs. during term time, also closed weekends Oct.–mid-Nov. Check Web site for details.*

WHERE TO EAT

£ ✗ **Two Brewers.** Two small, low-ceiling rooms make up this 17th-century
BRITISH pub where locals congregate and palace staff unwind after work. Children are not welcome, but adults will find a suitable collection of wine, espresso, and local beer, plus an excellent little menu. Reservations are essential on Sunday, when the pub serves a traditional roast. ⊠ *34 Park St.* ☎ *01753/855426* ▭ *AE, MC, V* ☯ *No full dinner Fri. and Sat.*

UNDERSTANDING LONDON

LONDON AT-A-GLANCE

FAST FACTS

Type of government: Representative democracy. In 1999 the Greater London Authority Act reestablished a single local governing body for the Greater London area, consisting of an elected mayor and the 25-member London Assembly. Elections, first held in 2000, take place every four years.

Population: Inner city 3 million, Greater London 7.7 million

Population density: 12,331 people per square mi

Median age: 38.4

Infant mortality rate: 5 per 1,000 births

Language: English. More than 300 languages are spoken in London. All city government documents are translated into Arabic, Bengali, Chinese, Greek, Gujurati, Hindi, Punjabi, Turkish, Urdu, and Vietnamese.

Ethnic and racial groups: White British 70%, White Irish 3%, Other White 9%, Indian 6%, Bangladeshi 2%, Pakistani 2%, other Asian 2%, Black African 6%, Black Caribbean 5%, Chinese 1%, Other 3%.

Religion: Christian 58%, nonaffiliated 15%, Muslim 8%, Hindu 4%, Jewish 2%, Sikh 1%, other religion 1%, Buddhist 0.8%

When a man is tired of London, he is tired of life; for there is in London all that life can afford.

—Samuel Johnson

GEOGRAPHY AND ENVIRONMENT

Latitude: 51° N (same as Calgary, Canada; Kiev, Ukraine; Prague, Czech Republic)

Longitude: 0° (same as Accra, Ghana). A brass line in the ground in Greenwich marks the prime meridian (0° longitude).

Elevation: 49 feet

Land area: City, 67 square mi; metro area, 625 square mi

Terrain: River plain, rolling hills, and parkland

Natural hazards: Drought in warmer summers, minor localized flooding of the Thames caused by surge tides from the North Atlantic

Environmental issues: The city has been improving its air quality, but up to 1,600 people die each year from health problems related to London's polluted air. Only half of London's rivers and canals received passing grades for water quality from 1999 through 2001. More than £12 million ($22 million) is spent annually to ensure the city's food safety.

I'm leaving because the weather is too good. I hate London when it's not raining.

—Groucho Marx

ECONOMY

Workforce: 3.8 million; financial/real estate 28%, health care 10%, manufacturing 4%, education 7%, construction 5%, public administration 5%

Unemployment: 7.2%

Major industries: The arts, banking, government, insurance, tourism

London: a nation, not a city.

—Benjamin Disraeli, Lothair

ENGLISH VOCABULARY

You and a Londoner may speak the same language, but some phrases definitely get lost in translation once they cross the Atlantic.

BRITISH ENGLISH	AMERICAN ENGLISH

BASIC TERMS AND EVERYDAY ITEMS

bill	check
flat	apartment
lift	elevator
nappy	diaper
holiday	vacation
note	bill (currency)
plaster	Band-Aid
queue	line
row	argument
rubbish	trash
tin	can
toilet/loo/WC	bathroom

CLOTHING

braces	suspenders
bum bag	fanny pack
dressing gown	robe
jumper	sweater
pants/knickers	underpants/briefs
rucksack	backpack
suspender	garter
tights	pantyhose
trainers	sneakers
trousers	pants
vest	undershirt
waistcoat	vest

TRANSPORTATION

bonnet	hood
boot	trunk

coach	long-distance bus
pavement	sidewalk
petrol	gas
pram	baby carriage
puncture	flat
windscreen	windshield

FOOD

aubergine	eggplant
banger	sausage
biscuit	cookie
chips	fries
courgette	zucchini
crisps	potato chips
jam	jelly
main course (or main)	entrée
pudding	dessert
rocket	arugula
starter	appetizer
sweet	candy
tea	early dinner

SLANG

all right	hi there
cheers	thank you
chuffed	pleased
fit	attractive
geezer	dude
guv'nor, gaffer	boss
hard	tough
mate	buddy
sound	good
ta	thank you

BOOKS AND MOVIES

London has been the focus of countless books and essays. For sonorous eloquence, you still must reach back more than half a century to Henry James's *English Hours* and Virginia Woolf's *The London Scene*. Today most suggested reading lists begin with V. S. Pritchett's *London Perceived* and H. V. Morton's *In Search of London*, both decades old. Four more up-to-date books with a general compass are Peter Ackroyd's *Thames* and anecdotal *London: The Biography*, which traces the city's growth from the Druids to the 21st century; John Russell's *London*, a sumptuously illustrated art book; and Christopher Hibbert's *In London: The Biography of a City*. Stephen Inwood's *A History of London* explores the city from its Roman roots to its swinging '60s heyday. Piet Schreuders's *The Beatles' London* follows the footsteps of the Fab Four.

That noted, there are books galore on the various facets of the city. *The Art and Architecture of London* by Ann Saunders is fairly comprehensive. *Inside London: Discovering the Classic Interiors of London*, by Joe Friedman and Peter Aprahamian, has magnificent color photographs of hidden and overlooked shops, clubs, and town houses. For a wonderful take on the golden age of the city's regal mansions, see Christopher Simon Sykes's *Private Palaces: Life in the Great London Houses*. For various other aspects of the city, consult Mervyn Blatch's helpful *A Guide to London's Churches*, Andrew Crowe's *The Parks and Woodlands of London*, Sheila Fairfield's *The Streets of London*, Ann Saunders's *Regent's Park*, Ian Norrie's *Hampstead, Highgate Village, and Kenwood*, and Suzanne Ebel's *A Guide to London's Riverside: Hampton Court to Greenwich*. For keen walkers, there are two books by Andrew Duncan: *Secret London* and *Walking Village London*. *City Secrets: London*, edited by Robert Kahn, is a handsome book of anecdotes from London writers, artists, and historians about their favorite

places in the city. For the last word on just about every subject, see *The London Encyclopaedia*, edited by Ben Weinreb and Christopher Hibbert. HarperCollins's *London Photographic Atlas* has a plethora of bird's-eye images of the capital. For an alternative view of the city, it would be hard to better Iain Sinclair's witty and intelligent *London Orbital: A Walk Around the M25* in which he scrutinizes the history, mythology, and politics of London from the viewpoint of its ugly ring road. Sinclair is also the editor of *London: City of Disappearances*, an anthology exploring what has vanished.

Of course, the history and spirit of the city are also to be found in celebrations of great authors, British heroes, and architects. Peter Ackroyd's massive *Dickens* elucidates how the great author shaped today's view of the city; Martin Gilbert's magisterial, multivolume *Churchill* traces the city through some of its greatest trials; J. Mansbridge's *John Nash* details the London buildings of this great architect. Liza Picard evokes mid-18th-century London in *Dr. Johnson's London*. For musical theater buffs, Mike Leigh's *Gilbert and Sullivan's London* takes a romantic look at the two artists' lives and times in the capital's grand theaters and wild nightspots. *Rodinsky's Room* by Rachel Lichtenstein and Iain Sinclair is a fascinating exploration of East End Jewish London and the mysterious disappearance of one of its occupants.

Maureen Waller's *1700: Scenes from London Life* is a fascinating look at the daily life of Londoners in the 18th century. Nineteenth-century London—the city of Queen Victoria, Tennyson, and Dickens—comes alive through *Mayhew's London*, a massive study of the London poor by Henry Mayhew, and Gustave Doré's *London*, an unforgettable series of engravings of the city (often reprinted in modern editions) that detail its horrifying slums and grand avenues. When it comes to fiction, of course, Dickens's immortal works top the list. Stay-at-home detectives have long walked the streets of London, thanks to great mysteries by Dorothy L. Sayers, Agatha Christie, Ngaio Marsh, and Antonia Fraser. Cops and bad guys wind their way around 1960s London in Jake Arnott's pulp fiction books, *The Long Firm* and *He Kills Coppers*. Martin Amis's *London Fields* tracks a murder mystery through West London. For so-called "tart noir," pick up any Stella Duffy book. Marie Belloc-Lowndes's *The Lodger* is a fictional account of London's most deadly villain, Jack the Ripper. Victorian London was never so salacious as in Sarah Waters's story of a young girl who travels the theaters as a singer, the Soho squares as a male prostitute, and the East End as a communist in *Tipping the Velvet*. Late-20th-century London, with its diverse ethnic makeup, is the star of Zadie Smith's famed novel *White Teeth*. The vibrancy and cultural diversity of London's East End come to life in Monica Ali's *Brick Lane*.

Many films—from *Waterloo Bridge* and *Georgy Girl* to *Secrets and Lies* and *Notting Hill*—have used London as their setting. The great musicals Walt Disney's *Mary Poppins*, George Cukor's *My Fair Lady*, and Sir Carol Reed's *Oliver!* evoke the Hollywood soundstage version of London.

Children of all ages enjoy Stephen Herek's *101 Dalmatians*, with Glenn Close as fashion-savvy Cruella de Vil. King's Cross Station in London was shot to cinematic fame by the movie version of J.K. Rowling's *Harry Potter and the Philosopher's Stone*. Look for cameos by the city in all other *Harry Potter* films.

The swinging '60s are loosely portrayed in M. Jay Roach's *Austin Powers: International Man of Mystery*, full of references to British slang and some great opening scenes in London. For a truer picture of the '60s in London, Michelangelo Antonioni weaves a mystery plot around the world of a London fashion photographer in *Blow-Up*. British gangster films came into their own with Guy Ritchie's amusing tales of London thieves in *Lock, Stock, and Two Smoking Barrels*, filmed almost entirely in London, and the follow-up *Snatch*. More sobering portraits of London criminal life include Neil Jordan's *Mona Lisa*, Paul McGuigan's *Gangster No. 1*, and John Mackenzie's *The Long Good Friday*. Of course, the original tough guy is 007, and his best exploits in London are featured in the introductory chase scene in *The World Is Not Enough*.

Sir Arthur Conan Doyle knew the potential of London as a chilling setting, and John Landis's *An American Werewolf in London* and Hitchcock's *39 Steps* and *The Man Who Knew Too Much* exploit the Gothic and sinister qualities of the city. For a fascinating look at Renaissance London, watch John Madden's *Shakespeare in Love*. Dickens's London is indelibly depicted in David Lean's *Oliver Twist*.

Some modern-day romantic comedies that use London as a backdrop are Peter Howitt's *Sliding Doors* with Gwyneth Paltrow and the screen adaptations of Helen Fielding's *Bridget Jones's Diary* (and its sequel), starring Renée Zellweger, Hugh Grant, and Colin Firth. Glossy London is depicted in Woody Allen's *Match Point*, bohemian London in David Kane's *This Year's Love*, gritty London in Shane Meadow's *Somers Town*, and post-zombie London in Danny Boyle's *28 Days Later*, while Patrick Kellior's *London* offers a uniquely informed, idiosyncratic view of the city.

Travel Smart London

WORD OF MOUTH

"Having just got back from London, I'd recommend an Oyster travel card to anyone staying more than two days."

—khunwilko

"We LOVED the tube—always amazed at how spotless the cars and stations are kept. What a pleasure!"

—keemick

www.fodors.com/community

GETTING HERE AND AROUND

Central London and its surrounding districts are divided into 32 boroughs—33, counting the City of London. More useful for finding your way around, however, are the subdivisions of London into postal districts. Throughout the guide we've given the full postal code for some listings. The first one or two letters give the location: N means north, NW means northwest, and so on. Don't expect the numbering to be logical, however. You won't, for example, find W2 next to W3. The general rule is that the lower numbers, such as W1 or SW1, are closest to Buckingham Palace, but it is not consistent—SE17 is closer to the city center than E4, for example.

■ AIR TRAVEL

Flying time to London is about 6½ hours from New York, 7½ hours from Chicago, 11 hours from San Francisco, and 21½ hours from Sydney.

For flights out of London, the general rule is that you arrive one hour before your scheduled departure time for domestic flights and two hours before international flights for off-peak travel.

Airlines and Airports Airline and Airport Links.com (⊕ www.airlineandairportlinks.com)

Airline Security Issues Transportation Security Administration (⊕ www.tsa.gov)

AIRPORTS

International flights to London arrive at either Heathrow Airport (LHR), 15 mi west of London, or at Gatwick Airport (LGW), 27 mi south of the capital. Most flights from the United States go to Heathrow, which is the busiest and is divided into five terminals, with Terminals 3, 4, and 5 handling transatlantic flights. Gatwick is London's second gateway. It has grown from a European airport into an airport that also serves dozens of U.S. destinations. A smaller third airport, Stansted (STN), is 35 mi east of the city. It handles mainly European and domestic traffic, although there's also scheduled service from New York. Two smaller airports, Luton (LTN), 30 mi north of town, and business-oriented London City (in East London E16) mainly handle flights to Europe.

Airport Information Gatwick Airport (☎ 0870/000–2468 ⊕ www.gatwickairport. com). Heathrow Airport (☎ 0870/000–0123 ⊕ www.heathrowairport.com). London City Airport (☎ 020/7646–0088 ⊕ www. londoncityairport.com). Luton Airport (☎ 01582/405–100 ⊕ www.london-luton.co.uk). Stansted Airport (☎ 0870/000–0303 ⊕ www. stanstedairport.com).

GROUND TRANSPORTATION

London has excellent bus and train connections between its airports and downtown. If you're arriving at Heathrow, you can pick up a map and fare schedule at a Transport for London (TfL) Information Centre (in Terminals 1 and 2). Train service can be quick, but the downside (for trains from all airports) is that you must get yourself and your luggage to the train via a series of escalators and connecting trams. Airport link buses (generally National Express Airport buses) may ease the luggage factor and drop you closer to central hotels, but they're subject to London traffic, which can be horrendous and make the trip drag on for hours. Taxis can be more convenient than buses, but beware that prices can go through the roof. Airport Travel Line has additional transfer information and takes advance booking for transfers between airports and into London. The BAA (British Airport Authority) Web site is a useful resource, giving all transport options from Gatwick, Heathrow, and Stansted.

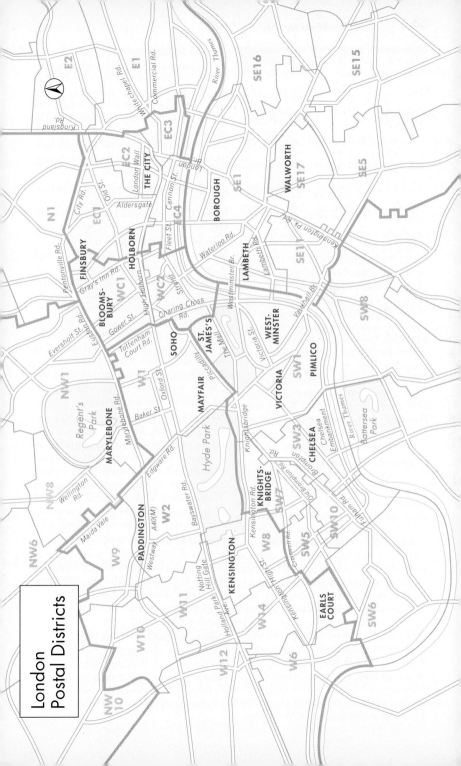

London Postal Districts

FROM HEATHROW TO CENTRAL LONDON		
Travel Mode	Time	Cost
Taxi	1 hour+	£50+
Heathrow Express Train	15 min	£16.50 (£32 round-trip) and £26 for first class
Underground	50 min	£4 one-way (less with Oyster card)
National Express Bus	1 hour	£4 one-way
Dot2Dot (door-to-door)	45 min	£21.50

Heathrow by Bus: National Express buses take one hour to reach the city center (Victoria) and costs £4 one-way and £8 round-trip. National Express has a new Dot2Dot door-to-door service taking you from Heathrow airport to any address in central London for £21.50 (journey time around 45 minutes, depending on traffic). The National Express Hotel Hoppa service runs from all airports to around 20 London hotels (£4). The N9 night bus runs every half hour from midnight to 5 AM to Trafalgar Square; it takes an hour and costs £4.

Heathrow by Train: The cheap, direct route into London is via the Piccadilly line of the Underground (London's extensive subway system, or "Tube"). Trains normally run every four to eight minutes from all terminals from early morning until just before midnight. The 50-minute trip into central London costs £4 one-way and connects with other central Tube lines. The Heathrow Express train is comfortable and very convenient, if costly, speeding into London's Paddington Station in 15 minutes. Standard one-way tickets cost £16.50 (£32 round-trip) and £26 for first class. Book ahead (online is the cheapest option, at a counter/kiosk less so), as tickets are more expensive to buy on board. There's daily service from 5:10 AM (5:50 AM on Sunday) to 11:25 PM (10:50 PM on Sunday), with departures every 15 minutes.

Gatwick by Bus: Hourly bus service runs from Gatwick's north and south terminals to Victoria Station with stops at Hooley, Coulsdon, Mitcham, Streatham, Stockwell, and Pimlico. The journey takes up to 90 minutes and costs £7.30 one-way. The easyBus service runs a service to west London (Fulham) from as little as £2; the later the ticket is booked online, the higher the price (up to £10 on board).

Gatwick by Train: The fast, nonstop Gatwick Express leaves for Victoria Station every 15 minutes 5:15 AM–midnight. The 30-minute trip costs £16.90 one-way, £28.80 round-trip. Book in advance, as tickets cost more on board. The First Capital Connect rail company's nonexpress services are cheaper; Capital Connect train runs regularly throughout the day until midnight to St. Pancras International, London Bridge, and Blackfriars stations; departures are every 15 to 30 minutes, and the journey takes almost one hour. Tickets are £10.90 one-way. FlyBy service to Victoria (£9 single) is not express, but the fare applies only on trains operated by Southern Trains.

Stansted by Bus: Hourly service on National Express Airport bus A6 (24 hours a day) to Victoria Coach Station costs £7.50 one-way, £14 round-trip, and takes about 1 hour and 40 minutes. Stops include Golders Green, Finchley Road, St. John's Wood, Baker Street, Marble Arch, and Hyde Park Corner. The easyBus service to Victoria via Baker Street costs from £2.

Stansted by Train: The Stansted Express to Liverpool Street Station (with a stop at Tottenham Hale) runs every 15 minutes 4:10 AM–11:25 PM daily. The 45-minute trip costs £18 one-way, £26.50 round-trip if booked online. Tickets cost more when purchased on board.

Luton by Bus and Train: A free airport shuttle runs from Luton Airport to the nearby Luton Airport Parkway Station, from which you can take a train or bus into London. From there, the First Capital Connect train service runs to St. Pancras,

Farringdon, Blackfriars, and London Bridge. The journey takes about 25 minutes. Trains leave every 10 minutes or so from 5 AM until midnight. Single tickets cost £13. The Green Line 757 bus service from Luton to Victoria Station runs three times an hour, takes about 90 minutes, and costs £13 (£14 return).

Heathrow, Gatwick, Stansted, and Luton by Taxi: This is an expensive and time-consuming option. The city's congestion charge (£8) will be added to the bill, you run the risk of getting stuck in traffic, and if you take a taxi from the stand, the price will be even more expensive (whereas a cab booked ahead is a set price). The trip from Heathrow, for example, can take more than an hour and cost more than £50. Checkercars offer cars from Gatwick, Heathrow, and Stansted for a flat fee—at this writing, a taxi trip to Victoria Station costs £42 from Heathrow, £93.50 from Gatwick, and £99 from Stansted.

TRANSFERS BETWEEN AIRPORTS

Allow at least two–three hours for an inter-airport transfer. The cheapest option—but most complicated—is public transport: from Gatwick to Stansted, for instance, you can catch the nonexpress commuter train from Gatwick to Victoria Station, take the Tube to Liverpool Street Station, then catch the train to Stansted from there. To get from Heathrow to Gatwick by public transport, take the Tube to King's Cross, then change to the Victoria Line, get to Victoria Station, and then take the commuter train to Gatwick.

The National Express Airport bus is the most direct option between Gatwick and Heathrow. Buses pick up passengers every 15 minutes from 5:20 AM to 11 PM from both airports. The trip takes around 70 minutes, and the fare is £19.50 one-way. It's advisable to book tickets in advance. National Express buses between Stansted and Gatwick depart every 30 to 45 minutes and take around 3 hours and 45 minutes. The adult single fare is £29.30. Some airlines may offer shuttle services

NAVIGATING LONDON

London is a confusing city to navigate, even for people who've visited it a few times. Its streets are arranged in medieval patterns that no longer make much sense, meaning that you can't always use logic to find your way around. A good map is essential, and public transportation can be a lifesaver: buses will take you magically from point A to point B, and the Tube is often the quickest way to reach your destination. Here are some basic tips to help you find your way around:

■ Although free tourist maps can be handy, they're usually quite basic and include only major streets. If you're going to be doing lots of wandering around, buy the pocket-size map book *London A–Z* sold in bookstores and Tube and train stations throughout the city. Its detailed maps are lifesavers.

■ To find your way, look for tall landmarks near where you are headed: the towering statue of Admiral Nelson in Trafalgar Square, for example, or the cross atop St. Paul's Cathedral—or the most obvious of all, Big Ben.

■ If you get properly lost, the best people to ask are the Londoners hustling by you, who know the area like nobody else. The worst people to ask are the people working in souvenir kiosks, and street vendors selling the local *Evening Standard* newspaper; they're famously rude and unhelpful to lost tourists.

■ The tourist hubs of Soho, Covent Garden, Leicester Square, and Trafalgar Square are separated from one another by only a few blocks. Taking the Tube from one to another actually takes longer than walking.

■ On the other hand, when you're lost, the Tube is often the shortest distance between two points. Don't hesitate to use it.

as well—check with your travel agent in advance of your journey.

Contacts BAA (⊕ www.baa.com). Checkercars (⊕ www.checkercars.com). easy-Bus (⊕ www.easybus.co.uk). First Capital Connect (⊕ www.firstcapitalconnect.co.uk). Gatwick Express (☎ 0870/530–1530 ⊕ www.gatwickexpress.com). Heathrow Express (☎ 0845/600–1515 ⊕ www.heathrowexpress.com). National Express (☎ 0870/580–8080 ⊕ www.nationalexpress.com). Stansted Express (☎ 0845/748–4950 ⊕ www.stanstedexpress.com).

Transfer Information Airport Travel Line (☎ 0870/574–7777).

FLIGHTS

British Airways is the national flagship carrier and offers mostly nonstop flights from 19 U.S. cities to Heathrow and Gatwick airports, along with flights to Manchester, Birmingham, and Glasgow.

Airline Contacts American Airlines (☎ 800/433–7300, 020/7365–0777 in London ⊕ www.aa.com). British Airways (☎ 800/247–9297, 0870/850–9850 in London ⊕ www.ba.com) to Heathrow, Gatwick. Continental Airlines (☎ 800/523–3273 for U.S. and Mexico reservations, 800/231–0856 for international reservations, 01293/776–464, 0845/607–6760 in London ⊕ www.continental.com). Delta Airlines (☎ 800/221–1212 for U.S. reservations, 800/241–4141 for international reservations, 0800/414–767 in London ⊕ www.delta.com). Northwest Airlines (☎ 800/225–2525, 0870/507–4074 in London ⊕ www.nwa.com). United Airlines (☎ 800/864–8331 for U.S. reservations, 800/538–2929 for international reservations, 0845/844–4777 in London ⊕ www.united.com). US Airways (☎ 800/428–4322 for U.S. and Canada reservations, 800/622–1015 for international reservations, 0845/600–3300 in London ⊕ www.usairways.com). Virgin Atlantic (☎ 800/862–8621, 01293/450–150 in London ⊕ www.virgin-atlantic.com).

❚ BUS TRAVEL

ARRIVING AND DEPARTING

National Express is the biggest British coach operator and the nearest equivalent to Greyhound. It's not as fast as traveling by train, but it's comfortable (with washroom facilities on board). Services depart mainly from Victoria Coach Station, a well-signposted short walk behind the Victoria mainline rail station. The departures point is on the corner of Buckingham Palace Road; this is also the main information point. The arrivals point is opposite at Elizabeth Bridge. National Express buses travel to all large and mid-size cities in southern England and the midlands. Scotland and the north are not as well served. The station is extremely busy around holidays and weekends. Arrive at least 30 minutes before departure so you can find the correct exit gate. Smoking is not permitted on board.

Another bus company, Megabus, has been packing in the budget travelers in recent years, since it offers cross-country fares for as little as £1 per person. The company's single- and double-decker buses serve an extensive array of cities across Great Britain with a cheerful budget attitude. In London, buses for all destinations depart from the Green Line bus stand at Victoria Station. Megabus does not accommodate wheelchairs, and the company strictly limits luggage to one piece per person checked, and one piece of hand luggage.

Green Line serves the counties surrounding London, as well as airports. Bus stops (there's no central bus station) are on Buckingham Palace Road, between the Victoria mainline station and Victoria Coach Station.

Tickets on some long-distance routes are cheaper if purchased in advance, and traveling midweek is cheaper than over weekends and at holiday periods.

GETTING AROUND LONDON

Private, as opposed to municipal, buses are known as coaches. Although London is famous for its double-decker buses, long articulated buses (locally known as "bendy buses") replaced the oldest buses—the beloved rattletrap Routemasters, which had the jump-on/off back platforms, under the previous mayor. However, these proved both unpopular and money-losing and are being phased out, to be replaced by a redesigned Routemaster in 2011. Two Routemaster "heritage" routes keep the old familiar double-decker buses working, however: the No. 9 travels through Piccadilly, Trafalgar Square, and Knightsbridge, and the No. 15 travels from Trafalgar Square down Fleet Street and on to St. Paul's Cathedral.

Bus stops are clearly indicated; signs at bus stops feature a red TfL symbol on a plain white background. You must flag the bus down at some stops. Each numbered route is listed on the main stop, and buses have a large number on the front with their end destination. Not all buses run the full route at all times; check with the driver to be sure. You can pick up a free bus guide at a TfL Travel Information Centre (at Euston, Liverpool Street, Piccadilly Circus, and Victoria Tube stations; and at Heathrow Airport).

Buses are a good way of seeing the town, particularly if you plan to hop on and off to cover many sights, but don't take a bus if you're in a hurry, as traffic can really slow them down. To get off, press the red STOP buttons mounted on poles near the doors. You will usually see a BUS STOPPING sign light up. Expect to get very squashed during rush hour, from 8 AM to 9:30 AM and 4:30 PM to 6:30 PM.

Night buses, denoted by an N before their route numbers, run from midnight to 5 AM on a more restricted route than day buses. However, some night bus routes should be approached with caution and the top deck avoided. All night buses run by request stop, so flag them down if you're waiting or push the button if you want to alight.

All journeys cost £2, and there are no transfers. If you plan to make a number of journeys in one day, consider buying a Travelcard (⇨ *Underground Tube Travel*), good for both Tube and bus travel. Also consider getting a prepaid Oyster card, as single journeys are less than a pound using a prepaid card. Travelcards are also available in one-, three-, or seven-day combinations. Visitor Oyster cards cost £2 and can be topped up. They are available from ticket desks at Gatwick and Stansted airports or at any Tube station and are transferable if you have money left over. Traveling without a valid ticket makes you liable for a fine (£20). Buses are supposed to swing by most stops every five or six minutes, but in reality, you can often expect to wait a bit longer, although those in the center of town are quite reliable.

In central London, if you don't have a prepaid Travel- or Oyster card, you must pay before you board the bus. Automated ticket machines are set up at these bus stops, which are clearly marked with a yellow sign BUY TICKETS BEFORE BOARDING. Otherwise, you can buy tickets at most central London Tube stations as well as at newsagents and shops that display the sign BUY YOUR TRAVELCARDS & BUS PASSES HERE. Outside the central zone, payment may be made to the driver as you board (exact change is best so as to avoid incurring the driver's wrath).

Bus Information Green Line (☎ 0870/608–7261 ⊕ www.greenline.co.uk). **Easy-Bus** (☎ www.easybus.com). **Megabus** (☎ 0900/160–0900 ⊕ www.megabus.com). **National Express** (☎ 0870/580–8080 ⊕ www.nationalexpress.com). **Transport for London** (☎ 020/7222–1234 ⊕ www.tfl.gov.uk). **Victoria Coach Station** (☎ 020/7730–3499).

❙ CAR TRAVEL

The best advice on driving in London is this: don't. London's streets are a winding mass of chaos, made worse by one-way roads. Parking is also restrictive and expensive, and traffic is tediously slow at most times of the day; during rush hours—from 8 AM to 9:30 AM and 4:30 PM to 6:30 PM—it often grinds to a standstill, particularly on Friday, when everyone wants to leave town. Avoid city-center shopping areas, including the roads feeding Oxford Street, Kensington, and Knightsbridge. Other main roads into the city center are also busy, such as King's Cross and Euston in the north. Watch out also for cyclists and motorcycle couriers who weave between cars and pedestrians and seem to come out of nowhere, and you may be fined heavily for straying into a bus lane.

If you are staying just in London on this trip, there's virtually no reason to rent a car since the city and its suburbs are widely covered by public transportation. However, you might want a car for day trips to castles or stately homes out in the countryside. Consider renting your car in a medium-size town in the area where you'll be traveling, and then journeying there by train and picking up the car once you arrive. Rental rates are generally reasonable, and insurance costs are lower than in comparable U.S. cities. Rates generally begin at £35 a day for a small economy car (such as a subcompact General Motors Vauxhall, Corsa, or Renault Clio), usually with manual transmission. Air-conditioning and unlimited mileage generally come with the larger-size automatic cars.

In London your U.S. driver's license is acceptable (as long as you are over 23 years old, with no endorsements or driving convictions). If you have a driver's license from a country other than the United States, it may not be recognized in the United Kingdom. An International Driver's Permit is a good idea no matter what; it's available from the American (AAA) or Canadian Automobile Association and, in the United Kingdom, from the Automobile Association (AA) or Royal Automobile Club (RAC). International permits are universally recognized, and

having one may save you a problem with the local authorities.

Remember that Britain drives on the left, and the rest of Europe on the right. Therefore, you may want to leave your rented car in Britain and pick up a left-side drive if you cross the Channel (⇨ *The Channel Tunnel*).

CONGESTION CHARGE

Designed to reduce traffic through central London, a congestion charge has been instituted. Vehicles (with some exemptions) entering central London on weekdays from 7 AM to 6:30 PM (excluding public holidays) have to pay an £8 daily fee; it can be paid up to 90 days in advance, or on the day you need it. Day-, week-, month-, and year-long passes are available on the Congestion Charging page of the Transport for London Web site, at gas stations, parking lots (car parks), by mail, by phone, and by SMS text message. Traffic signs designate the entrance to congestion areas, and cameras read car license plates and send the information to a database. Drivers who don't pay the congestion charge by midnight after the day of driving are penalized £80, which is reduced to £40 if paid within 14 days.

Information Congestion Charge Customer Service (✉ *Box 2985, Coventry CV7 8ZR* ☎ *0845/900–1234* ⊕ *www.cclondon.com*). **Transport for London** (⊕ *www.tfl.gov.uk*).

GASOLINE

Gasoline (petrol) is sold in liters and is expensive (about £1 per liter—around $6.50 per gallon—at this writing). Unleaded petrol, denoted by green pump lines, is predominant. Premium and Super Premium are the two varieties, and most cars run on regular Premium. Supermarket pumps usually offer the best value. You won't find many service stations in the center of town; these are generally on main, multilane trunk roads out of the center. Service is self-serve, except in small villages, where gas stations are likely to be closed on Sunday and late evening. Most stations accept major credit cards.

PARKING

During the day—and probably at all times—it's safest to believe that you can park nowhere except at a meter, in a pay-and-display bay, in a garage, or where you are sure there are no lines or signs; otherwise, you run the risk of an expensive ticket, plus possibly even more expensive clamping and towing fees (some boroughs are clamp-free). Restrictions are indicated by the NO WAITING parking signpost on the sidewalk (these restrictions vary from street to street), and restricted areas include single yellow lines or double yellow lines, and Residents' Parking bays. Parking at a bus stop or in a red-line bus lane is also restricted. It's illegal to park on the sidewalk, across entrances, or on white zigzag lines approaching a pedestrian crossing.

Meters have an insatiable hunger in the inner city—a 20p piece may buy just six minutes—and some will permit only a two-hour stay. Meters take 20p and £1 coins, pay-and-display machines 10p, 20p, 50p, £1 and £2 coins. Some take payment by credit card. In some parts of central London, meters have been almost entirely replaced by pay-and-display machines that require payment by phone. You will need to set up an account to do this (⊕ *www.westminster.gov.uk*). Meters are free after 6:30 or 8:30 in the evening, on Sunday, and on holidays. Always check the sign. In the evening, after restrictions end, meter bays are free. In the daytime, take advantage of the many NCP parking lots in the center of town (about £2.50–£3 per hour, up to eight hours).

Information NCP (☎ *0845/050–7080* ⊕ *www. ncp.co.uk*).

ROADSIDE EMERGENCIES

If your car is stolen, you're in a car accident, or your car breaks down and there's nobody around to help you, contact the police by dialing ☎ *999*.

The general procedure for a breakdown is the following: position the red hazard triangle (which should be in the trunk of the car) a few paces away from the rear of the car. Leave the hazard warning lights on. Along highways (motorways), emergency roadside telephone booths are positioned at intervals within walking distance. Contact the car-rental company or an auto club. The main auto clubs in the United Kingdom are the Automobile Association (AA) and the Royal Automobile Club (RAC). If you're a member of the American Automobile Association (AAA), check your membership details before you depart for Britain, as, under a reciprocal agreement, roadside assistance in the United Kingdom should cost you nothing. You can join and receive roadside assistance from the AA on the spot, but the charge is higher—around £75—than a simple membership fee.

Emergency Services American Automobile Association (☎ *800/564–6222*). **Automobile Association** (☎ *0870/550–0600, 44–161– 495–8945 from outside U.K., 0800/887–766 for emergency roadside assistance from mobile phones, 08457/887766*). **Royal Automobile Club** (☎ *0870/572–2722*).

RULES OF THE ROAD

London is a mass of narrow, one-way roads, and narrow, two-way streets that are no bigger than the one-way roads. If you must risk life and limb and drive in London, note that the speed limit is either 20 or 30 mph—unless you see the large 40 mph signs found only in the suburbs. Speed bumps are sprinkled about with abandon in case you forget. Speed is strictly controlled by cameras mounted absolutely everywhere, which ruthlessly photograph speeders for ticketing.

Medium-size intersections are often designed as "roundabouts" (marked by signs in which three arrows curve into a circle). On these, cars travel left in a circle and incoming cars must yield to those already on their way around from the right. Signal when about to leave the roundabout.

Jaywalking is not illegal in London and everybody does it, despite the fact that striped crossings with blinking yellow lights mounted on poles at either end—called "zebra crossings"—give pedestrians the right of way to cross. Cars should treat zebra crossings like stop signs if a pedestrian is waiting to cross or already starting to cross. It's illegal to pass another vehicle at a zebra crossing. At other crossings (including intersections) pedestrians must yield to traffic, but they do have the right-of-way over traffic turning left at controlled crossings—if they have the nerve.

Traffic lights sometimes have arrows directing left or right turns; try to catch a glimpse of the road markings in time, and don't get into the turn lane if you mean to go straight ahead. A right turn is not permitted on a red light. Signs at the beginning and end of designated bus lanes give the time restrictions for use (usually during peak hours); if you're caught driving on bus lanes during restricted hours, you could be fined. By law, seat belts must be worn in the front and back seats. Drunk-driving laws are strictly enforced, and it's safest to avoid alcohol altogether if you'll be driving. The legal limit is 80 milligrams of alcohol per 100 milliliters of blood, which roughly translated means two units of alcohol—two small glasses of wine, one pint of beer, or one glass of whiskey.

■ UNDERGROUND TRAVEL

London's extensive Underground train (Tube) system has color-coded routes, clear signage, and many connections. Trains run out into the suburbs, and all stations are marked with the London Underground circular symbol. (Do not be confused by similar-looking signs reading "subway"—in Britain, the word subway means "pedestrian underpass.") Trains are all one class; smoking is *not* allowed on board or in the stations. There is also

an Overground network serving the further reaches of Inner London. These now accept Oyster cards.

Some lines have multiple branches (Central, District, Northern, Metropolitan, and Piccadilly), so be sure to note which branch is needed for your particular destination. Do this by noting the end destination on the lighted sign on the platform, which also tells you how long you'll have to wait until the train arrives. Compare that with the end destination of the branch you want. When the two match, that's your train. ■ TIP→ Service on many Tube lines will be disrupted as a widespread improvements program continues before the 2012 Olympics. Check the TfL Web site for up-to-date information.

London is divided into six concentric zones (ask at Underground ticket booths for a map and booklet, which give details of the ticket options), so be sure to buy a ticket for the correct zone or you may be liable for an on-the-spot fine of £20. Don't panic if you do forget to buy a ticket for the right zone: just tell a station attendant that you need to buy an "extension" to your ticket. Although you're meant to do that in advance, generally if you're an out-of-towner, they don't give you a hard time.

For single fares, a flat £4 price per journey now applies across all six zones, whether you're traveling one stop or 12 stops. If you're planning several trips in one day, it's much cheaper to buy a tourist Oystercard or Travelcard, which is good for unrestricted travel on the Tube, buses, and some overground railways for the day. Bear in mind that Travelcards cost much more if purchased before the 9:30 AM rush-hour threshold. A one-day Travelcard for Zones 1–2 costs £7.20 if purchased before 9:30 AM, and £5.60 if bought after 9:30 AM. The more zones included in your travel, the more the Travelcard will cost. For example, Kew is Zone 4, and Heathrow is Zone 6. If you're going to be in town for several days, buy a three-day Travelcard (£18.40

for Zones 1–2, £42.40 for Zones 1–6). Children under 11 travel free on the Tube and buses after 9:30 AM, and children ages 11–15 travel free on buses as long as they order an Oyster card at least four weeks before they travel.

Oyster cards are "smart cards" that can be charged with a cash value and then used for discounted travel throughout the city. Each time you take the Tube or bus, you swipe the blue card across the yellow readers at the entrance and the amount of your fare is deducted. The London mayor is so eager to promote the cards that he set up a system in which those using Oyster cards pay lower rates. Oystercard Tube fares are £1.60–£2.20 if purchased during the off-peak hours of 9:30 AM–4 PM, £1.60–£3.80 if bought during peak rush hours. You can open an Oyster account online or pick up an Oyster card at any London Underground station, and then prepay any amount you wish for your expected travel while in the city. Using an Oyster card, bus fares are 90p instead of £2. If you make numerous journeys in a single day, your Oyster card deductions will always be capped at the standard price of a one-day Travelcard.

Trains begin running just after 5 AM Monday–Saturday; the last services leave central London between midnight and 12:30 AM. On Sunday, trains start two hours later and finish about an hour earlier. The frequency of trains depends on the route and the time of day, but normally you should not have to wait more than 10 minutes in central areas.

There are TfL Travel Information Centres at the following Tube stations: Euston, Liverpool Street, Piccadilly Circus, and Victoria, open 7:15 AM–9:15 PM; and at Heathrow Airport (in Terminals 1, 2, and 3), open 6:30 AM–10 PM.

Information Transport for London (☎ 020/7222-1234 ⊕ www.tfl.gov.uk).

▌TAXI

Universally known as "black cabs" (even though many of them now come in other colors), the traditional big black London taxicabs are as much a part of the city's streetscape as red double-decker buses, and for good reason: the unique, spacious taxis easily hold five people, plus luggage. To earn a taxi license, drivers must undergo intensive training on the history and geography of London. The course, and all that the drivers have learned in it, is known simply as "the Knowledge." There's almost nothing your taxi driver won't know about the city.

Hotels and main tourist areas have cab-stands (just take the first in line), but you can also flag one down from the roadside. If the yellow FOR HIRE sign on the top is lighted, the taxi is available. Cab-drivers often cruise at night with their signs unlighted so that they can choose their passengers and avoid those they think might cause trouble. If you see an unlighted, passengerless cab, hail it: you might be lucky.

Fares start at £2.20 and charge by the minute—a journey of a mile (which might take between 5 and 12 minutes) will cost anything from £4.40 to £8 (the fare goes up between 10 PM and 6 AM—a system designed to persuade more taxi drivers to work at night). A surcharge of £2 is applied to a telephone booking. At Christmas and New Year, there is an additional surcharge of £4. You can, but do not have to, tip taxi drivers 10%–15% of the tab.

Minicabs, which operate out of small, curbside offices throughout the city, are generally cheaper than black cabs, but are less reliable and trusted. These are usually unmarked passenger cars, and their drivers are often not native Londoners, and do not have to take or pass "the Knowledge" test. Still, Londoners use them in droves because they are plentiful and cheap. If you choose to use them, do not ever take an unlicensed cab: anyone who curb-crawls looking for customers is likely to be unlicensed. Unlicensed cabs have been associated with many crimes and can be dangerous. All cab companies with proper dispatch offices are likely to be licensed. Look out for a small purple version of the Underground logo on the front or rear windscreen with "private hire" written across it.

There are plenty of trustworthy and licensed minicab firms. For London-wide service try Lady Mini Cabs, which employs only women drivers, or Addison Lee, which uses comfortable minivans but requires that you know the full postal code for both your pickup location and your destination. When using a minicab, always ask the price in advance when you phone for the car, then verify with the driver before the journey begins.

Black Cabs Dial-a-Cab (☎ *0207/253–5000*). **Radio Taxis** (☎ *0207/272–0272*).

Minicabs Addison Lee (☎ *0844/800–6677*). **Lady Mini Cabs** (☎ *0207/272–3300*).

▌ DLR: DOCKLANDS LIGHT RAILWAY

For destinations in East London, the quiet, driverless Docklands Light Railway (DLR) is a good alternative, offering interesting views of the area.

The DLR connects with the Tube network at Bank and Tower Hill stations as well as at Canary Wharf. It goes to London City Airport, the Docklands financial district, and Greenwich, running 5:30 AM–12:30 AM Monday–Saturday, 7 AM–11:30 PM Sunday. The DLR takes Oyster cards and Travelcards, and fares are the same as those on the Tube. A £13.50 Rail & River Rover ticket combines one-day DLR travel with hop-on, hop-off travel on City Cruises riverboats between Westminster, Waterloo, Tower and Greenwich piers.

Information Transport for London (☎ *020/7222–1234* ⊕ *www.tfl.gov.uk*).

▌ RIVER BUS

In the run-up to the 2012 Olympics, a new push is being made to develop river travel as part of London's overall public transport system. The service stops at 10 piers between the London Eye/Waterloo and Greenwich, with peak-time extensions to Putney in the west and Woolwich Arsenal in the east. The Waterloo-Woolwich commuter service runs every 20 minutes from 6 AM–1 AM on weekdays, 8:30 AM–midnight on weekends. Tickets are £3–£5, with a one-third discount for Oyster card and Travelcard holders (full integration into the Oyster card system is expected in 2011). When there are events at the O2 (North Greenwich Arena), a half-hourly express service runs to and from Waterloo starting three hours before the event. There is also a special Tate-to-Tate express, a 20-minute trip between Tate Modern and Tate Britain that costs £5.30. Boats run every 40 minutes from 10–5. A £12 River Roamer ticket offers unlimited river travel from 10–10 weekdays and 8 AM–10 PM on weekends.

Contacts Thames Clippers (☎ *0870/781–5049* ⊕ *www.thamesclippers.com*). **London River Services** (☎ *020/941–2400* ⊕ *www.tfl. gov*).

▌ TRAIN TRAVEL

The National Rail Enquiries Web site is the clearinghouse for information on train times and fares as well as to book rail journeys around Britain—and the earlier the better. Tickets bought two to three weeks in advance can cost a quarter of the price of tickets bought on the day of travel. However, journeys within commuting distance of city centers are sold at unvarying set prices, and those can be purchased on the day you expect to make your journey without any financial penalty. Note that, in busy city centers such as London, all travel costs more during morning rush hour. You can purchase tickets online, by phone, or at any rail station in the United Kingdom. Check the Web site or call the National Rail Enquiries line to get details of the train company responsible for your journey and have them give you a breakdown of available ticket prices. Regardless of which train company is involved, many discount passes are available, such as the 16–25 Railcard (for which you must be under 26 and provide a passport-size photo) and the Family & Friends Travelcard, which can be bought from most mainline stations. But if you intend to make several long-distance rail journeys, it can be a good idea to invest in a BritRail Pass (which you must buy in the United States).

BritRail passes come in two basic varieties. The Classic pass allows travel on consecutive days, and the FlexiPass allows a number of travel days within a set period of time. The cost (in U.S. dollars) of a BritRail Consecutive Pass adult ticket for eight days is $399 standard and $576 first-class; for 15 days, $576 and $845; and for a month, $845 and $1,259. The cost of a BritRail FlexiPass adult ticket for four days' travel in two months is $315 standard and $465 first-class; for eight days' travel in two months, $459 and $715; and for 15 days' travel in two months, $689 and $1,025. Prices drop by about 25% for off-peak travel passes between November and February. Passes for students, seniors, and ages 16–25 are discounted, too.

Most long-distance trains have refreshment carriages, called buffet cars. Most trains these days also have "quiet cars" where use of cell phones and music devices is banned, but these rules are not enforced with any enthusiasm. Smoking is forbidden in all rail carriages.

Generally speaking, rail travel in the United Kingdom is expensive: for instance, a round-trip ticket to Bath from London can cost around £60 per person at peak times. The fee drops to around £35 at other times, so it's best to travel before or after the frantic business commuter rush (after 9:30 AM and before 4:30 PM). Credit cards are accepted for train fares paid both in person and by phone.

Delays are not uncommon, but they're rarely long. You almost always have to go to the station to find out if there's going to be one (because delays tend to happen at the last minute). Luckily, most stations have coffee shops, restaurants, and pubs where you can cool your heels while you wait for the train to get rolling. National Rail Enquiries provides an up-to-date state-of-the-railways schedule.

Most of the time, first-class train travel in England isn't particularly first-class. Some train companies don't offer at-seat service, so you still have to get up and go to the buffet car for food or drinks. First class is generally booked by business travelers on expense accounts because crying babies and noisy families are quite rare in first class, and quite common in standard class.

Short of flying, taking the Eurostar train through the channel tunnel is the fastest way to reach the continent: 35 minutes from Folkestone to Calais, 60 minutes from motorway to motorway, or 2 hours and 15 minutes from London's St. Pancras Station to Paris's Gare du Nord. The Belgian border is just a short drive northeast of Calais. High-speed Eurostar trains use the same tunnels to connect London's St. Pancras Station directly with Midi Station in Brussels in around two hours. If purchased in advance, round-trip tickets from London to Belgium or France cost between £90 and £125, cheaper in the very early or very late hours of the day.

Information BritRail Travel (☎ 1–866/274–8724 in U.S. ⊕ www.raileurope.com). **Eurostar** (☎ 0870/518–6186 in U.K. ⊕ www.eurostar. co.uk). **National Rail Enquiries** (☎ 0845/748–4950, 020/7278–5240 outside U.K. ⊕ www. nationalrail.co.uk).

Channel Tunnel Car Transport Eurotunnel (☎ 0870/535–3535 in U.K., 070/223–210 in Belgium, 03–21–00–61–00 in France ⊕ www. eurotunnel.com). **Rail Europe** (☎ 1–800/361–7245 in U.S., 0844/848–4064 in U.K. for inquiries and credit-card bookings ⊕ www. raileurope.com).

ESSENTIALS

■ BUSINESS SERVICES AND FACILITIES

There are several FedEx Kinko's and Mail Boxes Etc. locations in London to handle your photocopying, next-day mail, and packaging needs. Check their Web sites for more locations.

Contacts FedEx Kinko's (✉ 1 Curzon St., Mayfair, London ☎ 020/7717–4900 ⊕ www.kinkos. co.uk). **Mail Boxes Etc.** (✉ 19–21 Crawford St., Marylebone, London ☎ 020/7224–2666 ⊕ www.mbe.com).

■ COMMUNICATIONS

INTERNET

If you're traveling with a laptop, carry a spare battery and adapter: new batteries and replacement adapters are expensive; if you do need to replace them, head to Tottenham Court Road (W1), which is lined with computer specialists. For Macintosh computers, Micro Anvika is a good chain for parts and batteries, and the Apple Store on Regent Street off Oxford Street does repairs. John Lewis department store and Selfridges, on Oxford Street (W1), also carry a limited range of computer supplies.

Never plug your computer into any socket before asking about surge protection. Some hotels do not have built-in current stabilizers, and extreme electrical fluctuations and surges, although very rare, can short your adapter or even destroy your computer. IBM sells an invaluable pen-size modem tester that plugs into a telephone jack to check if the line is safe to use.

The United Kingdom is finally catching up to the United States in terms of the spread of broadband and Wi-Fi. In London, free Wi-Fi is increasingly available in hotels, pubs, coffee shops—even certain branches of McDonald's—and broadband coverage is widespread; generally speaking, the pricier the hotel, the more likely you are to find Wi-Fi there. To find your nearest free hot spot, see the Wi-Fi FreeSpot Web site.

Contacts Cybercafes (⊕ www.cybercafes. com) lists more than 4,000 Internet cafés worldwide. **Wi-Fi FreeSpot** (⊕ www. wififreespot.com).

PHONES

The good news is that you can now make a direct-dial telephone call from virtually any point on earth. The bad news? You can't always do so cheaply. Calling from a hotel is almost always the most expensive option; hotels usually add huge surcharges to all calls, particularly international ones. Calling cards usually keep costs to a minimum, but only if you purchase them locally. And then there are mobile phones, which are sometimes more prevalent—particularly in the developing world—than landlines; as expensive as mobile phone calls can be, they are still usually a much cheaper option than calling from your hotel.

The minimum charge from a public phone is 40p for a 110-second call. To make cheap calls it's a good idea to pick up an international phone card, available from newsstands, which can be used from residential, hotel, and public pay phones. With these, you can call the United States for as little as 5p per minute.

To dial from the United States or Canada, first dial 011, then Great Britain's country code, 44. Continue with the local area code, dropping the initial "0." The code for London is 020 (so from abroad you'd dial 20), followed by a 7 for numbers in central London, or an 8 for numbers in the Greater London area. Freephone (toll-free) numbers start with 0800 or 0808; national information numbers start with 0845.

A word of warning: 0870 numbers are *not* toll-free numbers; in fact, numbers beginning with this, 0871, or the 0900 prefix are "premium rate" numbers, and it costs extra to call them. The amount varies and is usually relatively small when dialed from within the country but can be excessive when dialed from outside the United Kingdom.

CALLING WITHIN BRITAIN

There are three types of phones: those that accept (1) only coins, (2) only British Telecom (BT) phone cards, or (3) BT phone cards and credit cards, although with the advent of mobiles, it's increasingly difficult to find any type of public phone.

The coin-operated phones are of the push-button variety; the workings of coin-operated telephones vary, but there are usually instructions on each unit. Most take 10p, 20p, 50p, and £1 coins. Insert the coins *before* dialing (the minimum charge is 10p). If you hear a repeated single tone after dialing, the line is busy; a continual tone means the number is unobtainable (or that you have dialed the wrong—or no—prefix). The indicator panel shows you how much money is left; add more whenever you like. If there is no answer, replace the receiver and your money will be returned.

There are several different directory-assistance providers. For information anywhere in Britain, try dialing 118–888 (49p per call, then 9p per minute) or 118–118 (49p per call, then 14p per minute); you'll need to know the town and the street (or at least the neighborhood) of the person or organization for which you're requesting information. For the operator, dial 100.

You don't have to dial London's central area code (020) if you are calling inside London itself—just the eight-digit telephone number. However, you do need to use it if you're dialing an 0207 (Inner London) number from an 0208 (Outer London) number, and vice versa.

For long-distance calls within Britain, dial the area code (which begins with 01), followed by the number. The area-code prefix is used only when you are dialing from outside the destination. In provincial areas, the dialing codes for nearby towns are often posted in the booth.

CALLING OUTSIDE BRITAIN

For assistance with international calls, dial 155.

To make an international call from London, dial 00, followed by the country code and the local number.

When calling from overseas to access a London telephone number, drop the first 0 from the prefix and dial only 20 (or any other British area code) and then the eight-digit phone number.

The United States country code is 1.

Access Codes **AT&T Direct** (☎ *0500/890–011*). **MCI** (☎ *0800/279–5088 in U.K., 800/444–4141 for U.S. and other areas*). **Sprint International Access** (☎ *0800/890–877*).

CALLING CARDS

Public card phones operate with either cash or with special cards that you can buy from post offices or newsstands. Ideal for longer calls, they are composed of units of 10p, and come in values of £3, £5, £10, and more. To use a card phone, lift the receiver, insert your card, and dial the number. An indicator panel shows the number of units used. At the end of your call, the card will be returned. Where credit cards are taken, slide the card through, as indicated.

MOBILE PHONES

If you have a multiband phone (Britain uses different frequencies from those used in the United States) and your service provider uses the world-standard GSM network (as do T-Mobile, AT&T, and Verizon), you can probably use your phone abroad. Roaming fees can be steep, however: 99¢ a minute is considered reasonable. And overseas you normally pay the toll charges for incoming calls. It's almost always cheaper to send a text message than to make a call, since text messages have a very low set fee (often less than 5¢).

If you just want to make local calls, consider buying a new SIM card (note that your provider may have to unlock your phone for you to use a different SIM card) and a prepaid service plan in London. You can top up your prepaid card at any ATM. You'll then have a local number and can make local calls at local rates. If your trip is extensive, you could also simply buy a new cell phone in your destination, as the initial cost will be offset over time.

■ TIP➜ If you travel internationally frequently, save one of your old mobile phones or buy a cheap one on the Internet; ask your cell phone company to unlock it for you, and take it with you as a travel phone, buying a new SIM card with pay-as-you-go service in each destination.

Any cell phone can be used in Britain if it's tri-band/GSM. Travelers should ask their cell phone company if their phone is tri-band and what network it uses, and make sure it is activated for international calling before leaving their home country.

You can rent a cell phone from most car-rental agencies in London. Some upscale hotels now provide loaner cell phones to their guests. Beware, however, of the per-minute rates charged, as these can be shockingly high.

Contacts Cellular Abroad (☎ 800/287–5072 ⊕ www.cellularabroad.com) rents and sells GMS phones and sells SIM cards that work in many countries. **Mobal** (☎ 888/888–9162 ⊕ www.mobalrental.com) rents mobiles and sells GSM phones (starting at $49) that will operate in 150 countries. Per-call rates vary throughout the world. **Planet Fone** (☎ 888/988–4777 ⊕ www.planetfone. com) rents cell phones, but the per-minute rates are expensive. **Rent a Mobile Phone** (☎ 0870/750–0770 ⊕ www.rent-mobile-phone. com) has phones with short contract.

■ CUSTOMS AND DUTIES

You're always allowed to bring goods of a certain value back home without having to pay any duty or import tax. But there's a limit on the amount of tobacco and liquor you can bring back duty-free,

and some countries have separate limits for perfumes; for exact figures, check with your customs department. The values of so-called "duty-free" goods are included in these amounts. When you shop abroad, save all your receipts, as customs inspectors may ask to see them as well as the items you purchased. If the total value of your goods is more than the duty-free limit, you'll have to pay a tax (most often a flat percentage) on the value of everything beyond that limit.

There are two levels of duty-free allowance for entering Britain: one for goods bought outside the European Union (EU) and the other for goods bought within the EU.

Of goods bought outside the EU you may import the following duty-free: 200 cigarettes or 100 cigarillos or 50 cigars or 250 grams of tobacco; 4 liters of table wine and 16 liters of beer and, in addition, either 1 liter of alcohol over 22% by volume (most spirits), or 2 liters of alcohol under 22% by volume (fortified or sparkling wine or liqueurs).

Of goods bought within the EU, you should not exceed the following (unless you can prove they are for personal use): 3,200 cigarettes, 400 cigarillos, 200 cigars, or 3 kilograms of tobacco, plus 10 liters of spirits, 20 liters of fortified wine, 90 liters of wine, or 110 liters of beer.

Pets (dogs and cats) can be brought into the United Kingdom from the United States without six months' quarantine, provided that the animal meets all the PETS (Pet Travel Scheme) requirements, including microchipping and vaccination. Other pets have to undergo a lengthy quarantine, and penalties for breaking this law are severe and strictly enforced.

Fresh meats, vegetables, plants, and dairy products may be imported from within the EU. Controlled drugs, flick knives, and self-defense sprays may not be brought into the United Kingdom, while firearms (both real and imitation) and ammunition, as well as souvenirs made from endangered plants or animals are barred except with relevant permits.

Information HM Revenue and Customs (⊠ *Portcullis House, 21 Cowbridge Rd. E, Cardiff* ☎ *0845/010–9000* ⊕ *www.hmrc.gov. uk*). **U.S. Customs and Border Protection** (⊕ *www.cbp.gov*).

▌ELECTRICITY

The electrical current in London is 220–240 volts (coming into line with the rest of Europe at 230 volts), 50 cycles alternating current (AC); wall outlets take three-pin plugs, and shaver sockets take two round, oversize prongs. For converters, adapters, and advice, stop in one of the many STA Travel shops around London or at Nomad Travel.

Consider making a small investment in a universal adapter, which has several types of plugs in one lightweight, compact unit. Most laptops and mobile phone chargers are dual voltage (i.e., they operate equally well on 110 and 220 volts), and thus require only an adapter. These days the same is true of small appliances such as hair dryers. Always check labels and manufacturer instructions to be sure. Don't use 110-volt outlets marked FOR SHAVERS ONLY for high-wattage appliances such as hair dryers.

Contacts Nomad Travel (⊠ *40 Bernard St., Bloomsbury* ☎ *020/7833–4114* ⊠ *52 Grosvenor Gardens, Victoria* ☎ *020/7823–5823*). **STA Travel** (⊕ *www.statravel.co.uk*). **Steve Kropla's Help for World Travelers** (⊕ *www. kropla.com*) has information on electrical and telephone plugs around the world. **Walkabout Travel Gear** (⊕ *www.walkabouttravelgear.com*) offers some helpful advice on electricity under ADAPTERS.

▌EMERGENCIES

London is a relatively safe city, though crime does happen. If you need to report a theft or an attack, head to the nearest police station (listed in the Yellow Pages or the local directory) or dial 999 for police, fire, or ambulance (be prepared to give the telephone number you're calling from). National Health Service hospitals, several of which are listed below, give free, round-the-clock treatment in Accident and Emergency sections, where waits can be an hour or more. Prescriptions are valid only if made out by doctors registered in the United Kingdom. All branches of Boots are dispensing pharmacies, and the one listed is open until midnight.

Doctors and Dentists Dental Emergency Care Service (☎ *020/7748–9365*). **UCL Eastman Dental Hospital** (⊠ *256 Gray's Inn Rd.* ☎ *020/7915–1000*). **Medical Express Clinic** (⊠ *117A Harley St.* ☎ *020/7499–1991*).

Foreign Embassies U.S. Embassy (⊠ *24 Grosvenor Sq., Mayfair* ☎ *020/7499–9000* ✉ *londonpassport@state.gov* ⊕ *www. usembassy.org.uk*).

General Emergency Contacts Ambulance, fire, police (☎ *999*).

Hospitals and Clinics Charing Cross Hospital (⊠ *Fulham Palace Rd., Fulham* ☎ *020/8846–1234*). **Royal Free Hospital** (⊠ *Pond St., Hampstead* ☎ *020/7794–0500*). **St. Thomas's Hospital** (⊠ *Westminster Bridge Rd., Lambeth* ☎ *020/7188–7188*). **University College Hospital** (⊠ *235 Euston Rd, Bloomsbury* ☎ *0845/155–5000*).

Hotlines Samaritans (☎ *0845/790–9090*) for counseling.

Pharmacies Boots (⊠ *44–46 Regent St., Piccadilly Circus* ☎ *020/7734–6126* ⊕ *www. boots.com*).

▌HEALTH

OVER-THE-COUNTER REMEDIES

Over-the-counter medications in Britain are similar to those in the United States, with a few significant differences. For one thing, medications are sold in boxes rather than bottles, and are sold in very small amounts—usually no more than 24 pills per package. There may also be fewer brands than you're likely to be used to. All headache medicine is usually filed

LOCAL DO'S AND TABOOS

CUSTOMS OF THE COUNTRY

In general, British and American rules of etiquette are much the same. Differences are subtle. British people find American and Canadian bluntness somewhat startling from time to time, but are charmed by their friendliness. Londoners tend to take politeness extremely seriously—they say "thank you" at every stage of a financial transaction, but they so value their isolation and personal space that they are unlikely to offer a "God bless you" should a stranger sneeze.

The famous British stiff upper lip is more relaxed these days, but on social occasions the best option is to observe what the others do, and then go with the flow. If you're visiting a family home, a gift of flowers is welcome, as is a bottle of wine, or maybe some candy for the children—but not all three.

GREETINGS

British people will shake hands on greeting old friends or acquaintances; female friends may greet each other with a kiss on the cheek. In Britain, you can never say please, thank you, or sorry too often; to thank your host, a phone call or card does nicely.

SIGHTSEEING

As in the United States, in public places it is considered polite to give up your seat to an elderly person, to a pregnant woman, or a burdened parent struggling with young children and bags—and there are also designated seats for them that should be vacated if necessary. Jaywalking is not illegal in England and everybody does it.

Out of town, British people take waiting in line (called "queuing") seriously (although these days London itself is more of a free-for-all)—if there is a visible queue, you should join at the end, as, even in polite London, "queue jumpers" who try to cut in line may be turned on with some ferocity. Complaining while waiting in line is considered wimpy. Enduring the wait with good humor is considered a sign of strong moral character.

OUT ON THE TOWN

Etiquette in restaurants is much the same in London as in any major U.S. city. In restaurants you hail a waiter by saying, "Excuse me..." as one passes by, or by trying to catch their eye by politely signaling with subtle hand signals. Friends and co-workers frequently gather in pubs, but you don't have to drink alcohol—you're allowed to drink juice or sodas. However, drunkenness is very common after about 9 PM—London has a serious binge-drinking culture—and many people avoid taking the Tube or bus late in the evening to avoid drunk travelers.

You're generally expected to dress "casually smart" for the theater (suits or nice jackets for men, skirts or nice slacks for women), and those going to nightclubs will dress just the same here as they would in New York or Chicago—the flashier the better. Pubs are very casual places, however, and jeans and sneakers are perfectly acceptable there.

The single thing you can do that will most mark you as a tourist—and an impolite one—is failing to observe the rule that, on virtually all escalators but especially those in Tube stations, you stand on the right side of the escalator and leave room for people to walk past you on the left. Commuters are far too impatient to wait for the escalator to make its way to the top or the bottom, and they need to be able to rush by you. If you're in their way, they'll never forgive you.

There is a ban on smoking in public, including all bars and restaurants.

DOING BUSINESS

In business, punctuality is of prime importance; if you anticipate a late arrival, call ahead. For business dinners, it's not assumed that spouses will attend unless prearranged, and if you proffered the invitation, it's usually assumed that you will pick up the tab. If you're the visitor, however, it's good form for the host to pay the bill. Alternatively, play it safe and offer to split the check.

under the heading of "painkillers." You can buy generic ibuprofen or a popular European brand of ibuprofen, Nurofen, which is sold everywhere. Tylenol is not sold in the United Kingdom, but its main ingredient, acetaminophen, is—although, confusingly, it's called paracetamol.

Among sinus and allergy medicines, Claritin is the main option here; it's the same brand sold in the United States. Some medicines are pretty much the same as brands sold in the United States—instead of Nyquil cold medicine, there's "Night Nurse." The most popular over-the-counter cough medicine is Benylin.

Drugstores are generally called pharmacies, but sometimes referred to as chemists. The biggest drugstore chain in the country is Boots. If you're in a rural area, look out for shops marked with a sign of a green cross; almost all small drugstores have one of these.

Supermarkets and newsagents all usually have a small supply of cold and headache medicines, often behind the cash register. As in the United States, large supermarkets will have a bigger supply on offer.

British people have more faith in herbal cures than Americans, and in some drugstores—including some Boots—you'll find as many herbal and vitamin offerings as actual medicine. If you can't find what you're looking for, just ask at the counter; many over-the-counter medicines are kept behind the cash register, whereas herbal remedies line the shelves. Pharmacy workers are trained to ensure you know basic safety issues with all drugs, so don't be surprised if you're asked a few questions about what else you're taking and how you're planning to use the medicine.

▌HOLIDAYS

Standard holidays are New Year's Day, Good Friday, Easter Monday, May Day (first Monday in May), spring and summer bank holidays (last Monday in May and August, respectively), Christmas, and Boxing Day (December 26). On Christmas Eve and New Year's Eve, some shops, restaurants, and businesses close early. Some museums and tourist attractions are also closed then.

▌MAIL

Stamps can be bought from post offices (generally open weekdays 9–5:30, Saturday 9–noon), from stamp machines outside post offices, and from newsagents' stores and newsstands. Mailboxes are known as post or letter boxes and are painted bright red; large tubular ones are set on the edge of sidewalks, whereas smaller boxes are set into post-office walls. Allow seven days for a letter to reach the United States. Check the Yellow Pages for a complete list of branches, though you cannot reach individual offices by phone.

Airmail letters up to 10 grams (0.35 ounce) to North America, Australia, and New Zealand cost 62p. Letters under 9.4 inches x 6.4 inches within Britain are from 39p for first class, 30p for second class. Large letters (over 9.4 inches x 6.4 inches, under 13.8 inches x 9.8 inches) cost from 61p first-class, 47p within the U.K., depending on weight. Airmail is assessed by weight alone.

If you're uncertain where you'll be staying, you can have mail sent to you at the London Main Post Office, c/o poste restante. The post office will hold international mail for one month.

Contact Royal Mail (☎ 0845/722–3344 ⊕ www.royalmail.com).

Main Branches London Main Post Office (✉ 24–28 William IV St., Trafalgar Sq., ⊕ www.postoffice.co.uk ✉ 43–44 Albemarle St., Mayfair 111 Baker St., Marylebone 1–5, Poland St., Soho ✉ 54 Great Portland St., Fitzrovia , 181 High Holborn, Holborn).

SHIPPING PACKAGES

Most department stores and retail outlets can ship your goods home. You should check your insurance for coverage of possible damage. Private delivery companies such as DHL, FedEx, and Parcelforce offer two-day delivery service to the United States, but you'll pay a considerable amount for the privilege.

Express Services DHL (☎ *0844/248–0808* ⊕ *www.dhl.com*). **FedEx** (☎ *08456/070809* ⊕ *www.fedex.com*). **Parcelforce** (☎ *0844/800–4466* ⊕ *www.parcelforce.com*).

∎ MONEY

No doubt about it, London is one of the most expensive cities in the world: getting around is expensive, eating can be expensive, travel is pricey, and hotels aren't cheap. However, for every yin there's a yang, and travelers do get a break in other places: most museums are free, for example, and Oyster cards help cut the price of travel.

ATMS AND BANKS

Your own bank will probably charge a fee for using ATMs abroad; the foreign bank you use may also charge a fee. Nevertheless, you'll usually get a better rate of exchange at an ATM than you will at a currency-exchange office or even when changing money in a bank. And extracting funds as you need them is a safer option than carrying around a large amount of cash.

∎ TIP➔ PIN numbers with more than four digits are not recognized at ATMs in many countries. If yours has five or more, remember to change it before you leave.

Credit cards or debit cards (also known as check cards) will get you cash advances at ATMs, which are widely available in London. To make sure that your Cirrus or Plus card (to cite just two of the leading names) works in European ATMs, have your bank reset it to use a four-digit PIN number before your departure.

CREDIT CARDS

Throughout this guide, the following abbreviations are used: **AE,** American Express; **DC,** Diners Club; **MC,** Master-Card; and **V,** Visa.

∎ TIP➔ Remember to inform your credit-card company before you travel, especially if you're going abroad and don't travel

internationally very often. Otherwise, the credit-card company might put a hold on your card owing to unusual activity—not a good thing halfway through your trip. Record all your credit-card numbers— as well as the phone numbers to call if your cards are lost or stolen—in a safe place, so you're prepared should something go wrong. Both MasterCard and Visa have general numbers you can call (collect if you're abroad) if your card is lost, but you're better off calling the number of your issuing bank, since Master-Card and Visa usually just transfer you to your bank; your bank's number is usually printed on your card.

If you plan to use your credit card for cash advances, you'll need to apply for a PIN at least two weeks before your trip. Although it's usually cheaper (and safer) to use a credit card abroad for large purchases (so you can cancel payments or be reimbursed if there's a problem), note that some credit-card companies *and* the banks that issue them add substantial percentages to all foreign transactions, whether they're in a foreign currency or not. Check on these fees before leaving home, so there won't be any surprises when you get the bill.

∎ TIP➔ Before you charge something, ask the merchant whether or not he or she plans to do a dynamic currency conversion (DCC). In such a transaction the credit-card *processor* (shop, restaurant, or hotel, not Visa or MasterCard) converts the currency and charges you in dollars. In most cases you'll pay the merchant a 3% fee for this service in addition to any credit-card company and issuing-bank foreign-transaction surcharges.

Dynamic currency conversion programs are becoming increasingly widespread. Merchants who participate in them are supposed to ask whether you want to be charged in dollars or the local currency, but they don't always do so. And even if they do offer you a choice, they may well avoid mentioning the additional surcharges. The good news is that you *do* have a choice. And if this practice really gets your goat, you can avoid it entirely thanks to American Express; with its cards, DCC simply isn't an option.

Credit cards are accepted virtually everywhere in London.

Reporting Lost Cards American Express (☎ 800/992–3404 in U.S., 01273/696–933 in U.K. ⊕ www.americanexpress.com). **Diners Club** (☎ 800/234–6377 in U.S., 0870/190–0011 in U.K. ⊕ www.dinersclub. com). **MasterCard** (☎ 800/627–8372 in U.S., 0800/964–767 in U.K. ⊕ www.mastercard.com). **Visa** (☎ 800/847–2911 in U.S., 0800/891–725 in U.K. ⊕ www.visa.com).

CURRENCY AND EXCHANGE

The units of currency in Great Britain are the pound sterling (£) and pence (p): £50, £20, £10, and £5 bills (called notes); £2, £1 (100p), 50p, 20p, 10p, 5p, 2p, and 1p coins. At this writing, the exchange rate was about Australian $2.20, Canadian $1.78, New Zealand $2.79, U.S. $1.42, and €1.12 to the pound (also known as quid).

Even if a currency-exchange booth has a sign promising no commission, rest assured that there's some kind of huge, hidden fee. (Oh . . . that's right. The sign didn't say no *fee*.) And as for rates, you're almost always better off getting foreign currency at an ATM or exchanging money at a bank.

■ TIP→ Banks never have every foreign currency on hand, and it may take as long as a week to order. If you're planning to exchange funds before leaving home, don't wait until the last minute.

Currency Conversion Google (⊕ www. google.com) does currency conversion. Just type in the amount you want to convert and an explanation of how you want it converted (e.g., "14 Swiss francs in dollars"), and then voilà. **Oanda.com** (⊕ www.oanda.com) also allows you to print out a handy table with the current day's conversion rates. **XE.com** (⊕ www.xe.com) is another good currency conversion Web site.

■ PACKING

London's weather is unpredictable. It can be cool, damp, and overcast, even in summer, but the odd summer day can be uncomfortable, as not very many public venues, theaters, or the Tube are air-conditioned. In general, you'll need a heavy coat for winter and light clothes for summer, along with a lightweight coat or jacket. Always pack a small umbrella that you can easily carry around with you. Pack as you would for any American city: jackets and ties for expensive restaurants and nightspots, casual clothes elsewhere. Jeans are popular in London and are perfectly acceptable for sightseeing and informal dining. Sports jackets are popular with men. In five-star hotels men can expect to be asked to wear a jacket and tie in the restaurant and bar, and women might feel out of place unless they're in smart clothes. Otherwise, for women, ordinary dress is acceptable just about everywhere.

■ PASSPORTS AND VISAS

U.S. citizens need only a valid passport to enter Great Britain for stays of up to six months. If you're within six months of your passport's expiration date, renew it before you leave—nearly extinct passports are not strictly banned, but they make immigration officials anxious, and may cause you problems.

PASSPORTS

We're always surprised at how few Americans have passports—only 25% at this writing. This number is expected to grow now that it is impossible to reenter the United States from trips to neighboring Canada or Mexico without one. Remember this: a passport verifies both your identity and nationality—a great reason to have one.

U.S. passports are valid for 10 years. You must apply in person if you're getting a passport for the first time; if your previous passport was lost, stolen, or damaged;

or if your previous passport has expired and was issued more than 15 years ago or when you were under 16. All children under 18 must appear in person to apply for or renew a passport. Both parents must accompany any child under 14 (or send a notarized statement with their permission) and provide proof of their relationship to the child.

There are 13 regional passport offices, as well as 7,000 passport acceptance facilities in post offices, public libraries, and other governmental offices. If you're renewing a passport, you can do so by mail. Forms are available at passport acceptance facilities and online.

The cost to apply for a new passport is $75 for adults, $60 for children under 16; renewals are $75. There is an additional "execution fee" of $25. Allow six weeks for processing, both for first-time passports and renewals. For an expediting fee of $60 you can reduce this time to about two weeks. If your trip is less than two weeks away, you can get a passport even more rapidly by going to a passport office with the necessary documentation. Private expediters can get things done in as little as 48 hours, but charge hefty fees for their services.

■**TIP→** Before your trip, make two copies of your passport's data page (one for someone at home and another for you to carry separately). Or scan the page and e-mail it to someone at home and/or yourself.

VISAS

A visa is essentially formal permission to enter a country. Visas allow countries to keep track of you and other visitors—and generate revenue (from application fees). You *always* need a visa to enter a foreign country; however, many countries routinely issue tourist visas on arrival, particularly to U.S. citizens. When your passport is stamped or scanned in the immigration line, you're actually being issued a visa. Sometimes you have to stand in a separate line and pay a small fee to get your stamp before going through immigration, but you can still do this at the airport on arrival. Getting a visa isn't always that easy. Some countries require that you arrange for one in advance of your trip. There's usually—but not always—a fee involved, and said fee may be nominal ($10 or less) or substantial ($100 or more).

If you must apply for a visa in advance, you can usually do it in person or by mail. When you apply by mail, you send your passport to a designated consulate, where your passport will be examined and the visa issued. Expediters—usually the same ones who handle expedited passport applications—can do all the work of obtaining your visa for you; however, there's always an additional cost (often more than $50 per visa).

Most visas limit you to a single trip—basically during the actual dates of your planned vacation. Other visas allow you to visit as many times as you wish for a specific period of time. Remember that requirements change, sometimes at the drop of a hat, and the burden is on you to make sure that you have the appropriate visas. Otherwise, you'll be turned away at the airport or, worse, deported after you arrive in the country. No company or travel insurer gives refunds if your travel plans are disrupted because you didn't have the correct visa.

U.S. Passport Information U.S. Department of State (☎ 877/487–2778 ⊕ travel.state.gov/passport).

U.S. Passport and Visa Expediters A. Briggs Passport & Visa Expeditors (☎ 800/806–0581 or 202/388–0111 ⊕ www.abriggs.com). **American Passport Express** (☎ 800/455–5166 or 603/559–9888 ⊕ www.americanpassport.com). **Passport Express** (☎ 800/362–8196 or 401/272–4612 ⊕ www.passportexpress.com). **Travel Document Systems** (☎ 800/874–5100 or 202/638–3800 ⊕ www.traveldocs.com). **Travel the World Visas** (☎ 866/886–8472 or 301/495–7700 ⊕ www.world-visa.com).

▌RESTROOMS

Restrooms in London are very similar to those in the United States, except they're not called restrooms or bathrooms, they're called any of the following: toilets, loos, ladies, or gents. Pay toilets are very rare. You'll see them largely in train stations, where you can expect to pay 30 pence to get in. Toilet attendants are extremely rare, and tip plates for them are even rarer. If you're desperate for a loo and there's no public toilet around, you can often pop into a nearby pub and slip into the restroom unnoticed. If the place is empty, though, you might need to buy a soft drink as an act of politeness.

▌SAFETY

The rules for safety in London are the same as in New York or any big city. If you're carrying a considerable amount of cash and do not have a safe in your hotel room, it's a good idea to keep it in something like a money belt or a neck pouch, but don't get cash out of it in public. Keep a small amount of cash for immediate purchases in your pocket or handbag.

Beyond that, use common sense. In central London, nobody will raise an eyebrow at tourists studying maps on street corners, and don't hesitate to ask for directions. However, outside of the center, exercise general caution about the neighborhoods you walk in: if they don't look safe, take a cab. After midnight, outside of the center, take cabs rather than waiting for a night bus. Although London has plenty of so-called "minicabs"—normal cars driven by self-employed drivers in a cab service—don't ever get into an unmarked car that pulls up offering you "cab service." Take a licensed minicab only from a cab office, or, preferably, a normal London "black cab," which you flag down on the street. Unlicensed minicab drivers have been associated with a slate of violent crimes in recent years.

If you carry a purse, choose one with a zipper and a thick strap that you can drape across your body; adjust the length so that the purse sits in front of you at or above hip level. Store only enough money in the purse to cover casual spending. Distribute the rest of your cash and any valuables among deep front pockets, inside jacket or vest pockets, and a concealed money pouch. Some pubs, restaurants, and bars have "Chelsea clips" under the tables where you can hang your handbag at your knee. These keep your bag safe, and make it hard for anybody to grab it. Never leave your bag beside your chair or hanging from the back of your chair. Be careful with backpacks, as pickpockets can unzip them on the Tube, or even as you're traveling up an escalator.

■ **TIP→** Distribute your cash, credit cards, IDs, and other valuables between a deep front pocket, an inside jacket or vest pocket, and a hidden money pouch. Don't reach for the money pouch once you're in public.

Advisories U.S. Department of State (⊕ *travel.state.gov*).

▌TAXES

An airport departure tax of £20 per person for flights within the United Kingdom and other EU countries is included in the price of your ticket. For long-haul flights, the amount varries according to destination. The fee is subject to government tax increases.

The British sales tax (V.A.T., value-added tax) returns to 17½% after January 2010. The tax is almost always included in quoted prices in shops, hotels, and restaurants.

Most travelers can get a V.A.T. refund by either the Retail Export or the more cumbersome Direct Export method. Many, but not all, large stores provide these services, but only if you request them; they will handle the paperwork. For the Retail Export method, you must ask the store for Form VAT 407 when making a purchase (you must have identification—passports are best). Have the form stamped like any customs form by customs officials when you leave the country or, if you're visiting several European Union countries, when you leave the EU. After you're through passport control, take the form to a refund-service counter for an on-the-spot refund (which is usually the quickest and easiest option), or mail it to the address on the form (or the envelope with it) after you arrive home. You receive the total refund stated on the form, but the processing time can be long, especially if you request a credit-card adjustment.

With the Direct Export method, the goods are shipped directly to your home. You must have a Form VAT 407 certified by customs, the police, or a notary public when you get home and then send it back to the store, which will refund your money. For inquiries, contact Her Majesty's Customs & Excise office.

Global Refund is a worldwide service with 240,000 affiliated stores and more than 700 refund counters at major airports and border crossings. Its refund form, called a Tax Free Check, is the most common across the European continent. The service issues refunds in the form of cash, check, or credit-card adjustment.

V.A.T. Refunds Global Refund (☎ 866/706–6090 in U.S., 800/321–1111 in U.K. ⊕ www.globalrefund.com). **Her Majesty's Customs & Excise office** (☎ 0845/010–9000 within U.K., 287/137–6200 from outside U.K. ⊕ customs.hmrc.gov.uk).

▌ TIME

London is five hours ahead of New York City. In other words, when it's 3 PM in New York (or noon in Los Angeles), it's 8 PM in London. Note that Great Britain and most European countries also move their clocks ahead for the one-hour differential when daylight saving time goes into effect (although they make the changeover several weeks after the United States).

Time Zones Timeanddate.com (⊕ www.timeanddate.com/worldclock) can help you figure out the correct time anywhere in the world.

▌ TIPPING

Tipping is done in Britain just as in the United States, but at a lower level. So, although it might make you uncomfortable, tipping less than you would back home in restaurants—and not tipping at all in pubs—is not only accepted, but standard. Tipping more can look like you're showing off. Do not tip movie or theater ushers, elevator operators, or bar staff in pubs—although you can always offer to buy them a drink.

TIPPING GUIDELINES FOR LONDON	
Bartender	In cocktail bars, on the other hand, if you see a tip plate, it's fine to leave £1 or £2. For table service, tip 10% of the cost of the bill. However, the gratuity is often included in the check at more expensive bars.
Bellhop	£1–£2 for carrying bags
Hotel Concierge	It is not necessary to tip your concierge and could be perceived as insulting.
Hotel Doorman	£1 for hailing taxis or for carrying bags to check-in desk
Hotel Maid	It's extremely rare for hotel maids to be tipped; £1 or £2 would be generous.
Porter at Airport or Train Station	£1 per bag
Skycap at Airport	£1–£3 per bag
Taxi Driver	Optional 10%–15%, perhaps a little more for a short ride
Tour Guide	Tipping optional; £1 or £2 would be generous.
Waiter	10%–15%, with 15% being the norm at high-end restaurants; nothing additional if a service charge is added to the bill.
Other	Restroom attendants in expensive restaurants expect some small change (20p or so).

∎ TOURS

BIKE TOURS

London's mayor, Boris Johnson, is a real cycling enthusiast and keen to make the capital more bike-friendly. However, the capital is still a busy metropolis, so the best way to see it on two wheels is to contact one of the excellent cycle tour companies that aim to take you around London, avoiding all the busy routes and traveling along cycle lanes and river paths, down quiet backstreets and through parks.

Tour Operators Cycle Tours of London (☎ *020/7738–6310* ⊕ *www.biketoursoflondon. com*). **Fat Tire Bike Tours** ☎ *0788/238–779* ⊕ *www.fattirebiketours.com*). **London Bicycle Tour Company** (☎ *020/7928–6838* ⊕ *www. londonbicycle.com*).

BOAT TOURS

Year-round, but more frequently from April to October, boats cruise the Thames, offering a different view of the London skyline. Most leave from Westminster Pier, Charing Cross Pier, and Tower Pier. Downstream routes go to the Tower of London, Greenwich, and the Thames Barrier via Canary Wharf. Upstream destinations include Kew, Richmond, and Hampton Court (mainly in summer). Most of the launches seat between 100 and 250 passengers, have a public-address system, and provide a running commentary on passing points of interest. Some include musical entertainment. Depending upon the destination, river trips may last from one to four hours.

Details on all other operators are available from London River Services.

River Cruise Operators Bateaux London (☎ *020/7695–1800* www.bateauxlondon. com*). **London Duck Tours** (☎ *020/7928–3132* www.londonducktours.co.uk*). **Thames Cruises** (☎ *020/928–9009* www. thamescruises.com*). **Westminster Passenger Boat Services** (☎ *020/7930–2062* www. wpsa.co.uk*).

BUS TOURS

Guided sightseeing tours from the top of double-decker buses, which are open-top in summer, are a good introduction to the city, as they cover all the main central sights. Numerous companies run daily bus tours that depart (usually between 8:30 and 9 AM) from central points. You may board or alight at any of the numerous stops to view the sights, and reboard on the next bus. Tickets can be bought from the driver and are good all day. Prices vary according to the type of tour, although £20 is the benchmark.

Bus Tour Operators Best Value Tours (⊕ *www.bestvaluetours.co.uk*). **Big Bus Tours** (☎ *020/7233–9533* ⊕ *www.bigbustours.com*). **Black Taxi Tour of London** (☎ *020/7935–9363* ⊕ *www.blacktaxitours.co.uk*). **Golden Tours** (☎ *0/844/880–6980 in U.K., 1–800/509–2507 in U.S.* ⊕ *www.goldentours. co.uk*). **Original London Sightseeing Tour** (☎ *020/8877–1722* ⊕ *www.theoriginaltour. com*). **Premium Tours** (☎ *020/7404–5100* ⊕ *www.premiumtours.co.uk*).

CANAL TOURS

The tranquil side of London can be found on narrow boats that cruise the city's two canals, the Grand Union and Regent's Canal; most vessels operate on the latter, which runs between Little Venice in the west (nearest Tube: Warwick Avenue on the Bakerloo Line) and Camden Lock (about 200 yards north of Camden Town Tube station). Fares start at about £8.50 for 1½-hour round-trip cruises.

Canal Tour Operators Canal Cruises (☎ *020/8440–8962* www.londoncanalcruises. com*). **Jason's Trip** (☎ *020/7286–3428* www. jasons.co.uk*). **London Waterbus Company** (☎ *020/7482–2660* www.londonwaterbus. co.uk*).

EXCURSIONS

Evan Evans, Green Line, and National Express all offer day excursions by bus to places within easy reach of London, such as Hampton Court, Oxford, Stratford, and Bath.

Tour Operators **Evan Evans** (☎ *020/7950–1777, 800/422–9022 in U.S.* ⊕ *www.evanevanstours.co.uk*). **Green Line** (☎ *0844/801–7261* ⊕ *www.greenline.co.uk*). **National Express** (☎ *0871/751–8181* ⊕ *www.nationalexpress.com*).

WALKING TOURS

One of the best ways to get to know London is on foot, and there are many guided and themed walking tours from which to choose. Richard Jones's London Walking Tours includes the Jack the Ripper Walk following in the footsteps of the titular killer, as does the Blood and Tears Walk. Other tours include Secret London, The West End with Dickens, and Hampstead—A Country Village. Context London's expert docents lead small groups on walks with art, architecture, and similar themes. The London Walks Company hosts more than 100 walks every week on a variety of themes, including a Thames pub walk, Literary Bloomsbury, and Spies and Spycatchers. For more options, pick up a copy of *Time Out* magazine and check the weekly listings for upcoming one-off tours.

Walking Tour Operators **Blood and Tears Walk** (☎ *07905/746–733* ⊕ *www.shockinglondon.com*). **Blue Badge** (☎ *020/7403–1115* ⊕ *www.blue-badge-guides.com*). **Context London** (☎ *020/193–9158, 800/691–6036 in U.S.* ⊕ *www.contexttravel.com/london*). **Richard Jones's London Walking Tours** (☎ *020/7928–2627* ⊕ *www.walksoflondon.co.uk*). **London Walks** (☎ *020/7624–3978* ⊕ *www.walks.com*).

Shakespeare City Walk (☎ *07905/746–733* ⊕ *www.shakespeareguide.com*).

▌ VISITOR INFORMATION

When you arrive in London, you can get good information at the London Visitor Centre near the Eurostar arrivals area at St. Pancras International train station and at Victoria Station. These are helpful if you're looking for brochures for London sights, or if something's gone horribly wrong with your hotel reservation—if, for example, you don't have one—as they have a useful reservations service. The Victoria Station center is open Monday–Saturday 7:15 AM–9:15 PM, Sunday 8:15 AM–8:15 PM. The St. Pancras center is open daily 9–7. The Britain and London Visitor Centre is a worthwhile stop for travel, hotel, and entertainment information. It's open 9–6 October–March and 9–6:30 April–September, weekends 10–4 October–May, and Saturday 9–5 June–September. The London Tourist Information Centre has a branch in Greenwich.

Official Web sites are ⊕ *www.visitbritain.com.* ⊕ *www.visitlondon.com.*

Other Web sites ⊕ *www.londontown.com*, the *Evening Standard's* online ⊕ *www.thisislondon.com*, No. 10 Downing Street (⊕ *www.number-10.gov.uk*), and the BBC (⊕ *www.bbc.co.uk*).

Entertainment Information ⊕ *www.timeout.com*, ⊕ *www.officiallondontheatre.co.uk*, and ⊕ *www.kidslovelondon.com*.

INDEX

PHOTO CREDITS

1, Richard Osbourne/Blue Pearl Photographic/Alamy. 2-3, Heeb Christian/age fotostock. 5, Rich B-S/Flickr. Chapter 1: Experience: 8-9, William Helsel/age fotostock. 10, Angelina Dimitrova/Shutterstock. 11 (left), British Tourist Authority. 11 (right), PCL/Alamy. 12, gary718/Shutterstock. 13 (left), Pres Panayotov/Shutterstock. 13 (right), Kathy deWitt/Alamy. 14, Jan Kranendonk/Shutterstock. 15 (left), Dominic Burke/Alamy. 15 (right), Doug Scott/age fotostock. 17, Marc Pinter/Shutterstock. 18 (right), Sean Nel/Shutterstock. 18 (top center), Vinicius Tupinamba/Shutterstock. 18 (bottom center), WH Chow/Shutterstock. 18 (top right), Jan Kranendonk/iStockphoto. 18 (bottom right), Thomas Sztanek/Shutterstock. 19 (top left), Bob Masters/Alamy. 19 (bottom left), Andrew Ward/Life File/Photodisc. 19 (top center), Jack Sullivan/Alamy. 19 (bottom center), Dominic Burke/Alamy. 19 (right), Walter Bibikow/viestiphoto.com. 20 (left), wikipedia.org. 20 (top center), The Print Collector/Alamy. 20 (bottom center and top right), wikipedia.org. 20 (bottom right), www.wga.hu. 21 (top left, bottom left, top center, and right), wikipedia.org. 22, Visit London. 23 (left), Danilo Donadoni/Marka/age fotostock. 23 (right), British Tourist Authority. 25 (left) British Tourist Authority (right), Christopher Steer/iStockphoto. 27 (right), Visit London. 27 (left), Lebrecht Music and Arts Photo Library/Alamy. 28, D.H. Snover/Shutterstock. 29, Sylvain Grandadam/age fotostock. 31 (left), Grant Pritchard/britainonview.com. 31 (right), 32 and 33, British Tourist Authority. 36, Jacqueline Abromeit/Shutterstock. 37, David Peta/Shutterstock. 38 (top left), UK21/Alamy. 38 (bottom left), wikipedia.org. 38 (right), Kobby Dagan/Shutterstock. 39 (left), Mike Booth/Alamy. 39 (top right), wikipedia.org. 39 (bottom right), INTER-FOTO Pressebildagentur/Alamy. 40 (top left), Robert Stainforth/Alamy. 40 (bottom left), Jeffrey Blackler/Alamy. 40 (right), Andrew Dunn/wikipedia.org. 41 (left), Eric Nathan/Alamy. 41 (right), Chris Batson/Alamy. 42 (left), Directphoto.org/Alamy. 42 (top right), Zaha Hadid/wikipedia.org. 42 (bottom right), Nigel Young/British Museum. Chapter 2: Westminster & Royal London: 43, British Tourist Authority. 45, Eric Nathan/ britainonview.com. 46, Peter Adams/age fotostock. 49, ktylerconk/Flickr. 50, Mark William Richardson/Shutterstock. 52, Pres Panayotov/Shutterstock. 56-57, Doug Pearson/age fotostock. 58, British Tourist Authority. 60, John Sturrock/Alamy. 63, Sean Nel/Shutterstock. 65 (left), F. Monheim/R. von Göt/Bildarchiv Monheim/age fotostock. 65 (top right), Dean and Chapter of Westminster. 65 (center right), Mark Thomas/Alamy. 65 (bottom right) and 67, Dean and Chapter of Westminster. 69, British Tourist Authority. Chapter 3: St. James's & Mayfair: 73, Doug McKinlay/britainonview.com. 75, British Tourist Authority. 76, David Noton Photography/Alamy. 78, PCL/Alamy. 79, Jess Moss. 81, Pawel Libera/Alamy. 82, Derek Croucher/Alamy. 85, Matthew Mawson/Alamy. Chapter 4: Soho & Covent Garden: 87, 89 and 90, British Tourist Authority. 91, Julian Love/John Warburton-Lee Photography/photolibrary.com. 92, Jon Arnold/age fotostock. 94, Ann Steer/iStockphoto. 97, British Tourist Authority. Chapter 5: Bloomsbury & Legal London: 99, Michael Jenner/Alamy. 101 and 102, British Tourist Authority. 104, Jarno Gonzalez Zarraonandia/Shutterstock. 105 and 106 (top), British Museum. 106 (bottom), Grant Rooney/Alamy. 108, British Museum. 109, James McCormick/britainonview.com. 110, Eric Nathan/Alamy. Chapter 6: The City: 115, PSL Images/Alamy. 117, Ryan Fox/age fotostock. 118-19, Jason Hawkes. 120, Jerry Millevoi/age fotostock. 123 (left), F. Monheim/R. von Göt/Bildarchiv Monheim/age fotostock. 123 (top right), Jeff Gynane/Shutterstock. 123 (center right), Ken Ross/viestiphoto.com. 123 (bottom right), Marcin Stalmach/iStockphoto. 125, Rene Ramos/Shutterstock. 127, Russ Merne/Alamy. 130, Imagestate/age fotostock.com. 133, iStockphoto. 135 (left), Walter Bibikow/viestiphoto.com. 135 (right), Tom Hanley/Alamy. 136 (top), Natasha Marie Brown/HRP/newsteam.co.uk. 137, Peter Phipp/Peter Phipp/age fotostock. 138 (left), Mary Evans Picture Library/Alamy. 138 (top center), Reflex Picture Library/Alamy. 138 (top right), Classic Image/Alamy. 139, Jan Kranendonk/iStockphoto. Chapter 7: The East End: 141, Janine Wiedel Photolibrary/Alamy. 143, Neil Setchfield/Alamy. 144, foybles/Alamy. 147, Jon Arnold/age fotostock. 150, Elly Godfroy/Alamy. Chapter 8: The South Bank: 153, Mike Peel/wikipedia.org. 155, Eric Nathan/britainonview.com. 156, PCL/Alamy. 159 (top), Shutterstock. 159 (bottom), Duncan Soar/Alamy. 160, Vehbi Koca/Alamy. 161 (top), Lebrecht Music and Arts Photo Library/Alamy. 161 (bottom), Eric Nathan/britainonview.com. 163, AA World Travel Library/Alamy. 165, Terry Walsh/Shutterstock. 166, Jess Moss. 169, David Pearson/Alamy. Chapter 9: Kensington, Chelsea & Knightsbridge: 171, Cahir Davitt/age fotostock. 173, British Tourist Authority. 174, Robert Harding Picture Library Ltd/Alamy. 176, John Warburton-Lee Photography/Alamy. 178, British Tourist Authority. 179, Londonstills.com/Alamy. 182, Ant Clausen/Shutterstock. 183, PCL/Alamy. Chapter 10: Notting Hill & Bayswater: 185, Dominic Burke/Alamy. 187, Doug Scott/age fotostock. 188, David H. Wells/age fotostock. 190, Peter Cook/age fotostock. 191, Corbis. 193, Joe Viesti/viestiphoto.com. 194, TNT MAGAZINE/Alamy. 195 (left), Andrew Holt/Alamy. 195 (top right), Dominic Burke/Alamy. 195 (bottom right), David Berry/Shutterstock. Chapter 11: Regent's Park & Hampstead: 197, Earl Patrick Lichfield/britainonview.com. 199, British Tourist Authority. 200, Bildarchiv Monheim GmbH/Alamy. 204,

ARCO/R. Kiedrowski/age fotostock. 206, PCL/Alamy. 209, Pictorial Press Ltd/Alamy. 212, PCL/Alamy. Chapter 12: Greenwich: 213, Michael Booth/Alamy. 215, Visit London. 216, one-image photography/Alamy. 218, Bartlomiej K. Kwieciszewski/Shutterstock. 219, Jon Arnold Images Ltd/Alamy. 221, Mcginnly/wikipedia.org. 222, Visit London. Chapter 13: The Thames Upstream: 225, britainonview.com. 227 and 228, Danilo Donadoni/Marka/age fotostock. 231 and 233, britainonview.com. 235, Rich B-S/Flickr. 236 (top), Mike Booth/Alamy. 236 (bottom), Danilo Donadoni/Marka/age fotostock. 237, wikipedia.org. 238, photogl/Shutterstock. 239 (top left), Roger Hutchings/Alamy. 239 (top right), Corbis. 239 (bottom), Lyndon Giffard/Alamy. 240, Rafael Campillo/age fotostock. 241 (top left), British Tourist Authority. 241 (top right), Danilo Donadoni/Marka/age fotostock. Chapter 14: Where to Eat: 243, John Angerson/Alamy. 244, Atlantide S.N.C./age fotostock. 249, Locanda Locatelli. 250, Duncan Hale-Sutton/Alamy. 251 (top), Alexandr Shebanov/Shutterstock. 251 (bottom), Fino. 252, British Tourist Authority. 253 (top), Amazing Space Ltd. 253 (bottom), Kathy de Witt/britainonview.com. 254, The Berkeley. 255 (top), Zuma. 255 (bottom), Tom Aikens. 256, Ken Ross/viestiphoto.com. 257(top), Ladbroke Arms. 257 (bottom), Four Seasons. 258, Angela Hartnett. 259 (top), Avenue. 259 (bottom), Neil Setchfield. 260, Gay Hussar. 261 (top), Massimiliano Pieraccini/Shutterstock. 261 (bottom), Herbert Ypma. Chapter 15: Where to Stay: 295, Danita Delimont/Alamy. 296, City Inn Westminster. 304 (top left), Generator Hostel London. 304 (top right), Marriott International. 304 (center left), VIEW Pictures Ltd/Alamy. 304 (center right), RayMain.co.uk. 304 (bottom left), The Hoxton. 304 (bottom right), Firmdale Hotels. 305 (top left), Mandarin Oriental. 305 (top right), Athenaeum Hotel and Apartments, London. 305 (center left), Damian Russell. 305 (center right), Claridge's Hotel. 305 (bottom left), The Stafford. 305 (bottom right), One Aldwych. Chapter 16: Pubs & Nightlife: 337, Jess Moss. 340, Everynight Images/Alamy. 344, Jess Moss. 349, Phillie Casablanca/Flickr. 353, Phillie Casablanca/Flickr. 356, British Tourist Authority. Chapter 17: Arts & Entertainment: 361, James McCormick/British Tourist Authority. 363, Grant Pritchard/British Tourist Authority. 364, Hugo Glendinning. 369, Lebrecht Music and Arts Photo Library/Alamy. 370, Lebrecht Music and Arts Photo Library/Alamy. 376, Tate Photography. 377, Jack Sullivan/Alamy. Chapter 18: Shopping: 379, Chris P. Batson/Alamy. 382, Heeb Christian/age fotostock. 383, Andrew Parker/Alamy. 384, Jim Batty/Alamy. 385, Andrew Parker/Alamy. 386, Ming Tang-Evans. 387, www.kohsamui.co.uk. 388, Ken Ross/viestiphoto.com. 415 and 416, British Tourist Authority. 417 and 418, Ingrid Rasmussen/ British Tourist Authority. 419 (top), Nigel Hicks/britainonview.com. 419-20, British Tourist Authority. Chapter 19: Side Trips from London: 421, Andrew Holt/Alamy. 423, Mark Sunderland/Alamy. 424, British Tourist Authority. 433, Atlantide S.N.C./age fotostock. 437, Daniel Bosworth/Tourism South East /British Tourist Authority. 442, John Martin/Alamy.

NOTES

ABOUT OUR WRITERS

Christi Daugherty updated the "Where to Stay" chapter of this book. A native Texan, she has lived in (and written about) England for nearly a decade. From her base just outside of London she regularly contributes to Fodor's England and London guides. She has also written books about Ireland and Paris. She misses long, straight American highways, outdoor swimming pools, and tacos.

Freelance writer **Kiki Deere** has written for the *Rough Guides* and *Time Out*, and updated the previous edition of Fodor's London. This year she worked on the "Shopping," "Arts and Entertainment," and "Pubs and Nightlife" chapters. When not scribbling away, Kiki tends to be roaming about some part or other of the world, her most recent fascination being with Russia. Currently you are most likely to find her pottering about a crumbling Soviet bunker or sipping chai in a café down one of Kitai Gorod's dinky side-streets.

Londoner and freelance writer **Damian Harper** has been authoring guidebooks (China, Malaysia, Great Britain) for more than a decade and lives in Honor Oak Park, southeast London. For this edition, Damian updated "Experience London."

Jan Fuscoe is a Londoner by birth and loves everything about the city, particularly the East End. To make a living she's worked in a bank, sold hats, run a soul/jazz club, reviewed films and these days makes art, is learning to plumb, and (for the money) works as a freelance editor and travel writer for such publications as *Time Out*, the *Guardian*, *Times*, and *Independent* newspapers. For this guide Jan updated "Bloomsbury and Legal London," "The City," "The East End," and the "South Bank."

A Londoner since public transport was cheap, **Jack Jewers** has reviewed pubs for *Time Out* and directed films for the BBC in addition to writing for several Fodors titles. In this book he updated the "Regent's Park and Hampstead," "Greenwich," and "Thames Upstream" chapters. Romantically, he met his American wife at the V&A, where they stood on a giant map of the world, looking for the midway point between their birthplaces. Unfortunately, it's called Labrador's Bottom.

Hertfordshire lass **Michelle Rosenberg** is a freelance writer, published author, and mother of two gorgeous gals. She has written for London's *Big Issue* magazine and her first book, *Inspiring Women,* focuses on women entrepreneurs. A baby-naming book and coffee shop business guide are being published in 2009. She loves being a tourist in her own city and spends most of her time (and money) at legendary Charing Cross bookstore Foyles. For this book, Michelle updated "Westminster and Royal London," "St. James's and Mayfair," and "Soho and Covent Garden" chapters.

Ellin Stein has written for publications on both sides of the Atlantic, including the *New York Times*, the *Times of London*, the *Guardian*, the *Telegraph*, the *Independent*, the *Village Voice*, *People* magazine, and *InStyle*, for whom she was European correspondent. Originally from Manhattan, she has lived in London for 15 years and is married to a native. For this edition, she updated the "Travel Smart London," "Understanding London" and "Kensington and Chelsea" chapters.

By day, Londoner and Shoalin kung fu enthusiast **Alex Wijeratna** works as a global hunger activist for ActionAid; by night, he hunts down the best food in town. With his mixed roots, Alex is well aware that London's restaurant boom is built on its ethnic diversity. He's written for the *Times* and *Daily Mail,* and for this edition, Alex updated the "Where to Eat" chapter.